RESEARCH HANDBOOK ON CORPORATE BANKRUPTCY LAW

RESEARCH HANDBOOKS IN CORPORATE LAW AND GOVERNANCE

Series Editor: Randall S. Thomas, John S. Beasley II Professor of Law and Business, Vanderbilt University Law School, USA

Elgar Research Handbooks are original reference works designed to provide a broad overview of research in a given field while at the same time creating a forum for more challenging, critical examination of complex and often under-explored issues within that field. Chapters by international teams of contributors are specially commissioned by editors who carefully balance breadth and depth. Often widely cited, individual chapters present expert scholarly analysis and offer a vital reference point for advanced research. Taken as a whole they achieve a wide-ranging picture of the state-of-the-art.

Making a major scholarly contribution to the field of corporate law and governance, the volumes in this series explore topics of current concern from a range of jurisdictions and perspectives, offering a comprehensive analysis that will inform researchers, practitioners and students alike. The Research Handbooks cover the fundamental aspects of corporate law, such as insolvency governance structures, as well as hot button areas such as executive compensation, insider trading, and directors' duties. The Research Handbooks, each edited by leading scholars in their respective fields, offer far-reaching examinations of current issues in corporate law and governance that are unrivalled in their blend of critical, substantive analysis, and in their synthesis of contemporary research.

Each Research Handbook stands alone as an invaluable source of reference for all scholars of corporate law, as well as for practicing lawyers who wish to engage with the discussion of ideas within the field. Whether used as an information resource on key topics or as a platform for advanced study, volumes in this series will become definitive scholarly reference works in the field.

Titles in this series include:

Research Handbook on Shareholder Power
Edited by Jennifer G. Hill and Randall S. Thomas

Research Handbook on Partnerships, LLCs and Alternative Forms of Business Organizations
Edited by Robert W. Hillman and Mark J. Loewenstein

Research Handbook on Mergers and Acquisitions
Edited by Claire A. Hill and Steven Davidoff Solomon

Research Handbook on the History of Corporate and Company Law
Edited by Harwell Wells

Research Handbook on Corporate Crime and Financial Misdealing
Edited by Jennifer Arlen

Research Handbook on Fiduciary Law
Edited by Gordon Smith and Andrew Gold

Research Handbook on the Regulation of Mutual Funds
Edited by William A. Birdthistle and John Morley

Research Handbook on Representative Shareholder Litigation
Edited by Sean Griffith, Jessica Erickson, David H. Webber and Verity Winship

Research Handbook on Corporate Bankruptcy Law
Edited by Barry E. Adler

Research Handbook on Corporate Bankruptcy Law

Edited by

Barry E. Adler

New York University, School of Law, USA

RESEARCH HANDBOOKS IN CORPORATE LAW AND GOVERNANCE

Edward Elgar PUBLISHING

Cheltenham, UK • Northampton, MA, USA

Published by
Edward Elgar Publishing Limited
The Lypiatts
15 Lansdown Road
Cheltenham
Glos GL50 2JA
UK

Edward Elgar Publishing, Inc.
William Pratt House
9 Dewey Court
Northampton
Massachusetts 01060
USA

A catalogue record for this book
is available from the British Library

Library of Congress Control Number: 2019956665

This book is available electronically in the **Elgar**online
Law subject collection
DOI 10.4337/9781781007884

MIX
Paper from
responsible sources
FSC www.fsc.org FSC® C013604

ISBN 978 1 78100 787 7 (cased)
ISBN 978 1 78100 788 4 (eBook)

Typeset by Servis Filmsetting Ltd, Stockport, Cheshire

Printed and bound by CPI Group (UK) Ltd, Croydon CR0 4YY

Contents

Figures and table

Figures

Table

Contributors

Kenneth Ayotte
University of California at Berkeley

Douglas G. Baird
University of Chicago

Anthony J. Casey
University of Chicago

Thomas H. Jackson
University of Rochester

Melissa B. Jacoby
University of North Carolina at Chapel Hill

Edward J. Janger
Brooklyn Law School

Stephen J. Lubben
Seton Hall University

Edward R. Morrison
Columbia University

John A.E. Pottow
University of Michigan

Robert K. Rasmussen
University of Southern California

Mark J. Roe
Harvard University

Alan Schwartz
Yale University

Michael Simkovic
University of Southern California

David Skeel
University of Pennsylvania

Richard Squire
Fordham University

George Triantis
Stanford University

Michelle J. White
University of California at San Diego

Todd J. Zywicki
George Mason University

Foreword: The creditors' bargain – past, present and future

Douglas G. Baird

This collection of essays is in many ways a celebration of the work of Thomas Jackson, and this foreword attempts to put his work into its proper context.[1] Jackson's ideas first took shape just after the 1978 Bankruptcy Code was enacted. Much of his focus was upon making sense of its provisions. The bankruptcy landscape has much changed since that time. Practices have emerged that the drafters of the Code never contemplated, and modern bankruptcy scholars have shifted their focus from provisions of the statute itself to more general principles. But Jackson's insights have become part of the way that the best practitioners think about bankruptcy, and they continue to be the starting place for modern bankruptcy scholars.

In his seminal paper on the creditors' bargain,[2] Jackson showed that although the creditors of a common debtor cannot negotiate with each other in advance, it makes sense to imagine the sort of bargain they would strike if they could. When a corporate debtor becomes insolvent, its creditors each have an incentive to advance her own interests at the expense of everyone else. Bankruptcy law exists to solve this collective action problem.

Jackson's work was revolutionary. His core idea—that bankruptcy solved a collective action problem by forcing creditors to work together—was not new. His innovation lay rather in his strikingly novel approach. Before Jackson, bankruptcy scholars focused on the mechanics of bankruptcy law. Instead of talking about theoretical problems, the leading academics focused on judicial opinions and statutory text. Jackson began with first principles.

Moreover, Jackson differed from previous bankruptcy scholars in his style and tone. His predecessors saw themselves as part of a fraternal organization like the Free Masons, Rotarians, or Shriners. They were part of a closely-knit community whose members believed that bankruptcy law worked for the social good and helped creditors and debtors alike. Even when these scholars talked about the great principles of bankruptcy, they sounded like they were giving after-dinner speeches. Jackson spoke the language of economics and finance. He cast a cold eye on the bankruptcy landscape. Gone were heartfelt homilies. Even when he talked about individual debtors, it was through the lens of behavioral economics.[3]

In this foreword, I try to make sense of the impact of Jackson's work, in the academy and elsewhere. On its face, this brand of scholarship was far removed from the rough-and-tumble world of practice. Indeed, to many bankruptcy lawyers and judges, it looked decidedly odd. A fine bankruptcy judge of the old school described the scholarship that followed in Jackson's wake as having "an eerie sort of abstraction." This judge felt about this new direction in bankruptcy scholarship, "a little like I feel about Henry James on love: remarkable stuff, but can you trust an author who doesn't seem to know how babies are made."[4]

In the end, however, Jackson's ideas resonated with judges and practitioners. He might not have seemed like someone who would be completely comfortable with the fraternal rituals of the National Bankruptcy Conference, but he was invited to join nevertheless.[5] His ideas have long since become part of the warp and woof of modern bankruptcy practice.

Jackson organized his bankruptcy work around two core ideas. First, he believed that bankruptcy law was largely procedural. It solved a collective action problem that creditors face, but did not otherwise change their nonbankruptcy rights. Second, he showed that, to understand the creditors' bargain, it was necessary to use the same tools of modern finance that others were bringing to the study of corporate law. These two ideas are the subject of this foreword's first two parts. The final part explores how modern discussions of bankruptcy rely on Jackson's work while at the same time it takes a critical look at both bankruptcy law and Jackson's understanding of it.

I. NONBANKRUPTCY RIGHTS

Earlier generations of bankruptcy judges, practitioners, and scholars were sometimes too willing to view bankruptcy courts as courts of equity. Rigorous adherence to principle gave way to softer notions of fairness, even as lip service was paid to such concepts as absolute priority. Jackson had none of this. His analysis always possessed hard edges.

Jackson began with the idea that bankruptcy law should respect nonbankruptcy rights unless some bankruptcy policy requires a different result. He based his argument on the Supreme Court's opinion in *Butner v. United States*.[6] On its face, this opinion was not particularly remarkable. The Court was interpreting an obscure provision of North Carolina real estate lien law in a case under the 1898 Act. It was handed down just a few months before the entirely new Bankruptcy Code was to go into effect and the old law would become a dead letter. But during the course of his opinion, Justice Stevens observed that "[p]roperty interests are created and defined by state law. Unless some federal interest requires a different result, there is no reason why such interests should be analysed differently simply because an interested party is involved in a bankruptcy proceeding."[7] Jackson's work did much to elevate this passing observation into a foundational principle. Bankruptcy lawyers today routinely invoke the *Butner* principle, something they never did until Jackson's work took hold.

Jackson's basic insight into the primacy of nonbankruptcy rights provides a set of intuitions that helps one to think about concrete problems. One can start with an easy example. Imagine that, before its bankruptcy, a debtor, acting in good faith, acquired a piece of property that had been stolen from its original owner. The original owner appears and asserts her right to the stolen property. Can the original owner reclaim her property? Most have the intuition that bankruptcy should not interfere with the original owner's ability to retrieve the property. Jackson offered an easy way to explain exactly why this was so.

One of the most firmly established principles in Anglo-American law is *nemo dat*. A person's title to a piece of property is no better than that of her transferor. This, of course, is only a starting point. There are exceptions. A bona fide purchaser for value can keep property bought from someone who acquired it by fraud. But these are the exceptions. No one, not even a good faith purchaser, can keep property that has been stolen from someone else. There is no bankruptcy policy that suggests that the outcome should be different merely because such a good faith purchaser finds herself in bankruptcy.

This intuition is useful to practitioners as well as to academics. It helps them orient themselves within the provisions of the Bankruptcy Code. The stolen property is not property of the estate within the meaning of §541 because it is not the debtor's outside of bankruptcy. Nor does it become part of the estate by virtue of §544, as outside of bankruptcy the creditors, after they reduced their claims to judgment and tried to levy on the debtor's property, would not have been able to seize the stolen property in the face of the original owner's claim.

Nor does §101(5) transform this right into a claim that is subject to discharge. To be sure, the original owner's conversion action against the debtor is discharged. It is a "claim" within the meaning of §101(5). But the original owner also has a replevin action, the right to compel the debtor to turn over the stolen property to her. A replevin action is not a claim, as it is not "an equitable remedy for breach of performance." Thus, the replevin action is not a "claim" and this is not discharged. The original owner can still assert it even after the bankruptcy is over.

This methodology is especially useful when one cannot rely on an idea as powerful as *nemo dat*. For example, imagine that a buyer pays the debtor for a picture, but the debtor files for bankruptcy before delivering it. The buyer has a right to specific performance outside of bankruptcy. Is she able to retrieve the painting in bankruptcy or is she merely a general creditor?

Jackson's methodology provides a straightforward way to think about the issue, one that is much easier than relying on intuition alone. The question is whether the creditors could reach the picture outside of bankruptcy. Even if the buyer had a right of specific performance, this right might give way under nonbankruptcy law. The relevant test is whether, notwithstanding the buyer's right of specific performance, a creditor outside of bankruptcy could have reduced her claim to judgment and levied on the painting notwithstanding the buyer's specific performance right.

As a matter of state law, much may turn on the picture still being in the buyer's possession. But, in any event, it is state law that determines the issue, not by abstract ideas about balancing competing equities.[8] In contrast to an earlier generation, Jackson did not believe that there was any bankruptcy policy that dictated whether the buyer received the painting or not. It turned on state law, and state law might vary from one jurisdiction to another.

This methodology did much to unscramble initial confusion about environmental tort liability and bankruptcy. Consider a debtor who runs a factory. The debtor allowed lubricating oil to leech into the ground. State environmental law requires the debtor to remediate the environmental damage it has caused. The debtor, facing other financial difficulties, files for bankruptcy. One of the creditors is a bank that has a security interest on the factory and the land beneath it. The bankruptcy must confront the question of how to sort out the environmental liability. The problem is hard because the state can impose liability in a number of different ways simultaneously.

Armed with Jackson's insights, one resists the temptation to go first to §554, a provision of the Bankruptcy Code that allows the trustee to abandon property. Being able to abandon an asset does not affect the liability of the estate for prepetition obligations. Disposing of an asset does not change a debtor's liability outside of bankruptcy, and nothing about bankruptcy changes this. The debtor remains liable to clean-up the land, just as the debtor would remain liable to an accident victim if its delivery truck had caused an accident and the debtor subsequently took the truck to the wrecking yard. Both are claims against the estate. Whether the state or the accident victim enjoys priority over other creditors against the assets of the debtor is a question of nonbankruptcy law.

But quite apart from the state's rights as a prepetition creditor, the state is also a postpetition regulator. The trustee in bankruptcy is obliged to follow state law. In that capacity, she (or the debtor in possession) may be obliged to clean up the polluted site by virtue of its status as a postpetition owner of the land. Environmental liability, unlike other sorts of liability, can arise from the fact of ownership. The fact that the debtor continues to own the land the moment after the bankruptcy is filed is sufficient to impose a postpetition obligation on the trustee to clean it up.

Such postpetition obligations are administrative expenses that must be paid before general creditors. The clean-up obligation takes precedence over the claims of the secured creditor as well. The secured creditor has no ability to reach the land without also being subject to the clean-up obligation outside of bankruptcy and should have none inside either. Debtors in bankruptcy and all who claim through them have to play by the same rules as everyone else.[9]

This part of Jackson's work, the one focused on the Bankruptcy Code itself, even as it discovered first principles, still had its foot firmly planted in the world of traditional bankruptcy scholarship, as it was tightly connected to disputes that were actively litigated. Much of it has been internalized by judges and the practicing bar, often without understanding his influence. The second aspect of Jackson's work—the part that connected bankruptcy to corporate finance—is the part that may have had the greatest influence in the academy.

II. CORPORATE REORGANIZATIONS, CORPORATE LAW, AND MODERN FINANCE

A. Bankruptcy and Its Related Disciplines

In addition to insisting that bankruptcy was in the first instance a procedure that vindicated rights based on nonbankruptcy law, Jackson looked at bankruptcy through the lens of corporate law and modern finance to understand its foundational principles. Earlier generations of academics came to bankruptcy as a result of their interest in fields such as consumer and debtor-creditor law. Their paradigm was the individual consumer debtor and the small-business owner, and their instincts were to apply this paradigm, centered as it was on the idea of the fresh start, to large corporations.

Jackson, by contrast, was grounded in corporate finance, and this provided a different perspective. When seen through the lens of corporate finance, a corporate debtor is merely an artifact of state law. It is a juridical entity, not a flesh-and-blood creature. This perspective subjected the homilies of the previous generation to tough interrogation.

Why should we care about a corporate charter as one might care about a human being? If one suggests that a corporate debtor deserves a fresh start, one cannot mean that preserving a particular corporate charter is a good thing in itself. Is one suggesting that a particular business continue? Rhetoric about the virtues of a fresh start might make this seem sensible for a flesh-and-blood individual, but why is a business like a person over this dimension? If a bad restaurant has poor food and surly waiters, why should it stay around?

One might want to help the owner of the business start again, but why is bankruptcy necessary? The owner of the corporation is not obliged for the debts of the business. This is the virtue of doing business in limited liability form. And if for some reason the individual debtor is liable for the debts of the business, is not the relevant bankruptcy that of the individual and not the corporation?

In addition, Jackson connected bankruptcy scholarship with what was happening in corporate law. In the 1980s, corporate law was undergoing a sea change. Traditional corporate scholars feared corporate raiders would prevent managers from doing their jobs. The new generation saw the market for corporate control as a force for good. The marketplace itself disciplined managers. Jackson followed a similar path. The players in a corporate reorganization were market actors who responded to incentives just like other market actors. And the tools of modern finance could be used to analyse what was going on.

A harbinger of the value of importing finance into thinking about bankruptcy came in a 1979 paper by Jackson and Anthony Kronman, an early collaborator (and later Yale Law School dean).[10] The paper explored the institution of secured credit and the benefits it brought. The paper, like Jackson's later paper on the creditors' bargain, was methodologically different from previous work on secured credit. Most of the scholarship on secured transactions accepted the value of secured credit without question. Jackson and Kronman did not. They asked exactly what benefits secured creditors brought. It is all well and good to say that a secured loan is safer than an unsecured loan, but when giving collateral one creditor takes assets away from the general creditors. One loan becomes safer, but others become more risky. Why is the greater safety for the secured creditor not exactly offset by the greater risk borne by everyone else?

Jackson and Kronman drew on the work of Franco Modigliani and Merton Miller. Modigliani and Miller had shown that, once one makes a handful of simple assumptions, the value of a firm is independent of how much debt it carries relative to the amount of debt.[11] Jackson and Kronman applied the same logic to different layers of debt in the capital structure. If Modigliani and Miller irrelevance propositions held, a firm's value was independent of how much senior and junior debt it carried. To explain why secured credit made creditors as a group better off, Jackson and Kronman attempted to identify which of those axioms did not hold and to suggest how secured credit was therefore able to bring net benefits to the creditors as a group. Quite apart from the success for their own explanation, they opened lines of inquiry for many others.[12]

Looking at bankruptcy through the lens of corporate finance provides a clearer window onto large reorganization practice far better than using the flesh-and-blood individual and the small business as paradigms. In the typical modern large reorganization, business with trade creditors goes on as usual, tort victims are fully compensated, and workers are paid as before.[13] The only ones the reorganization affects are professional investors, most of whom acquired their positions only after the firm was already financially distressed. Importing the idea of sharing into cases in which hedge funds would be the only beneficiaries requires something more than homilies about fairness.

Senior creditors, junior creditors, and shareholders who hold diversified portfolios all receive the market return on their capital. This idea has taken hold among practitioners and judges. Consider the *Delphi* bankruptcy, where the bankruptcy judge pushed back against a debtor that favored a sale to a particular bidder. He asked, "What's so special about Platinum? They're just guys in suits. Why can't the other guys in suits just pay more?"[14] One would not have found this sort of language in an earlier era.

B. Agency Costs

Taking their cue from corporate finance, Jackson saw agency costs as one of the principal challenges a bankruptcy regime confronted.[15] The problem was not exactly the same in the bankruptcy as in corporate law. In corporate law, the principal agency problem was the one between the shareholders of large corporations and the professional managers who ran them. In Chapter 11, the interests of managers and shareholders, at least in the 1980s, seemed aligned in bankruptcy. Instead, the tension in bankruptcy was between senior and junior investors.

Seen through this lens, the ambition of bankruptcy is to ensure that the assets of the bankruptcy estate are put to their highest-valued use even as individual investors groups push for courses of action that advance their own interests. There are several ways to go about solving this problem. The initial instinct of Jackson and others was to follow the lead of corporate law scholars and focus on the residual owner.

Easterbrook and Fischel's pathbreaking work on corporate law argued that, when business is good, control over decision making ought to lie with shareholders. They usually stand to gain or lose from a given course of action because, when the firm is solvent, they are the residual owners with respect to most decisions.[16] The Bankruptcy Code is built around the idea that in the typical reorganization, the general creditors stand in a position analogous to the shareholders. The firm is worth enough to pay the senior creditors, but what remains is not enough to pay the general creditors in full. As a result, they are the firm's residual owners. They are the ones who stand to gain or lose, depending on whether the bankruptcy succeeds or fails.

For this reason, Jackson argued that the Bankruptcy Code should be interpreted to allow the general creditors to exercise control, provided that they take steps to ensure that those senior to them would be paid in full. By requiring general creditors to protect the senior creditors, bankruptcy law could ensure that, when the general creditors controlled the case, they were in fact the residual owners of the firm and thus possessed the right set of incentives.[17]

But the agency problem in bankruptcy cannot be solved merely by focusing on residual owners. The residual owners may be hard to identify, and, even if they can be identified, they will not necessarily be the general creditors. A particularly vivid example arose in the bankruptcy of the Central Ice Cream Co.[18]

The Central Ice Cream Company owed its general creditors about $12 million. It had closed its doors, and its only asset was a lawsuit against McDonald's. Central Ice Cream prevailed at trial and received a $52 million judgment. At this point, McDonald's made a settlement offer of $16 million. This presented a conflict between the general creditors and the shareholders. The general creditors are senior in the capital structure to shareholders, and, as one might expect, the general creditors of Central Ice Cream wanted the settlement offer accepted post haste. If Central Ice Cream took the offer, the general creditors would be paid the entire $12 million they were owed. By contrast, if Central turned it down, the judgment might be reversed on appeal and leave them with nothing.

The shareholders, again none too surprisingly, wanted the offer rejected. They would receive only $4 million if the settlement offer were accepted, but they would get $40 million if Central Ice Cream refused to settle and ultimately prevailed on appeal. Getting the $40 million was not certain, but risking $4 million to get $40 million with reasonable odds was a good bet.

Neither group will act with the interest of the other in mind. There is a tension here that is inherent in any enterprise that has a hierarchical capital structure, and this tension is magnified in bankruptcy as, by definition, there is not enough money to pay everyone in full. In many contemporary bankruptcies, this problem of identifying a single residual owner manifests itself. The tension typically, however, is not between general creditors and shareholders as in *Central Ice Cream*, but rather in other parts of the capital structure.

In many large corporations, there are multiple levels of secured debt. The residual claimant is somewhere among the secured creditors, but it is not clear exactly where. The general creditors should not be calling the shots, as they are out of the money, but it does not make sense to dismiss the bankruptcy entirely. Even though the Bankruptcy Code was not designed with such cases in mind, bankruptcy may be useful for sorting out problems among multiple tiers of secured creditors.

Indeed, bankruptcy's origins lie in part in equity receiverships of the nineteenth century, and these involved railroads that had almost exclusively secured debt in their capital structure. Having a reorganization that works exclusively for the benefit of the secured creditor is completely consistent with Chapter 11's roots. But one still needs to sort out the rights among the secured creditors and ensure that those in control have the right incentives.

These changes in capital structure became manifest by the start of the twenty-first century, and they had the effect of changing the way academics and lawyers thought about the agency problem. In the 1980s, it was assumed that the interests of the managers corresponded with the interests of shareholders even in bankruptcy. But in the typical large bankruptcy today, shareholders receive nothing at the end of the case, and managers have little incentive to pay any attention to them. Instead, the managers worry about their own reputations and pleasing those who will end up with control of the business at the end of the case.

Sorting out exactly how to think about this problem became an arena in which academics and practitioners engaged in vigorous debate.[19] Instead of focusing on Jackson's notion of empowering the residual owner, however, the debate shifted to finding the best way to account for the various biases of the different parties who can exercise control over the debtor.

The bankruptcy judge faces the largest challenges at the start of the case. Not all the players have been assembled. The secured creditor might be willing to advance the funds that the debtor needs to make the next day's payroll in exchange for various protections for its prepetition loan. The judge is the only one who can push back. If she does not push back hard enough, the junior investors are worse off. But if she pushes too hard, the secured creditor might refuse postpetition lending and the business might collapse.

There is no magic formula for solving such problems. Nevertheless, the basic approach remains one of ensuring that the agency problem is overcome and that the value of the firm as a whole is maximized. The tools that are used remain those of corporate finance.

C. Going-concern Sales

Those who shaped the law of corporate reorganizations generally assumed that actual sales were not possible. At the time the law of corporate reorganizations emerged in the late-nineteenth century, it was a reasonable assumption. The firms being reorganized were giant railroads. Even though they were financially distressed, the railroads had considerable value as going concerns. They operated on thousands of miles of track and were worth many millions of dollars. The capital markets of the day were not equipped to handle the sale of such large enterprises.

There was also a separate strand of bankruptcy practice that focused on the problems of small businesses. These were on the other end of the spectrum, but here too going-concern sales were not in the cards. These firms often had no identity separate from the owner-managers who ran them. They could not be sold as going concerns. Separating the manager from the business was tantamount to liquidating it.

For the generation of scholars who linked corporate reorganizations with corporate law more generally and who, in the first instance, looked to the market as a disciplining force, it was natural enough to revisit the question of whether actual sales were possible. If there was an actual sale of the firm in bankruptcy, the sale would transform the debtor's assets into cash, and this cash would be distributed to the creditors in exchange for their old claims against the firm. In a reorganization, the same thing happens, except that instead of cash, old creditors receive interests in the reorganized firm. The recognition of the connection between reorganizations and sale opened a new line of thought for those who followed in Jackson's footsteps.[20]

Once a reorganization is equated with an actual sale, it becomes clear that one of the central challenges in any reorganization is determining the value of the firm. When a firm is sold on the market, its value is the price that a buyer is willing and able to pay for it. The value of a firm sold in a hypothetical sale must be established through some other mechanism. One could, for example, value a firm by selling equity in the reorganized company in the marketplace.[21] If one knows the price equity can fetch on the market, it is possible to value the firm as a whole.

Alternatively, one could simply require a sale of the business outright for cash.[22] In the 1980s, in contrast to the late-nineteenth century, the capital markets were sufficiently robust to enable buyers to raise the necessary funds. Sales of firms as going concerns regularly took place outside of bankruptcy. If a large firm had value as a going concern, someone should be willing to buy it. Traditional bankruptcy lawyers feared that many firms would not find buyers if they were put up for auction. No one would be willing to buy them as going concerns, and they would have to be liquidated. But the inability to sell a firm as a going concern might simply show instead that the firm in fact had no value as a going concern.

If equity could not be floated or if the sale of the business was not possible, market mechanisms could still be used. The creditors could bid for the firm themselves. A junior creditor has what is, in effect, a right to buy out the senior creditor for the amount that the senior creditor is owed. The right to buy a piece of property at a fixed price at a fixed time is a right well understood in finance. It is a call option, and such call options are a component of every financial instrument. One can argue that, when a firm is in bankruptcy, the call option is the only attribute of a junior creditor's investment instrument that matters.

The junior creditors are entitled to the firm only if it is worth more than the senior creditors are owed. They have, what is in effect, a call option, and the exercise date of the call option is the date of the petition. It makes sense, therefore, to put junior creditors to their proof. If they are unwilling to buy out the senior creditors, their reluctance is powerful evidence that their claims on the firm have no value. Their call options are out of the money. One could structure reorganization law along these lines. The hypothetical sale mechanism, which required a judicial valuation, could be replaced with a process in which the junior investors had an opportunity to exercise their options.[23]

This mechanism relies on the forces of the market, but does not require a sale of the entire firm. There are a number of ways to import market mechanisms into valuations in Chapter 11, and quite a number were proposed.[24] Quite apart from whether these proposals were feasible as a practical matter, they had the effect of introducing the language of finance to discussions of bankruptcy policy.

At the same time that academics looked towards bringing market mechanisms into bankruptcy law, the number of going-concern sales in bankruptcy practice exploded. Bankruptcy practice became a mergers-and-acquisitions practice.[25] In part due to what seemed at the time a minor change in the Bankruptcy Rules, it became much easier to acquire claims in bankruptcy. Someone who wanted to become owner of a firm could acquire control of the class of debt that would allow it to gain control of the reorganization and put through a plan in which it would end up as the equityholder of the reorganized firm. Once the dust settled, there was little difference between such a person and someone who acquired a solvent company by making a tender offer for its equity.

The changes transformed bankruptcy by the end of the 1990s. Going-concern sales became commonplace in large Chapter 11 practice. Just as M&A lawyers became more familiar with modern finance, so too did Chapter 11 lawyers. The link between options and junior investors that became part of academic conversation in the 1980s became the lingua franca of reorganization lawyers by the end of the century.

Instead of debating whether going-concern sales were possible, the ground shifted to debating how they should be conducted. Nonbankruptcy sales of going concerns are far from being either instantaneous or costless. Sales in bankruptcy might be sometimes desirable, but not always. The market may be illiquid. The most likely purchasers of the firm may be other businesses in the same industry. When a firm is distressed, these other firms may be distressed as well. They may not have the resources to take part in an auction. When those who value the firm the most are not able to bid, the auction will not yield what the firm is worth.[26]

Even if an industry is flourishing and the potential buyers lie outside the industry, there is another problem that limits one's ability to sell a firm.[27] By the time a distressed firm is sold, the investors have organized themselves. They have hired experts and spent time reviewing and assessing the quality of the managers and their plans for the business going forward. As a result, they may know much more about the value of the business than any potential buyer. Buyers may fear that the firm is being sold only because the current owners know it is going to fail and want to rid themselves of a lemon.[28]

The illiquidity of the market and the presence of private information suggests that reorganization regimes should accommodate both going-concern sales as well as reorganizations. The Bankruptcy Code is sufficiently open-ended that it allowed such a dual regime to emerge, but little in the text of the Bankruptcy Code or traditional legal analysis offers much in the way of specific guidance. This has pushed academics and practitioners further from the doctrinal analysis that was the hallmark of traditional bankruptcy scholarship. When a firm is to be sold in Chapter 11, the answers to the question of which sale procedures were appropriate lie not in statutory interpretation of the Bankruptcy Code, but rather in the application of auction theory. Many controversies, such as whether there are fire sales in bankruptcy, become empirical questions.[29]

III. REASSESSING THE CREDITORS' BARGAIN

The contemporary bankruptcy judge is economically sophisticated. She is completely open to the possibility of market sales and completely at ease with how the tools of finance can be used to value firms. She is familiar with auction theory. Nevertheless, she must confront the reality that markets are imperfect and valuations are always approximate. The costs of bankruptcy itself can be staggering. In a large case such as *Energy Future Holdings*, the direct costs alone can exceed a billion dollars. For the latest generation of bankruptcy scholars, ensuring that the value of the estate's assets is maximized at the lowest cost is the major institutional objective of the law of corporate reorganizations.

Once one fixes on the cost of bankruptcy itself as the central problem, one might question the importance that Jackson and others gave to the nonbankruptcy baseline and the absolute priority rule.[30] Shifting the focus to the costs of bankruptcy, however, is completely consistent with the spirit of Jackson's creditors' bargain model. If bankruptcy costs loom large enough, creditors as part of the ex ante bargain will care about minimizing them, perhaps to the exclusion of other concerns.

A. Nonbankruptcy Priority

Jackson's approach to bankruptcy begins, as noted, with the idea that bankruptcy's first ambition is to recognize nonbankruptcy rights in bankruptcy's collective proceeding. But there is no exact parallel to bankruptcy in ordinary debt collection procedures, and this makes it hard to identify exactly what the nonbankruptcy rights are.

The common law made it hard for creditors to take priority over a debtor's assets. Before the Uniform Commercial Code, a creditor that wanted to take priority over another had to navigate multiple legal regimes for equipment, inventory, and accounts receivable. Even at the time the 1978 Bankruptcy Code was enacted, the typical firm did not have an institutional lender with a blanket security interest over all of its assets. There might be multiple secured creditors, each of whom held priority with respect to different assets. One secured creditor might have financed the purchase of a piece of equipment. Another might have made a loan on the basis of accounts receivable.

In such a world, each secured creditor enjoys a right to its collateral, but is not a stakeholder in the firm as a going concern. A secured creditor whose collateral is a discrete asset should not receive anything less than the value of this asset, but she should not receive anything more either. The value that the firm has as a going concern is not something to which she lays claim. The general creditors are entitled to the synergy created by bringing the various assets together, and, as long as they protect the secured creditor from declines in the value of her collateral, the general creditors are the ones entitled to whatever incremental value the firm has over and above the piecemeal liquidation value of the assets.

But in the four decades since the Bankruptcy Code was enacted, secured credit has been radically transformed. Lenders commonly attempt to take first priority positions in all of a firm's assets. From the perspective of finance, hierarchical capital structures are perfectly ordinary. That they need to be assembled in pieces is a bug, not a feature of nonbankruptcy law.

Creating priority by bundling security interests together presents a problem, however. There are always some assets in which secured creditors fail to take security interests. Mistakes are easy to make and obtaining priority in some types of assets is especially hard—intellectual property and government licenses being two conspicuous examples. In a nontrivial minority of cases, perhaps as much as twenty percent, there is an important asset in which the senior creditor does not have priority.

A key issue is what to do when these gaps appear. If one is tied to nonbankruptcy entitlements, it might seem that the structure of Anglo-American law reveals something fundamental about the nature of the senior position. For practitioners and academics of the old school, it validates their intuition that bankruptcy should not make life easy for those who seek seniority.[31] They remain tied to old notions that bankruptcy proceedings are equitable in nature, and they are pulled towards the idea that equality is a good in its own right.

For someone steeped in corporate finance, the defects in the collateral package are a sideshow. They should not play a role in how one thinks about how a sensible bankruptcy law should operate. Of course, if a senior creditor wants to acquire the entire firm in Chapter 11, she must contribute cash to make up for gaps in her collateral package. But the fact that her senior position is incomplete in one respect is not a justification for reallocating the going-concern value of the firm—the value that it has over-and-above the value of each of the discrete assets—to the junior creditors.

This gap between the way that seniority is conceived in finance and the way it plays out on the ground as a technical matter is of no great moment to the latest generation of bankruptcy academics, even if does stand in tension with Jackson's emphasis on nonbankruptcy entitlements. For them, the problem of corporate restructuring is not tied to specific features of Anglo-American law. It makes more sense to start with a coherent theory of the firm and of corporate finance. The challenge that still remains is reconciling Modigliani and Miller's irrelevance propositions with Coase's theory of the firm.

B. Absolute Priority and the Creditors' Bargain

The original purpose of the absolute priority rule was to protect unsophisticated outside investors. It was put in place in the 1930s over the objection of investment bankers and the lawyers who represented them. In those days, outsiders held the most senior positions. Government regulators at the SEC believed that these investors were subject to the mercy of insiders and investment bankers. To protect them, the law should ensure these investors were paid first in full, before anyone junior received anything. Only in this fashion would outsiders enjoy a fair return on their investment. The SEC tried to persuade the Supreme Court to interpret the bankruptcy law in this fashion, and it was successful in large part because the Court's newest Justice came from the SEC and had indeed pushed for this form of priority, absolute priority, while he was there.[32]

The rationale that absolute priority protects unsophisticated senior investors from advantage-taking makes no sense when one approaches reorganization law with an awareness of how well-functioning capital markets work. Investors take into account how they will be treated in bad states of the world and will demand an interest rate that protects them. As long as they buy and hold a diversified portfolio over the long term, they will enjoy at least the market rate of return, even if investment bankers and insiders appropriate assets during a restructuring. Indeed, the bondholders of the 1930s that the SEC thought needed protecting enjoyed above-market returns.[33]

Given its origins, the enthusiasm that Jackson and others had for the absolute priority might seem hard to fathom. But there are several reasons why they embraced it. The absolute priority rule follows naturally from their assumption that a bankruptcy reorganization is the equivalent of a nonbankruptcy sale. A sale by its nature is a recognition event. It collapses all future possibilities to the present and requires all positions to be cashed out and all accounts squared.

Absolute priority has other important virtues. It is simple. Moreover, it aligns ex ante incentives correctly. When junior investors have control and there is private information, they should bear the maximum losses in bad states of the world.[34] For these reasons, the absolute priority rule was a natural starting place.

At the time Jackson wrote, arguments against absolute priority tended to be oblique and sloppy. Rather than asking whether absolute priority was indeed part of the creditors' bargain, its critics offered what were ungrounded and sentimental arguments that gave lip service to absolute priority, but undermined it in practice. Many of these arguments were too clever by half, and were often made with a smug satisfaction that their cleverness had once again secured a win for the good guys against the forces of evil. Through the lens of finance, the impulse behind this style of argument was mystifying. In a world of professional investors holding diversified portfolios, it is incoherent to think that sharing losses equally is a good idea in its own right.

With respect to all of this, Jackson and contemporary bankruptcy scholars share common ground. Nevertheless, there are reasons not to accept absolute priority uncritically. Many nonbankruptcy restructurings are not treated as recognition events by those involved. When venture capitalists need to refinance a start-up, underwater interests are not cashed out. Venture capital contracts provide for dilution of junior interests in bad states of the world, not their extinction. Intercreditor agreements involving loans to mature corporations can and do provide for payments to such junior interests in the event of a restructuring through what are known as x-clauses.[35] One can make a respectable argument, firmly grounded in the creditors' bargain, in favor of a reorganization regime that recognizes the option value of junior interests.[36] This idea emerged from the academy in recent years and has quickly become part of the law reform agenda among judges and practitioners.[37] And all speak the language of finance.

CONCLUSION

Contemporary bankruptcy scholarship finds itself moving in two strikingly different directions. On the one hand, it is trying to sort out the dynamics of bankruptcy cases and understand the effects on the ground. It models new practices and engages in empirical inquiry. This approach is deeply connected to the day-to-day practice even though it is relatively removed from doctrine. At the same time, contemporary scholarship has returned to foundational debates. The law journals of the 1920s and 1930s were filled with arguments about optimal priority rules in bankruptcy. The difference, however, is that instead of informal discussion of vague ideas, it is now captured formally in the language of options and is firmly rooted in the creditors' bargain. In both enterprises, there is engagement with the practicing bar and the origins can be traced back to Thomas Jackson.

NOTES

1. Jackson's conception of bankruptcy is set forth in a one-volume monograph, a classic that still bears careful reading. See Thomas H. Jackson, *The Logic and Limits of Bankruptcy Law* (Harvard University Press 1986). Nothing in this retrospective look at Jackson's work, however, is intended to suggest that Jackson's contributions to bankruptcy are behind him. Among other things, he has been among the most compelling voices in debates about how bankruptcy law should govern the insolvency of systemically important financial institutions. On a personal note, I would be remiss not to acknowledge my own debt to Jackson, who first became my mentor while I was in law

school and whose insight and generous spirit has done much to illuminate my own work in the decades since. I also want to thank The Frank Greenberg Fund and the John M. Olin Fund for their research support.

2. Thomas H. Jackson, Bankruptcy, Non-Bankruptcy Entitlements, and the Creditors' Bargain, 91 Yale L.J. 857 (1982).
3. Indeed, Jackson's paper on the individual discharge in bankruptcy is one of the first examples of behavioral law and economics. See Thomas H. Jackson, The Fresh Start Policy in Bankruptcy Law, 98 Harv. L. Rev. 1393 (1985).
4. John D. Ayer, The New Face of Douglas Baird, 12 Am. Bankr. Inst. L. Rev. 101 (2004).
5. The National Bankruptcy Conference is a small group (never more than seventy) of bankruptcy lawyers, judges, and academics dedicated to bankruptcy reform. It meets at least once a year, and it has had a hand in all major bankruptcy legislation since the 1930s.
6. *Butner v. United States*, 440 U.S. 48 (1979). Some have questioned whether the case itself can bear the weight that Jackson and others placed on it. See, e.g., Barry E. Adler, The Questionable Axiom of *Butner v. United States*, in *Bankruptcy Law Stories* 11 (Robert K. Rasmussen, ed. 2007).
7. Id. at 55.
8. This approach, one that uses state law as its benchmark, now permeates judicial opinions. For an example of a court applying this methodology in the context of a common-law bailment, see In re Mississippi Valley Livestock, Inc., 745 F.3d 299 (7th Cir. 2014).
9. In re CMC Heartland Partners, 966 F.2d 1143 (7th Cir. 1992).
10. Thomas H. Jackson & Anthony T. Kronman, Secured Financing and Priorities Among Creditors, 88 Yale L.J. 1143 (1979).
11. Franco Modigliani & Merton H. Miller, The Cost of Capital, Corporation Finance and the Theory of Investment, 48 Am. Econ. Rev. 261, 268–71 (1958).
12. See, e.g., Barry E. Adler, An Equity-Agency Solution to the Bankruptcy-Priority Puzzle, 22 J. Legal Stud. 73 (1993); George Triantis, Secured Debt under Conditions of Imperfect Information, 21 J. Leg. Stud. 225 (1992).
13. There are, of course, some bankruptcy cases, particularly those involving mass torts, in which the players are not financial professionals. The appropriate treatment of such creditors spawned considerable debate. There is, however, more or less agreement on the need to provide tort victims and the like with priority. The fighting issue is whether the priority should be located in nonbankruptcy law or should be a special bankruptcy policy. For Jackson and those who followed him, the former course made the most sense. For a lively debate joining this issue, see Elizabeth Warren, Bankruptcy Policy, 54 U. Chi. L. Rev. 775 (1987); Douglas G. Baird, Loss Distribution, Forum Shopping, and Bankruptcy: A Reply to Warren, 54 U. Chi. L. Rev. 815 (1987). The fighting issue in Delaware has been the conditions under which creditors can challenge the decision making of the board.
14. See Peter Lattman, Judge Orders Auction in a Rebuke to Delphi Plan, *Wall Street Journal*, June 12, 2009.
15. The foundational paper in corporate finance on agency costs remains Michael C. Jensen & William H. Meckling, Theory of the Firm: Managerial Behavior, Agency Costs and Ownership Structure, 3 J. Fin. Econ. 305 (1976).
16. These are set out in Frank H. Easterbrook & Daniel R. Fischel, *The Economic Structure of Corporate Law* (Harvard University Press 1991). The book brings together the core insights laid out in a series of articles in the early 1980s.
17. Douglas G. Baird & Thomas H. Jackson, Corporate Reorganizations and the Treatment of Diverse Ownership Interests: A Comment on Adequate Protection of Secured Creditors in Bankruptcy, 51 U. Chi. L. Rev. 97, 108 (1984).
18. In re Central Ice Cream Co., 836 F.2d 1068 (7th Cir. 1987). The same tension can exist in corporate law as well, and it is for this reason that Central Ice Cream led the courts in Delaware to revise the standard view that directors were obliged to maximize the value of

the shareholders' stake in the firm to the modern view that they are obliged to maximize the value of the firm for the benefit of all the stakeholders. See *Credit Lyonnais Bank Nederland, N.V. v. Pathe Commc'ns Corp.*, No. 12150, 1991 WL 277613 (Del. Ch. Dec. 30, 1991); *Quadrant Structured Products Co. v. Vertin*, 102 A.3d 155 (Del. Ch. 2014).

19. Douglas G. Baird & Robert K. Rasmussen, The End of Bankruptcy, 55 Stan. L. Rev. 751 (2002); Harvey R. Miller, Shai Y. Waisman, Does Chapter 11 Reorganization Remain A Viable Option for Distressed Businesses for the Twenty-First Century?, 78 Am. Bankr. L.J. 153, 153 (2004).
20. The idea of using a hypothetical sales as a paradigm for thinking about corporate reorganizations advanced by Jackson can be traced to Robert C. Clark, The Interdisciplinary Study of Legal Evolution, 90 Yale L.J. 1238, 1250–54 (1981).
21. Mark J. Roe, Bankruptcy and Debt: A New Model for Corporate Reorganization, 83 Colum. L. Rev. 527 (1983).
22. Douglas G. Baird, The Uneasy Case for Corporate Reorganizations, 15 J. Legal Stud. 127 (1986).
23. Lucian Bebchuk, A New Approach to Corporate Reorganizations, 101 Harv. L. Rev. 775 (1988).
24. See, e.g., Philippe Aghion, Oliver Hart & John Moore, The Economics of Bankruptcy Reform, 8 J.L. Econ. & Org. 523 (1992); Barry E. Adler & Ian Ayres, A Dilution Mechanism for Valuing Corporations in Bankruptcy, 111 Yale L.J. 83 (2001).
25. For a colorful account of the battle for Marvel Entertainment between Ronald Perelman and Carl Icahn while it was in Chapter 11, see Dan Raviv, *Comic Wars: How Two Tycoons Battled over the Marvel Comics Empire—And Both Lost* (Broadway 2002).
26. Shleifer and Vishny developed this explanation for the way in which illiquidity can limit the effectiveness of sales. Andrei Shleifer & Robert W. Vishny, Liquidation Values and Debt Capacity: A Market Equilibrium Approach, 47 J. Fin. 1343 (1992).
27. This justification for reorganizations sometimes being superior to sales is put forward in Douglas G. Baird & Donald S. Bernstein, Absolute Priority, Valuation Uncertainty, and the Reorganization Bargain, 115 Yale L.J. 1930, 1949 (2006).
28. For the iconic discussion of this problem, using the example of used cars that are "lemons," see generally George A. Akerlof, The Market for "Lemons": Quality Uncertainty and the Market Mechanism, 84 Q.J. Econ. 488 (1970).
29. Kenneth Ayotte & Edward R. Morrison, Creditor Control and Conflict in Chapter 11, 1 J. Legal Analysis 511 (2009).
30. See, e.g., Douglas G. Baird & Thomas H. Jackson, Bargaining After the Fall and the Contours of the Absolute Priority Rule, 55 U. Chi. L. Rev. 738 (1988).
31. See, e.g., Edward J. Janger, The Logic and Limits of Liens, 2015 U. Ill. L. Rev. 589, 612.
32. For a discussion of this history, see Douglas G. Baird, Present at the Creation: The SEC and the Origins of the Absolute Priority Rule, 18 Am. Bankr. L. Rev. 591 (2010).
33. W. Braddock Hickman, Corporate Bond Quality and Investor Experience 338, 509 (Princeton Univ. Press 1958).
34. See, e.g., Alan Schwartz, Bankruptcy Contracting Reviewed, 109 Yale L.J. 343 (1999).
35. See, e.g., In re Metromedia Fiber Network, Inc., 416 F.3d 136, 139–40 (2d Cir. 2005).
36. See Anthony J. Casey, The Creditors' Bargain and Option-Preservation Priority in Chapter 11, 78 U. Chi. L. Rev. 759, 765 (2011).
37. See Am. Bankr. Institute, Commission to Study the Reform of Chapter 11 2012–2014: Final Report and Recommendations, 207–24 (2014).

EDITOR'S NOTES

Professor Baird's foreword attributes much of modern bankruptcy scholarship, including the contributions of this volume, to a paradigm created by Thomas Jackson. This observation is proper and is echoed by the Introduction that follows. But Baird is too modest.

In addition to his redoubtable individual work in bankruptcy law, contracts law, and beyond, Baird was a frequent co-author with Jackson of articles that established and inhabited the Jacksonian bankruptcy framework. One needs no more evidence of Baird's importance to the field than the numerous citations to Baird's work in the chapters of this book.

Introduction to the *Research Handbook on Corporate Bankruptcy Law*

Barry E. Adler

More than thirty years ago, Thomas Jackson wrote *The Logic and Limits of Bankruptcy Law*, which describes bankruptcy as the implementation of a hypothetical bargain among creditors. Under the terms of such a bargain, bankruptcy's automatic stay on each creditor's individual collection rights prohibits a potentially destructive grab race and allows for a collectivized proceeding that can maintain a debtor's going-concern value for the benefits of the creditors as a group. Among both academics and practitioners, Jackson's hypothetical bargain has become the dominant paradigm in assessing bankruptcy, a true feat for a scholarly work.

Much has changed since Jackson wrote his classic treatise, particularly in the world of large-firm corporate bankruptcy, which is the primary focus of this handbook. Creditors have taken control of the corporate reorganization process, previously the domain of debtor management (the "debtor in possession" or "DIP"). Creditor control has been solidified over time by an expanded use of secured credit and prebankruptcy contractual arrangements that allow principal creditors to speak with a single voice in the bankruptcy process.

To the extent honored by the bankruptcy courts, such coordination among principal creditors largely replaces Jackson's hypothetical creditors' bargain with an actual bargain. That actual bargain has important consequences for the bankruptcy process including a financial stranglehold that restricts a bankruptcy court's ability to have the process fully honor the entitlement of creditors not part of the coalition. Full adherence to entitlement—known in some contexts as "absolute priority"—has, thus, become difficult to achieve for new reasons. Now, it is dominant creditors who may manage bankruptcy for their own advantage while in the past it was the debtor's shareholders who, despite holding options that were out of the money, had their managers run the bankruptcy process toward achieving some return to equity.

Another consequence of principal creditor coordination in bankruptcy is that large-firm debtors are today, more than in the past, sold in bankruptcy. Fewer firms now undergo traditional reorganization, with new claims and interests issued against the debtor's assets. In principle, this trend toward market resolution of financial distress can cure valuation problems that plagued traditional reorganization. But control of the process still matters because the sale of a large, complex company, such as automakers, for example, are not as simple as depicted on a law professor's chalk board (or PowerPoint slide). The auction process—how assets are marketed and to whom—can determine winners and losers and so there is a new front in the bankruptcy battles, one not typically fought back when Jackson first wrote on the topic.

More than just bankruptcy practice has changed; the economy has changed as well in ways that affect corporate bankruptcy. Large corporations have become increasingly global, rendering more important the international coordination of bankruptcy laws.

Also, as we learned painfully more than a decade ago, enormous financial institutions such as bank holding companies have become too big safely to fail and yet vulnerable to failure. This dangerous circumstance prompted Congress to pass the Dodd-Frank Act, which both regulates systemically important financial institutions ("SIFIs") and provides for their demise, including through bankruptcy. Such regulation, considered onerous by some, and the systemic consequences of bankruptcy for such debtors has prompted proposed deregulation in the Financial Choice Act and a proposed special chapter of the Bankruptcy Code for SIFIs in the Financial Institutions Bankruptcy Act. Although Congress enacted modest revision in 2018, an overhaul of Dodd-Frank is currently in limbo at least until the 2020 federal elections. Any such overhaul could have dramatic consequences for the failure of large financial institutions.

A related change in recent years is the burgeoning market for derivatives, which can be described, though not entirely accurately, as bets on the future value of securities and commodities. As financial, and other, large firms heavily issue or invest in these derivatives, exposure to market changes becomes acute, enhancing the risk and suddenness of collapse beyond what could have been imagined years ago when financial firms more simply transformed maturity while industrial firms were seen more simply as manufacturers and sellers of goods and services. Bankruptcy law has changed to account for the growth of derivatives but it's not clear the change has been for the better.

The chapters of this handbook touch on all these changes, as well as on other matters. That said, the chapters are not fundamentally chronologies or histories. Where relevant, each chapter provides the reader with a comparison between its topic today and in the past. But most of the chapters are centrally current analyses of their topics. Through the use of past as prologue, this volume is intended to be, in part, an update to the Jacksonian paradigm, which, while still relevant, has changed with the times.

In the book's Chapter 1, *Bankruptcy Logic and Limits in the 21st Century: Some Thoughts on Chapter 11's Evolution and Future*, Tom Jackson traces the past and predicted future of corporate bankruptcy, addressing many of the issues already discussed in this Introduction, including the application of the creditors' bargain model to systemically important financial institutions. The content of this chapter, which was drafted prior to the recent legislative developments mentioned above, has already proven influential.

Next, Chapter 2, Robert Rasmussen's *The End of Bankruptcy Revisited* also traces the history of corporate bankruptcy, emphasizing the shift from a debtor-driven reorganization process to a creditor-driven auction block. In this chapter, Rasmussen updates an influential series of articles he wrote on the topic with Douglas Baird, a long-time co-author of Rasmussen (and, separately, of Jackson).

In Chapter 3, *Bankruptcy Sales*, Melissa Jacoby and Ted Janger take on the much-debated issue of whether auctions in the practice of modern corporate bankruptcy are properly structured to maximize the debtor's value and to honor absolute priority among a debtor's claims and interests. The authors suggest that the current system is less than ideal but possible to reform.

Chapter 4 is David Skeel's *The New Synthesis of Bank Regulation and Bankruptcy in the Dodd-Frank Era*. This chapter, the title of which is largely self-explanatory, expands on Jackson's original insights and explores the perhaps vanishing distinctions between the resolution of bank and industrial firm financial distress.

In Chapter 5, *Derivatives and Repos in Bankruptcy*, Mark Roe explores the brave new world of bankrupt debtors, potentially including bank debtors, and their network of counterparties, saddled by obligations on derivatives. Among other matters, Roe speculates that the Bankruptcy Code's treatment of derivatives has been in approach exactly backwards.

Chapter 6, Richard Squire's *Distress-Triggered Liabilities and the Agency-Cost of Debt*, continues with the derivatives' theme and explains how investors in these instruments can manipulate risk to gain advantage over others in a firm's insolvency. Squire describes how the prospect of such strategic behavior creates perverse incentives.

The next two chapters address the modern fundamentals of what might be described as durational bankruptcy issues. Were the corporate bankruptcy process to begin and end in the same instant, no special rules would be required for the management and finance of the debtor during the bankruptcy process and this would be so whether the process reorganized a debtor's capital structure or sold its assets and distributed the proceeds. In fact, however, bankruptcy takes time. To preserve a debtor's potential going-concern value for the duration of the process, assets may need protection from piecemeal liquidation by creditor collection. (This is, as noted, central to Jackson's hypothetical bargain among creditors.) And the business of the debtor must be financed (referred to as "DIP" finance) so that the debtor can continue until disposition.

In Chapter 7, *On the Mandatory Stay of Secured Creditors in Bankruptcy*, Kenneth Ayotte newly considers, and critiques, the merits of bankruptcy's automatic stay as protection against a creditor grab race. In Chapter 8, *Debtor-in-Possession Financing in Bankruptcy*, George Triantis updates his own pioneering work on DIP finance, which is carefully assessed on efficiency terms.

Continuing the theme of efficiency, the following two chapters summarize and enter a debate on what may be the central question brought to the fore by recent changes, and proposed changes, in the bankruptcy process, namely: Should corporate bankruptcy honor traditional notions of absolute priority? In Chapter 9, Anthony Casey and Ed Morrison's *Beyond Options*, and in Chapter 10, Michelle J. White's *The Treatment of Secured Credit in Bankruptcy*, the authors respectively explain why they believe the traditional answer of simply "yes" is insufficiently nuanced.

Chapter 11, Michael Simkowic's *Making Fraudulent Conveyance Law More Predictable*, also addresses absolute priority, but in the indirect context of fraudulent conveyance laws, which along with related rules on voidable preferences, importantly determine priority in fact. In this chapter, Simkovic takes a new look at these rules.

The next chapters address an important current controversy on the direct and indirect costs of the bankruptcy process. In Chapter 12, *The Costs of Corporate Bankruptcy: How Little We Know*, Stephen Lubben summarizes and assesses the current evidence on the direct costs of corporate bankruptcy proceedings, while in Chapter 13, *The Chrysler and General Motors Bankruptcies*, Todd Zywicki uses the U.S. automaker cases to illustrate what he views as a costly manipulation of the bankruptcy process (including indirect costs as a result of deviations from absolute priority).

Chapter 14, John Pottow's *Cross-Border Corporate Insolvency in the Era of Soft(ish) Law*, shifts focus from exclusively U.S. bankruptcy cases to cross-border cases. In this chapter, Pottow takes account of increasing globalization to update a longstanding debate between universalists and territorialists on choice-of-law. Since this chapter was drafted, the United Nations Commission on International Trade Law ("UNCITRAL") has supplemented its Model Law on Cross-border Insolvency, discussed in the chapter, with The Model Law on the Recognition and Enforcement of Insolvency-related Judgments. The supplement is consistent with, and evinces the insights of, the approach to cross-border insolvency described in the chapter.

The final chapter of the book is a thought experiment by a leading bankruptcy theorist. In Chapter 15, *Bankruptcy Related Contracting and Bankruptcy Functions*, Alan Schwartz compares statutory rule to contractual alternatives and imagines how the world might change if the former were altered so that bankruptcy law addressed only those functions creditors need as determined by the capital structures that debtors adopt. This chapter questions the premises of the Jacksonian creditors' bargain and serves also as a rebuttal of sorts to earlier chapters that question the efficacy of absolute priority. The role of contract in bankruptcy is a topic to which Schwartz has importantly contributed in the past, but in this chapter he adds significant new observations.

1. Bankruptcy's logic and limits in the 21st century: some thoughts on Chapter 11's evolution and future

*Thomas H. Jackson**

I. INTRODUCTION

Now past the second decade of the 21st century, it is a sobering reminder that the Bankruptcy Code of 1978—the just-enacted statute when I first taught bankruptcy law in 1978–79—is beyond its 40th year. In recent U.S. history, that has been the life-cycle of significant bankruptcy enactments: The 1898 Bankruptcy Act; the 1938 Chandler Act; and, of course, the Bankruptcy Code of 1978. In many ways, one might have thought that the Bankruptcy Code of 1978 would be even *more* overdue for an overhaul, since bankruptcy has become, since 1978, a major topic for academic scholarship in a way that was not true (at least for an extended period) before, as well as a major growth area not just for "boutique" bankruptcy firms, but the country's major law firms as well.[1] More irons in the fire; more opportunities—or pressures—for reform.

Yet, while the Bankruptcy Code of 1978 has had several significant amendments, mostly in the area of consumer debtors[2]—and, on the business side, in qualified financial contracts[3]—there seems to be little urgency to engage in the kind of wholesale re-imagining of bankruptcy law that resulted in the major legislations of 1898, 1938, and 1978. I attribute that to three things (and from here on, I'm going to be focusing particularly on firms, not consumers, and their use of bankruptcy[4]). First, the growing experience and precedent by the time of the enactment of the 1978 Bankruptcy Code: It was, in many respects, a "mature" legal area. Second, the generally bipartisan nature of the enactment of the Bankruptcy Code of 1978[5] that is unlikely to be replicated any time soon and that dampens responsible calls for reform. Third, and perhaps most important, the remarkable *de facto* change in bankruptcy practice that has occurred since 1978 *within* the structure of the Bankruptcy Code of 1978, and particularly reorganization practice, that has been blessed by the courts. Unlike the 1898 Act (our first "permanent" bankruptcy law), the 1938 Chandler Act (the formalization of corporate reorganizations, together with its bifurcation and insertion of the Securities and Exchange

Commission into Chapter X for larger companies), and the 1978 Code (essentially, reversing both that bifurcation *and* the role of the SEC),[6] there is no looming *structural* reason to replace the Bankruptcy Code of 1978. That Code has shown an ability to adapt, within its existing statutory structure, to a number of major academic and practitioner developments since 1978, particularly in the use of going-concern sales and the reliance on market valuations in the context of Chapter 11.

As one who engaged—intensively—in scholarship following the Bankruptcy Code of 1978 for what now seems a remarkably brief period,[7] then largely was absent from the discussion and debate for essentially 20 years, I would like to accomplish several things in this piece. First, is to reflect on the original premises that framed my work. Second, to discuss three academic developments that took issue with, as well as (sometimes) built on those premises, and their relevance to issues we face today. Third, to note the rather remarkable change in reorganization practice that suggests that while those premises never won the legislative war, a number of them essentially overtook reorganization practice.[8] Fourth, to note the continued relevance of those premises to current issues—specifically, focusing on the treatment of qualified financial contracts in bankruptcy and on the role that bankruptcy law might play in the resolution of systemically important financial institutions. And, with the latter, I suggest that the ability of Chapter 11, originally designed as a negotiation framework that studiously avoided the market, to largely absorb market-based ideas through going-concern sales, may also have the ability today to absorb—or converge with—the contractarian proponents who powerfully argue that, for many firms, one can recapitalize a firm facing financial difficulties without needing bankruptcy. My conclusion then attempts to generalize from this analysis and imagine the statutory reforms that might currently be necessary or desirable. Perhaps because we do not need a major *structural* change, wholesale revision of our bankruptcy system is probably unnecessary in or around 2018—which may be a good thing given the unlikelihood of the replication of the generally bipartisan nature of the work that led to the 1978 Bankruptcy Code[9]—there may be a need to both codify, and place intelligent constraints around, generally welcome judicial developments since 1978 as well as realistically enact provisions making bankruptcy more suitable for financial institutions and what has been called the "new finance." One need not reinvent the wheel to recognize that bankruptcy will always be a "work in progress" (a good thing for bankruptcy scholars!). At the same time, we can applaud the flexibility that has been shown to have been built into the 1978 Bankruptcy Code, together with the impact, over time, of bankruptcy scholarship on bankruptcy practice under that Code, including judicial decisions.

II. THE PREMISES BEHIND "THE LOGIC AND LIMITS OF BANKRUPTCY LAW" INSOFAR AS IT CONCERNED FIRMS

Since my focus is on the role of bankruptcy for firms, I set aside the important, but in my view, wholly independent, "fresh start" policy for individuals.[10] Using "fresh start" to describe bankruptcy policy for both individuals and firms is unfortunate in the confusion it engenders—because they mean fundamentally different things. For individuals, the core of the fresh-start policy concerns the debtor keeping assets from exiting creditors.[11] For firms, a fresh-start policy means something entirely different: It means ensuring that financial failure does not lead to inappropriate liquidation.[12] But the "debtor" (often a corporate charter) does not get to free-up assets from its preexisting claimants and interest holders.

My focus here is on firms—paradigmatically, corporations—in financial distress,[13] and not just *all* corporations, but those with more than a single claim or interest holder.[14] In that context, my work started with the question of why bankruptcy law was needed at all, given that we already had a defined and robust mechanism for debt collection outside of bankruptcy, and answered that question by seeing multiple creditors going after a debtor's assets during a time of insolvency (or potential insolvency)—when the order in which one "reached" assets would matter in terms of recovery—as a form of a collective action problem:

> The grab rules of nonbankruptcy law and their allocation of assets on the basis of first-come, first-served create an incentive on the part of the individual creditors, when they sense that a debtor may have more liabilities than assets, to get in line today (by, for example, getting a sheriff to execute on the debtor's equipment), because if they do not, they run the risk of getting nothing. This decision by numerous individual creditors, however, may be the wrong decision for the creditors as a group. Even though the debtor is insolvent, they might be better off if they held the assets together. Bankruptcy provides a way to make these diverse individuals act as one, by imposing a *collective* and *compulsory* proceeding on them. Unlike a typical common pool solution, however, the compulsory solution of bankruptcy law does not apply in all places at all times. Instead, it runs parallel with a system of individual debt-collection rules and is available to supplant them when and if needed.[15]

This analogy—and description—is, however, by itself, incomplete. To be sure, like most common pool examples—fishing in a lake or drilling for oil—it is a solution designed to separate what to do with assets from the question of who owns the assets. In doing that, it is also necessary to distinguish economic failure (the assets should be doing something else)—classically a liquidation—from financial failure (the assets are doing just what they should be doing, but one needs to keep them from being pulled apart because of the incentives of creditors when a firm has too much debt (financial insolvency). At the time of writing, and still today, a classic example of this is Johns Manville's 1982 bankruptcy. Manville was hopelessly insolvent at that time, due to significant, but latent, tort liability for asbestosis products manufactured by Manville during and after the Second World War. But, at the time of its bankruptcy, Manville didn't produce asbestos-based products and, as far as one could tell, seemed to be a successful building supply company, whose assets were put to their highest and best use. But without a collective remedy such as bankruptcy, Manville would have been destroyed, turning the financial failure into the wrong asset-deployment decision.[16]

While that is one goal of bankruptcy, captured well by the imagery of a common pool, that imagery is incomplete in that there is a second feature of bankruptcy, also derived from its multiple ownership claims against a common pool of assets, but distinguished from most common pool problems by the fact that the multiple ownership claims have, themselves, different priority rights. The one of most interest for bankruptcy law is the distinction between debt and equity. The equity interests, who have the legal characteristic not only of claiming 100 percent of the value of the firm in excess of its liabilities but also suffering no further liability beyond the loss of the value of their interests once the firm is, in fact, insolvent. For clearly solvent companies, the equity interests legally are, and should be, the relevant decision-makers as to what to do with the assets.[17] But for insolvent companies,[18] equity interests are unlikely to make decisions that are in the interests of the owners (debt as well as equity) as a group. The economic incentives of equity interests in an insolvent company is to take excessive risks, since the equity interests do not have anything to lose, and a fair amount to gain, by such strategy. While it is possible to shift the decision-making interests from equity interests to creditors without a collective proceeding such as bankruptcy—and one would want to do so even if there were not multiple creditors where there was the risk of a common pool race—since bankruptcy is designed to handle the common situation of multiple creditors, it makes perfect sense to also have it be a mechanism for the transfer of decision-making rights (and equity ownership) from the old equity interests to the creditors.[19]

Since both of these notions—one central to bankruptcy law's existence, the other a logical corollary to the use of bankruptcy law, so created—serve the interests of creditors, I originally described bankruptcy as a "creditors' bargain."[20] In retrospect, although the imagery was correct, the term was infelicitous. It could be—and often was—taken as a bias in favor of creditors over debtors or other interests.[21] At some level, that was never true. In the corporate context, creditors are the only ones with relevant ownership claims vis-à-vis an insolvent entity. And non-ownership "interests," as I address next, involve a nuanced understanding of rights under nonbankruptcy law.[22]

What *is* correct is that I saw bankruptcy law for firms as limited to the two purposes noted above, and not as a forum to give rights to parties that would not have such rights outside of bankruptcy.[23] If workers, or a town, could not (legally) object to a firm with a single owner from shutting down, or moving operations, it struck me as *a fortiori* that the fact that bankruptcy was instituted to solve a collective action problem meant that it was an inappropriate forum to give those workers, or a town, a say in what was to be done with the debtor's assets.

This original vision—both in its positive nature (bankruptcy's "logic") and in its insistence on narrowly hewing to those purposes (bankruptcy's "limits"), ultimately spawned three distinct developments. First, there was—and remains today—a strong push-back against the view that bankruptcy was so limited. This is probably best framed, and remembered, in the now-classic "debate" between my occasional co-author, Douglas Baird, and Professor (now Senator) Elizabeth Warren.[24] I, stubbornly, continue to view this response as fundamentally wrong, and will develop that argument in Part IV of this chapter.

Second, there was a growing movement that markets could do much of what Chapter 11 was designed to do—value assets and decide on their optimal deployment—better than the lengthy negotiations that dominated the early days of Chapter 11.[25]

Third, and coming at this from a related but nonetheless distinct direction, scholars raised the question as to whether bankruptcy, even infused with market-oriented features, was needed at all, or rather the identified issues could be solved by other contractual devices.[26] For example, scholars proposed using convertible debt ("bail-in debt") that would be converted to equity upon certain triggering events related to potential insolvency, as a way of both solving the issue of optimal decision-making and, at least some of the time, the issue of financial failure not leading to inappropriate economic failure.[27] I agree with much of this work, and indeed think it is enjoying a renaissance today in light of the current discussion about the appropriate resolution mechanism for systemically important financial institutions, but also both think its advantages over bankruptcy are muted by finding the appropriate trigger as well as not really ultimately opposed to bankruptcy as much as a new tool that can make bankruptcy more productive and efficient.[28] I will develop that argument, particularly in conjunction with bankruptcy as a resolution mechanism for systemically important financial institutions, in Part VI of this chapter.

III. THE IMPACT OF THE THINKING BEHIND THE LOGIC AND LIMITS OF BANKRUPTCY LAW ON BANKRUPTCY LAW AND PRACTICE

As David Skeel correctly observed in 2001, "[a]lthough the law and economics proposals have had little legislative influence, market forces play an increasingly prominent role in the Chapter 11 process, as law and economics scholars have long advocated."[29] The Bankruptcy Code, itself, shows little change in its major provisions since its enactment in 1978 that can be attributed to any of the ideas I advanced. Indeed, in a number of respects, the changes that were made since then were more likely setbacks rather than advances. (I think here, particularly, of the writing into the Bankruptcy Code of numerous special, bankruptcy-only, protections for counterparties on qualified financial contracts.[30]) And, many prominent arguments I advanced fared little better in authoritative constructions of the Bankruptcy Code's statutory provisions. For example, I was a strong advocate for the idea that, as a part of adequate protection, secured creditors were entitled to compensation for the time value of money (an issue of some prominence in the early 1980s, and a time of high inflation). I even wrote an amicus brief in *Timbers of Inwood Forest* to make the argument,[31] complete with reasoning as to why it was the preferred way of reading the relevant statutory sections. The argument, and the reasoning underlying it, went nowhere (at least, a 9–0 loss at the Supreme Court sure looks as though the argument went nowhere).[32]

But in other respects—more incremental (as case law tends to be)—some of the arguments made by academics such as myself began to be reflected in changes in Chapter 11 practice. As originally designed by the Bankruptcy Code, Chapter 11 was clearly intended as a framework for negotiation, overseen by a bankruptcy judge who would be deciding important issues of rights, and valuations (both of assets and of claims).[33] The ownership shift from equity to creditors occurred, if at all, only at the end[34]—a notion sharply reinforced by extended "exclusivity" periods during which time only the debtor-in-possession could file a plan of reorganization.[35] The idea of what a "class" of claimants could agree to, and what protections a dissenting member of that class might be entitled to, was driven by a strong distinction between a "going concern" value and a "liquidation" value.[36] Indeed, this distinction was thought to be at the center of the negotiations over a plan.

I suggested this model was wrong:

> The key conceptual difference between a reorganization and a liquidation is that in a reorganization the firm's assets (or most of them) are sold to the creditors

> themselves rather than to third parties. The principal distinction is *not* that the assets are kept together in a reorganization; they can be kept together in a chapter 7 liquidation proceeding as well if they are sold as a unit to a third-party buyer.[37]

Because of that, I suggested that the principal difference was that, in the third-party sale, the asset valuation issues were far easier to determine than in the situation of the assets being "sold" to the creditors themselves in a negotiated plan. "It is principally these valuation issues that lie at the core of the reorganization chapter's provisions."[38] And I went further and suggested that the distinction between the rights of a class and the rights of a dissenting creditor were unlikely to be nearly as large as seemed to be contemplated by the 1978 Bankruptcy Code itself:

> "the extra value attributable to selling the business back to the prebankruptcy claimants is the difference in the value of the firm owned by them and what a third party would be willing to pay for it. . . . It is improper, even accepting this rationale for the reorganization process, to establish the baseline protection for an individual claimant as that of a piecemeal liquidation standard."[39]

From this, I made the (then) somewhat radical suggestion that the negotiation framework of Chapter 11 caused far more problems than it solved. Building off an idea by Mark Roe that proposed requiring a Chapter 11 reorganization to make a stock issuance to the public of 10 percent of the total stock the firm will ultimately issue, so as to gain a market valuation that would drive the distribution of those proceeds, and the remaining stock, to the prebankruptcy claimants in accordance with their priority entitlements,[40] I suggested one could eliminate Chapter 11 entirely and rely exclusively on Chapter 7:

> The premises for negotiation in a Chapter 11 process seem unproven and unpromising. Roe is probably correct in suggesting that they should be eliminated. Once that point is reached, however, there seems to be no remaining justification for Chapter 11 at all . . . . There is no reason why Chapter 7 could not be used as the vehicle to sell the firm as a going concern in the same way that companies go public. The assets of the firm could be transferred to a new corporation. This new corporation could have a capital structure placed on it. A public offering of the shares in the various classes of that corporation could then be made. Such a solution avoids the interclass conflicts about distribution that pervade Chapter 11.. .[41]

At the time, the idea seemed far-fetched (or, perhaps, heretical).[42] And, it had no influence on the statutory provisions themselves. As written, the Bankruptcy Code provisions regarding Chapter 11 look much the same today as they did upon enactment in 1978. But there *was* a revolution of practice. Whether in response to creative lawyering, academic criticism, or judicial awareness—or, very probably, all three—while the formal structure of the Bankruptcy Code of 1978 as it applied to reorganizations, did not change in significant respects, practices pursuant to it did.[43] Creditors began to push for "going-concern sales" of the firm—and hence for market-based valuations of the assets of the firm. A general bankruptcy provision, almost certainly originally thought to apply generally in Chapter 7 and to the sale of stray, unwanted, assets in Chapter 11,[44] began to be used in Chapter 11 as a vehicle for the sale of the firm as a whole.[45] Almost simultaneously—and indeed, in a practical sense, related—lenders began to exert increasing control over the case by including stringent covenants in their loan agreements with the debtor. Indirectly and at times directly, these covenants effectively cut back on a debtor's exclusivity period.

Together, these two changes had several dramatic effects. First and foremost, they severed the decision about what to do with the assets from the fights over how to distribute the value of those assets. The assets could now be sold early in a bankruptcy process, even while some fights over the validity of claims or priorities had not yet been resolved.[46] Second, and equally important, they substituted judicial valuations of the assets with market valuations. If the assets were worth more alive than dead, it was expected that the market bids would reflect this. And, finally, without asset valuations to fight about, there was no longer much room to argue about the impact of the decision concerning what to do with assets or workers or the community. A shift in practice had accomplished what market-based proponents had been unable to accomplish through legislative input.

IV. REFLECTIONS ON THE CURRENT USES (AND POTENTIAL USES) AND ABUSES OF BANKRUPTCY: THE CONTINUING RELEVANCE OF THE "LOGIC" AS WELL AS THE "LIMITS" OF BANKRUPTCY LAW

I would like to examine, from the perspective of my work now 30 years ago, as well as some of the trends I have commented on, how I believe that analysis, incorporating, of course, important work since that time, can help us understand and design a bankruptcy system that accommodates what David Skeel and I called "the new finance in bankruptcy," through a brief examination of what *The Logic and Limits of Bankruptcy Law*[47] might have to say about the "new finance" of qualified financial contracts (repos, swaps, and derivatives) and about the optimal way to resolve systemically important financial institutions while minimizing spill-over effects to other institutions. The first relies on understanding, in context, the attributes of "new" forms of contracts, such as repos, swaps, and derivatives; here, as before, there is an enormous amount to learn by a careful analysis of the nonbankruptcy attributes of things that are being transported into the bankruptcy forum. The second draws on the insights, and subsequent development in practice, of a Chapter 11 proceeding as involving a going-concern sale of assets, together with the strategic advantages of using, in bankruptcy, contractarian ideas such as convertible securities as both aiding in the process and providing a regulatory trigger mechanism.

Before turning to those, however, I would like to start with a cautionary tale about how the perennial perspective concerning how bankruptcy serves nonbankruptcy goals, such as job preservation, still introduces, in my view, unfortunate complications—and results. One of the premises for the model of corporate bankruptcy law that pervaded my early work was that it was essential to not ask bankruptcy law to do too much. Solving a common pool problem, shifting ownership and control, and respecting oftentimes complicated and nuanced priority issues,[48] were both important and difficult. Mixing in other policies—bankruptcy-specific policies because they did not attempt to implement, but augment, these three areas—inevitably weakened bankruptcy law's ability as its core mission was a core part of recognizing the "limits" as well as the "logic" of bankruptcy law. That concern is probably heightened, not reduced, by more recent scholarship—and practice—that suggests debtors and creditors could devise contractual schemes to avoid bankruptcy (and thus its policies) altogether.[49]

Much, but not all, of the early focus of this was on the somewhat careless use of a "fresh start" notion that bankruptcy law, and reorganization law specifically, was designed to enable firms to stay in business, thus saving jobs and the communities around them. I believe the wisdom of rejecting that notion in implementing bankruptcy law remains sound today, although I also believe that it remains engrained in the system, sometimes upending bankruptcy's clear goals and priorities, as was the case with the Chrysler reorganization of 2008 (with the significant help of the federal government in accomplishing this distortion of bankruptcy principles). As David Skeel and I wrote in 2013, in analysing the Chrysler bankruptcy:

> Throwing into bankruptcy an explicit focus on jobs, at least as an independent policy (or one that takes on a life of its own), we believe, more often than not, causes an unintended conflict with the issue of asset deployment that, at least for firms, bankruptcy is so uniquely suited to address. While we believe the concern about jobs—and job preservation—is pervasive and almost impossible to keep out of bankruptcy at one level or another as an independent focus or policy, we also think that paying heightened attention to its disruptive effects when used as an independent focus of bankruptcy is at least worthwhile, albeit

> partial, palliative. To be sure, in the case of a successful reorganization, the two policies—economic efficiency and job preservation (if not growth)—tend to merge. But where the economic decision about what to do with a firm's assets points to a possible liquidation, the two policies tend to come into conflict.
>
> We take seriously the issue of job creation—and the dislocations caused by job termination—but think that pressing this into bankruptcy as an independent policy along with asset deployment asks too much of bankruptcy. The issue of jobs, if inconsistent with the issue of asset deployment, should generally be addressed transparently and humanely through other vehicles. Bankruptcy's solutions for the use of assets are necessarily "micro," whereas too often the focus on "jobs" in bankruptcy has unintended, and indeed perverse, "macro" implications.[50]

My concern today for this is exacerbated—perhaps not in the case of a huge corporation such as Chrysler with multiple constituencies and the federal government as large players both in terms of the lenders as well as Chrysler itself[51]—but the important, but smaller, corporations that can devise nonbankruptcy solutions that, while perhaps not optimal, are better for the participants than emergence into this bankruptcy potpourri.[52] So, on this "big picture" issue, I remain convinced that bankruptcy law has both its "logic" *and* its "limits."

Recently, in an interesting and perceptive article, after noting that the model I outlined in this chapter (self-consciously focused on firms) was, itself, developed in the context of corporate bankruptcies and not individual bankruptcies (a point on which I agree), it went on to suggest:

> Politics is hardly missing from business bankruptcy. The Bankruptcy Code is replete with explicit special-interest provisions relating to business bankruptcy (e.g., the treatment of certain financial contracts, shopping center leases, airplane leases, utilities, collective bargaining agreements, as well as numerous implicit special interest provisions), but these provisions have been largely ignored by the creditors' bargain literature.[53]

While I agree that not every "special interest" provision of the Bankruptcy Code has been given rigorous analysis[54]—and I agree there are many provisions that are the result primarily of special interests—I continue to believe that some of the heuristic devices developed thirty years ago *are* useful for examining these provisions, some of which, because of the complicated details of nonbankruptcy priorities, are in fact justified, and others that are not.

To show the continued relevance of paying attention to how nonbankruptcy attributes are mapped into the bankruptcy forum (and goals), and how those attributes remain relevant to "new" forms of contracts, I'd like to look specifically at the first of Professor Levitin's list of special-interest provisions: The "treatment of certain financial contracts," which I take to be a reference to the numerous provisions added since the 1980s insulating these contracts from many of bankruptcy law's core provisions.[55] I do so through a look at their attributes, and whether there are any special features that bankruptcy law appropriately takes into account. In doing so, I conclude—and give a summary of the analysis leading to that conclusion—that the Bankruptcy Code's current treatment of qualified financial contracts indeed demonstrates "special interest" legislation, but that not all of it is necessarily inappropriate (while much of it assuredly is).

V. THE ATTRIBUTES OF LIABILITIES AND EXECUTORY CONTRACTS: AN ANALYSIS OF THE TREATMENT OF QUALIFIED FINANCIAL CONTRACTS IN BANKRUPTCY[56]

Prominent financial innovations of the past thirty years—most particularly, swaps and other derivatives contracts[57] and repurchase agreements (repos)[58]—were insulated from core bankruptcy provisions such as the automatic stay, which prohibits creditors from terminating their contracts or seizing and selling collateral,[59] thanks to a series of legislative amendments creating what are often described as "safe harbors" or "exemptions" for these contracts.[60] To understand my critique of these provisions, one needs, I believe, to start with my original work on assets, liabilities, and executory contracts, and their relationship to "contracts" more broadly.

Bankruptcy, of course, does not treat all contracts "the same" either in terms of the application of the automatic stay or in terms of the estate's ability to assume. Contracts that have been completed by one party or another are either "assets" (if completed by the debtor)[61] or "liabilities" (if completed by the other party).[62] And if the contracts remain materially uncompleted by both parties—and thus have elements of both assets and liabilities—they fall into a third category: executory contracts.[63] It is, for that reason, only for executory contracts that it makes conceptual sense to talk about the debtor's "choice" between assumption (i.e., a belief that the asset value exceeds the liability) or rejection (i.e., a belief that the asset value is less than the liability) of the contract.

Loans to a debtor are, effectively, "breached" upon the filing of a petition in bankruptcy by the debtor. The value of the breached loan is calculated as of that moment—as is the value of any collateral that may be securing the loan. With respect to the typical executory contract under Bankruptcy Code Section 365, the debtor may either "assume" or "reject" the contract,[64] and may do so at any time during the bankruptcy case unless, on motion, the court orders the decision to be made at an earlier point.[65] If the debtor rejects the contract, it is presumably because the debtor views the contract as a net burden. If the debtor assumes the contract, it is presumably because the debtor views the contract as valuable on net and the contract is treated as if it is one made by the debtor-in-possession (an "expense of administration"). This assumption[66] can be accomplished despite any contractual provision that is considered to be an "ipso facto" clause; that is, a clause providing that the contract is breached (or terminated) because of "the insolvency or financial condition of the debtor at any time before the closing of the case" or "the commencement of a case under this title."[67] These provisions may not be perfect—they seem, for example, to give the debtor a one-way option during the bankruptcy proceeding to see if the contract turns out to be valuable—and the other party to the contract may be faced during this interregnum with a decision whether to continue to work on the contract at some expense to that party.[68] But for present purposes, my point is more basic: For this kind of contract, these rules, whether properly part of the creditors' bargain or not, are clear and apply across the board.[69]

To be complete, there is a third category—a variation on the second—that is exemplified by classic insurance contracts as well as real estate leases. In these contracts, even if the debtor does not ultimately assume the contract, the debtor receives a "use" benefit during the period between the commencement of the bankruptcy case and a decision to assume or reject the contract. A debtor that uses real property during a bankruptcy proceeding should, and under the Bankruptcy Code would, be required to pay for that use, irrespective of any ultimate decision to assume or reject.[70] Similarly, a debtor whose building is insured should be required to pay for that insurance coverage during a bankruptcy proceeding, again irrespective of any ultimate decision to assume or reject.

With this as background, it is now possible to examine, for bankruptcy purposes, repos, swaps, and derivatives. As a matter of attributes, repos are essentially secured loans. Under the analysis above, they would accordingly belong in the category of classic loans. A second, conceptually quite different, type of contract is epitomized by swaps and various other forms of derivatives. At their core, they ordinarily are hedges—analytically indistinguishable from a contract to purchase widgets on June 1st at a certain price—and comfortably fit within the category of classic executory contracts. As executory contracts, their attributes would suggest, accordingly, that the debtor can choose to assume or reject them and the decision to assume can be made irrespective of "ipso facto" clauses. Those that function like an insurance policy would be given the additional protection of payments for the use of the "insurance" during the pendency of the bankruptcy case.

Using a rough look at attributes *does* suggest that the wholesale exemption of qualified financial contracts from bankruptcy's core provisions is not justified. But that is not to say that they do not have additional attributes that warrant attention, and perhaps statutory protection. Start with repos. As mentioned earlier, repos, in common with other loans, would be automatically "breached" as of the filing of the petition in bankruptcy, and the claim and the value of the collateral would be determined as of that moment. From that point forward, the debtor would have no further obligation to post collateral, but would need to provide adequate protection for the collateral's value as of the filing of the petition.[71] The counterparty could exercise recoupment rights, and would have rights of setoff, although it would need relief from the automatic stay in order to exercise the statutorily-recognized setoff right.[72]

With the possible exception of requiring the counterparty to gain court permission before exercising its setoff rights, this treatment strikes me as unexceptional. To the extent the collateral was insufficient, the counterparty would be unsecured, and would need to stand in line with other unsecured creditors. The essential point is that the counterparty knows its situation as of the moment of bankruptcy, and can proceed accordingly.

That said, I do think the Bankruptcy Code's automatic stay is, in some respects, overbroad. For example, to the extent the repo buyer is in possession of collateral, it should be able to quickly realize on this collateral. In most cases, the collateral is either cash or cash-like, highly liquid, assets for which there is almost no firm-specific value.[73] In those cases, there are few, if any, reasons, for delay. Valuation disputes are minimal to nonexistent when the collateral is cash or cash-like, and there is nothing "firm-specific" about the collateral, meaning that the ordinary justification for the automatic stay as applied to secured creditors simply does not exist. Indeed, if done as a matter of recoupment—that is, closing out on a single repo contract itself—the Bankruptcy Code would allow the counterparty to proceed without first going to court. For repo creditors that do not have a right of recoupment, there could be either an exception for such contracts from first needing court permission or a presumption of a quick determination upon a motion being made. In either case, the "exceptions," if such they are, to current bankruptcy rules are, at most, minor—and probably should be approached not by creating a "special" rule for repo counterparties, but using the occasion to examine, more generally, the application of the automatic stay to collateral (especially cash-like and other non-firm-specific collateral) in possession of a secured party—a place where the use of markets is not reflective of bankruptcy law language or practice.

Because of the range of functions they serve, the treatment of swaps and derivatives under core bankruptcy principles would be more variegated than with repos. While most swaps would be characterized as ordinary executory contracts, swaps also are used for financing and different kinds of insurance purposes (in which case they would be insurance-like executory contracts).

Most swaps, because they entail ongoing obligations by both sides, are simply ordinary executory contracts for bankruptcy purposes. The most troublesome feature of this result is that, as noted earlier, it may give a debtor time to speculate without consequence (if the hedge turns out to be "in the money," the debtor assumes; if the hedge turns out to be a bad deal, the debtor rejects).

While strategic use of the debtor's executory contract powers is a conceptual concern with *all* classic executory contracts, it may have particular bite in transactions that are themselves designed, explicitly, as hedges rather than as the buying and selling of a good. The Bankruptcy Code is not wholly consistent in how it currently treats this concern with respect to executory contracts in other contexts. For example, even though much of the undesirable nature of the delay option is mitigated by a requirement of compliance with the terms of the lease prior to assumption or rejection, Section 365(d) sets time limits on the debtor's decision in cases of unexpired leases of nonresidential real property where the debtor is the lessee.[74] Given the likely reality that the parties to swaps and derivatives are sophisticated players, a short period in which to assume or reject may be a desirable modification,[75] there is no particular reason for an extended stay on hedge contracts while the debtor is given an extended opportunity to choose whether to assume.

Title II of the Dodd-Frank Act includes a one-plus day halt on termination (which will function similarly to a stay in this context) in resolution proceedings.[76] I believe that a similarly truncated stay—perhaps three business days—should be workable in bankruptcy even in complex cases. It is important to recognize that the managers of a troubled financial institution will not begin thinking about which swaps to assume and which to reject for the first time the day they file for bankruptcy. Knowing that they only have three days to work with, a debtor's managers will have an incentive to plot their executory contract decisions long before they actually file. Moreover, the Dodd-Frank Act's requirement that systemically important financial institutions prepare wind-down plans on a regular basis, even while they are healthy, will aid in the ability quickly to sort out which swaps to assume, as will the increased transparency the new regulation should bring to the derivatives markets.[77]

VI. CHAPTER 11, GOING CONCERN SALES, CONVERTIBLE SECURITIES, AND BANKRUPTCY AS A RESPONSE TO TROUBLED FINANCIAL INSTITUTIONS

While, as discussed above, it is almost certainly the case that the original intent of Section 363 of the Bankruptcy Code—a provision providing for the use, sale, and lease of property of the estate—was to permit piecemeal sales of unwanted property, following the enactment of the Bankruptcy Code of 1978, Chapter 11 practice began, over time, to move in the direction of both (a) pre-packaged plans and (b) plans whose essential device was a going-concern sale of some or all of the business, leaving the original equity and much of the debt behind—with the proceeds of the sale forming the basis of their distribution according to the absolute priority rule.[78] It doesn't fit perfectly, but it has been used, repeatedly, as a way of creating a viable business outside of bankruptcy while the claimants, left behind, wind up as the owners of the estate of the former business entity.

But at the time of, and following, the 2008 financial crisis, American bankruptcy law was thought to be wholly inadequate to deal with the financial failure—and resulting systemic consequences—of a large financial institution. This built on a longstanding exclusion from bankruptcy of major financial institutions—banks and insurance companies[79] (albeit for very different reasons).[80] Indeed, the exclusion of qualified financial contracts from most of bankruptcy's essential provisions may have been fueled by a similar view that such financial contracts, often used by financial institutions (and thus not familiar to bankruptcy practitioners who were not prepared to oppose those amendments), were simply beyond the purview or competence of bankruptcy law.[81]

Thus, it isn't surprising, when Congress turned to deal with the repercussions of the 2008 financial crisis, bankruptcy largely wasn't a player in those discussions. Rather, based on a not-altogether appropriate analogy to depository banks,[82] the FDIC was thought to be the obvious entity to deal with the resolution of a troubled systemically important financial institution. This was reinforced, in part, by the international scope of those institutions and the unfortunate reality (borne in part from not really understanding the mature dynamics of U.S. bankruptcy law vis-à-vis bankruptcy systems in their own countries) that foreign regulatory authorities defaulted to a view that regulatory, rather than bankruptcy-induced, market-based solutions, were obviously preferable.

As a result—or I think substantially as a result—the U.S. "solution" became Title II of the Dodd-Frank Act, which borrowed many bankruptcy provisions and concepts, but left resolution firmly in the hands of the FDIC. But, then, an interesting development began to occur.

Two dominant—but, in actuality, very similar—proposals began to be developed, one in Europe, the other by the FDIC in the United States. Europe has focused on a "one-entity" recapitalization via bail-in[83] while the FDIC has focused in its "single point of entry" (SPOE) proposal for Title II of the Dodd-Frank Act on a "two-entity" recapitalization.[84] Under the FDIC's approach, a financial institution's holding company (the single point of entry) is effectively "recapitalized" virtually overnight by the transfer of its assets, contracts, and liabilities, *except* for certain long-term unsecured liabilities, to a new bridge institution. The bridge institution then forgives intercompany liabilities or contributes assets to recapitalize its operating subsidiaries.[85] Because of the splitting off of the long-term unsecured debt, the bridge institution, in the FDIC's model, looks very much like a financial institution holding company following a European-like "bail in"; the major difference is that in the "bail in," the financial institution holding company before and after the recapitalization is the same entity (thus, the one-entity recapitalization), whereas in the FDIC's SPOE proposal, the "recapitalized" bridge institution is legally different than the pre-SPOE financial institution holding company (thus, the two-entity recapitalization).

Both solutions involve a rapid recapitalization of a financial institution at the holding company level (or, indeed, the rapid recapitalization of an operating covered financial corporation, although the focus has been on financial institutions with a holding company structure), in which—in the course of a very short period of time—it is intended that the financial institution, through the recapitalization, would (a) likely be solvent, (b) appear so to market-participants, and (c) be subject to market discipline, although that third point is mitigated somewhat by the FDIC's continued authority over the bridge institution and its decisions.[86]

I believe this approach is a significant break-through, most prominently because, in a very short period, it promises the ability to accomplish both the substantive—a recapitalization that makes (under all but extreme circumstances) the holding company (or its replacement) solvent again—and the informational—an immediate ability for the market to recognize, and react to, the resulting entity's solvency (in terms of liquidity provision, ordinary dealings, and the like).[87]

But it also brings back into play what I view to be a natural question of whether bankruptcy law could be revised so as to make it a sensible alternative to either SPOE under Title II of the Dodd-Frank Act or bail-in—and thus bring about substantial convergence. After all, as outlined above, it seemed to me the "bones" of a responsible bankruptcy structure was already embedded in bankruptcy law and practice. Once again, while Section 363 of the Bankruptcy Code, permitting the "sale" of assets, may not have been envisioned in 1978 as a mechanism for a going-concern sale of some or all of a business, over the ensuing 30 (plus) years, it had become such a mechanism. While it doesn't fit perfectly, without modification, to the situation of complex systemically important financial institutions, it has been used, repeatedly, as a way of continuing a business outside of bankruptcy while the claimants, left behind, wind up as the owners of the estate of the former business entity.

Its current use differs in two key, and interrelated, ways from an envisioned response to the FDIC's rapid recapitalization under its SPOE proposal for Title II of the Dodd-Frank Act. First, current practice using going concern sales effectively transfers assets (and assumed executory contracts) to a new owner under Bankruptcy Code Section 363. Liabilities are, presumptively, left with the estate and, indeed, the core of the reorganization process following the sale is the sorting out of disputed claims and the allocation, pursuant to the absolute priority rule, of the proceeds of the sale (presumptively cash or marketable securities). To be sure, liabilities *can* be transferred. For example, secured debt might go with the assets. And, under the "doctrine of necessity," *some* unsecured claims may be transferred.[88] But the assumption of liabilities is the exception, not the rule.[89] This is in sharp contrast with the rapid recapitalization envisioned by something such as the FDIC's SPOE proposal, where virtually *all* assets, contracts, and liabilities—except for pre-identified capital structure debt—*are* transferred to the new entity.

Second, unlike current practice, the FDIC's SPOE proposal's "sale" isn't to an existing third-party, and it doesn't follow an auction. But this difference, rather than being troublesome, is actually a natural consequence of the idea of a recapitalization. However problematic going-concern sales may be when the buyer is one of the parties,[90] or when an auction isn't used, in cases where the assets are largely being severed from the liabilities, here the *essence* of the transfer is a recreation of the debtor that existed the moment *before* bankruptcy in a new entity that is identical *except* for the pre-identified debt that is left behind in the debtor's estate together with the former equity holders. The payment, at least originally, for the transfer is in the equity ownership of the *new* entity. There is little room for strategic manipulation because it really *is* the replication, albeit formally using two entities, of a one-entity recapitalization.[91]

Through this "expanded" sale concept, bankruptcy law—with certain regulatory or contractual preconditions—could do everything the FDIC is proposing under the Dodd-Frank Act's Title II with SPOE and, perhaps, could do it better.[92] That is, it could accomplish, via a "quick sale" of a financial institution holding company to a bridge company[93] (with market valuations postponed until later) a recapitalization that would be (a) quick, (b) with the resulting bridge company in a much stronger financial position that (c) would be recognized as such by the market. In addition, it could immediately provide the assurance as well that the bridge company (not itself in bankruptcy) was subject to market discipline and was not under the control of a judge overseeing the bankruptcy of the original holding company.

Bankruptcy law is, in my view, indeed up to the task, although implementing this "quick sale" will, in turn, depend on either regulatorily-required or contractually-based "bail in" or subordinated debt (that can be left behind without doing violence to the absolute priority rule) and by specific provisions in the Bankruptcy Code itself designed to implement a transfer to a new entity over a weekend. Among them are provisions—expansions, really, on rules already existing with respect to executory contracts under Section 365 and property of the estate under Section 541. But the rules need refinement so as to permit assets, liabilities, contracts, and permits to be transferred to the bridge company notwithstanding restrictions on transfer, or change-of-control provisions, or the like. In essence, a number of rules need to be in place to ensure that, but for the recapitalization, the bridge company has all of the rights and liabilities that the holding company had the moment before the commencement of the bankruptcy case.[94]

To be a credible alternative to SPOE under Title II, I believe at least three major changes or clarifications are essential. First, there must be sufficient loss-absorbency built into the capital structure of the holding company.[95] That is, there must be debt, known in advance, that can be "left behind" in any going-concern sale to a new entity, and thereby effectively converted into a potentially equity-like claim against the residual value of that new entity. It can be identified unsecured debt, bail-in debt, or subordinated debt. This requires legal or regulatory rules that will require such loss-absorbency capital *or* the realization (in its own self-interest) by financial institution holding companies, that to create "credible" resolution plans ("living wills") under Title I of the Dodd-Frank Act,[96] they will need to hold either contractually subordinated or "bail-in" debt—or comparable regulatorily-identified and required unsecured debt—that can be left behind (or converted) upon the transfer to the bridge company. Second, there needs to be change, or clarity, in any such recapitalization transfer, that not just assets, but executory contracts, debts (other than those scheduled to be "left behind"), and operating licenses and permits can be transferred to the new company notwithstanding "ipso facto" clauses, anti-assignment clauses, change-of-control provisions, and the like—and that those same rules apply to comparable assets, liabilities, and rights of subsidiaries that are not in bankruptcy but are "assets" of the holding company that are transferred in the recapitalization sale.[97] This particularly, but not exclusively, requires changes in the existing Bankruptcy Code provisions regarding qualified financial contracts along the lines of what was previously discussed.[98] Third, there needs to be a mechanism, known in advance, to have this recapitalization transfer occur within a very short period, such as within 48 hours of the filing of the petition.[99]

All of this takes place without wholesale revision of the Bankruptcy Code, and draws, albeit in a different context, upon the now-commonplace use of going concern sales in Chapter 11 via the use of Section 363. To be sure, the sale is not a market-based sale to a third party (following an auction), but, rather, a judicially-authorized transfer of all of the debtor's assets, liabilities, and contracts (excepting pre-identified debt) to a new entity that "pays" for the transfer by giving full equity ownership of the new entity to the debtor's estate. That said, the potential abuses of a sale to "oneself" are largely dealt with by pre-announced priority rules that, in essence, leave everything in place *except* for the convertible debt, and the resulting impact on the equity ownership of the firm.

Having gone this far, why stop here? This "quick sale" approach, while drawing on the vast change in corporate reorganization practice since the enactment of the Bankruptcy Code in 1978, may, in light of Europe's bail-in proposals, overcomplicate things. In essence, the bankruptcy recapitalization proposal I just outlined—like the FDIC's proposal for use of "single point of entry" under Title II of the Dodd-Frank Act—accomplishes a recapitalization through the use of two entities (i.e., the "continuing" entity is a new corporation), whereas European bail-in proposals, following much more closely earlier academic proposals for the use of convertible securities as a way to reorganize *outside* of bankruptcy,[100] essentially are designed to accomplish a one-entity recapitalization (i.e., the continuing entity is the same legal entity as before). Returning to those convertible debt proposals as an alternative to bankruptcy, it is possible to imagine bankruptcy being a system designed to (a) be the triggering mechanism for the conversion of the debt to equity itself and (b) ensure that contractual provisions of others in a relationship with the debtor do not trigger a withdrawal right upon that conversion. In that world, no new entity is needed, and there is essentially no need for either a "sale" *or* a reorganization process. In its extreme form, a financial institution would enter bankruptcy at one instant, have the conversion of debt to equity simultaneously occur (as well as the override of ipso-facto provisions, change-of-control provisions, cross-default clauses and the like), with the financial institution exiting bankruptcy at the next instant. It follows the nonbankruptcy convertible debt proposals, but uses a quick "bath" in bankruptcy as the legal mechanism to tie up loose ends and ensure everyone is bound.[101]

Whether this is desirable is debatable. It puts three distinct ideas (or alternatives) in play: (1) a two entity bankruptcy-based solution;[102] (2) a single-entity bankruptcy-based solution;[103] and (3) a nonbankruptcy contractually-based single-entity solution.[104] The resolution of that issue depends on how one feels about several factors. Ones that come to mind include: First, the relative merits of a nonbankruptcy trigger to the conversion versus using a bankruptcy filing; second, the need to have bankruptcy law be the mechanism that overrides the ability of other entities to declare default and "run" (versus contractual or other nonbankruptcy mechanisms that accomplish this);[105] and, third, whether the external world would view a two entity recapitalization differently than a one entity recapitalization (i.e., would the emergence of a "new" company give more confidence to third parties than a recapitalized "old" company?). Whatever its resolution, what it suggests to me is how much bankruptcy practice has evolved since 1978, and how the interplay between new ideas for handling insolvent firms, such as convertible debt, and the bankruptcy process should not be viewed as an "either"–"or" choice, but a more complex dynamic in which both processes might co-exist alongside each other, with a debtor (or regulator) making an initial choice between them through contract terms (or, in the case of regulatory oversight, devices such as the Dodd-Frank Act Title I's "living wills").

VII. CONCLUSION

The Bankruptcy Code of 1978 got a lot of things right, and also introduced a framework in Chapter 11 that, pretty much unbeknownst to its drafters at that time, could be adopted to a sale-based, as well as a negotiation-based, model of reorganization that meshed well with academic and practitioner shifts. Has the increasing focus on contractually-based ways of accomplishing a reorganization (or recapitalization) outside of bankruptcy rendered Chapter 11 significantly less important? In some ways, at least for certain firms, the answer may be "yes." But there is still a significant role for Chapter 11. Some firms aren't going to be suitable for recapitalization using a form of convertible debt.[106] Other firms are going to need a mechanism to bind various parties, or clean up loose ends that can't easily be dealt with contractually, and thus need bankruptcy's Chapter 11 as a short-term process.[107] And others, yet, may find judicial supervision of certain aspects preferable than hard-to-define nonbankruptcy triggering mechanisms.

The growth of those nonbankruptcy reorganization/recapitalization alternatives, however, makes more urgent understanding of bankruptcy law's limited purposes. Placing other policies in bankruptcy when they do not apply to sole owners, or to firms that have in place contractual mechanisms to reorganize/recapitalize outside of bankruptcy, reduces its ability to be successfully used when necessary (and leads to perhaps inefficient avoidances of it).

But while we don't need, from the perspective of a firm's use of bankruptcy, a 2020 "overhaul" of bankruptcy law, since there is no structural shift such as existed at the time of the 1978 Bankruptcy Code that isn't already largely embraced by current practices, there are useful changes that could be made. Some are in the nature of cleaning up "special interest" exceptions to devices of the new finance that, at the time those provisions were added to the Bankruptcy Code, were little understood, but now can be analysed, with some clarity, in terms of fundamental attributes and their bankruptcy consequences.[108] Some are in the nature of both statutorily-validating and constraining in various ways the nature of going concern sales as a primary mechanism of the reorganization of firms under Chapter 11.[109] And some may be not just considering how to make bankruptcy work as a part of the resolution framework for financial institutions, but how some of those ideas (in particular, a rapid one-or two-entity recapitalization that relies on convertible or subordinated debt) may be yet another alternative for *any* firm that wishes, contractually, to so structure itself through the use of convertible or subordinated debt as to be a candidate for such a rapid recapitalization.

All of these would be facilitated, in my view, by careful amendments to the current Bankruptcy Code. The resulting Code, even more so than today's, would bear little resemblance in practice, at least for publicly-traded and other larger firms, to the structure and process that was envisioned in the design of Chapter 11 in 1978. But it is the genius of those 1978 revisions, and a testament to the burgeoning academic focus on reorganization and its alternatives since then, that so much has been accomplished *within* the existing structure of Chapter 11—and more can be accommodated without wholesale revision. For a statute nearing its 40th birthday, that is a remarkable accomplishment, indeed.

NOTES

* Distinguished University Professor and President Emeritus, University of Rochester.

1. This is painting with a broad brush. The rise of major firms such as Cravath, Swaine & Moore was due in significant part to its work in railroad restructuring 100 years ago,

R. Swaine, The Cravath Firm and its Predecessors (Vol 2) 169–75 (1948); *see generally* Douglas Baird, Elements of Bankruptcy 64–74 (3rd ed. 2001), and scholarly debates over absolute versus relative priority was an important part of the literature around 1930, *see* James Bonbright & Milton Bergerman, *Two Rival Theories of Priority Rights of Security Holders in a Corporate Reorganization*, 28 Colum. L. Rev. 127 (1928). But there was a clear "return" of bankruptcy to mainstream (or main street) practice following the 1978 Bankruptcy Code. David Skeel, Debt's Dominion: A History of Bankruptcy Law in America 221 (2001) (hereafter David Skeel, Debt's Dominion) ('[i]n stark contrast to the bankruptcy bar under the old Bankruptcy Act, most of the honorees [in a 1992 article of the *National Law Journal*] now worked for the nation's most prestigious law firms.'). And that was true in the academy as well, *id.*, 228 ('[i]n the law schools, bankruptcy had for many years been as much a backwater as bankruptcy practice. . . . All of this changed in the wake of the 1978 Code.').

2. Some amendments were made in 1984; significantly greater amendments were made with the Bankruptcy Abuse Prevention and Consumer Protection Act of 2005.
3. *See* Part V, *infra*.
4. And, even there, on larger (often publicly-traded) firms for the most part. Without reintroducing a Chapter X-Chapter XI-like division, many of the developments I will be talking about here do not really apply to a "mom and pop" store, even when it is in corporate form.
5. Putting aside, perhaps, the issue about the status of bankruptcy judges. See *infra*, note 9.
6. All of these developments are recounted in David Skeel's definitive book, David Skeel, Debt's Dominion, *supra* note 1.
7. Starting with Thomas Jackson, *Bankruptcy, Non-Bankruptcy Entitlements, and the Creditors' Bargain*, 91 Yale L.J. 857 (1982) (hereafter Thomas Jackson, *Creditors' Bargain*) and (symbolically, although not actually) culminating with Thomas Jackson, The Logic and Limits of Bankruptcy Law (Harvard 1986) (hereafter Thomas Jackson, Logic and Limits).
8. As David Skeel correctly noted, David Skeel, Debt's Dominion, *supra* note 1, at 213: 'Law-and-economics scholars and their insights had remarkably little influence on [legislative reform], but actual bankruptcy practice has taken on many of the market-oriented characteristics that these scholars had advocated.'
9. *Id.*, at 132 ('the [National Bankruptcy Conference] and the other reform proponents achieved sweeping reform with remarkably little controversy. Although the Democrats controlled both Congress and the presidency, the legislation had widespread support on both sides of the aisle. Only on the question of whether bankruptcy judges should be given Article III status . . . did tempers frequently flare.').
10. Which has become increasingly controversial, and is likely to be the first place bipartisanship would break down in any overhaul of bankruptcy law today. Again, David Skeel's recounting of the difference between the 1978 Bankruptcy Code and subsequent debates over consumer bankruptcy reforms is a useful starting point. *Id.*, at 187 ('[t]he congressional debates on the 1978 Code seem almost Zen-like in their tranquility from our vantage point more than two decades later. . . . [T]he vast majority of the debates and hearings drew little attention. . . . The debates over consumer bankruptcy at the dawn of the new century could not be more different.').
11. Via discharge, which frees up human capital, and exemptions. *See* 11 U.S.C. §727(a)(1) (hereinafter, Bankruptcy Code) (limiting Chapter 7 discharge to individuals); §522 (listing exempt property).
12. Thomas Jackson, Logic and Limits, *supra* note 7, at 4. The language used sometimes seemed to conflate the ideas. For example, consider the prominent statement in the 1978 House report: 'The purpose of a business reorganization case . . . is to restructure a business's finances so that it may continue to operate, provide its employees with jobs, pay its creditors, and produce a return for its stockholders.' H.R. Rep. No. 95-595, at 220 (1978). I would add "yes, but only in cases where there was financial

failure but not economic failure." *See* Barry Adler, Douglas Baird & Thomas Jackson, Cases, Problems, and Materials on Bankruptcy 28 (4th ed. 2007) (hereafter, Barry Adler, Douglas Baird & Thomas Jackson, 4th Ed.) ('Understanding that financial and economic distress are conceptually distinct from each other is fundamental to understanding Chapter 11 of the Bankruptcy Code.'). While the "rights" of corporations in particular areas has become a contentious issue in recent years—e.g., campaign financing (see *Citizens United v. Federal Election Commission*, 558 U.S. 310 (2010)) or religious free exercise rights (*see Burwell v. Hobby Lobby Stores, Inc.*, 573 U.S. ___ (2014))—none of these issues translates over to the question of freeing up human capital, which is the essence of what the fresh-start policy does for individuals.

13. Thus, I agree in general contours with the notion that "the creditors' bargain has been developed by scholars whose primary focus is business bankruptcy, whereas the theory's critics have tended to focus on consumer bankruptcy, where social policy issues are more pronounced," Adam Levitin, *Bankrupt Politics and the Politics of Bankruptcy*, 97 Cornell L. Rev. 1399, 1455 (2012). When looking at individual bankruptcy issues, as I did in Thomas Jackson, *The Fresh-Start Policy in Bankruptcy Law*, 98 Harv. L. Rev. 1393 (1985) (hereafter, Thomas Jackson *Fresh-Start*), I would not wish to describe its outcome principally in terms of a "creditors' bargain" (nor do I think I did).
14. A corporation with one equity owner and no debt will, obviously, never face insolvency and thus will never use bankruptcy—another way of saying, as I discuss later, that while the corporation may face economic failure (the assets should be doing something else), it will never—as long as it stays in a debt-free condition—face financial failure. And a firm with multiple equity owners and no debt also has no business in bankruptcy as a place to resolve ownership disputes among the equity owners (although, since voluntary petitions have no preconditions, Bankruptcy Code §301, in theory such a case could end up, inappropriately in my view, in bankruptcy; presumably, the underlying dispute would be decided by nonbankruptcy law).
15. Thomas Jackson, Logic and Limits, *supra* note 7, at 12–13.
16. Many, including me, wrote about the issues, particularly dealing with the latent, unknown, claimants, raised by the Johns Manville bankruptcy. See Mark Roe, *Bankruptcy and Mass Tort*, 84 Colum. L. Rev. 846 (1984); Thomas Jackson, *Translating Assets and Liabilities to the Bankruptcy Forum*, 14 J. Legal Studies 73 (1985) (hereafter, Thomas Jackson, *Translating*); David Skeel, Debt's Dominion, *supra* note 1, at 217–21.
17. Subject, of course, to governing laws, contracts, and debt instruments.
18. As well as nearly insolvent companies.
19. See Robert Clark, *The Interdisciplinary Study of Legal Evolution*, 90 Yale L.J. 1238, 1250–54 (1981). This reflects nonbankruptcy policy. *Credit Lyonnais Bank Nederland v. Pathe Communications Corp.*, 1991 Del. Ch. LEXIS 215 (Del. Ch. Dec. 30, 1991). It is oftentimes, however, not easy to enform these rights outside of an insolvency proceeding. *See North American Catholic Educational Programming Foundation, Inc. v. Gheewalla*, 930 A.2d 92 (Del. 2007); Thomas Jackson & David Skeel, *Bankruptcy and Economic Recovery*, in Martin Baily, Richard Herring & Yuta Seki, Financial Restructuring to Sustain Recovery 97, 102 (Brookings 2013) (hereafter, Thomas Jackson & David Skeel, *Economic Recovery*). Because bankruptcy almost certainly will result in this shift, optimal timing of bankruptcy is another area of concern. See Barry Adler, Vedran Capkun & Lawrence Weiss, *Value Destruction in the New Era of Chapter 11*, 29 J. Law Econ. Organ. 461 (2013); Thomas Jackson & David Skeel, *Economic Recovery*, *supra* note 19, at 101–10. I raised this problem in Thomas Jackson, Logic and Limits, *supra* note 7, at 193–208.
20. Thomas Jackson, *Creditors' Bargain*, *supra* note 7.
21. Perhaps aided by my vigorous support for the absolute priority rule, including my visible defense of full economic compensation for secured creditors, seeming to suggest to some that I favored *secured* creditors. *See infra* notes 31–2.
22. See, e.g., my early work criticizing the use of bankruptcy to reject collective bargaining agreements originally approved by *National Labor Relations Board v. Bildisco*

& Bildisco, 465 U.S. 513 (1984). My criticism first appeared in Thomas Jackson, *Translating*, *supra* note 16. And my analysis of the "fresh-start policy" for individuals was driven by a vastly different heuristic—that of cognative and volitional psychology. *See* Thomas Jackson, *Fresh-Start*, *supra* note 13.

23. Even for parties that *do* have rights within bankruptcy, academic scholarship continues to debate whether the absolute priority rule accurately reflects those rights. *See* Anthony Casey, *The Creditors' Bargain and Option-Preservation Priority in Chapter 11*, 78 U. Chi. L. Rev. 759 (2011); Douglas Baird & Donald Bernstein, *Absolute Priority, Valuation Uncertainty, and the Reorganization Bargain*, 115 Yale L.J. 1930 (2006).
24. Elizabeth Warren, *Bankruptcy Policy*, 54 U. Chi. L. Rev. 775 (1987); Douglas Baird, *Loss Distribution, Forum Shopping, and Bankruptcy: A Reply to Warren*, 54 U. Chi. L. Rev. 815 (1987) (hereafter Douglas Baird, *Reply to Warren*). While Elizabeth Warren was, early on, the most visible critic (and the passage of time made her even more so), there were many other critics. *See*, e.g., Karen Gross, *Taking Community Interests into Account in Bankruptcy: An Essay*, 72 Wash. U.L.Q. 1031 (1994); Donald Korobkin, *Rehabilitating Values: A Jurisprudence of Bankruptcy*, 91 Colum. L. Rev. 717 (1991).
25. *See infra*, Part III.
26. Alan Schwartz, *A Contract Theory Approach to Business Bankruptcy*, 107 Yale L.J. 1807 (1998); Alan Schwartz, *Bankruptcy Workouts and Debt Contracts*, 36 J. Law & Econ. 595 (1993). *See also infra* Part IV.
27. *See* Viral Acharya, Barry Adler, Matthew Richardson & Nouriel Roubins, *Resolution Authority*, in Viral Acharya, Thomas Cooley, Matthew Richardson & Ingo Walter (eds), Regulating Wall Street: The Dodd-Frank Act and the New Architecture of Global Finance (Wiley 2011) (hereinafter "Acharya, Adler (etc.), *Resolution Authority*"); Barry Adler, *Financial and Political Theories of American Corporate Bankruptcy*, 45 Stan. L. Rev. 311 (1993); Michael Bradley & Michael Rosenzweig, *The Untenable Case for Chapter 11*, 101 Yale L.J. 1043 (1992).
28. David Skeel, *Markets, Courts & the Brave New World of Bankruptcy Theory*, 1993 Wis. L. Rev. 465 (1993). Some can be imported directly into bankruptcy, as I propose *infra* Part VI with respect to a "quick sale" resolution of a troubled systemically important financial institution. And, even when bankruptcy can be avoided altogether through some of these new contractual devices, it will remain important to have bankruptcy rules as efficient and clear as possible, as the effectiveness of the out-of-court devices may well take place "in the shadow" of what *would* occur in bankruptcy. *See* University of Rochester Roundtable on Preserving Value in Chapter 11, 16(2–3) J. Applied Corp. Fin. 8, 14 (2004) (comments of Thomas Jackson) (hereafter Rochester Roundable).
29. David Skeel, Debt's Dominion, *supra* note 1, at 227.
30. Notably, Bankruptcy Code §§362(b)(6), (7), (17), (27); 546(e), (f), (g), (j); 555; 556; 559; 560; 561.
31. Thomas Jackson, Brief for Amicus Curiae in *United Savings Associates of Texas v. Timbers of Inwood Forest Associates, Ltd.* (1987).
32. *United Savings Association of Texas v. Timbers of Inwood Forest Associates, Ltd.*, 484 U.S. 365 (1988).
33. Bankruptcy Code §1129.
34. *Id.*, §1141.
35. *Id.*, §1121(b), (c).
36. *Id.*, §1129(a)(7)(A)(ii) (a plan can be confirmed if dissenting claimants receive or retain value that is not less than it would retain "if the debtor were liquidated under Chapter 7"); §1129(b)(1), (2) (a plan can be confirmed over the objection of a class, §1129(a)(8), if the court determines that the class is receiving value that equals the full amount of their claims or no junior class receives anything on account of its claims or interests).
37. Thomas Jackson, Logic and Limits, *supra* note 7, at 211. Here, I was being consistent with my law student note, in which I suggested a reorganization, like any liquidation procedure, involves two steps: First, the assets of the firm are sold; second, the claims

against the debtor are paid out of the proceeds of this sale, *see* Note, *Giving Substance to the Bonus Rule in Corporate Reorganizations: The Investment Value Doctrine Analogy*, 84 Yale L.J. 932, 943–6 (1975).

38. Thomas Jackson, Logic and Limits, *supra* note 7, at 212.
39. *Id.*, at 214–15.
40. Mark Roe, *Bankruptcy and Debt: A New Model for Corporate Reorganization*, 83 Colum. L. Rev. 527 (1983).
41. Thomas Jackson, Logic and Limits, *supra* note 7, at 223. This, obviously, refers particularly to publicly-traded and other sizeable firms—the target of Professor Roe's proposal.
42. Although I was far from the only voice suggesting a market-based approach to, or replacement for, Chapter 11. Others, both from the legal side, *e.g.*, Mark Roe, *supra* note 40; Douglas Baird, *The Uneasy Case for Corporate Reorganizations*, 15 J. Legal Studies 127 (1986), and from the economic side, *see* Lucian Bebchuk, *A New Approach to Corporate Reorganizations*, 101 Harv. L. Rev. 775 (1988); Michael Jensen, *Corporate Control and the Politics of Finance*, 4(2) J. Applied Corp. Fin. 12 (1991), were making similar arguments.
43. *See* David Skeel, Debt's Dominion, *supra* note 1, at 213: 'Law-and-economics scholars and their insights had remarkably little influence on the 1994 commission . . . but actual bankruptcy practice has taken on many of the market-oriented characteristics that these scholars have advocated.' *See* also Rochester Rountable, *supra* note 28, at 14 (comments of Thomas Jackson); Douglas Baird & Robert Rasmussen, *The End of Bankruptcy*, 55 Stan. L. Rev. 751 (2002) (hereafter Douglas Baird & Robert Rasmussen, *End*).
44. David Skeel, *From Chrysler and General Motors to Detroit*, http://ssrn.com/abstract-2491022 at 5 (2014) (hereafter David Skeel, *Detroit*) ("The drafters of the Bankruptcy Code assumed that debtors might use [section 363(b)] to sell a few of their assets—say, a piece of equipment the debtor no longer needs. They did not seem to have imagined that a debtor might use section 363 to sell *all* of its assets.").
45. The provision is Bankruptcy Code §363, providing for the "use, sale, or lease of property" of the estate. The major cases heralding the new era were *In re Lionel Corp.*, 722 F.2d 1063 (2nd Cir. 1983) and *In re Braniff Airways*, 700 F.2d 935 (5th Cir. 1983). *See* David Skeel, *Detroit*, *supra* note 44, at 4 ('After the current bankruptcy laws were enacted in 1978, debtors were restructured through a traditional reorganization process, not by sales. . . . By the mid-1990s, however, sales became an increasingly routine strategy for resolving financial distress.'); Douglas Baird & Robert Rasmussen, *Chapter 11 at Twilight*, 56 Stan. L. Rev. 673 (2003) (hereafter Douglas Baird & Robert Rasmussen, *Twilight*); *see also* Douglas Baird, *The New Face of Chapter 11*, 12 Am. Bankr. Inst. L. Rev. 69 (2004); Douglas Baird & Robert Rasmussen, *End*, *supra* note 43.
46. The Bankruptcy Code explicitly allows the assets to be sold "free and clear" of many, if not most, claims; Bankruptcy Code §363(f). For an argument that overriding doctrines of successor liability may make sense under certain circumstances, *see* Thomas Jackson, *Translating*, *supra* note 16, at 94–7.
47. Thomas Jackson, Logic and Limits, *supra* note 7.
48. *See*, for example, my discussion of state law that created rights that were "like a lien," even though never called anything like that, such as in *Chicago Board of Trade v. Johnson*, 264 U.S. 1 (1924), analysed in Thomas Jackson, *Translating*, *supra* note 16. In 1986, I criticized much of Bankruptcy Code §365(f), as then written, Thomas Jackson, Logic and Limits, *supra* note 7, at 113–18. Similarly, several years later, Douglas Baird and I analysed issues around technology licensing agreements, the decision in *Lubrizol Enterprises v. Richmond Metal Finishers*, 756 F.2d 1043 (4th Cir. 1985) (holding such an agreement as executory in its entirety), and Congress' 1988 response in enacting Section 365(n). Douglas Baird & Thomas Jackson, Cases, Problems, and Materials on Bankruptcy Law 247–58 (2nd ed. 1990) (hereafter Douglas Baird & Thomas Jackson, 2d Ed.)

49. *See* sources cited *supra* notes 26–7.
50. Thomas Jackson & David Skeel, *Economic Recovery*, *supra* note 19, at 110–11. This article contains greater detail about the relationship between "saving" Chrysler jobs (but not necessarily jobs overall, given the overcapacity in the automobile industry) and the abuses of the bankruptcy process. On the latter, *see* Mark Roe & David Skeel, *Assessing the Chrysler Bankruptcy*, 108 Mich. L. Rev. 727 (2009) (hereafter Mark Roe & David Skeel, *Chrysler Bankruptcy*); Todd Zwicki, *Chrysler and the Rule of Law*, Wall Street Journal (May 13, 2009); *See* Barry Adler, *A Reassessment of Bankruptcy Reorganization after Chrysler and General Motors*, 18 Amer. Bankr. Inst. L. Rev. 205 (2010) (hereafter Barry Adler, *Reassessment*) (with a proposed amendment to Bankruptcy Code §363); see *also* www.scribd,com/doc/14952818/Objection-to-Chrysler-Sale-Motion (brief filed on May 4, 2009 in the Southern District of New York bankruptcy court by Chrysler's non-TARP secured lenders).
51. Interestingly, in Chrysler itself, it is unclear how much damage to bankruptcy principles I advocate was ultimately done. While the bankruptcy judge's opinion permitting the sale under dubious procedures and restrictions was affirmed in a hasty decision by the Second Circuit, *In re Chrysler LLC*, 576 F.3d 108 (2d Cir. 2009) (argued on June 5, 2009, decided on June 5, 2009, with an opinion issued after-the-fact on August 5, 2009—when its reasoning could hardly contradict its already-issued judgment), the Supreme Court, on December 14, 2010, granted certiorari, vacated the Second Circuit's opinion and directed that the Second Circuit dismiss the suit as moot. *Ind. State Police Pension Trust* v. *Chrysler LLC*, 130 S.Ct. 1015 (2010). As a consequence, the Second Circuit's opinion has no precedential value. *United States* v. *Munsingwear*, 340 U.S. 36 (1950). This rather remarkable step—since the Supreme Court in July had issued, and then lifted, a stay, following the Second Circuit's ruling (and prior to the Second Circuit's written opinion justifying that ruling), allowing the sale to be consummated, 129 S.Ct. 2275 (2009)—has led some to speculate that the Supreme Court's vacating the Second Circuit opinion six months after the court lifted the stay allowing the sale to go forward "was an expression of its disagreement with the Second Circuit's interpretation of the requirements of §363(b)," Fred David, *Interpreting the Supreme Court's Treatment of the Chrysler Bankruptcy and Its Impact on Future Business Reorganizations*, 27 Emory Bankr. Dev. J. (2010). This is at least plausible, since at the time the Supreme Court lifted the stay and allowed the transaction to be consummated, the Second Circuit had not yet written its opinion explaining its reasons for affirming the bankruptcy judge's decision to allow the sale to go forward as then structured.
52. Thirty years ago, citing *Butner v. United States*, 440 U.S. 48, 54–5 (1978) ('[u]niform treatment of property interests . . . serves . . . to discourage forum shopping, and to prevent a party from receiving "a windfall merely by reason of the happenstance of bankruptcy",' I talked about this in terms of "forum shopping," Thomas Jackson, Logic and Limits, *supra* note 7; *see also* Douglas Baird, *Reply to Warren*, *supra* note 24, but it is clear to me now that it isn't just alternative *judicial* forums that are in play. Rather, and perhaps more important, is "bailout" shopping, particularly where the federal government is a creditor, or otherwise interested party (for whatever reason), of an insolvent firm—such as in the case of Chrysler's 2008 bankruptcy.
53. Adam Levitin, *supra* note 13, at 1455.
54. But many *were* questioned using exactly the same heuristic. *See supra* note 22.
55. These provisions are listed *supra* note 30.
56. The arguments here are more fully fleshed out in David Skeel & Thomas Jackson, *Transaction Consistency and the New Finance in Bankruptcy*, 112 Colum. L. Rev. 152 (2012) (hereafter David Skeel & Thomas Jackson, *Transaction Consistency*). *See also* Thomas Jackson, *Bankruptcy Code Chapter 14: A Proposal*, Kenneth Scott & John Taylor (eds), Bankruptcy *Not* Bailout 25 (2012) (hereafter Thomas Jackson, *Chapter 14 1.0*); Darrell Duffie & David Skeel, *A Dialogue on the Costs and Benefits of Automatic Stays for Derivatives and Repurchase Agreements*, in Kenneth Scott & John Taylor, (eds), *infra*, at 133.

57. The major forms of swaps include credit default swaps, interest rate swaps, and currency swaps. A credit default swap functions like insurance, with one party (the protection seller) promising the other party (the protection buyer) a payment in the event a third party (the reference entity) that is the subject of the contract experiences a "credit event" such as default or bankruptcy. With an interest rate swap, one party agrees to pay one form of interest (such as a fixed interest rate) and the other pays a different rate (such as an interest rate that varies based on the prime rate). With a currency swap, one party agrees to pay a specified amount of one currency (such as dollars) and the other promises a different currency (such as euros). In each case, the obligations are usually netted out at the end of the contract, and one party pays the other the difference.
58. In a repurchase or "repo" transaction, one party sells securities to the other, and promises to buy them back at a specified time in the future. Repos are generally used for financing, and are very similar to a secured loan with securities as collateral.
59. Bankruptcy Code §362(a).
60. *Supra* note 30.
61. Bankruptcy Code §541.
62. Or, in bankruptcy terms, "claims," Bankruptcy Code §101(5).
63. The classic definition is that of Vern Countryman, *Executory Contracts in Bankruptcy (pt. 1)*, 57 Minn. L. Rev. 439, 460 (1973) (an executory contract is 'a contract under which the obligation of both the bankrupt and the other party to the contract are so far unperformed that the failure of either to complete performance would constitute a material breach excusing the performance of the other'); *see also* Thomas Jackson, Logic and Limits, *supra* note 7, at 105–18.
64. Bankruptcy Code §365(a). If the debtor wishes to assume a contract or lease, it must "cure[], or provide[] adequate assurance that [it] will promptly cure" any default, compensate the other party for any losses, and "provide[] adequate assurance of future performance." Bankruptcy Code §365(b).
65. Bankruptcy Code §365(d). The debtor generally has considerable discretion when it makes its decision whether to assume or reject a contract or lease. One of the few exceptions is nonresidential leases, which are subject to a 210-day limit. Bankruptcy Code §365(d)(4).
66. As well as assignment.
67. Bankruptcy Code §365(e).
68. *See* Douglas Baird & Thomas Jackson, (2nd ed.), *supra* note 48, at 278 (describing the parties' incentives during this period).
69. In these situations, the other party's major remedy is to seek a court order requiring the debtor to assume or reject the contract.
70. *See, e.g.*, *In re Thompson*, 788 F.2d 560, 563 (9th Cir. 1986).
71. Adequate protection is required by Bankruptcy Code §362(d)(1) and defined by Bankruptcy Code §361.
72. Bankruptcy Code §362(a)(7) (the filing of the petition operates as a stay of "the setoff of any debt owing to the debtor that arose before the commencement of the case under this title against any claim against the debtor"). While the setoff is *stayed* (absent court permission), the *right* of setoff is expressly recognized, as tantamount to a secured claim, by Bankruptcy Code §553. If the off-set arises out of the same transaction, it has been considered "recoupment," not "setoff," and thus not subject to the rules of Bankruptcy Code §553 (or §362(a)(7) as well). *See In re Holyoke Nursing Home, Inc.*, 372 F.3d 1, 3 (1st Cir. 2004).
73. This is particularly so in the wake of the 2008 financial crisis, which has prompted a shift back to cash-like collateral for derivatives, and sharply diminished repos based on mortgage-backed securities and other less liquidate collateral. If there are exceptions to the example in the text—for example, a concern of a cascade of defaults upon the removal of a financial institution's securities, they should be articulated and debated.
74. Under Bankruptcy Code §365(d)(4), 120 days. There are also time limits for such a

decision on residential real property or personal property in Chapter 7, Bankruptcy Code §365(d)(1).

75. If rejected, the discussion about counterparty rights regarding collateral for repos would apply here as well.
76. P. Law No. 111–203, Stat. 1376 (hereafter Dodd-Frank Act) §210(c)(10)(B).
77. The Dodd-Frank Act requirement of wind-down plans ("living wills") is Dodd-Frank Act §167(d). The Dodd-Frank Act also pushes towards a regime in which most swaps would be traded on an exchange of "swap execution facility" and cleared on a clearing house. Such a move would almost certainly permit rapid valuations of swaps, again facilitating the ability to make decisions regarding such swaps within a three-day stay period.
78. David Skeel, Debt's Dominion, *supra* note 1, at 227; Barry Adler, Douglas Baird & Thomas Jackson, 4th Ed., *supra* note 12, at 466–7 ('between [1983 and 2003] a sea change occurred through which an auction of the debtor's assets has become a commonplace alternative to a traditional corporate reorganization').
79. Bankruptcy Code §109(b)(2).
80. Depository banks are resolved by FDIC processes. *See* Federal Deposit Insurance Corporation Improvement Act of 1991, Pub. L. No. 102-242, 105 Stat. 2236 (1991) (codified as amended in scattered sections of 12 U.S.C.). The FDIC acts as a guarantor of the vast majority of a bank's claims and is, in effect, the residual owner of the bank's assets, so lodging resolution with it is, at least, defensible. The exclusion of insurance companies seems to stem from a (shaky) notion that they should be resolved by state insurance regulators. *See* David Skeel, *The Law and Finance of Bank and Insurance Insolvency Regulation*, 76 Tex. L. Rev. 723 (1998).
81. David Skeel & Thomas Jackson, *Transaction Consistency*, *supra* note 56, at 158–62 (recounting the parade of amendments, their rationale, and lack of opposition); Edward Morrison & Joerg Riegel, *Financial Contracts and the New Bankruptcy Code: Insulating Markets from Bankruptcy Debtors and Bankruptcy Judges*, 13 Am. Bankr. Inst. L. Rev. 641, 644–5 (2005).
82. *See* Thomas Jackson & David Skeel, *Bankruptcy, Banks, and Non-Bank Financial Institutions* (Wharton Fin. Inst. Cent. Workshop, Feb. 8, 2010); Thomas Jackson & David Skeel, *Dynamic Resolution of Large Financial Institutions*, 2 Harv. Bus. L. Rev. 435 (2012).
83. *See generally*, Financial Stability Board, *Progress and the Next Steps Towards Ending "Too-Big-to-Fail,"* Report of the Financial Stability Board to the G-20 at www.financialstabilityboard.org/publications/r_130902.pdf (Sept. 2013); Thomas Huertas, Vice Chairman, Comm. of European Banking Supervisors and Dir., Banking Sector, U.K. Fin. Services Autho., *The Road to Better Resolution: From Bail-Out to Bail-In*, speech at The Euro and the Financial Crisis Conference (Sept. 6, 2010); Clifford Chance, *Legal Aspects of Bank Bail-Ins* (2011). In part, this difference in focus is driven by general differences in financial institution capital structures between Europe and the United States.
84. Federal Deposit Insurance Corporation, *The Resolution of Systemically Important Financial Institutions: The Single Point of Entry Strategy*, 78 Fed. Reg. 76614 (Dec. 18, 2013).
85. *Id.*
86. *Id.*, at 76616–76618.
87. *See* John Bovenzi, Randall Guynn & Thomas Jackson, Too Big to Fail: The Path to a Solution (Bipartisan Policy Center, Failure Resolution Task Force May 2013).
88. *See In re KMart Corp.*, 359 F.3d 866 (7th Cir. 2004); *Miltenberger v. Logansport, C. & S.W. Railway Co.*, 106 U.S. 286 (1882). Here, in particular, this transfer is a priority-enhancing action for those unsecured claimants of an insolvent entity. Thus, the doctrine needs to be closely policed to ensure that the transfer is in the interest of the other unsecured creditors. *See* Barry Adler, Douglas Baird & Thomas Jackson, 4th Ed., *supra* note 12, at 446 ("the payment is made because of the benefit that will

accrue to the estate as a whole"). The prototype case may be the transfer of consumer warranty claims in the case of a durable-goods manufacturer.

89. David Skeel, *Detroit*, *supra* note 44, at 6 ('[i]n most cases, . . . the portion of the overall price paid by the buyer that consists of the assumption of debt is comparatively small').
90. Kenneth Ayotte & David Skeel, *An Efficiency-Based Explanation for Current Corporate Reorganization Practice*, 73 U. Chi. L. Rev. 425, 465–7 (2006).
91. There may be a particular concern with improving the position of an undersecured creditor in either situation. My own suggested "remedy" for this is to have secured claims transferred on a non-recourse basis to the new entity, and any deficiency claim also "left behind" in the debtor's estate. This is spelled out in greater detail in Thomas Jackson, *Building on Bankruptcy: A Revised Chapter 14 Proposal for the Recapitalization, Reorganization, or Liquidation of Financial Institutions*, in Kenneth Scott, Thomas Jackson & John Taylor, (eds), Making Failure Feasible: How Bankruptcy Can End "too Big to Fail" (Hoover Institution Press 2015) (hereafter Thomas Jackson, *Chapter 14 2.0*).
92. Thomas Jackson, *Resolving Financial Institutions: A Proposed Bankruptcy Code Alternative*, Vol. 1, Issue 1, Banking Perspective (2014).
93. Which may not be strictly necessary, *see infra* text at notes 100–101.
94. Details of the kinds of rules I envision are spelled out in Thomas Jackson, *Chapter 14 2.0*, *supra* note 91.
95. This is a point emphasized in John Bovenzi, Randall Guynn, Thomas Jackson, *supra* note 87. *See also* Daniel Tarullo *Toward Building a More Effective Resolution Regime: Progress and Challenges* (Oct. 2013) at 10–12; Acharya, Adler (etc.), *Resolution Authority*, *supra* note 27, http://www.federalreserve.gov/newsevents/speech/tarullo20131018a.htm; Financial Stability Board *Progress and the Next Steps Towards Ending "Too-Big-to-Fail,"* Report of the Financial Stability Board to the G-20 at www.financialstabilityboard.org/publications/r_130902.pdf (Sept. 2013). In my view, this is equally necessary for an effective use of a single point of entry strategy under Title II of the Dodd-Frank Act; FDIC ex post discretion is the other (not very palatable) alternative.
96. Dodd-Frank Act §165(d).
97. Existing Bankruptcy Code §§365 and 541 cover some, but not all, of these areas.
98. *See* Daniel Tarullo *supra* note 95, at 10–12.
99. A 2013 Senate Bill, which, among other things, proposes a new Chapter 14 for the Bankruptcy Code to handle a rapid recapitalization sale (a Section 1406 "special transfer"), provides detailed implementation provisions for the second and third points. *See* S. 1861 (Dec. 2013). A House Judiciary Subcommittee introduced a similar bill in 2014, H. 5421, that passed the House late in 2014 on a voice vote. After minor modifications, a similar bill, H. 2947, again passed the House in 2016. The Hoover Institution's Resolution Project has made a comprehensive proposal (dubbed "Chapter 14 2.0") that picks up many of the ideas from its original proposal, Thomas Jackson, *Chapter 14 1.0*), and adds to it features necessary to implement a rapid recapitalization sale. *See* Thomas Jackson, *Chapter 14 2.0*, *supra* note 91.
100. *See supra*, notes 26–8.
101. Think of it as a legally-devised "pre-package plan" on steroids!
102. Such as described in Thomas Jackson, *Chapter 14 2.0*, *supra* note 91; and proposed in S. 1861 (Dec. 2013), H. 5421 (Sept. 2014), and H. 2947 (Feb. 2016).
103. Such as just described.
104. Such as proposed (in a different context) in sources cited *supra* notes 26–7. *See also* John Coffee, *Systemic Risk After Dodd-Frank: Contingent Capital and the Need for Regulatory Strategies Beyond Oversight*, 111 Colum. L. Rev. 795 (2011).
105. A "blended" approach—melding contractual provisions with regulatory "muscle"—seems to be emerging with respect to staying cross-default and early termination rights in cases of qualified financial contracts of G-18 firms when one of them is subject to a resolution action. *See* http://www2.isda.org/newsroom/press-releases (Oct. 11, 2014)

announced by The International Swaps and Derivatives Association of its Resolution Stay Protocol. While this, by its current terms, would not apply to a private resolution, the idea could certainly be expanded to cover that context.

106. For example, a firm overwhelmed by tort liability, particularly historically-based tort liability, as was the case in Johns Manville's bankruptcy of 1982. It isn't clear to me whether a Chrysler or a General Motors could have contractually held enough convertible or subordinated debt, or bound enough parties, to make a nonbankruptcy resolution possible.
107. Even if an enlightened debtor can avoid contractually committing to "ipso facto," cross-default, or change-of-control provisions, there may be certain situations where it cannot avoid facing such provisions (such as, perhaps, in a government-issued regulatory permit with a change-of-control provision). The latter question is whether these restrictions are "lien like" and thus survive bankruptcy, or whether they are inapplicable to the kind of change-of-control outcomes envisioned here. And, sales that guarantee clean title may be desirable, and difficult to achieve outside of bankruptcy. *See* Douglas Baird & Robert Rasmussen, *Private Debt and the Missing Lever of Corporate Governance*, 154 U. Pa. L. Rev. 1209, 1251 n. 128 (2006) ("Similar [clean title] assurances are harder to provide outside of bankruptcy. To be sure, Chapter 11 was never intended to be a forum for senior lenders to sell assets and ensure buyers that they would receive clean title. Nevertheless, having some such forum seems a sensible idea."). With respect to this last point, *see supra* note 46.
108. *See supra*, Part V.
109. *See*, for example, Barry Adler's proposed amendment to Bankruptcy Code §363 in light of Chrysler's bankruptcy, Barry Adler, *Reassessment*, *supra* note 50, Mark Roe & David Skeel's proposal for required auctions, Mark Roe & David Skeel, *Chrysler Bankruptcy*, *supra* note 50, at 767, Kenneth Ayotte's and David Skeel's concerns about sales in which the same party serves as both lender and buyer, Kenneth Ayotte & David Skeel, *supra* note 90, at 465–7, or Douglas Baird's suggested limits on "gifting" and other procedural safeguards, Douglas Baird, *Lessons from the Automobile Reorganizations*, 4 J. Leg. Anal. 271 (2012).

EDITOR'S NOTES

The content of this chapter was drafted prior to the United States House of Representatives' proposed deregulation of systemically important financial institutions ("SIFIs") in the Financial Choice Act and proposed special chapter of the Bankruptcy Code for SIFIs in the Financial Institutions Bankruptcy Act.

The latter Act, at least, is testament to the influence of ideas developed by Jackson and summarized in this chapter.

2. The end of bankruptcy revisited

*Robert K. Rasmussen**

In 2002, Douglas Baird and I published *The End of Bankruptcy*.[1] The piece had two main aspirations. The first was to articulate the conditions necessary for a Chapter 11 proceeding to serve its traditional goal of protecting a business's going-concern surplus through a negotiation among its stakeholders; the second was to then use this understanding as a basis to take stock of existing bankruptcy practice, especially as it grappled with the financial distress of large enterprises.[2] Despite the absence of major amendments to Chapter 11, bankruptcy practice had changed in fundamental ways. Chapter 11 proceedings had shifted from their historical use to something quite different. The two points are linked. It is only by articulating how a business can have a going-concern surplus and how such a surplus can be preserved that enables one to provide insight into the forces driving changes in extant Chapter 11 practice, as well as others that were sure to come. In this essay, I want to revisit *The End of Bankruptcy* and take stock of what we have learned, and how bankruptcy practice has continued to evolve in the intervening years.

I. THE END OF BANKRUPTCY

The accepted understanding of Chapter 11 of the Bankruptcy Code was that it enhanced social welfare by creating a forum where businesses and their owners could address the challenges of financial distress.[3] Specifically, bankruptcy solved a collection action problem among the firm's creditors. Left to their own devices, the creditors – realizing that there were insufficient assets to satisfy all of the firm's obligations – would tear the firm apart as each sought to get paid in full. Chapter 11 called a halt to these individual collection efforts and replaced them with a forum where the stakeholders of the firm could make decisions collectively. The basic alternatives that they had were either to shut down the business or to revamp the capital structure and possibly the operation of the enterprise. The centerpiece of the proceeding was the negotiations that led to a plan of reorganization. It was through this process that the various stakeholders – the managers, the creditors, the equity holders – decided the future of the business. If the bargaining environment was set up correctly, the governing wisdom was that Chapter 11 could provide value by saving companies that would have otherwise been liquidated.[4]

But what are the principles by which one determines whether any given business that files for Chapter 11 should be reorganized through a negotiation among its various stakeholders? No one thinks that Chapter 11 should offer rehabilitation to every business that files for bankruptcy. Some enterprises should not continue. Moreover, the rise of a robust takeover market for even the largest of businesses meant that the sale of a troubled business was now possible. This burgeoning market for distressed businesses meant that a reorganization that struck a deal among the business's extant investors was no longer the only way to prevent a liquidation of the enterprise. In sum, Chapter 11 rested on a theory of valuation preservation without an operative theory as to where that value was coming from.

What the conventional story lacked was a robust theory of the firm.[5] Theories of the firm explain why we see economic activity inside of a firm as opposed to in the market. While economists have wrestled with the question of "why a firm?" for decades, they tend to slight legal boundaries when they describe firms. They focus on functional, rather than legal, demarcations. Bankruptcy law, on the other hand, operates on legal entities.[6] Thus, in moving from the economic literature to the bankruptcy setting, it is necessary to articulate why the legal entity that is in bankruptcy had value above and beyond the alternative uses for its assets. In short, "[R]eorganization law ought to begin by ascertaining the value of keeping *particular* assets together inside a *given* firm."[7]

> Connecting the theory of the firm with corporate reorganization reveals that [t]he traditional account of corporate reorganization assumes a financially distressed business faces three conditions simultaneously: (1) It has substantial value as a going concern; (2) its investors cannot sort out the financial distress through ordinary bargaining and instead require Chapter 11's collective forum; and (3) the business cannot be readily sold in the market as a going concern.[8]

To the extent that any one of these conditions failed to hold for a given entity, it made little sense to resort to Chapter 11's bargaining process. Changes in the marketplace had made it less likely that any, let alone all, of these conditions would obtain for any given firm.

That does not mean that when these three elements were lacking, it did not make strategic sense for a firm to file for bankruptcy. By "End of Bankruptcy," Baird and I did not mean that Chapter 11 would be stricken from the Code or that companies would cease to use its provisions. Quite the contrary; the powers that reside in Chapter 11 to alter relationships among various parties meant that it would still play a role in resolving the problems that arise when a business encounters financial distress. Rather, the essential point is that because of changes in the market and in bankruptcy practice, Chapter 11 would no longer be operating in the fashion intended by those who drafted it.

To see why this is the case, it is helpful to start with the observation that the cost of rearranging the assets in the marketplace places an upper limit on the value of the corporation. If the assets can be easily and cheaply reassembled outside of bankruptcy, the value that bankruptcy can save is only the cost of putting together the new operation. Thus, any role for corporate reorganization to play requires that the firm have a going-concern surplus, as defined by the inability to recreate the enterprise at a cost that is less than the cost of a bankruptcy proceeding. A necessary implication of this observation is that as transaction costs decline, and it becomes easier and cheaper to reassemble assets outside of bankruptcy, the value of the bankruptcy proceeding declines as well.

Even if a business has going concern value, the case for addressing the business's financial distress through a Chapter 11 proceeding remains incomplete. A going concern surplus is a necessary but not sufficient condition for a traditional Chapter 11 reorganization. By definition, bankruptcy is only a possibility when a business is experiencing financial distress that cannot be otherwise resolved. Traditional accounts of Chapter 11 assume that the disparate owners of the company cannot work together outside of a bankruptcy proceeding to solve the problem of financial distress. Indeed, it is the fear that the owners will rush to dismember the business that is the canonical justification behind Chapter 11. Put differently, control rights are not parceled out in a coherent manner.[9] To the extent that control rights are assigned sensibly such that they adjust as the financial condition of the business deteriorates, there is less work for bankruptcy law to do.

Current law places some impediments in the way of ensuring that a business's control rights and capital structure can be adjusted outside of bankruptcy. Even if the firm's creditors could come to agreement amongst themselves and with the debtor as to a new capital structure, such an agreement would be difficult to implement without a bankruptcy proceeding. The Trust Indenture Act prohibits changing the basic terms of a debt holder's financial instrument without that party's consent. For firms that have issued public debt, the free-rider problems created by this prohibition stand in the way of efforts to resolve the debtor's financial distress.[10] The collective forum is needed because there is no way to effectuate the value-enhancing agreement outside of bankruptcy.[11]

Finally, even if a firm has going-concern value, and even if its owners cannot strike a deal amongst themselves outside of bankruptcy to resolve the problem of financial distress, the traditional account of Chapter 11 only makes sense if a market sale is not an option. A market sale both provides a valuation of the company and vests control rights over the business in the buyer. A traditional Chapter 11 proceeding, in contrast, requires the valuation of the enterprise and a negotiation over how control rights are going to be assigned over the reorganized entity. In deciding who owns what in the new company, the parties have to agree on the value of the company. Assigning a value is a time-consuming process, and an inaccurate one at that. The valuation process then affects how control over the business is going to be parceled out. Thus, as a matter of procedure, a sale may be cheaper than a negotiated reorganization.[12]

The poster child for reorganization law has always been the railroad.[13] It is the paradigmatic case where the conditions necessary for a reorganization existed. Indeed, the history of our law of corporate reorganizations is tied up in the history of the railroads. The railroads were the first major American corporations. In laying down track, the company building the road would often underestimate the cost of construction. New rounds of financing would be needed to continue construction, with the company returning again and again to the debt markets. This method of building coupled with repeated borrowings often created a situation where the railroad was hopelessly insolvent. The railroad could never hope to generate enough revenue to pay off the debt that it accumulated in building the road. Yet, on an operating basis, the railroad was making money; its current revenues exceeded its current expenses. Finally, the relationships among the various bondholders was such that each group of bondholders had its own separate collateral, but each piece of collateral was worth little unless it was combined with the collateral that was owned by the other bondholders.

It was in this environment that the American law of corporate reorganization took root. There are very few alternative uses for railroad track. You can run a railroad over it if it is profitable to do so, or you could turn it into scrap. There is little else in between. For roads that generated current revenue in excess of current expense, it made little sense to shut them down. The railroad, albeit insolvent, had a substantial going-concern surplus.

This surplus, however, could not be captured through negotiation amongst the various bondholders. The problem was reaching agreement both among those who held a given issue of bonds and between the various groups of bondholders. The bondholders themselves were dispersed, living both in the United States and Europe, and there was no procedure in place that would allow the bondholders to work together. Moreover, a sale of the road was impossible. The value of the railroads exceeded what the capital markets at that time could hope to raise.

For those roads that were cash flow positive but insolvent, the only choice was to revamp the capital structure. The dedicated assets, the lack of a coherent capital structure and the lack of a market alternative required that the financial distress of railroads be handled in a negotiation among the various investors. Reorganization lawyers grabbed hold of the equity receivership, and modified it so as to provide a forum in which the various owners of the railroad could hammer out a new capital structure.[14]

While corporate reorganization grew out of the financial distress of the railroads, it is often overlooked that the railroads were, even at the time, an unusual case. Most businesses do not rely on assets that only have value to that operation. Indeed, even in industries where specialized assets were important, they often moved among different businesses within the industry. This is especially true of human capital and intangible assets. If anything, these trends have accelerated in the modern economy.

Understanding the theory of the firm on which bankruptcy rests helps to explain the fundamental changes that occurred in the practice of bankruptcy law, especially as it affected the reorganization of large companies. To understand the magnitude of these changes, it is helpful to recall the academic understanding of Chapter 11 at the start of the twenty-first century.

Chapter 11 of the Bankruptcy Code replaced Chapter XI of the Bankruptcy Act in 1979. The first years of the new provision's operation alarmed many. There were concerns that the debtor's old management remained in control of the firm; that they (and shareholders as well as unsecured creditors who were out of the money) had a bias towards continuing the business basically in its current form in hopes of a turnaround in the debtor's fortunes; and that money was being extracted from senior lenders to pay for this effort. The fear was that good money was going to be thrown after bad in a search for a turnaround that would never come. In short, asset allocation decisions were being poorly made.[15] On top of this, the priority of claims established outside of bankruptcy was not being respected.[16] Despite the Bankruptcy Code's commitment to absolute priority, equity holders were able to secure part of the reorganized company for themselves, often at the expense of senior lenders.[17] While the actual violations of absolute priority were modest, the direct and indirect costs of negotiating over the fate of the business loomed large. The reason for these problems lay in the fact that the Code gave substantial power to the managers of the corporation, and they could use that power to keep creditors at bay. Lenders confronted with this state of affairs had to contribute to the reorganization efforts, basically buying off the hold-up power given to the debtor.[18]

Things had change dramatically by 2000. Two trends stood out. The first was the increasing use of prearranged bankruptcies. As noted earlier, the Trust Indenture Act makes out-of-court debt adjustments difficult.

The more widely the debt is held, the more difficult a workout becomes. The drafters of Chapter 11 were well aware of this impediment, and they created the possibility of using Chapter 11 to implement a deal that the parties reached before a bankruptcy petition was filed. The new Code allowed for debtors to solicit consents to a plan of reorganization prior to a petition being filed.[19] The debtor would file the petition and the plan of reorganization at the same time, with the goal of having the proceeding wrapped up in a few months. This would be a "prepackaged" bankruptcy.

This device did not catch on quickly. From 1986 to 1990, there were a total of eight prepackaged bankruptcies. Their use, however, increased during the 1990s.[20] At the same time, creditors and debtors developed a modified version of a prepackaged bankruptcy. In a "pre-negotiated bankruptcy" the debtor and the lead creditor group or groups would negotiate a debt restructuring, but not sign up sufficient creditors to guarantee success. The parties fully expected sufficient consent would be rounded up shortly after the petition was filed.

These prearranged bankruptcies use Chapter 11 to implement a deal that the parties strike before the bankruptcy case begins. They use the power to bind dissident creditors to combat the problem created by the Trust Indenture Act. Looking at the cases of large, publicly-held companies that completed their Chapter 11 case in 2002, of cases where there was not a sale of company (more on that below), a majority implemented a deal that had been reached prior to bankruptcy. Specifically, this happened in 26 out of 41 cases.[21]

As dramatic as the increase in the number of prearranged deals was, even more dramatic was the rise in the use of Chapter 11 as a vehicle to sell the company. Indeed, what was once just an academic idea – the sale of a large company as part of the bankruptcy process[22] – was becoming commonplace. Market sales were replacing traditional reorganizations. Indeed, over half of the cases that end in 2002 were sales. There were 93 cases of large, publicly-held companies that exited Chapter 11 in that year. Fifty-two of these were sales of one sort or another. Some of the sales occurred under Section 363 of the Code, while others were implemented though a plan of reorganization. Either way, companies were being acquired inside the Chapter 11 process. This was definitely not the negotiated solution contemplated by the drafters of Chapter 11. Combining the prearranged deals and the sales, well over 80% of the cases from 2002 could not be classified as traditional Chapter 11 cases.

The trend was unmistakable. Chapter 11 had, in the main, ceased to be the collective forum where parties negotiated a plan of reorganization. Rather, it had become a vehicle to implement a deal struck before the petition was filed or a venue to sell the company to the highest bidder. While there were a few cases that bore the hallmarks of a traditional Chapter 11, it was easy to conclude that "[t]he end of bankruptcy is indeed upon us."[23]

What accounted for this new regime? Control rights over the firm had become much more dynamic.[24] No longer were they vested firmly in the hands of management. The dynamics had shifted from one where the debtor was in control of the bankruptcy process from beginning to end to one where the creditors dominated. No longer did the managers of the debtor have unfettered ability to run the business while in bankruptcy. Even before a bankruptcy petition was filed, control in many cases would shift from the debtor to the senior lender. The bankruptcy forum offered no relief. While some had talked about Chapter 11 providing a breathing space from a firm's creditors, now creditors were firmly in charge.

The shift in control was caused by a number of factors. Certainly, changes in finance were a contributing factor. New types of investors began appearing on the scene.[25] These professional investors began to explore ways to profit from firms in financial distress. Starting in the 1990s, a market in the claims against the company developed.[26] This activity was fueled in part by the rise of hedge funds, especially those funds that specialized in dealing in distress debt. The effect of this change was that a single creditor or a group of creditors could get control of a class of claims. The rise of this market also had the effect of granting an exit option to those who did not want to maintain their relationship with the debtor. If a lender who was part of a syndicate became uncomfortable as the debtor's fortunes declined, it could sell its interest in the secondary market. Small creditors and those who did not want to participate in the resolution of financial distress could sell their claim to a willing investor, an investor well schooled in the dynamics of today's reorganizations.[27]

Another factor was recent amendments to Article 9 of the UCC. The 1998 amendments made it easier for lender (or more accurately a group of lenders[28]) to obtain a blanket security interest in all the business's assets. Rather than disparate secured creditors each holding different collateral, new lending syndicates could lock up virtually all the business's assets. In particular, it became easier to get a direct security interest in the debtor's cash. Through lending covenants, the senior lender could control the debtor's access to the cash in its accounts.

The combination of these changes gave creditors and their lawyers room to innovate, both inside and outside of bankruptcy.[29] Capital structures become more attuned to the possibility of financial distress. The changes to Article 9 meant that the senior lending group could control the debtor's access to cash, thus allowing the lender to exert pressure on the company even before a bankruptcy proceeding is in the offing.[30] For example, rather than having to be beholden to current managers to steer the company, lenders could engineer the installation of a chief restructuring officer.[31] The CRO is not a typical part of the leadership team, owing fealty to the CEO. Rather, the CRO's allegiance is more with the senior lenders.

Bankruptcy offered no haven from the oversight of the senior lender. When the corporation filed for bankruptcy, it would often need cash to finance its operation, so-called "debtor-in-possession" financing.[32] The debtor could either reach an agreement with its existing lender to use cash collateral, or get a new loan, usually from the same group of lenders. Either way, these agreements came with strict terms. Covenants would require the debtor to hit certain targets. Failure to meet these targets could lead to putting the business on the auction block.

When the Bankruptcy Code first took effect, those who extend credit to the debtor were the ones who showed up in the bankruptcy proceeding. When a Chapter 11 was filed, the reorganization plan was negotiated among the debtor's senior bank, its trade creditors, and its unpaid landlord; these were all players who often had a long-term relationship with the debtor. They had often extended credit in good times, and were now stuck with the bad. Few had made an investment in the debtor with the expectation that they were going to be faced with a Chapter 11 proceeding. After the changes in financing the debtor both outside and inside of bankruptcy, the debt was held, both before and during bankruptcy, by debt trading professionals. These are people who wanted a seat at the table and only came on the scene after the debtor had hit financial headwinds. They often pushed for a quick sale or a quick restructuring of the debtor's capital structure. The rise of hedge funds created pools of liquidity whereby there could be a cash sale for hundreds of millions of dollars.

Whereas in the past, bankruptcy was a procedure to be avoided if at all possible, it had become just another tool in the toolbox of sophisticated investors. Indeed, there arose a group of investors known as the "loan to own" crowd. Such investors would either make a new loan to a distressed debtor, taking a first position in all of its assets, or buy into the existing debt. Regardless of the method, the goal was to have a claim against the debtor that both gave the lender control over the debtor and, if the debtor stumbled, allowed the lender to take over the debtor as part of the Chapter 11 case.[33]

This shift to creditor control was not a boon to managers. One would expect managerial turnover to increase during this period. Senior creditors could engineer the ouster of the current leader, and there is no reason to suggest that they would be overly sympathetic to managers in which they had lost faith. While there does not seem to be a comprehensive study on this matter, the evidence does at least suggest that managers were facing worse in the era of creditor control. For example, in looking at cases where a bankruptcy petition was filed in 2001, Ayotte and Morrison found that CEOs were replaced 70% of the time before the petition was filed.[34] This compared to a replacement rate of roughly 55% prior to the era of creditor control.[35] While these two studies differ somewhat in their methodologies, it is safe to say that by the year 2000, bankruptcy was not a sanctuary for underperforming CEOs.

Nor was the shift to creditor control beneficial to shareholders, at least in terms of what they could expect to receive at the end of the Chapter 11 proceeding. In the cases that concluded in 2002, there was little distribution to equity holders. Ayotte and Morrison found the same pattern, as did Adler, et al. To the extent that deviations from the absolute priority were commonplace in the 1980s, this practice had ended with the rise of creditor control in the 2000s.

II. THE END OF BANKRUPTCY TODAY

Bankruptcy case filings fluctuate depending on broad economic conditions. The last two decades have seen dramatic swings in the economy, and, not surprisingly, dramatic shifts in the number of Chapter 11 cases filed. While there has been variation in the number of Chapter 11 cases, the dominance of sales and prearranged deals has remained constant. From 2001 to 2007, there was a dramatic decline in the number of large Chapter 11 cases. In 2001, 263 public companies filed for bankruptcy, and by 2006 this number had dropped to 78. Looking only at the large, public companies, there were 97 cases filed in 2001 and only 13 in 2007.[36] Bankruptcy practice during this period continued largely the same as it had been in the immediate past, with creditors in control and a dominance of sales and prearranged deals. Then, financial Armageddon hit. Beginning in 2008, there was a financial upheaval unlike anything that we have witnessed before. The Great Recession shook the country's financial architecture to the core. Unprecedented government action was necessary to save the banking system. Assets plunged in value. Iconic companies such as General Motors and Chrysler encountered financial distress, and had that distress resolved in unprecedented fashion.

We are now on the backside of the Great Recession. A quick snapshot of recent cases shows that today's outcomes are not much different from what they were prior to 2008. It is still the case that traditional Chapter 11 cases are few and far between. One way to see this is to look at the cases that emerged from Chapter 11 in 2014 and compare the pattern that exists today with the one that obtained before the financial crisis.[37] In 2002, there were 93 cases of large, publicly held companies that completed their bankruptcy proceedings. Of these, 78 were either sales or pre-arranged deals. Of the remaining 15, at most four had going-concern value that could be saved through a traditional Chapter 11. Other studies found a similar pattern. Ayotte and Morrison examined a sample of 153 large privately and publicly-held firms that filed for bankruptcy in 2001. They found that two-thirds of these firms were either sold or liquidated.[38]Another nine percent of these cases were pre-negotiated deals.[39]

The same general pattern still holds. In 2014, 21 cases that began with the filing of a Chapter 11 petition by a large, publicly held company were completed.[40] Sixteen (76%) of these were either going concern sales or pre-arranged deals.[41] Just as was the case a decade ago, the lion's share of the cases of large public companies that enter Chapter 11 are either sold or implement a deal that the creditors had reached prior to filing. Indeed, it is now widely accepted that sales are a common occurrence in Chapter 11.[42]

Even when we look at the five cases from 2014 that were neither a sale nor prearranged deal, we do not see traditional reorganizations across the board. Of the five cases that were not sales or pre-arranged deals, three had no going concern value. Two (ATP Oil and Gas and China Natural Gas) ended up being converted to Chapter 7 for liquidation, and a third (Team Financial) – a bank holding company with no assets – was dismissed.

There remained two cases, one (MModal) was a restructuring of a leveraged buyout. The company had been taken private in August, 2012. It soon became apparent that it could not service its debt. Negotiations began well before the bankruptcy petition was filed, and though there is no indication that a final agreement on each and every detail had been reached at the time of filing, it seems to be the case that the parties were close to a deal when the company entered Chapter 11.

The last case (Overseas Shipholding Group) comes closest to a traditional Chapter 11 case. The debtor was the world's largest owner of oil tankers. It had an existing credit facility that it had entered into in 2006 that was due to be refinanced in the near future. Before it could do so, however, the debtor disclosed that, due to tax issues that had arisen, investors could not rely on the company's financial statements for the past three years. This announcement, and a subsequent downgrade by the rating agencies, had the effect of closing the capital markets to the company, and it could not replace its expiring credit facility. It filed for bankruptcy to prevent creditors from seizing collateral – the company's ships – should it default on its obligations. The company had sufficient cash flow from its operations to fund the bankruptcy case itself. The case lasted a bit more than a year and a half. The debtor rejected over 25 contracts that had become burdensome, and relocated its company headquarters. All the creditors were either paid in full or had their claims unimpaired.

While the outcomes of the cases today remain roughly the same as they were a decade and a half ago, there have been some developments worth noting. As sales have continued to be a regular occurrence in Chapter 11, more and more attention has been given to how they are handled by the bankruptcy court. Currently, the Bankruptcy Code does not provide any guidance as to how a sale should be run. There is a legitimate concern with the process. Sales can be conducted well or conducted poorly. Moreover, a sale carries the potential for abuse, as a party in control could orchestrate a quick sale at a reduced price, especially where it is part of the successful bidding group. What we have seen, however, is the development of standard protocols.[43] Along these same lines, the American Bankruptcy Institute Chapter 11 Reform Commission recommended that auction procedures be placed in the Code. For example, the Commission proposes that to ensure a robust auction, such a proceeding should not take place within the first 60 days of the proceeding, unless there is a clear and convincing showing that delay will result in a significant decrease in the value of the debtor's assets.[44]

While bankruptcy activity today, at least in terms of sales and prearranged deals, is roughly similar to what it was fifteen years earlier, the pattern was notably different during the Great Recession.[45] It is instructive to look at the pattern of cases that were handled during the Recession, as this provides some purchase on the factors that drive the bankruptcy practice in the modern era.

Sales and prearranged deals still took place during this period, but with a noticeable shift from sales to prearranged deals. The years 2007 and 2008, immediately prior to the Recession, still saw the dominance of sales. In 2007, nine out of 13 cases of large, publicly-held corporations that were filed that year were either sales or prearranged deals, with sales outnumbering deals five to four. In 2008, 22 out of 35 cases filed were one of these two types, with 16 sales and six prearranged deals. 2009 saw a noticeable shift in the relative mix of sales and prearranged deals. That year was by far the peak year for Chapter 11 filings during the Recession, with 84 cases being filed. While sales and prearranged deals still constituted a large majority of these cases, the relative proportion of each changed radically. Of these 84 cases, there were only 19 sales, but there were 31 prearranged deals. This trend of the dominance of prearranged deals continued for the next two years. In 2010, there were 28 cases filed, with six sales and 13 prearranged deals. Finally, in 2011, of 21 cases filed that year, three were sales and nine were prearranged deals. Once the pressures of the Great Recession receded, the pattern that existed prior to 2008 returned, with sales again taking the lead, and sales and prearranged deals accounting for the bulk of Chapter 11 cases, at least those involving large, publicly held companies.

The shift away from sales towards deals during the Great Recession should not be a surprise. As Shleifer and Vishny pointed out, at times the market may be illiquid. It could be that there is a general liquidity shortage, or that the most valuable buyer is another company in the industry and the entire industry is experiencing financial pressure.[46] Certainly the Recession reduced the overall amount of liquidity in the economy and put tremendous pressure on a number of sectors. Faced with this state of affairs, one should expect a decrease in the number of sales, at least until more benign conditions return.

Consider in this vein American Airlines. American Airlines was the last of the legacy carriers that was still in existence (Pan Am, TWA and Eastern had all ceased flying by 2001) and had not filed for Chapter 11 (US Airways and United filed in 2002, and Delta and Northwest filed in 2005). American finally joined its brethren and filed in November of 2011. At the time, American had the highest operating costs in the industry, and it filed for bankruptcy so that it could use the provisions of Chapter 11, especially Section 1113, to lower these costs. The airline industry, which had been hard hit by the Recession, was in a wave of consolidation. The best partner for American was likely another airline. During the Recession, however, it is unclear whether any of its competitors had the financial resources to buy American at auction. The CEO of US Airways approached the CEO of American, expressing interest in a merger. American's CEO rebuffed these efforts. The leader of US Airways then approached American's unions (70% of American's workforce was unionized). He was able to reach a deal for new contracts with the unions, contingent on American merging with US Airways. This tactic forced American's hand, and US Airways essentially took over American, including its name.

This takeover of American by US Airways cannot be confused with a traditional reorganization. This was a competitor using Chapter 11 to engineer a hostile takeover of a rival. While there may not have been sufficient liquidity for US Airways to buy American for cash at an auction, another mechanism was found to have American taken over by its rival. While the Great Recession may have constrained the ability to sell companies as part of a Chapter 11 reorganization throughout the period, lawyers were still able to adapt its procedures to facilitate moving assets from the debtor to other entities.

Of course, it would be hard to look back over the past decade and a half and not have at least a brief mention of the automotive bankruptcies.[47] In 2009, we saw two of the largest Chapter 11 cases ever, General Motors and Chrysler. Both were structured as sales, and to this extent they both illustrate the current use of sales as a routine part of Chapter 11 and raise the issue of how sales should be structured. Of course, they were more than this. What we saw here was the unprecedented involvement of the government in the insolvency process. GM and Chrysler were on shaky financial ground prior to the Recession. With the Recession, which led to a dramatic slow down in car buying, they were hopelessly insolvent. Prior attempts to stabilize the industry had left the government as a major creditor of both companies. In GM, the government had the senior position, whereas in Chrysler the government's loan was behind that of a syndicate of secured lenders. In February 2009, President Obama established a Presidential Task Force to examine these two companies. The government decided to rescue them, using funds from the Troubled Asset Relief Program (TARP). The government used the mechanism of a 363 sale as a way to accomplish the goal. In essence, GM was recapitalized and Chrysler was sold to Fiat. The goal may have been enlightened or misguided, but it certainly was not your father's Chapter 11.

Interestingly enough, in recent years cases that bear some of the hallmarks of traditional bankruptcies have reappeared, though in a very different context. They can be found in Chapter 9 rather than Chapter 11. The recent spate of municipal bankruptcies resembles the traditional free-fall bankruptcy much more than does today's modern corporate reorganization. There is no question that a city has a going-concern value. A city is a place where people live, and one does not redeploy a city's assets in the market through a liquidation. Similarly, it makes little sense to talk of a going concern sale when it comes to a city. The city is a dedicated jurisdiction that is going to remain in existence going forward. What is needed is a new capital structure, one that will allow the city to provide basic services to its residents. Here is a situation well suited to bankruptcy's vision of a negotiated reorganization among relevant stakeholders.

Consider Detroit. It had years of mismanagement as well as a shrinking manufacturing base due to the decline of the auto industry. These factors resulted in a declining population and deteriorating services. Indeed, from the high point in the 1950s to its bankruptcy filing, Detroit had lost over half of its population. Various obligations meant that it was hopelessly insolvent. The city owed $18 billion in total, more than it could ever pay back. Over half of this amount was owed to retirees through unfunded health and pension liabilities.[48] The relationships among the creditors were fraught. The financial creditors were adamant that whatever adjustments were needed had to respect the priority structure of the debt. Moreover, within any priority level, they insisted that it needed to be share and share alike. Union leaders were equally adamant that their retirees, who depended extensively on their modest pension, be shielded from as much pain as possible. Here, the only feasible option is a negotiated settlement among the parties.[49]

In the end, Detroit was able to use the Chapter 9 process to lop off about \$7 billion in debt. It was also able to procure \$1.7 billion to invest over the next 10 years in rebuilding the city. Detroit is a case where the bankruptcy forum was used to give the city a breathing spell where the various parties in interest could sketch out a course for the future.[50]

Still, the fact the one has to look to the municipal setting to find traditional bankruptcies underscores how much bankruptcy practice has changed in the last twenty years. Few question that we now live in a world of creditor control (even when they fight amongst themselves) where sales and prearranged deals are the norm. It remains uncertain, however, as to whether these changes have improved the operation of Chapter 11. Indeed, the biggest challenge in corporate bankruptcy law may be in trying to answer this question.

It is one thing to describe this system, a system that takes place far away from the pages of appellate reporters. Equally pressing is the evaluative question – did the changes improve the efficacy of the system? This is a pressing question, but it is difficult to address satisfactorily in an empirical analysis for a number of reasons. The ideal Chapter 11 would, as a matter of first order, deploy the debtor's assets to their highest valued use. It may be that the debtor should be shut down because it lacks any going concern value. Alternatively, it may be that selling the debtor to the highest bidder would bring the best returns. Finally, there may be situations where a negotiated solution is the right course. While we can observe what happens in any given case, we cannot observe the counter-factual – what would have happened to any given firm had another path been followed.

To be sure, one can run comparisons across companies, but here there are challenges. In any given year, there may not be that many cases. Also, what happens to a debtor is not a random event. It is not as if businesses are randomly chosen to be sold while others are selected for a more traditional reorganization. Those in charge (usually the creditors) select what option they view as best for them. They could, of course, be wrong in their judgment. Moreover, they could have interests that run counter to the group as a whole. On the other hand, there are cases where maximizing the value of the business maximizes their return. It is difficult to resolve this question based on either theory or empirical analysis.

Even if one could assess whether Chapter 11 is disposing of assets in the best manner possible, one would still have to assess how Chapter 11 affects behavior in advance of bankruptcy. As Adler et al. have pointed out, a regime that terminates managers quickly and eliminates equity's interest in full may induce some managers to try to take exorbitant risks to avoid bankruptcy at all costs. If so, one would have to balance this potential value destruction against the better deployment of the assets. Even that would not complete the analysis, of course. It may be that a regime that quickly terminates managers, while inducing them to take reckless gambles once they are in financial distress, may also make them so wary of the consequences of financial distress that they lean towards efficient investments so as to avoid financial distress in the first instance.[51]

Finally, there is the cost of the system itself. Commentators have questioned the cost of Chapter 11 for years.[52] Whether the evolution of Chapter 11 has led to a reduction of the actual cost of the proceeding is part, admittedly small, of assessing the overall impact of this change.

There have been attempts to address some of these issues. LoPucki, in looking at cases from 2000 to 2004, found that sales brought lower prices than reorganizations.[53] He had no way of concluding that this was a treatment effect – quick sales fetch less than market value, or a selection effect, those in control sell the poorer performing companies but reorganize the more valuable ones. Ayotte and Morrison found that when senior lenders were in control, they were more likely to sell than to reorganize the business, a finding that is consistent with senior lenders selling only to get what they are owed rather than maximizing the overall price.[54] Adler et al. found that debtors in the new era come into bankruptcy more heavily indebted.[55] They conjecture that the managers, knowing that they are not going to fare well in today's Chapter 11, borrow as much as possible as they try to turn things around outside of bankruptcy. They acknowledge that this finding is ambiguous as to whether this implies that Chapter 11 has become more or less efficient in the new era.

CONCLUSION

Chapter 11 marches on. The number of cases filed in any given year ebbs and flows with the economy, though the long-term trend remains downward. Creditors continue to use it as they see fit. Whatever Chapter 11 once was, it is now something else. It has become another venue where those with the financial wherewithal scour the landscape looking for ways to increase their returns. Bankruptcy has come and gone.

NOTES

* J. Thomas McCarthy Trustee Chair in Law and Political Science. My thanks to Barry Adler and Douglas Baird for helpful comments on this chapter.

1. Douglas G. Baird & Robert K. Rasmussen, *The End of Bankruptcy*, 55 Stan. L. Rev. 752 (2002).

2. We did, however, offer some thoughts on the reorganization of smaller companies. See *id.* at 788–9.
3. The best articulation of this justification for Chapter 11 remains Thomas H. Jackson, The Logic and Limits of Bankruptcy Law (1986). *See also* United States v. Whiting Pools, Inc., 462 U.S. 198, 203 (1983) ("In proceedings under the reorganization provisions of the Bankruptcy Code, a troubled enterprise may be restructured to enable it to operate successfully in the future. Congress presumed that the assets of the debtor would be more valuable if used in a rehabilitated business than if 'sold for scrap.'").
4. To the extent that there was a disagreement over the normative goals of Chapter 11, it was not a disagreement over whether the proceeding should preserve going-concern surplus via collection action. Rather, it was whether it should do more than this, such as having a bias towards reorganization, *see* Harvey R. Miller & Shai Y. Waisman, *Is Chapter 11 Bankrupt?,* 47 B.C.L. Rev. 129, 149 (2005) ("rehabilitation and reorganization were the policy goals underlying the enactment of the Bankruptcy Code"), or reallocating the losses caused by financial distress, *see* Elizabeth Warren, *Bankruptcy Policy*, 54 U. Chi. L. Rev. 775, 778 (1987) ("bankruptcy policy becomes a composite of factors that bear on a better answer to the question, 'How shall the losses be distributed?'").
5. Trying to articulate why a firm exists traces back to Ronald Coase's seminal work. Ronald H. Coase, *The Nature of the Firm,* 4 Economica 386 (1937).
6. The importance of the legal boundaries inside a business is receiving renewed attention these days, especially in the work of Tony Casey. *See* Anthony J. Casey, *The New Corporate Web: Tailored Entity Partitions and Creditors' Selective Enforcement*, 124 Yale L.J. 2680 (2015); Douglas G. Baird & Anthony J. Casey, *No Exit? Withdrawal Rights and the Law of Corporate Reorganizations,* 113 Colum. L. Rev. 1 (2013).
7. Baird & Rasmussen, *supra* note 1, at 758.
8. Douglas G. Baird & Robert K. Rasmussen, *Chapter 11 at Twilight*, 56 Stan. L. Rev. 673, 673–4 (2003).
9. On the need to focus on control rights in articulating the role that bankruptcy law plays, see Douglas G. Baird & Robert K. Rasmussen, *Control Rights, Priority Rights, and the Conceptual Foundations of Corporate Reorganizations*, 87 Va. L. Rev. 921 (2001). For an early recognition of the way in which adroit assignment of control can lessen the need for a Chapter 11 reorganization, see Barry E. Adler, *A Theory of Corporate Insolvency*, 72 N.Y.U. L. Rev. 343, 345, 367–75 (1997).
10. *See* Mark J. Roe, *The Voting Prohibition in Bond Workouts,* 97 Yale L.J. 232 (1987).
11. To the extent that the Trust Indenture Act prevents terms such as collective action clauses, it should be repealed. In the area of sovereign distress, where the Trust Indenture Act does not apply, it is now common for countries to issue bonds that contain collective action clauses. *See* Mitu Gulati & Mark C. Weidemaier, *A People's History of Collective Action Clauses*, 54 Va. J. Int'l L. 1 (2014).
12. As Baird has pointed out, the need for a valuation in the negotiation context is a consequence of respecting absolute priority. A system that embraced relative priority could engineer a reorganization without having to value the business as a whole. *See* Douglas G. Baird, *Priority Matters: Absolute Priority, Relative Priority, and the Costs of Bankruptcy*, 165 Pa. L. Rev. 785 (2016).
13. See David A. Skeel, Jr., Debt's Dominion: A History of Bankruptcy Law in America 48–70 (2001); Baird & Rasmussen, *Control Rights*, *supra* note 9, at 925–36.
14. In this bargaining environment, the deal that was struck tended to follow relative priority. *See* Douglas G. Baird & Robert K. Rasmussen, *Boyd's Legacy and Blackstone's Ghost*, 1999 S. Ct. Rev. 393, 401–08. It was Justice Douglas who later enshrined absolute priority into the law of corporate reorganizations. *See* Robert K. Rasmussen, *The Story of* Case v. Los Angeles Lumber Products*: Old Equity Holders and the Reorganized Corporation*, in Bankruptcy Law Stories 147 (Robert K. Rasmussen (ed.), 2007).
15. *See* Adler, *supra* note 9, at 358–67; Christopher W. Frost, *Running the Asylum: Governance Problems in Bankruptcy Reorganizations,* 34 Ariz. L. Rev. 89 (1992); Lynn

M. LoPucki, *The Debtor in Full Control – Systems Failure Under Chapter 11 of the Bankruptcy Code? (First Installment)*, 57 Am. Bankr. L.J. 99 (1983).
16. *See* Lynn M. LoPucki & William C. Whitford, *Bargaining Over Equity's Share in the Bankruptcy Reorganization of Large, Publicly Held Companies*, 139 U. Pa. L. Rev. 125 (1990).
17. *See* Michael Bradley & Michael Rosenzweig, *The Untenable Case for Chapter 11*, 101 Yale L.J. 1043 (1992); LoPucki & Whitford, *supra* note 16.
18. *See* Barry E. Adler, *Bankruptcy and Risk Allocation,* 77 Cornell L. Rev. 439, 448–9 (1992).
19. *See* 11 U.S.C. 1125(g) (2012).
20. *See* Robert K. Rasmussen & Randall S. Thomas, *Timing Matters: Promoting Forum Shopping by Insolvent Corporations,* 94 Nw. L. Rev. 1357, 1388 (2000).
21. *See* Baird & Rasmussen, *Twilight*, *supra* note 8, at 679.
22. *See* Douglas G. Baird, *The Uneasy Case for Corporate Reorganization,* 15 J. Legal Stud. 127 (1986).
23. Baird & Rasmussen, *Twilight*, *supra* note 8, at 699.
24. *See* Douglas G. Baird & Robert K. Rasmussen, *Private Debt and the Missing Lever of Corporate Governance*, 154 U. Pa. L. Rev. 1209 (2006).
25. Hedge funds that operate with an eye towards distress companies are only a part of the more general rise of hedge funds and their effects on corporations. *See generally* Institutional Investor Activism (William W. Bratton & Joseph A. McCahery (eds), 2015).
26. *See* Miller & Waisman, *supra* note 4, at 152–3.
27. *See* Douglas G. Baird & Robert K. Rasmussen, *Antibankruptcy*, 119 Yale L.J. 648, 660-61 (2010).
28. Most large loans are syndicated loans. *See* Steven C. Miller, A Syndicated Loan Primer 3 (2014).
29. As David Skeel has shown, the evolution of bankruptcy law in the United States has often been driven by bankruptcy lawyers. *See* Skeel, *supra* note 13.
30. *See* Baird & Rasmussen, *Missing Lever*, *supra* note 24, at 1223–36.
31. *See id.*
32. *See* 11 U.S.C. 364 (2012).
33. *See* David A. Skeel, Jr., *Creditor's Ball: The "New" New Corporate Governance in Chapter 11*, 152 U. Pa. L. Rev. 917 (2003).
34. *See* Kenneth M. Ayotte & Edward M. Morrison, *Creditor Control and Conflict in Chapter 11*, 1 J. Legal Analysis 511, 522 (2009).
35. See Stuart C. Gilson, *Management Turnover and Financial Distress*, 25 J. Fin. Econ. 241 (1989).
36. There was a similar decline in all Chapter 11 cases as well. In 2001, there were 11, 424 Chapter 11 cases nationwide; in 2007, the number was 6,352. 2015 Bankruptcy Yearbook & Almanac 3 (2015). In 1991, there had been 23,989 such cases. *Id.*
37. In terms of the total number of Chapter 11 cases filed, the number for 2014 was a tad higher than it had been in 2007, with 7,234 Chapter 11 cases filed in 2014. *Id.*
38. Ayotte & Morrison, *supra* note 34, at 520.
39. *Id.* at 520, 520 n.12.
40. These cases come from Lynn LoPucki's database. One thing that has not changed is the usefulness of this project. It remains the leading source of information on large firm bankruptcies.
41. These cases are Capital Bankcorp, Coldwater Creek, First Mariner Bancorp, Furniture Brands International, Global Aviation Holdings, Lifecore Holdings, Mercantile Bancorp, Tweeter Home Entertainment Group, Edison Mission Energy, Fiber Tower Corporation, GMX Resources, Momentum Performance Materials, USEC, Dolan Company, Eagle Bulk Shipping, and Genco Shipping and Trading Limited.
42. *See, e.g.*, Daniel S. Zazove, *Confidentiality Issues Arising Under Section 363 of the Bankruptcy Code*, Bus. L. Today, Aug. 2015, at 1 ("the majority of recently filed Chapter 11 cases have resulted in going-concern sales").

43. *See, e.g.*, *In re* Adoption of Amended Guidelines for the Conduct of Asset Sales, General Order Amending M-331, M-383 (Bankr. S.D.N.Y. Nov. 18, 2009).
44. *See* Comm'n to Study the Reform of Chapter 11, Am. Bankr. Inst., Final Report and Recommendations 83–7 (2014).
45. One change is that there was a rise in the Chapter 7 filing of bank holding companies, with four in 2008, seven in 2009, and eight in 2010.
46. *See* Andrei Shleifer & Robert W. Vishny, *Liquidation Values and Debt Capacity: A Market Equilibrium Approach*, 47 J. Fin. 1343 (1992).
47. Insightful work on these cases includes Barry E. Adler, *Reassessment of Bankruptcy Reorganization after Chrysler and General Motors*, 18 Am. Bankr. Inst. L. Rev. 305 (2010); Douglas G. Baird, *Lessons from the Automotive Reorganizations*, 4 J. Legal Analysis 271 (2012); Mark J. Roe & David Skeel, *Assessing the Chrysler Bankruptcy*, 108 Mich. L. Rev. 727 (2010).
48. The challenge of dealing with legacy pension obligations is straining the finances of many cities. Whether these pensions can or should be adjusted in a Chapter 9 proceeding is perhaps the most contentious issue surrounding municipal bankruptcy today.
49. To be sure, the city did have some assets that could in theory be sold, most notably its art museum. The city was able to keep the museum, as outside groups donated funds equal to the value of the museum.
50. For a description of the complex negotiation and maneuvering that took place in Detroit's bankruptcy proceeding, *see* David A. Skeel, Jr., *From Chrysler to General Motors to Detroit*, 24 Widner L.J. 121, 136–46 (2015).
51. *See* Adler, *supra* note 18; Lucian A. Bebchuk, *Ex Ante Costs of Violating Absolute Priority in Bankruptcy*, 57 J. Fin. 445 (2002).
52. *See, e.g.*, Edward I. Altman, *A Further Empirical Investigation of the Bankruptcy Cost Question*, 39 J. Fin. 1067 (1984); Arturo Bris, Ivo Welch & Ning Zhu, *The Costs of Bankruptcy: Chapter 7 Liquidation versus Chapter 11 Reorganization*, 66 J. Fin. 1253 (2006); Lynn M. LoPucki & Joseph W. Doherty, *Professional Overcharging in Large Bankruptcy Reorganization Cases*, 5 J. Empirical Legal Stud. 983 (2008).
53. Lynn M. LoPucki & Joseph W. Doherty, *Bankruptcy Fire Sales*, 106 Mich. L. Rev. 1 (2008).
54. Ayotte & Morrison, *supra* note 34, at 539.
55. Barry E. Adler, Vedran Capkun & Lawrence A. Weiss, *Value Destruction in the New Era of Chapter 11*, 29 J. L. Econ. & Org. 461, 465–78 (2013).

3. Bankruptcy sales

*Melissa B. Jacoby and Edward J. Janger**

INTRODUCTION

Asset sales in Chapter 11 bankruptcies exist along a continuum, within a variety of procedural contexts. The continuum ranges from selling a single unencumbered asset in the ordinary course of business to selling an entire firm as a going concern. The contexts are shaped by the relationship between state property law and federal bankruptcy law, as well as by the timing of the sale, whether before bankruptcy, during bankruptcy, or as part of a confirmed Chapter 11 plan.

A pressing question that must be answered is, "why bankruptcy?" Liquidation and the winding up of a firm can be accomplished under state law, so what does a federal bankruptcy forum add? When a company is seeking to reorganize, the value added by bankruptcy law is fairly obvious. A global estate, a broad stay on collection, and a discharge of debt, all of which operate across geographic boundaries, are necessary to effectuate a restructuring that binds holdouts. If a going-concern sale is the centerpiece of the bankruptcy, the value added by bankruptcy is less obvious.

To answer this question, one needs to retreat to some of the first principles of bankruptcy generally, and Chapter 11 specifically. In this chapter, we look at how disputes over sale-related hot topics flow from differing interpretations of these first principles. We describe the forms that bankruptcy sales can take, and the contexts in which they occur. Next, we explore the manner in which sales through the federal bankruptcy process can create value over and above what can be realized under contract or under a compulsory state process. We then explore concerns about these sales, and describe our recent proposal, the Ice Cube Bond, to address these concerns. Finally, we discuss the related issues of credit bidding and the scope of sales "free and clear."

I. THE SALE SPECTRUM IN CONTEXT

The Bankruptcy Code grants the debtor the power to "use or sell" property of the estate. At a very simple level, this power reflects the historic function of bankruptcy courts – to liquidate or wind up a debtor.

Bankruptcy courts can, and frequently do, authorize the debtor to liquidate assets piecemeal. Modern bankruptcy practice, however, raises the possibility of reorganization and going concern sales. Section 363 of the Bankruptcy Code permits the debtor-in-possession to liquidate by selling assets outside the ordinary course of business, if that is the best way to realize on the value of the estate. Such sales require court approval after notice and a hearing or can be conducted under a confirmed Chapter 11 plan.[1] As reflected in the law's dependence on court supervision *ex ante*, the debtor's business decisions are subject to constraints beyond those of ordinary corporate law.[2] The sales at issue might involve a single asset, such as a corporate car or jet, entire subsidiaries of the debtor, or substantially all of a debtor's assets. A sale may be part of an overall liquidation, or incidental to reorganization. While the stakes of approval or rejection of a sale rise with the centrality of the asset to the debtor's business, the Bankruptcy Code provides no more specific guidance for a going-concern sale of a whole restaurant than it does for the sale of a spare pizza oven. Section 363 is a provision of general applicability to all kinds of bankruptcies, untailored to specific types of cases, circumstances or assets.

The context of a sale relates in a complex way with the nature of the asset being sold. If the debtor is selling a spare company car, early in the case, one wishes to see value maximized, but it is probably sufficient that the transaction be at arm's length and that notice be given of the terms of the proposed sale. By contrast, if the debtor is selling a large piece of real estate or a division of the firm, questions might arise about whether the manner of sale will maximize the value of the asset.[3] Where some of the assets are subject to liens, issues of distribution may arise as well, particularly where the secured creditor seeks to receive the proceeds directly after the sale. Finally, where the firm is sold as a going concern, these issues expand exponentially, implicating questions of property law, securities law and corporate governance. The Chapter 11 plan deals with these issues through a well-developed process of disclosure and voting against the background of statutory priorities and baseline legal entitlements. If the sale occurs outside a confirmed plan, those procedures do not come into play, or do so only after the sale has rendered them largely irrelevant. This dichotomy creates various opportunities for abuse, particularly when the sale is held on an accelerated timetable.[4]

As one moves along the asset spectrum the costs and benefits of a federal bankruptcy forum shift, but the need to evaluate proposed bankruptcy outcomes against a state law baseline remains constant. This contextualization of bankruptcy sales is important for two reasons. First, state law determines whether the federal bankruptcy process is helping or harming a particular claimant. Second, it highlights global efficiencies created by sales in bankruptcy. We will discuss these questions in reverse order.

II. BANKRUPTCY SALES AND BANKRUPTCY-CREATED VALUE

The classic economic justification for bankruptcy reorganizations turns on the concern that coordination problems among creditors using state law compulsory remedies will lead to liquidations that are inefficient, sometimes because the firm would be more valuable as a going-concern, and sometimes because state compulsory remedies are not an effective method for realizing on assets. Both of these premises arise in the sale context as well. Sometimes the goal of a bankruptcy sale is to preserve property synergies, and sometimes the efficiency may arise solely due to speed, because an asset is perishable. In this section we tease apart the various "superpowers" of bankruptcy that apply to sales.

First, procedural devices available in the Bankruptcy Code have made bankruptcy courts a congenial forum for selling assets. The bankruptcy estate is global,[5] and supported by nationwide service of process. Also, the Bankruptcy Code provides for an automatic stay of creditor collection activities.[6] Together, these tools allow a period of reflection to determine how best to maximize the value of assets.

Second, as we discuss again in Part IV.C, the Bankruptcy Code provides special powers for transferring good title to purchasers. Section 363(f) of the Bankruptcy Code gives debtors the power to sell assets free and clear of liens and interests of various types. Courts also have interpreted this provision to authorize sales free and clear of unsecured successor liability claims.[7] The buyer obtains better title in bankruptcy than at a foreclosure sale under state law, and perhaps better than in consensual private transactions. In bankruptcy, the asset can be sold free of a secured creditor's lien regardless of whether the creditor consents. The lien is transferred instead to the proceeds of sale. This ability to strip off liens limits the hostage value that inheres in property-based claims against a debtor's assets. For example, ten pieces of real estate may be worth more together than apart. However, if encumbered by different creditors, holdout and coordination problems may limit the debtor's ability to realize that value of the assemblage outside of bankruptcy. In bankruptcy, the sale can be accomplished, so long as each lienholder receives the value of its collateral.[8]

The power to transfer good title is important for another reason. Debtors hold property in many forms. Sometimes realizing value is quite straightforward, but sometimes not. A customer list may be worthless unless sold quickly and with the right to actually use it. Bankruptcy law provides a mechanism to accomplish this objective. Alternatively, in a company with a complex capital structure, selling off a division might be impossible due to intracorporate guaranties. Bankruptcy facilitates such sales to the extent the debtor convinces the court that they are in the best interest of the bankruptcy estate. It is important to recognize that this sale power is not a matter of judicial or statutory fiat. The Bankruptcy Code and related rules of procedure are meant to ensure that the process of sale is open and transparent, and that the holders of interests in the property are adequately protected.

Third, financial distress can force premature realization on assets. As creditors rush to grab assets, or the debtor liquidates assets to stay afloat, sales may occur at the worst possible moments. Chapter 11 is designed to remove the time pressure imposed by insolvency and to give the debtor and its creditors a chance to consider how best to maximize asset value.[9] Value maximization sometimes depends on an accelerated process because the debtor is a "melting ice cube." In other contexts, though, realization should be delayed, and option value preserved, to the extent the debtor has considerable going-concern value or when unusual market forces or financial distress of the debtor suggest that the market will undervalue the debtor's assets. As we will discuss below, the benefits of speed do not apply in all situations; and speed imposes costs of its own. The advantage, or at least a goal, of bankruptcy is to allow decisions about timing to be made with an eye toward value maximization, rather than to be driven by the exigencies of the debtor's financial distress.

III. PROPERTY-BASED ENTITLEMENTS AND GOVERNANCE

Chapter 11 permits the state law governance regime to continue, but with an overlay of creditors' rights. Creditor governance largely supplants shareholder governance when a firm files for bankruptcy. A prime example is the right of creditors holding impaired claims to vote on a restructuring plan.[10] This is consistent with mainstream theories of corporate governance, as the unsecured creditors, not the shareholders, are likely to be the residual claimants. Recently, as a practical matter, governance rights have become more property-based. Creditors asserting liens on key assets, or substantially all assets, sometimes argue that those liens give them the right to dictate the direction of the bankruptcy. To the extent that liens confer control over the sale decision, the Bankruptcy Code's allocation of governance rights may be distorted. A secured creditor or other sale proponent is likely to seek to maximize its own interests at the expense of other stakeholders and the bankruptcy estate. For example, a purchaser might push for an expedited sale to capitalize on a low valuation of an asset. A secured creditor might push for an expedited sale of a firm to quickly satisfy its claim, gain control of the asset through credit bidding, or cut its losses even though a quick sale is not in the best interest of the bankruptcy estate. The problem inheres in the fact that power over property means that governance decisions are made by creditors with senior claims over particular assets rather than by residual claimants to the value of the firm as a whole.

Undersecured creditors frequently argue that these concerns are irrelevant, because they hold blanket liens on all of the assets of the debtor, and they *are*, therefore, the residual claimants. If they are not being paid in full, then the unsecured creditors have no interest in the firm worth protecting. This naked claim of, "it's all mine," deserves to be examined more closely. A consensual lien is not a straight distributional priority (as one might see with preferred equity, or debt over equity).[11] Lien priorities, derived from state property law, are asset specific and depend on the particulars of various statutes, typically Article 9 of the Uniform Commercial Code or the state law of real property mortgages. Much bankruptcy scholarship and many judicial opinions operate from the assumption that the secured creditor is the "fulcrum security" in cases in which the value of the firm is less than the amount of the secured creditor's debt. This make it appropriate to entrust to that lien holder the decision to sell, to identify the buyer, and to set the terms of sale. Our careful focus on the nature of security, and its asset-based nature, has caused us to question whether a secured claim can ever be the fulcrum security.[12] The secured creditor has a claim against particular assets, not a distributional priority against the firm. This conceptualization adds a layer of complexity to bankruptcy sales that we discuss more fully in other work.

Secured creditors also argue that any additional value created during the bankruptcy process constitutes "proceeds" of their collateral and thus is encumbered by their security interests as well. Although scholars and professionals dispute whether the law should allow for this as a normative matter, this position warrants further scrutiny as a descriptive claim. Even an interest in proceeds must rest on a perfected security interest in property. State law security interest regimes have scope limitations and thus cannot themselves be all-inclusive. They also contain procedural requirements that may make it difficult, if not impossible, for the creditor to actually have a lien on "everything." Bankruptcy law cuts off floating liens as of the date of the bankruptcy filing, so new inventory, cash or other assets acquired after the petition are not automatically encumbered.[13]

The Bankruptcy Code preserves the value of the prepetition security by granting a replacement lien on proceeds postpetition, but directs the court to limit the extent of those proceeds based on the secured creditors' relative contributions.[14] Together, sections 552(a) and 552(b) of the Bankruptcy Code protect the value of a secured claim in relation to other claims against the estate through changes in form, while preventing the expansion of collateral through an unduly liberal interpretation of proceeds.

Nonetheless, secured creditors frequently use practical leverage over the sale process, early in the case, to assert and lock-in a blanket lien over the sale proceeds.[15] Rushed sales may give a distorted view of the scope of the creditors' entitlement, where, if subjected to closer scrutiny, it might become apparent that some of the firm's value is unencumbered. There might be gaps in perfection or the scope of their property right. But more importantly, much of the value of the firm may not exist because of their "property" but from other inputs or the bankruptcy process itself. At the same time, once assets have been sold, and sale proceeds distributed, other creditors will not have an incentive or even a reasonable opportunity to challenge the secured creditor's claim to the debtor's value. As we discuss below, these claims of entitlement need careful scrutiny to ensure that secured creditors do not appropriate bankruptcy-created value that they do not own.

A court did give this scrutiny to a secured creditor's claims in the Residential Capital bankruptcy.[16] ResCap was a collapsed mortgage originator and servicer, and its Chapter 11 featured two significant section 363 sales of its assets. After those sales, junior secured noteholders objected to the allocation of sale proceeds under the plan. The plan, proposed jointly by the debtor and the creditors' committee, treated those noteholders as undersecured, whereas the noteholders contended they were oversecured. The parties were about $350 million apart in their estimates of the noteholders' entitlement. In a lengthy published decision, the bankruptcy court held that the junior noteholders were, in fact, undersecured by around $318 million.[17] Although the court recognized goodwill as an intangible asset subject to the noteholders' security agreement, it addressed two important subsidiary questions. First, should goodwill existing on the petition date be included in the secured creditor's allowed secured claim? And second, to the extent that there was goodwill on the effective date of the plan, was it proceeds of prepetition collateral?

As to the first question, the court rejected the methods proffered by the noteholders to value goodwill on the filing date, essentially assigning it a value of $0.[18] As to the second, with regard to goodwill that existed on the effective date of the plan, the court held that the noteholders had failed to show it was proceeds of their prepetition collateral.[19] The court highlighted the role of the debtors' time, effort, and expense in generating going-concern surplus. The court pointed to section 552(b), which limits the expansion of proceeds and preserves the relationship between asset-based claims and value-based claims during the case, and found that goodwill on the effective date of the plan belonged to the estate as a whole. The court also rejected the noteholders' argument that they had a lien on refinancing opportunities as general intangibles because those opportunities were not severable from ResCap's mortgage servicing rights to which the noteholders' security interest did not extend.[20]

Cases like *ResCap* demonstrate that, to the extent that firm value derives from asset synergies or labor rather than collateral per se, quick sales must adopt further procedural safeguards to ensure proper allocation and distribution of that surplus.

IV. ADDRESSING THE CONCERNS

The preceding sections raise questions about distortion of both governance incentives and distributional entitlements associated with "all-asset" bankruptcy sales. While the court in *ResCap* was able to explore the question of secured creditor entitlement after the sale, allocation in many other cases has occurred at the time of sale. Indeed, time pressure and the absence of the plan process protections may also reduce the information available with regard to firm value.

A. Ice Cube Bond

We recently proposed a mechanism called an Ice Cube Bond to address these concerns in the context of hurry-up sales of substantially all of a debtor's assets outside a plan.[21] We proposed that, in such sales, the court should routinely withhold a portion of sale proceeds from claimants who would otherwise receive a distribution—usually, but not always, a secured creditor. To recover those funds, a beneficiary would need to establish that the quick sale did not harm the bankruptcy estate, and that the claimant would be entitled to the reserved funds under the otherwise applicable bankruptcy priority rules or under an agreement reached through post-sale plan negotiations.[22] Our goal is to retain quick sales under section 363 as a useful tool to preserve value in moments of true crisis, while preserving opportunities for judicial and stakeholder deliberation to ensure that value is properly allocated.

Outside of bankruptcy, it is standard practice for courts to require an injunction bond to help preserve issues for later litigation. Existing bankruptcy law could be used to authorize such a bond or holdback—the essence of the Ice Cube Bond concept in the sale context. Indeed, bankruptcy courts are no stranger to disputed claims reserves or holdbacks to preserve the issues of priority or entitlement for later resolution. For reasons we discuss elsewhere, courts generally do not raise concerns about harm to the estate *sua sponte*, and assertions of crisis sometimes deter parties from asking them to do so. We would therefore reverse the burden, on the theory that a quick all-asset sale under section 363 should be understood as a procedurally irregular disposition of the estate. Again, Chapter 11 contemplates going-concern sales, but pursuant to a confirmed plan with its associated procedural protections, or pursuant to a prepackaged plan with votes already solicited in a manner that complies with applicable securities laws. A sale early in the case, without disclosure or voting, is a different matter entirely.

Under state law, the "rebuttable presumption" rule applies to procedurally irregular sales of personal property collateral under Article 9 of the Uniform Commercial Code.[23] When a lender disposes of collateral in a manner that does not comply with Article 9, the lender loses its claim to a deficiency judgment unless it can show that the irregularity did not depress the sale price. The Ice Cube Bond essentially mirrors this approach for all-asset sales under section 363. A portion of the quick-sale price could be reserved as presumptively unencumbered funds, to preserve issues of valuation and allocation for later determination.

The Ice Cube Bond limits the extent to which sale beneficiaries can externalize the increased risk associated with quick all-asset sales. It also limits the extent to which negotiations about distribution must be completed before the sale can occur. Our approach reinforces the separation between governance decisions about value maximization from those about value distribution. It also preserves the finality of the sale, as the purchaser gets clear title to the assets.

In sum, the Ice Cube Bond gives courts a procedural tool to sort hurry-up sales that are necessary from those that are opportunistic. While some details about the Ice Cube Bond, such as the percentage holdback, might be established by local rules of procedure, some may worry about onerous ex post judicial fact finding to determine when and how to release the funds. In practice, we predict that post-sale negotiations will dispense with many of these issues. Moreover, it should be noted, the cost of the Ice Cube Bond can be avoided entirely: the debtor (and its lenders behind the scenes) simply must conduct the sale pursuant to a plan, prepackaged or otherwise. In a world in which Ice Cube Bonds are routine, hurry-up sales would occur only in cases in which the value of speed exceeds the anticipated harm to the estate or other claimants.

The Ice Cube Bond addresses concerns about attempts to realize on the value of assets through sales outside the context of a plan of reorganization. It preserves the ability to resolve disputes about entitlement to sale proceeds and valuation by setting aside a portion of the sale proceeds for later distribution. And it recognizes that the plan process gives an option to the creditors of the estate to determine how best to realize on the value of the firm upon plan confirmation. As a result, an Ice Cube Bond is not necessary for sales conducted *pursuant* to a plan of reorganization. Our proposal should, therefore, be distinguished from Anthony Casey's argument that even a sale pursuant to a plan operates to foreclose the option value still held by out-of-the-money unsecured creditors at the time of plan confirmation.[24] Our view is that plan confirmation constitutes a realization of claims of both the secured creditor and the unsecured creditors, and that the plan process, by design, is meant to provide sufficient protection of this option value.

B. Credit Bidding

Our discussion of sales has not yet distinguished among methods a buyer might use to pay the sale price. Under both state law and bankruptcy law, a secured creditor may seek to bid on the assets. Both state law and bankruptcy law permit secured creditors to bid their debt rather than new money to purchase their own collateral.

Under state law, the foreclosure sale is, axiomatically, limited to a sale of the creditor's collateral. In bankruptcy, by contrast, the trustee or debtor-in-possession may seek to bundle and sell the estate's assets in any manner that is calculated to maximize value. These bundles may not be coextensive with a particular creditor's security interest. To the extent that the property is an assemblage of assets or is a going-concern business, some of the assets being sold may be unencumbered; there may be multiple creditors with secured claims; or other challenges may exist to the scope of a secured creditor's collateral that might justify qualifications or limits on credit bidding, consistent with these secured creditors' state law rights.

Thus, independent of the need for an Ice Cube Bond in any given situation, it is axiomatic that secured creditors should be allowed to credit bid only on their own collateral. Ensuring that result requires a preliminary evaluation of the scope of the allowed secured claim before a creditor is permitted to credit bid on assets or value that may not be its collateral. Two recent cases illustrate the point even though they primarily have received attention for findings of creditor misbehavior. In *Fisker Automotive Holdings*, the bankruptcy court capped a secured creditor's credit bid at the amount that creditor recently had paid for the debt.[25] Although the court's decision details aggressive behavior by the secured creditor, a major element contributing to the ruling was a stipulation between the debtor and the creditors' committee that some of the assets being sold were not the secured creditor's collateral.[26] Selling collateral and non-collateral together maximized the sale price, as the Bankruptcy Code contemplates. Such a strategy is consistent with the Bankruptcy Code, however, only if credit-bidding rights are limited to the value of the secured creditor's collateral. In *Free Lance-Star Publishing*, a case shortly after *Fisker*, the court also limited a credit bid due to a confluence of circumstances, including a finding that the secured creditor had not properly perfected security interests in all of the assets being sold.[27]

In response to these court decisions, some expressed fears that credit bid capping will leak into other settings and affect the market for debt. Notably, though, the limits on the power to credit bid in *Fisker* and *Free Lance-Star* did not limit the secured creditors' other rights or set the value of the secured claim for other purposes. Moving beyond these court decisions, we recognize the settled role of credit bidding, but also the need for credit bidding to be consistent with the secured creditor's state law property rights. Sometimes that means a secured creditor cannot credit bid the full amount of its debt.

C. Sales Free and Clear

One aspect of bankruptcy-created value discussed above, the power to transfer clean title, raises a variety of additional questions. Transferring clean title often means selling the assets free of claims and interests, stripping property interests away from the assets. These interests are respected through the granting of a lien on the proceeds of sale. Not all interests in property have value that can be reduced to money. One example can be found in section 363(b): when a debtor seeks to sell a customer list subject to a privacy policy, the ability to sell is conditioned on respect of reasonable expectations of privacy embodied in the policy. In an all-asset sale, there may also be claims of successor liability for future tort claims that would attach to the assets. Environmental claims may or may not transfer with the assets in a sale, depending on when they are deemed to arise. How to address these claims has bedeviled courts. General Motor's experience with faulty ignition switches highlights how the allocation of these claims to the estate or to the purchaser can fundamentally affect questions of firm value.[28]

The structured negotiation and voting requirements embodied in the Chapter 11 plan process allows for the various constituencies to allocate the risks associated with these uncertainties. Fast-track disposition of assets through 363 sales is particularly risky where such uncertainties exist, including whether a quick sale maximized value in the first place. These concerns offer another reason why quick 363 sales make sense only when the benefits of speed outweigh such risks.

CONCLUSION

The simple power to sell assets in bankruptcy has evolved into a powerful tool for right-sizing a firm and achieving value-maximizing sales of assets, or even the firm as a whole. This tool is widely recognized as a positive feature of the U.S. bankruptcy regime. But without careful attention to the legal limits of liens and other pre-bankruptcy entitlements, as well as the distorting effects of situational leverage, the tool presents opportunities for abuse and misallocation of value.

NOTES

* Graham Kenan Professor of Law at University of North Carolina at Chapel Hill, and David Barse Professor of Law at Brooklyn Law School, respectively. Thanks to Barry Adler for comments on an earlier draft and to Caleb Johnson for research and editorial assistance.

1. 11 U.S.C. §§ 363(b), 1123(a)(5) (2016).
2. *In re* Lionel Corp., 722 F.2d 1063, 1071 (2nd Cir. 1983).
3. *In re* Curlew Valley Assoc., 14 B.R. 506, 508 (Bankr. D. Utah. 1981) (reporting on debtor's disagreement with a trustee's substitution of hay baling for hay cubing in preparation for liquidating the debtor business).
4. Melissa B. Jacoby & Edward J. Janger, *Ice Cube Bonds: Allocating the Price of Process in Chapter 11 Bankruptcy*, 123 Yale L.J. 865, 871 (2014).
5. 11 U.S.C. § 541(a) (2016).
6. 11 U.S.C. § 362 (2016).
7. *In re* Trans World Airlines, Inc., 322 F.3d 283, 288 (3d Cir. 2003); *In re* Leckie Smokeless Coal Co., 99 F.3d 573, 585 (4th Cir. 1996).
8. 11 U.S.C. § 1129(b)(2)(A) (2016).
9. Jacoby & Janger, *supra* note 4, at 896.
10. 11 U.S.C. § 1126 (2016).
11. Jacoby & Janger, *supra* note 4, at 936.
12. Edward J. Janger, *The Logic and Limits of Liens*, 2015 U. Ill. L. Rev. 589 (2015).
13. 11 U.S.C. § 552(a) (2016).
14. *Id.* § 552(b).
15. Jacoby & Janger, *supra* note 4, at 909, 915 (discussing how this is sometimes attempted through the terms of a proposed sale order, or through the terms of a post-petition financing order, as the two are often closely connected).
16. *In re* Residential Cap., 501 B.R. 549 (2013).
17. *Id.* at 623.
18. *Id.* at 611.
19. *Id.* at 612.
20. *Id.* at 610.

21. Jacoby & Janger, *supra* note 4, at 926.
22. *Id.* at 936.
23. U.C.C. § 9-626.
24. Anthony J. Casey, *The Creditor's Bargain and Option-Preservation Priority in Chapter 11*, 78 U. Chi. L. Rev. 759, 760 (2011).
25. *In re* Fisker Auto. Holdings, Inc., 510 B.R. 55, 61 (Bankr. D. Del. 2014).
26. *Id.*
27. *In re* Free Lance-Star Pub. Co., 512 B.R. 798, 800 (Bankr. E.D. Va. 2014), *appeal denied* 512 B.R. 808 (Bankr. E.D. Va. 2014).
28. Elliott et al. v. General Motors LLC, 15-2844-bk(L) (2nd Cir. July 13, 2016).

4. The new synthesis of bank regulation and bankruptcy in the Dodd-Frank era

*David Skeel**

INTRODUCTION

Although they briefly came together during the savings & loan (S&L) crisis of the 1980s—creating serious frictions as they did—banking and bankruptcy have long occupied nonoverlapping magisteria in the United States, with separate regulators, starkly different insolvency resolution processes and divergent terms for some of the same creditors and claims.[1] When a commercial bank fails, bank regulators determine how the failure will be resolved, exercising broad discretion that is subject to very little second guessing. In bankruptcy, by contrast, the parties themselves make many of the key decisions, the process is slower and more transparent, and priority rules are more closely adhered to.

Since the enactment of the Dodd-Frank Act in 2010, bank regulation and bankruptcy have become far more closely intertwined. Thanks to the powers they are given under Title II—also known as the Orderly Liquidation Authority—bank regulators now can take over the holding company of a systemically important financial institution ("SIFI") and most of its subsidiaries, not just its commercial banking subsidiaries.[2] Dodd-Frank thus has significantly expanded the domain of the administratively-oriented bank resolution process. Yet Title I of Dodd-Frank—which gives bank regulators the power to designate SIFIs and subject them to special regulation—requires the SIFIs to produce "living wills" explaining how the SIFI could be resolved in *bankruptcy*, not under Title II.[3] Additionally, Title II prohibits bank regulators from invoking their new resolution powers unless they first determine that bankruptcy would not be effective.[4]

Additional frictions arise in the specific details of Title II, which depart from bankruptcy law at key junctures. The rules that apply to derivatives and financial contracts if regulators invoke Title II are quite different than the rules in bankruptcy, for instance; Title II requires that a SIFI's managers be ousted whereas bankruptcy does not.[5] It is of course possible that the divergences between OLA and bankruptcy are warranted. At the very least, however, the inconsistencies underscore the need to consider whether the new synthesis of bank regulation and bankruptcy is coherent, and whether it is likely to prove effective. That is the task that I attempt to undertake in this chapter.

I will begin (in Parts I and II) by exploring some of the basic differences between bank resolution, which is a highly administrative process in the U.S., and bankruptcy, which relies more on courts and the parties themselves. For the purposes of this comparison, I will consider how the two insolvency frameworks address four basic issues: ensuring timely initiation of insolvency proceedings, allocating losses among shareholders and creditors, maximizing the value of the firm's assets, and minimizing any externalities of the insolvency process. The striking differences between bank resolution's and bankruptcy's handling of these issues raises the question why bank resolution is so different than ordinary bankruptcy, and whether its deviations from ordinary rule of law principles are justified. I conclude that they are, at least for small and medium-sized banks whose balance sheets are dominated by deposit liabilities, but that the issues that arise in the two contexts are less distinct than is often assumed.

My second general focus in the chapter (Parts IV, V, and VI, after a brief overview of the new Dodd-Frank synthesis in Part III) is on a series of remarkable new innovations designed to facilitate the rapid recapitalization of a troubled financial institution. The first, which would take effect outside of any resolution or bankruptcy process, is convertible contingent capital securities, or CoCos. These are not a new idea, and they remain rare in the United States, but their use is rapidly expanding in Europe. I focus primarily on the question of how best to structure the trigger that would convert a CoCo into equity, endorsing the early trigger advocated by Charles Calomiris, Richard Herring and others. Although I am optimistic about the potential effectiveness of CoCos, I conclude that they are best seen as a supplement to the formal resolution and bankruptcy frameworks, not a replacement for them.

Turning to resolution and bankruptcy, I describe and critique the single point of entry strategy for recapitalizing SIFIs in Title II, which the Federal Deposit Insurance Corporation devised several years after the Dodd-Frank Act was enacted, and a more recent proposal to use an analogous technique in Chapter 11.[6] Since single point of entry and the bankruptcy alternative lie at the heart of current thinking about the new synthesis, I explore each at some length. As we shall we, although both have significant limitations, and the bankruptcy alternative would require several amendments to the Bankruptcy Code, they hold genuine promise.

I conclude the chapter by assessing (in Part VII) the general coherence of the new synthesis. Some commentators have argued that Title I and Title II have inconsistent objectives, with Title I attempting to remove the risk that a SIFI will default, based on an assumption that the largest financial institutions are too big to fail, while Title II requires regulators to shut down a troubled SIFI. The advent of single point of entry has significantly diminished the force of this objection. The remaining concerns about coherence lie not within Dodd-Frank itself, but in the relationship between Title II of Dodd-Frank and bankruptcy—or so I will argue.

I. BANK INSOLVENCY AND BANKRUPTCY: A BRIEF COMPARISON

To begin our consideration of the new regulatory synthesis, it may be useful to briefly describe the somewhat different answers that traditional bank insolvency law and the Bankruptcy Code give to the core questions that insolvency law must address. For present purposes, we can group many of the key issues into four basic categories: initiation of the insolvency proceedings; maximizing the value of the debtor's assets; determining which obligations to restructure and to what extent; and minimizing the spillover effects of the insolvency proceeding on third parties. In the discussion that follows, I briefly describe each, and note how bankruptcy and bank insolvency law address them.[7]

The first issue is ensuring that insolvency proceedings are triggered in a timely fashion.[8] Because insolvency proceedings do not hold much upside for them, the managers of a troubled firm may delay initiating these proceedings. Considerable value may be destroyed as the firm's financial fortunes deteriorate. Chapter 11 addresses this concern by permitting the firm's current managers to continue running the business after it files for bankruptcy, rather than requiring that they immediately be displaced. The soft landing reduces managers' disincentive to file for bankruptcy.[9]

Banking regulation looks to bank regulators rather than bank managers to make the initiation decision. Although regulators' relationship to a bank is quite different than managers', they too have a tendency to wait too long to trigger insolvency proceedings. According to the conventional wisdom, which is confirmed by historical patterns, regulators have an incentive to postpone intervention so that the consequences will be borne by future regulators.[10] To encourage more timely initiation, Congress enacted "prompt corrective action" requirements after the S&L crisis of the 1980s. The prompt corrective action rules require regulators to intervene in increasingly intrusive fashion as a bank's financial condition deteriorates.[11]

The second issue is maximizing the value of the debtor's assets. According to the best known normative theory of bankruptcy—the creditor's bargain theory—an effective insolvency regime addresses this concern by providing a collective forum for determining whether the assets should be reorganized or liquidated.[12] The automatic stay brings a halt to the "race to the courthouse" that could lead to the dismembering of an otherwise viable firm, and Chapter 11's voting rules give creditors a voice in the decision of how to allocate the debtor's assets. The Bankruptcy Code includes a variety of other provisions that are designed to enhance liquidity during the bankruptcy.[13]

As with initiation, bank insolvency law leaves the asset allocation decision in the hands of bank regulators. Regulators have broad discretion how to resolve a bank's financial distress, subject to the general statutory command that they choose the strategy that will best protect the deposit insurance fund. In a substantial majority of resolutions, the FDIC identifies a buyer for some or all of the bank's assets, and resolves the bank through a purchase and assumption transaction that takes place after the close of business on Friday and is completed before the end of the weekend.[14]

The third issue is the restructuring of the debtor's obligations. If creditors expect to bear losses in the event the firm falls into financial distress, they will have an incentive to monitor the debtor; by contrast, if debtors are confident they will be bailed out, they may be too willing to lend and have too little incentive to monitor the debtor.[15]

The Bankruptcy Code assumes that creditors will bear losses, and allocates them according to a soft version of the absolute priority rule. If a class of creditors objects to a proposed reorganization plan that will not pay the class in full, no lower priority class of creditors is permitted to receive anything.[16] A class of creditors can waive its right under the absolute priority rule, however, by agreeing to a proposed reorganization that deviates from strict absolute priority.[17]

The bank priority scheme differs in several significant ways. First, and most importantly, it fully protects up to $250,000 in deposits even though depositors traditionally would have been general unsecured creditors.[18] This protection is intended to discourage depositor runs. The protection against runs is thought to outweigh the risk of moral hazard created by the assurance that depositors will be paid in full. Second, bank insolvency law authorizes the FDIC to alter the priority rules.

The final objective is minimizing the potential externalities of the insolvency process. The concern that the insolvency framework may have effects on third parties was the principal justification for exempting derivatives, repurchase agreements and other financial contracts from the automatic stay and other core bankruptcy provisions.[19] If derivatives counterparties were subject to the automatic stay, the reasoning went, the counterparty's stability might be jeopardized by the delay in enforcing its contractual rights, and this might bode ill for the counterparties' counterparties. In banking, concern for spillover effects figures even more strongly. In addition to protecting depositors, bank insolvency law explicitly authorizes bank regulators to take systemic risks into account in its bank resolutions.

Overall, bank resolution is much more discretionary and does not honor rule of law virtues such as transparency and clear priorities. It also is more concerned with curbing potential spillover effects.[20]

II. WHY IS BANK INSOLVENCY LAW SEPARATE?

As the overview in the last part made clear, bank insolvency is subject to a different regulatory framework and has addressed the core questions quite differently than the bankruptcy laws that apply to other firms. This raises the question *why* bank insolvency is regulated separately and whether this is inevitable or desirable.

The first thing to note is that only the commercial banking subsidiary itself is excluded from bankruptcy.[21] Many banks—especially large and medium-sized banks—are part of a bank holding company framework. A systemically important financial institution like Citigroup or J.P. Morgan Chase may consist of a holding company, commercial banking subsidiaries, investment banking subsidiaries, and subsidiaries of other kinds. If the SIFI fell into financial distress, the holding company could file for bankruptcy, as could the investment banking subsidiaries and other subsidiaries (except insurance subsidiaries).[22] Only the commercial bankruptcy subsidiaries are barred from bankruptcy.

One answer to the question why bank insolvency law is separate is historical. The earliest American bankruptcy laws did not always distinguish between banks and other firms. Only during the Civil War era did bank regulation and the regulation of other firms decisively part ways. This suggests that separation may have been historically contingent rather than inevitable. Indeed, in some countries, such as the United Kingdom, banks are subject to the same insolvency framework as other businesses.[23]

The observation that the hiving off of bank insolvency regulation from bankruptcy does not appear to have been inevitable deepens the question of whether it is desirable. Is it? The conventional answer is yes—that banks need a special, administrative insolvency framework because bank resolution needs to take place extremely quickly to preserve the value of bank assets, to assure that depositors have continuous access to their deposits, and to prevent disruptions to the payment system. Given its ongoing involvement in oversight, the FDIC is well-positioned to intervene quickly, and bank insolvency law gives the FDIC the flexible authority it needs to achieve an effective resolution. By contrast, a bankruptcy judge would have no particular expertise or knowledge about a bank prior to its failure, and the bankruptcy process is too slow, requiring that creditors be notified and given the opportunity to object before a firm's assets could be sold or other major decisions made.[24]

It is perhaps worth noting that these benefits do not require the separate treatment of bank insolvency and bankruptcy. Lawmakers could incorporate the administrative features of bank resolution into a bankruptcy law if they wished, giving bank regulators the same powers in bankruptcy that they currently have under bank insolvency law. Since the initial objective of insolvency regulation is the same in both contexts—preventing destructive runs—there is nothing far-fetched about the suggestion that bankruptcy and bank resolution could be combined. But the current bank insolvency framework is administrative in nature, whereas the bankruptcy laws leave much more of the process to the parties themselves. Relatedly, the bank insolvency process emphasizes administrative flexibility rather than rule of law virtues such as clear rules and transparency, whereas the bankruptcy rules place more emphasis on rule of law virtues.

The FDIC's sweeping discretion leaves a bank's non-depositor creditors with very little protection. In theory, a disgruntled creditor can challenge either the resolution or the FDIC's treatment of its particular claim. But such a challenge is fraught with obstacles. Because the FDIC acts secretly, creditors cannot question an FDIC action in advance. Any challenge must thus come after the fact. Moreover, the banking laws constrain the grounds for recovery in important respects—limiting it to damages, for instance, and to the difference between the claimant's payout and its likely treatment in a liquidation—and the FDIC's determinations are given de facto deference. In the words of one former FDIC official, in an email to one of my co-authors, "there are few cases and changes in the outcome are rare."[25]

Despite these shortcomings, the current framework is probably worth retaining. First, preserving continuous access to deposits and protecting the payment system are indeed important concerns. Although these benefits could be replicated in a framework that paid more heed to rule of law virtues, the quick, secretive FDIC process achieves these objectives effectively.

Second, and more importantly, the vast majority of the liabilities of small and medium-sized banks are deposits (and deposits are entitled to first priority, thanks to a depositor preference law enacted in 1993). More than 96% of the liabilities of banks with less than $100 million in assets that failed between 1995 and 2009 were deposits.[26] For banks with between $100 and $500 million in liabilities the percentage was 92.85%; it was roughly 88% for banks up to $5 billion.[27] Because deposits make up such a large percentage of a bank's liabilities, and because the FDIC is responsible for making sure that depositors are paid, it makes sense to let the FDIC decide what to do with the bank's assets. The FDIC and the deposit insurance fund are, in a sense, the only creditors with a real interest in the outcome. Even if the FDIC does not handle the resolution effectively, the harm to the bank's other creditors (or the windfall, in the event the FDIC decides to protect them) is quite limited in most cases.[28]

Notice how context-specific this endorsement of the bank insolvency framework is. When banks' liabilities are nearly all deposits, and the government has guaranteed the deposits, the case for an administrative resolution framework is strong. For banks and other financial institutions that do not fit this profile—as the largest holding companies do not—administrative resolution needs to be justified on other grounds. It does not make sense to argue, as advocates of the new Dodd-Frank resolution rules did, that the FDIC's seventy-five-year track record of effectively resolving small and medium-sized banks demonstrates the virtues of expanding administrative resolution to the largest financial institutions.[29] This observation will prove important as we explore Dodd-Frank's reconfiguration of banking regulation and the ways the new rules are being worked out.

III. DODD-FRANK'S RECONFIGURATION OF BANKING REGULATION

As noted in the last part, prior to the Dodd-Frank Act, bank regulators had nearly unbridled discretion to resolve a failed commercial bank, but no particular insolvency authority over the other entities in a bank holding company structure. In this part, I begin by describing the pre-Dodd-Frank structure in slightly more detail. I then show how the Dodd-Frank Act reconfigured the regulatory framework, highlighting several underappreciated features of the new rules.

A. Bank and Bank Insolvency Regulation before Dodd-Frank

To appreciate the pre-Dodd-Frank structure, consider the largest bank holding companies. A holding company like Citigroup or J.P. Morgan Chase has a parent corporation, commercial banking subsidiaries, investment banking subsidiaries, insurance subsidiaries, and numerous other subsidiaries including (especially prior to Dodd-Frank) interests in hedge funds and other funds.[30] The different entities are subject to a variety of different regulators. The Federal Reserve regulates the holding company. Commercial banks may be regulated either by state regulators or, if it is a federal bank, the Office of the Comptroller of the Currency.

If a giant financial institution fell into financial distress prior to Dodd-Frank, the holding company itself and any subsidiary other than a commercial bank or insurance company could file for bankruptcy.[31] As noted earlier, most of these subsidiaries could file either in Chapter 11, which generally contemplates reorganization, or Chapter 7, which provides for liquidation.[32] The principal exception is investment banks, which can file for Chapter 7 but are not permitted to file for Chapter 11.[33] The exclusion of investment banks from Chapter 11—which now seems anachronistic—explains why Lehman Brothers' holding company and some of its subsidiaries filed for bankruptcy on September 15, 2008, but its investment banking subsidiary did not.[34]

Commercial banks and insurance companies are both excluded from bankruptcy. If a commercial bank falls into distress, either the FDIC or a state regulator can initiate insolvency proceedings; and the FDIC steps in as receiver (or much less often, conservator). Insurance insolvency is handled by state insurance regulators.

When a bank holding company files for bankruptcy, bank regulators have much less regulatory authority over the bankruptcy proceedings than they would in a bank resolution. This caused great consternation during the S&L crisis of the late 1980s. In a number of cases, bank regulators argued that the holding company needed to serve as a "source of strength" for its commercial bank subsidiary after the holding company filed for bankruptcy, but the holding company refused, insisting that its principal responsibility was to the holding company's own creditors and shareholders. Bank regulators won a partial victory in the Supreme Court's *MCorp* decision, although the Court concluded that it did not need to explicitly determine the legitimacy of the source of strength doctrine.[35]

After the 2008 crisis, bank regulators once again complained about the limitations of their authority. Henry Paulson, Ben Bernanke and Timothy Geithner—who were the Treasury Secretary, Federal Reserve Chair and President of the New York Federal Reserve at the time—have each insisted that they were precluded by the constraints on emergency Federal Reserve intervention from rescuing Lehman Brothers.[36] Although these post-crisis statements appear to have been revisionist history, enhancing bank regulators' ability to take control of the entire bank holding company structure—not just the commercial bank subsidiaries—was a central aim of the Dodd-Frank financial reforms.

B. The Dodd-Frank Framework

The Dodd-Frank reconfiguration of the pre-crisis regulatory framework has two major parts, each aimed at systemically important financial institutions.[37] In addition to creating a new financial regulator—the Financial Stability Oversight Council, comprised of the heads of the major financial regulators[38]—Title I singles out systemically important financial institutions for heightened capital requirements and regulatory oversight. A bank holding company that has $250 billion or more in assets (originally, $50 billion) automatically qualifies as systemically important for the purposes of Title I. Additionally, the FSOC has the authority to designate other, nonbank financial institutions as systemically important. In the first few years after the Dodd-Frank Act was enacted, the FSOC designated AIG, GE Capital, Prudential, and Metropolitan Life, but each of these designations was later withdrawn or, in the case of Metropolitan Life, successfully challenged.[39]

Title I requires each of the financial institutions subject to its enhanced oversight to prepare an annual "rapid resolution plan"—or living will—explaining how it could be resolved without causing systemic damage in the event it fell into financial distress.[40] Title I also authorized regulators to force large banks and nonbank financial institutions that have been designated under Title I to sell assets if there is a danger of systemic harm,[41] and instructed regulators to prepare studies of contingent capital securities and repurchase agreements.[42]

Dodd-Frank's other major contribution comes in Title II, which houses the new rules for resolving systemically important financial institutions. The U.S. Treasury is the quarterback of the new resolution process. If the Treasury, backed by two-thirds votes of the Federal Reserve Board of Governors and the FDIC board, concludes that a financial company is on the verge of default, or has defaulted, and that its failure "would have serious adverse effect on financial stability in the United States," it can trigger resolution by filing a petition in the federal court in Washington, D.C.[43] Judicial review is extremely limited. So long as it was not arbitrary and capricious for regulators to determine that the company was in danger of default, the court must sign off on the petition.[44] If the Treasury persuades the company to accept the petition, it can avoid review altogether.

If the petition is approved, the FDIC is appointed receiver (other than with investment banks, where the SEC is receiver), and is given extensive authority to borrow money and to take over the company's operations during the receivership. Under the Orderly Liquidation Fund provisions of Title II, the FDIC can borrow up to 10% of the pre-resolution asset value of the troubled institution or 90% of the fair value of its assets in resolution from the U.S. Treasury, no questions asked.[45]

Lest resolution have the appearance of a pleasant landing, the FDIC is instructed to kick out any managers of the company who were "substantially responsible for its financial distress," to wipe out shareholders' interests, and to impose losses on creditors whose claims are not assumed.[46] Unlike ordinary bank resolution, which permits the FDIC to reorganize a bank through a "conservatorship," Title II provides only for receivership, which in bank resolutions under the FDI Act is nearly always used to liquidate the troubled bank. A late amendment proposed by Senator Barbara Boxer added an exclamation point, stating that any company in resolution must be liquidated.[47]

One somewhat surprising feature of the Title II resolution rules is the absence of a formal relationship between Title II resolution and Title I oversight. It would be natural to assume that regulators cannot put a financial institution into Title II unless it has first been identified as systemically important for the purposes of Title I. But there is no explicit connection between the two titles. Any financial company—that is, a company that derives at least 85% of its earnings from financial activities[48]—can be labeled as a "covered company" and thrown into resolution if the regulators believe that its default would cause financial instability. Surely the two sets of companies will overlap significantly, but regulators' failure to have designated a company as systemically important for the purposes of Title I does not preclude them from subjecting it to a Title II resolution.

Equally surprising is the relationship between Title II resolution and bankruptcy. Despite regulators' profound distrust of bankruptcy in 2008, both Title I and Title II strongly emphasize that bankruptcy should be the insolvency framework of first resort. The Dodd-Frank Act signals its preference for bankruptcy at two key junctures. First, under Title I's living will requirement, systemically important financial institutions must explain how their financial distress could be resolved in bankruptcy without causing systemic harm.[49] Bankruptcy is the focus, not resolution under Title II. Second, before invoking Title II, regulators must first determine that the troubled financial institution cannot be resolved effectively in bankruptcy.[50] Once again, the Dodd-Frank Act instructs regulators to focus first on bankruptcy.

The principal limitation of this robust endorsement of bankruptcy is that regulators' authority to invoke Title II would trump bankruptcy if regulators wished to invoke their Title II powers.[51] Regulators are authorized to remove a financial institution from bankruptcy and put it in Title II at any time. Moreover, although the regulators must first conclude that the institution cannot be effectively resolved in bankruptcy, their conclusion that bankruptcy is not adequate is not subject to any judicial review at all. As noted earlier, the only issues that are subject to review are the questions whether the institution is a financial institution and whether it is in default or in danger of default.

C. Key Limitations of Title II as Enacted

As enacted,[52] Title II's handling of each of the key resolution issues appeared to be seriously deficient. If Title II requires regulators to liquidate any institution they take over (as the "thou shalt liquidate" provision suggests), they would have a strong disincentive to invoke it, especially with the largest financial institutions. And unlike ordinary bank insolvency law, the Dodd-Frank Act does not include any provisions that are designed to force regulators to intervene in a timely fashion. The managers of a troubled financial institution would have equally strong incentives to resist Title II, since Title II requires the removal of any who are "substantially responsible" for its decline.

Second, for those financial institutions that do wind up in Title II, liquidation may not always maximize the value of the estate. For well over a century, American corporate bankruptcy law has assumed that some form of reorganization will often preserve more value for creditors than liquidation. It is hard to imagine that this would never be true for large financial institutions.

Third, while Title II does require that shareholders and creditors take losses, its priority rules apply only to creditors whose contracts regulators choose not to fulfill. Shareholders would almost certainly be wiped out, but regulators have only one day to decide whether to assume the institution's derivatives contracts. It seems likely that regulators would assume most or all of the derivatives and pay them in full.

Finally, Title II does give regulators both the authority and the funding to ensure that a Title II resolution does not cause spillover effects. This is the one objective Title II is best designed to achieve. But the benefit would be quite limited if regulators were forced to liquidate any institution they took over, and thus had a strong disincentive to invoke Title II.

An insolvency framework that calls for liquidation is not necessarily inefficient. The prospect of harsh treatment in bankruptcy can strengthen creditors' ability to monitor outside of bankruptcy.[53] Where government regulators rather than creditors are the principal monitors, however, this approach is much less likely to be efficient. One solution to regulators' shortcomings is to impose additional requirements that are designed to overcome their flawed incentives. This is the strategy reflected in the prompt corrective requirements in banking law. As it turns out, bank regulators have responded to the regulatory delay concern themselves, albeit in a very different way, adopting a recapitalization strategy known as single point of entry that is designed to circumvent Title II's liquidation requirement. I turn to single point of entry below, after first considering another recapitalization strategy: contingent capital.

IV. THE CONTINGENT CONVERTIBLE CAPITAL ALTERNATIVE

For the past three decades, scholars have dreamed about approaches to bank insolvency that might make key features of the formal insolvency framework unnecessary. The most promising of these is the issuance of securities that would convert into equity in the event that a bank fell into financial distress. In the wake of the 2008 crisis, convertible contingent capital securities, or CoCos, are in wide circulation for the first time. In Europe, more than 100 billion euros of CoCos have been issued. After briefly describing the scholarly literature on these securities and their predecessors, I highlight the key design issues they raise and consider the relationship between these securities and the formal resolution rules.

During the S&L crisis of the 1980s and the early 1990s, several scholars proposed an early version of these contingent securities. Under the most prominent of the proposals, a bank would be required to issue a specified amount of puttable subordinated debt.[54] Holders of puttable subdebt could, and presumably would, put their debt back to the bank if its value fell below par. If lawmakers tied initiation to investors' exercise of their put options, insolvency proceedings might routinely be triggered as soon as a bank's net worth fell below zero.[55]

In the corporate bankruptcy literature, Barry Adler proposed that corporations issue debt, which he called "chameleon equity," that would automatically convert to equity if the firm defaulted.[56] Unlike the puttable subdebt proposal, which was designed to push troubled banks into insolvency proceedings, Adler's chameleon equity approach would recapitalize a troubled company after it had defaulted. If the company's distress were temporary, it might dramatically simplify the formal insolvency proceedings or even obviate the need for bankruptcy altogether.[57]

More recently, banking scholars have advocated that bank holding companies issue a very similar form of security that has become known as convertible contingent capital, or a CoCo.[58] Like chameleon equity, CoCos would convert to equity as the bank holding company's condition deteriorated. With CoCos, the conversion would come prior to a default. If effective, CoCos would quickly recapitalize a company, making formal resolution proceedings unnecessary.

The most difficult design issue is the trigger: Should an administrative official decide when the CoCo converts to equity, or should a market signal such as a drop in the market value of the securities or a decline in bank capital trigger the conversion? Both approaches have significant downsides. Administrators often wait too long to intervene and may be subject to political pressures. Some market triggers may be subject to manipulation. Banks may have the ability to manipulate the amount of capital they report, for instance. If conversion is triggered by a decline in the market price of the CoCos, and the bonds would sharply diminish in value after conversion, the prospect of conversion could create a feedback effect that prevents the trigger from occurring. If the bonds will retain their value and significantly dilute the bank's common stock in the event of conversion, by contrast, a stock price decline could snowball toward the conversion trigger and the trigger might invite manipulation.[59]

The most promising recent proposals rely on a market trigger that would occur much earlier in a bank's decline than the traditional approach. Charles Calomiris and Richard Herring propose, for instance, CoCos that would be triggered when the market value of a SIFI's equity, divided by the sum of the market value of the equity and the face value of its debt, dropped to 8%.[60] To avoid manipulation, Calomiris and Herring would base the value of the SIFI's equity on a 90-day moving average of its price.[61] To ensure that the CoCos would significantly dilute the value of the SIFI's equity, thus giving its managers a strong incentive to avoid conversion by maintaining a strong equity buffer, Calomiris and Herring advocate that SIFI's be required to issue CoCos with a face amount equal to or greater than 10% of the book value of the SIFI's assets; and that the conversion ratio ensure that equity would be diluted by at least 5%.[62] While many scholars would use the equity prices in their trigger, as Calomiris and Herring do,[63] other scholars have proposed triggers based on credit default swap spreads.[64]

Although CoCos were largely hypothetical before the recent crisis, European banks have now issued 100 billion euros of CoCos. In Switzerland, regulators required the two largest banks, UBS and Credit Suisse, to issue CoCos due to concerns that the banks would be "too big to save" if they failed. The Swiss vote of approval seems to have magnified the perceived legitimacy of CoCos.

In contrast to Europe, CoCos are still quite uncommon in the U.S. Why is this? The principal reason for SIFIs' failure to issue CoCos in the U.S. seems to be the disfavored tax and regulatory status of CoCos. Because CoCos convert to equity, they may not qualify as debt for tax purposes, which would preclude the issuing bank from deducting its interest payments on the CoCos.[65] CoCos also do not receive favorable regulatory treatment for the purpose of the bank's capital requirements.

Suppose that these obstacles disappear once CoCos fully take hold in Europe. How would they shape bank regulation and resolution? If bank SIFIs issued market-based CoCos, they might counteract the regulatory hesitancy that delayed intervention in 2008. Although Citigroup appeared to be insolvent, for instance, bondholders rightly assumed that regulators would not be willing to let Citigroup fail.[66] If Citigroup had issued CoCos, the CoCos might have triggered a recapitalization and possibly even avoided the need for the massive bailout that regulators funneled to Citigroup through the TARP program.

Yet even the best-designed CoCos would not serve as a substitute for a resolution framework, as advocates for CoCos acknowledge. "[I]f an institution waits too long [to replenish its equity]," as Calomiris and Herring put it, "or experiences a sudden, dramatic loss of market confidence (as in the Enron collapse), it may find that it can sell assets only at distressed prices."[67] Relatedly, CoCos are limited by the fact that they only dilute the financial institution's equity; unlike Chameleon Equity and related proposals, CoCos do not cancel the existing stock, even if the financial institution is clearly insolvent. CoCos may make insolvency less likely, but they do not fully resolve the distress of a financial institution that does become insolvent.

One can imagine at least two responses to these limitations. The first is to require financial institutions to hold much higher amounts of true equity, so that insolvency is unlikely. In a sense, lawmakers might require pure equity, rather than the conditional equity of a CoCo.[68] The second alternative is to permit or encourage CoCos but also provide a bankruptcy or resolution framework as a backstop. Since the financial crisis, regulators have ratcheted up equity requirements, but not to the levels that equity proponents advocate. The bankruptcy and resolution rules are therefore essential to the overall framework. It is to those rules that we now turn.

V. THE SINGLE POINT OF ENTRY STRATEGY FOR RESOLVING SIFIS

As enacted, Title II is a strategy for liquidating SIFIs that fall into financial distress. As we saw earlier, if a genuine liquidation were the only option under Title II, regulators would be extremely reluctant to use it. After Title II was enacted, the FDIC developed a more promising strategy for implementing Title known as single point of entry.[69] Single point of entry would recapitalize a troubled SIFI rather than liquidating it. It is, in a sense, a more thorough-going version of the recapitalization that CoCos are designed to provide.

The new approach is called single point of entry because the holding company atop a financial institution's corporate structure would be put into receivership but most if not all of the affiliated entities would not.[70] The restructuring would occur primarily at the holding company level, with liquidity down-streamed to affiliates as necessary.

In a single-point-of-entry resolution, the FDIC would transfer all of the holding company's assets, any short-term unsecured debt, and any secured debt to a newly created bridge institution. The holding company's stock and long-term unsecured debt would be left behind, leaving the bridge institution with a more sustainable capital structure. At some point thereafter, the FDIC would (probably) wipe out the old stock and would convert at least some of the long-term debt to stock in the bridge entity. If one or more subsidiaries were facing a solvency issue, the holding company could inject capital by converting obligations owed by the subsidiary to the bridge entity into stock or by contributing other holding company assets (including receivables from other subsidiaries) to the needy subsidiary.[71]

The single point of entry approach is far from foolproof, and I will consider some of its limitations below. But single point of entry is considerably more promising than the structure envisioned by the rules as enacted.[72]

A. Benefits of Single Point of Entry

Start with the uncertainty as to whether and how regulators will intervene.[73] With a well-defined single point of entry strategy in place, it is at least possible that regulators would invoke the resolution rules if a systemically important financial institution threatened to fail. The uncertainty would not be dispelled altogether, but it is more plausible that regulators would use Title II to effect a single-point-of-entry restructuring than it is that they would take over a giant financial institution and wind it down.

Second, because single point of entry promises that the financial institution's derivatives and other short-term debt will be fully protected, it diminishes the likelihood of runs in the event a financial institution threatens to default. (There are costs as well as benefits to the protection of derivatives, but I save the costs for the next section.) The risk of runs will not disappear altogether; repo lenders may still refuse to roll over their repo loans, for instance. But single point of entry reduces the downside consequences of failure for a financial institution's short-term creditors and as a result should dampen the incentive to run.

Finally, if the single point of entry plan works as intended, it addresses the global consequences of a failure by limiting the consequences of default to the U.S. holding company. Foreign subsidiaries theoretically will be insulated from the failure and will continue to operate on normal terms. So long as the crisis is limited to the U.S. holding company, or to the holding company and one or more U.S. subsidiaries, the effects of a financial institution's default outside the United States will be much less serious than with Lehman.[74]

B. Potential Problems with Single Point of Entry

The first concern with single point of entry is simply that regulators won't use it. The decision whether to invoke Title II is entirely discretionary, and the U.S. Treasury, Federal Reserve and FDIC all must agree to the intervention. Although single point of entry will make regulators more comfortable intervening than they would be if their only option were to liquidate the SIFI, regulators still will be tempted to delay, rather than take responsibility for the potential collapse of a large financial institution. The longer the time lag between the last crisis and the next one, the greater the temptation may be, since regulators' heightened state of readiness for the next crisis will inevitably erode with time. In part for this reason, the Federal Reserve and FDIC have recently developed potential triggers that are designed to force a struggling SIFI to replenish its capital and liquidity, and if this is not sufficient, to prompt regulators to intervene.[75] If the triggers are effective, they may counteract the temptation to delay. But there is a risk the triggers will prove subject to manipulation, will not function effectively, or will be weakened over time, or that regulators will delay initiation even if the triggers signal that Title II should be invoked.

Second, even if regulators are willing to intervene, single point of entry could prove problematic if one or more of the SIFI's subsidiaries is deeply insolvent. Although the FDIC has considered ways of down-streaming capital and liquidity to troubled subsidiaries, capital and liquidity alone may not be enough to solve the problems. The risk of subsidiary-level complications could be particularly acute if there are problems with a non-U.S. subsidiary. U.S. regulators would not have any control over the restructuring or liquidation of a non-U.S. subsidiary.

A third problem stems from the prospect that, if SIFIs were left to their own devices, they might have very little long-term holding company debt left when the time came to effect a single point of entry restructuring. Because the long term holding company debt will be written down in a restructuring, whereas other debt will be protected, holding company debt may become more costly and subsidiary debt comparatively cheap. Other things equal, SIFIs might therefore shift away from long-term holding company debt, leaving too little to recapitalize the SIFI effectively if it fell into financial distress.

Regulators are of course well aware of these incentives; they have responded by mandating that SIFI holding companies retain substantial amounts of long-term debt. In November 2014, the Financial Stability Board (FSB) issued a proposal for imposing new total loss-absorbing capacity (TLAC) requirements on global systemically important banking groups (G-SIBs) that would supplement Basel III regulatory capital requirements.[76] The Fed released a proposed rule for U.S. SIFIs in 2015,[77] and it was subsequently finalized. Even if the restrictions prove effective, regulators will be forced to police yet another dimension of SIFIs' capital restructure. The risk of evasion is especially high given the clash between the SIFIs' incentives and the regulatory objective of ensuring that SIFIs have enough long-term debt for an effective recapitalization.

With derivatives and other financial contracts, single point of entry creates precisely the opposite problem. Since derivatives and other short-term obligations will be fully protected, SIFIs have an incentive to use more of them. Given the problems with these financial contracts in 2008, the added incentive to use fragile forms of financing could have dangerous unintended consequences. To be sure, the risks are mitigated somewhat by the increased clearing and exchange trading of derivatives. But a substantial percentage of derivatives still are not cleared; and with cleared derivatives, the protection may have a dampening effort on the clearinghouses' monitoring incentives.

An additional complication is the uncertainty whether regulators will in fact use single point of entry rather than bankruptcy if a SIFI falls into financial distress, and whether they will put a SIFI's bank into bank resolution rather than protecting the bank's shareholders and creditors.[78] To invoke Title II, regulators must conclude that the SIFI's failure could cause systemic harm. In many cases, it will not. Derivatives are protected under single point of entry but not in bankruptcy, which may induce derivatives counterparties to run if they are uncertain which resolution mechanism will be used. Creditors of a bank subsidiary will be paid in full under single point of entry but will bear significant losses in a traditional bank resolution, a risk they may pass on to the bank in the form of higher credit costs.

Finally, single point of entry violates the spirit—and arguably the letter—of Title II's liquidation requirement. The new strategy's objective is to reorganize a troubled SIFI through a quick recapitalization. Although it is possible to characterize single point of entry as a liquidation—the SIFI's assets technically are transferred to a new entity, and the old entity is eventually liquidated—the effect is indistinguishable from a reorganization. This could subject regulators' intervention to legal challenge.

VI. THE BANKRUPTCY ALTERNATIVE TO TITLE II

Although bankruptcy is central to the new synthesis of banking regulation and bankruptcy, and the word bankruptcy appears sixty times (by my count) in the Dodd-Frank Act, Dodd-Frank left the Bankruptcy Code untouched. Lawmakers steered clear of bankruptcy for political reasons, not because they thought that the bankruptcy laws are just right in their current condition.[79] Indeed, advocates of the Dodd-Frank Act argued that bankruptcy is inadequate to the task of resolving the largest troubled SIFI. In my view, defended at length elsewhere, the current bankruptcy rules are far more effective than critics (and the conventional wisdom) suggest.[80] But in several areas, such as the special privileges given to derivatives and other financial contracts, the current rules undermine bankruptcy's effectiveness.

The discussion that follows begins by critiquing the current treatment of derivatives and other financial contracts. I then describe Chapter 14, the most comprehensive recent package of proposed bankruptcy reforms, both as initially proposed and as modified to authorize a quick sale modeled on Title II's single point of entry strategy.

A. Bankruptcy's Flaw: The Safe Harbors for Derivatives and Repos

Over the past thirty years, regulators have steadily expanded a set of exceptions for derivatives, repos and other financial contracts from a variety of core bankruptcy provisions.[81] The automatic stay prevents ordinary creditors from cancelling their contracts or seizing collateral from a financial institution that has filed for bankruptcy. If the debtor gave new collateral to a creditor or made a large payment shortly before bankruptcy, it may be able to retrieve these assets in bankruptcy. Derivatives and repo counterparties are not subject to any of these provisions. They can cancel their contracts and sell any collateral they hold whenever they wish.

Although a variety of justifications have been advanced for the departure from the ordinary rules, the principal rationale was that the impeding derivatives counterparties' ability to exit their contracts and re-hedge their position could jeopardize the financial stability of the counterparties themselves. Permitting the counterparties to terminate their contracts would reduce the risk that a financial institution's failure would cause systemic harm. The 2008 crisis revealed a serious shortcoming of this rationale: the safe harbors can make it impossible for a financial institution to halt its deterioration even briefly, thus exacerbating the effects of its financial distress.[82] They also make it harder for a troubled institution to arrange for sales or other distributions of its assets in bankruptcy, since counterparties cannot be prevented from fleeing before the sale takes place. The safe harbors also have deleterious ex ante effects, diminishing the counterparties' incentive to monitor the debtor and increasing a financial institution's incentive to use this form of funding rather than less fragile sources of funds.

The most promising response to these concerns is to partially reverse the safe harbors.[83] Fully reversing the safe harbors, and imposing an automatic stay of potentially unlimited duration, would sharply increase counterparties' incentive to run when a SIFI encountered financial distress. A counterparty that failed to exit before bankruptcy could be trapped in the bankruptcy process. Although even a brief stay would increase the incentive to run, the effect would be less dramatic. Title II provides a one day stay for derivatives, which is one plausible approach; a somewhat longer stay—such as three days—seems preferable, given the difficulty of making an immediate decision which derivatives portfolios to assume and which to reject.[84] Although even this seems too short to some, a short stay should prove sufficient for a financial institution that prepares for its bankruptcy before filing (unlike Lehman Brothers, which made almost no advance preparation for its bankruptcy).

The calculus is somewhat different for repos, which are often very short term and function like secured loans. If the collateral for the repo is treasury bills or other liquid securities, the risk of disruption is limited, even in the absence of a stay. If the collateral is mortgage-backed securities or other illiquid assets, however, as with Bear Stearns and Lehman, the absence of a stay may lead to fire sales as the debtor's counterparties sell the collateral. Repos with illiquid collateral should therefore be subject to a stay.[85]

Mark Roe and Stephen Adams have recently advocated an additional change to the treatment of derivatives in bankruptcy.[86] They argue, persuasively in my view, that a debtor should be permitted to retain or sell its entire portfolio of a particular derivatives product. Thus, the debtor could sell its portfolio of interest rate swaps or foreign exchange derivatives as a single package. Under existing law, a debtor often enters into a master agreement with a particular counterparty, and may include different derivatives products in the same agreement. If a buyer wished to buy the debtor's interest rate swaps, for instance, but not its other derivatives, the debtor could not easily preserve and transfer only that portion of its derivatives portfolio. Under current law, the debtor might need to transfer derivatives counterparty by counterparty, or simply transfer its entire portfolio. Permitting the debtor to assume and sell its derivatives by product line could significantly enhance the debtor's ability to arrange sales, since buyers might be more interested in a particular derivatives product than the debtor's entire derivatives book.

B. The Chapter 14 Proposal

Starting in 2009, a working group at the Hoover Institution devised a set of proposals that are designed to make bankruptcy better able to handle the financial distress of large financial institutions.[87] In addition to safe harbor reforms similar to those described above, the initial Chapter 14 proposal included a variety of other changes. I briefly describe several of the most important proposals in original Chapter 14 in this section; in the section that follows, I take up the group's subsequent proposal for a bankruptcy analogue to the FDIC's single point of entry strategy.[88]

Start with the role of regulators. In an ordinary Chapter 11 case, the regulators' ability to participate is quite constrained. Perhaps most importantly, they cannot initiate the bankruptcy case. The Chapter 14 proposal would explicitly authorize regulators to file an involuntary bankruptcy case against an insolvent financial institution that was of sufficient financial size;[89] and it would give regulators standing to appear and be heard on any issue in the case. Although regulators have traditionally been slow to take action, this proposal would enable them to file a case if managers failed to do so, and it provides a mechanism for tapping the information regulators have as a result of their ongoing supervisory role. In addition, it ensures a voice for systemic consequences in the bankruptcy proceeding.

Chapter 14 also would alter bankruptcy's debtor-in-possession financing provision to permit the debtor to make immediate, partial payments from any new financing to creditors (such as derivatives counterparties) with time sensitive claims. If the initial payment gives these creditors more than other general creditors eventually receive, the difference could be clawed back. But any clawback would occur much later, after the initial crisis had passed.[90]

A third innovation of Chapter 14 is its proposed judicial framework. Under Chapter 14, the case would be overseen by a federal district court judge selected by the chief judge of the federal court of appeals from a panel of judges with financial expertise. This would address any concerns about independence or jurisdictional scope. Chapter 14 also would explicitly authorize the judge to make use of special masters if he wished to bring additional expertise into the case.

If fully implemented, Chapter 14 would make a number of other adjustments as well. Chapter 14 would remove the outdated exclusion of brokerage operations from Chapter 11, for instance, and would permit insurance companies to file for bankruptcy.

Critics of Chapter 14 have questioned whether Chapter 14 would prove effective for the largest SIFIs, arguing that a much more robust source of funding would be needed and questioning whether a negotiated resolution of a SIFI's financial distress would work.[91] In part in response to these concerns, the Chapter 14 group developed an alternative resolution strategy that is closely analogous to the FDIC's single point of entry innovation. Since that proposal has subsumed the original proposal, I turn to it now, before providing a fuller assessment.

C. The Quick Sale Strategy for SIFIs in Bankruptcy

Under the most recent Chapter 14 proposal, the holding company of a troubled SIFI would file for bankruptcy and immediately propose under section 363 to transfer its assets and short-term liabilities to a newly created corporation, leaving its stock and long-term debt behind.[92] Unlike with an ordinary section 363 sale, which usually includes an auction period lasting at least thirty days, the new Chapter 14 proposes that the bankruptcy judge approve or disapprove the sale within two days, after notice to the holding company's largest creditors. The transfer would quickly recapitalize the debtor, much as with single point of entry under Title II.

In theory, a bankruptcy court could approve a quick sale that took this form under current bankruptcy law, although the parties could not be certain in advance that the judge would agree to act so quickly. Even if judges were willing to give or withhold their approval quickly, however, three potential problems could stymy such a sale under current law.

One potential problem is the derivatives safe harbors. Under current U.S. bankruptcy law, there is no stay at all on derivatives, as we have seen. Because the holding companies of most American SIFIs do not have significant derivatives portfolios, the absence of a stay on holding company derivatives is not as problematic as it might initially seem. The more pressing issue is the absence of a stay on termination of derivatives held by the SIFI's subsidiaries, especially commercial banking subsidiaries. Of particular concern are so-called cross-default provisions—that is, provisions in derivatives and other contracts that have been entered into by a SIFI holding company's affiliates that give the affiliate's counterparties the right to terminate their contracts if the holding company defaults or files for bankruptcy. Even if U.S. lawmakers were to enact legislation preventing affiliate counterparties from terminating their contracts, the U.S. law would not be binding in other countries; the creditors of a non-U.S. affiliate (such as Lehman's U.K. subsidiaries) might therefore terminate their derivatives if the holding company filed for Chapter 11, even if U.S. law prohibited the counterparties of U.S. affiliates from terminating.

In late 2014, the International Swaps and Derivatives Association promulgated the ISDA 2014 Resolution Stay Protocol, which provides a partial contractual solution to the cross-default problem.[93] By agreeing to adhere to the ISDA Protocol, a financial institution commits to honor the restrictions on its default and termination rights that are imposed by the resolution framework that governs a parent or affiliate of the counterparty with whom it has contracted.[94] The ISDA Protocol also covers U.S. bankruptcy proceedings, but in a more limited fashion than with Title II and other bank resolution regimes. The Protocol prevents the counterparties of an affiliate from terminating their derivatives for two business days after a Chapter 11 filing, but does not apply to counterparties of an entity that itself files for bankruptcy. A year after the initial Protocol, the ISDA adopted an expanded version.[95]

In its current form, the ISDA Protocol only partially addresses the need for a stay on cross default provisions in the context of a quick sale. The Protocol's first limitation is simply that it does not apply unless a financial institution voluntarily agrees to adhere to the Protocol. The Fed and FDIC can close this gap by threatening to take enforcement action against any SIFI that refuses to agree to the Protocol's strictures, and they have already essentially done this.[96] But institutions over which bank regulators have less authority may evade the reach of the Protocol. More importantly, the absence of a stay on an affiliate's counterparties if the affiliate itself files for bankruptcy could prove to be a serious limitation.[97] If it is necessary to put both the holding company and a troubled subsidiary into bankruptcy, and the subsidiary has a significant derivatives portfolio, the Protocol will not prevent counterparties of the subsidiary from terminating their contracts. The Protocol may thus prove helpful in simple quick sale cases—cases in which only the holding company needs to file for bankruptcy—but not in messier cases. To more fully close the circle, lawmakers need to reverse the existing derivatives safe harbors.

In addition to a more complete stay on derivatives, a second adjustment that would be needed is a provision assuring that any licenses that are transferred in the initial sale would continue to be valid, so that the company did not risk a disruption in its ability to do business as a result of the sale. Although bank regulators may be able to ensure the continuity of banking charters even under existing law, an explicit statutory protection of existing licenses would remove the risk that a license might be terminated when the holding company transferred its assets to a new entity as part of a quick sale resolution.[98]

The other major issue is funding. As discussed earlier, Title II makes huge amounts of funding available from the U.S. Treasury for a Dodd-Frank resolution. Although the financing provisions of U.S. bankruptcy law are extremely generous by international standards, they rely on financing by private lenders.[99] There are serious questions whether private financing could be raised quickly enough in the midst of a SIFI's distress to satisfy its liquidity needs. Many commentators who have followed the bank resolution discussions do not believe that it could be. Although I agree that at least limited access to public funding is needed, a SIFI's existing funding options seem much more substantial, and its liquidity needs less extensive, than is often recognized. Given the centrality of the funding issue, it warrants separate, more extensive discussion.

D. Funding a SIFI Bankruptcy[100]

Start with the SIFI's likely access to private funding. The new entity created by the quick sale will be a much better candidate for funding than the pre-bankruptcy SIFI, since it will have left its long-term debt behind, with the expectation that much or all of the debt will be converted into equity in the new entity. It is possible that this cleansing of its capital structure would enable the new entity to very quickly arrange funding from private lenders, especially if the SIFI arranges the funding in advance. Because the new entity will not be in bankruptcy, the funding would not even require bankruptcy court approval.[101]

The magnitude of the SIFI's financing needs may also be manageable. If the new capital and liquidity requirements imposed by Dodd-Frank and other new regulatory efforts are at all effective, a SIFI's capital and liquidity condition may be better when it fails than would have been true in previous years. "Better" doesn't mean good, of course. But SIFIs might not be quite so far gone when they file for bankruptcy in the new regulatory order, particularly if they think that regulators may otherwise take over the SIFI and put it in Title II resolution.

The quick sale itself also should further limit the SIFI's initial liquidity needs. The quick sale is quite similar to a prepackaged bankruptcy in this regard.[102] Because prepackaged bankruptcies quickly recapitalize the troubled company, they require much less DIP financing than other Chapter 11 cases. SIFIs are quite different than the companies that generally file prepackaged bankruptcy cases; their liquidity can disappear much more quickly, and liquidity is central to their business model.[103] But the general pattern should hold true.

It is also important to keep in mind that if the SIFI fell into distress during a period of market-wide crisis, as in 2008, and private financing disappeared, the Federal Reserve could fill in the gap.[104] Although the Dodd-Frank Act restricted the Federal Reserve's emergency lending authority under section 13(3) of the Federal Reserve Act— prohibiting it from making emergency loans to individual institutions[105]—the Fed still has the authority to create industry-wide lending programs. In the event of market-wide crisis, the Fed could set up an industry-wide borrowing mechanism.

If one were to conclude that an additional form of funding is necessary due to the uncertainty of private-market funding, what form should that funding take? One obvious alternative would be to replicate the funding terms of Dodd-Frank. A troubled financial institution could be given access to Treasury funding in the same or similar amounts. The principal concern with this approach is that it seems to put too much funding at the new entity's disposal. In theory, this need not have distortive effects, but it is impossible to avoid the suspicion that it would. In my view, these concerns counsel in favor of a more carefully calibrated approach.

The most plausible approach might be to explicitly extend the Fed's section 13(3) lending authority to cover an individual SIFI that has filed for bankruptcy and its successor entity.[106] Fed lending is limited to financial institutions that are solvent and are capable of providing adequate collateral, and is only available if the Fed determines that the loan is needed to avoid systemic harm.[107] The new financial institution that acquired a troubled SIFI's assets should be able to meet both requirements, but a troubled financial institution that used the ordinary bankruptcy process could not, since it would almost certainly be insolvent. As a result, access to the funds would be tightly constrained. The risk of a disguised bailout would be significantly lower than with Title II-style liquidity.

The systemic harm prerequisite to funding under section 13(3) would effectively limit governmental funding to bankruptcies of the largest SIFIs, but this is as it should be. The ordinary bankruptcy liquidity options should be adequate for effective resolution of financial institutions that are not systemically important.

The Federal Reserve backstop isn't foolproof. The presence or absence of adequate security is to some extent in the eye of the beholder, especially with a complicated financial institution whose assets are not easily valued. The Fed could manipulate access, much as it is thought by many to have manipulated its emergency lending powers in 2008. But it is subject to significantly more constraints than Title II-style funding.

If the FDIC took a more assertive role in facilitating bankruptcy funding, it could pre-arrange a source of liquidity even in the absence of formal legislative authority such as an amendment to the Fed's emergency lending powers. Under the systemic risk exception to the ordinary bank resolution rules, the FDIC has broad authority to provide funding for a commercial bank subsidiary that it has put in receivership.[108] As Howell Jackson and Stephanie Massman have pointed out, this authority could be used to inject liquidity into a SIFI's commercial bank subsidiary if the bank were put into receivership as regulators put the holding company into bankruptcy. The FDIC could ensure its availability for nonbank subsidiaries through a framework of guarantees by the SIFI's holding company, commercial bank and nonbank subsidiaries.[109] The principal limitation of the funding, as with an expansion of the Fed's emergency lending powers, is that it is only available for institutions whose failure could produce a systemic crisis.

Overall, the problem of ensuring adequate funding for a quick sale in bankruptcy seems more tractable than critics have contended. It is plausible that a troubled SIFI could arrange financing even as things currently stand. The FDIC could provide an additional source of funding for a SIFI, at least for SIFIs that truly are systemically important, even if Congress does not amend the Fed's emergency lending powers.

VII. IS THE NEW REGULATORY SYNTHESIS COHERENT?

In the final substantive Part of this chapter, I take a step back, and briefly consider how the major pieces of the new regulatory synthesis fit together. I focus first on the relationship between Title I and Title II of the Dodd-Frank Act, and then on the more problematic relationship between Title II and bankruptcy.

A. Tensions Within the Dodd-Frank Framework

Dodd-Frank has come in for criticism as 1) needlessly complex and 2) internally incoherent. The first part of this criticism—needless complexity—would be hard to deny. The Volcker Rule, which bans most proprietary trading by commercial banks, is hundreds of pages long. Even before regulators finally released the final rule, many of the largest banks had added numerous regulatory compliance officers whose primary responsibility is managing Volcker Rule compliance. The regulatory burden might be justified if the Volcker Rule enhances the safety of the largest banks, but there is little reason to believe that it will. It and other new regulatory obligations have steeply increased the compliance burdens of all banks, not just the largest institutions. Ironically, Dodd-Frank's complexity solidifies the pre-eminence of the largest banks, since they enjoy economies of scale in handling regulatory compliance costs.

The second, internal incoherence claim is more subtle and more directly relevant to my concerns in this chapter. Prominent banking consultant Karen Petrou Shaw has argued that the regulatory objectives of Titles I and II of Dodd-Frank are directly at odds with one another. "On the one hand," as a *New York Times* columnist summarized her diagnosis, Title II "is very clear that if a big bank becomes insolvent, there can be no taxpayer bailout. It must be wound down, just like any other bank."[110] Yet, as they implement Title I, regulators "are adding a host of special Too Big to Fail capital requirements and rules. 'They are acting as if these institutions are still too big to fail. The two thrusts are incompatible.'"[111]

Before asking whether these two key titles can be reconciled, let me first note a tension within Title I itself. Although Title I's designation process and capital requirements can be seen as entrenching Too Big to

Fail, several other features have an opposing thrust. Regulators can refuse to approve acquisitions by the largest banks, for instance, and even force them to downsize;[112] the Volcker Rule fits the break up theme. Whether or not the tension was intended, it reinforces the corporatist tendencies of the Dodd-Frank Act.[113] Absent a successful populist legislative intervention, the size restrictions and Volcker Rule will serve as leverage to reinforce the implicit partnership between the government and the largest banks. The TBTF orientation of Title I will be reinforced rather than undermined.

Absent single point of entry, the tension between Titles I and II—Petrou's particular concern—almost certainly would have been resolved the same way. Regulators would bail out a struggling SIFI rather than risking a messy liquidation under Title II. At least for the largest banks, Title II would be a dead letter.[114] Although Dodd-Frank prohibits rescue loans to a single institution, as we have seen, regulators could sidestep the restriction by putting an industry-wide program in place. Bailouts would be nearly as likely as before the Dodd-Frank Act.

The relationship between Titles I and II looks quite different in a world with single point of entry. Regulators might actually use single point of entry. If single point of entry worked as envisioned, the troubled bank would be recapitalized; it would not receive a 2008-style bailout. The bank would, however, remain nearly as large, and the banking industry would be just as concentrated, as before the single point of entry resolution.

As a matter of semantics, one might still claim that Title II is in tension with Title I, since Title I protects the largest institutions and tries to prevent them from defaulting, whereas Title II is triggered by a looming default. But the regulatory framework really is quite consistent. Title I is the first line of defense, and single point of entry is the backup; there is redundancy, perhaps, but a single objective: Both aim to preserve the current structure of the banking industry.

One can debate whether the current structure is desirable. In my view, the concentration of the U.S. banking industry is problematic, potentially chilling innovation and diminishing the access of small and medium-sized businesses to financing. If the largest banks were forced to downsize—or better yet, rewarded for downsizing[115]—these distortions might be reduced. The current framework is thus problematic, in my view, but it is nevertheless coherent.

The still-awkward relationship between Title II and bankruptcy, by contrast, raises questions of coherence. Once they are identified, both proponents and critics of the new synthesis should agree that at least some of the frictions need to be addressed. These frictions will occupy the rest of our discussion.

B. Frictions in the Title II–Bankruptcy Framework

1. Frictions in the basic framework

As noted earlier, the new regulatory synthesis takes a contradictory stance on the relationship between Title II and bankruptcy. The Dodd-Frank Act consistently prioritizes bankruptcy. The living will requirement instructs SIFIs to explain how they can be resolved in an orderly fashion in bankruptcy, not Title II; and Title II identifies bankruptcy as the preferred option, regulators are not permitted to invoke Title II unless they conclude that bankruptcy would prove systemically disruptive. Yet Title II explicitly trumps bankruptcy in the new regulatory scheme. If a SIFI files for bankruptcy, bank regulators can invoke Title II and take over the SIFI at any time, displacing the ongoing bankruptcy proceedings.[116]

Frictions also exist at the level of individual provisions. Although lawmakers incorporated a number of bankruptcy provisions into the Title II framework,[117] Title II is based primarily on the FDIC's bank resolution powers. Like bank resolution, but unlike bankruptcy, Title II imposes a one-plus day stay on derivatives, freezes cross default provisions, and invalidates walkaway provisions—which allow a derivatives counterparty to terminate a contract without making any payments to the SIFI debtor, even if the debtor is in the money.[118] Bankruptcy does not give a SIFI debtor any of these protections.

The treatment of SIFI managers is similarly divergent. Although the absence of a stay on derivatives reduces the benefits of bankruptcy, the managers of a troubled SIFI still may be willing to plan for and use bankruptcy, since they will continue to run the business at the outset of the bankruptcy case; the managers can effectuate their plans. Yet the managers cannot be certain that the resolution will in fact take place in bankruptcy. Regulators can move the proceedings to Title II.[119] If they do, the top managers lose control, will be promptly replaced, and may have their pre-default compensation clawed back.[120] Given the threat of Title II, managers may postpone bankruptcy and perhaps resist a bankruptcy filing altogether, much as Lehman Brothers did.

What could be done to resolve these frictions? One obvious step is to better coordinate the two frameworks. At the very least, lawmakers should amend the bankruptcy laws to provide the same limited stay and other protections in bankruptcy that a SIFI is given in Title II. Although this would not reduce counterparties' incentives to run, it would not substantially increase the likelihood of runs; and the stay would enhance bankruptcy's effectiveness in halting a run and would facilitate more effective resolution in bankruptcy.

The same logic might counsel in favor of either removing the manager penalties from Title II or adding them to bankruptcy, so that managers would receive the same treatment under both frameworks. Here, however, I would propose a different solution. Rather than equalizing the treatment, regulators could commit to leave a SIFI that has filed for bankruptcy in bankruptcy. From this perspective, bankruptcy's softer landing might strengthen managers' incentive to prepare and file for bankruptcy rather than waiting for regulators to intervene.[121]

2. Frictions created by single point of entry

The frictions we have considered thus far have been created by the Dodd-Frank framework itself. The single point of entry and bankruptcy quick sale strategies have introduced still another set of potential frictions. Under single point of entry, the bondholders and other long-term creditors of a SIFI's holding company will bear the burden of the SIFI's recapitalization. By contrast, if regulators put a SIFI's bank subsidiary into an ordinary bank receivership, bondholders of the bank, rather than holding company bondholders, may bear much of the cost of the restructuring. The incidence of the burden will be very different, depending on the resolution technique that regulators employ. One potential cost of the uncertainty may be difficulty issuing new bond debt at either the holding company or the subsidiary level as a SIFI's condition declines, since it is not clear which will bear the losses in the event of a default. Both sets of creditors need to assume that they will bear the brunt of the restructuring.

I do not think there is a fully satisfying solution to this problem. The Federal Reserve's TLAC requirements mandate that bank SIFIs maintain adequate buffers of long term debt, which theoretically will set a floor on the holding company's and banking subsidiary's issuance of long-term debt. If bank regulators are clear about what to expect if they intervene, they can further reduce the amount of uncertainty. Significant uncertainty is likely to remain, however. And the strategic incentives created by single point of entry—to issue debt at the entity that is less likely to be restructured—will require bank regulators to actively monitor SIFIs' capital structure. Given the mismatch between regulators' objective of ensuring an adequate buffer of long term debt, and the SIFI's incentives—minimizing its debt costs by raising money at entities whose debt will not be restructured—SPOE will invite the kinds of regulatory arbitrage that have long bedeviled capital regulation.

The difficulty SIFIs may have raising funds as their financial condition deteriorates does have one silver lining: it will strengthen their managers' incentive to file for bankruptcy sooner than might otherwise be the case—perhaps soon enough to enhance the prospects for an effective resolution.

CONCLUSION

Over the past ten years, the Dodd-Frank Act has reshaped the relationship between banking regulation and bankruptcy. In one sense, it dramatically expanded the reach of banking-style resolution, since the legislation gives bank regulators resolution authority over bank holding companies and investment banking operations that previously were subject solely to bankruptcy in the event of financial distress. But the Act also incorporates bankruptcy into bank regulation, as with the requirement that SIFIs' living wills outline how the SIFI could be resolved in an orderly fashion in bankruptcy.

The more effective the bankruptcy process is, the less necessary Title II will be. Even in its current configuration, bankruptcy law is a much better resolution mechanism than many commentators have recognized. With a handful of additional changes—most importantly, the reintroduction of a stay on derivatives—bankruptcy law would be a credible resolution strategy for nearly any SIFI. Given the benefits of bankruptcy as compared to Title II, this is a consummation devoutly to be wished. Title II will work best if it is available if necessary, but rarely or never used in practice.

Only in passing have I addressed the debate over whether the largest banks should be broken up. If this were actually to happen, my principal recommendations would not change. As noted earlier, I personally would favor a less concentrated banking industry, due to the detrimental effects of concentration on innovation and lending to small and medium-sized businesses. But I leave that particular debate for another day and other work.

NOTES

* S. Samuel Arsht Professor, University of Pennsylvania. Thanks to Barry Adler and Anat Admati for helpful comments on earlier drafts.
1. One obvious illustration: derivatives are defined as "qualified financial contracts" in banking, and as "swaps" in bankruptcy.
2. *See, e.g.*, Dodd-Frank Act § 203(b) (providing rules for taking over a "covered financial company"); § 201(a)(11) defining "financial company" (to include bank holding companies and other companies that are predominately engaged in financial activities).
3. *Id.* § 165(d).
4. *Id.* § 203(b).
5. *Id.* § 206.
6. A working group (of which I am a member) at the Hoover Institution has developed the most detailed proposal for implementing the bankruptcy strategy, which the group calls Chapter 14 2.0 or the "quick sale" strategy. Chapter 14 2.0 revises and supplements the group's earlier proposal for a new Chapter 14, a set of amendments to the Bankruptcy Code that are designed to enhance its effectiveness for SIFIs. *See* Thomas

H. Jackson, *Bankruptcy Code Chapter 14: A Proposal*, *in* BANKRUPTCY *NOT* BAILOUT: A SPECIAL CHAPTER 14, at 25 (Kenneth E. Scott & John B. Taylor, (eds), 2012).

7. These issues are addressed in somewhat more detail in DAVID SKEEL, THE NEW FINANCIAL DEAL: UNDERSTANDING THE DODD-FRANK ACT AND ITS (UNINTENDED) CONSEQUENCES (2010).
8. The best and most complete analysis of initiation issues in the bankruptcy literature is Douglas G. Baird, *The Initiation Problem in Bankruptcy*, 11 INT'L REV. L. & ECON. 223 (1991).
9. In the 1980s and early 1990s, deviations from absolute priority that resulted in recoveries for shareholders in many Chapter 11 cases may also have contributed to the soft landing for managers, since managers generally hold significant amounts of stock. *See, e.g.*, Thomas H. Jackson & Robert E. Scott, *On the Nature of Bankruptcy: An Essay on Bankruptcy Sharing and the Creditors' Bargain*, 75 VA. L. REV. 155 (1989). *But see* Barry E. Adler, *Bankruptcy and Risk Allocation*, 77 CORNELL L. REV. 439 (1992) (pointing out that the soft landing may distort decision-making incentives). But stockholders currently are less likely to receive a recovery.
10. *See, e.g.*, Jonathan R. Macey & Geoffrey P. Miller, *Kaye, Scholer, FIRREA, and the Desirability of Early Closure: A View of the Kaye, Scholer Case from the Perspective of Bank Regulatory Policy*, 66 S. CAL. L. REV. 1115, 1140 (1993).
11. For a brief overview of the requirements, *see* David A. Skeel, Jr., *The Law and Finance of Bank and Insurance Insolvency Regulation*, 76 TEX. L. REV. 723, 740-41 (1998).
12. *See* THOMAS H. JACKSON, THE LOGIC AND LIMITS OF BANKRUPTCY LAW (1986).
13. For discussion of bankruptcy's liquidity-enhancing features, *see* Kenneth Ayotte & David A. Skeel, Jr., *Bankruptcy Law as a Liquidity Provider*, 80 U. CHI. L. REV. 1557 (2013).
14. *See generally* CLIFFORD CHANCE, LEGAL ASPECTS OF BANK BAIL-INS 6 (2011).
15. For detailed discussion, *see* Kenneth Ayotte & David A. Skeel, Jr., *Bankruptcy or Bailouts?*, 35 J. CORP. L. 469, 495 (2009).
16. 11 U.S.C. § 1129(b).
17. The absolute priority rule in § 1129(b) only applies to classes that have not voted in favor of the plan.
18. I say "traditionally" because U.S. law also has given priority to U.S. (but not foreign) deposit claims since the enactment of the National Depositor Preference statute in 1993. 12 U.S.C. § 1821(d)(11)(A).
19. *See, e.g.*, David A. Skeel, Jr. & Thomas H. Jackson, *Transaction Consistency and the New Finance in Bankruptcy*, 112 COLUM. L. REV. 152 (2012); Mark J. Roe, *The Derivatives Market's Payment Priorities as Financial Crisis Accelerator*, 63 STAN. L. REV. 539 (2011); Franklin R. Edwards & Edward R. Morrison, *Derivatives and the Bankruptcy Code: Why the Special Treatment?*, 22 YALE J. REG. 92 (2005).
20. For discussion of this last point, *see* Randall D. Guynn, *Are Bailouts Inevitable?*, 29 YALE J. REG. 121 (2012).
21. 11 U.S.C. § 109(b) (excluding commercial banks and insurance companies from Chapter 7); 11 U.S.C. § 109(d) (excluding persons and entities that cannot file for Chapter 7 from Chapter 11).
22. 11 U.S.C. § 109(b) (excluding insurance companies from Chapter 7). One other important qualification is that investment banks can file for Chapter 7 but cannot file for Chapter 11. 11 U.S.C. § 109(d) (excluding "stockbroker" or "commodity broker" from Chapter 11).
23. *See generally* THOMAS F. HUERTAS, SAFE TO FAIL: HOW RESOLUTION WILL REVOLUTIONISE BANKING (2014).
24. *See, e.g*, Guynn, *supra* note 20.
25. Email correspondence from William Kroener to Thomas Jackson (August 2010).

26. These figures are cited in Richard Hynes & Steven Walt, *Why Banks are Not Allowed in Bankruptcy*, 67 WASH. & LEE L. REV. 985 (2010).
27. *Id.*
28. Hynes and Walt reach a similar conclusion. *Id.*
29. This theme was emphasized in the White Paper that served as the original foundation for the Dodd-Frank Act, *see* U.S. DEPT. OF TREASURY, FINANCIAL REFORM: A NEW FOUNDATION 76 (June 2009), and was repeated throughout the legislative debates.
30. The Volcker Rule enacted as part of the Dodd-Frank Act has sharply reduced the stake a bank holding company can hold in hedge funds or equity funds. Dodd-Frank Act § 619 (limiting holdings to 3% of fund).
31. 11 U.S.C. § 109(b) (excluding commercial banks and insurance companies from filing for bankruptcy, but not holding companies).
32. *See supra* note 22.
33. *Id.* (citing § 109(d)).
34. *See, e.g.*, David A. Skeel, Jr., *Bankruptcy Boundary Games*, 4 BROOK. J. CORP., FIN. & COMM'L L. 1, 3–6 (2009) (criticizing the exclusion of investment banks).
35. Board of Governors v. MCorp Financial, Inc., 502 U.S. 32 (1991). For a useful contemporaneous discussion of *MCorp*, see Craig L. Brown, Note, *Board of Governors v. MCorp Financial, Inc.: Evaluating the Source-of-Strength Doctrine*, 21 HOFSTRA L. REV. 235 (1992). Congress codified source of strength in the Dodd-Frank Act. Dodd-Frank Act § 616.
36. *See, e.g.*, HENRY M. PAULSON, ON THE BRINK: INSIDE THE RACE TO STOP THE COLLAPSE OF THE GLOBAL FINANCIAL SYSTEM (2010).
37. The discussion that follows draws from SKEEL, THE NEW FINANCIAL DEAL, *supra* note 7, which describes the framework in more detail.
38. Dodd-Frank Act § 111.
39. MetLife, Inc. v. Financial Stability Oversight Council, 177 F. Supp. 3d 219 (D.D.C. Mar. 30, 2016).
40. Dodd-Frank Act § 165(d).
41. *Id.* § 121(a)(5).
42. *Id.* § 115(c).
43. *Id.* § 202.
44. *Id.*
45. *Id.* § 210(n). It is worth noting that, in theory, the U.S. Treasury could decline to provide the funding requested by the FDIC in Title II, so the funding is not entirely automatic.
46. *Id.* § 206.
47. *Id.* § 214.
48. *Id.* § 201.
49. Dodd-Frank Act § 165(d).
50. Dodd-Frank Act § 203(b) prohibits regulators from invoking Title II unless the Secretary of the Treasury determines that "the failure of the financial company and its resolution under [other law, e.g., the Bankruptcy Code] would have serious adverse effects on financial stability in the United States."
51. *Id.* § 208.
52. I say "as enacted" to distinguish the literal language of Title II from the single point of entry strategy discussed in Part V below. Single point of entry stands in tension with the literal language of Title II but is in my view a more promising strategy.
53. *See, e.g.*, David A. Skeel, Jr., *An Evolutionary Theory of Corporate Law and Corporate Bankruptcy*, 51 VAND. L. REV. 1325 (1998) (contrasting ex ante and ex post governance approaches). *See also* Barry E. Adler, *A Theory of Corporate Insolvency*, 72 N.Y.U. L. REV. 343 (1997) (demonstrating that capital structure arrangements designed to leave little salvageable value in the event of failure could be efficient).
54. *See, e.g.*, Larry D. Wall, *A Plan for Reducing Future Deposit Insurance Losses: Puttable*

Subordinated Debt, ECON. REV. (Federal Reserve Bank of Atlanta), July/Aug. 1989, at 2–3; Charles W. Calomiris & Charles M. Kahn, *The Role of Demandable Debt in Structuring Optimal Banking Arrangements*, 81 AM. ECON. REV. 497, 500–01 (1991).

55. Puttable subdebt obviously would prove ineffective if regulators propped up the value of the subdebt by implicitly or explicitly promising a bailout in the event of distress, as was done with the biggest banks other than Lehman in 2008.
56. Barry E. Adler, *Financial and Political Theories of American Corporate Bankruptcy*, 45 STAN. L. REV. 311 (1993).
57. For a more complete description and critique of chameleon equity, *see* David A. Skeel, Jr., *Markets, Courts, and the Brave New World of Bankruptcy Theory*, 1993 WISC. L. REV. More recently, Adler has advocated that a similar approach be used in connection with the Dodd-Frank Act's living will requirement. Viral V. Acharya, Barry Adler, Matthew Richardson, and Nouriel Roubini, *Resolution Authority*, in REGULATING WALL STREET: THE DODD-FRANK ACT AND THE NEW ARCHITECTURE OF GLOBAL FINANCE 213, 235 (Viral V. Acharya et al, (eds) 2011) ("In the event of an uncured default (after ample opportunity for cure) on a firm's debt obligation, the equity of the firm would be eliminated and the lowest-priority debt tranche would be converted to equity").
58. *See, e.g.*, Charles W. Calomiris and Richard J. Herring, *How to Design a Contingent Convertible Debt Requirement that Helps Solve Our Too-Big-To-Fail Problem*, 25 J. APPLIED CORP. FIN. 21 (2013); Mark J. Flannery, *"No Pain, No Gain": Effecting Market Discipline via "Reverse Convertible Debentures," in* CAPITAL ADEQUACY BEYOND BASEL: BANKING, SECURITIES, AND INSURANCE (Hal Scott ed. 2005); Mark J. Flannery, *Stabilizing Large Financial Institutions with Contingent Capital Certificates*, Federal Reserve Bank of New York Working Paper (Oct. 5, 2009); Darrell Duffie, *A Contractual Approach to Restructuring Financial Institutions*, in ENDING GOVERNMENT BAILOUTS AS WE KNOW THEM (George P. Schultz, Kenneth E. Scott, & John B. Taylor, (eds) 2010).
59. Relatedly, Sundaresan and Wang show that dilutative CoCos can in theory give rise to a multiple equilibria problem, in which two potential values of the bank's stock are potential equilibria, one reflecting the value of the stock in the absence of conversion and the other reflecting its value after conversion. Suresh Sundaresan & Zhenyu Wang, *Design of Contingent Capital with Stock Price Trigger for Conversion*, Working Paper (April 23, 2010). Their analysis assumes that the bank's managers will not take steps to forestall conversion, such as issuing new equity. Calomiris & Herring, *supra* note 58, at 52.
60. Calomiris and Herring call their ratio the "quasi-market-value-of-equity" ratio, or QMVER. Calomiris & Herring, *supra* note 58, at 47.
61. *Id.*
62. *Id.* at 50–51.
63. John Coffee advocates a two-part trigger consisting of the price of the SIFI's stock as well as a market index. John C. Coffee, Jr., *Systemic Risk After Dodd-Frank: Contingent Capital and the Need for Regulatory Strategies Beyond Oversight*, 111 COLUM. L. REV. 795, 841 (2011). Under Coffee's approach, the CoCo would convert to preferred stock with significant voting rights after conversion. *Id.* at 828–33. Coffee's proposal seems to parallel Calomiris and Herring's in many respects, but would introduce additional complications and is unspecified in many of its details.
64. Calomiris and Herring conclude that CDS spreads are "less desirable" as triggers, because the markets are somewhat thin and they price risk differently at different points in time. Calomiris & Herring, *supra* note 58, at 47.
65. John Coffee has argued that CoCos would in fact qualify as debt for tax purposes, since neither managers nor shareholders would wish for the conversion to occur. Coffee, *supra* note 63, at 835–6.
66. Citigroup's travails before and during the crisis also illustrate the limitations of capital requirements as a gauge of a bank's condition. Darrell Duffie has pointed out that

Citibank "had a Tier 1 capital ratio that never fell below 7% during the crisis, and was measured at 11.8% at roughly its weakest moment in December 2008, when the stock-market capitalization of Citibank's holding company fell to . . . about 1% of its total accounting assets." Darrell Duffie, *Contractual Methods for Out-of-Court Restructuring of Systemically Important Financial Institutions*, at 4 (2009) (memorandum for U.S. Treasury Working Group on Bank Capital).

67. Calomiris & Herring, *supra* note 58, at 46.
68. The leading advocates of this approach are Anat Admati and Martin Helwig. *See* ANAT ADMATI & MARTIN HELWIG, THE BANKERS' NEW CLOTHES: WHAT'S WRONG WITH BANKING AND WHAT TO DO ABOUT IT (2013).
69. For early descriptions of this strategy, before it was dubbed single-point-of-entry, *see* Guynn, *supra* note 20, at 147–50; and comment letter from the Securities Industry and Financial Markets Association and The Clearing House Association to FDIC on its second notice of proposed rulemaking under Title II of the Dodd-Frank Act, May 23, 2011, http://www.fdic.gov/regulatios/laws/federal/2011/11c16Ad73.PDF. Douglas Baird and Ed Morrison also pointed out early on that Title II could be used to recapitalize a systemically important financial institution. *See* Douglas G. Baird & Edward R. Morrison, *Dodd-Frank for Bankruptcy Lawyers*, 19 AM. BANKR. INST. L. REV. 287 (2011). The FDIC formally endorsed and outlined single point of entry in Federal Deposit Insurance Corporation, The Resolution of Systemically Important Financial Institutions: The Single Point of Entry Strategy, 78 Fed. Reg. 76614 (Dec. 18, 2013).
70. The strategy is outlined in detail in John Bovenzi, Randall Guynn, and Thomas Jackson, Too Big to Fail: The Path to a Solution 26–7 (Bipartisan Policy Center, May 14, 2013).
71. *Id.* at 27. If one or more subsidiaries continued to face a liquidity crisis after being recapitalized, the bridge entity theoretically could make a secured loan to the needy subsidiary and re-pledge the collateral received from the subsidiary to the FDIC in return for a matching secured loan from the FDIC's orderly liquidation fund (which is borrowed from the U.S. Treasury).
72. For an argument that the single point of entry approach should be adopted in Europe, *see* Jeffrey N. Gordon & Wolf-Georg Ringe, *Bank Resolution in the European Banking Union: A Transatlantic Perspective on What it Would Take*, 115 COLUM. L. REV. 1297 (2015).
73. For further discussion of the points raised in this section, *see* David Skeel, *Single Point of Entry and the Bankruptcy Alternative*, in ACROSS THE GREAT DIVIDE: NEW PERSPECTIVES ON THE FINANCIAL CRISIS (John B. Taylor & Martin Neal Baily (eds) 2014).
74. U.S. and U.K. regulators have attempted to signal their confidence in the likely effectiveness of this approach through a joint statement endorsing the general framework. *See* Martin J. Gruenberg (chairman, FDIC) and Paul Tucker (deputy governor, financial stability, Bank of England), *Global Banks Need Global Solutions When They Fail,* FIN. TIMES, Dec. 10, 2012.
75. Guidance for 2017 § 165(d) Annual Resolution Plan Submissions by Domestic Covered Companies that Submitted Resolution Plans in July 2015, published by the FDIC and the Board of Governors of the Federal Reserve System.
76. Financial Stability Board, *Adequacy of loss-absorbing capacity of global systemically important banks in resolution*, Consultative Document (Nov. 10, 2014).
77. Board of Governors of the Federal Reserve System, Proposed Rules: Total Loss-Absorbing Capacity, Long-Term Debt, and Clean Holding Company Requirements for Systemically Important U.S. Bank Holding Companies and Intermediate Holding Companies of Systemically Important Foreign Banking Organizations; Regulatory Capital Deduction for Investments in Certain Unsecured Debt of Systemically Important U.S. Bank Holding Companies (Nov. 30, 2015).
78. Paul Kupiec and Peter Wallison emphasize uncertainty concerns in their critique of single point of entry. Paul Kupiec & Peter Wallison, *Can the "Single Point of Entry"*

Strategy be Used to Recapitalize a Failing Bank?, AEI Economic Working Paper 2014-08 (December 3, 2014).

79. The sponsors of the Dodd-Frank Act apparently were reluctant to include bankruptcy changes because bankruptcy comes within the jurisdiction of the Judiciary Committee, whereas financial reform is overseen by the Senate Banking and House Financial Services committees.
80. *See, e.g.*, Ayotte & Skeel, *supra* note 15.
81. The "safe harbors" are described in detail in Skeel & Jackson, *supra* note 19.
82. *See, e.g., id.*; Darrell Duffie & David Skeel, *A Dialogue on the Costs and Benefits of Automatic Stays for Derivatives and Repurchase Agreements*, *in* BANKRUPTCY *NOT* BAILOUT, *supra* note 6.
83. The arguments in this paragraph are defended more fully in Skeel & Jackson, *supra* note 19.
84. *Id.* at 184–5.
85. This would entail rolling back the extension of the repo safe harbor to illiquid collateral in 2005, and also amending the safe harbor for securities loans (which arguably protected repos based on mortgage-backed securities even before 2005). *Id.* at 177–9; Edward R. Morrison, Mark J. Roe & Hon. Christopher S. Sontchi, *Rolling Back the Repo Safe Harbors*, 69 BUS. L. 1015 (2014).
86. Mark J. Roe & Stephen D. Adams, *Restructuring Failed Financial Firms in Bankruptcy: Selling Lehman's Derivatives Portfolio*, 32 YALE J. on REG. 363 (2015).
87. Thomas Jackson outlines the original Chapter 14 proposal in Jackson, *supra* note 6.
88. The discussion that follows draws from Thomas H. Jackson & David A. Skeel, Jr., *Dynamic Resolution of Large Financial Institutions*, 2 HARV. BUS. L. REV. 435 (2012).
89. The Chapter 14 proposal is limited to financial institutions with at least $100 billion in assets.
90. For a similar proposal, *see* George G. Kaufman, *A Proposal for Efficiently Resolving Out-of-the-Money Swap Positions at large Insolvent Banks*, 9 J. BANKING REG. 3 (2003).
91. Stephen Lubben is among those who have voiced concerns of this kind. Stephen J. Lubben, *Resolution, Orderly and Otherwise: B of A in OLA*, 81 U. CINN. L. REV. 485, 517 (2012) (arguing that the "key difficulty" with Chapter 14 "rests on funding," and concluding that "something like" the Title II funding mechanism "is a prerequisite to a viable resolution authority"). *See also* Stephen J. Lubben, *What's Wrong with the Chapter 14 Proposal*, N.Y. TIMES.COM, April 10, 2013 (questioning "the dubious assumption in Chapter 14 that private debtor-in-possession financing will be available in times of financial distress, especially in the size a large financial institution would need"), http://dealbook.nytimes.com/2013/04/10/whats-wrong-with-the-chapter-14-proposal/?_r=0.
92. *See* Randall D. Guynn, *Framing the TBTF Problem: The Path to a Solution*, in ACROSS THE GREAT DIVIDE: NEW PERSPECTIVES ON THE FINANCIAL CRISIS (Hoover Institution Press 2014) (John B. Taylor and Martin Neal Baily, eds); John Bovenzi, Randall Guynn & Thomas Jackson, *Too Big to Fail: The Path to a Solution* (Bipartisan Policy Center, May 2013).
93. ISDA 2014 Resolution Stay Protocol (November 4, 2014).
94. Attachment to the ISDA 2014 Resolution Stay Protocol, section 1(a)(i)(A).
95. ISDA 2015 Universal Resolution Stay Protocol (November 12, 2015).
96. The Fed and FDIC have signaled that they intend to use the living will process to ensure that the largest banks are subject to an effective resolution process. *See, e.g.*, Joint Press Release, Board of Governors of the Federal Reserve System and Federal Deposit Insurance Corporation, *Agencies Provide Feedback on Second Round Resolution Plans of "First-Wave" Filers* (August 5, 2014), https://www.fdic.gov/news/news/press/2014/pr14067.html.
97. The stay also would not apply to counterparties of a holding company that files for bankruptcy. This arguably is less of a concern, because holding companies generally

do not have significant amounts of derivatives or other short-term debt. There is a risk that holding companies will begin using more short-term debt in response to the gap in the protocol's coverage; regulators have attempted to anticipate this risk by including "clean holding company" requirements in the new TLAC rule.

98. The proposed legislation currently pending in Congress includes a provision that would protect existing licenses.
99. The rules for debtor-in-possession financing are set forth in 11 U.S.C. § 364.
100. The issues discussed in this section are explored at greater length in David A. Skeel, Jr., *Financing a Systemically Important Financial Institution in Bankruptcy*, in MAKING FAILURE FEASIBLE, at 59 (Thomas Jackson, Kenneth E. Scott & John B. Taylor, (eds), 2015).
101. The Chapter 14 2.0 proposal would authorize the debtor to seek bankruptcy court approval if it wished.
102. In a typical prepackaged bankruptcy, a corporation that wishes to restructure its bond debt files its Chapter 11 petition and its proposed reorganization plan at the same time.
103. Interestingly, banks do sometimes recapitalize through a prepackaged bankruptcy. Anchor Bancorp Wisconsin Inc. did precisely this, recapitalizing its secured debt and its TARP obligations through a prepackaged bankruptcy that took only eighteen days. *See, e.g.*, Brian D. Christiansen, Van C. Durrer II & Sven G. Mickisch, *The Use of Pre-Packs in Bank Restructuring and M&A,* Financier Worldwide (Jan. 2014).
104. At least under existing law or under the Subchapter V proposal that was recently approved by the House. Legislation introduced in the Senate in late 2013 would have precluded the federal government from providing financing in connection with a SIFI restructuring.
105. Dodd-Frank Act § 1101(a) (extraordinary loans must be part of a "program or facility with broad-based eligibility").
106. This would require a partial shift from the current rule that the Fed is only permitted to adopt industry-wide emergency loan programs; but a requirement that the SIFI file for bankruptcy before the Fed could authorize funding might make it more palatable.
107. Extending the Fed's discount window would be an alternative strategy. The principal difference between § 13(3) lending and the discount window is that discount window loans are available even in the absence of systemic risk concerns.
108. 12 U.S.C. § 1823(c)(4)(G) (authorizing the FDIC to "take other action or provide assistance . . . as necessary to avoid or mitigate [serious adverse effects on economic conditions or financial stability]" if the Fed, Treasury and FDIC agree that there is an emergency].
109. Under Jackson and Massman's proposal, the commercial bank would guarantee the holding company's obligation to serve as a source of strength for a troubled nonbank subsidiary, and the holding company would then commit to indemnify the commercial bank for any losses on the guarantee. Howell E. Jackson & Stephanie Massman, *The Resolution of Distressed Financial Conglomerates* (unpublished manuscript, April 11, 2016).
110. Joe Nocera, *Keep it Simple*, N.Y. TIMES, Jan. 17, 2012, at A23.
111. *Id.*
112. Dodd-Frank Act § 121.
113. *See* SKEEL, NEW FINANCIAL DEAL, *supra* note 7.
114. A catch 22: Title II wouldn't be used for the big banks; yet regulators theoretically could not use it for smaller banks because it requires a finding that failure could cause systemic harm.
115. The proposed Brown-Vitter legislation, which would have imposed much higher capital requirements on bank holding companies with $700 billion or more in assets, might have had something like this effect if it had been adopted.
116. Dodd-Frank Act § 208.

117. The most obvious illustration is the incorporation into Title II of significant portions of the preference, fraudulent conveyance and setoff rules that apply in bankruptcy.
118. Dodd-Frank Act § 210(c)(10)(B) (one day restriction on ipso facto clauses); § 210(c)(8)(F) (walkaway provisions).
119. *Id.* § 208 (Title II displaces any prior bankruptcy case).
120. *Id.* § 206 (managers removed); § 210(s)(clawback).
121. I proposed a somewhat analogous strategy for bank resolution many years ago. Skeel, *Law and Finance*, *supra* note 11.

5. Derivatives and repos in bankruptcy

*Mark J. Roe**

INTRODUCTION

One of the more important bankruptcy developments of recent decades has been the widening extent of financial contracts that are exempt from bankruptcy. Holders of the exempt, safe-harbored contracts are exempt from the basic bankruptcy institutions, such as the stay, fraudulent conveyance law, and preference law. These wide exemptions were increasingly used in the run-up to the financial crisis, in which they played a role, which seems to have been a negative one. While the exemptions have several important positive characteristics in promoting liquidity (for holders of repurchase agreements) during stable economic times, they also have negative features (in encouraging short-term financing and facilitating crisis-centered runs and economy-wide collateral liquidation). The value to the economy overall of these exemptions from bankruptcy must, therefore, be questioned and the negative experience with the safe-harbored financial contracts during the financial crisis suggests the possibility, perhaps even the likelihood, that the overall costs of the full package of exemptions from ordinary bankruptcy outweigh their benefits.

* * *

Chapter 11 of the Bankruptcy Code bars bankrupt debtors from immediately repaying most of their creditors, including their secured creditors so that the bankrupt firm can reorganize without creditors forcing an otherwise viable business to liquidate. There are, however, exceptions to Chapter 11's reorganization orientation, with one of the most important being that according to the bankrupt's derivatives and financial repurchase (known to all involved as "repo") counterparties, who, unlike typical creditors, can seize and liquidate collateral, terminate their contracts with the bankrupt, and keep both preferential eve-of-bankruptcy payments and the most common types of fraudulent conveyances obtained from debtors, which other creditors would have to return to the bankrupt.

The impact of this favorable treatment is to graft a fast liquidation-oriented system onto a traditionally reorganization-oriented Chapter 11, but only for repos and derivatives. This grafting has benefits in that the rapid liquidation of these claims, particularly from repo financing, promotes liquidity, but it also has costs, in encouraging short-term repo financing in vital financial sectors during strong economic times and in facilitating collateral fire sales during downturns. Those fire sales, if widespread in a major market like that of mortgage-backed securities, can facilitate market-wide panic and financial contagion. The repo safe harbors protect repo on U.S. Treasuries, which maintained their fundamental value during the crisis, as well as mortgage-backed securities, which did not. Yet it is the *prevention* of financial contagion that has been the core raison d'être for the safe harbors. Their justifying rationale was not borne out in the crisis.

Derivatives' and repos' power under bankruptcy law to leap-frog other creditors, including other secured creditors, reduces their pre-bankruptcy incentives for market discipline in dealing with counterparties. Because the derivatives and repo players need not be as concerned about a counterparty's failure as with an ordinary debtor's failure, they have less incentive to ration their dealings with derivatives and repo debtors as carefully. If they were made to account for repo and derivatives counterparty risk in ways similar to how they must account for other counterparty risks, they would be more likely to insist that there be stronger counterparties than otherwise on the other side of their derivatives bets and they would substitute at the margin away from short-term derivatives and repo financing into more stable financing, thereby insisting for their own good on strengthening the financial system. Bankruptcy rules thereby affect financial markets' stability and discipline. Here they do so unfavorably for financial stability, as they encourage more short-term financing than would otherwise be the case.

True, if derivatives and repo counterparties bear less risk because of the Bankruptcy Code's favoritism, then other creditors that are poorly prioritized concerning repos and derivatives concomitantly bear more risk and thus have more incentive for market discipline. This is a basic application of the well-known Modigliani-Miller framework. But the other creditors—such as the United States of America as a guarantor of too-big-to-fail institutions—are poorly positioned contractually to consistently anticipate problems and to react quickly and well when problems arise anyway. A worthwhile policy agenda to consider is for bankruptcy institutions to harness private incentives for market discipline by cutting back on the large advantages that Chapter 11 and related insolvency legislation, such as Dodd-Frank's resolution regime, bestow on these investment channels. Below I outline how best to reconfigure these bankruptcy exemptions, often called the bankruptcy "safe harbors." The two fundamental changes that are warranted are first, to bestow the full range of safe harbors only on U.S. Treasury repo, not repo of mortgage-backed securities, and second, to bring back the bankruptcy stay for derivatives for a period long enough to break up and sell off the major financial institution's derivatives book in an orderly way.

When we favor derivatives and repo via bankruptcy benefits unavailable to other creditors, we get more of that subsidized activity than we otherwise would. Because instability in these two channels can seriously degrade overall financial stability, the bankruptcy rules facilitate unsafe financing and risk-transfer channels. Bringing these bankruptcy benefits for repo and derivatives down would induce the derivatives and repo markets to better recognize the risks of counterparty financial failure, which in turn should dampen the possibility of another AIG/Bear/Lehman financial melt-down, such as that which occurred in 2007 and 2008. American and worldwide financial stability would be enhanced. Moreover, quick contract-by-contract liquidation by counterparties of a failed financial firm's derivatives book will make it harder to quickly reposition divisions and product lines without large losses, as it did in the Lehman bankruptcy. Regulatory action could move the system in that direction—cutting the safe harbors for mortgage-backed repo and putting a short stay back in place for derivatives—and has done so somewhat. Bankruptcy could do more.

I. DERIVATIVES PRIORITIES AND THE FINANCIAL CRISIS

The AIG, Bear Stearns, and Lehman Brothers failures were at the heart of the 2008–2009 financial crisis and economic downturn. Some said their failure fueled a financial panic and exacerbated the consequent economic downturn. Some said they transmitted financial troubles emanating elsewhere in the economy—largely in the subprime mortgage market—in a way that exacerbated financial damage.[1] Quite plausibly, the latter scenario was not peripheral, with financial weakness in the housing and mortgage markets then affecting financial institutions that, due to their derivatives and repo market exposures, were less able to sail through the financial storm than they otherwise would have been.

The Bankruptcy Code's favored treatment of these firms' massive derivatives and financial repurchase contracts facilitated these firms' failures, by undermining market discipline in both the derivatives and repurchase markets in the years before these firms failed. It did so by sapping the failed firms' counterparties' incentives to account well for counterparty risk—the risk that their financial trading partner would fail (as AIG, Bear, and Lehman eventually did). Policymakers at the highest levels expected private monitoring to substitute for public monitoring, apparently unaware that bankruptcy rules reduced those private incentives. Alan Greenspan, who chaired the Federal Reserve, extolled the derivatives players'

> strong incentives to monitor and control [counterparty risk]. . . . [P]rudential regulation is supplied by the market through counterparty evaluation and monitoring rather than by authorities. . .. Private regulation generally has proved far better at constraining excessive risk-taking than has government regulation.[2]

As late as 2008, Greenspan praised "counterparties' surveillance" as "the first and most effective line of defense against fraud and insolvency." "JP Morgan," he said, "thoroughly scrutinizes the balance sheet of Merrill Lynch before it lends. It does not look to the SEC to verify Merrill's solvency."[3] That expected scrutiny was less thorough than Greenspan expected and a look at the incentives arising from the safe harbors suggests why: the safe harbors make the "counterparty evaluation and monitoring" that Greenspan expected superfluous for the safe harbor beneficiaries. The safe harbored counterparties want the safe harbors so that they are *not* subject to counterparty risk so that they can rapidly liquidate collateral and end their financial relationship with a bankrupt debtor. Greenspan may have been correct about incentives for monitoring and evaluation in other markets, but the explicit goal of safe-harbored counterparties is to exempt themselves from the kind of counterparty risk that would make them monitor and evaluate.

In the end, the financial sector relied on the government for more than just verifying counterparty solvency, as it eventually in the crisis obtained the Federal Reserve's and U.S. Treasury's cash to bail out the seriously insolvent. Indeed, the Federal Reserve backed up the repo market with a huge financial facility, one that was not well-publicized during the crisis or since it. The alternative view to Greenspan's is that bankruptcy priority discourages such counterparty surveillance in the derivatives and repo markets. Because the Code has not been amended since the crisis and because the leading restructuring mechanism under Dodd-Frank—the so-called single point of entry—contemplates that the safe harbored channels be fully paid, it is possible that some players are making similar mistaken judgments.

Were the Bankruptcy Code priorities narrower, the failed firms' financial trading partners would have anticipated that they might not be fully paid if weak counterparties failed. Understanding this—or more realistically, raising their estimate of the chance of bearing major losses if a counterparty failed—they would have been more incentivized to lower their exposure to a potential failure of Lehman, AIG, or Bear. Were these priorities not in the Code, each failed firm would itself have been incentivized to substitute away from risky, typically overnight, financing and toward a stronger balance sheet, to better attract trading partners. Were the priorities not in the Code, the three firms' counterparties would have had reason to substitute away from some trades with the failed firms, into trades with the next tier of financial firms. Failure of a big firm with major derivatives and repo positions could disrupt these markets in ways that implicate the general economy; financial firms with heavy repo and derivatives positions become too-big-to-fail because of those positions. Failed financial firms that gather funding from plain vanilla deposits or long-term debt are not as disruptive to the economy and, hence, are less likely to be seen as too-big-to-fail. If the derivatives and repo safe harbors were not available, Lehman, AIG, and Bear would have had less repo and a smaller derivatives book, in all likelihood and, as such, these firms would have been less financially central, less interconnected, and less costly to the economy if they failed. The financial system should accordingly have been more resilient.

These bankruptcy-based problems are not small. When Bear failed, a quarter of its capital came from the "repo" market via short-term, often overnight borrowings, amounting to eight times its capital at risk.[4] The proportion of its funding coming from short-term repo had been increasing in the years and decades before its failure. Without the Code's priorities, such a precarious capital structure would not have been viable. Additionally, when AIG failed, its excessive credit default derivatives exposure destabilized it further. Without the Code's priorities for AIG's derivatives-trading partners, such a precarious position for AIG would not have been so easily viable. Without the Code's priorities, they would have had reason to pay more attention to the identity and solvency of their counterparties earlier. AIG's potential precariousness and potential to fail to make good on its derivatives obligations would have been more subject to the market discipline that Greenspan had hoped for.

Weakened incentives is one major downside of favoring the derivatives and repo markets in bankruptcy. The difficulty of repositioning the failed firm's portfolio when its counterparties can immediately liquidate parts of that portfolio is another major downside. But risk-free investments with super-high bankruptcy priorities have major efficiency potential. Highly prioritized investment channels can lower information and negotiation costs for lenders and borrowers, facilitating financing flows that otherwise would not occur. Such efficient flows, if they could proceed without imposing costs on other parties or the financial system, deserve a supportive legal framework. The repo market can provide near-money-like channels that some financial parties would like to have; indeed, their benefit in liquidity and the absence of the need to understand counterparty risk are the mirror images of their costs. And transferring risk via derivatives with minimal need to consider counterparty risk has similar efficiency benefits because those trading risks do not then need to incur the costs of evaluating and bearing counterparty risk.

The problem, though, is that this lower risk for derivatives traders and repo investors comes at the expense not just of other financial creditors who price and monitor the debtor. The advantages are embedded in systemically vital businesses, institutions, and markets, with the short-term repo funding market and the derivatives market two of the biggest and potentially most fragile. As such, the failure of a systemically-vital financial firm calls forth a government bailout or degrades financial and economic results generally if financial markets deteriorate. Hence, the cost of this low-risk environment for derivatives traders and repo investors is not fully borne, and not fully priced, by those doing the trading and investing. The economy as a whole bears the risk of a melt-down and the taxpayers bear the risks of a bailout. In the 2007–2009 financial crisis, both costs were imposed on outsiders to these two safe-harbored markets.

If we can separate efficient flows from systemically-dangerous flows—and then allow the first, while restricting, regulating and pricing the second—we could strengthen finance in two dimensions. But if we cannot separate the efficient from the dangerous, and if we cannot price either, then we need to choose which policy package makes the most sense: better bankruptcy treatment for derivatives and repo creditors, which gives them trading efficiencies, or equal treatment for them and other secured creditors. Given our recent poor experience in 2007 and 2008, the best choice may well be to strengthen the system in the more important dimension of systemic stability. To do so, policymakers would need to cut back the priority package for derivatives and repos. The best-targeted cutbacks would leave the no-stay policy in place for U.S. Treasury repo but have a longer although not endless stay in place for mortgage-backed securities. For derivatives, a longer than the safe-harbor no-stay makes sense to reposition the derivatives book in an orderly sale over a few weeks, if the current restructuring mechanisms—the so-called single-point-of-entry—fail.

Overall, these are policy issues that reflect not just the problems of local, minor financial structures that unfortunately failed: When the financial crisis began in June 2007, the United States had $2.5 trillion in overnight repos, while the aggregate insured bank deposits in the United States were only twice as much. Overnight repo is intrinsic to the now-famous "shadow" banking system. Just one type of derivative market—the interest rate swap—grew to more than $400 trillion by December 2008, with $4 trillion of collateral backing up the derivatives market overall.[5]

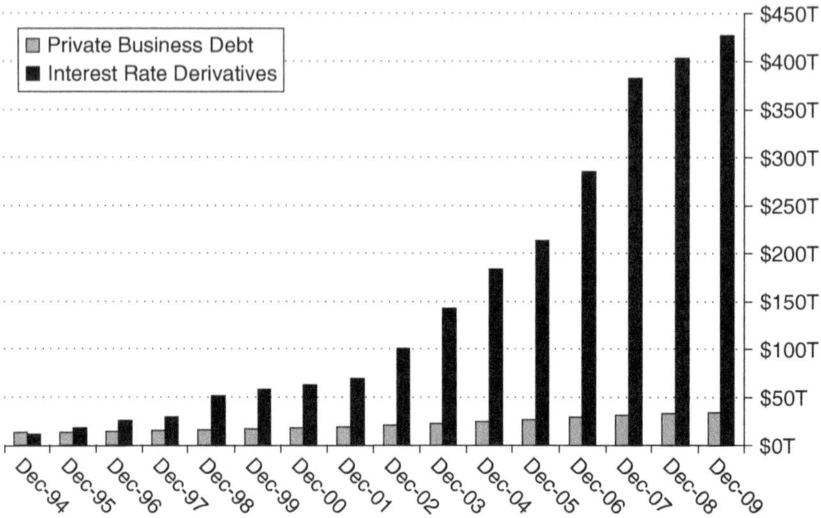

Figure 5.1 *Growth in the markets for interest rate derivatives, compared with growth in the markets for all business debt, 1994–2009*[6]

Figure 5.1 illustrates the market's explosive growth in the dozen years preceding the financial crisis. In 1994, the private business debt and interest rate derivatives markets were about the same size, at $13 trillion for the first and $11 trillion for the second. In the subsequent 15 years, the business debt market tripled in size to $34 trillion, while the interest rate derivatives markets increased nearly 40-fold to $430 trillion. Combine the overnight repo market with the collateralized portion of the derivatives markets and we have a financial market *bigger* than the FDIC-insured banking system. If there's a failure in these markets, the first set of governing rules come from the Bankruptcy Code. (For some financial institutions, like the banks embedded in bank holding companies, the reorganization rules emanate from laws other than the Bankruptcy Code, such as the banking laws most recently updated via Dodd-Frank; but the safe-harbor treatment under the other laws is substantially similar to the treatment under the Bankruptcy Code.) Academic supporters of the derivatives and repo markets indicate that these markets' growth would not have been possible without the bankruptcy safe harbors.[7] Those safe harbors can be viewed less neutrally, as I do here, as subsidies at the expense of other creditors.

* * *

In the next few pages, in Part II, I describe the counterparties' Code-based advantages. Although several are conceptually sound, most go far beyond wise bankruptcy and financial policy. Some remedy defects in the Code, but do so only for safe-harbored creditors; the better policy would be to fix the Code for all creditors. In Part III, I show how the Code's advantages weaken counterparties' incentives for market discipline. The Code thereby discourages financial resiliency. Better bankruptcy law could create better incentives than it does now for counterparties to more efficiently structure their trillion-dollar derivatives and repo books to *avoid* an eventual counterparty collapse, rather than to avoid the *consequences* of an actual collapse. This lost potential for enhanced market discipline is where, I argue, the central bankruptcy priority costs of the derivatives and repo markets lie.

Then, in Part IV, I apply Modigliani-Miller's irrelevance hypothesis to show how the bankruptcy rules shift risks from inside the derivatives and repo markets to outside it. Although creditors' lawyers here often like to think of the structure as reducing risk, and it does reduce it for the immediate parties, it does not necessarily reduce it system-wide and may, in fact, increase that risk. Code priorities that *reduce* the derivatives counterparties' risks and monitoring incentives thereby *raise* risks that the financial firm's other creditors face. Risk is transferred, not eliminated. And, if the system is destabilized, because run propensity and collateral fire sales increase, economy-wide risk is increased.

Conceptually, those other creditors can reduce their exposure to a risky debtor, raise their prices, or monitor more closely. But the relevant players here are not always the best informed and best skilled at reducing resulting risks because they often are not themselves derivatives and repo professionals. The largest affected creditor is the United States as de facto guarantor of weak, too-big-to-fail financial debtors. But the United States has no contract unless we conceptualize the Bankruptcy Code rules and financial regulation as its de facto contract. If we do so, that contract needs to be revised going forward.

In Part V, I examine the core arguments favoring derivatives and repo priorities, as well as glance at some of the major recent regulatory reactions. Although several bankruptcy advantages for each instrument are functional and ought to be kept, the full range is far too broad. In particular, I examine the contagion argument again and point to two negative, perhaps serious, macro-economic implications of derivatives priorities.

* * *

Overall, the Bankruptcy Code's safe-harbor, strong priorities for those with derivatives contracts or repurchase agreements above a bankrupt's other creditors are too strong for sound policy governing major, systemically important financial institutions. Not only do the provisions facilitate runs on financial institutions during financial crises, but they also seriously weaken counterparties' ex ante incentives for financial stability. The Code priorities decrease the derivatives players' ex ante monitoring incentives and decrease their incentives to use stronger financing channels. If these other, systemically stronger financial channels lack the derivatives and repo channels' private priorities, one should ordinarily expect players to substitute away from the systemically stronger into the systemically weaker but privately attractive other financing channels. Moreover, these safe-harbored channels make the quick repositioning of ongoing bundles of a failed financial firm's portfolio impossible, as the counterparties can, unlike secured creditors generally, immediately liquidate their safe-harbored positions, shredding the portfolio.

The Code thereby encourages risky, knife's edge financing, and complex, difficult-to-reposition financial books. When this kind of financing and these kinds of investment books are pursued in financially central firms, the pursuit transfers risk to the United States as the ultimate guarantor of the key firms' solvency. Financial resiliency is thereby drained; market discipline forgone.

II. THE PROBLEM: SHORT-RUN SUPERPRIORITY IN THE DERIVATIVES AND REPO MARKETS

A bankruptcy filing strips creditors of contractual rights that they would otherwise have.

First, bankruptcy law bars the bankrupt's creditors from suing the debtor for repayment, bars them from trying otherwise to collect debts due from the bankrupt, and bars secured creditors from immediately seizing and liquidating their security. Inventory financiers, for example, cannot seize the inventory they have financed, but must ask the court for permission to do so and typically must wait, while the business is reorganized. Later on, they all collect their security, if it's still available, or what's due them (equal to the amount of their security), oftentimes when a plan of reorganization is completed. The purpose of this bar on collection is to do the best the bankruptcy system can to reorganize the failed firm into a viable enterprise, on the theory that many bankrupt firms remain viable, albeit in a reduced state.

Second, bankruptcy law treats safe harbored creditors more favorably in other dimensions. A bedrock principle for bankruptcy is preference law, designed to reduce an eve-of-bankruptcy rush by creditors to grab the failing firm's assets. Preference law requires that creditors who were repaid within 90 days of the bankruptcy filing be made to return their repayments under wide conditions, thereby allowing all creditors to share in that value. The preference remedy is a weak one[8]—the grasping creditor typically only has to return what it took—but it discourages creditors from investing heavily in eve-of-bankruptcy collection since it may well have to return what it got anyway.

Third, creditors and suppliers generally cannot terminate an open contract with the bankrupt solely because the debtor filed for bankruptcy.

For creditors of the bankrupt that are derivatives or repo players, these rules are reversed to favor the derivatives and repo creditors, who are "safe-harbored" from basic bankruptcy institutions. The safe harbors pull these favored creditors out from the bankruptcy process, exempting them from the reorganization. First, they can immediately collect on their debts. Second, they do not need to return payments they received within the 90 days prior to bankruptcy as do regular creditors. Third, the safe-harbored derivatives and repo players can decide to terminate their contracts with the debtor, as opposed to the usual bankruptcy rule that gives this option to the bankrupt debtor. Collectively, these rules highly prioritize derivatives and repo creditors over other creditors.

Several of these baseline American bankruptcy rules are, in the view of bankruptcy analysts (including this author) flawed. Indeed, were these baseline rules improved, the demand for safe-harbored repos and derivatives would decline because some of that demand comes from a desire to escape bankruptcy rules that are unwisely too costly to creditors. But, flawed or not, it is poor policy to have some rules favor contracts that are derivatives or repo contracts over all other kinds of pre-bankruptcy credit contracts, principally because the favored contracts come with significant risks to the overall economy. The impact of favoring one class of credits is to drive more credit transactions into such shorter-term financial contracts, like repo, from other kinds of credit channels. At the moment of failure, this increasingly widely used exemption-from-bankruptcy reduces the chances of a successful restructuring by motivating creditors owning core credit positions in the derivatives and repo markets to liquidate their positions quickly to pull as much cash out of failing financial firms as they can, thereby hastening the firms' demise. Some creditors are using these liquidation-oriented instruments not because the creditors and the debtor want such a run, but because these instruments are exempt from undesirable bankruptcy rules. The rules thereby enhance run potential.

III. UNDERMINING MARKET DISCIPLINE

The major damage done by the safe harbors is that they weaken the derivatives and repo markets incentives for market discipline and widen these markets beyond the size they would naturally reach. The priorities' systemic impact is important at two different times. The first is when the economy is suffering an ongoing crisis. At that time one question is whether the safe harbor priorities facilitate or impede the repositioning of a failed financial firm and its portfolio. The second question at that time is whether the priorities dampen or exacerbate a financial crisis. Although safe harbors supporters justified their exemption from bankruptcy with the supposition that the safe harbor priorities and exemptions would dampen or prevent a financial crisis, the experience during the recent crisis suggests the contrary—that the safe harbors do not dampen runs, and that they, in fact, exacerbate a crisis by propelling more runs and deeper, wider fire sales of volatile financial collateral, like mortgage-backed securities.

To be sure, it is conceptually possible that the availability of repo financing can stave off a run in many, but not all, instances. So even though the repo safe harbors worked poorly in the crisis, we cannot from that alone reject the possibility that the safe harbors provided financing that staved off many other crises. One can profitably analogize to detrimental side effects from a drug. If we observe that a patient died from a drug's side effect we cannot by that observation alone conclude that the drug is detrimental. After all, the drug saved hundreds of others' lives. But if we observe some deaths and no saves, then there's reason to doubt the value of the drug in practice. For financial runs, we can observe one major safe-harbor-associated run; actual on-the-ground examples of their benefits in staving off runs have not been brought forward.

The second time the priorities have an important impact is well before the crisis hits, during ordinary financial times. During that period, these safe harbor priorities sap market discipline and thereby increase the chance that, when a financial crisis occurs, it will be worse than it otherwise would have been. The two safe-harbored markets—repo and derivatives, where much systemic risk resides—become larger than they would otherwise be, and the counterparties do not police one another's riskiness and financial stability, notwithstanding Greenspan's view.

There are multiple channels for market discipline and each deserves more analysis than it will get here.[9] But the persistent overall impact of the Code's priorities' channels for derivatives and repos is to weaken discipline in each channel. The most obvious weakening of market discipline comes from the safe harbor priorities' weakening of the counterparties' incentives to monitor one another—the kind of market discipline Greenspan was looking for. True, the full derivatives book for a counterparty is opaque and difficult to monitor. But if the counterparties were made to bear more of the risk of counterparty failure, some would raise prices and some would seek better collective monitoring channels. Others would deal only with the strongest counterparties.[10] Still, others would reduce their exposure to a single counterparty or require that their counterparties substitute into a stronger financial structure. Weaker counterparties, if faced with higher prices or reluctant counterparties, would have incentives to strengthen their own balance sheet, such as by substituting more long-term financing for the short-term derivatives and repo financing.

The systemic justification usually given for the safe harbor priorities is, as we have seen, that they reduce contagion during a crisis. Firm A fails to pay B, so B fails to pay C, in the common story. But if B can immediately collect on its safe-harbored debt from A, then it, B, can pay C. A fails, but if it was going to fail regardless, then the safe harbors at least assure that C can be paid by B, thereby keeping B and C stable. Even if this anti-contagion story is true—and the 2009 experience suggests the contrary, since the relevant repo market was flooded with Federal Reserve lending and *that* held back contagion, not the safe harbors—any such benefit could be more than balanced conceptually by two heavy counterweights. Even if the safe harbor priorities reduce contagion during a crisis, they also induce runs during that crisis. Maybe A would not have failed if B could not immediately collect from A. And even if the safe harbors reduce contagion more than they induce runs (which is by no means proven), they also have the large ex ante systemic costs of sapping market discipline and facilitating a larger financially-fragile market.

The contagion idea is that if one institution is weakening and its counterparties cannot take their derivatives and repo investments out, then these counterparties will also fail. Then, like a row of dominoes, the financial system will topple, as one party after another fails. A difficulty with this view is that it's unclear why only derivatives and repo counterparties need to be protected from financial contagion. That is, one must ask whether all counterparties everywhere should get that protection of exemption from bankruptcy, to stop runs and domino-like collapse.

But, worse yet as a logical matter, by permitting safe-harbored, prioritized derivatives and repo creditors to take their money out immediately from a weakening financial institution, but not permitting any other creditor to do so, the safe harbors can shift the channel for contagion potential when the other, nonprioritized creditors bear the losses that the favored creditors do not bear. Will the nonprioritized creditors—themselves financial institutions—thereby weaken and, perhaps, fail? The safe harbors allow counterparties to remove their asset from the bankrupt quickly, and that can be beneficial to financial stability; but removal has costs, first to the bankrupt debtor's other counterparties and then to the financial system overall.[11]

A second difficulty with the contagion analytic is that the same process that reduces contagion also creates runs: the strong counterparty who sees its trading counterparty weakening then considers that, via the superpriorities and bankruptcy exemptions, it has the incentives and means to pull its cash out of the weakening financial institution, like AIG, Lehman, and Bear Stearns. This strength that the strong safe-harbored creditors have, but the other creditors lack, can induce a run on the weakening institution, bringing about the weakened financial firm's failure when, if financial heads were made to cool down, they might have survived or been disposed of in a more systemically sound way.[12] A third difficulty with the contagion analytic is that it focuses on "old-school" contagion: the parties have interconnected obligations, such that A's inability to pay B affects B's ability to pay C, and so on. In the prior paragraph, we noted that B's safe-harbor ability to be repaid quickly from A may hurt A's other counterparties, who presumably collect less. (This resembles the failure of the Reserve Primary Fund due to its holding of ordinary Lehman debt when Lehman failed; Lehman's safe harbored creditors took much of Lehman's value for themselves.) But there is another contagion channel that the safe harbors do not help, that they probably exacerbate, and that was heavily in play during the financial crisis. If the safe harbored financial contract between A and B is, say, a mortgage-backed security, and B quickly liquidates that security (as the safe harbors allow it to do), then, if enough of the economy's "B's" are doing the same, the market price of these securities could well decline (as it did). This liquidation affects other financial institutions, J, K, and L, that have no dealing with either A or B. Institution J, for example, finds that the market value of its portfolio has declined (due to the heavy selling of mortgage-backed securities by the B's, and it is nearly rendered insolvent. Institution J then sells its own portfolio off, to raise cash to keep itself stable. With many J's selling and no one buying, the safe harbors have induced (or supported) a downward price spiral, a fire sale, and a financial panic. On their books, J, K, and L are less well-capitalized (because their mortgage-backed securities are worth less) and they cut back on their lending. Without the safe harbors, A's bankruptcy would not have led to B immediately selling the mortgage-backed securities it had traded with A. The panic would not have happened and J, K, and L's lending cutbacks would not have been as severe.

IV. MODIGLIANI-MILLER APPLIED

Applying one of the finance theory's central insights helps us to better understand the mixed impact of the safe harbor priorities for derivatives and repo contracts.

The risks of loss that bankruptcy law's safe harbors lift from the shoulders of the derivatives and repo players do not disappear. Rather, they shift to others' shoulders. Hence, priority proponents' arguments that derivatives and repo priorities reduce risk must be qualified, or ignored as incorrect: Although the safe harbors do indeed reduce the risk for derivatives and repo players, they do so in the first instance by transferring those risks to other financial players. In the first instance, the risk is not directly reduced by financial manipulation, but only shifted from shoulder to shoulder. For such insights and development, Modigliani and Miller[13] won their Nobel Prizes.

But the M-M risk transfer analysis also rebuts some of the market discipline analytics I have thus far offered. By transferring the risk, yes, the bankruptcy rules do not reduce overall risk. They reduce the derivatives and repo players' incentives for market discipline, as I have indicated. But they concomitantly raise the incentives of *other* creditors for more market discipline.

The reason this M-M–style rebuttal fails—that is, the reason that the risk transfer is not a simple wash for market discipline—is that a major creditor of systemically central financial firms affected by American bankruptcy law is the United States as contingent guarantor. The United States does not ordinarily react like a contract creditor. It could, in principle, regulate the financial institutions more tightly and effectively, and the M-M analysis indicates why it should and why leaving the results to marketplace monitoring, as so enamored Alan Greenspan, is mistaken if the monitors are bankruptcy-favored.

The better next step in the analysis is not to rely solely, or even primarily, on governmental prudential regulation. Rather, the better step is to hybridize by using bankruptcy rules to better harness market discipline than before, because governments will often be late to realize the risks that are emanating from one market or another to threaten financial stability.

V. FURTHER CONSIDERATIONS

A. Reducing and Increasing Contagion

1. Ordinary contagion

The Code's superpriorities were first justified as measures to reduce contagion. One institution fails and another, unable to get its cash out of the failed firm, is rendered illiquid and fails itself. As we have seen, while this contagion-prevention scenario is theoretically possible, on an ex ante basis it is offset by the possibility that the first institution, although weak, would not have failed were it not for the second institution's bankruptcy rights to pull cash out of the weak but potentially survivable firm.

Hence, we have a conceptual reason to believe that the bankruptcy safe harbor priorities could be as likely to spread contagion as they are to contain it.

2. Information and collateral contagion

These priorities also facilitate information contagion and encourage simultaneous liquidation of collateral in a financial crisis, as we have seen. Both difficulties were strongly in play in the financial crisis and the Code's priorities exacerbate both. Information contagion comes when lending markets discover they do not understand counterparty financial strength and stop lending until they acquire enough information; bankruptcy superpriority discourages early information acquisition. Collateral value contagion comes when financiers simultaneously sell similar collateral, depressing its price, thereby compromising the immediate value of other collateral. The lowering of other collateral value induces other lenders to themselves declare a default, seize collateral, and liquidate that collateral. The Bankruptcy Code allows derivatives and repo creditors, but not most others, to immediately seize and sell off their collateral, thereby facilitating collateral contagion. These two effects—information contagion and collateral-value contagion—are run-*enhancing* consequences of the priority rules we have. Prior analysis has not, as far as I know, shown the logical links between bankruptcy's payment priorities and these two crisis-exacerbating difficulties, a gap that I suggested earlier in 2011.[14]

B. Clearinghouses

Clearinghouses and collateral have been a major focus of reforms. Much of this effort is helpful, but much of it must be incomplete, as applying the M-M hypothesis to the setting shows us. Clearinghouses can enhance transparency, which is good here, especially in that it might alert government players to a problem earlier than otherwise. But much of the justification for the clearinghouses, as well as for strong collateral requirements, is that they are thought to reduce systemic risk. On this level, the argument is weak or at least not self-evident.[15]

Yes, the clearinghouse enables participants to net contracts and this reduces the risk for those inside the clearinghouse system. But the risk is not assuredly eliminated. It can be and often is, just transferred to creditors outside the insider clearinghouse system. The next paragraph suggests how.

A weak financial institution, say, Bank of America, has two separate contracts, one with AIG and one with Citibank. BoA owes $100 million to AIG and another $100 million to Citibank. The contract with AIG is a derivatives contract, which goes through the clearinghouse; the contract with Citibank is another kind of contract, maybe just a regular loan, and does not go through the clearinghouse. BoA also has a contract with, say, Bear Stearns, through the clearinghouse for $100 million, with Bear on the losing end.

Without a clearinghouse, BoA has a $100 million asset (the $100 million that Bear owes it) and owes $200 million. Having only $100 million (if these are its only assets and liabilities), BoA would have to pay AIG and Citibank each $50 million and each of those two would suffer a $50 million loss.

If AIG is systemically vital, its inability to collect the full $100 million could drive it to fail. This is where the clearinghouse protects AIG. AIG's winning contract with BoA nets against Bear's losing contract with BoA. The clearinghouse here eliminates counterparty risk for these three players, *but only by transferring the loss to Citibank*, which instead of losing $50 million, ends up losing the full $100 million.

Regulators have celebrated the clearinghouse. Among its most important advertised features is that it reduces the risk for its participants. Which, as advertised, it does—but *only* for its participants. Citibank, however, now loses $50 million more, since it can't crack into the clearinghouse's assets. If that extra loss pushes a systemically vital Citibank over the precipice, the clearinghouse has not, as it has been advertised to do, reduced systemic risk.

Whether or not the clearinghouse reduces systemic risk depends primarily on the relative systemic importance of AIG and Citibank in these renditions of the clearinghouse basics, and secondarily on whether the clearinghouse can settle out the transactions much faster than any alternatives, but *not* on the clearinghouse's capacity to reduce the underlying risk among its members.

Much recent regulatory activity has focused on enabling, enhancing, and requiring clearinghouses for these kinds of financing arrangements. As said, clearinghouses offer multiple benefits, including better transparency, better pricing, and better regulatory potential. But some of their central proposed benefits do not withstand a Modigliani-Miller analysis, as much of what gets justified as reducing systemic risk is just moving that risk somewhere else in the system.

Clearinghouses may well have other advantages. They may facilitate sound capital requirements behind the derivatives contract. They may well be a good window into the structure of the market. By taking some of the derivatives contracts away from financial firms, they may make it easier in a crisis for financial markets to ascertain which financial firms are truly at risk and which have such limited exposure to the riskiest markets that they can be seen to be safe and easy to deal with.

Clearinghouses have another effect on the analysis here: if more of the derivatives market moves into clearinghouses and little remains in banks and other financial institutions (we're far from that situation right now), then the positive or negative impact of the safe harbors becomes less important because the non-cleared market will be smaller.

C. The Dodd-Frank Uncertainties in Application

Congress reacted to the financial crisis with major financial reform legislation, which did not alter the bankruptcy rules but did potentially move a wider array of financial institutions out from under the Bankruptcy Code's repo rules and into a new financial resolution regime, which would be run by the Federal Deposit Insurance Corporation. For such financial institutions, Dodd-Frank's "Orderly Liquidation Authority" brings back the classic bankruptcy bar on counterparties immediately collecting on their derivatives and repos, but typically only for a single business day, and it then otherwise reaffirms the safe harbor superpriorities.[16] Although that bar on collection endures for a single business day, it is still more reorganization-oriented than the bankruptcy safe harbors, which contemplate no delay in the bankrupt's counterparties cashing out.

The Dodd-Frank one-day stay and the related single-point-of-entry plans would further protect repo and derivatives counterparties at the expense of the failed firm's other nondeposit creditors. That will tend to make such systemically-important markets bigger than they would otherwise be, and likely to call forth counter-regulation to limit their size and riskiness.

VI. THE APPROPRIATE SCOPE OF THE SAFE HARBORS

Three dimensions for the safe harbors are appropriate to reconfigure: scope, portfolio placement, and preference impact. The goal for such a reconfiguring would be to reduce the size of the market that would tend to be bailed out in a crisis, to make it easier for counterparties to assess, price, and act on the riskiness of their counterparties, and to reduce the severity of a run if a crisis comes to pass.

On scope, the repo safe harbors are too broad. They allow a repurchase agreement covering a U.S. Treasury security to be exempt from the bankruptcy of the repo borrower. This exemption makes sense in that financial markets have always run on the assumption that Treasury securities are the closest thing to money without being money. But other repo investments are also exempt from bankruptcy and they do not perform nearly as well in a financial crisis. The broadest of these are mortgage-backed securities whose poor performance was central in the financial crisis. When these declined sharply in value, financial institutions that had relied upon them, partly due to their safe-harbored status, were further weakened.[17]

On portfolio placement, the safe harbors stymie bankruptcy from being able to sensibly reposition a derivatives portfolio. A financial firm that has a balanced portfolio (selling euros under some contracts, and buying them under others, while making a profit on selling each contract) will find that the safe harbors rip apart the portfolio, as both counterparties terminate their contracts, liquidate the collateral, and charge the debtor for the cost of replacing their contract. Better to sell the portfolio off to a third party, intact; but the safe harbors do not permit that. We want that capacity as a matter of public policy, to avoid the excessive private costs of portfolio degradation and to avoid a disrupted market such as that which the world faced after Lehman filed for bankruptcy and its derivatives portfolio was liquidated via the safe harbor close-outs.

The Dodd-Frank Act provides more options for portfolio repositioning. While better than bankruptcy, the Dodd-Frank options are inadequate. First off, the regulatory prerequisites to invoking Dodd-Frank must be overcome. They might be overcome, but they might not. If they are not overcome, the firm will need to be reorganized in bankruptcy. Secondly, Dodd-Frank requires that the portfolio be transferred intact, along counterparty lines. That will typically be the best repositioning. But in a serious financial collapse, it may not be possible without a bailout. The firm and its financial portfolio may be too big to reposition and refinance in its entirety. That is, a counterparty that has multiple interest rate swaps and multiple foreign exchange deals with the debtor cannot have these contracts broken up. The better way to handle these is to allow the contracts to be transferred along product market lines, which is the natural way to break up the portfolio. Moreover, the derivatives market is highly concentrated. The regulatory move to have clearinghouses take over the plain vanilla trades will reduce but not eliminate this concentration in a handful of systemically-important financial institutions. Four dealers today have very large derivatives books, accounting for the bulk of derivatives trades in the United States. Public policymakers should want some mechanism to break-up these derivatives books if one of these institutions fails, and the most obvious way is for the book to be broken up and sold along product market lines.[18]

The safe harbors give the favored counterparties a blanket exemption from preference law. Preference law is basic to bankruptcy, requiring that creditors return any eve-of-bankruptcy repayments and collateral transfers that allowed them to get proportionately more from the bankrupt company than other creditors were obtaining, as long as a set of preference prerequisites are met. Preference law is often justified as reducing runs against a debtor that is better restructured and continued than liquidated piecemeal. One can immediately see the irony here: the safe harbors are touted as reducing systemic risk and the safe harbors exempt the favored from preference law. The experience from the financial crisis strongly suggests that the blanket exemption for favored creditors from preference law is unwise. AIG's failure was hastened and perhaps worsened when its counterparties obtained more collateral to back up their derivatives contracts with AIG (the famous credit default swaps). These transfers were conceptually preferential, as preference law is designed to reduce creditors' capacity to obtain more collateral when a debtor's financial situation deteriorates. Several alternatives to the blanket preference make sense, even if the Code is not returned to its standard state for currently safe-harbored contracts. For example, collateral posts under a contractual formula based on changes in the value of the underlying deal could be safe harbored, but transfers of collateral due to changes in the creditworthiness of the debtor would not be.

VII. BANKRUPTCY THEORY AND THE SAFE HARBORS

The core policy justification for a bankruptcy law with a collective proceeding replacing a baseline of creditors, one-by-one clearing out their contracts is that dispersed creditors would destroy going concern value as each raced to collect from the wounded debtor.[19] If creditors were concentrated and could coordinate their actions—think of a single creditor negotiating with the management of the debtor firm—then Coasian bargaining should lead to sound firms being restructured and unsound ones not, even without bankruptcy's collective proceeding. That Coasian concept has been used to criticize bankruptcy's collective proceeding as being too broad, as often applying to many modern firms that have a single dominant creditor who is well-positioned to make a Coasian bargain with the bankrupt debtor's owner.[20]

There is more than a little irony here in the result when we place the safe harbors exemption from a collective proceeding next to bankruptcy's core justifications. The irony is that the Code's widest exemption from bankruptcy's baseline collective proceeding is accorded not to such Coasian-friendly structures with concentrated creditors but the derivatives and repo markets. Those markets largely replicate the decentralized contracting market that bankruptcy theorists bring forward to *justify* bankruptcy's collective proceeding—many creditors, few with the incentive to preserve the debtor's going concern value, all with incentives to liquidate their position quickly, regardless.

Could bankruptcy rules have gotten the proper application of bankruptcy's core collective proceeding norm exactly backwards?

CONCLUSION

American bankruptcy law favors derivatives and repo contracts, at the expense of other debt, by moving them up on the bankruptcy repayment queue above other creditors of the failing firm. By favoring, safe-harboring, and prioritizing such short-term financial contracts, the rules weaken market discipline during ordinary financial times in ways that can leave financial institutions weaker than they would be otherwise. This weakness, in turn, exacerbates financial failure during an economic crisis. The crisis can emanate from elsewhere in the economy—as the 2007–2008 downturn emanated from the mortgage market—but then magnify its impact.

Because the strongest priorities in the Code are available only for short-term financing arrangements, they thereby favor short-term financing arrangements over more stable longer-term arrangements. While proponents of these priorities for derivatives and repos justify them as reducing contagion, there's good reason to think that they do not reduce contagion meaningfully, but contribute to runs and, most importantly, undermine market discipline ex ante. Basic application of the Modigliani-Miller framework suggests that the risks policymakers might hope the favored treatment would eliminate are principally shifted from inside the derivatives and repurchase agreement markets to creditors who are outside that market. The most important outside creditor is the United States, as de jure or de facto guarantor of too-big-to-fail financial institutions.

NOTES

* Professor, Harvard Law School. An earlier version of the argument I present here appeared in more extensive form in Stanford Law Review, as *The Derivative Market's Payments Priorities as Financial Crisis Accelerator*, 63 Stan. L. Rev. 539 (2011), and a related article appeared in Comparative Economic Studies, as *Derivatives Markets in Bankruptcy*, 55 Comp. Econ. Stud. 529 (2013).

1. *Compare* Thomas Ferguson & Robert Johnson, *The God that Failed: Free Market Fundamentalism and the Lehman Bankruptcy*, The Economists' Voice, Jan. 2010, at 1, *with* John Cochrane & Luigi Zingales, *Lehman and the Financial Crisis*, Wall St. J., Sept. 15, 2009, at A21. *Cf.* John Taylor, *Economic Policy and the Financial Crisis: An Empirical Analysis of What Went Wrong*, 21 Critical Rev. 341 (2009).
2. Alan Greenspan, Chairman, The Federal Reserve Board, Remarks at the 2003 Conference on Bank Structure and Competition (May 8, 2003) (transcript available at http://www.federalreserve.gov/boarddocs/speeches/2003/20030508/ default.htm).
3. Alan Greenspan, The Age of Turbulence 257 (2008).
4. Bear Stearns, *Form 10-Q* (Feb. 29, 2008), http://sec.gov/Archives/edgar/data/777001/0 000914121080003 45/be12550652-10q.txt.
5. *See ISDA Margin Survey 2009*, Int'l Swaps and Derivatives Ass'n (2009), http://www.isda.org/c_and_a/pdf/ISDA-Margin-Survey-2009.pdf; *Summaries of Market Survey Results*, Int'l Swaps and Derivatives Ass'n (2009), http://www.isda.org/statistics/recent.html. In an interest rate swap, one party trades a floating interest rate for a fixed one on, say, $100 million of debt that neither party has borrowed or lent. The $100 million "notional" amount is often reported as the transaction's size—with that notional amount totaling $400 trillion at year-end 2008. But it's the smaller interest payment obligation that is being swapped and the collateral transferred is even smaller. That lower collateral amount goes into the text's still-big $4 trillion number.
6. For sources and further information on the growth of the derivatives' market outstripping the growth of private business debt, see Roe, *infra* note 9, at 543–44.
7. Gary Gorton & Andrew Metrick, *Regulating the Shadow Banking System*, 2010 Brookings Papers on Econ. Activity 261, 266.
8. Barry E. Adler, *A Re-Examination of Near-Bankruptcy Investment Incentives*, 62 U. Chi. L. Rev. 575 (1995).
9. For more extensive analysis, *see* Mark J. Roe, *The Derivatives Market's Payment Priorities as Financial Crisis Accelerator*, 63 Stan. L. Rev. 539, 560–64 (2011).
10. This feature could weaken discipline, in that if there are still too-big-to-fail financial firms, these contracts could migrate to the too-big-to-fail. A policy of narrowing the safe harbors needs to work in tandem with more general financial regulation.
11. True, the baseline bankruptcy rule does not anticipate quick extraction of cash, while the safe harbors facilitate quick extraction for the favored. But this reservation suggests that the appropriate policy avenue should be to facilitate better sales of portfolios and firms, not necessarily favoring a liquidation-oriented, run-facilitating cash extraction channel.
12. *See* Franklin R. Edwards & Edward R. Morrison, *Derivatives and the Bankruptcy Code: Why the Special Treatment?*, 22 Yale J. Reg. 91, 101 (2005); Frank Partnoy & David A. Skeel, Jr., *The Promise and Perils of Credit Derivatives*, 75 U. Cin. L. Rev. 1019, 1049 (2007); Roe, *supra* note 9, at 564–9; David A. Skeel, *Bankruptcy Boundary Games*, 4 Brook. J. Corp. Fin. & Com. L. 1, 10–11 (2009).

13. Franco Modigliani & Merton H. Miller, *The Cost of Capital, Corporation Finance and the Theory of Investment*, 48.3 Am. Econ. Rev. 261 (1958).
14. Roe, *supra* note 9, at 567–9.
15. *See* Craig Pirrong, "The Economics of Clearing in Derivatives Markets: Netting, Asymmetric Information, and the Sharing of Default Risks Though a Central Counterparty" (Jan. 8, 2009) (unpublished manuscript) (http://www.ssrn.com/abstract=1340660); Mark J. Roe, *Clearinghouse Overconfidence*, 101 Cal. L. Rev. 1641 (2013); Mark J. Roe, *Derivatives Clearinghouses Are No Magic Bullet*, Wall St. J., May 6, 2010, at A19; Roe, *supra* note 9, at 586–7.
16. Dodd-Frank Wall Street Reform and Consumer Protection Act, H.R. 4173 111th Cong. § 210(c)(8)(C)(i) (2010).
17. This proposition is examined in greater analytic detail in Edward Morrison, Mark J. Roe & Christopher Sontchi, *Rolling Back the Repo Safe Harbor*, 69 Bus. Law. 1015 (2014).
18. These ideas are explored further in Mark J. Roe & Stephen D. Adams, *Restructuring Failed Financial Firms in Bankruptcy: Selling Lehman's Derivatives Portfolio,* 32 Yale J. Reg. 363 (2014).
19. *See* Thomas Jackson, The Logic and Limits of Bankruptcy Law (1986); Alan Schwartz, 2017. *Bankruptcy Related Contracting and Bankruptcy Functions*, *in* Corporate Bankruptcy (Barry Adler ed). This volume.
20. Schwartz, *supra* note 19.

6. Distress-triggered liabilities and the agency costs of debt

*Richard Squire**

INTRODUCTION

Firms with debt can take actions that benefit their shareholders not by creating value but by shifting risk onto creditors. Termed from the creditors' perspective, such acts of 'debtor misconduct'[1] range from aggressive dividend payments and piling on more debt[2] to subtler maneuvers, such as asset substitution (exchanging safe assets for risky ones).[3] Contractual creditors can anticipate debtor misconduct and demand higher interest rates *ex ante* as compensation. For this reason, misconduct is unlikely to change the division of wealth between debtors and most creditors.[4] But misconduct does generate costs that erode the joint surplus from credit arrangements, leaving debtors and creditors collectively worse off.

In an important 1976 article, Michael Jensen and William Meckling identified three types of cost attributable to debtor misconduct.[5] First, creditors incur monitoring costs to deter misconduct. Second, debtors incur bonding costs to appear more trustworthy and thus reduce the price they are charged for credit. Finally, undeterred misconduct induces debtors to overinvest, committing capital to projects that increase expected shareholder returns only because the projects are subsidized by value transfers from creditors.[6] Conceptualizing debtors as agents who manage (and sometimes mismanage) capital on behalf of creditors, Jensen and Meckling referred to these three types of cost as the agency costs of debt.[7]

In prior work, I have described a form of debtor misconduct, *correlation-seeking*,[8] that involves the sale of contingent claims. A claim is contingent if it becomes payable only upon the occurrence of an uncertain (that is, non-inevitable) future event. An example is a guarantee on a loan, which requires the guarantor to compensate the lender if the borrower defaults. The consideration for a contingent claim can be a direct payment, such as a premium paid by a lender to a guarantor in exchange for a loan guarantee. Or, as in the case of a loan prepayment penalty, the consideration can consist of an interest-rate discount on the loan to which the contingent claim is attached.[9]

Correlation-seeking occurs when a debtor sells a contingent claim against itself with a positive *internal correlation*, meaning that the risk the debtor will become insolvent correlates positively with the risk the claim will be triggered.[10] The consideration received by the debtor benefits its shareholders by increasing its equity value. The shareholders do not, however, bear a proportionate share of the claim's expected burden, as the claim is unlikely to be triggered unless the debtor has become insolvent, in which case the shareholders' interests will already be wiped out. Rather, the claim's expected burden falls disproportionately on the debtor's general creditors, the residual claimants when the debtor is insolvent. As a result, the sale of a contingent claim with a positive internal correlation shifts value from the debtor's general creditors to its equityholders. These value transfers, and the efforts parties undertake to prevent them, generate the agency costs of debt.[11]

This chapter discusses three prevalent contingent-claim arrangements that exemplify correlation-seeking. They are the loan default penalty, the loan prepayment fee (one variety of which is the make-whole premium), and the intragroup guarantee. What these arrangements have in common is that they create *distress-triggered liabilities*, which are contingent obligations of a corporate debtor that tend to be triggered by the debtor's own financial distress. Distress-triggered liabilities thus produce debt's agency costs, as they have high internal correlations inherent in their structures.

A loan default penalty is a contractual fine that a borrower must pay, on top of the regular loan balance, for missing a scheduled payment.[12] It can take the form of a fixed fee, a boosted interest rate, or both. Default penalties serve the economically beneficial function of deterring late payments, thereby reducing lenders' expected collection costs. But the penalties are also, from the borrowers' perspective, contingent liabilities with inherently high internal correlations, as borrowers are especially likely to miss loan payments and thus incur the penalties when insolvent.

A loan prepayment fee, in turn, is a contractual penalty a borrower must pay for electing to repay a loan before its maturity date.[13] The fee can serve the positive function of protecting the lender against the risk that the borrower will refinance a loan to take advantage of a drop in market interest rates. One variety of prepayment fee, the make-whole premium, has been the subject of several recent bankruptcy decisions.[14] A primary question in each case has been whether the automatic acceleration of loans upon the debtor's voluntary bankruptcy filing constituted, per the terms of the loan agreement, a prepayment event that triggered the premium. In loan agreements in which the answer to this question is yes, the make-whole premium is especially likely to be triggered by the borrower's own insolvency and therefore has a high internal correlation.

The third example of a distress-triggered liability is a guarantee issued by one member of a corporate group on the debt of another member.[15] Intragroup guarantees can reduce incentives for managers to play a shell game with the firm's assets, shuffling them among affiliated entities to keep them away from creditors. Because, however, the typical corporate group is in fact a single business firm, whose constituent entities thrive or fail in unison, the guarantor entity is likely to be insolvent when a claim on an intragroup guarantee is triggered.[16]

Bankruptcy courts could reduce the agency costs of debt by subordinating distress-triggered claims to general creditor claims. Subordination would eliminate the value transfers away from general creditors that cause parties to incur monitoring and bonding costs and that subsidize over-investment. But would subordination undermine the positive functions of distress-triggered claims? With respect to loan default penalties and prepayment fees, the answer clearly is no. These contingent claims serve to deter late payments and opportunistic prepayments by making them costly for the borrower (or its shareholders). But the claims serve no useful deterrence function if their burden instead falls on a borrower's general creditors. Therefore, a rule that subordinated such claims to general unsecured claims, while leaving them recoverable ahead of shareholder interests, would preserve their positive functions while preventing the value transfers that drive up the agency costs of debt.

The story is a bit more complicated for intragroup guarantees, which can serve a positive function even when enforceable at the expense of general creditors. That function is to shield lenders from debtor misconduct that reduces the net worth of their particular borrower entities. At the same time, however, intragroup guarantees reduce the monitoring incentives of the sophisticated lenders who typically receive them, and for this reason can make debtor misconduct more likely rather than less. Moreover, the issuance of such a guarantee itself typically shifts value from the guarantor's general creditors to the group's shareholders, increasing the agency costs of debt directly. The implication is that the costs of enforcing intragroup guarantees at the expense of the guarantor's general creditors usually outweigh the economic benefits. If claims on intragroup guarantees were subordinated, they would continue to be fully enforceable against solvent guarantors, the context in which the benefits of enforcing them unambiguously outweigh the social costs.

Currently, bankruptcy courts do not subordinate claims on most distress-triggered liabilities, nor do they analyze legal challenges to such claims in terms of the agency costs of debt. A consistently enforced subordination rule would reduce the overall cost of debt, which is a primary objective of the Bankruptcy Code; in most cases such a rule would accord with the text of the Code as well.[17]

I. DEBTOR MISCONDUCT AND THE AGENCY COSTS OF DEBT

The problem of debtor misconduct has been recognized for centuries. The first statute on fraudulent conveyances, enacted by the English Parliament in 1571, targeted the most flagrant form: eve-of-bankruptcy asset giveaways to friends, family members, and other accomplices.[18] In the last several decades, commentators have described subtler debtor maneuvers that take value from creditors by causing them to bear more risk. An example is correlation-seeking, which like other risk-shifting actions distorts investment incentives and induces parties to incur monitoring and bonding costs. Correlation-seeking is unusual, however, in its impact on equity volatility, potentially making it more attractive to shareholders than other misconduct types.

A. Debtor Misconduct: Prices and Incidence

Besides describing debtor misconduct's economic costs, Jensen and Meckling's 1976 article analyzed how misconduct affects the price of debt.[19] The price effect is important because it determines whether misconduct produces a net change in the distribution of value, and also whether price changes can make misconduct less likely. On the first question, Jensen and Meckling observed that contractual creditors can anticipate misconduct and factor their expected losses from it into the interest they charge.[20] For this reason, misconduct will not, on net, enrich debtors at the expense of most creditors.[21] On the second question, the authors observed that higher interest charged in anticipation of debtor misconduct does not, in itself, reduce the agency costs of debt.[22] Once a loan's interest rate is set, it is a fixed cost the debtor must pay regardless of how the debtor behaves before the loan comes due. The incentive to misbehave persists: the debtor pays the same (heightened) interest rate either way, but its equity value will be higher if it shifts more risk onto creditors.

To see the relationship between misconduct incentives and price adjustments in a related context, consider the market for auto insurance. A driver with a collision policy has less incentive to drive cautiously, as the insurer will bear the costs of accidents. This moral hazard raises the expected cost of insuring against collisions and hence the premiums that insurers must charge to turn a profit.[23] The resulting increase in the price for insurance introduces a deadweight loss, causing fewer drivers to buy insurance than would otherwise. But for drivers who do buy insurance despite the higher prices, the general boosting of premiums on account of moral hazard does not deter reckless driving. Only if the premium charged to a particular driver will rise *ex post*, after he has actually driven recklessly, will the prospect of a price increase motivate him to drive safely. Analogizing to debt arrangements, drivers are debtors, insurers are creditors, and reckless driving is the misconduct made more likely by shifting risk from the former group to the latter. Just as *ex ante* changes in insurance premiums do not deter bad driving, *ex ante* interest-rate increases do not deter debtor misconduct.

To be sure, auto insurers do raise prices on drivers who get into accidents or receive traffic citations, which are proxies for reckless driving. Similarly, creditors often monitor debtors for misconduct and adjust interest rates or seek other relief when misconduct is detected. But monitoring a debtor is not always cost-effective, as the creditor must insist on loan covenants prohibiting specified acts and then keep an eye on the debtor to ensure compliance. Sometimes the costs of monitoring would exceed the expected cost to the creditor of the debtor misconduct the monitoring would prevent; the creditor then will rationally decline to monitor, and misconduct will still occur, producing value transfers that encourage overinvestment. In this chapter, I will refer to these value transfers as *distortive* transfers, as their important quality is not that they alter the overall division of wealth (frequently they do not), but rather that they distort incentives. Like subsidies, they make it profitable for firms to undertake some projects whose expected value, taking into account the impact on all parties, is negative.[24]

B. Traditional Debtor Misconduct: Fixed Debts and Risky Assets

There are a variety of ways that a debtor can, short of an outright asset giveaway, reduce the value of creditor claims. One type, first described by Jensen and Meckling,[25] is a tactic that scholars now call asset substitution.[26] It occurs when an indebted corporation sells a safe asset in order to buy a risky asset, with risk defined as the variance in the distribution of an asset's potential future values. Even if the riskier asset has a lower expected value, its substitution for the safe asset might benefit the corporation's equityholders. They will capture the incrementally higher profits if the riskier (higher-variance) asset appreciates, but they will not bear the incrementally deeper losses if it depreciates. The rule of limited shareholder liability concentrates those losses on the corporation's creditors.[27] In this way, asset substitution produces a distortive transfer from creditors to equityholders. Therefore, creditors will incur monitoring costs to prevent it, and corporations—to reduce the price they are charged for debt—will incur bonding costs to reassure creditors that they will not engage in it. If asset substitution occurs despite such efforts, and the riskier asset is in fact worth less than the safe asset, then the exchange reduces the firm's overall value.

Elazar Berkovitch and E. Han Kim have described a variation on asset substitution that I will refer to as *risk expansion*. It occurs when an indebted firm that already owns one asset issues debt to purchase a second asset.[28] The expansion of the firm's balance sheet produces a distortive transfer from the preexisting creditors to equityholders if (as in the case of asset substitution) it increases the variance of the distribution of the firm's potential asset values. For the addition of the second asset to have this effect, the asset must be riskier than the first and changes in their values must have a sufficiently high positive correlation.[29] Under such conditions, the firm's shareholders could benefit from the purchase of the second asset even its expected value is less than its purchase price.[30]

Both Jensen-Meckling asset substitution and Berkovitch-Kim risk expansion increase the variability of the debtor's asset value. Scholars have described other forms of risk-shifting that operate instead by increasing the debtor's debt-equity ratio. An example is debt dilution, which occurs when a debtor adds more debt to its balance sheet without also adding a proportionate amount of equity.[31] Because it spreads the debtor's equity cushion more thinly, debt dilution produces a distortive transfer away from preexisting creditors. The transfer, and hence the overinvestment risk, is greater if the new debt is secured and thus involuntarily subordinates the preexisting unsecured debt.[32]

C. Correlation-Seeking: Misconduct Through Contingent Debt

In most forms of debtor misconduct, the debtor either incurs no new debt (asset substitution) or incurs only fixed debt (risk expansion, debt dilution, involuntary subordination).[33] Correlation-seeking, by contrast, involves the incurring of contingent debt—in particular, contingent debt that is especially likely to become payable when the debtor is insolvent.

As an illustration of correlation-seeking, imagine that a firm borrows \$90 under the following terms: it will owe the lender \$100 in one year, unless the firm becomes insolvent before then, in which case it will owe the lender \$200. This arrangement consists of a fixed liability of \$100 plus a contingent liability, triggered by the borrower's insolvency, of another \$100. The contingent liability has a high internal correlation, as its triggering risk is perfectly positively correlated with the borrower's insolvency risk. To be sure, the lender is unlikely to recover the full \$200 if the borrower becomes insolvent. But as long as the claim on the contingent liability is enforceable on par with, or ahead of, the claims of the borrower's general creditors, it has some value to the lender, who therefore will be willing to pay for it, such as by charging less interest on the underlying loan. For example, without the $100 contingent claim, the lender might insist on being repaid $110 in one year, charging $20 in interest on the $90 loan rather than $10. In essence, the borrower uses the contingent claim to sell the lender a portion of the borrower's future bankruptcy estate that would otherwise go to other creditors. The sales price—in the form of an interest-rate discount—increases the borrower's equity value, and it also might augment the borrower's estate if bankruptcy ensues. However, it can readily be shown mathematically that the expected cost of the contingent claim to the borrower's general creditors will exceed any benefit they might derive from the sales price collected by the borrower.[34] As a consequence, the sale of the contingent claim will produce a distortive transfer from the borrower's general creditors to its shareholders.

There is a general sense in which correlation-seeking, asset substitution, and risk expansion operate by a common mechanism. As noted, asset substitution and risk expansion both increase the variance of the distribution of the debtor's potential asset values. Higher asset-value variability, in turn, produces wider swings in the debtor's net worth.[35] In this way, these forms of debtor misconduct are similar to correlation-seeking, which also increases the variance of the distribution of the debtor's potential net worth.[36] However, correlation-seeking produces this effect not by increasing asset-value variability, but rather by causing increases in a firm's payable liabilities to coincide with decreases in its asset value.

Given that most shareholders are risk-averse, increased net-worth variability might seem to be a negative side effect of these various forms of debtor misconduct. But what actually matters to corporate shareholders is not their firm's net worth per se, but rather the value of their equity interests—which, unlike their firm's net worth, cannot drop below zero. And, in terms of equity-value variability, most correlation-seeking has the opposite effect of other types of debtor misconduct.[37] Asset substitution, risk expansion, and debt dilution all have a positive relationship with equity volatility: the larger the distortive transfer, the greater the increase in equity volatility. Both asset substitution and risk expansion operate by increasing the variability of the debtor's asset value, which perforce increases equity volatility. Debt dilution also increases equity volatility, as it concentrates swings in a debtor's asset value onto a relatively narrower equity cushion. To risk-averse shareholders, higher equity volatility is a cost of these forms of misconduct, diminishing their appeal in terms of overall shareholder utility.[38]

Correlation-seeking defies the standard relationship between risk and return. As is true with fixed debt, the incurring of most contingent debt dilutes the debtor's equity cushion and thus increases equity volatility. However, as a contingent liability's internal correlation—and hence the distortive transfer—grows, the liability's impact on equity volatility typically shrinks.[39] To see why, imagine a contingent liability with a 50% chance of being triggered if the debtor remains solvent but no chance of being triggered if the debtor becomes insolvent.[40] This liability has a negative internal correlation and therefore does not transfer value from creditors to equityholders (rather, incurring the liability for consideration shifts value in the opposite direction[41]). The liability does, however, increase the variance of the distribution of the potential values of equity interests in the debtor. Now consider the converse contingent liability, with a 50% chance of being triggered if the debtor becomes insolvent but no chance of being triggered if the debtor remains solvent. This liability has a perfectly positive internal correlation and hence incurring it for consideration transfers value from the debtor's existing creditors to its equityholders. But the liability does not make shareholder equity more volatile, as it can be triggered only when equity interests have no value. The relationship between the size of the transfer and equity volatility is thus inverted: as the transfer grows, the impact on volatility shrinks. This unusual feature of correlation-seeking increases its attractiveness to shareholders relative to other misconduct types.[42]

II. DISTRESS-TRIGGERED LIABILITIES

It is rare for a contingent-claim arrangement to state explicitly that the debtor's insolvency triggers the claim. But contracts often do specify triggering events that the parties know are highly likely to coincide with the debtor's insolvency. In such arrangements, the contingent liability's internal correlation is positive, though not perfectly so. But a correlation coefficient of 1.0 is not necessary for a distortive transfer to result. As long as the coefficient is greater than zero, the arrangement will shift value away from the debtor's general creditors, thereby increasing the agency costs of debt.[43] And the internal correlation will reliably be positive if the debtor's own distress tends to trigger the liability, as is true with loan default penalties, prepayment fees triggered by bankruptcy, and intragroup guarantees.

A. Loan Default Penalties

A loan default penalty is a contractual contingent liability that a borrower incurs along with the fixed debt to which it is attached. It inherently has a high internal correlation, as a borrower is especially likely to miss a loan payment when insolvent. Therefore, a default penalty enforceable at the expense of the borrower's general creditors will increase the agency costs of debt.

For any loan that includes a default penalty, there is, in theory, a penalty-free loan that would provide the lender the same expected return. For example, if a loan has a regular (pre-default) interest rate of 5% and a penalty (post-default) rate of 10%, then a loan with a fixed rate of 6% and no penalty rate might have the same expected value. The fixed rate that would produce the return-equivalent loan will depend on the default probability and the lender's expected recovery if default occurs. Given that parties could always agree to such a return-equivalent, fixed-rate loan, why do they sometimes opt for a loan with a default penalty instead?

One answer is, of course, correlation-seeking. As long as a default penalty is recoverable (in whole or in part) at the expense of the borrower's other creditors when the borrower is insolvent, its inclusion in a loan agreement shifts expected value from those creditors to the borrower's shareholders. The shareholders reap most of the expected benefit of the lower, pre-default interest rate, while the penalty's expected burden falls primarily on the creditors.[44] The resulting incentive to include a default penalty in the loan agreement is present even if the borrower's creditors have anticipated the distortive transfer and priced their credit accordingly. Their *ex ante* interest-rate adjustment is a sunk cost the borrower must pay regardless of whether it subsequently takes out a loan with a penalty clause.

Default penalties also have a salutary function, which is to reduce expected collection costs. Dunning a tardy borrower entails efforts of escalating expensiveness, starting with late notices, moving to threatening lawyer letters, and culminating in a lawsuit and possible asset seizures. The expectation of such efforts leads lenders to charge more for credit. Default penalties avoid collection costs by encouraging borrowers to pay punctually. This is a value-creating rather than value-shifting function of penalties, as it prevents costs that would reduce the joint surplus from debt arrangements.

Notably, the prospect of a default penalty encourages timely payment only as long as the borrower is solvent. If the borrower becomes insolvent, a triggered penalty harms not its shareholders but rather its general creditors, because it cuts into their bankruptcy recoveries. Yet there is no positive economic rationale for permitting a lender to shift its collection costs, or a penalty meant to compensate the lender for those costs, onto other creditors, who (unlike the borrower) are in no position to avoid them, and who must, if the borrower is insolvent, undertake their own collection efforts. To the contrary, a default penalty recoverable at the expense of other creditors increases their information costs, requiring them to estimate the penalty's likely dilutive effect on their recoveries and adjust their loan terms accordingly. Therefore, the efficient rule for default penalties would be to subordinate them to general creditor claims, leaving them recoverable only at the expense of the borrower's equityholders. Subordination would preserve the penalties' positive economic function while preventing them from increasing creditor information costs and the agency costs of debt.

Currently, bankruptcy courts do not subordinate claims for most default penalties. If the lender is unsecured or undersecured, a penalty in the form of a fixed charge can be tacked onto the lender's unsecured claim unless the penalty would be unenforceable under state law.[45] The same is true of unpaid, pre-petition interest calculated at a higher, post-default rate. Unless, however, the debtor is solvent at the end of the bankruptcy case,[46] unsecured and undersecured creditors are not permitted to recover post-petition interest, regardless of the rate.[47] To the extent a lender is instead oversecured, section 506(b) of the Bankruptcy Code permits inclusion of a default penalty—whether in the form of a fixed charge or of accrued, penalty-rate interest (even if the interest accrued post-petition)—in the secured claim, as long as the court deems the penalty 'reasonable.'[48] Reasonableness is normally assessed in such cases with reference to industry practice.[49]

B. Prepayment Fees, Including Make-whole Premiums

Like a default penalty, a prepayment fee is a contingent claim tied to a loan. One variety is the make-whole premium, which has been the subject of several recent bankruptcy disputes.[50] A primary issue in the cases has been whether a make-whole was, per the terms of the applicable loan agreement, triggered by the automatic acceleration of debts upon the debtor's voluntary bankruptcy filing.[51] A make-whole that always becomes payable upon the borrower's bankruptcy filing necessarily has a high internal correlation, as it will be triggered almost whenever the borrower is insolvent. It therefore will, if enforceable at the expense of the borrower's general creditors,[52] produce a distortive transfer that increases the agency costs of debt.

The positive function of a prepayment fee is to protect the lender against reinvestment risk.[53] A borrower will exercise an option to prepay a loan if a drop in the market price of credit permits refinancing at a lower rate. Prepayment then harms the lender, who cannot relend the principal at the same interest rate except to a riskier borrower. Lenders could obviate reinvestment risk by prohibiting prepayment altogether, but doing so would hamstring borrowers who might wish to prepay their loans for reasons other than changes in market rates. For example, a borrower might want to prepay to avoid breaching a change-in-control covenant that would stymie a prospective merger.[54] Many loan agreements thus allow early redemption, but for a fee that deters strategic refinancing.

When a prepayment fee takes the form of a make-whole premium, the amount of the premium is determined by a contractual 'yield-maintenance' formula that typically awards the lender the present value of the future interest payments avoided by prepayment.[55] The formula usually employs a discount rate slightly above the risk-free rate. For example, the recent case *In re Energy Future Holdings Corp.* featured a yield-maintenance formula that used a discount rate equal to the yield on U.S. Treasury debt plus 50 basis points.[56] Such a formula fully serves its positive function, as it reliably awards a premium exceeding any savings the borrower could obtain by refinancing.[57] But the formula also makes the lender much more than 'whole,' because it disregards the lender's opportunity to reinvest the repaid principal. Indeed, if the market rate has risen above the contract rate, prepayment benefits the lender, and yet the standard yield-maintenance formula will still award the lender a premium.[58] By contrast, a formula that limited the lender's recovery to actual damages would subtract the market rate from the contract rate before discounting to present value, often resulting in no premium when market rates have risen.

As with other types of contingent liability, a prepayment fee produces a distortive transfer only if recoverable at the expense of the debtor's general creditors. But a fee need not be recoverable on par with, or ahead of, general creditor claims to serve its positive function of deterring strategic refinancing. As long as the fee is recoverable ahead of equity interests, it will prevent the borrower from enriching its shareholders by refinancing to exploit a drop in market rates. This will be true even if a solvent debtor tries to use bankruptcy to refinance, as allegedly occurred in the case *In re Energy Future Holdings Corp.*[59] If the fee has priority over equity interests, the debtor must still pay it in full before distributing any value to shareholders.

Under current law, the enforceability of a prepayment fee in bankruptcy depends on whether it is a fixed charge or instead is the product of a yield-maintenance formula. When the fee consists of a fixed charge, the analysis is the same as for a default penalty: assuming the fee is enforceable under state law, an unsecured creditor can add the fee to its allowed claim,[60] and an oversecured creditor can include the fee in its secured claim if the court deems the fee amount reasonable.[61] Matters become more complicated if the fee consists of a make-whole premium calculated through a yield-maintenance formula, as then the fee will likely be challenged as a claim for unmatured interest,[62] recovery for which is excluded by the Bankruptcy Code's section 502(b)(2). The lender might, however, be able to sidestep section 502(b)(2) by convincing the court that the premium represents liquidated damages rather than unmatured interest, as liquidated damages are normally recoverable in bankruptcy to the extent enforceable under state law.[63]

C. Intragroup Guarantees

The third common example of distress-triggered liability is the intragroup guarantee.[64] Courts often distinguish among three varieties: downstream (parent guarantees subsidiary's debt), upstream (subsidiary guarantees parent's debt), and cross-stream (one subsidiary guarantees the debt of another). The distinction is legally relevant because downstream guarantees, in particular, enjoy special protection under fraudulent-transfer law.[65] Economically, however, all three varieties have essentially the same impact: they all reliably have high internal correlations and thus produce distortive transfers when enforceable at the expense of the guarantor's general creditors. The correlation arises because a corporate group's constituent members usually produce the same or complementary goods or services, subjecting them to common supply and demand conditions.[66] Moreover, the members often make debt and equity investments in each other that further link their fates. Accordingly, the misfortunes that cause one group member to default on its debts also normally render insolvent any parent, subsidiary, or sibling entity that guaranteed that debt.

An intragroup guarantee's positive function is to reduce the lender's exposure to misconduct that makes the borrower entity less creditworthy.[67] As an illustration, suppose that a bank intends to lend to X, a subsidiary in a corporate group, but fears that the group's managers will subsequently shift X's assets to a sibling subsidiary, Y, to reduce Y's cost of credit. Such an asset shift would constitute debtor misconduct, producing a distortive transfer from X's general creditors to the group's shareholders, who would benefit from the reduction in Y's borrowing costs. To protect itself, the bank could demand a cross-stream guarantee from Y, which would leave the bank largely indifferent to the division of assets between the two entities.[68] The guarantee might also make the managers less likely to spirit assets from X to Y in the first place, as any such transfer would increase Y's exposure on the guarantee, which would be counterproductive to the goal of making Y more creditworthy. On the other hand, the guarantee might make such asset transfers *more* likely by removing the incentive for the bank—likely X's most sophisticated creditor—to monitor to prevent them. In other words, the bank might be the cheapest cost avoider, in which case shielding it from harms borne by X's creditors as a group could be inefficient. The implication is that the net effect of most intragroup guarantees is to increase the agency costs of debt. The distortive transfer away from the guarantor's general creditors occurs whenever the guarantor has preexisting unsecured debt, whereas any countervailing benefit from reduced debtor misconduct is speculative.

A comparison can be drawn to security interests. By granting a lien to one creditor, a debtor subordinates the claims of its other, unsecured creditors, producing a distortive transfer that promotes overinvestment.[69] But the lien also makes it harder for the debtor to profit from shifting risk onto the secured creditor. In this way, the lien makes debtor misconduct less likely, unless the secured creditor would otherwise monitor effectively to prevent it.[70] Thus, intragroup guarantees and security interests both have positive and negative implications for the agency costs of debt. As between the two, however, intragroup guarantees probably generate higher net costs.[71] This is because a security interest is a more effective bonding device: unlike an intragroup guarantee, a lien deters asset substitution, by making it difficult for the debtor to sell the encumbered assets and use the proceeds to buy riskier assets.[72] In addition, the distortive transfer produced by issuing a security interest is easier to detect. Perfecting a lien typically requires a public filing,[73] which reduces the cost of monitoring the debtor for compliance with a negative pledge covenant forbidding the incurring of secured debt. An (unsecured) intragroup guarantee, by contrast, is fully enforceable even when undisclosed.

An intragroup guarantee issued by a debtor in the years leading up to its bankruptcy filing will often be challenged as a fraudulent transfer. The challenge's likelihood of success will depend on the variety of guarantee: downstream guarantees are less vulnerable to disallowance than are the upstream and cross-stream varieties. The reason for the downstream guarantee's privileged status is the common practice whereby lenders pay for intragroup guarantees not by making a direct payment to the guarantor but rather by reducing the interest rate on the underlying loan. The lack of direct consideration for the guarantor is often cited to establish that the guarantor incurred the obligation without receiving 'a reasonably equivalent value' in exchange, one of the elements of a constructive fraudulent-transfer claim.[74] When the guarantee is upstream or cross-stream, this argument has a good chance of prevailing.[75] When, however, the guarantee is downstream, courts typically conclude that the parent benefitted from the guarantee indirectly, though the reduction in the subsidiary's cost of credit.[76]

The factors that courts consider when analyzing fraudulent-transfer challenges to intragroup guarantees bear little relation to whether the guarantees actually shift risk onto unsecured creditors and thus increase the agency costs of debt. When a contingent liability has a positive internal correlation, its incurrence produces a distortive transfer even if the debtor receives consideration equal to the claim's full expected value to the claimant.[77] Correlation, not the allocation of consideration, determines most of a contingent liability's expected impact on the debtor's general creditors. Indeed, a downstream guarantee—despite being the variety least vulnerable to fraudulent-transfer attack—typically produces a larger distortive transfer than an otherwise equivalent cross-stream guarantee, as the parent's equity stake in the subsidiary increases the correlation between the two entities' insolvency risks.[78]

III. DISTRESS-TRIGGERED LIABILITIES AND BANKRUPTCY LAW

The law of business bankruptcy can be understood as a device for reducing the cost of debt capital,[79] an important component of which are the agency costs resulting from the structural conflict of interests between creditors and equityholders. The implication is that courts could advance the Bankruptcy Code's purpose by subordinating distress-triggered claims, except to the extent that particular creditors have contractually waived the right to recover ahead of such claims.[80] A consistently applied subordination rule would prevent the distortive transfers that increase debt's agency costs. But should bankruptcy judges derive from the Code subordination rules that private parties could, in theory, write into contracts themselves? And would judicial subordination of distress-triggered liabilities be consistent not just with the purpose of the Code, but with its text as well?

A. Misconduct, Bankruptcy Law and Contract

Creditors can police debtor misconduct contractually, most obviously by insisting on loan covenants that forbid it. It thus could be argued that courts need not take an active role in reducing the agency costs of debt beyond simply enforcing loan covenants as written.[81] But loan covenants have drawbacks that limit their cost-effectiveness. The standard remedy for breach of a loan covenant is acceleration plus possible monetary damages. Yet a breach of a covenant forbidding, for example, the debtor from issuing an intragroup guarantee would not typically be evident until after the debtor has become insolvent and entered bankruptcy, at which point the creditor will be unable to force acceleration or recover adequate damages. Because such under-recovery is foreseeable, the covenant will not fully deter the misconduct it proscribes. Full deterrence depends upon monitoring the debtor over a loan's duration to catch breaches while the debtor is solvent and contractual remedies remain effective.[82] However, monitoring is expensive—often more expensive than the conduct it would prevent. Therefore, the more cost-effective remedy for breach of a covenant forbidding correlation-seeking would be to subordinate the claim on the offending contingent liability, as this remedy would not require ongoing monitoring to be effective. But this would be an equitable remedy against a third party, not normally available for breach of contract.[83]

Another drawback of loan covenants is under-enforcement due to the creditor collective-action problem.[84] Although a dollar spent on monitoring might deter two dollars' worth of debtor misconduct, the two-dollar benefit would often be spread among the debtor's general creditors, while the cost would fall entirely on the creditor who monitors. In other words, monitoring generates positive externalities and hence will be undersupplied unless creditors can coordinate to share the cost of monitoring along with its benefits. But coordination will, like monitoring, often be costlier than the misconduct it would deter, leading rational creditors to forgo active covenant enforcement.

Rules based in bankruptcy law lack these two drawbacks of covenants. The Bankruptcy Code can supply the valuable remedy that contract law does not: subordination of a third-party claim. Therefore, anti-misconduct rules derived from the Code do not require ongoing monitoring of the debtor, as they can effectively deter misconduct that would not be discovered until after the debtor has become insolvent and entered bankruptcy. In addition, the litigation expenses of the bankruptcy trustee (or debtor in possession) are paid by the estate, and thus, in effect, by the debtor's unsecured creditors as a group. Such cost-sharing alleviates the mismatch between private cost and collective gain that causes covenants to be underused and underenforced.

Another possible objection to judicial policing of debtor misconduct is that courts will make mistakes, condemning transactions that are actually value-creating. Consider, for example, the evidentiary challenges that would face a judge who decided to use the Code's fraudulent-transfer provisions to prevent asset substitution. The judge would have to determine not only whether a past asset exchange had the foreseeable effect of increasing the variance of the distribution of the debtor's potential asset values, but also whether the new asset's expected value exceeded that of the old asset. The necessary inquiries would raise complex factual questions debated by (presumably expensive) expert witnesses. And they would be subject to hindsight bias given that the debtor, by dint of being bankrupt, presumably suffered a steep loss of value after the exchange in question.

The prospect of expensive inquiries that often produce false positives argues against treating the Bankruptcy Code as a license for judges to hunt down all forms of debtor misconduct. But the specific type of misconduct of concern in this chapter—correlation-seeking through distress-triggered liabilities—does not present such a prospect. As an evidentiary matter, distress-triggered liabilities are easy to identify, thus presenting little risk of false positives. With default penalties, it is self-evident that a contingent liability triggered whenever a debtor defaults on its debts is especially likely to be triggered when the debtor is insolvent. No detailed analysis of the debtor's past financial condition is required. The same is true of any prepayment fee, including a make-whole premium, triggered by the debtor's bankruptcy filing. Therefore, courts would not have to investigate debtors' financial history to be confident that these types of contingent liabilities had high internal correlations when incurred.

Similar logic applies to intragroup guarantees. When, for example, a subsidiary has guaranteed a debt of its parent, a judge need not reconstruct the two entities' past balance sheets, nor evaluate the market conditions in which the entities operated, to know that the guarantee had a high internal correlation when issued. The mere fact of the parent's ownership of the subsidiary indicates a strong correlation between the risk the subsidiary would become insolvent and the risk the parent would also become insolvent, triggering the subsidiary's liability on the guarantee. If, as will often be the case, the parent and subsidiary produced the same goods or services—a fact that would typically be easy to ascertain, if not undisputed—then the internal correlation would be even higher. A distortive transfer from the guarantor's general creditors would then be easy to establish, with little risk of hindsight bias.

A further argument for judicial subordination of distress-triggered liabilities is that their main economic benefits do not normally depend on their being enforced at the expense of general creditors. The positive function of a loan default penalty is to promote punctuality by requiring the debtor to internalize the lender's collection costs, a function not served if those costs are shifted to the debtor's general creditors. Prepayment fees, in turn, serve no salutary function if enforced at the expense of general creditors, as their only wealth-creating (as opposed to wealth-shifting) purpose is to deter borrowers from refinancing debt at lower interest rates, a purpose requiring only that the borrowers' shareholders bear the fee. Finally, intragroup guarantees will, as described above, almost always produce a net increase in the agency costs of debt when enforceable at the expense of general creditors. Therefore, for all three types of distress-triggered liability, there is little risk that a subordination rule would destroy economic value by undermining their positive functions.[85]

B. Code Specifics

Turning from general considerations of bankruptcy law to the Bankruptcy Code's specific provisions, the most obvious statutory basis for a subordination rule is section 548, which enables bankruptcy trustees (and debtors in possession) to set aside claims resulting from fraudulent transfers.[86] The recognized purpose of fraudulent transfer law is to protect unsecured creditors against debtor conduct that was intended to harm them or that foreseeably had that effect.[87] Although section 548 speaks in terms of 'avoid[ing]' obligations,[88] the actual remedy is subordination, as a claim excluded under section 548 remains enforceable ahead of shareholder interests.[89]

One way to avoid an obligation under section 548 is to show that the debtor incurred it 'with actual intent to hinder, delay or defraud' creditors.[90] However, proving such intent is difficult in practice. If a transaction had a legitimate business purpose—and a contract creating a distress-triggered liability generally does—then courts are reluctant to deem it intentionally fraudulent.[91] Their reluctance suggests that courts read the statute to require proof that the debtor's *sole* intent in a transaction was to harm creditors. The statute's language, however, imposes no such restriction. Moreover, a transaction harmful to creditors can reflect dual intentions: for example, to deter certain debtor conduct while the debtor is solvent, and to shift losses onto general creditors when the debtor is insolvent. Courts that recognize the dual-intent nature of most distress-triggered liabilities should be more willing to allow subordination through section 548's actual-fraud provision.

As an alternative to establishing actual intent to harm creditors, a challenger can prevail under section 548 by proving the two elements of a constructive fraudulent transfer.[92] The first element is that the debtor transferred property or incurred an obligation without receiving 'a reasonably equivalent value' in exchange.[93] The second element is that the challenged transaction occurred under conditions, specified in section 548(a)(1)(B)(ii), when harm to creditors was especially likely.

With respect to the first element, the Code defines 'value' as 'property, or satisfaction or securing of a present or antecedent debt of the debtor.'[94] To determine whether a value received by a debtor reasonably equaled an obligation incurred, courts usually look for a conspicuous change in the debtor's net worth. For example, courts find a lack of equivalent value if the debtor simply gave assets away,[95] incurred a loan but did not receive the proceeds,[96] or issued an upstream or cross-stream guarantee but got no direct or indirect payment in exchange.[97] The common consequence of such transactions is a reduction in the simple difference between the debtor's asset value and the face value of its debts.

By contrast, the incurring of a distress-triggered liability does not produce the type of conspicuous reduction in the debtor's net worth that would show up on a standard balance sheet. Instead, the transaction reduces the expected value of general creditor claims against the debtor through a distortive transfer that increases the expected value of shareholder interests by a comparable amount. Therefore, to use fraudulent-transfer law to police distress-triggered liabilities, courts would have to define 'reasonably equivalent' in terms of value to creditors rather than debtor net worth. The inquiry would be whether the consideration received by the debtor had a value to the debtor's unsecured creditors comparable to the expected cost to them of the contingent liability. So far, courts have not framed their inquiries in such terms. Consequently, fraudulent-transfer doctrine is underinclusive as applied to contingent liabilities, providing no remedy in the large majority of cases in which the contingent liability has shifted risk onto general creditors and thus increased the agency costs of debt.

Although the Code does not define 'reasonably equivalent' or explain how to measure it, statutory structure indicates that a transaction's net impact on the debtor's unsecured creditors is the relevant inquiry. The subparagraph of section 548 that voids actual (rather than constructive) fraudulent transfers explicitly targets transactions intended to harm creditors.[98] The most natural reading of the next subparagraph—which voids constructive fraudulent transfers—is that it targets transactions whose *effect* was to harm creditors, regardless of intent.[99]

The high internal correlation inherent in a distress-triggered liability ensures that, even when the contingent claimant pays the debtor consideration equal to the claimant's full expected recovery on the claim, that consideration will be inadequate to offset the expected cost to the debtor's general creditors.[100] Therefore, fraudulent-transfer doctrine that reflected the true economics of distress-triggered liabilities would apply a strong presumption that the debtor did *not* receive a reasonably equivalent value when incurring such a liability. Merely showing that the debtor received consideration equal to the contingent claim's full expected value to the claimant would not be sufficient to rebut the presumption, as such consideration would not be large enough to prevent the value transfer that generates the agency costs of debt. Rather, the claimant should have to show that, for some reason, the debtor received consideration far exceeding the claim's value to the claimant. Because such instances will be rare (for why would a claimant deliberately overpay for a claim?), the first element in a constructive fraudulent-transfer challenge to a distress-triggered liability would almost always be satisfied. Moreover, the court's task in determining whether the debtor received equivalent value would be greatly simplified, because the liability's internal correlation would constitute prima facie evidence which the claimant in most cases could not plausibly rebut.[101]

Besides simplifying the analysis of the first element of constructive fraudulent-transfer challenges to distress-triggered liabilities, evidence of a high internal correlation could be used to simplify analysis of the second element as well. To satisfy the second element, the challenger must prove any one of the four conditions listed under section 548(a)(1)(B)(ii). Challengers normally try to prove the first listed condition, namely that the debtor was insolvent at the time it incurred the obligation or was made insolvent by it.[102] But proving past insolvency often entails a complicated factual inquiry that, given the fact of bankruptcy, is subject to hindsight bias. Challengers could instead use evidence of a high internal correlation to prove the third listed condition, which is that the debtor 'intended to incur, or believed that the debtor would incur, debts that would be beyond the debtor's ability to pay as such debts matured.'[103] A debtor does exactly this when it incurs a contingent liability with a high internal correlation: it takes on a (contingent) debt that it foreseeably will be unable to pay when the debt comes due, because the debt is especially likely to be triggered when the debtor is insolvent. In this way, the mere fact of a high internal correlation—inherent in the structure of all distress-triggered liabilities—could be used to prove the second element of a constructive fraudulent transfer, further simplifying the legal analysis.[104]

Beyond its fraudulent-transfer provisions, the Bankruptcy Code has two other provisions that courts could use to reduce the impact of distress-triggered liabilities on general creditors and thus lower the agency costs of debt. One is section 506(b), which, as noted, permits oversecured creditors to augment their secured claims by any 'reasonable fees, costs or charges' provided for in their loan agreements.[105] Lenders often rely on this provision to add default penalties and prepayment penalties to their secured claims. Importantly, the Code does not define 'reasonable,' leaving courts some latitude. Judges could reduce debt's agency costs by finding it unreasonable for a lender to recover a penalty that the debtor itself, so long as it remained solvent, was unlikely to have to pay, and that when combined with the lender's claim for principal and accrued interest would well exceed the funds the lender originally advanced to the debtor. Such an approach would be particularly justified as applied to make-whole premiums, which often enable lenders to earn, at the expense of general creditors, a much higher return on their loans than they would have earned had the debtor remained solvent.[106]

Another Code provision that bears on make-whole premiums in particular is section 502(b)(2), which disallows claims for unmatured interest.[107] A party seeking to block recovery of a make-whole often argues that it represents a claim for unmatured interest and thus should be disallowed per this provision. A contrary argument, which has convinced several courts, is that prepayment fees are not unmatured interest but rather are liquidated damages and hence are recoverable in bankruptcy to the extent enforceable under state law.[108] The argument is strained: as two commentators have noted, 'to disallow a claim for unmatured interest, but not a claim for the present value of that interest, is difficult to defend.'[109] Moreover, the argument seems to be premised on a false dichotomy. A contract can define liquidated damages in terms of unmatured interest; the resulting claim would then be for unmatured interest notwithstanding that it arises from a liquidated-damages clause. One bankruptcy court recently applied this logic to disallow recovery of a make-whole per section 502(b)(2).[110] Not only was this holding consistent with the text of the Code, but it also advanced the Code's purpose of reducing the cost of debt, in particular the component attributable to principal-agent conflict between creditors and debtors.

CONCLUSION

This chapter has described how distress-triggered liabilities contribute to the agency costs of debt, and how courts could employ the Bankruptcy Code to reduce those costs. Contingent liabilities generate agency costs through correlation-seeking, which occurs when a corporate debtor sells a contingent claim against itself whose risk of being triggered has a strong positive correlation with the risk that the debtor will become insolvent. Such a correlation is inherent in the structures of loan default penalties, prepayment fees such as make-whole premiums, and intragroup guarantees. The common element among these arrangements is that they create contingent liabilities that tend to be triggered by the debtor's own financial distress. When enforceable at the expense of the debtor's general creditors, distress-triggered claims generate distortive transfers from those creditors to shareholders that reduce economic wealth by encouraging overinvestment and inducing parties to incur monitoring and bonding costs.

Courts could block the distortive transfers, thereby preventing the costs they generate, by employing several provisions of the Bankruptcy Code to subordinate claims on distress-triggered liabilities. When correlation-seeking is inherent in a contingent liability's structure—as is true with distress-triggered liabilities—courts need not undertake complex factual inquiries to conclude that enforcing the resulting claim at the expense of the debtor's general creditors will increase the agency costs of debt. Judges also need not fear that subordinating distress-triggered claims would undermine their positive economic functions. The claims would continue to be collectable from solvent debtors, the only circumstance in which the economic benefits of enforcing them are likely to outweigh the costs.

NOTES

* Professor of Law and Alpin J. Cameron Chair in Law, Fordham Law School. I am grateful to the editor, Barry Adler, for helpful comments on an earlier draft of this chapter.

1. *See* Daniel R. Fischel, *The Economics of Lender Liability*, 99 Yale L.J. 131, 135–6 (1989) (defining 'debtor misconduct' as actions adverse to creditors that firms take after incurring debt).
2. Increasing a firm's debt-equity ratio makes its debt riskier, which shifts value from existing creditors to equityholders unless the creditors adjust by charging more interest. Alan Schwartz, *A Theory of Loan Priorities*, 18 J. Legal Stud. 209, 228 (1989).
3. Asset substitution shifts value from creditors to equityholders by increasing the variance in the distribution of the firm's potential asset values. Alan Schwartz, *Security Interests and Bankruptcy Priorities: A Review of Current Theories*, 10 J. Legal Stud. 1, 11 (1981).
4. Debtor misconduct probably does reduce net recoveries for involuntary tort claimants, who cannot adjust the interest rate payable on their claims. Lucian A. Bebchuk & Jesse M. Fried, *The Uneasy Case for the Priority of Secured Claims in Bankruptcy*, 105 Yale L.J. 857, 892 (1996).
5. Michael C. Jensen & William H. Meckling, *Theory of the Firm: Managerial Behavior, Agency Costs and Ownership Structure*, 3 J. Fin. Econ. 305 (1976).
6. Jensen and Meckling did not use the term 'overinvestment' but rather referred to the costs of undeterred misconduct as the 'residual loss.' *Id.* at 308.
7. *Id.*
8. Richard Squire, *Shareholder Opportunism in a World of Risky Debt*, 123 Harv. L. Rev. 1151, 1157 (2010) (defining 'correlation-seeking').
9. *Id.* at 1159.
10. *Id.*
11. *Id.* at 1180–82.
12. *See infra* Part II.A.
13. *See infra* Part II.B.
14. *See infra* note 50 and accompanying text.
15. *See infra* Part II.C.
16. Richard Squire, *Strategic Liability in the Corporate Group*, 78 U. Chi. L. Rev. 605, 626–7 (2011).
17. See *infra* Part III.
18. 13 Eliz. 1, c. 5.
19. Jensen & Meckling, *supra* note 5, at 336.
20. *Id.*
21. In the Jensen-Meckling model, the lender raises the interest rate to achieve the required return, with the consequence that the firm uses less capital than it would if there were no agency costs. *Id.* at 337.
22. *Id.* The debtor's desire to pay less for credit could induce it to incur bonding costs, but these are also economic costs that reduce the joint surplus from borrowing.
23. Steven Shavell, *On Moral Hazard and Insurance*, 93 Q.J. Econ. 541, 541 (1979) ('Moral hazard refers to the tendency of insurance protection to alter an individual's motive to prevent loss. This affects expenses for the insurer and therefore, ultimately, the cost of coverage for individuals.').

24. When Jensen and Meckling referred to a 'transfer' caused by debtor misconduct, they placed the term in quotation marks to indicate that creditors can neutralize the transfer *ex ante* by charging more for credit. Jensen & Meckling, *supra* note 5, at 337. Even with such an adjustment, however, the transfer is real in the sense that, once credit is extended and the terms of credit (including the interest rate) are fixed, creditor claims will be worth less, and equityholder interests worth more, if the debtor actually engages in misconduct.
25. Jensen & Meckling, *supra* note 5, at 334–7.
26. *See, e.g.*, Elazar Berkovitch & E. Han Kim, *Financial Contracting and Leverage Induced Over- and Under-Investment Incentives*, 45 J. Fin. 765 (1990) (referring to 'Jensen and Meckling's (1976) asset substitution effect').
27. The equityholders are, in effect, holders of a call option whose value increases with the variance in the distribution of the firm's potential values. Jensen & Meckling, *supra* note 5, at 336. The strike price is the face value of the firm's debt. If the firm's assets appreciate, the firm can pay off the debt and distribute the surplus to its shareholders; if they depreciate, it can let the option expire, leaving the creditors to bear the losses beyond the amount of the equityholders' original investment.
28. Berkovitch & Kim, *supra* note 26, at 767.
29. If a positive correlation is not present, then the second asset will diversify the risk from the first asset, shifting value in the opposite direction (from shareholders to creditors).
30. Berkovitch & Kim, *supra* note 26, at 771.
31. *See* Schwartz, *supra* note 2, at 228.
32. *See* Berkovitch & Kim, *supra* note 26, at 781.
33. *See id.* at 768 (modeling risk expansion using fixed debt); Jensen & Meckling, *supra* note 5, at 334–7 (modeling asset substitution using fixed debt).
34. *See* Squire, *supra* note 8, at 1163–75; Squire, *supra* note 16, at 664–9.
35. Comparably, debt dilution increases the relative standard deviation of the debtor's potential net-worth values.
36. Squire, *supra* note 8, at 1176 ("The thing that asset substitution and. . .correlation-seeking have in common is that both increase the volatility of a firm's net worth—meaning the simple arithmetic difference between the firm's assets and liabilities.").
37. *Id.*
38. Shareholders can diversify away the increased equity volatility only to the extent it is unsystematic. Debt dilution increases both systematic and unsystematic risk, while asset substitution and risk expansion increase systematic risk to the extent the volatility of the riskier asset is non-idiosyncratic.
39. Squire, *supra* note 8, at 1176–8. There are exceptions: an increase in the internal correlation will not decrease equity volatility if the contingent liability is especially small or especially likely to be triggered. The reason for the first exception is that a very small claim lacks the power to drive the direction of equity swings; the reason for the second is that a contingent liability which is highly likely to be triggered is more like a fixed debt and thus produces considerable debt dilution. *Id.* at 1179.
40. If the contingent claim is *always* triggered when equity has a positive value, then the sale of the claim will not increase the variance of the distribution of the debtor's potential equity values, as the claim will depress equity's value in all states of the world in which the debtor is solvent. The described effect on equity volatility requires that there be potential future states in which equity has a positive value and the contingent liability is not triggered.
41. Squire, *supra* note 8, at 1167.
42. *Id.* at 1178.
43. *Id.* at 1167.
44. *See* David G. Carlson, *Postdefault Interest Rates in Bankruptcy*, 2015 U. Ill. L. Rev. 617, 618 ('It is easy for debtors to agree to [higher post-default interest] rates. Typically, the price is paid not by debtors, who expect to be bankrupt in case of default, but by the unsecured creditors.').

45. Section 502(a) of the Bankruptcy Code provides that a 'claim' supported by proof is deemed allowed in bankruptcy unless an objection is filed. 11 U.S.C. § 502(a). Section 101(5)(A), in turn, defines 'claim' as a 'right to payment, whether or not such right is reduced to judgment. . ..' 11 U.S.C. § 101(5)(a). Section 502(b) lists grounds for excluding claims, but none squarely covers a fixed default penalty. 11 U.S.C. § 502(b).
46. *See In re* Dow Corning Corp., 456 F.3d 668, 680 (6th Cir. 2006).
47. *See* 11 U.S.C. § 502(b)(2) (disallowing claims for unmatured interest); Univ. Sav. Ass'n of Tex. v. Timbers of Inwood Forest Assocs., Ltd., 484 U.S. 365 (1988) (holding that undersecured creditors, unlike oversecured creditors, cannot recover post-petition interest on their secured claims).
48. The section reads:

    To the extent that an allowed secured claim is secured by property the value of which. . .is greater than the amount of such claim, there should be allowed the holder of such claim, interest on such claim, and any reasonable fees, costs, or charges provided for under the agreement. . .under which such claim arose.

    11 U.S.C. § 506(b).
49. See, e.g., *In re* SW Boston Hotel Venture, LLC, 748 F.3d 393 (1st Cir. 2014); *In re* Terry Ltd. P'ship, 27 F.3d 241 (7th Cir. 1994). A related question is whether, if an oversecured creditor's loan agreement specifies a higher, post-default interest rate, a reorganization plan must provide for payment at that higher rate in order for the debtor's default on the agreement to be deemed cured for purpose of reinstatement. *See In re* New Invs., Inc., 840 F.3d 1137, 1140 (9th Cir. 2016) (holding that Bankruptcy Code § 1123(d) requires payment at the contractual post-default rate for the default to be considered cured).
50. *See, e.g.*, *In re* Energy Future Holdings Corp., 842 F.3d 247, 257–8 (3d Cir. 2016) (holding that two make-whole agreements were contractually triggered by the debtors' voluntary bankruptcy filing); *In re* MPM Silicones, LLC, 531 B.R. 321, 325 (S.D.N.Y. 2015) (holding that, per the terms of an indenture, the acceleration of debt in bankruptcy did not trigger a make-whole premium); *In re* Sch. Specialty, Inc., No. 13-10125 KJC, 2013 WL 1838513 (Bankr. D. Del. Apr. 22, 2013) (holding that a make-whole premium was recoverable in bankruptcy if triggered by automatic acceleration of the loan and enforceable under controlling state law); *In re* Trico Marine Servs., Inc., 450 B.R. 474, 480 (Bankr. D. Del. 2011) (holding that a make-whole premium was a liquidated damages provision and therefore not excludable as a claim for unmatured interest).
51. *See, e.g.*, *In re* Energy Future Holdings Corp., 842 F.3d at 250–51; *In re* MPM Silicones, LLC, 531 B.R. at 325.
52. *See* discussion *infra* notes 62–6.
53. *See In re* Energy Future Holdings Corp., 533 B.R. 106, 114 (Bankr. D. Del. 2015) (explaining that make-whole provisions protect lenders against 'reinvestment risk,' namely the risk that, after prepayment of the loan, 'the investor would be unable to find in the market a bond of comparable credit quality and duration that would generate a comparable return').
54. Andrew Kalotay, *Making Sense of the Make-Whole, From its Origins to Babs*, The Bond Buyer (July 23, 2010), https://www.bondbuyer.com/opinion/making-sense-of-the-make-whole-call-from-its-origins-to-babs.
55. *See In re* Hidden Lake Ltd. P'ship, 247 B.R. 722, 727 (Bankr. S.D. Ohio 2000).
56. The loan agreement further required the borrower to pay a penalty equal to 1% of the principal if such penalty was greater than the present value of the foregone interest payments. *In re* Energy Future Holdings Corp., 527 B.R. 178, 186 (Bankr. D. Del. 2015). A similar fee was at issue in the case of *In re* School Specialty, Inc., No. 13-10125 KJC, 2013 WL 1838513 (Bankr. D. Del. April 22, 2013).
57. Suppose that a loan will mature in one year, at which point the borrower will owe $100 in principal and $10 in interest. Suppose further that the loan agreement contains a

make-whole provision whose yield-maintenance formula specifies a discount rate equal to the risk-free rate, which is currently 1%, plus 50 basis points. If the borrower prepays this loan now, it will owe the $100 principal plus a make-whole premium of $10 / 1.015 = $9.85. If the borrower borrows both the $100 principal and the $9.85 premium from a second lender, that second lender would have to charge annual interest of less than 0.14% for the borrower to owe the second lender less than $110 in one year, which of course is highly unlikely given a risk-free rate of 1%.

58. *See In re* Kroh Bros. Dev. Co., 88 B.R. 997, 1001 (Bankr. W.D. Mo. 1988).
59. *In re* Energy Future Holdings Corp., 842 F.3d 247, 251 (3d Cir. 2016).
60. *See supra* note 47.
61. 11 U.S.C. § 506(b).
62. *See In re* Doctors Hosp. of Hyde Park, Inc., 508 B.R. 697, 706 (Bankr. N.D. Ill. 2014); *In re* Chemtura Corp., 439 B.R. 561 (Bankr. S.D.N.Y. 2010); *In re* Ridgewood Apartments of DeKalb Cty., Ltd., 174 B.R. 712, 720 (Bankr. S.D. Ohio 1994); *In re* Skyler Ridge, 80 B.R. 500, 504 (Bankr. C.D. Cal. 1987).
63. *See, e.g.*, *In re* Sch. Specialty, Inc., No. 13-10125 KJC, 2013 WL 1838513, at *2; *In re* Trico Marine Servs., Inc., 450 B.R. 474, 480 (Bankr. D. Del. 2011).
64. Almost all public companies are organized as corporate groups. In 2010, the 100 largest American public companies by revenues (excluding Fannie Mae and Freddie Mac) reported an average of 245 major subsidiaries. Only five reported fewer than five major subsidiaries. Squire, *supra* note 16, at 601 n.1.
65. *See infra* notes 75–9 and accompanying text.
66. Squire, *supra* note 16, at 626.
67. *See* Avery W. Katz, *An Economic Analysis of the Guaranty Contract*, 66 U. Chi. L. Rev. 47, 73–4 (1999) (noting that a loan guarantee from a corporate affiliate of the borrower can protect the lender against asset transfers from the borrower to the guarantor).
68. Even with the guarantee, the bank will prefer that whichever subsidiary ends up with more assets be the one with less debt.
69. *See* Berkovitch & Kim, *supra* note 26, at 773 ('[I]f the new project is a risk-increasing type with a negative NPV, allowing stockholders to issue senior debt may exacerbate the over-investment incentive.').
70. For example, the lien protects against correlation-seeking: a fully secured creditor will not suffer a value transfer if the debtor subsequently issues an intragroup guarantee.
71. An intragroup guarantee can itself be secured, which increases the distortive transfer it produces. The remedy for guarantee-based correlation-seeking advocated in Part III—avoidance under fraudulent transfer law—would, by subordinating the claim on the guarantee, also nullify the distortive transfer resulting from the security interest.
72. Clifford W. Smith, Jr. & Jerold B. Warner, *On Financial Contracting: An Analysis of Bond Covenants*, 7 J. Fin. Econ. 117, 127 (1979).
73. Alternatively, the creditor could take possession of the collateral, but this is impractical when the collateral is a non-financial asset that the debtor uses for production.
74. 11 U.S.C. § 548(a)(1)(B)(i).
75. *See, e.g.*, *In re* Tousa, 680 F.3d 1298, 1302 (11th Cir. 2012).
76. *See, e.g.*, *In re* Royal Crown Bottlers of N. Ala., Inc., 23 B.R. 28, 30 (Bankr. N.D. Ala. 1982).
77. Squire, *supra* note 16, at 627, 664–9.
78. *Id.* at 636.
79. For an argument that reducing the cost of debt is the only proper function of a commercial bankruptcy regime, see Alan Schwartz, *A Contract Theory Approach to Business Bankruptcy*, 107 Yale L.J. 1807, 1840 (1998).
80. See note 85, *infra.*
81. For an argument that even small, nonfinancial contract creditors may not need extra-contractual protection, see Barry E. Adler & Marcel Kahan, *The Technology of Creditor Protection*, 161 U. Pa. L. Rev. 1773, 1807–08 (2013).
82. *Id.* at 1780.

83. To overcome the inadequacy of standard contractual remedies for covenant breaches, Barry Adler and Marcel Kahan have proposed a system in which loan covenants could be filed in public registries, after which they would be enforceable against third parties who enter into transactions with debtors that violate them. *Id.* at 1796–7. In other words, creditors would be able to give property-like protection to their contracts with debtors. The proposal has much to recommend it, especially if creditors were also contractually permitted to waive their statutory protections (which is not permitted now). Parties could then tailor property-like rules to the context, instead of relying on one-size-fits-all rules supplied by judges and legislatures. *Id.* at 1810. If the proposal were adopted, there would be less need for statutory creditor-protection rules, although Adler and Kahan stop short of concluding that such rules could then be dispensed with altogether. *See id.* (arguing that adoption of the covenant-registration proposal would reduce the need for fraudulent conveyance law 'in some contexts').
84. In theory, bond indenture trustees can mitigate the coordination problem among holders of debt securities (but not other general creditors such as trade creditors). Adding a trustee to act on behalf of bondholders does, however, introduce another principal-agent relationship that will generate its own agency costs.
85. The possibility of judicial mistakes does nonetheless suggest a more general problem with statutory creditor-protection rules, which is their mandatory nature. Accordingly, Adler and Kahan have argued that parties should be allowed to contract out of such rules. *See* Adler & Kahan, *supra* note 81, at 1810. Given the risk of false positives and other judicial errors, a system of voluntary opt-out would, at least in principle, constitute an improvement over the current system. With respect to distress-triggered liabilities, an opt-out system would permit a creditor to agree with the debtor that the creditor's bankruptcy recovery could be diluted by a lender's recovery on, for example, an intragroup guarantee—even if the guarantee were otherwise deemed a fraudulent transfer. The creditor would presumably charge more interest on account of the waiver, making the debtor unlikely to bargain for the right to issue intragroup guarantees enforceable at the expense of the creditor unless doing so were efficient.
86. Section 544 further allows the trustee or debtor in possession to use any available state-law avoidance statutes. 11 U.S.C. § 544(a).
87. *See* Mellon Bank, N.A. v. Metro Commc'ns, Inc., 945 F.2d 635, 646 (3d Cir. 1991) ('[T]he fraudulent conveyance laws are intended to protect the debtor's creditors.'); Rubin v. Mfrs. Hanover Tr. Co., 661 F.2d 979, 988–9 (2d Cir. 1981) (explaining that the purpose of the constructive fraudulent-transfer provision in the predecessor to the 1978 Code was to reverse transactions that 'deplete[d] the debtor's estate of valuable assets without bringing in property of similar value from which creditors' claims might be satisfied'). In addition, the official comments to the Uniform Fraudulent Transfer Act, which was adapted from § 548, describe the Act's purpose as 'protect[ing] a debtor's estate from being depleted to the prejudice of the debtor's unsecured creditors.' Unif. Fraud. Transf. Act § 3, cmt. 2 (1984).
88. 11 U.S.C. § 548(a)(1).
89. *See* Boyer v. Crown Stock Distrib., Inc., 587 F.3d 787, 797 (7th Cir. 2009).
90. 11. U.S.C. § 548(a)(1)(A).
91. *See* ASARCO LLC v. Ams. Mining Corp., 396 B.R. 278, 391 (Bankr. S.D. Tex, 2008) (noting that many courts permit a transferee to rebut a prima facie case of an intentional fraudulent transfer by showing that the transfer had a legitimate business purpose).
92. 11 U.S.C. § 548(a)(1)(B).
93. 11 U.S.C. § 548(a)(1)(B)(i).
94. 11 U.S.C. § 548(d)(2)(A).
95. *See, e.g., In re* Bernard L. Madoff Inv. Sec., LLC, 458 B.R. 87 (Bankr. S.D.N.Y. 2011) (holding that a complaint adequately alleged that loans purportedly extended to the debtor's officers were made for less than a reasonably equivalent value where promissory notes given in exchange for the loans were executed pro forma and without the

intention that they be repaid); *In re* Trafford Distrib. Ctr., Inc., 431 B.R. 263 (Bankr. S.D. Fla. 2010) (holding that prepetition payments made by the debtor to affiliated entities for overdue rent the debtor did not in fact owe were made for less than a reasonably equivalent value).

96. *See, e.g.*, Weiboldt Stores, Inc. v. Schottenstein, 94 B.R. 488 (N.D. Ill. 1988) (holding that the debtor did not receive a reasonably equivalent value in a leveraged buyout in which the loan proceeds were used to buy the debtor's shares).
97. *See, e.g.*, *In re* Tousa, 680 F.3d 1298, 1302 (11th Cir. 2012).
98. 11 U.S.C. § 548(a)(1)(A).
99. *Id.* at § 548(a)(1)(B).
100. *See supra* note 34.
101. In a challenge to a cross-stream intragroup guarantee in particular, courts could permit lenders to rebut the presumption of inadequate value by showing that the corporate group was a true conglomerate, with subsidiaries engaged in unrelated lines of business. In such a group, a guarantee issued by one subsidiary on the debt of another might not have a high internal correlation. To accommodate this possibility, courts could place the burden on the lender seeking recovery on the cross-stream guarantee to show that the borrower entity and the guarantor entity, despite common ownership, were not subject to correlated business risks. *See* Squire, *supra* note 16, at 656–8. This defense should be available only for cross-stream guarantees: if the guarantee is upstream or downstream, the ownership stake that one of the involved entities holds in the other would alone establish a high internal correlation and therefore that the guarantor did not receive a reasonably equivalent value.
102. 11 U.S.C. § 548(a)(1)(B)(ii)(I).
103. *Id.* at § 548(a)(1)(B)(ii)(III).
104. For a fuller discussion, see Squire, *supra* note 8, at 1209–10.
105. 11 U.S.C. § 506(b). The Supreme Court has held that the reference in this provision to the loan agreement, because set off by a comma, does not modify the phrase 'interest on such claim,' and therefore that the loan agreement does not dictate the post-petition interest rate to which the creditor is entitled. United States v. Ron Pair Enters., Inc., 489 U.S. 235, 241 (1989).
106. By deeming a claim for a prepayment fee unreasonable, the court would relegate it to unsecured status, where it might be further challenged under section 502(b) as a claim for unmatured interest.
107. 11 U.S.C. § 502(b)(2).
108. *See, e.g.*, *In re* Sch. Specialty, Inc., No. 13-10125 KJC, 2013 WL 1838513 (Bankr. D. Del. Apr. 22, 2013) (holding that a make-whole premium was recoverable in bankruptcy if triggered by automatic acceleration of the loan and enforceable under controlling state law); *In re* Trico Marine Servs., Inc., 450 B.R. 474, 480 (Bankr. D. Del. 2011) (holding that a make-whole premium was a liquidated damages provision and therefore not excludable as a claim for unmatured interest).
109. Scott K. Charles & Emil A. Kleinhaus, *Prepayment Clauses in Bankruptcy*, 15 Am. Bankr. Inst. L. Rev. 537, 581 (2007).
110. *In re* Doctors Hosp. of Hyde Park, Inc., 508 B.R. 697, 706 (Bankr. N.D. Ill. 2104). The court left open the question whether the lender was oversecured, which would make the premium potentially recoverable under § 506(b). *Id.* at 708. Notably, to the extent § 506(b) permits recovery of interest that was unmatured as of the petition date, it allows recovery only of post-petition interest—that is, interest that further accrues during the bankruptcy proceeding. A make-whole premium, by contrast, awards the present value of all unmatured interest through the loan's original maturity date. Therefore, § 506(b) should not be a basis for allowing full recovery of a make-whole unless the bankruptcy case has run past the point when the loan would normally have come due.

7. On the mandatory stay of secured creditors in bankruptcy

*Kenneth Ayotte**

1. INTRODUCTION

The automatic stay is one of the fundamental features of corporate reorganization. When a bankruptcy petition is filed, most rights against a debtor are temporarily suspended. The stay is most commonly justified as a way of defeating an unsecured creditor run due to a common pool problem. But, in practice, the stay operates more broadly than just preventing unsecured creditor runs. A secured creditor's right to seize and sell collateral is automatically stayed, even when the creditor is fully secured.[1]

The stay cannot be directly contracted around: attempts to waive the stay in loan contracts are not enforceable. But the stay is often contracted around indirectly. Baird and Casey (2013) give several examples suggesting that, in the modern firm, legal entity partitioning is used to create the same effective result. In some cases, the firm's core assets are involved. The Los Angeles Dodgers placed each of the baseball team's major assets (the team, the parking lot, and the stadium) in separate legal entities. While the baseball team entity filed for bankruptcy, a separate entity owning the team's parking lot did not. Creditors of the parking lot entity were free to exercise their contractual rights as a result, notwithstanding the team entity's bankruptcy case. The Dodgers case is not an isolated example: it has become common for firms with significant real estate exposure, such as retailers, nursing homes, and casinos, to separate their real estate into separate subsidiary entities that are separately financed ("OpCo-PropCo" structures).[2]

Baird and Casey (2013) argue that the ability to withdraw has ex-ante disciplinary benefits on management, and the observability of entity partitioning will likely lead to efficient creation of withdrawal rights. While this work and others explore the ex-ante benefits of secured creditor rights to seize collateral (Bolton and Scharfstein 1990, Hart and Moore 1994), the costs of these rights have not been fully developed. Doing so requires a theory explaining why a mandatory stay of secured creditors—a policy rarely questioned by practitioners and policy makers, yet not fully explained by bankruptcy theory—may be valuable in the first place.[3] The increasing use of subsidiaries to hold firm-specific assets brings this issue to the forefront.

In this chapter, I contrast a system of free withdrawal rights against the mandatory stay and structured bargaining that approximates the treatment of secured credit in bankruptcy. The main result of this chapter is to identify conditions under which a mandatory stay of secured creditor withdrawal can be efficient—that is, conditions under which the mandatory stay increases the overall ex-ante value of the company. These conditions are as follows: First, the collateral subject to the stay must be a firm-specific asset that is not easily or quickly replaceable, so that the firm's value can be affected by the withdrawal of the asset. Second, there must be some potential for bargaining inefficiencies at bankruptcy, when a withdrawal right would be triggered, that could produce either an inefficient withdrawal by the creditor or an inefficient retention of the collateral by the firm. Third, debt contracts must be sequential and incomplete: some other creditors whose recoveries are negatively affected by the presence of the withdrawal right are not able to prevent the debtor from granting it. These conditions together open the door to a negative externality: the debtor and the withdrawing creditor do not fully internalize the costs of creating a withdrawal right on the debtor's other creditors. I show that, because withdrawal rights lead to higher recoveries for the creditor holding the right, and hence a lower cost of funds for the debtor ex-post, the debtor and the creditor have a private incentive to create withdrawal rights even when they are inefficient.

2. RELATED LITERATURE

There is a large literature on the ex-ante benefits of secured credit, which allows the creditor to withdraw collateral in default. One branch focuses on preventing moral hazard, such as the diversion of cash flows (Bolton and Scharfstein 1990, Hart and Moore 2004). Secured debt can limit other moral hazard problems such as asset substitution and overinvestment in a way that limits monitoring costs associated with covenants in unsecured debt (Jackson and Kronman 1979, Triantis 1992). A second branch focuses on adverse selection. Collateral serves as a signal, thus limiting the need for creditors to be fully informed about firm value (Bester 1985, Besanko and Thakor 1987).

This chapter adds to a literature that analyses mandatory rules in bankruptcy. In the corporate context, mandatory rules are challenging to justify, as they may disturb efficient contractual bargains (Che and Schwartz 1999). Mandatory rules have been justified in environments where multiple creditors contract sequentially with the debtor, giving rise to potential externalities. Externalities are imposed on early creditors by later creditors to the extent that covenants cannot prevent subsequent dilutive contracts (Longhofer and Peters 2004) or imposed on late creditors by early creditors when information about existing rights is costly to verify (Ayotte and Bolton 2011). This chapter's approach is similar to Longhofer and Peters (2004) in focusing on externalities imposed by later creditors on earlier creditors. It adds to it by analysing a specific bankruptcy institution (the stay of secured creditors and the structured bargaining in the U.S. Bankruptcy Code) and contrasting it against the alternative of free withdrawal.

My model bears resemblance to the normative debate about whether secured credit should receive full priority with respect to their collateral (Bebchuk and Fried 1996, Schwartz 1996). Different from this literature, which analyses whether the substantive value of a secured creditor's collateral should be respected, I analyse how the choice of procedure (a mandatory stay and structured bargaining, or free withdrawal) affects efficiency. My model does not suggest that the substantive rights of secured creditors should be weakened by law; in fact, the tendency to grant withdrawal rights inefficiently in my model is driven by the assumption that secured creditors do not receive full value of their collateral under the stay.[4]

In contrasting the stay and free withdrawal, my model also relates to the bankruptcy literature that addresses the inherent tension between holdup and cramdown (Adler 2012). This chapter also relates to the maturity rat race in Brunnermeier and Oehmke (2013). In their model, short maturity is similar to a withdrawal right in my model; they show that maturity can be too short due to creditor externalities. Their paper does not model or discuss bankruptcy law, however. An important assumption in my model, as in Brunnermeier and Oehmke (2013), is that early creditors are limited in their ability to police the debtor's contracts with other creditors. Acknowledging this problem under existing law, Adler and Kahan (2013) propose allowing for property-like enforceability of creditor rights, such as negative pledge clauses, against later creditors.

Previous literature suggests several benefits of creating separate subsidiaries and free withdrawal rights. Giving lenders a claim that is targeted only to a particular asset, via a separate legal entity, limits problems of moral hazard and adverse selection by borrowers (Hill 1996, Iacobucci and Winter 2005). Creditors secured by collateral of a known value with free withdrawal rights can focus their monitoring efforts on their collateral; they need not be as concerned about the debtor's other assets, liabilities, and operations. Moreover, due to the fact that secured creditors are not entitled to the full economic value of their collateral when the firm reorganizes, the dilution of secured creditors can create a continuation subsidy that favors reorganization. Granting a withdrawal right through separate entities can reduce this continuation subsidy (Ayotte and Gaon 2011).

3. MODEL SETUP

3.0.1 Timeline

Consider a model that takes place over four relevant dates, 1, 2, 3, 4. At date 1, an owner/equity holder (E) starts a firm by issuing debt to a creditor (P1) to finance the purchase of asset A. At date 2, the owner needs continuation financing i_2 to finance a new asset B. The financing must be provided by a new creditor (P2). At date 3, an interim signal is realized and a continuation or liquidation decision must be made. At date 4, a final cash flow is realized and distributed.

3.0.2 States of the world

At date 3, the firm will either succeed or default. Success occurs with probability p. If success occurs, the firm will produce a large cash flow X_3 at date 3, sufficient to pay off all creditors in full and leave a surplus for the owner. If default occurs, with probability $(1 - p)$, the final cash flow will not be sufficient to pay creditors in full, so the owner will receive zero. The continuation/liquidation decision will affect the recoveries of P1 and P2. Importantly, assets A and B are assumed to be essential for the firm to continue.

In default, there are three possible states (high, medium and low) that represent the continuation value of the firm. Conditional on default, state $j \in \{h, m, l\}$ occurs with probability p_j, so $p_h + p_m + p_l = 1$. The liquidation value of the firm at date 3 is $L_3 = \alpha_3 + \beta_3$, where $\alpha_3(\beta_3)$ is the liquidation value of asset A (B) at date 3, and is the same in all states. If continuation is chosen, the firm may recover or fail. Failure produces $L_4 = \alpha_4 + \beta_4$, and recovery produces $X_4 > L_4$. The states are represented by the probability of recovery. Let π_j represent the probability of recovery in state j. The continuation value of the firm at date 3 in state j, then, is $C_j = \pi_j X_4 + (1 - \pi_j) L_4$. I assume that continuation is efficient in the high and medium states but not the low state: $C_h > C_m > L_3 > C_l$. For convenience, let $\bar{\pi}$ denote the ex-ante expected probability of recovery if all types continue: $\bar{\pi} = p_h\pi_h + p_m\pi_m + p_l\pi_l$, and let $\overline{C}$ represent the average continuation value if all types continue: $\overline{C} = \bar{\pi}X_4 + (1 - \bar{\pi})L_4$.

The timeline and project payoffs are represented in Figure 7.1.

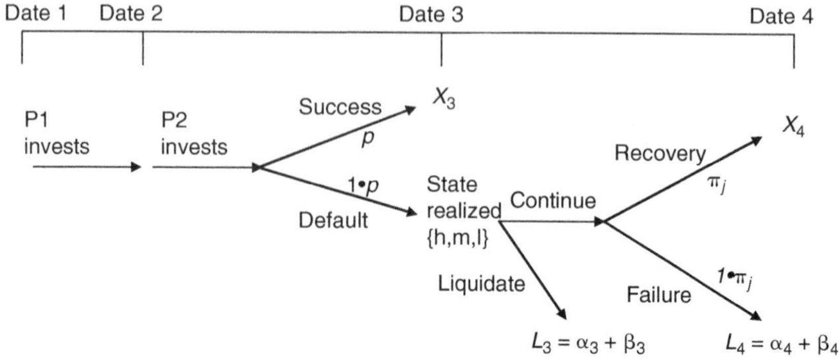

Figure 7.1 Timeline and project payoffs

3.0.3 Creditors, contracts and information

Though represented here as a single actor, P1 is intended to represent the general body of a firm's creditors other than P2. When we discuss bargaining under the stay, P1 will exercise control over and represent the interests of the bankruptcy estate. I assume that P1 has a debt claim, secured by asset A, that comes due no earlier than date 3. P2 also has a debt claim, secured by asset B.

I assume parameter values such that E will receive zero in default; because E is always out of the money, bargaining will take place between P1 and P2. This is justifiable empirically, as shareholders commonly receive nothing in Chapter 11 (Ayotte and Morrison 2009). I allow for bargaining imperfections by assuming that creditors may have asymmetries of information when they bargain. To model information asymmetries simply, I suppose that both *P*1 and *P*2 may be either informed or uninformed about the date 3 state of the world. I assume only that each of the possible information allocations for P1 and P2: <informed, informed>, <informed, uninformed>, <uninformed, informed>, and <uninformed, uninformed> occur with strictly positive probability. I also assume that P1 and P2 have knowledge of whether the other party is informed or not.

3.0.4 Bargaining

In borrowing at date 2, the owner has two choices of creditor rights (free withdrawal and stay). Under free withdrawal, P2 has the right to seize asset B. Because asset B is assumed to be essential, P1 and P2 must reach an agreement in bargaining or the firm will liquidate. I assume the following bargaining structure in default: nature chooses one of the two creditors to make a take-it-or-leave-it offer to the other.[5] The probability with which P1 is chosen is assumed to lie strictly between 0 and 1. Importantly (and realistically), because the firm is in financial distress, I assume that the players are liquidity-constrained when they bargain; thus, they can offer only a stake in the ongoing firm as currency. A player can either choose to make an offer of a state-contingent payoff in continuation or propose liquidation. Let $\{t_h, t_l\}$ denote the payoff of the party receiving the proposed offer, where $t_h \leq X_4$, $t_l \leq L_4$. Alternatively, the party making the offer can propose liquidation, which causes liquidation to occur automatically. If a continuation offer is refused, then liquidation also occurs.

Bargaining will proceed differently if withdrawal rights are stayed. The parties will participate in a bargaining stage as above, but in the absence of a bargain the collateral will be retained by the firm rather than seized, and the secured creditor will be entitled to adequate protection as determined by a judge, rather than the collateral itself. I postpone the discussion of adequate protection and bargaining in the shadow of the stay until Section 5 below.

3.1 Parameter Assumptions

I make the following parameter assumptions:

Assumptions 1 and 2:

$$X_3 > \overline{F}_{\max}$$

$$C_h < \overline{F}_{\min}$$

where $\overline{F}_{\max}$ ($\overline{F}_{\min}$) is the total face value of debt to all creditors when default is as inefficient (efficient) as possible.

$$p\overline{F}_{\max} + (1 - p)\{(p_h + p_m)L_3 + p_l C_l\} = i_1 + i_2$$

$$p\overline{F}_{\min} + (1 - p)\{p_h C_h + p_m C_m + p_l L_3\} = i_1 + i_2$$

The first assumption ensures that if success occurs, there will always be value left over for the owner. The second assumption ensures that debtor always gets nothing in default.

Assumption 3: It is always efficient to borrow at dates 1 and 2, no matter what choices are made in distress:

$$pX_3 + (1 - p)\{(p_h + p_m)L_3 + p_l C_l\} > i_1 + i_2$$

$$(p_h + p_m)L_3 + p_l C_l > i_2 + L_2$$

This assumption rules out credit rationing at dates 1 and 2. By doing so, it merely cabins the potential inefficiencies that might occur in the model. Relaxing these assumptions would increase the number of cases to consider without affecting any of the qualitative insights.

3.1.1 The maximization problem

The essence of this problem is that E cannot commit to its financing choices at date 2 when it contracts at date 1. Hence, we state the objective by working backward from date 2. E's objective at date 2 is to choose the withdrawal right ($w = \{1, 0\}$, where 1= free withdrawal, 0 = stay) and debt repayment obligation F_2 to maximize her own expected payoff subject to the creditor's participation constraint:

$$\max_{w,F_2} p(X_3 - F_1 - F_2)$$

subject to

$$pF_2 + (1 - p)R^{w}_{P2} \geq i_2$$

The R^{w}_{P2} term is P2's expected recovery in a default, which will depend on whether P2 has the right to withdraw. P2's participation constraint will always bind in equilibrium, so we can substitute the constraint into the objective. Eliminating parameters that are fixed as of date 2, the date 2 problem is equivalent to maximizing R^{w}_{P2}, P2's recovery in default. Maximizing R^{w}_{P2} allows E to borrow at the lowest cost, and hence maximize E's payoff in the success state.

3.1.2 The Date 1 problem

If we call the solution to this problem $\{w^*, F^*_2\}$, then E's date 1 problem is to maximize

$$\max_{F_1} p(X_3 - F_1 - F_2)$$

subject to

$$pF_1 + (1 - p)R_{P1}(w^*, F^*{}_2) \geq i_1$$

In our problem, F_1 does not affect F_2 or $R_{P1}(w^*, F^*_2)$. Hence, the period one problem is simply to minimize F_1 subject to the lender's participation constraint, which always binds. Solving using the binding participation constraint, we have $F^*_1 = \frac{i_1 - (1 - p)R_{P1}(w^*, F^*_2)}{p}$. Previous literature justifying mandatory features of bankruptcy focus heavily on "maladjusting" creditors who do not anticipate or respond to the debtor's subsequent actions (Warren and Westbrook 2005). This model, by contrast, will demonstrate that a mandatory stay can be optimal even if all creditors are "fully adjusting": they price all anticipated future actions into their interest rate. These early creditors only need to be limited in their ability to police the debtor's subsequent actions.

If we plug in the solutions to the date 1 and 2 maximization problems, the debtor's date 1 utility is

$$pX_3 + (1 - p)\{R_{P1}(w^*, F_2^*) + R_{P2}^{w*}\} - i_1 - i_2$$

Since $R_{P1}(w, F_2) + R_{P2}^{w}$ is the total value of the bankruptcy estate, it is clear that any inefficient outcomes in bankruptcy are fully borne by the debtor in equilibrium. Nevertheless, the debtor may not be able to eliminate inefficiencies, because it cannot commit at date 1 to excluding terms in P2's loan that will negatively affect P1's recovery.

Having set up E's problem, I will now examine outcomes under free withdrawal and the stay.

4. BARGAINING UNDER FREE WITHDRAWAL RIGHTS

To solve the model, I will work backward, starting from the date 3 bargaining game between P1 and P2 when P2 has the right to withdraw asset B in a default. For ease of exposition, I describe outcomes assuming that P1 is always the party who makes the offer to P2. Since the game is symmetric under withdrawal rights, all results are analogous when nature chooses P2 to offer to P1. I state the propositions with full generality.

4.0.1 Symmetric: both parties are informed

When both parties are informed, the bargaining game between P1 and P2 is a game of complete information; i.e. both parties know the continuation and liquidation values of the firm. Hence, ex-post efficiency will obtain. When both players are informed, it is irrelevant how surplus is shared across the recovery and failure outcomes; hence I simply focus on the division of the firm's expected continuation value C.

When nature chooses P1 to make the offer and the low state occurs, P1 can do no better than proposing liquidation, so the firm will liquidate and both parties receive their liquidation values, α_3 and β_3. In the medium and high states, P1 will make a continuation offer $\{t_h, t_l\}$ that gives P2 her liquidation payoff in expectation, β_3, and P1 will keep $C_j - \beta_3$.

4.0.2 Symmetric: both parties are uninformed

When both parties are uninformed, they also bargain under symmetric information. Though offers will not be state-contingent, ex-post efficiency will obtain, conditional on the parties' information. Continuation will occur if and only if the expected continuation value of the firm is higher than the liquidation value ($\overline{C} > L_3$). If $\overline{C} > L_3$, P2 will receive her liquidation value β_3, and P1 will receive $\overline{C} - \beta_3$. If $\overline{C} < L_3$, P1 will liquidate and the parties will receive their respective liquidation values, α_3 and β_3.

4.0.3 Asymmetric: more informed party makes the offer

Under incomplete information, the bargaining game is slightly more complicated and can result in inefficient continuation and liquidation.

When nature chooses the more informed party to make the offer, the offer can reveal information about the continuation value of the firm. I use Perfect Bayesian Equilibria (PBE) as the equilibrium concept: the uninformed party must form a belief about the continuation value of the firm for every offer the informed party might make, and this belief must be consistent with Bayes rule along the equilibrium path. It is well-known from the corporate finance literature that an informed party observing the high state prefers an equilibrium in which the uninformed party is offered the least information-sensitive claim possible, which is senior debt (Myers and Majluf 1984). That is, the informed P1 will load the uninformed P2's payoff into the failure outcome to the maximum extent possible, to minimize the payoff difference between recovery and failure to P2.[6] This occurs because in the high state, the informed party will want to minimize the cross-subsidy associated with offering a stake in the firm whose value is unknown.

I focus on PBE that take this form. I assume that P2's beliefs are as follows: any offer that is not senior debt is viewed skeptically: it is assumed to come from a low state P1. When senior debt is offered, P2's belief about the state is her prior belief, updated in a Bayesian way by assigning zero probability to states in which P1 would (weakly) prefer liquidation to continuation under that offer. More concretely, when the informed P1 offers the uninformed P2 a payoff function $\{t_h, t_l\}$ in the form of senior debt, P2's belief that the state is j is 0 if P1 would prefer liquidation to acceptance of the continuation offer in that state, and $\frac{p_j}{\Phi}$ otherwise, where $\Phi \leq 1$ is the sum of the probabilities of states in which P1 prefers acceptance of the offer to liquidation.[7] Since the liquidation payoff is known and independent of the state, it is clear that whenever P1 prefers continuation in a given state, he prefers continuation in any higher state as well.

This leads us to the following proposition, which shows that inefficient outcomes can occur under asymmetric information:

Proposition 1 *Suppose that an informed P1 makes the offer to an uninformed P2, and P2's beliefs are as described above.*

If $\beta_3 > L_4$ and $\pi_l(X_4 - \frac{\beta_3 - (1-\pi)L_4}{\bar{\pi}}) > \alpha_3$, then the unique PBE is a pooling equilibrium with inefficient continuation in the low state. All P1 types make a continuation offer $t^* = \{\frac{\beta_3 - (1-\pi)L_4}{\bar{\pi}}, L_4\}$ and P2 accepts. If these conditions do not hold, then the unique PBE involves efficient outcomes: the high state and medium state P1s make a continuation offer of senior debt to P2, and P2 accepts. The low state P1 proposes liquidation.

Suppose that an informed P2 makes the offer to an uninformed P1, and P1's beliefs are as described above.

If $\alpha_3 > L_4$ and $\pi_l(X_4 - \frac{\alpha_3 - (1-\pi)L_4}{\bar{\pi}}) > \beta_3$, then the unique PBE is a pooling equilibrium with inefficient continuation in the low state. All P2 types make a continuation offer $t^* = \{\frac{\alpha_3 - (1-\pi)L_4}{\bar{\pi}}, L_4\}$ and P1 accepts. If these conditions do not hold, then the unique PBE involves efficient outcomes: the high state and medium state P2s make a continuation offer of senior debt to P1, and P1 accepts. The low state P2 proposes liquidation.

All proofs are located in the appendix.

When the two inequalities hold, a PBE with inefficient continuation may occur because the informed low state P1 may try to mimic the higher type P1s, and the higher state P1s cross-subsidize the low state P1 in continuation. If this continuation cross-subsidy is large enough relative to the inefficiency of continuation in the low state, the low type P1 will make a continuation offer. The uninformed P2 has rational expectations in equilibrium, and knows that all types will propose continuation under the same terms. A high state or medium state P1 cannot improve on this pooling outcome, however, since any attempt to keep a larger share of the payoff (i.e. reduce t_h) will be rejected by P2, given her beliefs. Since low state P1s prefer continuation to liquidation, then higher types also prefer it.

An inefficient continuation is more likely to occur when the subsidy to the low state P1 is larger. When P2 can be given a risk-free claim ($\beta_3 < L_4$ when P1 offers and $\alpha_3 < L_4$ when P2 offers), there is no cross-subsidy from high and medium types to low. Hence, there is no inefficient continuation problem. If a risk-free claim cannot be given, then inefficient continuation is more likely to occur when the cross-subsidy is larger. If the degree of asymmetric information rises (specifically, if $\bar{\pi}$ rises, holding π_l fixed) then the low type receives a larger cross-subsidy, and thus inefficiency is more likely to occur.

If the inefficient pooling equilibrium results, P2's expected payoff is her liquidation value β_3, and P1 receives $\overline{C} - \beta_3$.

4.0.4 Asymmetric: less informed party makes the offer

I have shown that inefficient continuation can occur when an informed party makes an offer to an uninformed party. Next, consider the case where nature appoints the less informed party to make the offer. In this case, inefficient liquidation can result:

Proposition 2 *Suppose the less informed party makes the offer. Inefficient liquidation occurs in the medium state if*

a) P1 makes the offer and $p_h \frac{(\pi_h - \pi_m)}{\pi_m}(\beta_3 - L_4) > p_m(C_m - L_3)$

b) P2 makes the offer and $p_h \frac{(\pi_h - \pi_m)}{\pi_m}(\alpha_3 - L_4) > p_m(C_m - L_3)$.

If neither of these conditions holds, then efficient outcomes will result.

Intuitively, in making a take-it-or-leave-it offer, P1 tries to capture as much of the continuation surplus as possible from P2. If P2's date 3 liquidation value can be provided with certainty at date 4, then P1 can acquire the entire going concern surplus from both high and medium types by simply offering a risk-free debt claim on the firm that pays liquidation value, allowing P1 to keep the remainder.[8] If this is not possible, then P1 faces a trade-off. Because of P2's information advantage, P1 must choose between capturing all the surplus in the high state and risking rejection of the offer in the medium state, or capturing all the surplus in the medium state and leaving P2 with positive surplus in the high state. When the inequality holds, the high state is sufficiently attractive that P1 prefers to risk liquidation in the medium state for a greater share of the high state payoff.

By examining the inequalities in the proposition, we can see that inefficient liquidation is more likely when there is more uncertainty about the going-concern value, conditional on continuation being efficient (i.e. $\pi_h - \pi_m$ is higher). We can also see, similar to Proposition 1 above, that inefficient liquidation is more likely when P1 is forced to offer a more informationally sensitive claim. This happens when P2's date 3 liquidation value (α_3 or β_3) is large relative to L_4 (the maximum guarantee that can be offered in continuation).

In the next section, I consider an alternative to free withdrawal: a stay on withdrawal and structured bargaining, akin to the rights a secured creditor would have in bankruptcy.

5. PAYOFFS UNDER THE STAY

The bargaining process will proceed differently under the stay. Under the stay, the asset remains in possession of the bankrupt debtor, and the creditor cannot repossess the collateral unless the judge lifts the stay. Hence, I assume a bargaining process that leaves the Bankruptcy Code to determine the creditor's payoff in the absence of a bargaining agreement between P1 and P2.

As under withdrawal, I assume that P1 and P2 are each chosen with some positive probability to make a take-it-or-leave-it offer to the other.[9] If that offer is rejected, then the parties proceed to an *adequate protection (AP) subgame*. In this subgame, P1 is in control of the firm. He can either liquidate, or propose to the bankruptcy judge a continuation payoff for P2. The judge approves P2's treatment if and only if the judge is satisfied that P2's security interest is adequately protected.

Specifically, if P1 wishes to continue, he proposes a state-contingent date 4 payoff $\{t_h, t_l\}$ to P2. This allocation must give P2 an expected payoff that the judge believes is worth at least β_3, P2's date 3 liquidation value. The offer must also guarantee P2 her collateral value at date 4 after continuation and failure $(t_l \geq \beta_4)$.[10]

I assume that the judge is not aware of the state and the parties cannot credibly convey this information to the judge. The judge is only aware of the probabilities of the states and the payoffs in each state. As is common in the literature, I assume that the judge has a continuation bias. Specifically, the judge can always be convinced that the state is the high state. Assuming the high state will allow P1 to propose a state-contingent payoff that has lower expected value than β_3 if the true state is medium or low, and this facilitates continuation in those states. Under the stay, P2's payoff is not affected by its information: I do not allow P2 to influence the judge's perception of the state.

To understand bankruptcy payoffs under the stay, I will first solve for outcomes in the adequate protection subgame. I then offer a more general proposition comparing payoffs for P2 under the stay versus the withdrawal right for any equilibrium that might be feasible under the stay regime.

5.1 Adequate Protection Subgame (after offer is rejected)

5.1.1 Informed P1

First, consider the adequate protection subgame. Since P1 controls the outcome at this stage and makes a unilateral decision, the outcome does not depend on whether or not P2 is informed. If P1 is informed, then the bankruptcy subgame is straightforward. Whenever P1 favors continuation,

P1 will propose an allocation that would give P2 her liquidation value at date 4 in failure, and a payoff in recovery that would give P2 an expected value of β_3 *if the high state were the true state*. Formally, P1 proposes $t=\{t_h', \beta_4\}$ where t_h' solves $\pi_h t_h' + (1-\pi_h)\beta_4 = \beta_3$, or $t_h' = \frac{\beta_3 - (1-\pi_h)\beta_4}{\pi_h}$.[11] This will result in a dilution of P2's date 3 collateral values in the low and medium states: P2 will receive an expected payoff less than β_3. Let δ_j denote the amount of dilution of the secured claim in state j:

$$\delta_j = \beta_3 - \{\pi_j t_h' + (1-\pi_j)\beta_4\}$$

An informed P1 will always propose continuation in the high and medium states, because the going concern value is positive, and P2 receives no more than her liquidation value β_3. Hence, P1 always receives more than his liquidation value. In the low state, P1 may propose liquidation if the cost of inefficient liquidation exceeds the amount that P1 redistributes from P2 through dilution. Continuation will occur in the low state if and only if

$$\pi_l(X_4 - t_h') + (1 - \pi_l)\alpha_4 > \alpha_3. \tag{7.1}$$

or, equivalently, if and only if the amount of dilution of P2 exceeds the efficiency loss from continuation:

$$\delta_l > L_3 - C_l$$

5.1.2 Uninformed P1

If P1 is uninformed, P1 will make the same continuation terms to P2 if P1 believes it is optimal to continue. But since P1 is uninformed, P1 must assess whether continuation is superior to liquidation in expectation. This expected continuation value depends on P1's belief about the state of the world after an offer is rejected. Let $\hat{\pi}$ denote P1's updated belief about the expected probability of success after a rejected offer. Continuation will occur for a belief $\hat{\pi}$ if and only if P1's expected continuation value exceeds P1's liquidation value:

$$\hat{\pi}(X_4 - t_h') + (1 - \hat{\pi})\alpha_4 > \alpha_3. \tag{7.2}$$

or, equivalently, if the expected amount to be diverted from P2 exceeds the expected efficiency loss from continuation.

5.2 Bargaining Stage Under the Stay

Under a withdrawal right, I assumed beliefs were such that any offer of senior debt would be viewed skeptically by P2 when P1 has an information advantage. Under the stay, these same beliefs are not as straightforward to motivate and might change when bankruptcy is involved. As I have modeled adequate protection, P2 would be entitled to receive its own collateral after failure, but not P1's collateral. As a result, adequate protection does not provide the least information sensitive claim possible. Knowing this, would an uninformed P2 still react skeptically and assume the state is low when an informed P1 offers a payoff that replicates the adequate protection payoff? This is not obvious. Since choosing a single set of beliefs is less intuitive, I instead opt for more generality, and show that efficiency will pertain under the stay for some parameter values.

Proposition 3 *In any equilibrium, the stay approaches efficiency, conditional on the available information, as the probability of liquidation being efficient goes to 0* $(p_l \to 0)$.

Proposition 3 suggests that the stay regime will approach efficiency when the probability of efficient liquidation approaches zero. This is not always true in the withdrawal rights regime, as Proposition 2 illustrates. The stay eliminates the possibility of inefficient liquidation when an uninformed P1 makes an aggressive offer to an informed P2 that is rejected. Under the stay, if p_l approaches zero, continuation is always efficient. P1 knows this, and would always propose continuation in the AP subgame. And at the ex-ante bargaining stage, no liquidation offer would be acceptable to both P1 and P2.

6. FREE WITHDRAWAL VERSUS THE STAY

We are now in a position to compare the efficiency properties of withdrawal rights and the stay. Proposition 4 sets the stage by comparing P2's recoveries under the two regimes:

Proposition 4 *P2's expected payoff in default is strictly lower under the stay than under a withdrawal right.*

Key to Proposition 4 is the idea that under a withdrawal right, P2 is always guaranteed at least liquidation value β_3, and does strictly better in some states of the world. For example, when P2 is chosen to make the offer and both parties are informed, P2 can capture all the continuation surplus in the high and medium states and leave P1 with its liquidation value α_3. The bargaining is much different under the stay regime, because P1 always has the outside option of continuing and leaving P2 with its judicially valued claim, which is never worth more than β_3. Thus, in nearly all states of the world, P1 can hold P2 at or below β_3.[12]

Having shown that P2 does better under a withdrawal right, the ex-ante implications for capital structure are straightforward:

Proposition 5 *When E can choose between offering P2 a withdrawal right or a secured claim subject to a stay, E will always choose free withdrawal.*

When E and P2 contract, they will choose the option that maximizes P2's recovery in distress, because this allows E to borrow at a lower interest rate from P2, and a lower interest rate maximizes E's payoff in a success. P2 always does strictly better in withdrawal than under a stay, as the previous proposition illustrates.

The model's result is clearly stronger than we observe in reality, of course: debtors do not always place new assets in subsidiaries to create withdrawal rights. There are several reasons why this strong result emerges. First, I assume that E always receives zero in any bankruptcy. If this assumption is relaxed, E will internalize some of the inefficiency from withdrawal directly, and thus may seek to prevent it by contracting for a stay. Second, I have assumed that P1 controls the bankruptcy estate, and uses this control right to deny P2 any of the going-concern value in reorganization. If P2 were to receive some of this value, P2 might contract for a stay if sufficient value is put at risk through bargaining breakdown. Finally, I have assumed that creating a withdrawal right has no effect on E's payoff in a success. In reality, the creation of a separate subsidiary adds some legal constraints. In using assets A and B together, the subsidiary and the parent must transact as separate parties and this may impose some constraints on their operations (Iacobucci and Triantis 2007). Relaxing these assumptions would result in debtors subjecting some creditors to the stay voluntarily, but the debtors' tendency to grant withdrawal rights too often should be robust to these changes.

Though E and P2 always have a private incentive to create a withdrawal right, there are conditions under which it is inefficient to do so:

Proposition 6 *There exist parameter values under which a mandatory stay is efficient. In particular, a stay will result in efficiency but a withdrawal right would be chosen when:*

a) p_l approaches 0, and
b) the conditions for inefficient liquidation occur under a withdrawal right (i.e. if either inequality in Proposition 2 holds).

When the debtor gives a creditor a withdrawal right, asymmetries of information can lead to inefficient bargaining outcomes. Under a reasonable set of beliefs, both inefficient liquidation and inefficient continuation can occur. Though I have not fully described the inefficiencies that may arise under a stay, Lemma 4 reveals that there are parameters under which the stay will approach efficiency in any equilibrium. This occurs because P1 would always choose continuation in the adequate protection subgame, and this makes the ex-ante bargain between P1 and P2 merely one that divides the surplus.

In summary, I have shown that the higher recovery that P2 expects under a withdrawal right causes E to give P2 a withdrawal right, irrespective of the overall efficiency consequences. I have also shown conditions under which a stay is more efficient than a withdrawal right. Under those conditions, a mandatory stay can increase efficiency.

7. DISCUSSION

7.1 Contractual Alternatives to a Stay

The discussion suggests that the choice between free contracting for withdrawal rights and a mandatory stay is a nontrivial one. This happens because the contract between E and P2 creates externalities that can negatively affect early creditors (P1 in the model), to the detriment of overall efficiency. Early creditors will anticipate these inefficiencies and price them into their loan contracts, but this merely shifts the costs of inefficient use of assets onto the debtor. The debtor, then, will prefer a regime that allows for a commitment to efficient financing terms and efficient resolution of distress to the extent possible.

An important assumption underlying the analysis is that early creditors' contracts are long-term and not contingent on E's contract with P2. Thus, P1 cannot prevent any contracting externalities between E and P2. A possible objection to this assumption is that E and P1 have an incentive to include covenants that prevent subsequent inefficient contracts between E and P2. In a complete contracting world, P1 would include a covenant that would create an event of default any time an inefficient withdrawal right is created in favor of P2. This would deter any inefficiency, and would obviate the need for a mandatory stay since any permissible withdrawal right would be an efficient one.

To the extent that early lenders are comprised of lenders that actively monitor and can renegotiate with the debtor, covenants can be effective. Bank loan facilities to large corporate borrowers typically mention subsidiaries for the purposes of calculating liquidity and leverage ratios, and restrict activity between parent and subsidiaries. Some require the lender's permission to create new subsidiaries. There are costs to this strategy, as covenants that require lender permission to create new subsidiaries are probably over-broad; but to the extent that renegotiation is flexible, the costs of overly broad covenants (the risk of acceleration and bankruptcy and inefficient outcomes) are less severe.

The strongest case against covenants preventing all inefficiency is the existence of creditors that are not active monitors. Examples of these types of lenders include trade creditors, lessors and other executory contract counterparties, asset-based lenders (such as mortgage lenders), tax and tort creditors, and to a lesser extent, public bondholders. These creditors rarely require covenants that are sufficiently detailed to prevent withdrawal rights through subsidiaries. Empirical evidence suggests that these creditors are an economically significant part of a firm's capital structure.[13] If a borrower wanted to include an inefficient withdrawal right, they would likely need to compensate their active monitors for any costs imposed on them, but they would not need to compensate inactive monitors.

7.2 Withdrawal Rights in Contracts Versus Subsidiaries

Bankruptcy operates at the legal entity level, not at the corporate group or firm level. As a result, a withdrawal right created by placing an asset in a subsidiary is more likely to be enforceable than a withdrawal right created by contract in an ordinary loan agreement, which is clearly unenforceable. My model describes a potential inefficiency that can result from free contracting for withdrawal rights, but does not distinguish between these two possible ways a withdrawal right might be created. In this section, I consider whether the normative case for enforcing withdrawal through subsidiaries is stronger than the (hypothetical) case for enforcing a waiver of the stay in an ordinary secured credit contract.

The two mechanisms provide slightly different forms of public notice, but these differences are not substantial. In both a subsidiary withdrawal, and a hypothetical stay waiver, the law requires that the later creditor provide some form of public notice of its interest, which is only partially informative about the presence of a withdrawal right.[14] That is, the public notice available in either mechanism would make an actively monitoring lender aware that the debtor *may have* created a withdrawal right. The scope of that withdrawal right (whether the later lender has the right to freely withdraw, and the states of the world in which it is possible), however, would require knowledge of the specific details of the agreement between the later lender and the borrower (Ellias 2014). In the stay waiver case, the early creditor would need to observe the loan contract to observe the presence or absence of a stay waiver. In the case of subsidiary withdrawal, the loan must include a covenant that creates an event of default whenever the parent defaults. The subsidiary creditor's ability to withdraw also depends upon the parent's control over the subsidiary. If the parent controls the subsidiary, it could deny withdrawal by bringing the subsidiary into bankruptcy along with the parent. For early creditors to target and prevent only those transactions that create withdrawal rights, then, they must condition covenants on non-public information that the debtor must be willing to provide voluntarily.

With respect to the potential for better notice to control the inefficient withdrawal rights the model analyses, it is not clear that permitting withdrawal through subsidiaries is preferable to contractual withdrawals. A more important distinction is that subsidiaries are useful, and in some ways necessary, for making businesses distinct and separable from each other. Hence, the synergy between assets A and B assumed in the model are less likely true when A and B are in separate legal entities. Hansmann and Kraakman (2000) argue that legal entities are essential to create asset partitioning, which allows creditors to focus their monitoring efforts on a particular group of assets. Ayotte and Hansmann (2013) argue that subsidiary entities are useful in creating bundles of contracts that can be freely transferred as bundles. Casey (2013) suggests that separate entities can be useful in confining the consequences of default. All of these theories predict that those assets/contracts with greater value as stand-alone projects will be more likely found in separate subsidiaries than inside a given legal entity. This difference explains why a court might optimally give more deference to honoring a withdrawal right against assets in a separate entity: the assets in the separate entity are less likely to be essential to the bankrupt entity. But, assuming the asset is necessary to the bankrupt firm, there is no obvious reason to favor withdrawal just because the asset is in a separate entity. Doing so would only elevate form over substance.

7.3 Comparative Statistics and Principles

Baird and Casey (2013) note that bankruptcy judges have occasionally limited the attempt to exercise withdrawal rights through subsidiaries in an ad-hoc fashion, without a consistent framework. The model suggests that allowing a per se exception to the stay for subsidiary withdrawals can be inefficient, and there may be scope to allow for judges to apply a stay selectively to non-debtor subsidiaries to prevent particularly inefficient outcomes. In identifying a set of assumptions that are necessary to justify a stay, the model suggests some normative principles that can reduce the inefficiencies that the model identifies:

1. A withdrawal right is inefficient only to the extent that it redistributes value from early creditors. This suggests that a subsidiary stay should be applicable only to the extent that there were creditors who lent before the withdrawal right.
2. A withdrawal right is inefficient only if the asset has synergies with the rest of the firm. Thus, withdrawal rights to assets in a subsidiary that are not necessary to the reorganization of other entities in the group should be fully honored. Bankruptcy law might do this through language as in §362(d)(2): a judge can apply a subsidiary stay only if the asset is necessary to an effective reorganization of the debtor entity.[15] Judicial discretion could be further limited by providing a safe harbor for withdrawal rights over the types of non-specific assets that are typical in securitization transactions, such as accounts receivable or other cash-like assets.
3. The temptation to create an inefficient withdrawal right occurs because the later creditor's collateral value is diluted under the stay. This suggests that full protection of the substantive rights of secured creditors under a stay regime is desirable. While curing any judicial bias toward continuation might be difficult, there are some substantive rights that might be changed. Under current law, secured creditors do not receive compensation for the lost time value of money due to the delay inherent in reorganization.[16] A change to the Bankruptcy Code that eliminates this dilution of secured credit would result in less temptation to create withdrawal rights, and less breakdown in bargaining as a result.

8. CONCLUSION

This chapter adds to an ongoing debate about the use of subsidiaries in bankruptcy, and how an optimal bankruptcy law should respond to their use. As Baird and Casey (2013) show, financing through subsidiaries can be different from ordinary financing methods because bankruptcy operates at the level of the legal entity. Hence, when a parent company files for bankruptcy but its subsidiary does not, subsidiary assets are not subject to the automatic stay.

To answer whether bankruptcy should respect such arrangements, I construct a model that generates conditions under which a mandatory stay can be optimal. Three elements are necessary to generate a tradeoff, whereby a mandatory automatic stay can add value: 1) sequential, incomplete contracts that allow later lenders to redistribute from earlier lenders by giving a withdrawal right, 2) ex-post bargaining frictions, and 3) the financing of a complementary asset that is necessary to the going-concern value of the firm. When these elements are present, borrowers have the incentive to issue claims that give creditors free withdrawal rights even when these rights are inefficient.

One payoff from the model, then, is a set of principles to guide the application of a stay. When firms use subsidiaries to separate replaceable assets, like cash and receivables, or when subsidiaries are used to separate distinct businesses from each other, the case for respecting them is greater. Allowing debtors to use a stay might simply exacerbate ex-ante moral hazard and create ex-post inefficient continuation problems. But when a specific and necessary asset is separated via a subsidiary, staying withdrawal can reduce the probability of bargaining failure and prevent inefficient liquidations.

Another payoff from the model is the explicit identification of the assumptions required to justify the stay, which can be empirically tested. In particular, how much are financing patterns driven by the incentives to redistribute value from pre-existing debt? This is an important question for future empirical research.

NOTES

* Thanks to Barry Adler, Douglas Baird, Tony Casey, Ezra Friedman, William Hubbard, Alan Schwartz, David Skeel, and workshop participants at the 2013 Law and Economics Theory conference, the University of Chicago Creditors' Rights Conference, U.C. Berkeley, and University of Chicago for helpful comments.

1. 11 U.S.C. §362(a)(4)
2. The PropCo subsidiaries typically lease the assets back to the OpCo, and the lease payments form the backing assets for CMBS or other debt securities. ToysR'Us, Station Casinos, and Genesis Healthcare are recent examples. While I do not model leases between the subsidiary and the parent formally here, Ayotte and Gaon (2011) show that such leases are not a complete cure for inefficient liquidation/continuation problems when necessary assets are transferred to a subsidiary.
3. As an example, Baird and Jackson (1984) argue in favor a stay of secured creditors: "Because of the costs repossession and subsequent repurchase may bring, it is consistent with the purposes of bankruptcy to substitute for a secured creditor's actual substantive rights under nonbankruptcy law a requirement that the secured creditor accept the equivalent value of those rights."

   The contribution of this paper is to endogenize these repossession costs and explain the stay's mandatory nature: i.e., why it might be contracted around even when it is efficient.

4. The case for a mandatory stay is likely stronger than the case for weakening a secured creditors' substantive rights. First, the ex-ante benefits of secured debt (such as preventing debtor moral hazard) generally rely on protecting the substantive value of the creditors' claim, not the procedural right. Second, early creditors can protect themselves against inefficient subsequent security interests by taking a security interest themselves (Schwartz 1996). The same is not true for withdrawal in this model: early creditors *are* secured by all assets available at the initial date. An inefficient withdrawal right reduces the value of the early creditors' deficiency claim, which is harder to defend against redistribution.
5. This bargaining structure was chosen because it is a simple bargaining structure that generates bargaining inefficiencies in the presence of asymmetric information. The basic insights of the model should hold in alternative models of bargaining where asymmetric information leads to inefficiencies, such as costly delays.
6. Formally, senior debt means that P2 is promised a fixed payment F and receives a payoff $\min\{x, F\}$ where x is the date 4 cash flow. In this context $t_l = t_h$ if $t_h < L_4$, and $t_l = L_4$ for any $t_h > L_4$.
7. As an example, if P1 would prefer acceptance of a given offer to liqudation in the good and medium state but not the low state, then P2's belief that the state is {high, medium, low} is $\{\frac{p_h}{p_h + p_m}, \frac{p_m}{p_h + p_m}, 0\}$.
8. Strictly speaking, the offer would need to involve a small amount of risk for the offeror, so as to keep the low type offeree from accepting, but this risk could be made arbitrarily small.
9. The key result in this section is that the stay approaches efficiency as the probability of liquidation being efficient approaches zero. This result is not affected by the presence of the bargaining stage or the allocation of bargaining power.
10. The need to guarantee β_4 in failure is motivated by the practice of providing adequate protection. Secured creditors generally keep the security interest in their original collateral, and receive additional collateral to the extent that their collateral is depreciating. It is also akin to the requirement in a cramdown plan of reorganization in which the debtor keeps the collateral and gives the secured creditor a note, that the secured creditor's new claim must be backed by the original collateral. §1129(b)(2)(a)(i).
11. If P1 tries to keep more than this, P2 can convince the judge she is not receiving her liquidation value even if she is uninformed, since I assume that the judge is aware of the payoffs in the three possible states. Note that, in contrast to the problem above, P1 wants to maximize the difference between P2's high state and low state payoff, to maximize the information rents from continuation when the high state does not occur.
12. The only possible exception is when an uninformed P1 makes an offer to an informed P2. In that case, P1 may want to use the offer to screen out the medium and high types from the low types, to ensure that a very inefficient low type is liquidated, but the medium and high types are continued. In such cases, P1 may be forced to make a continuation offer that is accepted by both the medium and the high type P2, and this offer may result in the high state P2 receiving more than β_3. Importantly though, whenever this equilibrium would exist under the stay, I show that the outcome, and P2's payoff, would be the same under a withdrawal right.
13. Rajan and Zingales (1995) find that trade credit (as measured by accounts payable) are 22.7% of the total liabilities of public firms. Ayotte (2015) finds that capital and operating leases constitute 12% of assets and 21% of financial liabilities for large Chapter 11 filers in the year before the filing.
14. In the case of the typical secured loan, the creditor must make a notice filing that lists the debtor, creditor, and type of collateral. In the case of a subsidiary, the debtor must register the new entity, and any real property it owns will be publicly recorded.
15. §362(d)(2) does not require the judge to lift the stay even if the property is unnecessary to an effective reorganization of the debtor, if the debtor has equity in the property. This requirement might be removed with respect to a subsidiary stay.
16. United Sav. v. Timbers of Inwood Forest, 484 U.S. 365 (1988)

REFERENCES

Adler, B.E. (2012). "Game Theoretic Bankruptcy Valuation". 41 *Journal of Legal Studies* 209.

Adler, B.E. and M. Kahan. (2013). "The Technology of Creditor Protection". 161 U.Pa. L. Rev. 1773.

Ayotte, K. and P. Bolton. (2011). "Optimal Property Rights in Financial Contracting". 24 *Review of Financial Studies* 3401.

Ayotte, K. and S. Gaon. (2011). "Asset-Backed Securities: Costs and Benefits of Bankruptcy Remoteness. 24(4) *Review of Financial Studies*, 1299–335.

Ayotte, K. and H. Hansmann. (2013). "Legal Entities as Transferable Bundles of Contracts". 111 *Michigan Law Review* 715.

Ayotte, K.M. and E.R. Morrison. (2009). "Creditor Control and Conflict in Chapter 11". 1(2), *Journal of Legal Analysis* 511–51.

Ayotte, K. (2015). "Leases and Executory Contracts in Chapter 11". 12 *Journal of Empirical Legal Studies* 637–63.

Baird, D.G. and A.J. Casey. (2013). "No Exit? Withdrawal Rights and the Law of Corporate Reorganizations". 113 Colum. L. Rev. 1.

Baird, D.G. and T.H. Jackson. (1984). "Corporate Reorganization and the Treatment of Diverse Ownership Interests: A Comment on Adequate Protection of Secured Creditors in Bankruptcy". 51 U. Chi. L. Rev. 97.

Bebchuk, L.A. and J.M. Fried. (1996). "The Uneasy Case for the Priority of Secured Claims in Bankruptcy". 105, *Yale Law Journal* 857–934.

Besanko, D. and A.V. Thakor. (1987). "Collateral and Rationing: Sorting Equilibria in Monopolistic and Competitive Credit Markets". 28(3), *International Economic Review* 671–89.

Bester, H. (1985). "Screening vs. Rationing in Credit Markets with Imperfect Information". 75 *American Economic Review* 850–55.

Bolton, P. and D.S. Scharfstein. (1990). A theory of predation based on agency problems in financial contracting. 80 *American Economic Review* 93–106.

Brunnermeier, M.K. and M. Oehmke. (2013). "The Maturity Rat Race". 68 *Journal of Finance* 483.

Casey, A.J. (2013). "Tailoring the Corporate Web". Working Paper.

Che, Y.K. and A. Schwartz. (1999). "Section 365, Mandatory Bankruptcy Rules and Inefficient Continuance". 15 *Journal of Law, Economics and Organization* 441.

Ellias, J. (2014). "The Shadowy Contours of Bankruptcy Resistant Investments". 114 *Columbia Law Review Sidebar* 123–38.

Hansmann, H. and R. Kraakman. (2000). "The Essential Role of Organizational Law". 110 *Yale Law Journal* 387.

Hart, O. and J. Moore. (1994). "A theory of debt based on the inalienability of human capital", 109 *Quarterly Journal of Economics* 841–79.

Hill, C. (1996). "Securitization: A Low-Cost Sweetener for Lemons", 74 Wash. U. L. Q. 1061.

Iacobucci, E.M. and R.A. Winter. (2005). "Asset securitization and asymmetric information". *Journal of Legal Studies*, 161–206.

Iacobucci, E.M. and G.G. Triantis (2007). "Economic and Legal Boundaries of Firms". 93(3), *Virginia Law Review* 515–70

Jackson, T.H. and A.T. Kronman. (1979). "Secured Financing and Priorities Among Creditors", 88 Yale L.J. 1143.

Longhofer, S.D. and S.R. Peters. (2004). "Protection for Whom? Creditor Conflict and Bankruptcy". 6 *American Law and Economic Review* 249–84.

Myers, S.C. and N.S. Majluf. (1984). "Corporate Financing and Investment Decisions When Firms Have Information that Investors Do Not Have". 13 *Journal of Financial Economics* 187.

Rajan, R. and L. Zingales. (1995). "What Do We Know About Capital Structure? Some International Evidence". 50 *Journal of Finance* 1421.

Schwartz, A. (1996). "Priority Contracts and Priority in Bankruptcy". 82 Cornell L. Rev. 1396.
Triantis, G.G. (1992). "Secured Debt Under Conditions of Imperfect Information", 21 J. Legal Stud. 225.
Warren, E. and J. Westbrook. (2005). "Contracting Out of Bankruptcy: An Empirical Investigation". 118 Harvard L. Rev. 1197.

APPENDIX

Proof of Proposition 1:
I will prove the proposition for the case where an informed P1 offers to an uninformed P2; the second half of the proposition follows immediately due to the symmetry of P1 and P2.

First, note that an offer of anything except senior debt or liquidation will never be optimal, since P2 adopts the most pessimistic beliefs upon a continuation offer other than senior debt. Thus, we can restrict consideration to senior debt continuation offers and liquidation offers.

Suppose $\beta_3 > L_4$ and $\pi_l(X_4 - \frac{\beta_3 - (1 - \pi) L_4}{\bar{\pi}}) > \alpha_3$.

First, note that t^* is the offer that causes P2 to receive her liquidation value in expectation given that all P1 types offer it, so she weakly prefers to accept. When $\pi_l(X_4 - \frac{\beta_3 - (1 - \pi) L_4}{\bar{\pi}}) > \alpha_3$ holds, the low type P1 prefers acceptance of this offer to rejection, and hence the other types prefer acceptance as well. Any offer of a lower t_h would be rejected: P2 will maintain the belief $\bar{\pi}$ at any lower offer and thus, P2 expects to receive less than her liquidation value given her beliefs. This implies that, $t^* = \{\frac{\beta_3 - (1 - \pi) L_4}{\bar{\pi}}, L_4\}$ constitutes the unique offer made by all types in a pooling equilibrium.

I now show that efficiency holds when the conditions above do not hold. First, suppose $\beta_3 < L_4$. P2 will accept an offer of riskless senior debt $\{\beta_3, \beta_3\}$. Under this offer, the high and medium type P1s receive the entire going-concern surplus, so they can do no better than making this offer. A low type P1 can do no better than liquidate given P2's beliefs: an offer of riskless debt would be accepted, and P1 would receive a payoff $C_l - \beta_3 < \alpha_3$.

Next, suppose $\beta_3 > L_4$ and $\pi_l(X_4 - \frac{\beta_3 - (1 - \pi) L_4}{\bar{\pi}}) < \alpha_3$. Let $\pi' = \frac{p_m}{p_m + p_h}\pi_m + \frac{p_h}{p_m + p_h}\pi_h$, the updated probability of success if only the high types and medium types are included. The unique PBE involves the low type proposing liquidation, and the high and medium type P1s offering one of two possible offers: (i) if $\pi' X_4 - \pi' \frac{\alpha_3}{\pi_l} + (1 - \pi') L_4 > \beta_3$, an amount such that the low-type P1 is indifferent between making this offer and liquidation: $t = \{X_4 - \frac{\alpha_3}{\pi_l}, L_4\}$; (ii) if the converse is true ($\pi' X_4 - \pi' \frac{\alpha_3}{\pi_l} + (1 - \pi') L_4 < \beta_3$), an amount such that P2 is indifferent between acceptance and rejection, given that only the high and medium types make the offer: $t = \{\frac{\beta_3 - (1-\pi')L_4}{\pi'}, L_4\}$.

Under (i), it is clear by the construction of t that the low type P1 weakly prefers liquidation. Since the low type P1 is indifferent given the offer, the medium and high type P1s strictly prefer continuation. The expected value to P2 of this offer under a belief π' is $\pi' X_4 - \pi' \frac{\alpha_3}{\pi_l} + (1 - \pi')L_4$, which is greater than P2's liquidation value β_3 by condition (i), so P2 accepts. The high and medium types can do no better than make this offer, since any offer of a lower t_h will result in P2 having a belief $\bar{\pi}$. Note that $\pi_l(X_4 - \frac{\beta_3 - (1 - \bar{\pi})L_4}{\bar{\pi}}) < \alpha_3$, a required condition in the proposition, can be rewritten as $\bar{\pi}(X_4 - \frac{\alpha_3}{\pi_l}) + (1 - \bar{\pi})L_4 < \beta_3$. This implies that any t_h less than or equal to $X_4 - \frac{\alpha_3}{\pi_l}$ will be rejected by P2 under the belief $\bar{\pi}$.

Under (ii), it is clear by construction that P2 weakly prefers acceptance of the offer. The condition $\pi' X_4 - \pi' \frac{\alpha_3}{\pi_l} + (1-\pi')L_4 < \beta_3$ can be rewritten as $\pi_l(X_4 - \frac{\beta_3 - (1-\pi')L_4}{\pi'}) < \alpha_3$, implying that the low type P1 strictly prefers liquidation to making the offer. The high and medium type P1s can do no better, since a lower t_h pays P2 less than β_3 in expectation for any belief less than or equal to π'. Hence, P2 would reject.

Proof of Proposition 2:
As with Proposition 1, I focus on an uninformed P2 offering to an informed P1; with this in hand, proving the converse is straightforward due to symmetry. The only way for P2 to capture all the surplus from both medium and high types while avoiding liquidation is to offer P1 riskless debt; then the maximum riskless debt that can be offered is $t = \{L_4, L_4\}$. (To avoid indifference, P2 can add a small amount of risk to P1's claim so that low type P1 strictly prefers to reject). If this is not enough to compensate *P*1 (that is, if $\alpha_3 > L_4$), then the high type P1 will receive a greater expected payoff under a given offer than the medium type. Thus, P2 has to choose between reaching for all surplus from the high type or taking all surplus only from the medium type. To take all surplus from the medium type in a way that draws in the most value from the high type, P2 will offer P1 senior debt; i.e. make $t_h - t_l$ as small as possible, which means setting $t_l = L_4$.

To capture all surplus in the high state, P2 will offer t_h such that P1 gets his liquidation value in the high state: $\pi_h(t_h) + (1 - \pi_h)L_4 = \alpha_3$. Solving for t_h, $t_h = \frac{1}{\pi_h}\{\alpha_3 - (1 - \pi_h)L_4\}$.

To capture all surplus in the medium state, P2 will offer t_h such that $\pi_m t_h + (1 - \pi_m)L_4 = \alpha_3$.

This implies that to capture all surplus in the medium state, set $t_h = \frac{1}{\pi_m}\{\alpha_3 - (1 - \pi_m)L_4\}$.

Comparing P2's expected payoffs, P2 will choose to capture all surplus in the high state, thus resulting in liquidation in the medium state, if and only if $p_h(C_h - \alpha_3) + p_m\beta_3 > p_h\pi_h(X_4 - \frac{1}{\pi_m}\{\alpha_3 - (1 - \pi_m)L_4\}) + p_m(C_m - \alpha_3)$. This expression reduces to $p_h\frac{(\pi_h - \pi_m)}{\pi_m}(\alpha_3 - L_4) > p_m(C_m - L_3)$.

Proof of Proposition 3:
For p_l sufficiently close to 0, P1's optimal strategy in the AP subgame is to always choose continuation. Since continuation is also efficient in the medium and high states, there is no liquidating offer that one party can make at the bargaining stage that would increase the offeror's payoff relative to the AP subgame outcome without decreasing the offeree's payoff.

Proof of Proposition 4:
First, note that under a withdrawal right, there is no equilibrium in which P2 receives less than her liquidation payoff β_3, since she can always unilaterally choose liquidation and get β_3. Moreover, when both P1 and P2 are informed and P2 makes the offer, P1 receives liquidation value and P2 gets all continuation surplus. Hence, there are states that occur with positive probability in which P2 receives more than liquidation value.

Next, consider the stay regime. In all information states other than {*P*1 is uninformed; P2 is informed}, P2 will receive no more than liquidation value and P2 receives strictly less in some states.

1. P1 is informed. In the good and medium states, any offer that P1 either makes or accepts in equilibrium must give P1 at least his adequate protection payoff $C_j - \beta_3 + \delta_j$. Thus, in any accepted offer in those states, P2 would get no more than $\beta_3 - \delta_j$. Since $\delta_h = 0$ and $\delta_m > 0$, P2 receives strictly less than liquidation value in the medium state and no more than liquidation value in the high state. In the low state AP subgame, P1 would prefer continuation if and only if $C_l - \beta_3 + \delta_j > \alpha_3$, or, equivalently, if $\delta_j > L_3 - C_l$. If this condition holds, then any continuation offer made or accepted by P1 will give P1 at least $C_l - \beta_3 + \delta_j$, which implies that P2 receives no more than $\beta_3 - \delta_j$. And any liquidation offer made or accepted by P1 will also give P1 at least $C_l - \beta_3 + \delta_j$, so P2 gets no more than $L_3 - (C_l - \beta_3 + \delta_j) = \beta_3 + (L_3 - C_l) - \delta_j < \beta_3$. If the condition does not hold ($C_l - \beta_3 + \delta_j \leq \alpha_3$), then P1 would choose liquidation in the AP subgame and get α_3. Thus, in any liquidation offer, P2 would get no more than $L_3 - \alpha_3 = \beta_3$. And in any continuation offer, P2 would get no more than $C_l - \alpha_3 \leq \beta_3 - \delta_l$.
2. P1 and P2 are uninformed. In the AP subgame, P1 would continue if and only if $\overline{C} - \beta_3 + p_m\delta_m + p_l\delta_l > \alpha_3$, or equivalently, if $\overline{C} + p_m\delta_m + p_l\delta_l > L_3$. If this inequality holds but $\overline{C} < L_3$, then there is scope for a mutually beneficial liquidation offer. If P1 offers, then P2

is held to $\beta_3 - p_m\delta_m - p_l\delta_l$ and P1 will receive $\alpha_3 + p_m\delta_m + p_l\delta_l$. If P2 offers, then P1 receives his outside option $\overline{C} - \beta_3 + p_m\delta_m + p_l\delta_l$ and P2 will receive $\beta_3 - p_m\delta_m - p_l\delta_l + (L_3 - \overline{C})$. Since $L_3 - \overline{C} - p_m\delta_m - p_l\delta_l < 0$, this is less than β_3.

If $\overline{C} > L_3$, then there is no scope for bargaining, and P2 will receive its AP subgame payoff $\beta_3 - p_m\delta_m - p_l\delta_l$. If $\overline{C} < L_3 + p_m\delta_m + p_l\delta_l$, then P1 does not have a credible threat to continue, so P2 will get β_3 irrespective of who offers.

3a. P1 is uninformed and P2 is informed. First suppose that P2 offers. If P2 makes a liquidation offer, P1 would never accept less than α_3 under any belief since P1 can liquidate unilaterally and get α_3, so P2 can get no more than β_3. In any continuation offer, P1 will form a belief that must be correct in equilibrium. Let the belief about the states given the offer be $\hat{p} = \langle \hat{p}_h, \hat{p}_m, \hat{p}_l \rangle$. The offer of continuation must be worth to P1 at least $\hat{p}_h(C_h - \beta_3) + \hat{p}_m(C_m - \beta_3 + \delta_m) + \hat{p}_l(C_l - \beta_3 + \delta_l)$, since P1 could get this payoff in expectation in the AP subgame. This implies that the value of the continuation offer to P2 is no more than $\hat{p}_h(\beta_3) + \hat{p}_m(\beta_3 - \delta_m) + \hat{p}_l(\beta_3 - \delta_l)$, which is weakly less than β_3 and strictly less than β_3 if $\hat{p}_h < 1$. For any types that remain following a rejected offer, P1 will choose either continuation or liquidation under the AP subgame, which gives P2 no more than β_3.

3b. The remaining case to consider is one where P1 is uninformed, P2 is informed, and P1 makes the offer. In this case, there may be an equilibrium in which P1 makes a continuation offer of $\langle t_h, t_l \rangle = \langle \frac{1}{\pi_m} \{\beta_3 - (1 - \pi_m)L_4, L_4\}$, and liquidates any type that rejects the offer; the high and medium type P2s accept the offer and the low type rejects. Following Proposition 2, this offer is worth β_3 to P2 in the medium state and more than β_3 in the high state.

Necessary conditions for this to constitute an equilibrium include the necessary and sufficient condition under which this outcome is an equilibrium under a withdrawal right: P1 must get a higher payoff under this outcome than offering $\langle t_h, t_l \rangle = \langle \frac{1}{\pi_h} \{\beta_3 - (1 - \pi_m)L_4, L_4\}$, which takes all the surplus from the high type and lets the medium type liquidate. This condition is $p_h \frac{(\pi_h - \pi_m)}{\pi_m} (\beta_3 - L_4) > p_m(C_m - L_3)$. (Under the stay regime, it also must be the case that P1 is better off under this outcome than continuing all types in the AP subgame.)

Thus, I have shown that in all cases except case 3b, P2 gets no more than β_3 and in some states, P2 gets strictly less. And in case 3b, if there is an equilibrium in which P2 gets strictly more than β_3, then P2 gets the same payoff under the withdrawal right. Hence, in expectation, P2 gets strictly more under a withdrawal right.

Proposition 5: This follows immediately from Proposition 4 and E's maximization problem, which is equivalent to minimizing R^{w}_{P2}, P2's recovery in default.

Proposition 6: This follows immediately from Proposition 2, which shows that inefficient liquidation can occur under a withdrawal right under the specified parameters, which are independent of p_l; Proposition 3, which shows that outcomes under a stay are efficient as p_l approaches 0; and Proposition 5, which shows that a withdrawal right will always be chosen by E and P2.

8. Debtor-in-possession financing in bankruptcy

George Triantis

I. INTRODUCTION

Though its origins date back to the equity receiverships of railroads in the late 19th and early 20th centuries,[1] debtor-in-possession (DIP) financing has emerged over the past few decades as an essential component of corporate bankruptcy reorganization. Most debtors who file for bankruptcy do so because they lack the liquidity with which to continue to operate – that is, they neither have liquid assets nor readily available credit. By the conclusion of the bankruptcy process, this liquidity problem is addressed by the financial reorganization of the debtor, the sale of its assets, or both. However, this process takes time and during this time, the debtor needs working capital to continue to operate and preserve its value. Upon the filing of the petition, the automatic stay on creditor enforcement provides relief from the threats of asset removal by creditors and contract termination. In addition, the bankruptcy court may authorize the debtor to use cash in its possession or control, such as its checking account, despite the objection of the lender holding a lien against such collateral. These forms of relief, however, are often insufficient because the debtor needs fresh financing to continue to operate. In other words, although the bankruptcy process itself is designed to yield ultimately a solvent and liquid debtor, most debtors cannot wait for this process to develop without having access to liquid assets or credit. The typical debtor has an immediate need for working capital and liquidity at the outset of the case, in order to finance the reorganization process and avoid value-destroying piecemeal liquidation. Not surprisingly, therefore, judicial authorization of interim DIP financing is among the common first-day motions of a Chapter 11 case and is often followed by at least one more round of authorized financing before the debtor emerges from bankruptcy.[2] Indeed, obtaining a line of credit shortly after filing is a favorable signal of the debtor's prospects in bankruptcy and many debtors get larger credit lines than they expect to draw on.

Under the governance scheme of the Bankruptcy Code, the bankruptcy court must authorize decisions made out of the ordinary course of business. Section 364 gives the bankruptcy court discretion over DIP financing. The provision allows the court to facilitate new borrowing by authorizing the debtor to grant the DIP lender priority ranging from administrative expense to junior and senior secured credit. However, the statute permits secured borrowing only if the court finds that credit would be unavailable without such priority. If the secured credit is senior to a prepetition lien, then the debtor must also ensure "adequate protection" of the subordinated prepetition lien – that is, the debtor must provide assurance that the granting of the superior lien does not harm the economic interest of the subordinated prepetition lienholder.

Over the four decades since §364 was enacted in the 1978 Bankruptcy Code, the liabilities of corporations and the nature of liquidity constraints have become much more complex, as have the structures of DIP lending. Credit markets have grown much more diverse and sophisticated. The drafters of §364 envisaged that it would occasionally encourage existing creditors to loan new funds to the insolvent debtor in bankruptcy, but the current practice is much different. In the 1980s and early 1990s, fewer than one-third of the publicly-held debtors filing in Chapter 11 obtained DIP financing and this was mostly from prepetition lenders.[3] During the 1990s, a growing number of financial institutions began to look at DIP financing as a new business opportunity with low risk and profitable returns. The syndications market also matured and syndicated DIP loans became more common in this period. These market trends opened up further options. The proportion of debtors in bankruptcy taking DIP loans grew to about a half by the end of the decade and up to 70% range in the 2000s.[4]

DIP lending also became a tool by which some creditors have increased their control over bankrupt firms. Over the past decades, lenders have been taking broader security interests covering almost all assets of distressed debtors, thereby tightening constraints on liquidity and heightening the urgency for DIP financing in a larger proportion of bankruptcy cases. DIP loan terms contain restrictive negative and affirmative covenants, similar to – but often more intrusive than – those that address moral hazard concerns in debt relationships outside of bankruptcy. In fact, DIP covenants commonly set budgets, targets and deadlines that constrain the debtor's discretion and influence over the course of the bankruptcy process, especially given that the debtor can and does typically waive the bankruptcy stay on acceleration and enforcement of postpetition loans. Also, since the turn of the century, some DIP lenders have been motivated to lend in order to improve their prospects for acquiring the debtor's assets or ownership interests in the reorganized company. The contracts with such "loan-to-own" lenders often include deadlines for auctions or closings of asset sales or for the filing of a reorganization plan and disclosure statement.

The bankruptcy court has the important discretion to order or deny authorization for the DIP financing arrangement proposed by the debtor. Although most DIP financing arrangements are made with the consent of the unsecured creditors' committee and principal secured creditors, the judicial determination of contested motions sets the defaults for these negotiations. The language of section 364 instructs the court to authorize a §364(d) loan only if credit would be unavailable otherwise and the prepetition lien subordinated (or "primed") by the proposed DIP loan is adequately protected. As discussed in Part II below, new credit for a debtor is not always a good thing and it is inefficient if it props up a nonviable operation (sometimes referred to as "overinvestment"). The court must ensure that funding is authorized when, and only when, it is efficient – in other words, when value is created or preserved so that no party is made worse off as a result of the DIP financing.[5] A related objective is ensuring that the terms of DIP finance are as competitive as possible. Outside bankruptcy, the presence of a prepetition secured creditor can deter other prospective lenders from offering new credit under a subordinate lien. By permitting the priming of the prebankruptcy lien, §364(d) encourages bids by new lenders and thereby reduces the ability of the prebankruptcy secured creditor lender to extract a supernormal rate of return in return for new financing.

As discussed below, courts should bear in mind these objectives in deciding, for example, whether to permit extraordinary terms such as cross-collateralization and roll-ups. Moreover, although the language in §364 focuses on priority, the court must also assess whether all the significant terms of the DIP loan are in the best interests of the estate. Thus, bearing in mind the two objectives identified above (permitting only value-creating new finance and at a competitive rate of return), the court must scrutinize the rate of interest and contractual events of default, as well as the priority. To date, bankruptcy courts have not ordered explicit bidding contests among prospective lenders, in the way that they order auctions of assets under §363(b) or of the equity interest in the reorganized debtor in a cramdown, as instructed by the U.S. Supreme Court opinion in *North LaSalle*.[6]

The acceptable conditions and terms for DIP loans have been subject to a considerable policy debate. This discussion has been informed by some empirical study of DIP financing patterns and their relationships to bankruptcy outcomes. A number of studies suggest a positive correlation between DIP financing and the emergence from Chapter 11, particularly in the important jurisdictions of Delaware and the Southern District of New York.[7] The mechanics of the relationship between financing and outcome, however, are unclear. Even if DIP lending has been beneficial overall, there remains an unresolved debate as to the effect of certain specific features.

In 2014, the American Bankruptcy Institute's Commission to Study the Reform of Chapter 11 proposed significant restrictions on several types of provisions that can be included in DIP financing arrangements, particularly at the interim order stage.[8] These provisions include cross-collateralization, roll-ups, liens in avoidance actions, waiver of avoidance claims against the DIP lender, deadlines for the sale of assets or the filing of a reorganization plan. The Commission's position was that these provisions are not necessary for a robust supply of DIP financing and each can lead to inefficient decisions that inflict losses on prebankruptcy creditors. In an opposing submission to the Commission, the Loan Syndications and Trading Association argued that the proposed limitations would raise the cost of DIP loans for some debtors and make them unavailable for others. These conflicting and core assumptions have not been tested and are difficult to prove empirically.

II. LIQUIDITY, FINANCIAL SLACK AND DEBT OVERHANG

Liquidation priority is a core feature of debt contracts. Creditors have the right to be paid before stockholders, and priority among debt claims is hierarchical as against either individual assets or the debtor as a whole. The priority ranking among creditors may be created by contract or the grant of a property interest. In the contractual form, one creditor consents to be subordinate to another in its claim against the debtor. A debtor's promise to cap its borrowing or refrain from granting future liens on its assets (known as a negative pledge covenant) is a weaker contractual provision because it is only binding against the debtor and not the future lien creditor who would assert its priority. Shorter-maturity debt – whether short-term liability or debt maturity that can be accelerated under tight covenants or cross-default clauses – has effective priority over longer-term debt because it comes due earlier.

The debtor may give priority to a creditor by granting a property interest: specifically, a lien, mortgage or security interest in some of its assets (collateral). Article 9 of the Uniform Commercial Code enables security interests in a broad range of personal property, including bank deposits and cash. The secured creditor or lienholder enjoys a superior claim to the value of the collateral asset, and the right to be paid from this asset before all unsecured creditors. Among competing liens in the same collateral, priority is determined generally according to the time at which each creditor publicizes her lien by possession or registration. Another property-based form of priority is created in a parent-subsidiary corporate group structure, where the creditor of an operating subsidiary has structural priority over the creditors of the holding company. The latter creditors have rights against the parent's stock in the subsidiary, which is subordinate to the subsidiary's creditors.

Debt – and particularly secured debt – constrains the debtor's ability to fund its operations or new projects in various ways.[9] The repayment obligations remove cash from the debtor periodically and if the debtor defaults, a secured creditor can move quickly to freeze the debtor's access to liquid assets. In addition, security interests make it difficult to convert illiquid into liquid assets because, in a sale outside the ordinary course of business, the lien follows the asset into the hands of the transferee. Thus, prospective purchasers are reluctant to buy encumbered assets.

A highly levered company will find it more difficult to raise new financing than a similarly situated firm with less debt. A company with a larger share of assets encumbered by liens will find it more difficult than one whose debt is largely unsecured, all else equal. The term "debt overhang" describes the condition in which the debtor cannot raise new capital to finance a profitable and low-risk project because the payoffs from that project will be absorbed first by (or in the case of unsecured debt, shared with) the earlier creditors who cannot be paid their return out of the value of existing assets. This leaves an inadequate return for the new investor.[10] The overhang problem can be overcome if the firm can issue debt with higher priority than its existing liabilities,[11] but this is difficult to do if the debtor has encumbered most or all its assets with security interests that rank in priority on a first-in-time basis. A better regime might provide that the later-in-time lender has priority only to the extent that she contributes new value. This can and is achieved when the new lender finances the acquisition of a discrete asset (through a "purchase money security interest"), but not when it adds value to existing assets (such as by paying the utility bills).[12]

Liquidity can be a good or bad condition depending on contextual variables. In a company with abundant profitable investment opportunities, liquidity is good because it enables the firm to exploit those projects promptly, especially in an environment when cash flow is otherwise volatile. In a company with few or no profitable opportunities, liquidity provides management with financial slack to promote its self-interest rather than maximizing firm value (for example, through perquisite consumption or as a forgiving buffer for poor or inattentive management). Debt – and particularly debt secured by broad security interests – serves the function of constraining financial slack[13] (Triantis 1995[14]), but it can also constrain the liquidity necessary to invest in profitable opportunities, such as the continuation of efficient operations. Outside of bankruptcy, security interests that are publicized (usually by registration) have priority over later security interests and thereby constrain future financing prospects. The principal exception to this general first-in-time priority rule is the purchase money security interest, but it applies narrowly to the financing of a specific discrete asset as opposed to working capital. So, a blanket lien over the debtor's assets has an indiscriminate effect on future financial prospects: it can discourage either efficient or inefficient future financing[15] (Triantis 1995[16]). Optimally, a company would set the amount and priority of debt in the capital structure of a firm to preserve the liquidity needed to make all profitable investments but no more. However, over time, circumstances change, causing the liquidity settings to be looser or tighter than optimal. If a leveraged company has a lower cash flow than expected but its operations continue to be profitable, for example, it faces a liquidity problem that can lead to inefficient cessation of operations.

A debtor that files for bankruptcy is typically one that cannot fund its ongoing operations. Over the past few decades, illiquidity and debt overhang have become more severe among these firms. The proportion of asset value covered by liens has grown so that many firms entering into bankruptcy have few if any unencumbered assets.[17] Many have postponed bankruptcy filing by drawing down on revolving credit facilities secured by blanket liens.[18] One of the fundamental goals of bankruptcy is to relieve the overhang of existing obligations and restore desirable levels of liquidity.[19] Reorganization under the Chapter 11 process reduces the debt obligations of the debtor so that it emerges from bankruptcy solvent and with adequate liquidity. This is accomplished largely by forcing the recapitalization on dissenting creditors through supermajority voting and judicial cram down. In light of the fact that Chapter 11 cases take time and liquidity needs are typically urgent, the Bankruptcy Code enables the funding of operations during the process, with financing that is repaid when the debtor emerges from bankruptcy. These provisions give the bankruptcy court important discretion to authorize and condition the new funding when it is efficient and in the interests of the estate.

Before turning to the authorization of DIP financing, two related provisions in the Bankruptcy Code are worth mentioning in addressing the liquidity constraints of debtors. First, blanket security interests that extend to proceeds or products from collateral are enforceable in bankruptcy but section 552(b) of the Bankruptcy Code authorizes the court to limit this coverage, after notice and a hearing, "based on the equities of the case." The court may use this provision to limit the reach of prepetition liens if the proceeds and products are created by a mix of the existing collateral and new investment. This liberates assets to support new credit that would fund the operations.[20] Second, security interests often cover the debtor's bank deposits and cash holdings, subject of course to the aforementioned "equities" limit in §552(b). The ability of the secured party to take possession of these liquid assets, by set-off or otherwise, is frozen by the automatic stay in §362(a)(3) and debtors often move to authorize the use of such cash collateral.[21] This loosens the debtor's liquidity compared to what it would have been outside of bankruptcy.

"Adequate protection" plays a central role in bankruptcy as a condition of the debtor's continued use of collateral assets: such as in the judicial determination to continue the automatic stay or to authorize the use of cash collateral. Adequate protection vindicates the economic value of the property interests, particularly liens, of prepetition creditors. In addition, it provides a check to ensure that the debtor's use of the collateral is efficient. After all, if the use of the collateral creates value in the debtor's enterprise, the debtor should be able to ensure that the lienholder is no worse off. Section 361 of the Bankruptcy Code lists three ways by which the debtor could provide adequate protection. The first two – cash payment (§361(1)) and an additional or replacement lien in another asset (§361(2)) – are unlikely to be feasible because debtors typically file for bankruptcy with insufficient cash and little, if any, value in unencumbered assets. The courts have interpreted the third option (§361(3)) – such other relief as would result in the realization of the indubitable equivalent of the protected lien – as being satisfied by the presence of a significant equity cushion in the value of the collateral, particularly with prospects that the value will increase in bankruptcy. A common justification is that the debtor's use of the collateral will create sufficient value to ensure that the prepetition secured claimant is left no worse off, while the junior creditors benefit.

III. DIP FINANCING UNDER SECTION 364

a. DIP Financing Priorities and Priming Liens

Section 364 of the Bankruptcy Code provides a ladder of priority debt that the bankruptcy court can authorize if financing cannot be otherwise obtained. Under subsections 364(a) and (b), the debtor may obtain unsecured credit as an administrative expense in the ordinary course of business (unless the court orders otherwise) or, with judicial authorization after notice and a hearing, outside the ordinary course. Administrative expenses are paid prior to unsecured claims in liquidation, and they must be satisfied in full to confirm a reorganization plan. Under §364(c), after notice and a hearing, the court can authorize debt secured by an interest in unencumbered assets or by an interest junior to an existing lien in encumbered property, but only if the debtor is unable to obtain unsecured credit as an administrative expense.[22]

Finally, under §364(d), the court may authorize a lien that is senior or equal to an existing lien, but only if the debtor is unable to obtain such credit otherwise and the debtor demonstrates that the subordinated (or equal) prepetition interest is adequately protected. As noted earlier, debtors can demonstrate that lienholder interests are adequately protected by an equity cushion in the collateral value, particularly if the new financing will also enhance the value of the collateral. However, the two requirements for priming liens under §364(d) are in tension with each other. If a prebankruptcy secured claim can be adequately protected notwithstanding the priming of its lien, this begs the question of why the new financing could not have been obtained by offering a junior lien. For instance, if the prebankruptcy creditor has a claim of $60 secured by collateral worth $100, the DIP might propose a new priming loan for $20 and point to the $20 remaining cushion as adequate protection. However, the DIP must also argue that this cushion would have been inadequate to induce a new lender to provide $20 in credit with a junior lien. Similarly, if the DIP offers adequate protection in the form of a replacement or additional lien in unencumbered assets, it begs the question – and warrants some skepticism – as to why this collateral could not have supported the new DIP loan. This gives rise to the concern that the DIP financing authorization compels the primed lienholder to accept a risk that the debtor could not sell to a new lender.

Most DIP loans are secured by blanket liens over the debtor's assets and around two-thirds enjoy a §364(d) security interest.[23] As noted earlier, the two core objectives for the court in authorizing DIP financing are to ensure that the financing (a) creates rather than simply redistributes wealth and (b) is made on competitive terms. With the relaxation of the adequate protection requirement under the "indubitable equivalent" provision of §361, the first objective calls on the authorizing court to also assess the viability of the debtor and the efficiency of the use to which the funds will be put, including the debtor's business plan and the intended use of proceeds. The court performs a critical service in distinguishing between the two possibilities of value creation and expropriation: Does DIP financing correct underinvestment and create value or produce overinvestment and expropriate value from prebankruptcy creditors who are compelled to accept a higher risk without compensation?[24] The risk of overinvestment and expropriation of value is significant, especially when the DIP lender takes a higher priority. After all, from the DIP lender's perspective, a priming lien in all the debtor's assets is a relatively low risk irrespective of the feasibility of the debtor's operations and plans: the DIP lender is insulated from losses due to inefficient investment.[25] Overinvestment in risky projects enriches the shareholders, managers and underwater junior creditors who would gain if the project is successful, but compromises the expected payoff of the fulcrum or marginal creditors, who bear the cost of failure. The sharing of the benefit depends on the financial condition of the company, the risk profile of the project and the relative bargaining power of the DIP and the DIP lender.

The evidence of the relationship between DIP financing and bankruptcy outcomes is tentative. Several empirical studies find in their respective samples that companies with DIP financing were more likely to survive as going concerns, suggesting that the courts are performing their screening function well.[26] However, the causal link, if any, remains unclear. Are firms receiving DIP financing those that were already more likely to emerge in the first place, or does the DIP lender contribute screening or monitoring that materially improves those prospects? Are some features of DIP financing more likely to lead to emergence by funding value-creating expenditures and others more likely to redistribute wealth away from other creditors by continuing inefficient operations? The mechanism by which DIP financing creates value, if any, in bankruptcy is critical to the question of whether courts should allow certain controversial features of DIP financing that are discussed below.

The second objective of judicial oversight under §364 is to promote DIP lending on competitive terms, which should entail both ensuring that the debtor has sufficiently shopped the financing and examining the proposed lending arrangement.[27] In the majority of cases, the DIP lender presented to the court is also a prebankruptcy secured lender.[28] These creditors enjoy an advantage over other potential lenders because of their relationship and superior information about the debtor, and this may skew the court's determination. A debtor-in-possession is required to present evidence that it has sought out financing from several sources, but courts generally do not require a formal bidding process from prospective lenders. Although auctions have been increasingly used in other bankruptcy proceedings – such as asset sales under §363(b) – this has yet to become a requirement for §364 DIP financing authorizations. While a market test is required under the doctrine of the Supreme Court in North LaSalle before allowing the new capital from prebankruptcy owners to effectively "prime" prebankruptcy creditor claims in a reorganization plan, this is not required under analogous circumstances during bankruptcy under §364 authorizations.[29] In addition, as the supply of DIP financing expands, prospective DIP lenders may compete across different terms (priorities, interest, covenants, and so on), so that courts will be called upon to consider trade-offs across these term types. For example, they may need to compare the desirability of a priming lien against an alternative debt obligation with lower priority and a higher rate of interest. Although the lower interest rate offered with a more senior lien can be seductive, the courts should not ignore the implicit cost borne by the junior primed lienholder whose risk has increased.

b. Cross-collateralization, Roll-ups and Avoidance Protection for Prepetition DIP Lenders

Cross-collateralization and roll-ups are two features that debtors commonly propose and that entice prepetition creditors to provide DIP financing.[30] As discussed above, the priming of liens may mitigate underinvestment or exacerbate overinvestment, and the court plays an essential screening role in authorizing §364(d) priority. Cross-collateralization and roll-ups raise more severe concerns about overinvestment and there is controversy as to whether these features are needed to attract new funding for efficient investments, as opposed to those with negative expected net present values. Both features benefit DIP lenders by improving the return on their prepetition claims at the expense of other claimants.[31] Under cross-collateralization, the DIP provides a lien that secures in the agreement not only the new funds but also the prepetition claims held by the lender. Under a roll-up, the DIP loan provides funding to satisfy prepetition claims – often claims of the DIP lender – and to fund operations. The benefit to a DIP lender with an undersecured prepetition claim, and the corresponding loss to other unsecured creditors, is clear. It can also benefit the DIP lender with a secured prepetition claim if its prepetition lien is subject to a possible avoidance action or other challenges in bankruptcy, or to a crammed-down adjustment under a reorganization plan. Indeed, a DIP might alternatively waive its right to challenge liens or payments preceding bankruptcy or make representations to acknowledge the validity of the existing lien.

Cross-collateralization, roll-ups and avoidance protection encourage DIP lending through the benefit they confer onto prepetition claims, as opposed to the return on the new funding. To the extent that they are retroactive in adding value to prepetition claims, they might improve the value of the prepetition debt in order to induce DIP financing of an unprofitable project in a distressed firm (i.e., overinvestment) by the gain in the value of the prepetition debt. The DIP financing thereby causes a redistribution from unsecured creditors to the DIP lender, who can often capture most of these rents because of its privileged position as a lender with prebankruptcy exposure to the debtor.

Although the 11th Circuit Court of Appeals held that cross-collateralization is not within the equitable authority of the bankruptcy court under §364,[32] most other courts regard it as disfavored but permissible, particularly if the DIP shows that it is necessary to obtain credit. The influential courts in Delaware and the Southern District of New York have issued guidelines relating to the authorization of cross-collateralization and roll-ups which require conspicuous disclosure of the terms and the justification, and provide that, barring compelling circumstances, they should not be approved without notice and hearing.[33]

The concern about cross-collateralization and roll-ups is reflected also in legal scholarship and reform proposals. The ABI's Chapter 11 Commission expressed skepticism that cross-collateralization and roll-ups are needed for debtors to obtain postpetition credit and that they are not costly to existing claimants.[34] The Commission recommended that these provisions – as well as debtor's concessions as to the validity of prepetition liens – not be permitted in interim DIP financing orders. It also proposed that roll-ups be limited even in final orders to exceptional cases in which the debtor shows that the terms with roll-up are better than the alternative financing arrangements and that the roll-up loan is in the best interest of the estate. In its response to the Commission's Report, the Loan Syndication and Trading Association argued that these provisions 'help debtors preserve their going-concern value by offering nonmonetary inducements to lend. . . . Prohibiting such provisions would impede debtors from obtaining DIP financing, to the detriment of all stakeholders.'[35] Although this empirical premise is difficult to prove, the LSTA's argument would have been strengthened if it pointed to a market failure that would prevent debtors from offering their DIP lenders a sufficiently enticing return prospectively out of the value created by their investment, rather than through cross-collateralization, roll-ups or other protections of their prebankruptcy liens.

IV. CONTROL PROVISIONS IN DIP LOANS

Priority and interest rates are key features of debt, but increasing scholarly attention has been paid to other contract terms, particularly control rights. As in the controversies over priming liens, cross-collateralization and roll-ups, a fundamental issue is whether common control rights are needed to tackle the overinvestment problem of insolvent debtors. The concern about some control features is that they are both unnecessary and inefficient. As discussed above, there is a contrast between the way that debt priority is determined outside and inside bankruptcy. Priority is determined outside of bankruptcy predominantly by rules that implement a first-in-time, first-in-right principle; in bankruptcy, courts authorize priority under a standard that depends on the facts of each case. The courts are called upon to police the assignment of priority to new financing on a case-by-case basis. It is similarly useful to compare the control rights of debtholders outside and inside bankruptcy. Creditor control rights are created contractually outside of bankruptcy through combinations of covenants, events of default clauses, acceleration provisions and enforcement rights. The covenants are drafted to constrain the decision making discretion of the debtor – such as the ability to acquire or dispose of assets or to make distributions to shareholders – and to impose trip-wires for default – such as the violation of certain financial ratio tests or the instigation of significant civil or regulatory legal actions against the debtor. The violation of a covenant and an event of default gives the lender the right to accelerate, and the lender can credibly threaten enforcement in order to gain even more influence in the decisions of the debtor.

These control provisions and the associated monitoring activity of lenders together play an important role in corporate governance, that benefits investors by reducing agency costs.[36] They form an important complement to the governance rights of shareholders and other stakeholders. A lender's control rights are problematic when the debtor becomes financially distressed or insolvent, and the lender's interests turn sharply toward the distribution rather than the size of the pie. The filing of bankruptcy and the onset of the automatic stay replaces the prebankruptcy control rights with a different governance system that relies more heavily on judicial oversight. For example, the debtor must first obtain court approval, after notice and a hearing, before using or disposing of any asset outside the ordinary course of business.

DIP loans likewise contain covenants to protect the DIP lender's expected return from agency costs.[37] Since they are postpetition agreements, they typically provide that they are not subject to the stay. In fact, in the case of a DIP loan by a prepetition creditor, they also protect the existing credit exposure. Over the past couple of decades, DIP financing agreements have included more and tighter covenants and events of default to constrain the decisions of the debtor. Three-quarters contain specific line item budget limits, over half limit monthly or quarterly capital expenditures and over half set profitability targets such as minimum monthly EBITDA.[38] The DIP loans commonly require frequent reporting of financial numbers including cash flow forecasts and demand a continuing cash management system.

Although §364 does not explicitly instruct the court to approve the events of default (or the interest rate and fees), courts do scrutinize these terms, especially if they are out of the ordinary and give the lender undue influence over the course of the bankruptcy case.[39] Some types of debt covenants are the subject of controversy, largely along the same lines as the features of cross-collateralization, roll-up and anti-avoidance protection: namely, are they necessary to attract DIP financing of efficient projects, do they enable overinvestment, and do they inflict costs on existing creditors?

Bankruptcy courts are now faced with a category of covenants that confer advantages to DIP lenders who seek to acquire assets or controlling interests over the debtor enterprise through bankruptcy auctions or reorganization.[40] The acquirers are often private equity or hedge funds, and they tend to lend to debtors with weaker financial conditions than their pure lender counterparts.[41] The loan-to-own strategy grew in the 2000s[42] and was particularly pronounced during and in the aftermath of the financial crisis of 2008–09. Of the seventy-four private-equity-sponsored companies filing for bankruptcy in 2009, for instance, forty-three (58%) received DIP financing and, in 53% of that subset, the DIP lenders emerged as owners of the debtor or purchasers of its assets.[43] In a study of large bankruptcy cases between 2000 and 2013 in which the debtor was acquired by a fund, the purchaser was a prepetition stakeholder 54% of the time and a DIP lender at least 19% of the time.[44]

The Chapter 11 Commission expressed concern about milestones and deadlines that relate 'in a material or significant way to the debtor's operations . . . or to the resolution of the case,' such as setting deadlines for the holding of an auction, closing of a sale or proposing a plan and filing of a disclosure statement in connection with a plan. One study suggests that these covenants appear in almost a quarter of DIP financing agreements.[45] The Commission's concern was that these loan covenants accelerate asset sales and lead to loss of value that would have been realized through either reorganization or an extended sale process. While bank-provided DIP lending is correlated with emergence of a going concern from Chapter 11,[46] it appears that DIP lending by other institutions is associated with more asset sales. The Commission did not propose a ban on milestones and deadlines in DIP loan covenants but instead recommended (a) a prohibition on such provisions in interim orders and (b) a 60-day moratorium from the petition date on the effective date of such covenants.

V. CONCLUSION

New debt in bankruptcy is subject to a very different governance regime than debt issuance outside of bankruptcy, largely because of the debtor's insolvency. The rules that apply outside of bankruptcy are replaced by judicially applied standards that address the debt overhang problem without exacerbating the debtor's incentive to overinvest in risky projects with negative expected net present value. The assignment of priority is different: outside bankruptcy, it is largely a property-based, first-in-time rule or priority across liens, while a bankruptcy court can authorize later-in-time priority if necessary to resolve the debt overhang in the particular debtor. Outside of bankruptcy, parties enjoy greater freedom of contract: they can grant liens in a broad range of assets, cross-collateralize and roll-up debt if they choose to, and are free to include covenants and events of default that give control to lenders over the decisions of the debtor. Inside bankruptcy, this freedom in either contracting or enforcing is subject to judicial oversight because of the policy concern that the debtor-in-possession will not be a faithful agent of its principals in bankruptcy, namely its marginal creditors. How far the courts can or should go in their oversight is a matter of current debate, as described in this chapter. As the opposing sides in the policy debates examine DIP loan contracts on a term-by-term basis, the dispute largely boils down to two empirical questions. Is the contract term in question necessary to induce new lending and does it distort the efficient decisions of the debtor regarding asset deployment? One can anticipate two helpful developments in the next few years: first, further evolution in the market for DIP loans and second, more empirical insights derived from the availability of digital court records and dockets.

NOTES

1. Peter Tufano, *Business Failure, Judicial Innovation, and Financial Innovation: Restructuring U.S. Railroads in the Nineteenth Century*, 71 Bus. Hist. Rev. 1 (1997); David A. Skeel, Jr., *The Past, Present, and Future of Debtor-in-Possession Financing*, 25 Cardozo L. Rev. 1905 (2004).
2. Under Bankruptcy Rule 4001(c)(2), the court may hold a hearing on motion to authorize credit no earlier than 14 days after service of the motion, but it may waive the notice and authorize the financing earlier only to the extent necessary to avoid immediate and irreparable harm to the estate pending a final hearing.
3. Sandeep Dahiya, John Kose, Puri Manju & Gabriel Ramirez, *Debtor-in-Possession Financing and Bankruptcy Resolution: Empirical Evidence*, 69 J. Fin. Econ. 259 (2003) (finding an increase from 10.42% of their sample in 1989 to 48.2% in 1996); Siris Chatterjee, Upinder S. Dhillon and Gabriel G. Ramirez, Debtor-in-Possession Financing, 28 J. Bank. & Fin. 3097 (2004) (observing a similar growth from 27% in early 1990s to 46% in late 1990s).
4. Maria Carapeto, *Does Debtor-in-Possession Financing Add Value?* (October 28, 2004) (unpublished manuscript on file with the author); Kenneth Ayotte & Edward R. Morrison, *Creditor Control and Conflict in Chapter 11*, 1 J. Legal Analysis 511 (2009); Lynn M. LoPucki & Joseph W. Doherty, Bankruptcy Survival, 62, UCLA L. Rev. 970 (2015); Stuart Gilson, Edith S. Hotchkiss & Matthew Osborn, *Cashing Out: The Rise of M&A in Bankruptcy* (August 15, 2015) (unpublished manuscript) http://ssrncom/abstract=2547168); Kai Li & Wei Wang.
5. George Triantis, *A Theory of the Regulation of Debtor-in-Possession Financing*, 46 Vand. L. Rev. 901 (1993); George Triantis, *A Free Cash-flow Theory of Secured Debt and*

Creditor Priorities, 80 Va. L. Rev. 2155 (1994); George Triantis, *Financial Slack Policy and the Laws of Secured Transactions*, 29 J. Legal Stud. 35 (2000).

6. Bank of Am. v. 203 N. LaSalle St. P'ship, 526 U.S. 434 (1999).
7. Dahiya, Kose, Manju & Ramirez, *supra* note 3; Carapeto, *supra* note 4; Stuart C. Gilson, *Coming Through in a Crisis, How Chapter 11 and the Debt Restructuring Industry are Helping to Revive the U.S. Economy*, 24 J. Applied Corp. Fin. 23 (2012); Loan Syndications and Trading Assoc., The Trouble with Unneeded Bankruptcy Reform: The LSTA's Response to the ABI Chapter 11 Commission Report (2015); LoPucki and Doherty, *supra* note 4.
8. Comm'n to Study the Reform of Chapter 11, Am. Bankr. Inst., 2012–2014 Final Report and Recommendations (2014).
9. Triantis, George (1994), *supra* note 5; Triantis, George (2000), *supra* note 5.
10. Stuart C. Myers, *The Determinants of Corporate Borrowing*, 5 J. Fin. Econ. 147 (1977).
11. Rene M. Stulz & Herb Johnson, *An Analysis of Secured Debt*, 14 J. Fin. Econ. 501 (1985).
12. Triantis, George (1994), *supra* note 5; Triantis, George (2000), *supra* note 5.
13. Id.
14. Triantis, George (1994), *supra* note 5; Oliver Hart and John Moore, *Debt and Seniority: An Analysis of the Role of Hard Claims in Constraining Management*, 85 Am. Econ. Rev. 567 (1995).
15. Triantis, George (1994), *supra* note 5.
16. Triantis, George (1994), *supra* note 5; Triantis, George (2000), *supra* note 5.
17. Ayotte & Morrison, *supra* note 4 (finding a 35% drop in asset value and eleven-fold increase in secured debt during the year or two before bankruptcy); Jay L. Westbrook, *Secured Creditor Control and Bankruptcy Sales: An Empirical View*, 2015 U. Ill. L. Rev. 831 (finding that the amount of secured debt exceeded the total scheduled asset value in 29% of the filed cases in 2006).
18. Barry Adler, Vedran Capkun & Lawrence A. Weiss, *Value Destruction in the New Era of Chapter 11*, 29 J.L. Econ. & Org. 461 (2013); Gilson, Hotchkiss & Osborn, *supra* note 4.
19. Triantis, George (2000), *supra* note 5; Kenneth Ayotte and David A. Skeel, Jr., *Bankruptcy Law as a Liquidity Provider*, 80 U. Chi. L. Rev. 1557 (2013).
20. Triantis, George (2000), *supra* note 5.
21. The debtor applies for authorization to use cash collateral under Bankruptcy Code §363(c)(2) (in the ordinary course of business) or §363(b)(1) (outside the ordinary course). Debtors often apply for a preliminary order at the beginning of the case and the court may authorize the use of cash collateral on such an interim basis only if there is a reasonable likelihood that the debtor will prevail at the final hearing. Bankruptcy Code §363(c)(3).
22. The authorization of a lien in avoidance actions or proceeds therefrom is controversial and the Chapter 11 Commission proposed that it be discontinued. This chapter suggests that efficiency is most likely promoted when the collateral assets are those created as a result of the new financing. In contrast, avoidance actions are existing assets of the estate.
23. Empirical studies have found a range: for example, from 65% in the 2001 sample of Ayotte and Morrison, Ayotte & Morrison, *supra* note 4, to almost 90% in the 2009 sample of Coyne, Daniel J. Coyne, *Debtor-in-Possession Financing Agreements* in *Private Equity-Sponsored Companies in Bankruptcy* in 2009 (July 2012) (unpublished manuscript) (on file with author).
24. These effects of DIP financing priority on over- and under-investment are discussed in Triantis, George (1992). See Robert Gertner and David Scharfstein, *A Theory of Workouts and the Effects of Reorganization Law*, 46 J. Fin. 1189 (1991).
25. A study published by Moody's confirms that the default risk of DIP lenders to large public companies has been low. Moody's examined the default and loss experience of facilities in its DIP database including 297 bankruptcy cases that were resolved, either through emergence or liquidation of the DIP. Of the 297 cases, only two DIP facilities

experienced defaults involving missed payments of scheduled principal or interest, suggesting a default probability of about 0.5%. William Fahy, Moody's Comments On Debtor-In-Possession Lending 4 (Oct. 2008), https://www.moodys.com/sites/products/DefaultResearch/2007300000539803.pdf.

26. Dahiya, Kose, Manju & Ramirez, *supra* note 3; Carapeto, *supra* note 4; LoPucki & Doherty, *supra* note 4 (finding no statistically significant difference in the key districts of Delaware and the SDNY).
27. The ABI Chapter 11 Commission Report noted that intercreditor agreements between junior and senior secured creditor groups often contain clauses that prohibit the junior secured creditors from offering DIP financing without the consent of the senior secured creditors. The Commission was concerned about the possible reduction in competition for credit and proposed to limit the enforcement of these agreements to provisions that prohibit the priming of the senior secured creditor and that gave the senior secured creditor the right to lend on the same terms offered by the junior lender and approved by the court. Am. Bankr. Inst., *supra* note 8.
28. Dahiya, Kose, Manju & Ramirez, *supra* note 3 (finding that the DIP lender is a prepetition secured lender in 58% of cases in their sample).
29. In fact, while priming liens are particularly common when the DIP lender is a prepetition creditor (or the lending syndicates overlap, the loans often prime the DIP lender's own prepetition lien. Dahiya, Kose, Manju & Ramirez, *supra* note 3; Ayotte & Morrison, *supra* note 4.
30. *See, e.g.*, Gilson, Hotchkiss & Osborn, *supra* note 4.
31. Another term having a similar distributional effect grants a lien to the new DIP lender on avoidance actions and proceeds therefrom. Bankruptcy Rule 4001(c)(1)(B)(xi). The ABI Chapter 11 Commission proposed that such DIP liens be banned. Am. Bankr. Inst., *supra* note 8.
32. *In re* Saybrook Mfg. Co., 963 F.2d 1490 (11th Cir. 1992); David A. Skeel, Jr., *The Story of Saybrook: Defining the Limits of Debtor-in-Possession Financing*, in R.K. Rasmussen, (ed.), Bankruptcy Law Stories (2007).
33. Del. L. Bankr. R. 4001-2(a)(i)(2002); S.D.N.Y. L. Bankr. R. 4001-2.
34. Am. Bankr. Inst., *supra* note 8, at 75–9.
35. Loan Syndications and Trading Assoc., *supra* note 7.
36. George Triantis & Ronald J. Daniels, *The Role of Debt in Interactive Corporate Governance*, 83 Cal. L. Rev. 1073 (1995); George Triantis, *Debt Financing, Corporate Decision Making, and Security Design*, 26 Can. Bus. L. J. 93 (1995); Clifford W. Smith, Jr. & Jerold B. Warner, *On Financial Contracting: An Analysis of Bond Covenants*, 7 J. Fin. Econ. 117 (1979).
37. Chatterjee, Dhillon & Ramirez, *supra* note 3.
38. Ayotte & Morrison, *supra* note 4; Chatterjee, Dhillon & Ramirez, *supra* note 3.
39. The guidelines for approval of DIP financing motions in the Southern District of New York refers to these terms as extraordinary and requires that they be clearly disclosed. S.D.N.Y. L. Bankr. R. 4001–02.
40. Paul M. Goldschmid, *More Phoenix than Vulture: The Case for Distressed Investor Presence in the Bankruptcy Process*, 2005 Colum. Bus. L. Rev. 191 (2005); David A. Skeel, Jr., *Creditors' Ball: The 'New' New Corporate Governance in Chapter 11*, 152 Pa. L. Rev. 917 (2003); Skeel, *supra* note 1.
41. Li & Wang, *supra* note 4.
42. *Id.*
43. Coyne, *supra* note 23.
44. Michelle M. Harner et al., *Activist Investors, Distressed Companies and Value Uncertainty*, 22 Am. Bankr. Inst. L. Rev. 167 (2014).
45. Ayotte & Morrison, *supra* note 4.
46. Gilson, *supra* note 7.

9. Beyond options

*Anthony J. Casey and Edward R. Morrison**

INTRODUCTION

For many decades, it has been well understood that options are embedded within the debt and equity issued by a corporation. Equity is implicitly a call option on the firm's assets, with a strike price equal to the firm's liabilities.[1] Senior (secured) debt is equivalent to owning the firm's assets and selling a call option with a strike price equal to the face value of the senior debt. And unsecured debt is a combination of two options—a long call option on the firm's assets, with a strike price equal to senior debt, plus a short call option, entitling equityholders to buy the assets from unsecured creditors at a price equal to total firm liabilities.

Under current law, a bankruptcy filing is analogous to a common expiration date – imposed by law – for all options embedded within the firm's securities.[2] All debts come due and the present value of the firm is distributed as if the firm were being liquidated. By function of the Bankruptcy Code's absolute priority rule (APR) – which forbids payouts of any kind to junior creditors[3] when senior creditors have not been paid in full – the distribution collapses all future possibilities and effectively destroys the options held by junior creditors and equityholders. They must exercise their options immediately or lose them forever.

This options-based perspective highlights the extent to which the Code implicitly impairs junior stakeholders' options during the bankruptcy process. It also highlights the extent to which the bankruptcy process itself creates new options.[4] Because confirmation takes time and asset values are volatile, the value of the bankruptcy estate can change substantially between filing and plan confirmation. For junior stakeholders, this volatility creates a payoff profile identical to the payoffs from a call option. As with any option, the longer the time until the option expires (the delay from filing to confirmation), the greater the option value. Moreover, the firm's value at confirmation is determined by a judge, not the market. The greater the variance in judicial valuation, the greater the option value created by a process that relies on that valuation.[5]

These insights have prompted recent re-evaluation of the APR. The central goals of a well-functioning bankruptcy system include minimizing the deadweight costs of financial distress and maximizing creditor recoveries. Both goals reduce costs of capital *ex ante*. The focus on options reveals that current bankruptcy law preserves and destroys options in ways that can increase the costs of financial distress and permit some creditors to benefit at the expense of others. Because the APR causes the expiration of all junior-creditor options, for example, it creates an incentive for junior creditors to agitate for a lengthier bankruptcy proceeding, especially a reorganization, which exposes the parties to greater judicial variance. For the same reason, the APR induces secured creditors to push for quick sales, even at fire-sale prices.

Recent scholarship has advocated reforms that unwind these adverse effects. For example, scholars have advocated a return to "relative priority," requiring senior lenders to buy out the options of junior lenders when seniors advocate a quick sale, or at least to compensate the junior lenders for the value of those options.[6] The primary goal of a "relative priority" regime is to preserve, as much as possible, the options held by creditors outside bankruptcy. A bankruptcy filing would no longer represent a common expiration date for options.[7] Instead, junior creditors and investors would retain options allowing them to capture future appreciation in firm value, if the debtor is reorganized. If the debtor is instead sold off, they might (depending on the specific proposal) retain the right to compensation for the value of these options, which are extinguished by the sale.

These proposals make sense if our primary concern is the APR and its degrading effect on the options of junior creditors. This concern, we argue here, is too narrow. It ignores the many other options that are altered by bankruptcy proceedings. For example, valuable real options held by senior creditors are impaired both by the bankruptcy code's automatic stay and its lien stripping rules. Equally important, the focus on junior creditors' options exalts options for options sake without considering whether or not protecting those options is necessary for advancing the goals of a well-functioning bankruptcy system.

We argue here that protecting options is, ultimately, neither necessary nor sufficient for that purpose. What is necessary and sufficient is a regime that cashes out the rights of junior investors (creditors and equityholders) at market prices. To illustrate this, we propose an "automatic bankruptcy procedure" that gives senior creditors an option to restructure the firm's debt or sell its assets at any time after a default, with or without a bankruptcy filing. If the option is exercised, the senior creditor must choose between two types of restructurings. One is to sell the firm's assets free and clear of all interests but allow junior creditors and equityholders to demand an appraisal, which guarantees that they receive no less than they would have received from the going-concern value in a reorganization. Alternatively, the senior creditor can sell the firm subject to warrant-like instruments that are distributed to all creditors and equityholders who are not paid in full on the sale date. These instruments ensure that these junior stakeholders benefit from future appreciation in the value of the assets. The warrants would have a strike price equal to the face value of the senior claims and an expiration date set at somewhere around five or ten years after the restructuring date.

The most important feature of this mechanism is that no judicial intervention would be needed to implement our procedure. To be sure, judicial involvement is needed if creditors or shareholders demand an appraisal. But this remedy is no different from the one available to minority shareholders in any corporate control transaction. Indeed, our proposal can be seen as an effort to design a formalized restructuring procedure that borrows from traditional state law governing corporate-control transactions.

Our proposal also draws on prior work by Adler. Like Adler, we advocate a procedure that automatically adjusts the firm's capital structure. But the trigger for adjustment is not the advent of distress, as in Adler's proposal. It is instead the decision of the senior lender to exercise an option.

1. OPTIONS IN AND OUT OF BANKRUPTCY

1.1 Non-bankruptcy Options in the Shadow of Bankruptcy

Every firm is a collection of assets with uncertain future cash flows. The volatility of those cash flows generates option value for junior creditors and shareholders: if the firm thrives, they enjoy cash flows; if the firm fails and merits liquidation, they can leave the firm to the senior creditors and walk away. The greater the uncertainty about future cash flows, the more valuable the option becomes.

Outside bankruptcy, this option is constrained by the senior creditor's right (also an option) to demand an immediate liquidation in the event of default. The senior creditor has the right to capture the value it can recover in a foreclosure sale. Thus, a default on senior debt accelerates the maturity of junior investors' options. Of course, if the senior creditor wants to keep the firm alive – to recover something more than foreclosure value – it must negotiate with junior creditors, who otherwise have the option to obtain and enforce judgment liens.[8]

The problem is that such bargaining is, with large enterprises,[9] often impossible. A firm might have thousands of creditors (some identifiable and some not) with different (and unknown) incentives with regard to the future of the firm. Moreover, their incentives to maximize their individual returns create a classic common pool where creditors fail to coordinate action, race to the assets, and destroy the value of the estate for all stakeholders.

Bankruptcy law is intended to solve this problem by forcing creditors to forebear their rights and enter a collective bargaining process. The driving theory behind all of this is that bankruptcy should be "designed to mirror the agreement one would expect the creditors to form among themselves were they to negotiate such an agreement from an *ex ante* position."[10] And – somewhat obviously – that hypothetical ex ante agreement cannot be known with certainty but it is assumed to be the one that maximizes collective value for all stakeholders.

This raises a key point: In the absence of bankruptcy law, the fate of a firm after default would depend on the ex-ante agreements the senior and junior creditors have negotiated and their ex post decisions with regard to enforcing those agreements. But we don't know what rights the creditors would have bargained for in such a world. And even if senior creditors had bargained for the right—on paper—to accelerate the loan and liquidate the firm's assets, whether they would exercise that option would depend on further negotiations with other creditors. Put differently, we can read and re-read acceleration clauses into eternity and still have no clue how creditors would respond to the firm's default in a world that has no bankruptcy rules and no bargaining costs because we don't live in that world.[11] In a world with bankruptcy, the terms of existing lending contracts are not only uninformative, but may even be socially inefficient.[12]

Because the terms of existing contracts tell us little if anything about negotiations (efficient or otherwise) in a world without the current bankruptcy code, it is surprising that some scholars, including Adler and Triantis, as expressed in the Editor's Notes at the end of this chapter, implicitly assume that *no* negotiation would occur and contracts (as they are written today) would be enforced mechanically according to their terms. What's the sense in that? This amounts to assuming away the very problem that bankruptcy law is trying to solve. Bankruptcy law should construct (or get as close as possible to) the counterfactual bargain that would have been struck by creditors in a world of complete contracts and no transaction costs – the bargain that maximizes the value of the estate as a whole and minimizes costs of credit ex ante. Even Adler and Triantis agree with this proposition. Yet their assumption runs contrary to the fundamental point. For example, non-bankruptcy liquidation values are often much lower than the value that can be recovered through a going concern sale in bankruptcy. That is precisely why many senior creditors cooperate with or push for a bankruptcy filing in order to achieve a free-and-clear sale rather than exercising their foreclosure rights outside of bankruptcy.[13] Why, then, should we assume that those same creditors would bargain for a right to accelerate their loans in bankruptcy even if doing so destroys estate value?

A simple example can demonstrate the point. Imagine the debtor has two assets, A & B. Secured Creditor A is owed $100 and has a security interest in asset A. Secured Creditor B is owed $100 and has an interest in asset B. Debtor also has several unsecured creditors. Assets A and B can be sold in a foreclosure sale for $50 each, but the firm can be sold in bankruptcy for $210. What are Secured Creditor A's contractual rights outside of bankruptcy? The only thing the contractual acceleration and foreclosure rights tell us is that Secured Creditor A can foreclose and get $50.

But to answer the priority question we want to know what to do with the additional $110 in surplus that is created by the bankruptcy process. And, herein, lies the circularity problem with the entire priority debate. Bankruptcy is a non-contractual process by which creditors forbear on their enforcement rights, *force* others to do the same, and facilitate a sale or reorganization that increases their recovery. Bankruptcy law, in other words, is implementing a "hypothetical bargain" that we might observe in a counterfactual universe with complete contracts and no transaction costs. Conventional theories tell us that such a hypothetical bargain will be the one that maximizes the surplus value of the whole estate. But what does that bargain look like?

Nothing in existing debt contracts answers that question. These contracts already assume the existence of a bankruptcy law that imposes a mandatory bargain that may or may not be the optimal one.[14] Thus, it is a non-sequitur to argue that, simply because debt contracts contain acceleration clauses, any value created by bankruptcy belongs to the senior creditors, or that the junior creditors' options expire with the bankruptcy filing. Senior loan agreements may indeed *say* these very things, but these agreements were drafted with the full knowledge that these very things will *never* happen if a bankruptcy filing occurs. More fundamentally, we have *no way* to know whether the counterfactual world with complete contracts and no transaction costs would implement the bargain described in the debt contracts that we observe in a world with incomplete contracts and high transaction costs.

Of course, the opposite claim is also fallacious. There is no theoretical principle that tells us, as Jacoby and Janger suggest, that the going concern value of a firm belongs to the junior creditors. Indeed, our central point in this chapter is that the value does not *belong* to anyone and any attempt to *correctly allocate* it is a fool's errand. Instead, we focus on designing the most efficient reorganization system with whatever priority scheme happens to go along with it.[15] In a sense, we are calling for a return to the first principles of the creditors-bargain theory. The priority rule that the parties would have bargained for is the rule that maximizes the value of reorganization for the estate, and the parties are "entitled" to whatever such a rule would provide them.[16]

1.2 What Happens to Options in Bankruptcy?

As noted, inside bankruptcy, contractual terms are replaced by a mandatory process. In practice, this process forces parties to lobby the judge to protect their options. The lobbying is intense, and is the source of substantial deadweight loss, because the bankruptcy code contains many rules that undermine or destroy investors' options outside bankruptcy.

Some of these rules have attracted attention. Scholars and policymakers have focused recently on the effects of the APR, which treats the bankruptcy filing as a common expiration date for all options. This tends to benefit senior lenders: If the present value of the firm's future cash flows (as measured in a sale or by a judge in a reorganization) is less than the value of the senior claims, they receive that present value. Junior interests are wiped out. If the firm's value increases in the future, even if it increases sufficiently to repay the senior debt in full, the senior lenders keep the entire firm value. This occurs because the APR forces a valuation of the firm at the filing date;[17] subsequent volatility in firm value is irrelevant. Contrast this with what happens outside bankruptcy. There, senior lenders face asymmetric claims on the firm: When firm cash flows are low (lower than debt service), senior lenders capture all flows. But when cash flows are high (higher than debt service), senior lenders share these flows with junior investors. That asymmetry (sharing the highs, but capturing the lows) is replaced with a symmetry in bankruptcy (capturing the highs and the lows), which benefits the senior lenders, induces costly strategic behavior by all creditors, and has prompted various reform proposals.[18]

But this is only one of many ways that the bankruptcy code rewrites options. For example, secured creditors hold an implicit real option in the event of default, allowing them to choose between immediate recovery (via market-based liquidation of collateral) or postponed realization (via debt restructuring).[19] Many scholars have noted that this option is *devalued* by the code's "adequate protection" rules, which systematically undercompensate secured creditors for the delay in payment caused by lengthy bankruptcy proceedings.[20] The option is further devalued by the judge's role (and potential error) in computing the amount of compensation payable to secured creditors as "adequate protection."

Less obviously, the option can be *destroyed* (not merely devalued) by the interplay of bankruptcy's automatic stay, which prevents immediate liquidation, and bankruptcy's lien-stripping rules, which force the creditor to accept payment equal to the current, judicially-appraised value of the collateral. To see this, begin with the fundamental rule for valuing the claims of a secured creditor: The creditor has a secured claim equal to the lesser of (a) the judge-determined value of the collateral and (b) the debt owed to the creditor.[21] This is called "lien stripping" because the creditor's lien is reduced to the current value of the collateral if the total debt exceeds the collateral value. When lien stripping occurs, the creditor receives an unsecured claim equal to the deficiency.

This process makes sense if the judicial valuation is derived from an auction of the collateral.[22] The process makes less sense if the collateral will be retained pursuant to a plan of reorganization. In that case, the judge must first estimate the collateral's value. Then the secured creditor will receive either cash or a lien plus a promise of future payments equal to the collateral's judicially determined value. This promise of future payment—where a new lien is crammed down on the creditors—destroys option value. Indeed, the promise of payment is often worth less—sometimes far less—than the present value of the collateral. This is true even if the judge's estimate is perfectly accurate in the sense that it pinpoints the collateral's present value.[23]

To illustrate, assume Debtor enters bankruptcy with $1,000 of unsecured debt and $150 of secured debt. Secured creditor has a lien on a key asset (perhaps the debtor's only asset) with uncertain value. There is an equal chance that the asset will be worth $140 or $60 in the future. If it were sold at auction, the asset would likely fetch its present value of $100. But Debtor plans to retain the asset pursuant to a plan of reorganization, and it is the judge's job—not the market's—to value the asset. Debtor proposes, and the judge confirms, a reorganization plan that promises to pay the secured creditor $100 over time.[24] Secured creditor also gets an unsecured deficiency claim, worth $50, but this claim has an expected value near zero because it is severely diluted by the $1,000 owed to unsecured creditors.[25]

Debtor's promise to pay the $100 is, of course, not really worth $100. The promise is risky. Suppose Debtor will honor this promise only if, post-bankruptcy, the value of the asset is revealed to be $140. If the value of the asset turns out to be only $60, Debtor will default with certainty. Assume that, if this happens, the asset is sold at foreclosure and that secured creditor's deficiency claim ($40) is worthless.

Under these assumptions, even if the judge appraises the collateral at $100, the expected value of Debtor's promise is only $80. If the collateral rises in value to $140, Debtor will pay only $100 to secured creditor (plus a trivial recovery on account of its deficiency claim). If the collateral falls in value to \$60, secured creditor receives that amount from the foreclosure sale. Because these outcomes—\$100 and \$60—occur with equal probability, secured creditor's expected recovery is \$80. Thus, a combination of lien stripping and the ability to cram the new lien down on the lender forces secured claimants to receive less than the market value of the collateral. If lien stripping were forbidden, the secured creditor in our hypothetical would receive \$140 when the asset rises in value and \$60 when it falls. The expected recovery would be \$100, the same amount that the creditor expects from an immediate auction of the collateral.

The key problem, of course, is that the judge in our hypothetical is not discounting the promised future payments at a rate that reflects the risk of default. Under existing law, a secured creditor can demand an interest rate that compensates for this risk. But what interest rate would offer sufficient compensation? The rate must ensure that the present value of Debtor's future payments is equal to the current value of the collateral (\$100). There are two potential outcomes in our case. One is that Debtor defaults and Secured Creditor forecloses, recovering \$60. The present value of that recovery is \$30. Nothing can be done to increase the foreclosure recovery. The other, equally likely outcome is that Debtor honors its promise. How large should that promise be in order to ensure that Secured Creditor receives \$100 in present value? The answer is \$140. The present value of that promise—honored half of the time—is \$70. If we sum the creditor's expected recoveries in both potential outcomes (\$30 + \$70), we obtain a net present value equal to \$100. If the time for repayment is one year, this implies that the appropriate interest rate is 40%. As long as Debtor promises to pay \$100 plus 40% interest, Secured Creditor will receive deferred cash payments with a present value equal to the current value of the collateral (\$100).

The appropriate interest rate is therefore a rate that *reverses* lien stripping.[26] At a 40% interest rate, Secured Creditor is capturing the full future appreciation in collateral value. This undoes the effects of lien stripping and provides the creditor with a lien that is at or above the level of the original lien. Thus, any bankruptcy code that is committed to the notion of lien stripping is also a regime that systematically destroys the secured creditor's non-bankruptcy option to exercise foreclosure rights immediately and capture the full present value of the collateral.[27] This destruction is costly not only to the secured creditor, but can be inefficient as well because it diverts value to junior classes.[28] Although this redistribution occurs *ex post* (during a bankruptcy), it will distort *ex ante* capital structure decisions of borrowing corporations. As secured debt becomes more expensive in response to the possibility of *ex post* redistribution, some firms may find themselves unable to borrow (or borrow as much) on a secured basis. If secured debt has efficiency properties, as many scholars hypothesize, these distortions almost certainly bring costs.[29]

2. TRADING OFF OPTIONS IN BANKRUPTCY

The point of the foregoing discussion is to illustrate how the bankruptcy code implicitly re-allocates option value between junior and senior investors. In our view, any effort to protect junior investor options necessarily entails a reduction in protection for senior investor options, and any effort to protect senior investors will reduce the protection for junior investors. This trade-off is inherent in the nature of bankruptcy. A system that alters non-bankruptcy rights to preserve value will, by definition, alter the rights and options of the various stakeholders. To select one option for protection, as much of the literature does, is to ignore the various other options and the dynamic interplay between them all.

One reaction to this trade-off is to ignore it, or at least be unconcerned about *ex post* reallocations of rights unless they create deadweight costs. It's not necessarily problematic that the bankruptcy process causes a significant reallocation of value between junior and senior investors because the parties can take steps *ex ante* to protect themselves. Junior investors can demand a higher rate of return as compensation for any *ex post* diversion of value to senior investors (and vice versa). The parties can also design capital structures that minimize the need for bankruptcy and the extent of value diversion *ex post*.[30]

Under this view, the only ex-post reallocations that matter are those that generate value destruction. Critics of the APR see the rule as just such a source of value destruction. The rule announces a common expiration date for all options and directs the bankruptcy judge to value the firm. Because everything hinges on the judicial valuation, the parties jockey to avoid or exploit valuation variance. In some cases, we get fire sales, induced by senior creditors seeking to avoid variance in judicial valuations. In others, we get inefficiently drawn-out reorganizations, induced by junior stakeholders seeking to exploit that variance. When scholars and policymakers advocate a "relative priority" regime, they are arguing for a regime that allocates options in a way that may reduce the risk of fire sales and drawn-out reorganizations.

In our view, this is only an indirect way to avoid fire sales and inefficient reorganizations. It seems better, we think, to focus on the root problem: *The bankruptcy process is run by judges.* If asset sales were timed to avoid fire sales, if secured creditors were compensated fully for delay, and if asset valuations were unbiased and had low (or no) variance, we wouldn't care about what the bankruptcy process does to the parties' nonbankruptcy options. But assets can fetch fire sale prices when judges are convinced to conduct premature sales. And secured creditors can be undercompensated for delay when judges make errors in computing adequate protection. And, of course, judicial valuations are error-prone and volatile. But if we had an automatic system, that minimized judicial involvement, many of these problems would go away. Senior and junior investors would be cashed out of their positions at market values. If doing so destroys option value, the parties would make *ex ante* adjustments to their contracts. The key is not the preservation of the rights of the stakeholders. The key is the preservation of the value of the estate. These intuitions—that it is impossible (and unnecessary) to protect all options in bankruptcy and that fire sales and valuation are problems *only* when judges run the process—motivate the following proposal for an automatic process that minimizes judicial involvement.[31]

3. AN AUTOMATIC PROCESS

We propose a restructuring process in which parties can elect *ex post* between a regime of relative priority and one of absolute priority. Bankruptcy judges are involved only if the parties invoke the absolute priority regime. The threat of a judicial valuation, if it is indeed a threat, can induce the parties to restructure the firm via a relative priority regime with minimal (or no) judicial oversight. Although we cannot identify the optimal "hypothetical bargain" that would have been struck by creditors and the debtor in a world with complete contracts and no transaction costs, our proposal creates a process that allows the parties to negotiate toward an optimal bargain while minimizing the costs (including errors) of the judicial process.

Under our proposal, the firm's senior creditors hold the option to restructure the firm's debt at any time after a contractually-defined default.[32] If the restructuring option is exercised, the firm must be sold as a going concern immediately, as described below. If the option is not exercised, ordinary bankruptcy rules apply but the firm cannot be sold in bankruptcy: The debtor is either reorganized or liquidated piecemeal.[33] Thus, our proposal can be seen as a supplement to traditional bankruptcy law. It provides a new process for the going-concern sale procedures ("363 Sales") that have evolved over the last two decades, but otherwise leaves bankruptcy law unchanged.

If the restructuring option is exercised, the senior lenders choose between two types of going-concern sales:[34] (i) a sale subject to warrants, or (ii) a sale subject to appraisal. The first type pays junior investors in full or distributes warrants allowing them to capture future appreciation in the sold-off firm's assets ("sale subject to warrants"). There is little need for judicial oversight of this type of sale process, though it would not be problematic to allow for high-level judicial oversight of the bidding procedures. The problems generated by judicial error arise not from procedural oversight, but rather from substantive decision-making. Our proposal eliminates the latter.

The other type of sale—"sale subject to appraisal"—is a process in which the buyer takes the assets free and clear of investors' claims, but the proceeds are distributed to senior and junior investors after a judicial appraisal hearing. The hearing would be similar to that used in conventional sale-of-control cases outside of bankruptcy. If the sale price is lower than the appraised going-concern value, senior investors must compensate juniors for the loss. A judge is therefore involved in the appraisal hearing, not the sale (though, once again, there could be a high-level role for hearing objections to egregious sale procedures).

By placing the restructuring option in the hands of senior lenders, our proposal not only preserves their non-bankruptcy option to liquidate or offer forbearance, but permits restructuring in advance of the kind of financial meltdown that often precedes a bankruptcy filing. Although senior lenders retain their non-bankruptcy option to accelerate the indebtedness, the payoffs from exercising that restructuring option—a sale subject to warrants or a sale subject to appraisal—are designed to reduce the risk of fire sales that harm junior investors.

Suppose, for example, that senior lenders are considering whether to exercise the restructuring option. If they opt for a sale subject to warrants, the price paid by the buyer will be discounted by the value of those warrants. Senior investors, in other words, must pay a premium to engage in a fire sale. They give up their absolute priority rights and transfer the option value to the junior creditors in the form of warrants. This translates to a reduction in the price that a buyer is willing to pay. Because the juniors are retaining their option value and thus getting the same as they would under a full reorganization, the senior creditors bear the full cost of a fire sale. Every dollar of discount in the value of the firm relative to a full reorganization is borne by the senior creditors, forcing them to internalize fully the cost of the sale.[35]

Alternatively, senior investors can opt for a sale subject to appraisal. This preserves absolute priority. Here too, however, senior creditors can expect to pay compensation to juniors if the judge determines that the sale price was below the going-concern value of the firm. Because seniors must compensate juniors after the fact, it will be unattractive to exercise the restructuring option when it exposes the firm to a fire sale.

If the sale is subject to warrants, these securities should entitle junior investors to buy the firm's assets at a price equal to the value of the senior investors' claims, regardless of the purchase price. The warrants would have a long duration, perhaps five or ten years or perhaps they could be perpetual. This effectively preserves the junior investors' non-bankruptcy call option. If the sale price is below the seniors' claim, the buyer captures any appreciation up to the value of the seniors' claim. Further appreciation can be enjoyed by the buyer only after buying the juniors' warrants. In this way, the warrants permit a two-step sale: When the seniors exercise their restructuring option, the firm is sold subject to warrants (step 1). Later, the buyer can obtain full ownership of the firm by buying the juniors' warrants (step 2).

Of course, some may argue that the warrants create a governance problem. The firm is sold to a new owner who has control but does not hold the rights to residual value of the firm. This introduces agency costs where ownership and control are separated.[36] It is likely that this problem will loom large for some companies, but not others. The more out-of-the-money the warrants are, the less the buyer should care that the warrants exist, especially if the volatility of asset value is low.

But the appraisal option addresses this problem. When agency costs are expected to be large, senior lenders will be more likely to favor a sale subject to appraisal. This choice places a cap on the costs that the warrants can impose. If the agency costs exceed the cost of appraisal, they won't be incurred.

On the other side of the equation, our proposal mitigates key problems under current law—appraisal variance and junior creditors taking advantage of judicial error. Because senior lenders choose which cases go to appraisal, the choice to invoke the procedure is taken out of the hands of those who have the incentive to exploit judicial error. And because the senior lender has the option to skip appraisal by using warrants, we place a ceiling on the harm caused by judicial error and valuation variance. When error is likely or when judicial valuation is expected to have high variance, the senior creditors will opt for a sale subject to warrants.

One might object that where the warrants introduce high costs and variance from judicial error is high, the senior lenders will find themselves stuck between a rock and a hard place. A sale subject to warrants is costly, but a sale subject to appraisal is vulnerable to judicial error. This dilemma may induce senior lenders to opt for a traditional reorganization rather than a sale. That is true. But it may be a good thing. Cases where assets are so volatile that out-of-the-money warrants might actually pay out (otherwise a buyer wouldn't care) *and* where a judge's valuation is expected to have high variance are also the cases most likely to result in a fire sale if the assets are sold off. The value of those firms, both to the market and to judges is highly uncertain or highly volatile. The higher the volatility of an asset, the more likely a senior creditor will want to sell cheap and reduce its risk at the cost of the junior creditors. Put another way, when a senior creditor is particularly worried that both the market and the judge think that the firm is likely to be worth more than the senior debt, there may be good reason to think that the firm is in fact likely to be worth more than the senior debt.

In all of this it should be noted that a sale without appraisal requires the senior creditor to forgo its APR rights. This is likely a significant cost to the creditor. But it is the price that a creditor would pay to avoid judicial valuation. In that way, it places an outer-bound on the distortions that can be imposed by valuation. Thus, our proposal both reduces the variance of judicial involvement by permitting an after-the-fact appraisal hearing and gives creditors an escape valve for cases where that variance remains significant. The senior creditor then gets to choose the lesser of the evils that are necessary to avoid fire sales.

Our "automatic procedure" resembles Adler's "chameleon equity" proposal (and "bail-in," more generally) because a restructuring occurs without judicial intervention. It also resembles the proposals of Casey as well as Jacoby and Janger because the senior investors must compensate juniors for fire sales. Our procedure differs from prior proposals because it puts decision-making authority in the hands of senior investors. Whereas most prior work advocates limiting the power of senior lenders, ours would increase it in order to leverage the informational advantages of senior investors. Additionally, unlike prior proposals, ours integrates an out-of-court procedure (sale subject to warrants) with a judicial appraisal (sale subject to appraisal). The judicial appraisal, which is central to the Jacoby and Janger proposal, is invoked here to function as a threat-point for the out-of-court restructuring.[37]

NOTES

* University of Chicago and Columbia University. We thank Barry Adler and Richard Squire for their help. We are grateful for generous financial support from the Richard Weil Faculty Research Fund and The Paul H. Leffmann Fund (Casey) and the Charles Evans Gerber Transactional Studies Program Fund (Morrison).

1. Fischer Black & Myron Scholes, *The Pricing of Options and Corporate Liabilities*, 81 J. Pol. Econ. 637 (1973); Robert C. Merton, *On the Pricing of Corporate Debt: The Risk Structure of Interest Rates*, 29 J.Fin. 449 (1974).
2. Bo Huang, *Absolute Priority Rule and Option Theory* (2011) http://papers.ssrn.com/sol3/papers.cfm?abstract_id=1930404.
3. Following convention, for most of this article we refer to equity and other classes of junior creditors interchangeably.
4. *See, e.g.*, Douglas G. Baird and Edward R. Morrison, *Bankruptcy Decision Making*, 17

J. L. Econ. & Org. 356 (2001) (modeling the decision-making of the bankruptcy judge using real-options theory).

5. Senior and junior creditors can change the value of these bankruptcy options by filing sale motions (speeding up the case, thereby reducing option value) or demanding judicial valuation prior to cramdown (slowing down the case, increasing option value). Anthony J. Casey, *The Creditors' Bargain and Option Preservation Priority in Chapter 11*, 78 U.Chi. L. Rev. 759 (2011). Incentives to engage in such strategic behavior will depend on the expected volatility in asset values during the reorganization period and the variance inherent in the judicial valuation of the firm's assets ("appraisal variance"). Douglas G. Baird & Donald S. Bernstein, *Absolute Priority, Valuation Uncertainty, and the Reorganization Bargain*, 115 Yale L. J. 1930, 1937 (2006).
6. *See* Douglas G. Baird and Donald S. Bernstein, *Absolute Priority, Valuation Uncertainty, and the Reorganization Bargain*, 115 Yale L. J. 1930 (2006); Casey *supra* note 5; Melissa Jacoby and Edward Janger, *Ice Cube Bonds: Allocating the Price of Process in Chapter 11 Bankruptcy*, 123 Yale L. J. 862 (2013); American Bankruptcy Institute Commission to Study the Reform of Chapter 11, Final Report and Recommendations (2015) (hereinafter, "ABI Commission Report").
7. For a lucid exploration of how a relative priority regime would work, *see* Douglas G. Baird, *Bankruptcy's Lost Paradigm*, working paper (2015).
8. Casey, *supra* note 5, at 775–7.
9. It is sometimes possible with smaller enterprises, as discussed in Edward R. Morrison, *Bargaining around Bankruptcy: Small Business Distress and State Law*, 38 J. Legal Stud. 255 (2009).
10. *See* Thomas H. Jackson, *Bankruptcy, Non-bankruptcy Entitlements, and the Creditors' Bargain*, 91 Yale L. J. 857, 860 (1982).
11. The range of potential post-default outcomes is vast (as most recently noted by Baird). Douglas G. Baird, *The Rights of Secured Creditors After Rescap*, 2015 Univ. Ill. L. Rev. 849, 853.
12. *See, e.g.*, Kenneth M. Ayotte, "On the Mandatory Stay of Secured Creditors in Bankruptcy," working paper (2016)
13. This concept is discussed more fully in Casey *supra* note 5, at 770–78.
14. And, under plausible assumptions, is likely to be suboptimal. *See* Ayotte, *supra* note 12.
15. The claim on the going concern value that is preserved though the bankruptcy process is highly controversial. Some believe that the senior creditor's lien on the firm covers going concern value. Barry E. Adler and Ian Ayres, *A Dilution Mechanism for Valuing Corporations in Bankruptcy*, 111 Yale L. J. 83 (2001). Others argue that the going concern value belongs to the junior creditors. Jacoby & Janger, *supra* note 6. In reality, there is nothing about the non-bankruptcy relationship between debtors and creditors that tells us anything about who is entitled to going concern value. Casey *supra* note 5. The most we can say with certainty is that it belongs to whomever the bankruptcy code says it belongs to. Similarly, those who claim that the parties have agreed that the junior creditor's option expires upon the filing of bankruptcy have conflated bankruptcy's mandatory rules with the rights for which the parties have bargained. *Id.* at 766. Under the APR, bankruptcy terminates the junior creditor's option. But the relevant question is whether or not the APR *should* do that. It is not a sufficient response to say that bankruptcy should terminate the option because bankruptcy terminates the option.
16. Any objection that any single creditor is being underpaid, of course, goes away with the well-rehearsed point that such a creditor can adjust its ex ante interest rate. See Alan Schwartz, *Security Interests and Bankruptcy Priorities: A Review of Current Theories,* 10 J. Legal. Stud. 1, 7–9 (1981); Thomas H. Jackson and Anthony J. Kronman, *Secured Financing and Priorities among Creditors,* 88 Yale L. J. 1143 (1979). Nonadjusting creditors are another matter that do not fit well into the creditors' bargain and may justify a special carve out. But such creditors play a much smaller role in major corporate reorganizations and are beyond the scope of this chapter.
17. In practice, though, valuation more often occurs at the confirmation date. On this

dissonance between doctrine and practice, see Douglas G. Baird, *The Rights of Secured Creditors after* Rescap, 2015 Ill. L. Rev. 849 (2015).

18. See, e.g., the ABI Commission Report. Scholars have advocated mechanisms for protecting junior investors against the risk of judicial error in asset sales and in firm valuation during the plan confirmation process. *See* Casey, *supra* note 5 (on the former); Jacoby & Janger, *supra* note 6 (on the former); and Baird & Bernstein, *supra* note 5 (on the latter).
19. Robert K. Rasmussen, *Secured Credit, Control Rights, and Options*, 25 Cardozo L. Rev. 1935, 1941–50 (2004).
20. *See*, e.g., Douglas Baird, *The Rights of Secured Creditors after* ResCap, 2015 U. Ill. L. Rev. 849 (2015).
21. Section 506(a) requires a judicial valuation: a creditor has a secured claim "to the extent of the value of such creditor's interest in the estate's interest" in the collateral.
22. When collateral is sold for cash at a well-conducted foreclosure or bankruptcy sale, the lender receives a market estimate of the present value of that collateral. Assuming an efficient market, the lender should be indifferent between a sale now and a sale in the future.
23. This is not a problem if the reorganization plan will pay secured claims in cash in full at confirmation; in that case, the creditor can invest the proceeds and capture appreciation in the investment.
24. We are putting aside collateral valuation error, which generates the strategic behavior studied by Adler. Barry E. Adler, *Creditor Rights After Johnson and Dewsnup*, 10 Bankr. Dev. J. 1, 3–9 (1993/1994).
25. Here we are assuming a Debtor that resembles the typical firm we see in Chapter 11: Highly insolvent, with trivial expected recoveries to unsecured creditors even in the best scenarios. The problems we document can disappear if the reorganization plan gives Secured Creditor a continuing claim against the firm on account of its deficiency claim, and if the payoff to this continuing claim is sufficiently high in good states of the world that Secured Creditor is compensated for the losses it faces in bad states. Our understanding is that these happy conditions rarely obtain, and indeed that senior creditors don't always benefit from happy conditions (a plan can cash out the deficiency claim for a small sum while giving equity to other unsecured creditors).
26. In some cases, the interest rate would even raise the lien to a level higher than it was before it was stripped. In practice, it is difficult to know whether a judge would apply a discount rate that has this effect on lien stripping. As a matter of doctrine, the caselaw instruct courts to apply a discount rate that includes an appropriate "risk adjustment" or, if possible, to apply a rate that would be applied in market settings. *See*, e.g., *Till v. SCS Credit Corp.*, 541 U.S. 465, 479 (2004) (a Chapter 13 case); *In re Gramercy Twins Assoc.*, 187 B.R. 112, 123–4 (Bankr. SDNY 1995) (Chapter 11 case); *In re American HomePatient, Inc.*, 420 F.3d 559, 568 (6th Cir. 2005). But it seems unlikely that the risk adjustment will be sufficient to compensate secured creditors for the risk of default. Not only is the adjustment complex and controversial, but it appears that many courts favor an adjustment equal between one and three percent (above the prime rate). Gary W. Marsh & Matthew M. Weiss, *Chapter 11 Interest Rates After Till*, 84 Am. Bankr. L.J. 209, 231 (2010). This will be undercompensatory in many cases. *See*, e.g., *Till*, *supra*, at 488 ("The dissent might be correct that the use of the prime rate, even with a small risk adjustment, 'will systematically undercompensate secured creditors for the true risks of default.' . . . This systematic undercompensation might seem problematic as a matter of policy. But, it raises no problem as a matter of statutory interpretation. Thus, although there is always some risk of nonpayment when A promises to repay a debt to B through a stream of payments over time rather than through an immediate lump-sum payment, § 1325(a)(5)(B)(ii) does not take this risk into account.").
27. We can take steps to protect senior creditors' options. One is the §1111(b) election, which allows the creditor to give up its unsecured deficiency claim in exchange for a secured claim that is equal to the value of the collateral but supported by a lien equal to the

original indebtedness. Even though the §1111(b) election increases the value of the creditor's lien it does not increase the real value of the payments required in a cramdown. This is useful to a creditor only if the debtor defaults when the value of the collateral has *appreciated*. Then the creditor can use the lien to capture that appreciation. But the risk of default will be relatively low when collateral appreciates. The real danger to a secured creditor is a default when collateral values have depreciated, and the §1111(b) election does nothing to address that danger.

28. The inefficiency might be justified by other policies, such as preservation of viable going-concerns. That policy could be invoked in situations in which multiple lenders have liens against a single asset. These situations arise, for example, when a secured loan has been securitized: multiple investors will have claims (with the same or differing priority) against a single asset. Unless the intercreditor agreement has a collective action clause or other device for creditor cooperation, a distressed debtor will face high or prohibitive costs to negotiate a modification. Cramdown could have positive efficiency effects in these multi-creditor situations. When a lien has been securitized, bankruptcy law may be needed to solve the collective action problem that arises from competition across multiple creditors. Some kind of agreement must be imposed on the creditors. Cramdown can be seen as a simple solution with low administrative cost. In many situations, however, there are only one or two liens against a piece of collateral and the costs of negotiation are low. In these situations, the inefficiency of lien stripping is high.

29. Suppose, for example, that secured debt serves as a commitment device for financially weak firms that cannot otherwise convince investors to commit capital (e.g., by issuing unsecured debt with financial covenants). The secured debt protects the lender against the risk that the borrower will subsequently engage in conduct that reduces the lender's expected payment ("dilution"). *See* Alan Schwartz, *Priority Contracts and Priority in Bankruptcy*, 82 Cornell L. Rev. 1396 (1997), for a model along these lines. Lien stripping and cramdown, working in tandem, weaken the ability of secured debt to serve as a commitment device because they expose secured creditors to "dilution" in bankruptcy. In response, secured lenders may increase the price of secured credit. Assuming borrowing firms know how likely they are to enter bankruptcy, but secured lenders cannot verify this, "low-risk" firms will face a price of secured credit that is too high relative to their risk level. Facing such a high price, these firms may not make productive investments. That is inefficient. The inefficiency could be even more severe in equilibrium. As low-risk firms drop out of the market, secured lenders will see a riskier set of borrowers and therefore further increase the price of secured credit. A lemons equilibrium could arise. Alternatively, a rationing equilibrium could result, with secured lenders offering a low price but randomly loaning to only a subset of borrowers. At such a low price, the applicant borrowers will include a mix of low-risk and high-risk types. Randomly choosing from this group may be more profitable than charging a high rate to only the high-risk types. *See* Joseph E. Stiglitz & Andrew Weiss, *Credit Rationing in Markets with Imperfect Information*, 71 Am. Econ. Rev. 393 (1981).

30. This is really just a restatement of the Modigliani-Miller Theorem. Franco Modigliani and Merton H. Miller, *The Cost of Capital, Corporation Finance and the Theory of Investment*, 48 Am Econ Rev 261, 268–71 (1958); *see also* Casey, *supra* note 5, at 778–89 (exploring arguments why the Modigliani-Miller Theorem may or may not hold in this context).

31. We are, of course, not the first to advocate a system that minimizes the role of the judge. *See, e.g.*, Douglas G. Baird, *The Uneasy Case for Corporate Reorganizations*, 15 J. Legal Stud. 127 (1986) and Lucian A. Bebchuk, *A New Approach to Corporate Reorganizations*, 101 Harv. L. Rev. 775 (1988). Our proposal departs from prior proposals like these because it envisions a process that commences *before* bankruptcy.

32. We acknowledge that such a proposal would require either a change to state law (likely through Article 9 of the UCC) or a much broader scope for the bankruptcy code.

33. The senior creditor could respond to a filing by exercising its restructuring option within a certain time frame. That way, the debtor cannot threaten to use liquidation as a means to thwart a going concern sale.

34. If a piecemeal liquidation is thought optimal, the firm should be liquidated in a Chapter 7 or a traditional foreclosure proceeding, which our proposal would retain.
35. *See* Casey, *supra* note 5 (modeling out the creditors incentives in a fire sale subject to warrants).
36. *See* Casey, *supra* note 5, at 805 (discussing the possible agency costs introduced by granting non-expiring options to junior investors).
37. One other feature that many have highlighted in the Jacoby and Janger proposal is the requirement that the senior creditors post a bond. This bond is, in our view, of little consequence because senior creditors are unlikely to be judgment proof even without the bonds.

EDITOR'S NOTES

Professors Casey and Morrison refer to work by Adler and Triantis that disagrees with their approach to options in bankruptcy. Our point is that the debtor and its lenders have good reason to, and in fact often do, agree that the commencement of the debtor's bankruptcy case is both a default and, thus, the date of maturity (expiration) for the debtor's option. In the absence of externalities, there is no reason to interfere with the freedom to contract and investors should be permitted to demand whatever rights against a debtor they choose as a condition of their investment. We are sanguine, despite the Casey-Morrison misgivings, that current capital structures provide reliable indication of sound financial judgment by investors collectively and debtors who so limit the exercise of junior options.

Readers desirous of an elaboration are referred to Barry E. Adler and George G. Triantis, *Debt Priority and Options in Bankruptcy: A Policy Intervention*, 91 Am. Bankr. L.J. (2017). That article includes an extensive discussion of the debate described in this chapter.

10. The treatment of secured credit in bankruptcy: a unified model

Michelle J. White

Secured credit is a loan in which the creditor has the right to claim some specific property—the collateral—if the debtor defaults on the loan. Collateral can take the form of real property, personal property, inventory, or accounts receivable. Unsecured credit, in contrast, is a loan in which the creditor has a claim to be repaid, but no right to claim any specific property. Secured loans are safer than unsecured loans for creditors, because the right to claim and sell the collateral when borrowers default assures creditors of a minimum return equal to the value of the collateral minus transactions costs. Secured loans make unsecured loans riskier because the latter are repaid only if the defaulting firm has assets remaining after secured creditors take their collateral. However, a bankruptcy filing may change secured creditors' rights. If the debtor firm liquidates in bankruptcy, secured creditors' rights are respected and they are allowed to claim their collateral. But if the firm files to reorganize in bankruptcy under Chapter 11, secured creditors lose their right to claim their collateral. This is to prevent them from shutting the firm down, allowing managers an opportunity to save the firm by reorganizing it.[1]

In this chapter, I re-examine the general question of how secured credit affects economic efficiency and the specific question of how strongly secured creditors' claims should be protected in bankruptcy. The issue of whether secured credit increases efficiency has generated a substantial literature in law and economics, including several proposals for reform of bankruptcy law. But it has not generated a consensus answer. Economists agree that the rules for use of secured credit and the rules of bankruptcy priority should be constructed so as to maximize economic efficiency, which we can think of as choosing rules that maximize the size of the pie regardless of how it is divided among claimants. Thus, secured credit is economically efficient if it increases the value of firms in bankruptcy (a larger pie) and, if so, then secured creditors' high priority should be respected in bankruptcy. But if secured credit reduces the value of firms in bankruptcy (a smaller pie) while increasing secured creditors' return (a larger slice of the pie for these creditors), then it is economically inefficient. In this case, it is best to reduce the strength of secured creditors' position in bankruptcy.

An important part of the confusion concerning secured credit is that economic efficiency in the bankruptcy context has many dimensions and different authors focus on different aspects of the problem. Among the efficiency dimensions that are potentially affected by the use of secured credit are: (1) whether it reduces firms' total cost of borrowing net of transactions costs, (2) whether it affects managers' incentives to select only economically efficient investment projects, (3) whether it affects managers' incentives to shirk in managing their firms, (4) whether it affects creditors' incentive to race to the courthouse when they think the firm might default, which can lead to too many financially distressed firms shutting down, (5) whether it affects managers' incentives to reduce the external harm caused by firms' operations, (6) whether it affects managers' decisions to file for bankruptcy at the most economically efficient time, and (7) whether it affects the efficiency of bankruptcy screening, i.e., do firms that are economically inefficient liquidate in bankruptcy and firms that are economically efficient (despite their financial distress) get saved in bankruptcy?

What this essay does is to selectively survey the literature on secured credit and bankruptcy and then present a simple model that re-evaluates the various arguments in favor and against secured credit. I focus, in particular, on what I consider to be the most important economic function of bankruptcy law: saving financially distressed firms that are economically efficient and shutting down financially distressed firms that are economically inefficient. Firms are economically efficient despite their financial distress when the value of their assets is highest in its current use: these firms should continue operating either in bankruptcy reorganization or by remaining outside of bankruptcy. Firms are economically inefficient when the value of their assets is higher in some alternative use: these firms should be liquidated. Efficient screening of financially distressed firms in bankruptcy is important because when economically efficient firms shut down in bankruptcy, their going concern value is lost. And when economically inefficient firms are saved in bankruptcy, economic growth falls and new job creation slows because resources remain in outdated industries and obsolete technologies.[2]

My conclusions are mainly negative—no single treatment of secured creditors in bankruptcy always improves the efficiency of bankruptcy screening. Neither the existing treatment of secured creditors in bankruptcy nor the proposed reforms unambiguously improves the efficiency of bankruptcy screening. Instead, different treatments of secured credit have the effect of changing the proportions of firms that are inefficiently liquidated versus inefficiently saved.

I. SELECTIVE LITERATURE REVIEW

Consider how secured debt affects firms' total borrowing costs when they have a mixture of secured versus unsecured debt. An important paper on this topic was Schwartz (1981), who showed a neutrality result: that under certain conditions, how a firm's debt is divided between secured versus unsecured has no effect on firms' total cost of capital. Schwartz's article was written as an extension of the Modigliani-Miller (M-M) (1958) theorem, which holds that how a firm's capital is divided between debt versus equity has no effect on firms' total cost of capital. The two results mean that firms' decisions to finance themselves using debt versus equity or using secured versus unsecured debt are both independent of their operational decisions. The theorem requires a long menu of strong assumptions, including no corporate taxes, no transactions costs, no bankruptcy costs, competitive loan markets, risk-neutral lenders, and the fact that the firm raises a fixed total amount of capital from all sources. Schwartz's paper makes the same set of assumptions. Suppose that, initially, none of the firm's loans is secured. Now suppose some of the firm's loans become secured, but the total amount the firm borrows remains the same. The change makes the loans that become secured safer because secured creditors can claim their collateral if the firm defaults, but the remaining loans that are unsecured become riskier because the firm has fewer assets to repay these loans when default occurs. In response to the changes in risk, secured creditors lower their interest rate, while unsecured creditors raise their interest rate. Overall, these changes fully offset each other, since the reduction in the cost of the loans that become secured just equals the increase in the cost of the loans that remain unsecured. Thus, there is no change in the firm's total cost of capital.[3]

A problem with the Schwartz model is that secured debt is inefficient. This is because firms do not benefit from making some of their debt secured, because their total cost of capital remains the same. But Schwartz argued that using secured debt actually raises firms' cost of capital, since secured debt has higher transactions costs than unsecured debt due to the need to negotiate over the collateral and register (perfect) secured creditors' liens. This means that for use of secured debt to be economically efficient, it must generate some efficiency gain that offsets the increase in transactions costs. Schwartz hypothesized that use of secured credit might reduce the total cost of monitoring by creditors or increase the probability that managers choose efficient projects for their firms by reducing information asymmetries between managers and creditors. These hypotheses led other researchers to explore possible efficiency gains from use of secured credit.

Among these, Triantis (1992) presented a model in which the higher transactions cost of secured debt generates efficiency gains by reducing the cost of asymmetric information. In his model, managers choose between efficient/safe projects versus inefficient/risky projects. Some managers choose risky projects even though they are inefficient, because these projects benefit shareholders at the expense of creditors and creditors cannot determine at the time they make their loans which firms will choose which projects. Triantis showed that using secured credit allows firms to credibly signal that they will choose safe/efficient projects, since firms that choose safe projects make higher profit and are therefore better able to bear the higher cost of secured debt. Secured debt therefore allows loan markets to function more efficiently, since creditors can identify firms that choose safe/efficient projects and they reward these firms by charging lower interest rates.

Picker (1992) presents a model in which the benefit of using secured debt is that creditors' cost of monitoring the firm is lower. In his model, managers have an incentive to choose an inefficient/risky project over an efficient/safe project, so that creditors gain from monitoring that steers managers toward safe projects. Picker assumes that monitoring is sometimes a public good with spillover benefits, in which case it is efficient for only one creditor to monitor the firm. He presents several versions of his model. In one, all creditors are unsecured and, in equilibrium, all of them choose to monitor the firm and total transactions costs are high. In a second version, all creditors are secured and each can monitor only its own collateral, so that monitoring has no spillover benefits. In equilibrium, all creditors again monitor the firm, although each creditor now monitors only the firm's use of its own collateral. Total monitoring costs are again high, although they may be lower than when all creditors are unsecured. But in a third model, monitoring by one secured creditor has spillover effects for all other creditors by preventing managers from misbehaving. In this model, it is efficient for only one secured creditor to do all the monitoring and this solution minimizes total transactions costs. However, in practice, it is not clear how frequently monitoring has spillover benefits or how often the specialized monitoring equilibrium would prevail. In addition, it is unclear why a secured creditor is the best monitor in a specialized monitoring equilibrium.[4]

Now turn to literature that examines how use of secured credit affects the screening of firms in bankruptcy. In the "creditors' bargain" model, Jackson (1982) and Baird and Jackson (1984) argue that the role of bankruptcy law is to force creditors to act collectively so as to maximize the value of the firm's assets, regardless of how the assets are divided. This means that firms in bankruptcy should reorganize if the value of their assets is higher when they continue to operate and should liquidate if the value of their assets is higher in some alternate use. The question then is whether use of secured debt improves the efficiency of firms' bankruptcy choices. In particular, when firms file for bankruptcy, there is a conflict between high-priority creditors, who generally prefer liquidation so that they receive their repayment quickly, versus low-priority creditors, who generally prefer to save the firm since their claims will be worth little in liquidation, but may be worth more if the firm reorganizes and succeeds. How does the use of secured credit affect the outcome of this conflict?

Jackson and Baird posit a hypothetical bargaining process that all creditors participate in before making their loans to the firm, which would result in agreement on priority rules that lead to efficient liquidation versus reorganization decisions. If all creditors were unsecured, they argue that the bargain would call for a priority rule in which all creditors have equal priority and are treated equally in bankruptcy, because equal treatment both reduces total transactions costs and reduces individual creditors' incentives to race to be first to collect whenever they fear that the firm might default. But if some creditors are secured, these creditors have an incentive to quickly seize their collateral once the firm defaults, even if seizure reduces the value of the firm's assets by forcing it to shut down. Jackson argues that in this situation, creditors would adopt a priority rule that prevents secured creditors from seizing their collateral, but protects them with payments equal to their loss from depreciation of the assets and foregone interest during the delay. The payments may come from the firm's cash, from a new lender or from the old unsecured creditors, but in any case, the cost of the payments is borne by unsecured creditors. Under this priority rule, unsecured creditors, as a whole, would choose to keep their firms running when the gains from avoiding liquidation exceed the costs of compensating secured creditors and would choose liquidation otherwise. In contrast, if unsecured creditors were not required to compensate secured creditors for delay in seizing their collateral, then firms in bankruptcy would choose reorganization even when it is more efficient for them to liquidate. Thus, Baird and Jackson argue that respecting secured creditors' priority in bankruptcy improves efficiency because it results in efficient bankruptcy screening.

I analyse this argument more formally in the next section, but some weaknesses are worth noting here. One is the fact that unsecured creditors have to get together after the firm files for bankruptcy and decide whether to compensate the secured creditors and, if so, to raise the funds. They also must bargain separately with each individual secured creditor to determine an amount that each is willing to accept in return for giving up the right to seize collateral. But these negotiations are likely to fail because some unsecured creditors will act as free-riders and refuse to contribute and some secured creditors will act as hold-outs and demand extra-high compensation. An alternative is that managers pay off secured creditors using a loan from a new lender or from cash on hand, which is likely to result in more reorganizations because it avoids the free-rider problem. But the hold-out problem is not eliminated, so that the number of firms that reorganize may still be inefficiently low. Another problem is that unsecured creditors are not in a good position to evaluate whether the firm is more valuable if it shuts down versus continues to operate, since this decision requires determining how much the firm's assets would be worth if they were sold to a different firm in possibly a different industry. But each creditor is likely to know only a small part of the firm's operations. Thus, negotiations among creditors when the firm is in bankruptcy seem unlikely to result in efficient liquidation versus reorganization decisions.

An extension of this approach concerns the issue of "involuntary" or "non-adjusting" claims against the firm, i.e., claims of creditors that never had an opportunity to negotiate their contracts with the firm. Involuntary claims include tort claims by individuals harmed by the firm, government claims for unpaid taxes and fines, and claims for environmental damage caused by the firm. Non-adjusting claims also include claims of contract creditors who have extended loans to the firm on fixed terms and small claims of all types. Non-adjusting creditors do not re-negotiate the interest rates they charge in response to changes in the firm's risk. Under an extension of the creditors' bargain approach, these claimants should be represented in the hypothetical bargaining that determines the bankruptcy payoff rule, even if, in reality, they never have an opportunity to bargain with the firm. However, in practice, bankruptcy law treats these claims as unsecured and they receive little or no compensation in bankruptcy (although claims for unpaid taxes have priority over general unsecured claims).

This causes various inefficiencies in firms' behavior. Hansmann and Kraakman (1991) point out that low payoff rates on involuntary claims in bankruptcy encourage firms to engage in projects that cause high levels of environmental and tort damage, to strip the corporation of assets that could be used to pay these claims, to buy too little liability insurance, and to avoid making investments that would mitigate the damage. Bebchuk and Fried (1996) argue non-adjusting claims give managers an incentive to make their "adjusting" creditors secured, since non-adjusting creditors cannot respond by raising the interest rates they charge. As a result, making adjusting creditors' claims secured lowers firms' total cost of capital. The existence of non-adjusting claims gives managers an incentive to choose inefficiently risky investments, since the cost of taking on extra risk is lower, capital is lower.[5]

Both sets of authors propose changes in bankruptcy law to take account of involuntary or non-adjusting claims. Hansmann and Kraakman (1991) propose that corporate shareholders have unlimited liability for external damage. Bebchuk and Fried (1996) propose that secured creditors' claims be treated as secured for only 75 percent of the liquidation value of their collateral, with the remaining 25 percent treated as unsecured.[6] Thus, secured creditors would receive only partial rather than full priority over unsecured creditors. I discuss both of their proposals below.

There is also a more general literature in economics that deals with how debt contracts should be structured to reduce inefficient behavior by managers. The central problem here is that once firms borrow, managers have an incentive to behave inefficiently by defaulting even when their firms are doing well ("strategic default"), because creditors may agree to accept a reduced payoff rather than forcing the firm to liquidate. In one of these papers, Bester (1994) examines whether use of secured debt reduces the probability of strategic default. He argues that managers are less likely to default strategically when the firm has secured rather than unsecured debt, because secured creditors are better off when the firm liquidates and are therefore less likely to agree to a reduced payoff. Use of secured debt thus may be worthwhile despite its higher transactions costs because it reduces the probability of strategic default.[7]

II. MODEL

In this section, I develop a model that examines how secured credit affects the efficiency of firms' bankruptcy decisions and use it to evaluate the two proposals discussed above. Why is it useful to examine another model? One reason is that the model focuses on the same efficiency objective as in Baird and Jackson: that of using bankruptcy to liquidate inefficient firms while saving firms that are economically efficient despite their financial distress. But my model uses a more realistic set of assumptions in which not all creditors are equally represented in the bargaining over the treatment of different types of claims in bankruptcy. The model also allows me to evaluate whether the reform proposals discussed above result in more economically efficient bankruptcy decisions.

The model has two periods. In period 1, firms are financially distressed, but may be either economically efficient or inefficient. Managers are assumed to have three alternatives: continue operating outside of bankruptcy for another period, file for Chapter 7 bankruptcy and liquidate, or file for Chapter 11 bankruptcy and reorganize. Both continuing to operate outside of bankruptcy and reorganizing under Chapter 11 are alternative methods of saving firms.

Small versus large firms in financial distress are likely to face different choices among these alternatives. Managers of small firms usually choose between continuing to operate outside of bankruptcy versus liquidating in Chapter 7 bankruptcy, because they cannot afford the high transactions costs of reorganization. But managers of large firms typically choose between filing to liquidate versus reorganize in bankruptcy. This is because larger firms are more closely monitored by creditors, so that they make their bankruptcy decisions when their firms are in better financial condition and can afford the transactions costs of reorganizing.[8]

Prior to the start of the model, firms borrow from at least two creditors. By period 1, some of these firms are in financial distress and managers must make bankruptcy decisions. If firms liquidate in bankruptcy in period 1, the liquidation value of their assets is assumed to be V_1. If firms continue to operate in period 1, either outside of bankruptcy or in Chapter 11, then in period 2 the value of their assets is assumed to be V_2. V_2 is assumed to be known with certainty, but may take a range of (positive) values from low to high. The model ends in period 2 with liquidation of firms' assets. Both V_1 and V_2 represent the market value of all of the firm's assets in their best alternative use, sold either piecemeal or as going concerns to buyers in the same or other industries. Because we wish to consider the possibility that firms cause environmental and/or accidental damage when they operate, firms that continue to operate from period 1 to period 2 are assumed to cause external harm of X_2. X_2 includes all types of external harm, regardless of whether victims receive compensation.[9]

It is unusual in discussing firms' bankruptcy decisions to assume that future earnings are certain rather than uncertain. I make this assumption partly for convenience, since it simplifies the notation and makes the model simpler. However, the main reason for this assumption is to show that managers make inefficient bankruptcy decisions regardless of whether their firms' future earnings are certain or uncertain; in other words, uncertainty is not necessary for managers to make inefficient bankruptcy decisions. If earnings were assumed to be uncertain rather than certain, then it is straightforward to show that more firms would choose continuation or reorganization even when the best outcome is liquidation. Thus, inefficient continuations or inefficient reorganizations would occur more often.[10]

The economically efficient treatment of firms in bankruptcy is straightforward: firms should continue operating if the increase in the value of their assets between periods 1 and 2 exceeds their external harm, or if $V_2 - V_1 > X_2$, and they should liquidate in period 1 otherwise.[11] Thus, saving the firm is more likely to be efficient if the increase in the firm's value $V_2 - V_1$ is high and/or if external harm X_2 is small. Only future external harm affects whether it is efficient for the firm to continue operating versus liquidate; past external harm is a sunk cost. Making the economically efficient choice between saving versus liquidating the firm is equivalent to choosing the alternative that maximizes the size of the pie, regardless of how it is divided.

The firm is assumed to have no cash on hand as of period 1. As a result, in order for it to continue operating or reorganize in period 1, it must receive a new loan that allows it to pay all of its debt obligations that are due in period 1.

Now turn to the question of how firms make their bankruptcy decisions. Unlike Baird and Jackson, I do not assume that a grand "creditors' bargain" made in advance determines the decision. Instead, I assume that the decision is made in period 1 by a sub-group of parties: managers—who represent themselves and equity—and a single creditor called the bank that may or may not be willing to make a new loan to the firm. These parties collectively are referred to as the coalition. The coalition excludes creditors who are not willing to make new loans to the firm when it is in financial distress, because these creditors are assumed to have no bargaining power at the time of the bankruptcy decision. Non-coalition creditors include holders of damage claims, government and trade creditors, and adjusting or non-adjusting creditors of the firm that are unwilling to extend new credit. As discussed below, the bank's new loan can be either secured or unsecured.[12]

In period 1, the coalition chooses between continuing to operate outside of bankruptcy versus liquidating in Chapter 7 (below, I consider the coalition's choice between reorganizing in Chapter 11 versus liquidating in Chapter 7). Because the model has only two periods, the choice of continuation delays liquidation of the firm from period 1 until period 2. Since I assume that equity would be wiped out if liquidation occurred in period 1, shareholders are assumed to be willing to give up part or all of their equity in order to induce the bank to make the new loan. The coalition makes the bankruptcy decision by picking the alternative that maximizes the size of its pie slice. This decision may be inefficient because the choice that maximizes the size of the coalition's pie slice may not be the choice that maximizes the size of the pie.

The firm is assumed to have three groups of existing creditors: secured creditors who are owed S_1 in period 1 and S_2 in period 2, unsecured creditors who are owed U_1 in period 1 and U_2 in period 2, and creditors with damage claims who are owed T_1 in period 1 and T_2 in period 2.[13] Because the firm is in financial distress, the total value of claims is assumed to exceed the liquidation value of the firm's assets in period 1, V_1. Thus, $S_1 + S_2 + U_1 + U_2 + T_1 + T_2 > V_1$.

If the firm liquidates in Chapter 7 bankruptcy in period 1, the value of its assets V_1 will be used to pay creditors' claims according to the absolute priority rule. I assume that secured creditors' claims are backed by collateral that is equal in value to the amount of their claims and, in liquidation, they take their collateral and are therefore paid first. The remaining assets of the firm are liquidated and used to pay unsecured and damage claims. All of these are assumed to have equal priority and thus are paid the same proportion of their face value. The fractional payment rate to unsecured and damage claims is $(V_1 - S_1 - S_2)/(U_1 + U_2 + T_1 + T_2)$. Shareholders receive nothing.

In contrast, if the firm continues to operate outside of bankruptcy, it must repay all claims due in period 1, $S_1 + U_1 + T_1$, in full. The firm is assumed to have no cash on hand in period 1, so that all of the funds for repayment of these claims must come from a new loan from the bank. The interest rate on the new loan is assumed to be r. The amount that the firm must repay in period 2 if it avoids bankruptcy and continues operating in period 1—referred to as the continuation loan—is therefore $B_2^C = (S_1 + U_1 + T_1)(1 + r)$. Here, the superscript C refers to continuation and the subscript 2 refers to period 2 when the loan must be repaid.

How much does the coalition receive under continuation? In period 2, the total amount available to be distributed is V_2, which may be high or low. Secured creditors claim their collateral, so that the first S_2 dollars go to them. If $V_2 > S_2$, then the next payment goes to the bank to repay the continuation loan, since the continuation loan is assumed to take priority over unsecured and damage creditors' claims.[14] Thus, increases in V_2 up to $S_2 + B_2^C$ go to the coalition. If $V_2 > S_2 + B_2^C$, then the next payment goes to unsecured and damage creditors and, finally, if $V_2 > S_2 + B_2^C + U_2 + T_2$, anything else goes to the coalition. The coalition's return under continuation is therefore $\max[V_2 - S_2, 0]$ if $V_2 \leq S_2 + B_2^C + U_2 + T_2$ plus $V_2 - (B_2^C + S_2 + U_2 + T_2)$ if $V_2 > S_2 + B_2^C + U_2 + T_2$. Since shareholders' return if liquidation is chosen in period 1 is zero, shareholders therefore prefer continuation over liquidation in period 1 whenever the firm's future value is large enough to repay the continuation loan in full, or if $V_2 \geq S_2 + B_2^C$. The condition for the coalition to form is the same, since the bank is willing to provide the continuation loan as long as it will be repaid, or if $V_2 \geq S_2 + B_2^C$.

Figure 10.1 shows the coalition's return on the vertical axis and the range of values of V_2 on the horizontal axis. The coalition receives nothing unless V_2 exceeds S_2, then it receives all of the increase in V_2 up to $S_2 + B_2^C$, at which point the continuation loan has been repaid in full. Past this point,

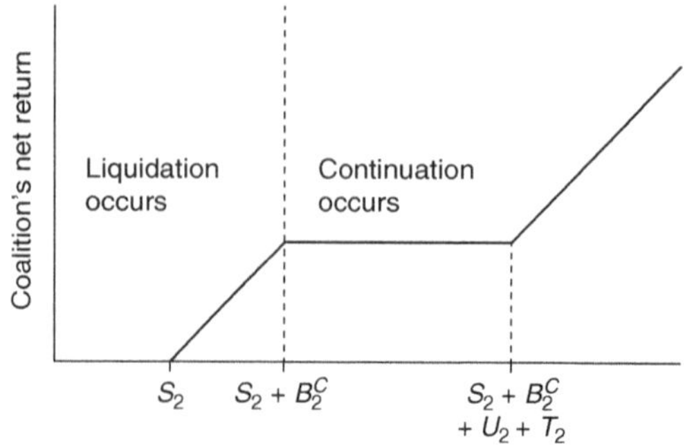

Figure 10.1 *The coalition's choice between continuation and liquidation*

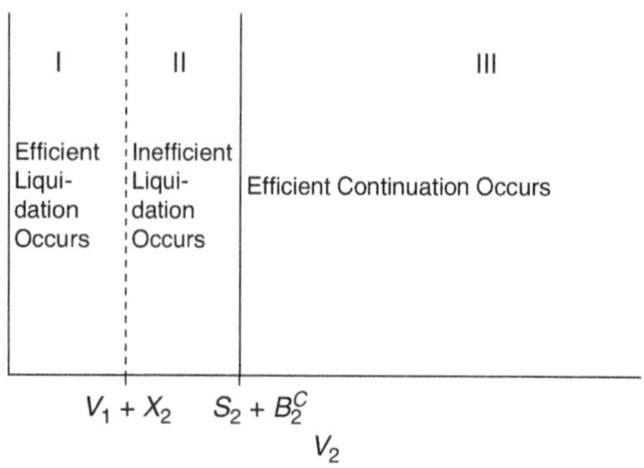

Figure 10.2A *Conditions for inefficient liquidation to occur*

the coalition receives nothing more until unsecured creditors and damage claimants have been paid in full, and finally, it receives all of the firm's value above $S_2 + B_2^C + U_2 + T_2$. The vertical line at $S_2 + B_2^C$ is the boundary between the regions where the coalition does not form and liquidation occurs and where the coalition forms and chooses continuation. To the left of the vertical line, the coalition does not form and liquidation occurs because V_2 is not high enough to repay the continuation loan in full, so the bank would lose money if it made the loan. To the right of the vertical line, the coalition forms and continuation occurs because V_2 is high enough to repay the continuation loan in full and possibly more.

Now turn to question of whether the coalition's bankruptcy decision is economically efficient. Figure 10.2A again shows values of V_2 along the horizontal axis. The solid vertical line delineates the regions on either side of

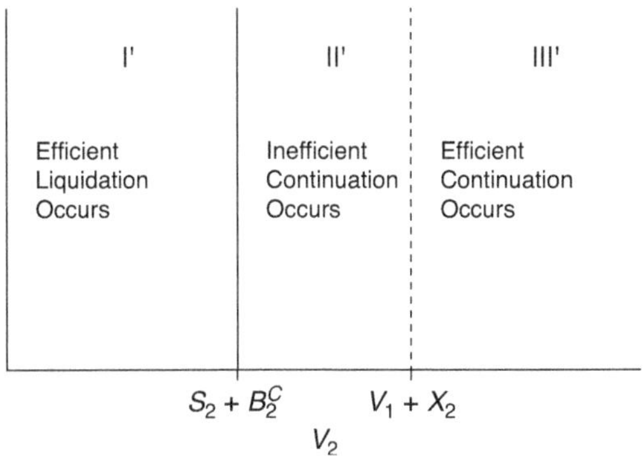

Figure 10.2B Conditions for inefficient continuation to occur

$S_2 + B_2^C$ where the coalition chooses liquidation versus continuation. But now there is also a dotted vertical line at $V_1 + X_2$. This line separates the region where $V_2 < V_1 + X_2$ and liquidation is economically efficient (to the left of the dotted line) from the region where $V_2 > V_1 + X_2$ and continuation is economically efficient (to the right of the dotted line). The two vertical lines together delineate three regions, labelled regions I, II and III. In region I, the coalition chooses liquidation because $V_2 < S_2 + B_2^C$ and liquidation is also economically efficient because $V_2 < V_1 + X_2$. Thus, liquidation occurs and is the efficient choice. In region III, the coalition chooses continuation outside of bankruptcy because $V_2 > S_2 + B_2^C$ and this choice is also economically efficient because $V_2 > V_1 + X_2$. Thus, continuation occurs and is the efficient choice. However, in region II, the coalition chooses liquidation because $V_2 < S_2 + B_2^C$, but continuation is economically efficient because $V_2 > V_1 + X_2$. Thus liquidation occurs but continuation is economically efficient. The coalition makes economically inefficient decisions in region II because, while the firm is worth more if it continues to operate, the coalition prefers liquidation since creditors' claims in period 1 are too large for the bank to make the continuation loan. Although the pie would be bigger if the firm continued to operate in region II, the coalition makes the wrong choice because its pie slice in liquidation is larger.[15]

In Figure 10.2B, the situation is reversed because $S_2 + B_2^C$ is assumed to be smaller than $V_1 + X_2$, rather than larger. This means that the dotted vertical line is to the right of the solid vertical line, rather than the reverse. The resulting three regions are now labelled I', II', and III'. In regions I' and III', liquidation or continuation is economically efficient and the coalition again makes the economically efficient choice. But now in the middle region, region II', liquidation is economically efficient because $V_2 < V_1 + X_2$, but the coalition chooses continuation because

$V_2 > S_2 + B_2^C$. Thus, continuation occurs in this region even though liquidation is economically efficient. The difference between the two figures is that either creditors' claims $S_2 + B_2^C$ are smaller, which increases the coalition's return from continuation, and/or the economic costs of continuing the firm's operations, $V_1 + X_2$, are higher. Thus, rather than too much liquidation occurring, instead, too much continuation may occur.[16]

Overall, the model shows that the coalition of shareholders and the bank does not generally make economically efficient bankruptcy decisions and that, depending on individual firms' characteristics, either too much continuation or too much liquidation may occur. The only situation in which the coalition always makes economically efficient bankruptcy decisions is the special case when $V_1 + X_2 = S_2 + B_2^C$. In this case, the inefficient regions II in Figure 10.2A and II' in Figure 10.2B both disappear. But this special case is unlikely to occur in practice.

Now consider whether treating secured creditors less favorably in bankruptcy improves the efficiency of the coalition's bankruptcy decisions. In particular, suppose now that if continuation is chosen in period 1, secured creditors' claims become unsecured.

Because the coalition, rather than secured creditors, now receives the first S_2 dollars of the firm's period 2 value, the coalition now chooses continuation whenever $V_2 \geq B_2^C$, rather than when $V_2 \geq S_2 + B_2^C$. Because the former inequality is more likely to hold than the latter, the coalition chooses continuation more often. In Figure 10.1, the curve showing the coalition's net return shifts to the left, so that the coalition's return begins to rise starting at zero rather than starting from S_2. Also, the line between the regions where liquidation versus continuation is chosen shifts leftward from $S_2 + B_2^C$ to B_2^C, making the coalition choose continuation more often and liquidation less often.

In Figure 10.2A, the solid vertical line shifts to the left by the same amount, but the dotted vertical line remains in the same position, because changing the treatment of secured creditors has no effect on economic efficiency. The leftward shift of the solid vertical line makes region II in Figure 10.2A smaller and region III in Figure 10.2A larger. As a result, inefficient liquidation is less likely to occur. However, in Figure 10.2B, the same leftward shift of the solid vertical line occurs and this causes region II' to increase in size and region I' to become smaller, making inefficient continuation more likely to occur. Thus, treating secured creditors less favorably causes the coalition to choose continuation more often, reducing the probability of inefficient liquidation but increasing the probability of inefficient continuation. This is because the coalition is more likely to choose continuation, but the efficiency of continuation remains unaffected. Treating secured creditors more favorably has the opposite effect. In general, no treatment of secured creditors in bankruptcy always results in the coalition making economically efficient bankruptcy decisions.

Now assume that the coalition's choice in period 1 is between liquidation under Chapter 7 versus reorganization under Chapter 11, rather than between liquidation versus continuation outside of bankruptcy—the typical bankruptcy choice for large corporations. If the firm reorganizes under Chapter 11, assume that it must pay transactions costs of C in period 1, which include lawyers' fees, professional fees and court costs. Also, managers must make an agreement with creditors on the terms of a reorganization plan that will go into effect in period 2. Suppose the reorganization plan that satisfies the requirements for approval by creditors has the following characteristics. It pays all unsecured creditors and damage claimants a fraction u of the face value of their claims in period 2, while the remaining fraction (1-u) of these claims is discharged. Also, secured creditors are not allowed to foreclose on their collateral in period 1, but they may receive interest on their loans and/or compensation for loss of the value of their collateral during the reorganization procedure. This payment is assumed to equal a fraction s of the face value of their claims, while the remaining fraction (1-s) of their claims is discharged. Secured creditors are assumed to receive this payment in period 1, regardless of whether their claims are due in period 1 or period 2. Note that the coalition benefits from choosing reorganization in period 1 both because reorganizing delays the firm's obligation to repay unsecured claims that are due in period 1 and because it partially discharges both unsecured and secured claims. These features of reorganization provide both temporary and permanent financial relief to financially distressed firms.[17]

The amount of the bank loan needed to finance reorganization in period 1 is denoted B_2^R, where the R superscript denotes reorganization and the 2 subscript again denotes the amount to be repaid in period 2. The reorganization loan equals the transactions costs of reorganizing plus the cost of payments to secured creditors in period 1.[18] The interest rate on the loan is again assumed to be r, so that $B_2^R = (C + s(S_1 + S_2))(1 + r)$. Assume that the reorganization loan takes highest priority as an "administrative expense" of Chapter 11 bankruptcy and is repaid in period 2 before all other creditors' claims.

Now consider the coalition's choice between liquidation versus reorganization in period 1. If the coalition chooses liquidation, it receives nothing. If it chooses reorganization in period 1, again I assume that the firm's assets will be sold for the amount V_2 in period 2. (This means that the value of the firm continuing to operate between periods 1 and 2 is assumed to be the same regardless of whether it remains outside of bankruptcy or reorganizes in Chapter 11.) In period 2, the first B_2^R dollars of V_2 go to

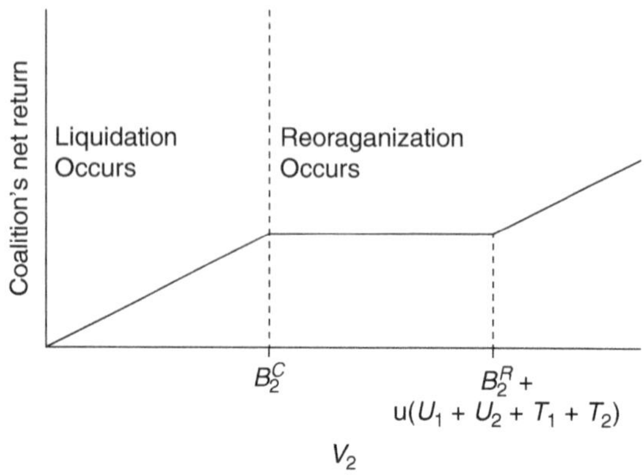

Figure 10.3 The coalition's choice between reorganization and liquidation

the coalition to repay the reorganization loan. Then the coalition receives nothing more until all payments to unsecured and damage claimants owed under the reorganization plan are made, and finally it receives all of the firm's additional value beyond $B_2^R + u(U_1 + U_2 + T_1 + T_2)$, if any. As shown in Figure 10.3, the coalition chooses reorganization over liquidation whenever $V_2 \geq B_2^R$ and it chooses liquidation whenever this condition is reversed. This inequality is also the condition for the bank to be willing to make the reorganization loan. Figure 10.3 shows the regions where the coalition chooses liquidation versus reorganization.

An interesting implication of the model is that the size of the payments promised to unsecured and damage creditors under the reorganization plan has no effect on the coalition's choice between reorganization versus liquidation. This is because all payments promised to these creditors under the plan take lower priority in period 2 than the bank's loan to finance reorganization and therefore the coalition ignores them in making its bankruptcy decision. Only the payments promised to secured creditors affect the coalition's choice.

If we compare Figure 10.3 to Figure 10.1, the coalition is more likely to choose reorganization over liquidation than it is to choose continuation over liquidation as long as $B_2^R < S_2 + B_2^C$. Ignoring interest payments, this condition is satisfied whenever $C < (1 - s)(S_1 + S_2) + U_1 + T_1$, or when the transactions costs of reorganizing are less than the value of claims that the coalition avoids repaying in period 1 when it chooses reorganization. This condition is likely to hold for many large firms.

Now turn to the efficiency effects of the reorganization choice, shown in Figures 10.4A and 10.4B. The solid vertical lines in both figures indicate the boundary between the regions where the coalition chooses

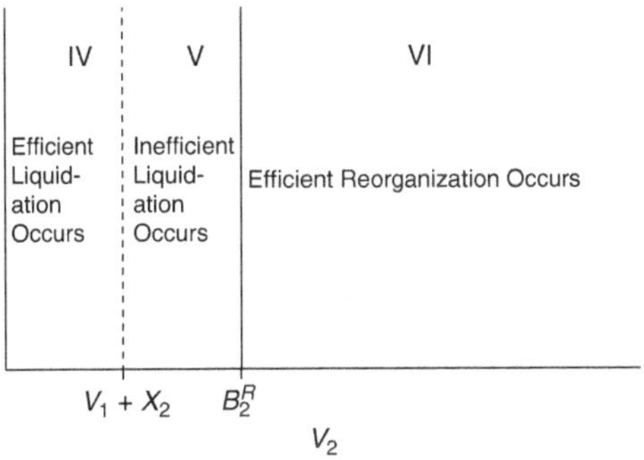

Figure 10.4A Conditions for inefficient liquidation to occur

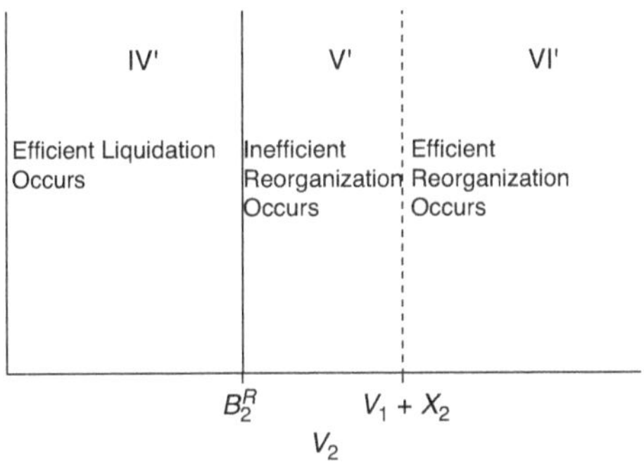

Figure 10.4B Conditions for inefficient reorganization to occur

liquidation versus reorganization, while the dotted vertical lines in both figures indicate the boundary between the regions where liquidation versus reorganization is economically efficient. (As in Figures 10.2A and 10.2B, liquidation is economically efficient when $V_2 < V_1 + X_2$ and reorganization is economically efficient otherwise.) In each figure, the two vertical lines delineate three regions, labelled IV, V, and VI in Figure 10.4A and IV', V', and VI' in Figure 10.4B. In regions IV and IV', liquidation is economically efficient and is chosen by the coalition and in regions VI and VI', reorganization is economically efficient and is chosen by the coalition. However, in region V of Figure 10.4A, the coalition chooses liquidation even though reorganization is economically efficient. Thus, liquidation occurs too often and some firms liquidate that should reorganize. Similarly in region V' in Figure 10.4B, the coalition chooses reorganization even though liquidation is more efficient. Thus reorganization occurs too often and some firms reorganize that should liquidate. In general, inefficient reorganization is more likely to occur when the economic cost of the firm operating until period 2, $V_1 + X_2$, is high and/or when the cost of the bank loan B_2^R required to finance reorganization is low. Inefficient liquidation is more likely in the opposite situations.

Now consider how changing the treatment of secured creditors in reorganization affects the efficiency of the coalition's reorganization versus liquidation choice. In particular, suppose secured creditors are treated worse in reorganization because the partial payment of their claims is deferred until the reorganization plan is adopted in period 2, rather than being paid when the firm files to reorganize in period 1. This change means that the bank loan required to finance reorganization falls by the amount $s(S_1 + S_2)(1+r)$ and the condition for the coalition to choose reorganization becomes $V_2 > C(1 + r)$, rather than $V_2 > (C + s(S_1 + S_2))(1 + r)$. In Figure 10.3, the reduction in the size of B_2^R causes the region where the coalition chooses reorganization to increase in size. In Figure 10.4A, the solid vertical line shifts to the left, while the dotted vertical line remains unchanged. This makes region V smaller, so that inefficient liquidation is less likely to occur. However, in Figure 10.4B, the same leftward shift of the solid vertical line makes region V' larger and means that inefficient reorganization is more likely to occur. These changes result from the fact that reducing the priority of secured creditors' claims makes reorganization more attractive to the coalition by increasing the size of its pie slice, but does not affect the efficiency of reorganization so that the size of the pie remains the same. Reducing the favorable treatment of secured creditors in reorganization thus has ambiguous effects on the economic efficiency of reorganization versus liquidation decisions: while fewer inefficient liquidations occur, there are more inefficient reorganizations.

Finally, it is useful to consider the economic efficiency implications of the bankruptcy choice if the coalition were choosing between continuation outside of bankruptcy versus reorganization under Chapter 11. In our model, reorganization has efficiency costs because it generates extra transactions costs of C, while its benefit to the coalition consists entirely of redistribution from non-coalition creditors to the coalition. Reorganization is therefore inefficient relative to continuation outside of bankruptcy unless it generates some efficiency improvement that is outside of the model.

A. Hansmann and Kraakman's Proposal for Unlimited Liability for Damage Claims

Now turn to Hansmann and Kraakman's (H-K) proposal for unlimited liability by shareholders for claims of damage by tort victims. One important consideration is that the priority rule in bankruptcy affects whether shareholders actually bear the cost of paying damage claims or whether they are able to transfer this cost to creditors. If damage claims take high priority in bankruptcy, then at least part of the cost of repayment may be shifted to creditors rather than borne by shareholders; while if these claims take low priority, then most or all of the cost of repayment falls on shareholders, but the claims are less likely to be paid. Another important consideration is that it may be difficult to enforce unlimited liability (or any liability) by shareholders, since enforcement may require that the bankruptcy trustee sue individual shareholders and these suits are time-consuming and uncertain. Because bankruptcy trustees are likely to sue the deepest-pocketed shareholders, unlimited liability may also discourage rich shareholders from investing in corporations that create tort damages and therefore reduce the benefits of diversification. In addition, individual shareholders' liability is limited by personal bankruptcy law, where shareholders may benefit from high exemptions levels.[19]

Assume that if the firm liquidates in period 1, secured creditors claim their collateral and are repaid in full. Also suppose that unsecured creditors have higher priority than damage creditors in bankruptcy. They therefore are repaid next, but I assume that they receive less than the full value of their claims, so that $V_1 - S_1 - S_2 < U_1 + U_2$.[20] As a result, if the firm liquidates in period 1, damage creditors receive nothing from the liquidation process and so the entire cost of repaying their claims falls on shareholders. Shareholders' return if the firm liquidates in period 1 is therefore $-(T_1 + T_2)$, rather than zero as in the previous discussion.

Now, suppose the firm instead continues to operate outside of bankruptcy in period 1. The amount of the continuation loan, $B_2^C = (S_1 + U_1 + T_1)(1 + r)$, remains the same as in the previous discussion and covers full repayment of all debts due in period 1. In period 2, the firm liquidates and its value is again assumed to be V_2. Suppose that in period 2, secured creditors are repaid first because they claim their collateral assets, the continuation loan is paid next, unsecured claims are paid next, and damage claims take lowest priority. However, unlike the discussion above, shareholders must now bear the remaining amount of damage claims that are not repaid in the liquidation process.

This means that secured creditors receive the first S_2 dollars of the firm's period 2 value, the bank receives the next B_2^C dollars, unsecured creditors receive the next U_2 dollars, and damage claimants receive the next T_2 dollars, until the value of the firm's assets V_2 is exhausted. Damage claimants therefore receive nothing unless the firm's value exceeds $S_2 + B_2^C + U_2$, they receive all of the firm's additional value from $V_2 = B_2^C + S_2 + U_2$ to $V_2 = B_2^C + S_2 + U_2 + T_2$, and they receive no additional payment if V_2 exceeds the latter amount. Thus, if V_2 is between $B_2^C + S_2 + U_2$ and $B_2^C + S_2 + U_2 + T_2$, damage claimants receive partial payment from the liquidation process. Call this amount P_2 (for partial payment of period 2 damage claims). Shareholders owe damage claimants the remaining amount $T_2 - P_2$, if this amount is positive. Shareholders' return if continuation is chosen in period 1 is therefore $-T_2$ if $P_2 = 0$, $-(T_2 - P_2)$ if $0 < P_2 < T_2$ and 0 if $P_2 = T_2$. Because this return is higher than shareholders' return of $-(T_1 + T_2)$ if the firm liquidates in period 1, they prefer that the firm continue to operate outside of bankruptcy. Intuitively, choosing continuation allows shareholders to escape liability for current damage claims T_1 and to partially or fully avoid liability for future damage claims T_2 as well. Although imposing unlimited liability for damage claims makes shareholders worse off under both liquidation and continuation, they are better off if the firm continues to operate in period 1.[21] Thus inefficient continuation decisions still would be expected to occur.

Turning to efficiency considerations, the change in shareholders' liability for damage claims has no effect on the efficiency of the bankruptcy decision, since the change is just a transfer from shareholders and/or debtholders to damage claimants. As in the discussion in the previous section, the increase in the probability that continuation is chosen by the coalition in period 1 causes the solid vertical line in Figure 10.2A to shift to the left. But because the efficiency of liquidation versus continuation is unaffected, the dotted vertical line in Figure 10.2A remains the same. As a result, region II becomes smaller and inefficient liquidation is less likely to occur. However, the change also causes the solid vertical line in Figure 10.2B to shift to the left, while the dotted vertical line remains the same. This means that region II' in Figure 10.2B becomes larger, so that inefficient continuation is more likely to occur. Thus, making shareholders liable for damage claims causes firms to continue operating more often, lowering the probability of inefficient liquidation, but raising the probability of inefficient continuation. Again, the efficiency effects of the change to unlimited liability are ambiguous.

Now turn to the effect of unlimited shareholder liability for damages on the efficiency of firms' decisions to reorganize in Chapter 11. H-K do not discuss whether their proposal would also apply unlimited liability for damage claims to shareholders of corporations that reorganize in Chapter 11. An issue with unlimited liability for damage claims is that it conflicts with the goal of Chapter 11 that all creditors take a "haircut" and receive partial payment of their claims in order to facilitate the failing firm's survival.

Suppose the coalition now chooses between liquidating versus reorganizing in period 1. Shareholders' return in liquidation remains the same as before, $-(T_1 + T_2)$. Assume that if reorganization is chosen instead, damage claims receive the same treatment as in the discussion of reorganization in the previous section. Thus, damage claimants, like unsecured claimants, are assumed to receive *u* percent of their claims, with the payment being made in period 2. Choosing reorganization rather than liquidation in period 1 thus allows the coalition to defer paying all damage claims and to reduce the amount they pay damage claimants by (1-*u*) percent. Because liquidation is now much less favorable to the coalition while reorganization remains equally favorable as before, the coalition has a stronger incentive to choose reorganization when liability for damage claims is unlimited in liquidation. But because the efficiency of the liquidation-reorganization choice is unaffected by the change to unlimited shareholder liability for damage claims, the result is that more inefficient reorganizations and fewer inefficient liquidations would occur.

These results suggest that if shareholders had unlimited liability for damage claims, they would choose to continue failing firms' operations—either outside of bankruptcy or in Chapter 11 reorganization—more often and would choose liquidation less often. Thus, fewer failing firms would liquidate in bankruptcy. But the efficiency effects of the change in liability are ambiguous, since some of the additional continuations and reorganizations would be economically inefficient.

B. Bebchuk and Fried's Proposal for 75 Percent Priority for Secured Claims

The Bebchuk and Fried (B-F) proposal is that secured claims take priority for only 75 percent of the face value of their claims in bankruptcy, with the remaining 25 percent of their claims treated as unsecured. How would this proposal affect bankruptcy decisions and the efficiency of bankruptcy choices?

Consider first how the change in the treatment of secured claims affects the efficiency of the coalition's choice between liquidation versus continuation outside of bankruptcy. The change does not affect the analysis of when it is economically efficient for the firm to liquidate, but it does affect the coalition's bankruptcy decision. Suppose T_1 and T_2 are now redefined to represent non-adjusting claims due in periods 1 and 2, while U_1 and U_2 are redefined to represent unsecured, but adjusting (negotiated) claims due in the two periods. The total amount of the firm's debt,

$S_1 + S_2 + U_1 + U_2 + T_1 + T_2$, remains the same and is again assumed to be greater than the period 1 value of the firm's assets, V_1.

If the firm chooses to liquidate in bankruptcy in period 1, shareholders' return is zero regardless of whether secured creditors have priority for 75 percent or 100 percent of their claims. This is because all creditors' claims must be repaid in full before equity receives anything.[22] Now consider the coalition's return if it chooses continuation outside of bankruptcy in period 1. Secured creditors are again assumed to take highest priority when the firm liquidates in period 2, but now their priority is only for 75 percent of their period 2 claims. The size of the new loan from the bank needed to finance continuation in period 1 remains the same as above, $B_2^C = (S_1 + U_1 + T_1)(1 + r)$. But the coalition's return under continuation rises as a result of the change, because secured creditors now take priority in period 2 only for 75 percent of their claims, with the remaining 25 percent becoming unsecured. This means that the first $.75S_2$ dollars of the firm's period 2 value goes to secured creditors, the next $B_2^C(1 + r)$ dollars go to the coalition, the next $.25\ S_2 + U_2 + T_2$ dollars go to creditors, and anything that remains goes to equity, until the firm's period 2 value V_2 is exhausted. The condition for the coalition to choose continuation over liquidation in period 1 therefore becomes $V_2 > .75S_2 + B_2^C$, rather than the previous condition of $V_2 > S_2 + B_2^C$ when secured creditors' claims took full priority in period 2. The coalition therefore chooses continuation more often.

In Figure 10.1, the change in secured creditors' priority causes the vertical line between the liquidation versus continuation regions to shift to the left, so that the coalition is more likely to choose continuation. Examining how this change affects efficiency, in Figure 10.2A the solid vertical line moves to the left, but the dotted vertical line remains in the same place. As a result, region II becomes smaller and inefficient liquidation is less likely to occur. But in Figure 10.2B, the solid vertical line also moves to the left, making region II' larger and inefficient continuation more likely to occur. Thus, reducing secured creditors' priority from 100 percent to 75 percent of their claims makes the coalition more likely to choose continuation outside of bankruptcy over liquidation in period 1, but does not make this choice more economically efficient. As a result, fewer inefficient liquidations occur under the reform, but there are more inefficient continuations. The change has ambiguous effects on the efficiency of firms' bankruptcy decisions.

Finally, examine the effect of B-F's proposed reform on the efficiency of firms' decisions to liquidate under Chapter 7 versus reorganize under Chapter 11. To do so, we return to the model of reorganization discussed above in which secured creditors are entitled to be paid s percent of their claims in period 1 when the firm reorganizes. Under the B-F proposal, suppose secured creditors are now entitled to be paid the fraction $.75s$ of their claims in period 1 and an additional fraction $.25s$ of their claims in period 2. (This assumes that the overall payoff rates to secured and unsecured creditors under the reorganization plan, s and u, remain the same as before.)[23] Under these assumptions if the coalition chooses reorganization, the reorganization loan from the bank becomes $(C+.75s(S_1 + S_2))(1 + r)$ and this loan is repaid first in period 2. Thus, the first $(C+.75s(S_1 + S_2))(1 + r)$ dollars of the firm's period 2 value go to the coalition to repay the reorganization loan, the next $u(U_1 + U_2 + T_1 + T_2 + .25(S_1 + S_2))$ dollars go to creditors as payments promised under the reorganization plan, and, if anything is left, it goes to equity. The condition for the coalition to choose reorganization over liquidation in period 1 therefore becomes $V_2 \geq (C+.75s(S_1+S_2))(1 + r)$. This condition is more likely to be satisfied than the previous condition, which was $V_2 \geq (C + s(S_1 + S_2))(1 + r)$.

These changes mean that under the B-F proposal, the vertical line forming the boundary between the regions of liquidation versus reorganization in Figure 10.3 shifts to the left, making the coalition choose reorganization more often. However, the efficiency of liquidation versus reorganization remains unchanged, because the reform only redistributes returns among creditor groups. Thus, in Figure 10.4A, the solid vertical line moves to the left while the dotted vertical line remains in the same position. This means that inefficient liquidation is less likely to occur. In Figure 10.4B, the solid vertical line also moves to the left while the dotted vertical line again remains in the same position. This means that inefficient reorganization is more likely to occur. Overall, adopting B-F's proposed reform means that more reorganization would occur, but some of the additional reorganizations would be of firms that should liquidate.

B-F's proposal to downgrade 25 percent of secured creditors' claims to unsecured status thus lowers the cost to the coalition of continuing to operate the firm, either by remaining outside of bankruptcy or filing to reorganize under Chapter 11. But the coalition's return when it chooses liquidation remains unchanged. The result is that continuation outside of bankruptcy and reorganization would occur more often under the proposal, while liquidation in Chapter 7 would occur less often. But because the proposal has no effect on the efficient outcome, the efficiency implications are ambiguous: while fewer economically efficient firms would liquidate, more economically inefficient firms would be saved.

III. CONCLUSION

This chapter re-examines an old controversy in the law and economics literature: whether use of secured credit is economically efficient and what treatment of secured credit in bankruptcy leads to economically efficient outcomes. The literature has not generated a consensus answer and several authors have proposed changes in the treatment of secured claims in bankruptcy that they argue would improve efficiency. But a problem with the literature is that bankruptcy law affects economic efficiency in many ways and different authors focus on particular economic efficiency goals in arguing for their proposed treatments of secured creditors in bankruptcy. In this chapter, I focus on the central economic function of bankruptcy law—that of screening of failing firms in bankruptcy so that economically inefficient firms liquidate and economically efficient (although financially distressed) firms are saved. I analyse various priority rules for secured credit in bankruptcy and two proposals for reform of the treatment of secured credit in bankruptcy, all using efficient screening in bankruptcy as the criterion for economic efficiency.

The overall result is that none of the actual or proposed rules for treatment of secured credit in bankruptcy always improve efficiency. All of the proposed changes increase the number of firms that are saved by reorganizing in Chapter 11 bankruptcy or by continuing to operate outside of bankruptcy. But while some of the additional firms saved should be saved, others that are saved should shut down. There appears to be no general rule for treatment of secured claims in bankruptcy that always results in economically inefficient firms shutting down in bankruptcy and economically efficient firms being saved.

NOTES

1. Secured creditors have the right to be compensated for the loss of value of their collateral during the reorganization process if the value of their collateral exceeds the face value of their claims. Another way that collateral protects secured creditors is that, in bankruptcy, unsecured creditors' claims receive payment only after the transactions costs of bankruptcy are paid and therefore may receive only partial or no payment. But secured creditors are paid in full as long as the value of their collateral equals the value of their claims. See Adler (1998) for general discussion of secured credit.
2. An important problem with efficient bankruptcy screening is that neither managers nor creditors of bankrupt firms are likely to know whether their firms are economically efficient or inefficient, since the answer depends on the value of firms' assets in alternative uses. See White (1989) and (2016) for discussion of bankruptcy screening and the multiple efficiency objectives of bankruptcy.
3. An earlier model of the effect of secured debt on the total cost of capital is Scott (1977). Unlike Schwartz (1981), Scott argues that use of secured credit reduces firms'

total cost of capital rather than leaving it unaffected. The difference between the two models is that Scott assumes that some of the unsecured creditors are tort claimants and government creditors that do not raise the interest rates they charge when firms issue secured debt, even though their claims become riskier. Scott's model thus anticipated the research both on the effect of secured debt on the total cost of capital and the effect of secured debt on unsecured claims that cannot adjust their loan terms when the firm becomes riskier (discussed below).

4. See Jackson and Kronman (1979), Levmore (1982) and Adler (1993) for additional discussion of whether/when using secured credit reduces the cost of monitoring. To the author's knowledge, there have been no empirical studies of monitoring costs and monitoring equilibria.
5. Bebchuk and Fried (1996) also discuss the fact that, when firms have more non-adjusting creditors, secured creditors have a reduced incentive to bargain with managers to adopt and enforce restrictive covenants that would improve the efficiency of the firm's behavior. This is because part of the cost of not adopting or enforcing covenants is borne by non-adjusting creditors. The more non-adjusting creditors the firm has, the more inefficient are managers' incentives.
6. This is Bebchuk and Fried's "fixed-fraction priority rule." They also discuss an "adjustable-priority rule" that would deny secured creditors priority over non-adjusting creditors, but allow them priority over other adjusting creditors. They show that, relative to full priority for secured creditors, both rules reduce the firm's incentive to invest in inefficiently risky projects and to create external harm, at the cost of raising the firm's total cost of capital and possibly preventing the firm from investing in economically efficient projects. But they do not address the effect of their priority rules on the efficiency of bankruptcy screening. Other proposals for super-priority of tort claims are discussed by Adler (1993) and LoPucki (1994).
7. Other papers in this literature show that strategic default by managers is reduced when firms borrow from multiple creditors rather than a single creditor (Bolton and Scharfstein, 1996) and when creditors hold a mixture of long-term and short-term debt rather than only short-term debt (Berglof and von Thadden, 1994). Berkovitch, Israel and Zender (1998), and Povel (1999) examine how features of bankruptcy law affect managers' level of effort in managing their firms.
8. For discussion of small firms' bankruptcy choices, see LoPucki (1983); for discussion of large firms' bankruptcy choices, see LoPucki and Whitford (1990), and Weiss (1990).
9. If a party sustains damage but has a contractual relationship with the firm, then the harm is not part of X_2 because the contract presumably includes compensation.
10. In particular, as uncertainty in future earnings increases, more firms choose to continue to operate outside of bankruptcy or reorganize even when liquidation is more efficient, because shareholders benefit disproportionately when firms' future earnings turn out to be high. See Stiglitz (1972) and White (1989) for discussion.
11. For simplicity, the discount rate is assumed to be zero.
12. Bebchuk and Fried (1996) use a similar model to analyse the effects of their proposed priority rules. Papers that discuss actual firms' bankruptcy decisions, such as LoPucki (1983), and LoPucki and Whitford (1990), also emphasize that these decisions are typically made by managers and a narrow group of creditors. Other coalition models of the bankruptcy decision include Bulow and Shoven (1978), White (1980 and 1989), and Ang and Chua (1980). Coalition creditors are assumed here not to have previously loaned money to the firm, but see Bizer and DeMarzo (1992) for a model in which creditors make sequential loans to a firm.
13. Damage claims may still be in litigation, so that their value could be uncertain. However, in the model, I assume here that they have fixed values.
14. The bank's new loan may take priority over unsecured claims and damage claims in period 2 for a variety of reasons, including that the continuation loan is secured or that the firm has an account at the bank and the bank can claim the funds in the account when default occurs. Other priority rules are discussed below. See Schwartz (1989) and

Bebchuk and Fried (1996) for discussion of the relationship between loan priority, whether loans are secured, and rules that give priority to earlier-in-time lenders.

15. Note that inefficient liquidation occurs here even though there is no race among creditors to be first to collect. In most models, when firms in financial distress liquidate too often, it is because of the race to be first. For an example, see Webb (1991).
16. If the firm's future earnings were uncertain rather than certain, then the coalition would be more likely to choose continuation. This means that region II' would become larger and region II would become smaller.
17. Secured creditors receive interest during the Chapter 11 procedure only if the liquidation value of their collateral exceeds the face value of their claims. Thus, the payment rate of s may represent a mixture of higher payments to some secured creditors and lower payments to others.
18. Liquidation clearly has transactions costs as well, but these are implicitly assumed to be smaller and are ignored here. The transactions costs of liquidation are limited by the fact that firms filing to liquidate often have very few assets not subject to secured creditors' liens and trustees' fees are a percentage of the value of assets they liquidate. It would be straightforward to add these costs to the model. See LoPucki (1983), White (1983), Weiss (1990), and Bris et al. (2006) for estimates of the transactions costs of reorganization versus liquidation for small and large corporations.
19. H-K also discuss whether individual shareholders should share liability for tort damages proportionate to the number of shares they own or whether liability should be joint and several. In this discussion, I ignore distributional issues and assume that all shareholders share equally in the cost paying damage claims, or that all shares are owned by a single owner. For discussion of real world problems concerning unlimited liability, see Hansmann and Kraakman (1991), and LoPucki (1994).
20. Damage claims often rank below other unsecured claims in bankruptcy, because they are involuntary claims that have not been negotiated with the firm. Unsecured creditors, in contrast, sometimes negotiate contractual provisions with the firm that give them higher priority in bankruptcy liquidation.
21. The bank is willing to provide the loan as long as $V_2 \geq S_2 + B_2^C$. However, if this inequality is not satisfied, then shareholders are willing to bribe the bank up to $T_1 + T_2$ to make the continuation loan, since they must pay this amount to damage claimants if the firm liquidates in period 1. Consequently, the bank is willing to make the continuation loan when the firm's period 2 value is as low as $S_2 + B_2^C - (T_1 + T_2)$.
22. Bebchuk and Fried (1996) assume that the 75 percent treatment of secured creditors' claims would not apply in bankruptcy liquidation, since secured creditors generally seize their collateral prior to the firm's Chapter 7 filing. They also argue that secured creditors in practice get only partial priority in Chapter 11 reorganizations, because they do not receive interest during the reorganization proceeding if their claims are undersecured and because their compensation under the reorganization plan may be in the form of a risky note rather than cash.
23. Changes in the bargaining power of creditors' groups might cause these payoff rates to change.

REFERENCES

Adler, B.E. (1993), "An Equity-Agency Solution to the Bankruptcy-Priority Puzzle," *J. of Legal Studies* 22:1, 73–98.

Adler, B.E. (1998), "Secured Credit Contracts," in *The New Palgrave Dictionary of Economics and The Law*, Peter Newman (ed.), vol. 3, pp. 405–10. London: Macmillan Reference Limited.

Ang, J.S. and J.H. Chua (1980), "Coalitions, the Me-First Rule, and the Liquidation Decision," *Bell Journal of Economics* 11:1, 355–9.

Baird, D. and T.H. Jackson (1984), "Treatment of Diverse Ownership Interests: A Comment on Adequate Protection of Secured Creditors in Bankruptcy," *Univ. of Chic. Law Review* 51, 9.
Bebchuk, L. and J. Fried (1996), "The Uneasy Case for the Priority of Secured Claims in Bankruptcy," *Yale Law Journal* 105, 857.
Berglof, E. and E.L. von Thadden (1994), "Short-term Versus Long-term Interests: Capital Structure with Multiple Investors," *Quarterly J. of Econ.* 109, 1055–84.
Berkovitch, E., R. Israel and J.F. Zender (1997), "Optimal Bankruptcy Law and Firm-specific Investments," *European Econ. Rev.* 41, 487–97.
Bester, H. (1994), "The Role of Collateral in a Model of Debt Renegotiation," *J. of Money, Credit, and Banking* 26, 72–85.
Bizer, D.S. and P.M. DeMarzo (1992), "Sequential Banking," *J. of Political Economy* 100:1, 41–61.
Bolton, P. and D. Scharfstein (1996), "Optimal Debt Structure and the Number of Creditors," *J. of Political Economy* 104, 1–25.
Bris, A., I. Welch and N. Zhu (2006), "The Costs of Bankruptcy: Chapter 7 Liquidation versus Chapter 11 Reorganization," *J. of Finance* 61:3, 1253–303.
Bulow, J. and J. Shoven (1978), "The Bankruptcy Decision," *Bell J. of Econ.* 9, 437–56.
Hansmann, H. and R. Kraakmann (1991), "Toward Unlimited Shareholder Liability for Corporate Torts," *Yale Law Journal* 100, 1879.
Jackson, T.H. (1982), "Bankruptcy, Non-Bankruptcy Entitlements, and the Creditors' Bargain," *Yale Law J.* 91, 857.
Jackson, T.H. and A. Kronman (1979), "Secured Financing and Priorities Among Creditors," *Yale Law J.* 88, 1143.
Levmore, S. (1982), "Monitors and Freeriders in Commercial and Corporate Settings," *Yale Law J.* 92, 49.
LoPucki, L.M. (1983), "The Debtor in Full Control: Systems Failure Under Chapter 11 of the Bankruptcy Code?" *American Bankruptcy Law J.* 57, 247–73.
LoPucki, L.M. (1994), "The Unsecured Creditors Bargain," *Virginia Law Rev.* 80, 1887.
LoPucki, L.M. and W. Whitford (1990), "Bargaining over Equity's Share in the Bankruptcy Reorganization of Large, Publicly-held Companies," *Univ. of Penn. Law Rev.* 139, 125–96.
Modigliani, F. and M.H. Miller, "The Cost of Capital, Corporation Finance and the Theory of Investment, *American Ec. Rev*. 48:3, 261–97 (1958).
Picker, R.C. (1992), "Security Interests, Misbehavior, and Common Pools," *U. Chic. L. Rev.* 59, 649–50.
Povel, P. (1999), "Optimal 'Soft' or 'Tough' Bankruptcy Procedures," *J. of Law, Econ. and Org.* 15, 659–84.
Schwartz, A. (1981), "Security Interests and Bankruptcy Priorities: A Review of Current Theories," *J. of Legal Studies* 10:1, 1–37.
Schwartz, A. (1989), "A Theory of Loan Priorities," *J. of Legal Studies* 18:2, 209–61.
Scott, J.H. (1977), "Bankruptcy, Secured Debt and Optimal Capital Structure," *J. of Finance* 32, 1–19.
Stiglitz, J.E. (1972), "Some Aspects of the Pure Theory of Corporate Finance: Bankruptcies and Take-overs," *Bell Journal of Economics* 3, 458–82.
Triantis, G. (1992), "Secured Debt under Conditions of Imperfect Information," *J. of Legal Studies* 21:1, 225–58.
Webb, D.C. (1991), "An Economic Evaluation of Insolvency Procedures in the United Kingdom: Does the 1986 Insolvency Act Satisfy the Creditors' Bargain?" *Oxford Econ. Papers* 43, 139–57.
Weiss, L.A. (1990), "Bankruptcy Resolution: Direct Costs and Violation of Priority of Claims," *J. of Financial Econ.* 27, 285–314.
White, Michelle J. (1980), "Public Policy Toward Bankruptcy: Me-First and Other Priority Rules," *Bell J. of Economics* 11:2, 550–64.
White, Michelle J. (1983), "Bankruptcy Costs and the New Bankruptcy Code," *J. of Finance* 38, 477–88.

White, Michelle J. (1989), "The Corporate Bankruptcy Decision," *J. of Economic Perspectives* 3, 129–52.

White, Michelle J. (2016), "Economics of Corporate and Personal Bankruptcy Law," in *Oxford Handbook of Law and Economics*, Francesco Parisi (ed.). Oxford, UK: Oxford University Press.

11. Making fraudulent transfer law more predictable

*Michael Simkovic**

I. INTRODUCTION AND BACKGROUND

Fraudulent transfer law fills an important gap in U.S. regulations of corporations. Although corporate law makes limited liability widely available and inexpensive for businesses, it has relatively few mechanisms to prevent excessive and socially destructive risk taking.[1] Although it may seem sensible to enforce minimum capital requirements before granting limited liability, such prospective minimum capital regulation is generally only applied to firms in the financial sector.[2] For most other firms, fraudulent transfer law is the closest thing to a minimum capital requirement.

Fraudulent transfer law enables bankruptcy courts to void certain prepetition transfers that depleted a debtor's estate. The standard of liability for constructive fraudulent transfer is that (1) the transfer was made for less than "reasonably equivalent value," and (2) the debtor either: (i) was insolvent at the time of the transfer or was rendered insolvent by the transfer; (ii) was inadequately capitalized; or (iii) believed it would be unable to pay its debts as they matured.[3]

Because the test for the financial condition of the debtor is disjunctive, constructive fraudulent transfer is less tolerant of risk to creditors than a simple standard of balance sheet solvency. For example, even though a debtor currently has assets that exceed the value of its liabilities, it could still be inadequately capitalized or unlikely to pay its debts as they mature.

For the sake of economy, the words "insolvent" or "insolvency" are used in this chapter to refer to any financial condition that is sufficient to satisfy the requirements for fraudulent transfer liability.[4]

If important counterparties determine that the risk of fraudulent transfer liability is too high, they can pressure the debtor corporation to raise equity, or refuse to extend credit or otherwise transact. Fraudulent transfer law[5] forces parties who deal with financially vulnerable institutions to tread cautiously.[6]

Unfortunately, the methods that bankruptcy courts have traditionally used to adjudicate fraudulent transfer claims have at times led to inconsistent, unpredictable, and inadvertently biased outcomes.

In leveraging transactions such as leveraged buyouts, dividend recapitalizations and corporate spin-offs, secured lenders are often targeted as defendants.[7]

Because such investors typically demand a premium for non-diversifiable risk, uncertainty and inconsistency created in adjudication of fraudulent transfer claims can unsettle lenders and drive up the cost of capital ex-ante without offering commensurate benefits in terms of recovery to unsecured creditors ex-post.[8]

There are two important causes of uncertainty and inconsistency. First, courts' reliance on experts introduces tremendous subjectivity and complexity into the process. Second, well-established features of human psychology—which cannot be overcome, despite the good intentions of bankruptcy judges—taint decision-making with legally impermissible hindsight bias.

However, recent legal and financial innovations may aid bankruptcy courts in assessing fraudulent transfer claims in large business bankruptcies. These innovations have the potential to diminish the importance of experts, increase consistency and predictability in fraudulent transfer law, de-bias and simplify judicial decision-making, and reduce the cost of capital for ex-ante value-creating leveraging transactions while deterring imprudent excess leverage.

Specifically, this chapter discusses the shift by bankruptcy courts toward market-implied probabilities of default and the growing sophistication of courts in applying these methods for purposes of solvency analysis. This new market-centered paradigm—coupled with recent innovations in the financial markets and finance theory—can enable fraudulent transfer law to more effectively achieve its historical policy objectives.

Although this chapter focuses on fraudulent transfer law, its potential applications are much broader. Market-implied probabilities of default can assist courts in deciding any controversy that requires a judicial determination of corporate solvency, whether the controversy pertains to fraudulent transfer, preference, or corporate directors' duties.[9] Market-implied probabilities of default can be calculated from any debt instrument that is traded in a liquid and reasonably informed market and for which a yield to maturity can be calculated, whether the instrument is a credit default swap, a corporate bond, or a bank loan. The applications are diverse and the ramifications are potentially vast.[10]

II. WHY LEVERAGING TRANSACTIONS?

LBOs became popular in the 1980s as a method of facilitating acquisitions.[11] They are credited with creating a market for corporate control by funding many potential buyers who would not otherwise have access to sufficient capital. By introducing competition for control, the prospect of an LBO can put performance pressure on incumbent management, which can benefit investors.[12] Changes in a firm's capital structure and ownership can also increase the value of the firm by improving corporate governance and reducing taxes.[13] Leverage in general may be an attractive way to convert the relationship between a corporation and its investors from one of amorphous fiduciary duties to one of clearly defined contractual rights, thereby reducing agency costs.[14] Most empirical studies suggest that, on average, LBOs create value for the firm as a whole but also transfer value from creditors to equity holders.[15]

An LBO resembles a nonrecourse mortgage, in which an acquirer buys an asset by borrowing funds against that asset.[16] In a typical LBO transaction, the acquirer creates a merger subsidiary. At the closing, the merger subsidiary borrows funds to purchase the equity of the target from the target's stockholders, often at a significant premium to market prices. Immediately after closing, the acquisition debt is secured by the target's assets (and often its equity).[17] After the LBO, the target's capital structure includes more debt and fewer unencumbered assets.[18] This change in capital structure may reduce the recovery of unsecured creditors if the company becomes insolvent.[19]

LBOs and other complex leveraging transactions are routinely challenged under fraudulent transfer law if the debtor files bankruptcy.[20] Plaintiffs allege that these transactions imprudently reduce the debtor's liquidity and capital adequacy, and that the borrowed funds cannot provide a reasonably equivalent value because they merely pass through the debtor to former shareholders. According to plaintiffs, the debtor is saddled with obligations while the lender effectively delivers the cash proceeds directly to shareholders.

A number of courts have established doctrines such as threshold knowledge or intent requirements[21] that excuse some stakeholders,[22] especially small shareholders from whom recovery would be impractical.

Once certain threshold knowledge or intent requirements are met,[23] liability generally turns on the financial condition of the debtor at the time of the challenged transaction.[24] The financial condition determination must be made without the benefit of hindsight.[25]

III. RECENT JUDICIAL DECISIONS CAN MAKE FRAUDULENT TRANSFER LAW FAIRER AND MORE EFFICIENT THROUGH THE USE OF FINANCIAL MARKET PRICES

Constructive fraud statutes leave it to bankruptcy courts to develop methodologies for measuring "solvency" and adequacy of "capital" and "ability to pay" debts as they mature.

The methodologies that bankruptcy courts developed drew on the methods of solvency analysis and valuation that were used by financial professionals.[26] These methods can roughly be divided into two categories: those used to measure cash-flow solvency (liquidity) and those used to measure balance sheet solvency (value).[27]

A. Dependence on Financial Experts, Increased Costs and Arbitrariness

Experts' methods of financial analysis, though quantitative and grounded in assumptions of efficient capital markets, largely depend on subjective judgments.[28] Although investors can legitimately differ on questions of value,[29] in the context of high-stakes litigation, experts who are motivated to serve the interest of the parties who pay their fees[30] often come to starkly different and predictably self-serving conclusions.[31] The problem is compounded by the lack of clear definition for "adequate capital." Adequate or inadequate capital means what courts say it means, and what courts say it means varies from case to case in ways that may not readily lend themselves to ex-ante prediction by those planning transactions.

The "hired gun" approach of many experts, and the difficulty courts face evaluating their testimony, have produced substantial injustice for litigants and embarrassment for courts.[32] In *In re Exide Technologies*, dueling experts for the debtor and the creditors' committee both used the three standard valuation methodologies—comparable company analysis, comparable transaction analysis, and discounted cash flow—yet arrived at very different results.[33] The Court sided with the creditors' committee expert,[34] but almost immediately after the debtor exited bankruptcy, the market showed that the Court was dead wrong.[35] *Exide* exemplifies why judges should not be placed in a situation where experts can mislead them.

The sections that follow highlight ways in which the most commonly used traditional measures of solvency and adequate capital—liquidity, discounted cash flow, comparable company multiples, and comparable transactions multiples—can be manipulated. The discussion also describes inconsistent application of these methods by different courts.

1. Cash flow projections are inherently subjective and prone to hindsight bias

Projected cash flows are probably the single most important component of solvency analysis because they are relevant to both a dynamic, cash-flow concept of solvency (can the company pay its debts as they become due?) and to a static, balance sheet approach to solvency (is the company currently worth more than it owes?). Projections are used both in liquidity analysis and in discounted cash flow ("DCF") analysis.

Projecting future cash flows involves making a subjective judgment about the future based on imperfect and limited information about the past and the present.[36] Although projections are generally based on a financial model, the complexity of sophisticated financial models may make it more difficult for bankruptcy judges to detect unreasonable subjective assumptions.[37]

DCF is a method of valuation that has three components: (1) projections of future cash flows of the debtor; (2) a discount rate that is used to convert future cash flows into their present value; and (3) a terminal value used to limit the necessary projection period.[38] Experts can manipulate the outcome of a DCF analysis,[39] either by constructing their own post hoc cash-flow projections or by selectively emphasizing certain projections that were created at the time of the allegedly fraudulent transaction.[40] Terminal value can similarly be manipulated because it depends on the last year of cash-flow projections and on a perpetual growth rate for the company. Experts can manipulate terminal value by choosing a growth rate that is similar to the historical growth rate of either the company, the industry, or the broader economy (U.S. or global)—whichever leads to the outcome they prefer.

In the fraudulent transfer context, where experts retroactively select cash-flow "projections" for the period between the challenged transaction and the bankruptcy, the credibility of cash-flow projections and growth rates depends on the apparent foreseeability of the business setbacks that derailed the debtor.

Foreseeability is determined on a case-by-case basis, but such an ad hoc approach to justice provides little guidance to counterparties structuring transactions. In many cases, courts have reached seemingly inconsistent determinations about whether a particular type of business setback is foreseeable. Low-cost competition is apparently foreseeable in the automotive industry,[41] but not in the mobile communications industry.[42] Loss of revenue is apparently foreseeable if it is due to the loss of a key customer,[43] but not if it is due to the loss of a key employee.[44] Financial crises are apparently not foreseeable if they are due to defaults by poor, formerly communist countries,[45] but they are foreseeable if they are due to defaults by poor subprime mortgage borrowers.[46]

In addition to contending with manipulations by expert witnesses and inconsistent precedent, judges must also contend with innate and universal psychological biases that affect all decision makers. An overwhelming amount of psychological research suggests that a judge will tend to believe that projections that closely match what actually happened are more reasonable than would a decision maker who did not have the benefit of hindsight.[47] In other words, the court will generally tend to believe that more negative projections are more reasonable because the debtor did in fact file for bankruptcy. Instructions to the contrary, and legal prohibitions against hindsight, are an ineffective prophylactic against such hindsight bias.

2. Discount rates can be manipulated because they depend on complicated math masking subjective assumptions

Discount rates are important for static balance sheet solvency analysis.[48] Experts can manipulate the discount rate by choosing from several methods of calculation.[49] In addition, within each method, experts can manipulate assumptions about financial arcana[50] such as equity risk premiums[51] and systemic risk (beta).[52]

All else being equal, higher projections should be accompanied by a higher discount rate because more extreme projections are less likely to materialize. In practice, however, plaintiffs' experts will typically use a high discount rate and low projections, while defense experts will typically use a low discount rate and high projections.[53]

3. Multiples methods can easily be manipulated unless the judge is an expert on several industries

Multiples analysis embraces market value as a reality check on DCF analysis.[54] However, rather than using market prices of the debtor, this approach uses market prices of similar firms.[55]

The problem with the multiples approach is that no two companies are ever perfectly comparable.[56] Some are more cost-efficient, some have better growth prospects, some have stronger brands, and some enjoy better relationships with the government. They may have a different mix of business lines or operate in different markets.

The selection of comparable companies is an art, not a science, with considerable room for manipulation by experts.[57] Defense experts tend to select guideline companies or transactions that will yield a high multiple, and therefore a high valuation of the debtor, while plaintiffs' experts tend to select guideline companies or transactions that will yield a low multiple.[58] Without extensive knowledge of many companies (and industries, given that large debtors often have multiple business lines), courts cannot easily evaluate which comparables are more appropriate than others.[59]

4. Experts can exploit judges' natural tendency to avoid extremes

Experts often provide a "sensitivity analysis" displayed as a table containing a range of possible assumptions and projections.[60] Such an analysis enhances the apparent sophistication of the projections and the credibility of the expert.[61] However, because judges, like most decision makers, tend to prefer to avoid extremes, courts will be inclined to believe that the most likely outcome is one that is in the middle.[62] By manipulating the endpoints of the range, and thereby moving the middle, the expert can guide the court toward a decision that is favorable to his client.[63] Judges may also want to split the difference between experts, which encourages experts to take extreme positions.

5. Traditional methods assume that capital markets are efficient

For all of their subjectivity and complexity, the traditional methods of solvency analysis still depend on the assumption that capital markets are efficient. The discount rate used in DCF analysis is almost always calculated using mathematical methods that require an assumption that capital markets are efficient.[64] Multiples methods rely on the capital markets to value comparable firms comparably.

If financial markets can be trusted to discount cash flows or value comparable firms, then one wonders why they cannot be trusted to value the debtor, thereby eliminating the need to determine which projections are appropriate or which firms are comparable. As discussed below, a number of recent decisions have suggested that not only can financial markets frequently be trusted, but they are in fact usually more trustworthy than litigation experts.

B. Delaware and New York Courts Have Started to Use Market Prices Instead of Experts

The Supreme Court has long embraced the belief, widely shared by many Anglo-American economists, that well-regulated financial markets effectively process available information and thereby fairly and appropriately value securities.[65] The Court suggested that the main sources of defects in market prices are inaccurate or incomplete information, or other concerted attempts to manipulate market prices, which market regulation seeks to prevent.[66]

The Supreme Court's insight about the use of market prices to perform valuation analysis has influenced fraudulent transfer analysis. The first judicial use of market prices as a substitute for, rather than as a supplement to, expert opinion was by the Delaware District Court in *VFB LLC v. Campbell Soup Co.* in 2005, affirmed by the Third Circuit in 2007.[67] The propriety of using financial market prices for fraudulent transfer analysis was further reinforced by Judge Peck of the U.S. Bankruptcy Court for the Southern District of New York in *In re Iridium Operating LLC*, 373 B.R. 283 (Bankr. S.D.N.Y. 2007).

Recently, the court in *Tronox Inc. v. Kerr McGee Corp. (In re Tronox Inc.*), 503 B.R. 239 (Bankr. S.D.N.Y. 2013), took a nuanced and skeptical approach to certain market-based defenses, but distinguished *VFB*.

1. *VFB LLC v. Campbell Soup Co.*

VFB is noteworthy for three reasons: first, the Delaware District Court relied heavily on market prices and essentially ignored the opinions of expert witnesses who used traditional methods of valuation and solvency analysis.[68] The district court attributed differences between the implicit judgment of the market and the opinion of plaintiffs' experts to the experts' "hindsight bias."[69] The Third Circuit went further, questioning the basic worth of expert opinion when market prices are available and trading is open, liquid, and informed.[70]

Second, the Third Circuit did not use the market prices of securities to simply value those securities, as the Supreme Court did in *Basic v. Levinson*, but instead used the price of securities to value and evaluate the solvency of a firm as a whole.[71]

Third, *VFB* is noteworthy because the Court developed a clever solution to the problem of imperfect public disclosure of relevant financial information. Rather than use contemporaneous market prices that were based on manipulated accounting information, the court used delayed market prices from a time period after the correct financial information had been disclosed to the market.[72]

In *VFB*, Campbell Soup Company ("Campbell") spun off underperforming product lines through a leveraged transaction.[73] Campbell received $500 million in cash, while the new company, Vlasic Foods International ("VFI"), took on debt obligations.[74] About three years later, VFI filed bankruptcy.[75]

The spin-off transaction resembled an LBO with Campbell, as the pre-LBO equity holder, receiving cash for its equity stake, and the new company replacing equity with bank debt. However, unlike most LBOs, the spin-off was not a going-private transaction. The equity markets therefore continued to process and display information about the financial state of VFI after the transaction.

For two years before the spin-off, Campbell used a variety of dubious accounting techniques to improve the reported finances of the division that would become VFI without actually improving its long-term prospects.[76] These manipulations appear to have successfully misled both the securities markets and the banks that extended credit to finance the spin-off transaction.[77]

However, shortly after the spin-off, the court found that VFI's "inflated sales and earnings figures quickly corrected themselves."[78] The market presumably processed this new, more accurate information about VFI's past performance and future prospects, but VFI's market capitalization remained above $1.1 billion, and the company was able to raise $200 million in new unsecured debt.[79] The court interpreted equity market prices and bond market receptivity as a judgment by the capital markets that VFI was solvent as of the date of the spin-off, and therefore concluded that the spin-off could not be avoided as a fraudulent transfer.

The court suggested that the point at which the debtor became insolvent could be determined based on the time when the debtor's bonds began trading below par value.[80] Bond price relative to par is a flawed measure of the financial condition of a debtor,[81] but the court correctly concluded that credit market prices contain information that is relevant to a fraudulent transfer analysis. Notably, at the time VFI filed for bankruptcy, its bonds were generally traded on over-the-counter markets with very little public disclosure of transaction pricing or trade volumes[82]—unlike the liquid, transparent, exchange-traded stock markets discussed by the Supreme Court in *Basic v. Levinson*. The court nevertheless deferred to bond market prices.

2. *In re Iridium Operating LLC*

The Third Circuit's reasoning in *VFB*, that market prices are the best indicator of valuation and solvency, was accepted and extended by the bankruptcy court in *In re Iridium Operating LLC*.[83] *Iridium* is noteworthy because Judge Peck resisted the temptation to second-guess market participants' contemporaneous judgments, even though the market was so bad at predicting the future performance of the debtor that the market's valuation in this instance seems almost absurd—at least with the benefit of hindsight.[84] The court focused not on whether the market was a good predictor of the future in this particular instance, but on whether the market was 'reasonably well informed as to [the debtor's] operating characteristics and constraints. . . .'[85]

The key facts of *Iridium*, as described in the opinion, are as follows:

In 1990, Motorola established a Satellite Communications Division to design, develop, and implement a commercially viable satellite-based phone system that would provide worldwide coverage using a handheld, portable device.[86] In the early 1990s, Motorola transferred ownership of the Iridium system to Iridium, Inc. (later Iridium LLC), and ultimately to a group of private investors who bought shares in Iridium, Inc. through private placements of equity.[87] Motorola retained a significant equity stake, seats on the board, and, through a series of contracts, the rights to design, develop, and sell critical parts of the Iridium system.[88] In the late 1990s, an Iridium entity raised hundreds of millions in equity through an initial public offering (IPO) and subsequent sales of stock to the public.[89]

Pursuant to Iridium's contracts with Motorola, Iridium paid Motorola more than $3.7 billion.[90] To help finance the development of the Iridium System, Iridium borrowed billions of dollars.[91] Some, but not all, of these debts were guaranteed by Motorola. Throughout this period, stock market valuations and access to credit (including secured bank debt) suggested that Iridium was solvent and had a reasonably bright future.[92]

Iridium entered bankruptcy in 1999, less than a year after the commercial launch of the system. Subscriptions were far below projections. The disappointing results may have been due to technical limitations of the system, such as very large and heavy handsets and the need for a direct line of sight to the satellite (and therefore the inability to use the system reliably in cities).[93] The failure may also have been due to the high cost of subscriptions and rapid improvement in competing cellular telephone technology.[94]

To anyone who has used a mobile telephone in the last few years, it seems obvious that a large, heavy, and expensive device that does not work reliably inside buildings or moving cars would not be a serious contender. However, in the 1990s when the system was developed and competing technologies were in their infancy, this was far from obvious to many highly intelligent and well-informed market participants. As Judge Peck explained:

> The fact that Iridium failed in such a spectacular fashion stands out as a disturbing counterpoint to the market's optimistic predictions of present and future value for Iridium, but in the end, the market evidence could not be denied. The capital markets synthesized and distilled what all the smart people of the era knew or believed to be true about Iridium. Given the overwhelming weight of that market evidence, it may be that the burden of proving insolvency and unreasonably small capital simply could not be met under any circumstances, regardless of the evidence adduced, in the wake of the Third Circuit's VFB decision. . . .[95]

The court held for defendants, but suggested in dicta that the debtor 'may have been in the zone of insolvency or may have actually slipped into insolvency at some point between the date of commercial activation and the petition date.'[96] The court pointed out that plaintiffs might have been able to prove insolvency after the launch, given the 'inexorable and increasingly sharp decline' in the debtor's stock price if they had analysed the market data. However, the court did not discuss how a court would or could use a debtor's stock price to distinguish between a solvent debtor with declining fortunes and a debtor that had actually become insolvent.[97]

3. *In re Tronox, Inc.*

In *In re Tronox, Inc.*, the Chapter 11 trustee challenged the spinoff of a profitable oil subsidiary. The spinoff left behind substantial environmental and tort legacy liabilities, and the trustee argued that the transaction was both constructively and actually fraudulent. The value of the spun off subsidiary at the time of the lawsuit was much greater than the price received at the time of the sale. The court ultimately held that the spinoff was for less than reasonably equivalent value, and an important question was therefore whether, at the time of the spinoff, the holding company was adequately capitalized.

The *Tronox* court found that the debtors' ability to obtain secured credit from a sophisticated counterparty was irrelevant to a solvency determination, because the expected recovery rate for secured creditors is so high that the pricing on secured debt is not sensitive to the risk of default.[98] On the other hand, the *Tronox* court was impressed with the debtor's ability to raise unsecured debt and equity at the time it was allegedly insolvent.[99] However, the *Tronox* court, distinguishing *VFB*, found that the company failed to disclose certain material liabilities to the market, and that the market's assessment of the debtor's prospects was therefore unreliable.[100]

The court also considered evidence that sophisticated private investors with access to more accurate information had decided to invest in the company. However, the court concluded that because investment banks were lending on a secured basis, and because a private equity firm demanded substantial indemnification against legacy liabilities, those investors' willingness to invest did not provide much evidence of solvency.[101]

4. *In re American Classic Voyages, Co.*

In *In re American Classic Voyages, Co.*,[102] debtors brought an adversary proceeding against defendant banks, seeking to recover a payment of $29,500,000 made under a revolving line of credit. After trial, the Bankruptcy Court dismissed the complaint, finding that debtors were not insolvent at the time of the alleged preferential payment.

On appeal, debtors argued that the Third Circuit's *VFB* decision—issued a month prior to the Bankruptcy Court's decision but after the submission of post-trial briefs to the Bankruptcy Court—prohibited the use of discounted cash flow analysis for solvency analysis. According to appellant debtors, defendants' expert—who relied on DCF—had therefore failed to overcome the presumption of insolvency. Debtors argued that the matter should be remanded for a new trial because a 94 percent drop in equity value suggested that the debtor may have been insolvent.

The Delaware District court held that notwithstanding the *VFB* decision, DCF remained a viable method of establishing solvency. The Court noted that although the defense expert did not use market prices in his analysis, market prices appeared to be generally consistent with the defense expert's DCF analysis. The Court noted that the debtor was able to refinance debt and had access to revolving credit in spite of the drop in equity value.

Overall the opinion confirms that market-price-based analyses are helpful to include in a solvency or adequate capitalization analysis. However, a failure to include a market-price-based analysis is not necessarily fatal, particularly when a market-price-based analysis would likely lead to the same conclusions as a more traditional approach. It is possible that the District Court was reluctant to overturn the Bankruptcy Court as "clearly erroneous" in part because of the late timing of the *VFB* decision. Courts in the Third Circuit may insist on a market-based analysis in more recent cases litigated after the *VFB* decision.

IV. BENEFITS OF INCORPORATION OF ADDITIONAL INSIGHTS FROM FINANCE INTO THE LAW

The *VFB, Iridium,* and *Tronox* decisions represent major advances in how courts approach fraudulent transfer claims. It is important for courts to use market prices to assess solvency, to combat the dangers of expert manipulation and hindsight bias.

The legal consensus surrounding the Efficient Market Hypothesis has been modified since the financial crisis, as scholars and courts have increasingly recognized that in addition to outright manipulation, complexity and information costs may also reduce transparency and market efficiency.[103] However, under most circumstances, markets continue to offer a good guide to value.

VFB and *Iridium* leave important questions unanswered. How should courts decide close cases such as when a debtor's equity price is declining but still positive, when bonds are trading slightly below par, or when the debtor has access to credit but on unfavorable terms?

What about cases in which equity prices may reflect volatility instead of adequate capitalization? Or when equity prices cease to be available, such as in going-private transactions?

How can courts evaluate whether market prices in relatively lightly regulated, nontransparent markets reflect informed analysis or market manipulation? How can courts articulate clear standards that are applicable across time and across debtors?

The discussion that follows will try to answer some of these questions by explaining the methods that financial professionals and economists use to calculate the probability and severity of default implied by financial market prices. The discussion will also suggest relatively simple equations and rules of thumb to guide courts as they use market prices to evaluate solvency and adequate capitalization. The discussion will emphasize clarity and ease of use over technical precision, with the goal of providing courts with a practical tool they can readily use. The techniques are generally applicable, but particular emphasis will be placed on the fraudulent transfer and LBO contexts.

A. Equity Market Prices Provide a Noisy Signal of Default Probability Because They Reflect Option Value

For purposes of predicting default, equity market capitalization is not directly comparable to balance sheet equity[104] or to adequate liquidity. Instead, economists and financial professionals view equity as a call option on the assets and future cash flows of a firm.[105] The most important implication of this realization is that a firm can have a positive equity value even though it is highly likely that debt holders will incur steep losses, i.e., that the firm is insolvent, inadequately capitalized, or will be unable to pay its debts as they come due. Equity value in isolation is therefore an unreliable measure of solvency.[106]

However, equity market prices can provide a more robust measure of solvency when coupled with measures of volatility, capital structure, and debt market prices.[107] Unfortunately, the mathematics are complex, equity prices generally cease to be available after an LBO, and the models can easily be incorrectly calibrated or applied to situations in which the assumptions on which they depend do not hold true.[108] Simpler models, such as enterprise value—i.e., adding up the market values of tradable equity and debt—may be useful in some contexts, but when a large proportion of the debt is not tradable—such as pension, tort, or environmental liabilities—a robust market price for tradable high yield debt does not necessarily reflect a high likelihood that other unsecured creditors will be repaid in full. In a low interest rate environment, high yield debt might trade at a premium even if it carries substantial risk of default.

Instead of using equity or relying exclusively on enterprise value and equity in combination with bond prices, courts should use credit spreads, which provide more robust and reliable estimates of the financial condition of the debtor. Credit spreads are particularly useful with respect to the last two prongs of the test, adequate capitalization and ability to pay debts as they come due. These are generally referred to as "solvency" for purposes of the discussion that follows.

B. Credit Spreads Should Be Used to Measure Credit Market Implied Probabilities of Default

When courts apply fraudulent transfer law, they engage in an analysis similar to that used by fixed-income investors[109] who buy or sell corporate debt (bonds) or insurance on corporate debt (credit default swaps). Courts must determine whether, at the time of the alleged fraudulent transfer, the debtor was inadequately capitalized and likely to become unable to pay its debts based on reasonable projected future cash flows. Fixed-income investors must similarly determine the likelihood that the bond issuer (debtor) will default on its obligations and the likely severity of any default.

Courts face a more challenging task than fixed-income investors, however, because by law, courts must act without hindsight, even though they are fully aware that the debtor ultimately filed for bankruptcy. By contrast, investors need only act in the moment, based on the best information available to them at the time.

When bond market and CDS participants trade, they leave a record of the conclusions of their analysis. This record is prospective because market participants always act in the moment, without the benefit of hindsight. This record is also likely to reflect a reasonably good assessment of the probability of default because large fixed income market participants—such as investment managers at mutual funds, insurance companies, and pension funds and traders at hedge funds and investment banks—are generally sophisticated, well-informed, and data-driven.

Bond prices should not be used because bonds can trade above or below par because of factors that are unrelated to the probability or severity of default. These factors include current and expected fluctuations in prevailing interest rates, which affect yields and therefore prices.[110] Bond price movements can be dramatic if there is a sufficiently large change in the interest rate environment and if most of the payments on the bond are due far in the future (i.e., the bond has a high duration).

Instead of bond prices or yields, courts should focus on credit spreads. Credit spreads can be the difference between the yield on a bond with some risk of default and the yield on a risk-free instrument of equal maturity. Credit spreads can also be the fees paid by protection buyers who enter into contracts known as credit default swaps.

Credit default swaps are derivatives that economically resemble bond insurance but can be used to speculate (or place a "naked" bet) as well as to hedge (or place a "covered" bet).[111] Credit default swaps are designed specifically to permit bets on the likelihood of default of a particular company, and therefore, arguably provide an even clearer market-based indicator of the likelihood of default than bond spreads.[112] Several perceived limitations in the bond markets—such as limited liquidity and the difficulty of establishing a short position—are believed to have contributed to the growth of the market for credit default swaps.[113] It is also likely that increasing transparency in the bond market made the CDS market more attractive to market participants who preferred to keep their transactions secret.[114]

In a CDS transaction, there are two counterparties: a protection buyer and a protection seller.[115] The two counterparties place opposite bets on whether a third party will default on its debts (the "reference debt"). The protection seller agrees in the event of a "credit event"—a situation in which a third party defaults on its debt, restructures its debt, or files for bankruptcy—to pay the protection buyer an amount that is calculated based on losses that would be experienced by an investor who holds a "notional" amount of a third party's debt.[116] In return for this default protection, the protection buyer pays periodic fees to the protection seller.[117] The fees are quoted in basis points ("bps"; 100 bps = one percent) of the notional value.

When interpreting credit spreads, the most important concept to understand is that bankruptcies and defaults can involve different degrees of loss to bondholders. The probability of default and the severity of the default—the loss given default—are what drive credit spreads.[118] For a given spread, the probability of default and the loss given default are inversely related. In other words, if two investors both agree that a certain credit spread is appropriate, but the first investor believes that the probability of default is higher than the second investor, then the first investor must believe that the loss given default will be lower than the second investor.

The discussion that follows explains the relative advantages and disadvantages of bond market data and CDS data, and why courts should ideally consider data from both markets in their analyses. It also explains how courts (or those seeking to persuade them) can extract the probability of default and the expected loss given default that are implicit in bond credit spreads and CDS fees (also called spreads). The techniques we develop and present here are designed to be simple. Although professional fixed income traders—whose profits depend on fractions of a percent on every trade[119] and who may wish to make surgical bets about the timing of a default—may use more sophisticated techniques,[120] extracting market implied probabilities of default for our purposes does not require the same degree of precision. More complex techniques are more assumption-laden and therefore easier for experts to manipulate. In the legal context, simplicity is a virtue. The discussion also explains important caveats and precautions that should be taken when using the described approaches.

1. Market implied probabilities of default facilitate continuous solvency analysis

Bankruptcy courts sometimes conceived of insolvency as a state into which a debtor moved on some date before filing bankruptcy, and that once insolvent, a debtor remained insolvent until filing bankruptcy. This view was convenient because it was historically expensive and time-consuming for a court to determine a debtor's financial condition at each point in time, and a single bankruptcy might involve numerous alleged fraudulent transfers on different dates.

However, the truth is that a debtor can shift back and forth between insolvency and solvency several times before filing bankruptcy. The Bankruptcy Code explicitly contemplates this possibility because it refers to the financial condition of the debtor on "the date" of the alleged fraudulent transfer.

The output of our model—a line graph showing the probability of default across multiple dates—enables courts to make more fine-grained determinations about the pre-bankruptcy periods during which the debtor was solvent and those during which the debtor was insolvent.

Before diving into a discussion of the technical aspects of calculating market implied probabilities of default, it may be helpful for the reader to see examples of results of the analysis. The charts below illustrate the power of market implied probabilities of default as a tool for bankruptcy judges.

Figure 11.1 below shows CDS market participants' view of the solvency of General Motors. To those who are familiar with the company, it is probably unremarkable that General Motors's bankruptcy was no surprise to the market. Between General Motors's high labor costs, legacy liabilities, and stiff competition from leaner rivals—whose products the public often perceived to be of higher quality than General Motors's—CDS market participants could see bankruptcy coming years ahead.

By contrast, Lehman Brothers's bankruptcy came as surprise.

Figure 11.2 below shows CDS market participants' view of Lehman Brothers.

As long as market participants were informed, and the market was free of manipulation, these results suggest answers to fraudulent transfer questions.[121] Any transfer made by General Motors for several years before it filed bankruptcy may qualify as a constructively fraudulent transfer. Any

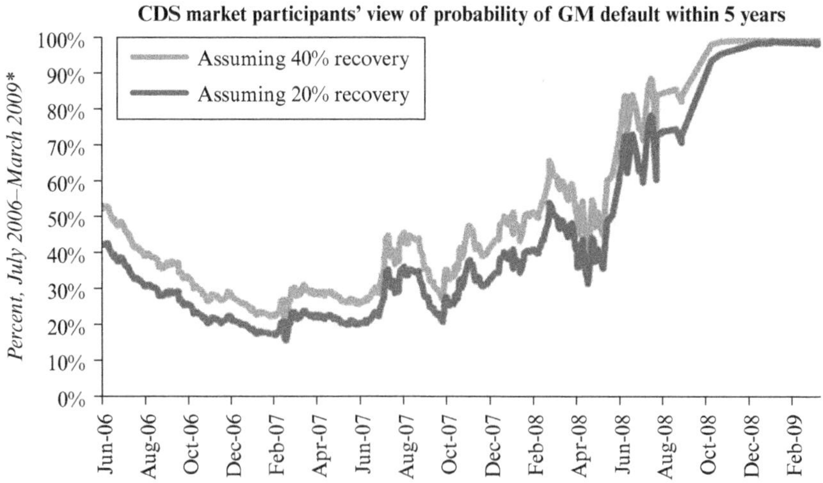

Note: *General Motors filed bankruptcy in July of 2009.

Source: Bloomberg, CMA,Equations 4 through 7.

Figure 11.1 CDS market predicted General Motors' bankruptcy years in advance

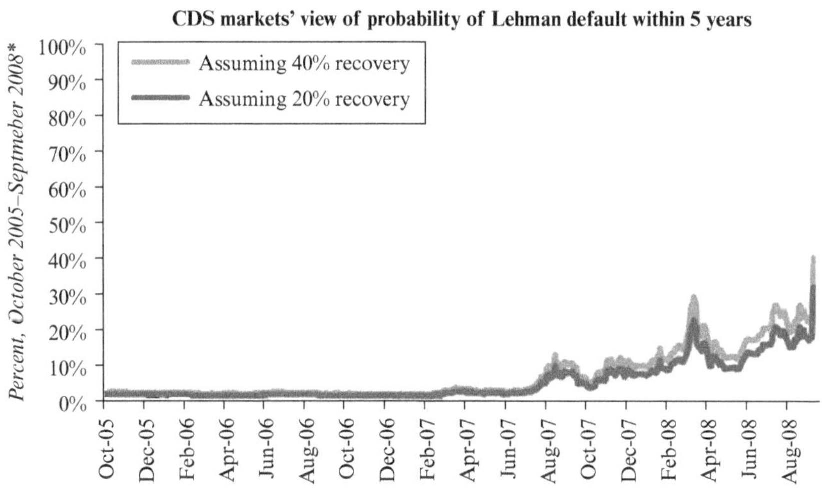

Note: *Lehman Brothers filed bankruptcy in September 2008.

Source: Bloomberg, CMA,Equations 4 through 7.

Figure 11.2 CDS market believed Lehman Brothers was solvent until shortly before bankruptcy

transfer made by Lehman Brothers before July 2007 almost certainly does not qualify.[122] Lehman transfers in March 2008 or after July 2008 may qualify as fraudulent transfers. The answers to these questions depend on judicial determinations of acceptable default probabilities.

2. CDS markets may often provide the best information about default risk

a. CDS markets may be more efficient because they are a haven for insider trading The smaller the information gap between management and market participants at the time of the allegedly fraudulent transfer, the more reliable market prices are as a gauge of the risk of default.

The information available to market participants at the time of an allegedly fraudulent transaction may not include all of the information that courts wish to consider in evaluating whether the company was insolvent. For example, management and banks conducting due diligence may have non-public information. In such situations, courts have considered market prices after the public disclosure of pertinent information rather than solely at the time of the alleged fraudulent transfer.[123]

However, if insider trading or sophisticated due diligence by investors are prevalent in a particular market, prices at the time of the fraudulent transfer may at least in part reflect information that is not generally available to the public.

The data suggests that CDS markets anticipate negative credit rating agency actions, including reviews for downgrade, negative outlooks, and downgrades.[124] Although equities markets and bond markets also anticipate negative credit rating agency actions, CDS markets move sooner than either bond or equities markets.[125] Empirical evidence strongly suggests the presence of insider trading in the CDS market: the CDS market anticipates the public release of negative news.[126]

There are strong reasons to believe that prices in the CDS market reflect insider information. The CDS market was historically lightly policed by regulators and was therefore an attractive venue for insider trading.[127] As U.S. regulation has tightened after the financial crisis, CDS trading has moved overseas.[128] Market participants are overwhelmingly large, sophisticated financial institutions[129] such as banks, securities firms, hedge funds, and insurance companies.[130] Many of these institutions may also be secured creditors or financiers of inventory or receivables, and therefore have access to critical information about the debtor that is not widely known.[131]

b. CDS markets are probably more "complete" than bond markets because credit default swaps facilitate shorting Market prices can be skewed if technical features of the market make it easier for investors with certain opinions to "vote" than others. A market is complete if it is possible to enter a trading position placing any bet with regard to the future state of the market.[132] Bond markets may be less than perfectly complete in part because it may be difficult and costly to bet that a bond will fall in value.[133] If an investor who does not already own a bond wishes to bet that the bond will fall in value, the investor may source the bond from a current bondholder who is willing to lend it, borrow the bond, sell it, and repurchase the bond later after the price has (hopefully) fallen. Transactions costs may in some cases be prohibitive, particularly where trading volumes are low and the bonds are difficult to source.[134]

If that is the case, then the bond market might reflect a somewhat more optimistic view than the prevailing view among sophisticated investors because of the technical difficulties such investors face in placing bets that the value of the bonds will fall.

Unlike the bond market, the CDS market likely reflects a neutral or perhaps even a pessimistic view. It is not necessary to source bonds to bet against them using credit default swaps. Rather, it is only necessary to find a sufficiently well-capitalized counterparty that is willing to make the opposite bet.

Considering probabilities of default implied by both bond spreads and CDS spreads should mitigate any problems caused by incompleteness in the bond market.

c. CDS markets may be more efficient because they are anonymous and reduce the risk of retaliation for shorting In addition to the technical difficulties and risks inherent in short-selling debt, there is an additional challenge facing would-be-shorts: retribution. Corporations that disclose sensitive information to financial advisers and vendors and that pay them hefty fees tend to be displeased when these advisers and vendors bet against their success.[135] In fact, firms that issue debt typically require underwriters to agree to retain a portion of that debt on their balance sheets as a sign of support and confidence in the debtor.

Credit default swaps can enable financial institutions and other market participants to offload all default risk (or go further and actually bet against the debtor) while continuing to hold a significant portion of the debt on their balance sheets.[136] In so doing, the financial institution appears to its client—and the outside world—to believe in the client's success, while its true opinion may be considerably less sanguine.[137]

Because credit default swaps are not disclosed on a balance sheet, through U.C.C. filings, through an exchange, or pursuant to any mandatory regulation, CDS trades are generally less transparent than bond trades.[138] In other words, whereas selling a large amount of bonds or bank debt may be the equivalent of stating one's vote during a roll call, buying credit default swap protection can more closely resemble casting a secret ballot.

However, the secrecy and anonymity of the CDS market could also make it an attractive vehicle for market manipulation.[139]

d. Courts can reduce the risk of market manipulation If courts or regulators rely heavily on a single indicator of the probability of default, such reliance will increase market participants' incentive to manipulate that indicator. For example, an activist hedge fund with a large position in an individual debtor's bonds might attempt to push down the price of those bonds (and thereby increase the bond spread) around the time of a leveraging transaction in order to establish a future claim for fraudulent transfer. Similarly, equity holders or banks that stand to benefit from such a transaction might attempt to support the price of the bonds temporarily in order to minimize the risk of a claim for fraudulent transfer. Market manipulation is generally prohibited by sections 9 and 10 of the Securities Exchange Act of 1934, as well as the U.S. Commodity Futures Trading Commission's rules and regulations, but it is probably safe to assume that enforcement is less than completely effective.[140]

Market prices of illiquid assets are less reliable than market prices of liquid assets because a relatively small transaction in an illiquid market can lead to a large change in the volume-weighted average price. To give a concrete example, if $10 million worth of bonds typically trade hands each day and an investor suddenly attempts to sell $50 million worth of bonds in one day, there will likely be an insufficient number of buyers at the most recent market price and the investor will have to accept a price significantly lower than the last market price. On the other hand, if $1 billion worth of bonds trades hands each day, the market can likely absorb the same $50 million transaction without a significant movement in price.

Higher trading volumes make market manipulation more difficult and more expensive because more capital must be deployed to move the market price. Financial market prices are also generally more reliable when trading volume is robust. Prices generated through low-volume trades are unlikely to represent the collective wisdom of market participants for the same reasons that election results with low voter turnouts are unlikely to reflect the will of the people—the results only reveal the opinions of a small minority of potential decision makers who participated. Higher trading volumes suggest that more firms put more capital at stake and expended more resources evaluating the price at which the debt should trade. Higher trading volumes also tend to reduce transactions costs and make markets more efficient.

Because price disclosure in the CDS market is voluntary, and volume-weighted average price data is generally not available, CDS markets are probably vulnerable to manipulation, even with higher volume. Regulation in OTC derivatives markets is also notoriously lax.[141]

To avoid the problems of low volume trades, it may be advisable to consider the volume-weighted average price over a period one to two weeks before or after the allegedly fraudulent transfer,[142] because the total trading volume will be higher than on the day of the alleged fraudulent transfer.

The dangers of market manipulation can also be reduced by considering market-based indicators of default suggested by multiple markets: different bonds or secured debt instruments of the same issuers, equity prices, and derivatives. The larger the universe, the more difficult it will be to manipulate.

Finally, courts can directly police and monitor manipulation by permitting discovery of trading records, emails, and other communications that might reveal the motives of large creditors—banks and hedge funds—who were trading bonds and credit default swaps around the time of the allegedly fraudulent transfer.[143]

3. High quality market data can be obtained within the context of litigation

a. Corporate bond markets are generally transparent Detailed corporate bond trade data—including price, volume, date, and time—is available through TRACE, the Trade Reporting and Compliance Engine. Limited data is available as far back as 2002, but coverage greatly expanded from 2003 through 2005.[144] Corporate bond trades must be disclosed within fifteen minutes of the trade under Financial Industry Regulatory Authority ("FINRA") rules.[145] TRACE data may be downloaded free of charge for personal use from the FINRA website, but it is also available in a more user-friendly format from financial data providers such as Bloomberg Professional Service and Markit.

b. Although CDS markets are generally not transparent, litigation can shed new light on their inner workings Historically, the CDS market was largely unregulated, and as a result, detailed and reliable data about pricing and volume is hard to obtain. However, several private entities currently aggregate, validate, and sell pricing information provided to them by private market participants.[146] The CDS market may become more transparent because the Dodd-Frank Wall Street Reform and Consumer Protection Act and new rules from the Securities and Exchange Commission and the Commodities Futures Trading Commission require real-time public reporting of swap transaction price and volume data.[147]

Two of the leading data providers of historical CDS pricing are Markit, which is affiliated with CDS dealers (large investment banks), and CME Group's CMA Datavision, which is affiliated with large derivatives buyers (hedge funds, mutual funds, insurance companies, pension funds, etc.).

4. Simple, robust, manipulation-resistant equations can be used to calculate market-implied probabilities of default based on credit market prices

a. How to calculate credit spreads from bond yields or CDS fees One relatively simple technique that helps to isolate default risk from other factors that affect bond yields is to subtract from the corporate bond yield the risk-free interest rate.[148] The risk-free rate is an interest rate paid by a hypothetical borrower who has zero chance of defaulting. Although no such borrower exists, there are borrowers with extremely low probabilities of default. For example, the U.S. government is perceived to have an extremely low probability of default.[149] Academic economists generally use yields on U.S. Treasuries as a benchmark risk-free rate for U.S. dollar denominated debts.[150] Finance professionals tend to use the London Interbank Offered Rate ("LIBOR"), the rate at which banks rated AA (or better) can borrow from other banks.[151] Although LIBOR is not as low risk as U.S. Treasuries (except during periods of distress in the financial system), LIBOR may be only slightly higher than Treasury yields.[152]

The difference between the corporate bond and the risk-free rate is called the "spread," "bond spread," or "credit spread." Credit spreads should be calculated using a risk-free instrument with a term structure that matches the corporate bond as closely as possible.[153] The term structure refers to the timing of interest and principal payments. Equation 11.1 below shows a simple technique to calculate a bond spread.

$$\textit{Credit spread} \cong \textit{Corporate bond yield} - \textit{risk free rate} \tag{11.1}$$

It is important to match the duration and term structure of the corporate bond and the risk-free instrument because yields vary by duration and term structure.[154] In practice, it may not always be possible to perfectly match the term structures.

There are more sophisticated techniques available that try to account for differences in the term structure of the corporate bond and the risk-free rate by constructing a yield curve, but in most cases in the judicial context, the marginal improvement in accuracy presented by these techniques is unlikely to justify the added complexity and potential for manipulation.

Credit default swaps have the advantage of not requiring any math to calculate a credit spread—the market has already done the math.[155] CDS annual fees are themselves a credit spread. The fees paid by CDS protection buyers to protection sellers—under ideal market conditions in which there are no transactions costs, taxes, counterparty risks among derivatives counterparties, or arbitrage opportunities—should be equivalent to the spread between the yield of the reference corporate bond and the risk-free interest rate.[156]

To understand why this is true, consider the following example. Investor A holds \$100 million worth of five-year corporate bonds yielding eight percent. Investor B holds \$100 million worth of five-year Treasuries yielding five percent. If Investor A wishes to eliminate the risk of default from his portfolio, he may do so either by purchasing a five-year credit default swap or by selling his corporate bonds yielding eight percent and purchasing Investor B's Treasuries yielding five percent.[157] In selling his corporate bonds for default-risk-free Treasuries, Investor A will sacrifice 300 basis points, or three percent. Therefore, if a five-year credit default swap would successfully eliminate all default risk, it should also cost 300 basis points. Because of this theoretical equivalence between CDS fees and bond spreads, the fees on credit default swaps are frequently referred to as the "CDS spread" or simply "the spread."

b. How to extract the one-year market implied probability of default from credit spreads The relationship between a credit spread and the perceived risk of default may be approximated by the following simplified equation:

$$(\textit{Risk neutral probability of default in } 1 \textit{ year}) \cong \frac{\textit{Credit spread}}{\textit{Expected loss rate given default}} \qquad (11.2)$$[158]

This simple equation is useful for illustrative purposes. As this equation demonstrates, an increase in the bond spread suggests either an increase in the perceived probability of default or an increase in the expected loss rate given default.

These relationships are directionally correct, but Equation 11.2 is mathematically only a rough approximation. Even under ideal conditions—a credit market that is rational, risk-neutral, transparent, liquid, and free of transactions costs, taxes, or market manipulation—a more complex equation is needed to precisely describe the relationship between perceived probability of default, expected recovery rate, corporate bond yields, and the risk-free rate. The following formula provides a more precise description of the relationship under idealized conditions

$$(\textit{Risk neutral probability of default in } 1 \textit{ year}) = \qquad (11.3)$$

$$\frac{1 - \dfrac{1 + \textit{Risk free rate}}{1 + \textit{Corporate bond yield}}}{\textit{Expected loss rate given default}}$$

If CDS spreads are used instead of bond spreads, Equation 11.3 may be rewritten as:

$$(\textit{Risk neutral probability of default in } 1 \textit{ year}) = \qquad (11.4)$$

$$\frac{1 - \dfrac{1 + \textit{Risk free rate}}{1 + \textit{CDS spread} + \textit{Risk free rate}}}{\textit{Expected loss rate given default}}$$

Equation (11.2), Equation (11.3), and Equation (11.4) all include the expected loss rate given default as a variable. The expected loss rate given default presents a challenge because unlike the corporate bond yield, CDS spread, and the risk-free rate, the expected loss rate given default cannot be directly observed in the market. By convention, financial professionals will sometimes assume a sixty percent expected loss rate given default (a forty percent expected recovery rate) when calculating the implied probability of default for senior unsecured bonds. However, it is possible to make a more well-informed assumption by using historical recovery rates.[159] Furthermore, recent finance research suggests that it may be possible to calculate recovery rates based on prices and rates that are observable in the CDS and equities markets.[160]

c. Credit spreads based on treasuries may overestimate default risk A recent empirical study suggests that, although the majority of the credit spread is due to default risk, other factors still play a role.[161] The credit spread is therefore a good first approximation of default risk, but the analysis can be improved by taking other factors into account.

Finance professionals routinely use credit spreads as a measure of the market perception of the creditworthiness of the debtor,[162] but a number of academic studies have suggested that Treasury-to-corporate bond spreads tend to be wider than can be justified by the real-world historical probability of default alone.[163] In fact, a few studies have even suggested that default risk may account for only a minority of the yield spread.[164]

It is likely that at least some of the bond spread is due to factors other than the probability of default, such as taxes and liquidity. Naïve use of bond spreads to calculate the probability of default will therefore tend, at least on the margin, to overestimate the implied probability of default.

Three approaches may be taken to account for the possibility that bond spreads may overestimate the probability of default.

One approach, frequently used by financial professionals, is to use LIBOR as a risk-free rate instead of Treasuries.[165] Because LIBOR is higher than Treasury yields, the calculated spread will be lower, and the probability of default will also be lower. At least one academic economist strongly favors this approach.[166] However, the use of LIBOR as a risk-free rate is inappropriate during times of distress in the financial system. When banks are perceived to be at risk of default, the spread between LIBOR and Treasuries widens and the impact of using LIBOR instead of Treasuries becomes large because banks are not risk-free.[167]

Another approach is to consider bond spreads, not only in isolation, but also relative to other bond spreads. For example, courts could consider bond spreads of both the debtor and comparable companies. Although an implied probability of default of twenty-five or thirty percent within five years may sound shockingly high in isolation, a comparison may reveal that it is in fact fairly typical for companies within a particular industry. Changes in bond spreads may also be considered over time, for example, shortly before and shortly after the allegedly fraudulent transfer. If the yield on a debtor's bonds increased relative to both the risk-free rate and to comparable companies that did not engage in a similar allegedly fraudulent transfer, then the increase in the spread over comparable companies suggests the extent to which the allegedly fraudulent transfer increased the debtor's risk of default.

Approaches similar to this are frequently used by finance professionals. Major benefits of this approach are that the math is straightforward and the analysis can be understood by viewing a simple line graph showing credit spreads of several companies over time and the timing of the allegedly fraudulent transfer. Although this approach entails subjectivity in the selection of "comparable" companies, it is no more subjective than the comparable companies multiples analysis currently used by the courts for valuation in the fraudulent transfer context.

A third approach, favored by academic economists, is to use mathematically complex models to attempt to isolate the portion of the bond spread that is due to default risk and the portions that are due to other factors. This approach is far more challenging, and probably no less subjective, given the sensitivity of the outcome to the selection of a model and the calibration of that model. Courts may simply wish to recognize that the true probability of default is likely somewhat lower than suggested by credit spreads.

d. How to calculate the multiyear cumulative probability of default Equation 11.2, Equation 11.3, and Equation 11.4 express the market-implied probability of default over one year. However, bankruptcy courts deciding fraudulent transfer cases will generally be concerned with the cumulative probability of default over a multi-year period. Under section 548 of the Bankruptcy Code, the clawback period for fraudulent transfer claims is two years. Under section 544, which incorporates state fraudulent transfer and fraudulent conveyance statutes, the clawback depends on state law but will often be four to six years. It therefore makes sense for courts deciding fraudulent transfer cases to consider the implied cumulative probability of default over the time period during which transferees may be liable under the relevant fraudulent transfer statute.

Thus, for a claim under section 548, the courts should consider the cumulative probability of default from the date of the alleged fraudulent transfer to two years after the alleged fraudulent transfer. For a claim under section 544 and New York fraudulent conveyance law, the courts should consider the cumulative probability of default from the date of the alleged fraudulent transfer to six years after the alleged fraudulent transfer.

The ideal way to calculate the market implied probability of default over such a multi-year period is to calculate the credit spread from corporate bonds or credit default swaps whose maturity date, at the date of the alleged fraudulent transfer, matched the relevant fraudulent transfer period. For example, suppose the alleged fraudulent transfer took place on January 1, 2009 and the applicable fraudulent transfer statute extended fraudulent transfer liability for two years. The court would ideally calculate the spread between the historical yield, on January 1, 2009, of a non-callable bond of the debtor set to mature on January 1, 2011 and an appropriate historical risk-free rate, such as a Treasury bond whose term structure matched the corporate bond and which was set to mature on January 1, 2011. Alternatively, the court could try to look at the spread on a two-year credit default swap set to mature on January 1, 2011.

To calculate the cumulative probability of default over a multi-year period based on a single year probability of default equation—such as Equation 11.2, Equation 11.3, or Equation 11.4—the following equation may be used:

$$\textit{Cumulative probability of default} \qquad (11.5)$$

$$= 1 - (1 - \textit{probability of default in } 1 \textit{ year})^{\textit{number of years}}$$

Using Equation 11.5, as long as the probability of default in each individual year is greater than zero but less than 100 percent, the cumulative probability of default will increase with additional years, approaching but never reaching 100 percent.

Caution should be exercised when extrapolating a cumulative probability of default over many years from a spread based on bonds or credit default swaps of a single, relatively short term. Caution is advised because the probability of default may be higher in some years than in others.

When it is necessary to extrapolate because bonds or credit default swaps of the desired term are not trading, the bankruptcy judge or financial analyst should consider bond spreads across multiple maturities and the timing of large, predictable future cash inflows and outflows.

The most liquid and frequently traded CDS contract is typically the five-year CDS contract for senior unsecured debt.[168] The five-year CDS contract is therefore the contract used most frequently by finance professionals as a benchmark for creditworthiness and default risk.[169] The one-year CDS contract is generally the second most frequently traded. CDS pricing on contracts of other terms is less likely to be available.

V. CONCLUSION: A SHIFT TO MARKET-BASED MEASURES OF SOLVENCY CAN EMPOWER RISK MANAGERS AT BANKS TO BLOCK DESTABILIZING TRANSACTIONS

The problems of hindsight bias and subjective financial analyses are among the most challenging—and most economically important—in bankruptcy law. By moving away from post-hoc expert opinion and toward objectively verifiable, contemporaneous market measures, courts can fundamentally transform fraudulent transfer law for the better. The methods we suggest will not eliminate the need for active judicial oversight aided by outside expertise because courts should still confirm that markets are informed and free of manipulation. However, market-based methods will greatly reduce the importance of experts, the danger of hindsight bias, and the burdens placed on judges. As courts begin to articulate acceptable and unacceptable market-implied probabilities of default, banks and other creditors will be able to plan and adjust their behavior before problems arise. Banks can choose to forego funding LBOs or other transactions that would create liability.

Clear, predictable judicial guidance will empower risk managers at banks to block imprudent transactions. When times are good, default rates are low, and leveraged deals are plentiful, risk management is at the nadir of its power. Front office bankers who source deals and generate revenue outrank back office risk managers who appear to generate nothing but costs.[170] Risk managers' best chance of prevailing comes when the data is clear and unambiguous.

When market prices become the best predictor of fraudulent transfer liability, banks can build contractual releases into their funding commitments that are tied to the relevant prices. With releases in place, if the condition of the debtor deteriorates between signing and closing, the bank need not face the Hobson's choice of either walking away empty handed and being sued immediately by the LBO sponsor for breach of contract,[171] or staying the course, collecting fees, and being sued later by bondholders under a theory of fraudulent transfer. In effect, bankruptcy courts and financial markets will jointly set minimum capital adequacy and liquidity standards for all non-financial firms, and large banks and other creditors will enforce those standards. As a result of their gate-keeping activities, the law will be more fair, predictable, and administratively efficient. With fewer ill-conceived leveraged transactions and fewer resulting business bankruptcies, the economy will be more stable. At the same time, greater certainty for investors should reduce the cost of capital and facilitate value-creating leveraged investments.

NOTES

* Michael Simkovic is a Professor of Law and Accounting at the University of Southern California. This chapter is adapted from Michael Simkovic & Benjamin Kaminetzky, *Leveraged Buyout Bankruptcies, the Problem of Hindsight Bias, and the Credit Default Swap Solution*, 2011 Colum. Bus. L. Rev. 118 (2011).

1. Stephen Bainbridge, The New Corporate Governance in Theory and Practice 115 (Oxford University Press 2008); Reinier Kraakman et al., The Anatomy of Corporate Law: A Functional Approach 9–11 (2nd ed. 2009).
2. Douglas G. Baird, *Legal Approaches to Restricting Distributions to Shareholders: The Role of Fraudulent Transfer Law*, 7 Eur. Bus. Org. L. Rev. 201, 205 (2006); *see generally* Bruce A. Markell, *Toward True and Plain Dealing: A Theory of Fraudulent Transfers Involving Unreasonably Small Capital*, 21 Ind. L. Rev. 469, 497–8 (1988).
3. 11 U.S.C. § 548(a)(1)(B)(ii). For the sake of economy, the words "insolvent" or "insolvency" are used in this chapter to refer to any financial condition that is sufficient to satisfy the requirements for fraudulent transfer liability under the Bankruptcy Code or liability under similar state law fraudulent transfer or fraudulent conveyance statutes.
4. This may be broader than the definition of "insolvency" under the Bankruptcy Code or under state law fraudulent transfer statutes.
5. At various points in this chapter, we use "fraudulent transfer" to mean both "fraudulent transfer" and "fraudulent conveyance" because the standards of liability and the available remedies are similar.
6. Henry F. Owsley & Peter S. Kaufman, Distressed Investment Banking: To the Abyss and Back 100 (2005); Corinne Ball, *Asset Dispositions in Chapter 11: Whether to Sell Through Section 363 or a Plan of Reorganization*, *in* Navigating Today's Environment: The Directors' and Officers' Guide to Restructuring 251, 251 (John Wm. Butler, Jr. & Nigel Page (eds), 2010).
7. Some have argued against the application of constructive fraudulent transfer to consensual arm's length transactions and restriction of its scope to actual fraud. Douglas G. Baird & Thomas H. Jackson, *Fraudulent Conveyance Law and Its Proper Domain*,

38 Vand. L. Rev. 829 (1985); *see also* Barry E. Adler, *Bankruptcy and Risk Allocation*, 77 Cornell L. Rev. 439 (1991). Such arguments have generally not been adopted by courts, although they may have influenced restrictions on the application of fraudulent transfer to shareholders through 11 U.S.C. § 545(e).

8. Kenneth M. Ayotte & Edward R. Morrison, *Creditor Control and Conflict in Chapter 11*, 1 J. Legal Analysis 511 (2009). Costs related to fraudulent transfer litigation may be difficult to diversify because defaults, bankruptcies, and resulting fraudulent transfer litigation tend to cluster in periods when many tradable assets are simultaneously declining in value. The beneficiaries of fraudulent transfer litigation—unsecured creditors—are still likely to incur substantial losses.
9. Under Delaware corporate law, the directors of an insolvent corporation owe fiduciary duties to the corporation for the benefit of its creditors, which require them to maximize the value of the firm as a whole rather than to maximize shareholder value. Frederick Tung, *The New Death of Contract: Creeping Corporate Fiduciary Duties for Creditors*, 57 Emory L. J. 809 (2007); Douglas G. Baird & M. Todd Henderson, *Other People's Money*, 60 Stan. L. Rev. 1309 (2008).
10. *See* Oliver Hart & Luigi Zingales, *A New Capital Regulation for Large Financial Institutions*, 13 Am. L. & Econ. Rev. 453 (2011) (arguing for the use of CDS prices in capital adequacy regulation of financial institutions).
11. Steven L. Schwarcz, *Rethinking a Corporation's Obligations to Creditors*, 17 Cardozo L. Rev. 647, 649 (1996).
12. *Id;* Guhan Subramanian, *Bargaining in the Shadow of Takeover Defenses*, 113 Yale L. J. 621 (2003).
13. Douglas G. Baird, *Fraudulent Conveyances, Agency Costs and Leveraged Buyouts*, 20 J. Legal Stud. 1, 5–7 (1991); Michael C. Jensen, *Agency Costs of Free Cash Flow, Corporate Finance, and Takeovers*, 76 Am. Econ. Rev. 323 (1986); Joanna M. Shepherd, Frederick Tung & Albert H. Yoon, *What Else Matters for Corporate Governance? The Case of Bank Monitoring*, 88 B.U. L. Rev. 991 (2008).
14. Alan Schwartz, *A Theory of Loan Priorities*, 18 J. Legal Stud. 209 (1989); Randal C. Picker, *Security Interests, Misbehavior, and Common Pools*, 59 U. Chi. L. Rev. 645 (1992); George G. Triantis, *Secured Debt Under Conditions of Imperfect Information*, 21 J. Legal Stud. 225 (1992); Barry E. Adler, *An Equity-Agency Solution to the Bankruptcy-Priority Puzzle*, 22 J. Legal Stud. 73 (1993); David G. Carlson, *On the Efficiency of Secured Lending*, 80 Va. L. Rev. 1393 (1994); Ronald J. Mann, *Explaining the Pattern of Secured Credit*, 626 Harv. L. Rev. 625 (1997); Robert E. Scott, *The Truth About Secured Financing*, 82 Cornell L. Rev. 1436 (1997); Claire A. Hill, *Is Secured Debt Efficient?* 80 Tex. L. Rev. 1117 (2002); Douglas G. Baird & Robert K. Rasmussen, *Private Debt and The Missing Lever of Corporate Governance*, 154 U. Pa. L. Rev. 1209 (2006); Kelli A. Alces, *Debunking the Corporate Fiduciary Myth*, 35 J. Corp. L. 240 (2009); Frederick Tung, *Leverage in the Board Room: The Unsung Influence of Private Lenders in Corporate Governance*, 57 UCLA L. Rev. 115 (2010); *cf.* Lucian Bebchuck & Jesse Fried, *The Uneasy Case for the Priority of Secured Claims in Bankruptcy*, 105 Yale L. J. 857 (1996); Jay Lawrence Westbrook, *The Control of Wealth in Bankruptcy*, 82 Tex. L. Rev. 795 (2004).
15. Shourun Guo, Edith S. Hotchkiss & Weihong Song, *Do Buyouts (Still) Create Value?*, 66 J. Fin. 479 (2011); Arthur Warga & Ivo Welch, *Bondholder Losses in Leveraged Buyouts*, 6 Rev. Fin. Stud. 960 (1993) (finding large stockholder gains and small bondholder losses shortly after LBO announcements); April Klein & Emanuael Zur, *The Impact of Hedge Fund Activism on the Target Firm's Existing Borrowers*, 24 Rev. Fin. Stud. 1735 (2011); Matthew D. Cain & Steven M. Davidoff, *Form over Substance? The Value of Corporate Process and Management Buy-outs*, 36 Del. J. Corp. Law 849 (2011).
16. *See* Barry L. Zaretsky, *Fraudulent Transfer Law as the Arbiter of Unreasonable Risk*, 46 S.C. L. Rev. 1165, 1178–9 (1995).
17. In addition to taking a security interest in all of the assets of the corporation, the

lender may also require the purchaser to grant a security interest in the equity because it is often easier to foreclose on corporate equity than on individual corporate assets, especially real estate,

18. *See, e.g.*, Mellon Bank, N.A. v. Metro Commc'ns, Inc., 945 F.2d 635, 645–6 (3d Cir. 1991).
19. *Id.;* Richard Squire, *The Case for Symmetry in Creditor's Rights,* 118 Yale L.J. 807 (2009); Richard Squire, *Strategic Liability in the Corporate Group,* 78 U. Chi. L. Rev. 605 (2011); *cf.* Steven L. Schwarcz, *The Easy Case for the Priority of Secured Claims in Bankruptcy,* 47 Duke L.J. 425 (1997); Yair Listokin, *Is Secured Debt Used to Redistribute Value from Tort Claimants in Bankruptcy? An Empirical Analysis*, 57 Duke L.J. 1037 (2008).
20. *See, e.g.*, *In re* Tribune Co., 418 B.R. 116 (Bankr. D. Del. 2009); V Capital Master Fund Ltd. v. Official Comm. of Unsecured Creditors of TOUSA, Inc. (*In re* TOUSA, Inc.), 444 B.R. 613 (S.D. Fla. 2011); and Complaint of the Official Comm. of Unsecured Creditors of Lyondell Chem. Co. *In re* Lyondell Chemical Co., No. 09-10023 (REG), 2009 WL 2350776 (Bankr. S.D.N.Y. July 22, 2009).
21. *See* Kupetz v. Wolf, 845 F.2d 842, 848 (9th Cir. 1988) (citing Baird & Jackson, *supra* note 7, at 852); *see also* Credit Managers Ass'n of S. Cal. v. Fed. Co., 629 F. Supp. 175, 181 (C.D. Cal. 1985); *In re* Ohio Corrugating Co., 91 B.R. 430, 440 (Bankr. N.D. Ohio 1988); *In re* Plassein Int'l Corp., 388 B.R. 46, 49 (D. Del. 2008), *aff'g*, *In re* Plassein Int'l Corp., 366 B.R. 318 (Bankr. D. Del. 2007); *In re* Sunbeam Corp., 284 B.R. 355, 373 (Bankr. S.D.N.Y. 2002).
22. The specific mechanism is that the transaction is only "collapsed"—viewed in substantive economic terms rather than formal terms—with respect to some investors. In *Wieboldt Stores, Inc. v. Schottenstein*, 94 B.R. 488 (N.D. Ill. 1988), the transaction was collapsed with respect to bank lenders and inside shareholders who understood and helped structure the transaction, but not with respect to passive shareholders. *Id.* at 503–04. Section 546(e) of the Bankruptcy Code has similarly been used to shield shareholders from fraudulent transfer liability, and 2006 amendments may extend this protection more broadly. *See* Lowenschuss v. Resorts Int'l, Inc. (*In re* Resorts Int'l, Inc.), 181 F.3d 505, 515–16 (3d Cir. 1999); Quality Stores, Inc. v. Alford (*In re* QSI Holdings, Inc.), 571 F.3d 545 (6th Cir. 2009), *cert. denied*, 130 S. Ct. 1141 (2010).
23. Not all courts require knowledge or intent. *See* MFS/Sun Life Tr.-High Yield Series v. Van Dusen Airport Servs. Co., 910 F. Supp. 913, 936 (S.D.N.Y. 1995); Liquidation Tr. of Hechinger Inv. Co. of Del. v. Fleet Retail Fin. Grp. (*In re* Hechinger Inv. Co. of Del.), 327 B.R. 537, 546–7, 551 (D. Del. 2005), *aff'd*, 278 F. App'x 125 (3d Cir. 2008). These courts move directly to an analysis of reasonably equivalent value and solvency.
24. Although plaintiffs must also prove that the debtor received "less than a reasonably equivalent value" in the challenged transfer, they can generally do so if the court is willing to "collapse" multiple steps of a leveraging transaction. *See, e.g.*, Mellon Bank, N.A. v. Metro Commc'ns, Inc., 945 F.2d 635, 645–6 (3d Cir. 1991). However, where borrowed funds are used to repay previous debts or retained as working capital, or where the transaction creates very substantial synergies, defendants may have a stronger defense independent of the financial condition of the debtor. *See Best Products*, 168 B.R. at 58; *Mellon Bank*, 945 F.2d at 635; *MFS/Sun Life*, 910 F. Supp. at 937.
25. Murphy v. Meritor Sav. Bank (*In re* O'Day Corp.), 126 B.R. 370, 404 (Bankr. D. Mass. 1991); *see also MFS/Sun Life*, 910 F. Supp. at 943–4.
26. Stan Bernstein, Susan H. Seabury & Jack F. Williams, *Squaring Bankruptcy Valuation Practice with* Daubert *Demands*, 16 Am. Bankr. Inst. L. Rev. 161, 175 n. 56 (2008).
27. *See* Moody v. Sec. Pac. Bus. Credit, 971 F.2d 1056, 1066 (3d Cir. 1992); *Murphy*, 126 B.R. at 397–403.
28. Tim Koller, Mark Goedhart & David Wessels, Valuation Measuring and Managing the Value of Companies 355 (4th ed. 2005); Iridium Capital Corp. v. Motorola, Inc. (*In re* Iridium Operating), 373 B.R. 283, 347–8 (Bankr. S.D.N.Y. 2007); *See* Peltz v.

Hatten, 279 B.R. 710, 737–8, (D. Del. 2002); Global GT LP v. Golden Telecom, Inc., 993 A.2d 497, 497 (Del. Ch. 2010); JPMorgan Chase Bank, N.A. v. Charter Commc'ns Operating, LLC (*In re* Charter Commc'ns), 419 B.R. 221, 236 (Bankr. S.D.N.Y. 2009); Bernstein, Seabury & Williams, *supra* note 26, at 171.

29. Douglas G. Baird & Donald S. Bernstein, *Absolute priority, valuation uncertainty, and the reorganization bargain,* 115 Yale L.J. 1930 (2006); Anthony J. Casey, *The Creditor's Bargain and Option–Preservation Priority in Chapter 11,* 78 U. Chi. L. Rev. 759 (2011); Basic v. Levinson, 485 U.S. 224, 246 (1988) ('The idea of a free and open public market is built upon the theory that competing judgments of buyers and sellers as to the fair price of a security brings . . . about a situation where the market price reflects as nearly as possible a just price.') (quoting H.R. Rep. No. 73-1383, at 11 (1934)).
30. As financial experts have become more influential, they have also become increasingly expensive. *See* Lynn M. LoPucki & Joseph W. Doherty, *Rise of the Financial Advisors: An Empirical Study of the Division of Professional Fees in Large Bankruptcies*, 82 Am. Bankr. L.J. 141, 142 (2008) (reporting that from 1998 to 2003, fees of financial advisers grew at the rate of about 25% per year, whereas professional fees and expenses as a whole grew only about 9% per year). As the number of financial advisers working on a case increases, so do their fees. *Id.* at 162–3.
31. Douglas Baird & Robert Rasmussen, *Anti-Bankruptcy,* 119 Yale L. J. 648, 671 (2010); *In re Iridium Operating*, 373 B.R. at 291, 293; Fidelity Bond & Mortg. Co. v. Brand (*In re* Fidelity Mortgage and Bond Corp.), 340 B.R. 266, 289 (Bankr. E.D. Pa. 2006), *aff'd*, 371 B.R. 708 (E.D. Pa. 2007) (finding that 'both [parties'] experts made various adjustments to the balance sheet line items to arrive at their starkly different conclusions regarding . . . solvency . . . .'); *In re Charter Commc'ns*, 419 B.R. at 236 n.11; *In re* Nellson Nutraceutical, Inc., 356 B.R. 364, 367 (Bankr. D. Del. 2006) (where expert's metric of value for determining the terminal value utilized a methodology not generally accepted by experts in the field of valuation and was, in fact, invented by the expert for use in the case).
32. *See* Harvey R. Miller & Shai Y. Waisman, *Is Chapter 11 Bankrupt?*, 47 B.C. L. Rev. 129, 174 n. 259 (2005).
33. *In re* Exide Techs., 303 B.R. 48, 59 (Bankr. D. Del. 2003). The expert financial adviser to the debtor submitted a valuation range of $950 million to $1.05 billion, while the expert financial adviser to the creditors' committee submitted a valuation range of $1.478 billion to $1.711 billion. *Exide* involved valuation for plan confirmation, not for fraudulent transfer.
34. *Id.* at 66. Judge Carey determined the debtor's valuation to be in the range of $1.4 billion to $1.6 billion.
35. When Exide emerged from bankruptcy in May 2004, the market set an enterprise value of $1.03 billion. By November 16, 2005, Exide's enterprise value had declined to $788 million. *See* Miller & Waisman, *supra* note 32.
36. Baird & Rasmussen, *supra* note 31, at 655; Koller, Goedhart & Wessels, *supra* note 28, at 159
37. Prescott Grp. Small Cap v. Coleman Co., No. 17802, 2004 WL 2059515, at *31 (Del. Ch. Sept. 8, 2004); Cede & Co. v. Technicolor, Inc., No. Civ. A. 7129, 2003 WL 23700218, at *2 (Del. Ch. Dec. 31, 2003).
38. Richard A. Brealey, Stewart C. Myers & Franklin Allen, Principles of Corporate Finance 65 (8th ed. 2006); Doft & Co. v. Travelocity.com, Inc., No. 19734, 2004 WL 1152338, at *5 (Del. Ch. May 20, 2004).
39. *See* To-Am Equip. Co. v. Mitsubishi Caterpillar Forklift Am., Inc., 953 F. Supp. 987, 996–7 (N.D. Ill. 1997), *aff'd*, 152 F.3d 658 (7th Cir. 1998); Iridium Capital Corp. v. Motorola, Inc. (*In re* Iridium Operating), 373 B.R. 283, 351 (Bankr. S.D.N.Y. 2007).
40. *To-Am Equip.*, 953 F. Supp. at 996 ('[A] skilled practitioner can come up with just about any [projected future cash-flow] value he wants . . . .'); *see also* Bernstein, Seabury & Williams, *supra* note 26, at 187–8. Management, lending banks, investors, and Wall Street research analysts will typically all have prepared projections for large companies,

often under several different scenarios and at several different points in time. Baird & Bernstein, *supra* note 29, at 1942–3.

41. *See* CNB Int'l, Inc. v. Kelleher (*In re* CNB Int'l, Inc.), 393 B.R. 306, 321 (Bankr. W.D.N.Y. 2008).
42. *See In re Iridium Operating*, 373 B.R. at 298.
43. *See In re CNB Int'l.*, 393 B.R. at 321.
44. *See* MFS/Sun Life Tr.-High Yield Series v. Van Dusen Airport Servs. Co., 910 F. Supp. 913, 944 (S.D.N.Y. 1995).
45. *See* Peltz v. Hatten, 279 B.R. 710, 734–47 (D. Del. 2002) (finding that collapse of the high-yield bond market following the Russian debt default in the late 1990s was not foreseeable).
46. *See* Official Comm. of Unsecured Creditors of Tousa, Inc. v. Citicorp N. Am., Inc. (*In re* TOUSA, Inc.), 422 B.R. 783, 813–14 (Bankr. S.D. Fla. 2009) (finding that the sharp decline in the housing market in August 2007 was foreseeable at least several months prior), *rev'd on other grounds*, *In re* TOUSA, Inc., Nos. 10-60017-CIV/GOLD, 10-61478, 10-62032, 10-62035, 10-62037, 2011 WL 522008 (S.D. Fla. Feb. 11, 2011).
47. Marianne M. Jennings, D. Jordan Love & Philip M.J. Reckers, *Causality as an Influence on Hindsight Bias: An Empirical Examination of Judges' Evaluation of Professional Audit Judgment*, 21 J. Acct. & Pub. Pol'y 143 (1998); John C. Anderson, Marianna M. Jennings, D. Jordan Lowe & Phillip M.J. Reckers, *The Mitigation of Hindsight Bias in Judges' Evaluation of Auditor Decisions*, 16 Auditing: J. Prac. & Theory 20 (1997).
48. *See* Brealey, Myers & Allen, *supra* note 38, at 16, 37, 222–4; Koller, Goedhart & Wessels, *supra* note 28, at 292–4; Bernstein, Seabury & Williams, *supra* note 26, at 190.
49. Brealey, Myers & Allen, *supra* note 38, at 66–7, 222–6; Bernstein, Seabury & Williams, *supra* note 26, at 191 n.102.
50. *See* Del. Open MRI Radiology Assocs. v. Kessler, 898 A.2d 290, 338 (Del. Ch. 2006) (noting that '[t]estimonial feuds about discount rates often have the quality of a debate about the relative merits of competing alchemists' and that "[o]nce the experts" techniques for coming up with their discount rates are closely analyzed, the court finds itself in an intellectual position more religious than empirical in nature, insofar as the court's decision to prefer one position over the other is more a matter of faith than reason.').
51. *See* Brealey, Myers & Allen, *supra* note 38, at 217 (noting that '[m]easuring differences in risk is difficult to do objectively'); Koller, Goedhart & Wessels, *supra* note 28,, at 297–8 ('Sizing the market risk premium . . . is arguably the most debated issue in finance.'); Bernstein, Seabury & Williams, *supra* note 26, at 190–93.
52. *See* Brealey, Myers & Allen, *supra* note 38, at 219–21; Koller, Goedhart & Wessels, *supra* note 28, at 307–08; Bernstein, Seabury & Williams, *supra* note 26, at 190–93.
53. *See* CNB Int'l, Inc. v. Kelleher (*In re* CNB Int'l, Inc.), 393 B.R. 306, 320 (Bankr. W.D.N.Y. 2008).
54. Koller, Goedhart & Wessels, *supra* note 28, at 361.
55. *Id.*
56. *Id.* at 366–8, 380; Brealey, Myers & Allen, *supra* note 38, at 511; Bernstein, Seabury & Williams, *supra* note 26, at 196; Prescott Grp. Small Cap, L.P. v. Coleman Co., No. 17802, 2004 WL 2059515, at *22 (Del. Ch. Sept. 8, 2004); *In re* Radiology Assocs., Inc., 611 A.2d 485, 490 (Del. Ch. 1991).
57. Koller, Goedhart & Wessels, *supra* note 28, at 362–3, 366–7.
58. *See* Peltz v. Hatten, 279 B.R. 710, 737–8 (D. Del. 2002); Lippe v. Bairnco Corp., 99 F. App'x 274, 279 (2d Cir. 2004); *In re* Oneida Ltd., 351 B.R. 79, 91 n.18 (Bankr. S.D.N.Y. 2006); *see also* Bernstein, Seabury & Williams, *supra* note 26, at 198–9.
59. *See, e.g.*, Global GT LP v. Golden Telecom, Inc., 993 A.2d 497, 510 (Del. Ch. 2010).
60. Brealey, Myers & Allen, *supra* note 38, at 248 ('Sensitivity analysis boils down to expressing cash flows in terms of key . . . variables and then calculating the consequences of misestimating the variables. . . . One drawback to sensitivity analysis is that it always gives somewhat ambiguous results.').

61. *See, e.g.*, *Lippe*, 288 B.R at 686–7, 689–90.
62. Cass R. Sunstein, *Social Norms and Social Roles*, 96 Colum. L. Rev. 903, 933 (1996) (citing Itamar Simonson & Amos Tversky, *Choice in Context: Tradeoff Contrast and Extremeness Aversion*, 29 J. Marketing Res. 281, 289–92 (1992)); Bernstein, Seabury & Williams, *supra* note 26, at 198–9.
63. Bernstein, Seabury & Williams, *supra* note 26, at 198–9.
64. Koller, Goedhart & Wessels, *supra* note 28, at 294–318; Del. Open MRI Radiology Assocs. v. Kessler, 898 A.2d 290, 338 (Del. Ch. 2006) ('[T]here is much dispute about how to calculate the discount rate to use in valuing their future cash flows, even when one tries to stick as closely as possible to the principles undergirding the capital asset pricing model and the semi-strong form of the efficient capital markets hypothesis.'); Bernstein, Seabury & Williams, *supra* note 26, at 190–92.
65. Basic v. Levinson, 485 U.S. 224, 244 (1988) ('[T]he market . . . ideally transmits information to the investor in the processed form of a market price. Thus, the market is performing a substantial part of the valuation process performed by the investor in a face-to-face transaction. The market is acting as the unpaid agent of the investor, informing him that given all the information available to it, the value of the stock is worth the market price.') (quoting, *In re* LVT Securities Litigation, 88 F.R.D. 134, 143 (N.D. Tex. 1980)); *id.* ('In an open and developed market . . . purchasers generally rely on the price of the stock as a reflection of its value.'); *see also* Bank of Am. Nat'l Tr. & Sav. Ass'n v. 203 N. LaSalle St. P'ship, 526 U.S. 434, 456–7 (1999) (finding that 'the best way to determine value is exposure to a market,' not through a 'determination . . . made by a judge in bankruptcy court.'). In the parlance of economists, the Supreme Court has accepted the semi-strong form of the Efficient Market Hypothesis.
66. *Basic*, 485 U.S. at 245–6 ('Just as artificial manipulation tends to upset the true function of an open market, so the hiding and secreting of important information obstructs the operation of the markets as indices of real value.') (quoting H.R. Rep. No. 1383, at 11).
67. VFB LLC v. Campbell Soup Co., No. Civ. A. 02-137, 2005 WL 2234606, at *22 (D. Del. Sept. 13, 2005), *aff'd*, 482 F.3d 624 (3d Cir. 2007).
68. VFB LLC v. Campbell Soup Co., 482 F. 3d 624, 629 (3d Cir. 2007) ('[B]asically, the district court regarded the hired expert valuations as a side-show to the disinterested evidence of VFI's capitalization in one of the most efficient capital markets in the world.') (internal quotations omitted).
69. *Id.* at 629.
70. *See id.* at 629–30, 633.
71. As discussed below, there are important differences between changes in the value of an equity investment and changes in the value of a firm as a whole.
72. *VFB*, 482 F.3d at 632.
73. *Id.* at 626–7.
74. *Id.* at 627, 629.
75. *Id.* at 628.
76. *Id.* at 627.
77. *Id.* at 627–8.
78. *Id.* at 628.
79. *Id.* at 628–9.
80. *Id.* at 633.
81. *See* section IV.B.
82. Bond markets became far more transparent in the mid-2000s due to mandatory disclosure through the Trade Reporting and Compliance Engine (TRACE). TRACE initially covered 500 bonds in July 2002, expanded to cover 4,600 bonds in April 2003, then expanded to 17,000 bonds in October 2004, and finally expanded to full coverage of virtually all corporate bonds—approximately 29,000 bonds—in February 2005. *See* News Release of *NASD's Fully Implemented "TRACE" Brings*

Unprecedented Transparency to Corporate Bond Market, FINRA, http://www.finra.org/Newsroom/NewsReleases/2005/P013274 (Feb. 7, 2005).

83. *In re* Iridium Capital Corp. v. Motorola, Inc. (*In re* Iridium Operating), 373 B.R. 283, 291, 352 (Bankr. S.D.N.Y. 2007).
84. *Id.* at 292–3.
85. *Id.* at 293.
86. *Id.* at 305.
87. *Id.* at 305.
88. *Id.* at 305–06.
89. *Id.* at 329–30.
90. *Id.* at 290.
91. *Id.* at 320–22.
92. *Id.* at 346–9.
93. *Id.* at 296–301.
94. *Id.* at 296–301.
95. *Id.* at 352.
96. *Id.* at 302.
97. *Id.* at 302–03.
98. *Tronox Inc. v. Kerr McGee Corp. (In re Tronox Inc.)*, 503 B.R. 239, 298 (Bankr. S.D.N.Y. 2013).
99. *Id.*
100. *Id.* at 301–03.
101. *Id.* at 303–07.
102. Am. Classic Voyages Co. v. JPMorgan Chase Bank (*In re* Am. Classic Voyages, Co.), 367 B.R. 500, 504 (Bankr. D. Del. 2007), *aff'd*, 384 B.R. 62 (D. Del. 2008).
103. Michael Simkovic, *Secret Liens and the Financial Crisis of 2008*, 83 Am. Bankr. L.J. 253 (2009); Robert P. Bartlett III, *Inefficiencies in the Information Thicket: A Case Study of Derivative Disclosures During the Financial Crisis,* 36 J. Corp. L. (2010); Kathryn Judge, *Fragmentation Nodes: A Study in Financial Innovation, Complexity & Systemic Risk,* 64 Stan. L. Rev. 657 (2012); Ronald J. Gilson & Renier Kraakman, *Market Efficiency after the Financial Crisis: It's Still A Matter of Information Costs,* 100 Va. L. Rev. 313 (20014).
104. Assets minus liabilities, also called "net worth."
105. *See* Fischer Black & Myron Scholes, *The Pricing of Options and Corporate Liabilities*, 81 J. Pol. Econ. 637 (1973); Robert C. Merton, *On The Pricing of Corporate Debt: The Risk Structure of Interest Rates*, 29 J. Fin. 449 (1974); Maria Vassalou & Yuhang Xing, *Default Risk in Equity Returns*, 59 J. Fin. 831 (2004); Antje Berndt, Rohan Douglas, Darrell Duffie, Mark Ferguson & David Schranz, *Measuring Default Risk Premia from Default Swap Rates and EDFs* (Bank for Int'l Settlements, Working Paper No. 173, 2005), http://ssrn.com/abstract=556080. If equity is a call option, then the strike price equals the firm's liabilities. If the firm is only worth as much as its debt, then equity is worth zero. If the firm is worth far less than its debt, equity is still worth zero—the downside is capped. If the firm is worth more than its debt, the option is in the money and equity is positive. Like all options, equity expires, but the expiration is not on a set date. Instead, equity expires when the firm runs out of cash and is forced to enter bankruptcy, at which point equity is wiped out.
106. Although the opinions in *VFB* and *Iridium* may reflect a misunderstanding of the relationship between equity prices and the likelihood of insolvency, the courts probably came to the correct conclusion regarding solvency of the debtor because they also considered indicators of solvency from the debt markets.
107. *See* Berndt, Douglas, Duffie, Ferguson & Schranz, *supra* note 105, at 7–8.
108. *See* Sreedhar T. Bharath & Tyler Shumway, *Forecasting Default with the KMV-Merton Model*, 1–3, 23 (AFA 2006 Boston Meetings Paper, 2004), *available at* http://ssrn.com/abstract=637342 (finding that the most widely applied equity-based model of implied probability of default, KMV-Merton, performs poorly as a predictor of default, possibly because of unrealistic assumptions and unnecessary mathematic complexity);

Vineet Agarwal & Richard Taffler, *Comparing the Performance of Market-Based and Accounting-Based Bankruptcy Prediction Models*, 32 J. of Banking & Fin. 1541–51, 304 (2008).

109. The phrases "traders" and "investors" are used interchangeably in this chapter.
110. "Yield" is a measure of the effective interest rate to an investor who buys a bond at a certain price, which may be above or below par (100 cents on the dollar), assuming no default. Most corporate bonds are coupon bonds initially issued at par and scheduled to pay a fixed coupon (or interest payment) periodically. Bonds may trade in the secondary market above or below par. An investor who buys a bond below par will receive a yield higher than the coupon rate, while an investor who buys a bond above par will receive a yield below the coupon rate. Secondary market yields inform pricing of new debt issuances.
111. *See* Frank Partnoy & David Skeel, Jr., *The Promise and Perils of Credit Derivatives*, 75 U. Cin. L. Rev. 1019, 1022, 1050 n.79 (2007); Stephen J. Lubben, *Credit Derivatives and the Future of Chapter 11*, 81 Am. Bankr. L.J. 405, 411–12 & n.49 (2007).
112. For most vanilla credit default swaps, the spread will depend both on the expected likelihood and severity of default (the inverse of the recovery rate), which is not directly observable. However, for digital default swaps that specificy a contractual payout in the event of default, which is often independent of the severity of default, it is easier to estimate the market-implied likelihood of default without making assumptions about severity.
113. *See* Robert F. Schwartz, *Risk Distribution in the Capital Markets: Credit Default Swaps, Insurance and a Theory of Demarcation*, 12 Fordham J. Corp. & Fin. L. 167, 169 (2007); Lubben, *supra* note 111, at 411 ('In addition, the growth of credit markets has allowed for 'shorting' of bonds, something that was often impossible beforehand due to the limited liquidity of the corporate bond markets.').
114. Simkovic, *supra* note 103, at 273–4.
115. *See* Lubben, *supra* note 111, at 411–12.
116. *Id.* A company that was technically solvent in a narrow, balance sheet sense theoretically could still trigger a credit event. For example, imagine a gold mine that could be sold at fire sale value for more than its debts but had mismanaged its cash and had to temporarily suspend bond payments. However, because bondholders would likely still recover 100 percent, it seems unlikely that such a credit event would cause a large spike in CDS premiums.
117. Although some contracts also require upfront fees, it is possible to calculate what periodic fees would be for such a contract if there were no upfront fee.
118. *See* Merton, *supra* note 105, at 449 (arguing that the risk of default is reflected in interest rates and noting that the value of a particular issue of corporate debt depends on three things: (1) the default-risk-free rate of return; (2) the term structure and seniority; and (3) the probability of default); Lawrence Fisher, *Determinants of Risk Premiums on Corporate Bonds*, 67 J. Pol. Econ. 217, 217 (1959) (hypothesizing that the difference between the market yield on the bond and the risk-free rate 'depends first on the risk that the firm will default on its bonds and second on their marketability').
119. *See* Michael Lewis, The Big Short: Inside the Doomsday Machine 208 (2010) ('On a $2 billion trade . . . the traders were arguing over interest payments amounting to $800,000 per year. Over that sum, the deal fell apart.').
120. Trading models are proprietary. *See* Gillian Tett, Fool's Gold 132–3 (2009). However, several economists have published sophisticated valuation models that influence many trading models. *See* John Hull & Alan White, *Valuing Credit Default Swaps I: No Counterparty Default Risk*, J. Derivatives, Fall 2000, at 29; John Hull & Alan White, *Valuing Credit Default Swaps II: Modeling Default Correlations*, J. Derivatives, Spring 2001, at 12; John Hull & Alan White, *The Valuation of Credit Default Swap Options*, J. Derivatives, Spring 2003, at 40; Darell Duffie, *Credit Swap Valuation*, 55 Fin. Analysts J. 73 (1999); Darrell Duffie, Jun Pan & Kenneth Singleton, *Transforming Analysis and Asset Pricing for Affine Jump-Diffusions*, 68 Econometrica 1343 (2000).

121. For purposes of the discussion in this paragraph, assume that the applicable fraudulent transfer statute reaches transfers within five years of bankruptcy, no defenses are available, and all challenged transfers were not for reasonably equivalent value.
122. With the benefit of hindsight, some might argue that this suggests problems with market-based indicators of default risk. However, in the lead up to the financial crisis of 2007–2009, credit spreads reflected risks in the financial sector earlier than many non-market based indicators such as credit ratings. Mark J. Flannery, Joel F. Houston & Frank Partnoy, *Credit Default Swap Spreads as Viable Substitutes for Credit Ratings*, 158 U. Pa. L. Rev. 2085 (2010). To be useful, credit spreads need not be perfectly predictive in each instance; any method of predicting credit risk will sometimes be mistaken. To be useful, credit spreads need only be about as predictive or more predictive than alternatives.
123. *See* VFB LLC v. Campbell Soup Co., 482 F. 3d 624, 632 (3d Cir. 2007).
124. John Hull, Mirela Predescu & Alan White, *The Relationship Between Credit Default Swap Spreads, Bond Yields, and Credit Rating Announcements*, 28 J. Banking Fin. 2789, 2801–03 (2004); Lars Norden & Martin Weber, *Informational Efficiency of Credit Default Swap and Stock Markets: The Impact of Credit Rating Announcements*, 28 J. Banking & Fin. 2813, 2837 (2004); Drew D. Creal, Robert B. Gramacy & Ruey S. Tsay, *Market-Based Credit Ratings*, 32 J. Bus. & Econ. Stat. 430 (2014).
125. Roberto Blanco, Simon Brennan & Ian W. Marsh, *An Empirical Analysis of the Dynamic Relationship Between Investment Grade Bonds and Credit Default Swaps*, 60 J. Fin. 2255, 2279 (2005); Norden & Weber, *supra* note 124, at 2838.
126. *See* Viral V. Acharya & Timothy C. Johnson, *Insider Trading in Credit Derivatives*, 84 J. Fin. Econ. 110 (2007); *see also* Lewis, *supra* note 119, at 197.
127. The SEC has acknowledged serious gaps in its ability to enforce insider trading and anti-manipulation regulations in derivatives markets. *See Over-the-Counter Derivatives Markets Act of 2009: Hearing Before the H. Comm. on Fin. Servs.*, 111th Cong. (Oct. 7, 2009) (statement of Henry T. C. Hu, Director of the SEC Division of Risk, Strategy, and Financial Innovation), http://www.sec.gov/news/testimony/2009/ts100709hh.htm.
128. Katy Burne, *Big U.S. Banks Make Swaps a Foreign Affair*, Wall St. J., Apr. 27, 2014, https://www.wsj.com/articles/big-u-s-banks-make-swaps-a-foreign-affair-1398627739.
129. There is a substantial and growing body of empirical research supporting the notion that institutions are well-informed investors who convey private information to the market through their trading activities, particularly in the equities markets. *See* Ashiq Ali, Cindy Durtschi, Baruch Lev & Mark A. Trombley, *Changes in Institutional Ownership and Subsequent Earnings Announcement Abnormal Returns*, 19 J. Acct. Auditing & Fin. 221, 222 (2004); Ekkehart Boehmer & Eric K. Kelley, *Institutional Investors and the Informational Efficiency of Prices*, 22 Rev. Fin. Stud. 3563, 3565 (2009); Hsiu-Lang Chen, Narasimhan Jegadeesh & Russ Wermers, *The Value of Active Mutual Fund Management: An Examination of the Stockholdings and Trades of Fund Managers*, 35 J. Fin. & Quantitative Analysis 343, 345 (2000); Joseph D. Piotroski & Darren T. Roulstone, *The Influence of Analysts, Institutional Investors, and Insiders on the Incorporation of Market, Industry, and Firm-Specific Information into Stock Prices*, 79 Acct. Rev. 1119, 1121–2 (2004); Xuemin Yan & Zhe Zhang, *Institutional Investors and Equity Returns: Are Short-term Institutions Better Informed?*, 22 Rev. Fin. Stud. 893, 895 (2009).
130. Francis A. Longstaff, Sanjay Mithal & Eric Neis, *Corporate Yield Spreads: Default Risk or Liquidity? New Evidence from the Credit Default Swap Market*, 60 J. Fin. 2213, 2217 (2005); *see also* British Bankers' Ass'n, Credit Derivatives Report 2003/2004 (2004).
131. *See* Norden & Weber, *supra* note 124, at 2818.
132. *See* Mark D. Flood, *An Introduction to Complete Markets*, 7 Fed. Res. Bank St. Louis Rev. 32, 34 (1991), http://research.stlouisfed.org/publications/review/91/03/Markets_Mar_Apr1991.pdf.
133. *See id.* at 48–50.

134. *See* Lewis, *supra* note 119, at 107; Vikas Bajaj, *Even as Dow Soars 11%, Skeptics Lurk*, N.Y. Times, Oct. 29, 2008, at B1.
135. *See* Tett, *supra* note 120, at 57; *see also* Jenny Strasburg, Aaron Lucchette & Liz Rappaport, *New Law Fuels a Shake-Up at Morgan Stanley*, Wall St. J., Aug. 5, 2010, at C1.
136. *See* Tett, *supra* note 120, at 57 (calling credit default swaps "a way to maintain 'client confidentiality' even while reshaping a bank's balance sheet").
137. *See* Simkovic, *supra* note 103, at 270 (noting that banks offloaded mortgage risk prior to the subprime crisis while appearing to hold mortgage-backed bonds on their balance sheet).
138. *See id.* at 271–9.
139. *See* Lewis, *supra* note 119, at 164–6, 184–6, 194–6, 219, 221.
140. *See, e.g.*, Franklin Allen, Lubomir Litov & Jianping Mei, *Large Investors, Price Manipulation, and the Limits to Arbitrage: An Anatomy of Market Corners*, 10 Rev. Fin. 645 (2006).
141. CDS have recently started trading on an exchange, although much of trading still appears to be OTC. Katy Burne, *ICE Launches Electronic Trading Network for Credit-Default Swaps*, Wall St. J., January 27, 2014, https://www.wsj.com/articles/ice-launches-electronic-trading-network-for-creditdefault-swaps-1390845869.
142. One would examine the period before the alleged fraudulent transfer to assess claims that the transfer was made at a time when the debtor was already insolvent, while one would examine the period after the alleged fraudulent transfer to assess claims that the debtor, though financially healthy before the alleged fraudulent transfer, was rendered insolvent as a result of the allegedly fraudulent transfer.
143. Bankruptcy Rule 2019 requires many groups, committees, and entities to provide enhanced disclosures of their economic interests in the debtor, including derivatives, in order to participate actively in a bankruptcy case.
144. *See* FINRA News Release, *supra* note 82.
145. FINRA Manual §6739(a) (2010), http://finra.complinet.com/en/display/display_main.html?rbid=2403&element_id=4402 (last visited Mar. 4, 2011). Until July 2005, dealers were required to disclose trades within thirty minutes. *See* FINRA News Release, *supra* note 82.
146. The discussion of private data providers that follows is based on a combination of those providers' marketing materials and conversations with employees and customers of those data providers.
147. Dodd-Frank Wall Street Reform and Consumer Protection Act, § 753(i) (to be codified at 15 U.S.C. § 78a).
148. *See* Jerome S. Fons, *The Default Premium and Corporate Bond Experience*, 42 J. Fin. 81, 81 (1987); Longstaff, Mithal & Neis, *supra* note 130, at 2214–18.
149. Merton, *supra* note 105, at 449; Joost Driessen, *Is Default Event Risk Priced in Corporate Bonds?*, 18 Rev. Fin. Stud. 165, 169 (2005).
150. *See* Longstaff, Mithal & Neis, *supra* note 130, at 2223. Finance professionals will sometimes use swap curves rather than Treasuries. *Id.*; John Hull, Mirela Predescu & Alan White, *Bond Prices, Default Probabilities and Risk Premiums*, J. Credit Risk, Spring 2005, at 53.
151. *See* Mohamed Bouzoubaa & Adel Osseiran, Exotic Options & Hybrids: A Guide to Structuring, Pricing and Trading 4 (2010).
152. The spread between Treasuries and LIBOR, known as the TED spread, serves as a measure of credit risk in the interbank market. *Id.*
153. *See, e.g.*, Fons, *supra* note 148, at 81–2; Longstaff, Mithal & Neis, *supra* note 130, at 2218; Merton, *supra* note 105, at 449; Gregory R. Duffee, *The Relation Between Treasury Yields and Corporate Bond Yield Spreads*, 53 J. Fin. 2225, 2225–6 (1998).
154. In general, long-term debt carries a higher yield than short-term debt from the same issuer, and zero-coupon debt carries a higher yield than coupon debt with the same maturity. This positive correlation between yield and maturity is known as the "upward

sloping yield curve," although yield curves are occasionally kinked, flat, or downward sloping. Historical yields for U.S. Treasuries of different maturities are freely available from the U.S. Treasury Department's website and from Federal Reserve statistical releases.

155. *See* Hull, Predescu & White, *supra* note 124, at 2792 ("CDS spreads . . . are already credit spreads.").
156. *See id.* at 2790; Duffie, Pan & Singleton, *supra* note 120.
157. Assuming no risk of default by the CDS seller.
158. The expected loss rate given default will almost always be less than 100 percent because even when a debtor defaults, creditors generally recover some portion of the amount owed to them. The expected recovery rate and the expected loss rate given default sum to 100 percent. In mathematical notation, (expected loss rate given default) = 1 – (expected recovery rate).
159. Moody's Investors Service publishes historical recovery rates of corporate bonds and loans from 1920 to the present, broken down by year, level of seniority, and letter rating, as well as recovery outlooks for the coming year. *See, e.g.*, Sharon Ou et al., Moody's Investors Service, Corporate Default and Recovery Rates, 1920–2014 (Mar. 2015), *available at* https://www.moodys.com/researchdocumentcontentpage.aspx?docid=PBC_179348.
160. *See* Sanjiv R. Das & Paul Hanouna, *Implied Recovery*, 33 J. Econ. Dynamics & Control 1837 (2009).
161. Longstaff et al., *supra* note 130, at 2215 (reporting that the nondefault component ranges from 0.2% to 1%, and is present in at least three-quarters of firms sampled).
162. *See* Robert L. Geske & Gordon Delianedis, *The Components of Corporate Credit Spreads: Default, Recovery, Tax, Jumps, Liquidity, and Market Factors* 2 (The Anderson Sch. at UCLA, Working Paper No. 22-01, 2001), http://ssrn.com/abstract=306479.
163. *See, e.g.*, Edwin J. Elton, Martin K. Gruber, Deepak Agrawal & Christopher Mann, *Explaining the Rate Spread on Corporate Bonds*, 56 J. Fin. 247, 272–3 (2001); Fons, *supra* note 148, at 96; Geske & Delianedis, *supra* note 162, at 3, 26; Hull, Predescu & White, *supra* note 150, at 53.
164. *See, e.g.*, Geske & Delianedis, *supra* note 162, at 26–7; Jing-zhi Huang & Ming Huang, *How Much of the Corporate-Treasury Yield Spread Is Due to Credit Risk? A New Calibration Approach,* 2 Rev. Asset Pricing Stud. 153 (2012).
165. *See supra* note 151 and accompanying text.
166. *See* Hull, Predescu & White., *supra* note 124, at 2795–800.
167. *See* Lorenzo Naranjo, *Implied Interest Rates in a Market with Frictions* 1–4, 8 (Feb. 2009) (unpublished manuscript) (http://ssrn.com/abstract=1308908); *supra* note 152 and accompanying text.
168. *See* Longstaff, *supra* note 130, at 2217.
169. The five-year CDS contract is also frequently used by researchers. *See id.* (using five-year CDS contract data).
170. *See* Tett, *supra* note 120, at 112, 114–15, 134–5, 138.
171. The vagueness of currently used materially adverse change clauses is an invitation to litigate. A contractual release tied to specific market indicators reaching specific levels would prevent litigation. Banks already use CDS spreads to adjust pricing on revolving credit facilities for risk. *See* Serena Ng, *Banks Get Tougher on Credit Line Provisions*, Wall St. J., May 4, 2009, at A1.

12. The costs of corporate bankruptcy: how little we know

*Stephen J. Lubben**

Complaints about unnecessarily high expenditures attendant upon liquidation proceedings are common in the history of American bankruptcy law. There is practically no period in the development of the institution at which such complaints were not expressed, resulting often in the enactment of provisions intended to increase and strengthen judicial control over expenses of administration.[1]

INTRODUCTION

For almost as long as there have been bankruptcy laws, there have been complaints that the primary beneficiaries of these laws are insiders who administer the bankruptcy system.[2] In recent decades, this line of criticism has carried with it an implicit criticism of bankruptcy courts, who are urged to more aggressively police the costs of bankruptcy. Indeed, at least one recent critic has unkindly suggested that the failure of the courts to control bankruptcy costs is the result of a corrupt bargain between bankruptcy courts and practitioners.[3]

Rarely addressed is why bankruptcy courts regulate professional costs at all.[4] In most areas of American law, a professional is accountable solely to its client.[5] Complaints about excessive cost might result in a separate malpractice action, but a client who thinks they have been overcharged for the defense of their speeding ticket will find little relief in traffic court. Why is bankruptcy different?

This chapter begins to look at this question with a brief overview of the concept of bankruptcy costs, traditionally divided between direct and indirect costs. I next turn to a consideration of the process for overseeing bankruptcy costs. I briefly trace the history of court control of compensation in corporate bankruptcy, and then detail the current legal structure. Approaching the costs of Chapter 11 from a historical approach makes it clear that the current system has developed in a manner than can only be termed accidental, perhaps even haphazard. That suggests that the *status quo* is not entitled to any particular deference, and indeed is arguably overdue for a comprehensive reevaluation.

The final part of the chapter then surveys the existing understanding of Chapter 11 cost, and concludes with some thoughts on the important questions that remain unanswered. In short, we know a bit about direct costs, but very little about any other sort of costs. Moreover, what we know is almost entirely lacking in context. This makes it quite hard to understand if the existing system of cost regulation is either useful or justified.

BANKRUPTCY COSTS

The costs of corporate bankruptcy or reorganization are often considered to encompass two concepts.[6] First, there are the direct costs, comprised chiefly of the professional fees associated with reorganization, but also including other lesser costs like court filing fees and, in the United States, quarterly fees due to the United States Trustee's office.[7] In addition, there are also indirect costs of a firm's bankruptcy, which are more abstract but include things like lost managerial time, lost revenues, lost opportunities, and lost goodwill. Some of these costs may be of concern to the firm's stakeholders, but not to policymakers if, for example, financial distress simply results in the shifting of sales from the distressed firm to a competitor firm – unless the competitor is abroad, and nationalism takes hold.

The indirect costs are not only difficult to measure generally, but it is also difficult to determine what portion of these costs is attributable to any particular bankruptcy system.[8] Firms that fail are likely to incur lost sales and the like even in a jurisdiction without a bankruptcy or insolvency system.[9] The indirect costs of a particular bankruptcy system like Chapter 11, as opposed to the indirect costs of financial distress generally, are in truth then the marginal difference in such costs between the system under study and some alternative, often a hypothetical world with no bankruptcy system.[10]

Although there have been some efforts to study indirect costs empirically,[11] and one recent study suggests that the total expected cost of financial distress may be as high as 4.5% of the firm's pre-distress assets,[12] more often efforts to examine these costs have been theoretical, particularly in the legal literature.[13] In addition, studies of indirect costs have been limited to publicly held companies, and it is unknown if the results found in that context will translate to privately held firms, which make up the vast majority of debtors.

Direct costs are much easier to measure, and thus unsurprisingly are the subject of many more studies. Under current law, professional fees in particular are subject to court oversight in the United States, and thus relatively transparent.

THE OVERSIGHT OF BANKRUPTCY COSTS

When first developed in England, bankruptcy involved no regulation of compensation of any of the parties involved.[14] Instead, commissioners, the rough equivalent of today's bankruptcy judges, simply instructed the assignee, the rough equivalent of today's trustees, to make payments from the estate. As might be expected, this proved problematic, especially with regard to payments the commissioners authorized to themselves.

In the United States, the literature on costs and the regulation thereof under the first bankruptcy law, in 1800, is rather sparse. Like its predecessor, the second American bankruptcy law, the 1841 Act, primarily followed a fixed fee for service model of cost, with the district court ultimately overseeing the cost of the bankruptcy process.

Section 6 of the 1841 Act provided that:

> the said courts shall, from time to time, prescribe a tariff or table of fees and charges to be taxed by the officers of the court or other persons, for services under this act, or any other on the subject of bankruptcy; which fees shall be as low as practicable, with reference to the nature and character of such services.

Samuel Owen's *Treatise on the Law and Practice of Bankruptcy* provided a Table of Fees prescribed by the Circuit and District Courts of the United States for the Southern District of New York under Section 6 of the Act. This table divided the prescribed fees into six categories: (1) Counsel or Attorney's Fees; (2) Fees of the Clerk of the Circuit Court; (3) Fees of the Clerk of the District Court; (4) Fees to the Circuit or District Clerk Performing the Following Services; (5) Commissioner's Fees; and (6) Witness' Fees.

The commissioner received payment for the performance of a variety of tasks, including

> taking proof of any debt or claim against the bankrupt, (by statute); taking evidence of witnesses to be used in hearing before the Court; Appointing time and place for taking testimony, (five hours to be a day's sitting, where more than one is charged); Drawing and copy of examination of witness or bankrupt, per folio of 100 words; Every copy furnished either party at request, per folio; Certificate to examination; Administering an oath; Every necessary summons to witnesses; Return of proofs and filing; For travel expenses for the purpose of taking proof of a debt or claim against a bankrupt, 5 cents per mile each way; and Making a report to the court of disorderly conduct, or the refusal of a witness to attend or submit to examination.[15]

The assignee was compensated "five per cent on all monies received and paid out not exceeding one thousand dollars: two and a half per cent for sums exceeding one thousand and not amounting to five thousand dollars, and one per cent for all sums above five thousand dollars."[16] The compensation of the assignee was limited to his work in executing the estate: "But the assignee, like any other trustee, will not be permitted to make a profit out of the bankrupt's estate."[17]

Federal judges did not receive any additional monetary payments for adjudicating bankruptcy matters under the Act. Instead, judges reaped the intangible benefits of political capital from the creation of patronage networks. Judges had the ability to appoint family and friends for the highly sought-after clerk and commissioner positions in the bankruptcy courts.[18]

After the 1841 Act's swift demise, it was eventually replaced with the 1867 Act. That provided two basic ways of controlling bankruptcy costs. First, the Act itself created a framework of fees to be paid to registers, clerks and administrators in Section 47. Second, in addition to the fees set forth in Section 47, Section 10 of the Act gave the Supreme Court the power to frame "general orders" for several enumerated purposes, including "[f]or regulating the fees payable and the charges and costs to be allowed, except such as are established by this act or by law with respect to all proceedings in bankruptcy before said courts."[19]

These General Orders substantially resembled the rules and regulations issued by individual circuit and district courts under the 1841 Act. The General Orders provided guidelines for compensation of the court Clerk, the Register, and payments to the Assignee, but these guidelines remained flexible.

Under General Order No. 30, judges retained discretion to decrease costs payable to the Clerk and the Register in the event that the debtor provided proof "to the Court's satisfaction" that he lacked the appropriate means to pay such costs. In one case under the 1867 Act, the judge informed the parties that he

> does not allow the fee unless satisfied that full value has been given in the services rendered. The estate of the creditors is thus protected against any possible sinister speculations of client and counsel, or any innocent fanciful valuation that counsel might attach to their services, and clients might be disposed to allow, if permitted without restraint to tax the estates of bankrupts.[20]

Under these early bankruptcy laws there was a great deal of political controversy over the large cost of administering estates. Thus, the 1898 Bankruptcy Act, which would remain in force (with amendments) until 1978, reflected Congress' desire to administer bankrupt estates at minimum expense.[21]

In 1898 there were more than 650 referees – the new name for those would become bankruptcy judges – appointed to administer the new law.[22] These referees were compensated on a commission basis, depending heavily on the amount of assets recovered in bankruptcy proceedings. Because of this, referees benefitted from seeking out cases with the greatest potential for asset recoveries, and there is some anecdotal evidence that supports the theory that referees did personally seek out these cases, on at least a few occasions.

Referees continued to be paid commissions until 1946 with the enactment of the Referee's Salary Act.[23]

Under section 48 of the original 1898 Bankruptcy Act trustees were compensated by "sums to be paid as dividends and commissions as may be allowed by the courts." Similar to section 40 referee compensation under the Act, courts limited the trustee's compensation base to unsecured claims only.[24] Although the statute never truly defined the term "dividend" it made it clear in its construction of sections 64b and 65a that dividends have no application whatsoever to priority claims, and thus trustee received no compensation for those sorts of distributions.[25]

For the first time, the 1898 Act also directly addressed the compensation of professionals. For example, language controlling the compensation of attorneys in bankruptcy proceedings, located in section 64b,[26] was introduced in the 1898 Act and subsequently amended[27] in 1926, 1934 and 1938.

Under the original 1898 Act, section 64b listed the debts that have priority over other claims and the order in which they should be paid. Section 64b(3) addressed the issue of compensating attorneys in bankruptcy proceedings, providing a third rank priority for:

> the cost of administration, including the fees and mileage payable to witnesses and now or hereafter provided by the laws of the United States, and one reasonable attorney's fee, for the professional services actually rendered, irrespective of the number of attorneys employed, to the petitioning creditors in involuntary cases, to the bankrupt in involuntary cases while performing the duties herein prescribed, and to the bankrupt in voluntary cases, as the court may allow.[28]

The language unambiguously stated that only one attorney's fee would be granted regardless of the number of attorneys actually employed and rendering service.[29]

The attorney had the burden of applying for compensation, and if he (they were almost always men then[30]) failed to do so, he would not be compensated.[31] In order for an attorney's fee to be granted, a detailed statement[32] was given to the court or referee who would then make the determination of what amount of compensation should be granted.[33] The birth of the modern fee application.

The Act separated attorney's fees into those who acted for the petitioning creditors and those who act for the bankrupt. In general, attorneys for petitioning creditors were entitled to compensation for the preparation and filing of the petition in bankruptcy.[34] In cases where a trustee was yet to be appointed and the attorney for petitioning creditors had taken on added responsibilities, sufficient additional compensation was allowed for these services.[35]

The Act defined separate standards for attorneys acting for the debtor in involuntary cases and those acting in voluntary cases. Attorneys acting for the bankrupt in involuntary cases would only receive compensation "while performing the duties herein prescribed."[36] If any of the listed duties were performed, the attorney, as a matter of right, was entitled to compensation.

The amount must have been reasonable, and in determining a reasonable amount the court looked to a list of characteristics in order to determine compensation, including: the nature of the service, the time necessarily employed therein, the amount involved, the responsibility assumed, and the result obtained.[37] Modern section 330(a)(3) is almost identical.[38]

Attorneys acting for the bankrupt in voluntary petitions were not guaranteed compensation.[39] The amount of compensation allowed to these attorneys, as with those in involuntary proceedings, was limited to services that benefit the estate; in no means would they be compensated for defending the bankrupt personally.[40] If at any point during the proceedings, the attorney for the bankrupt acted to defeat or delay the process, or created additional expenses, compensation would be refused.[41] It must have been found that the attorney rendered services in good faith in line with the purpose of the Act.[42]

In all cases, the watchword remained thrift. As one court explained, "in view of the policy of economy of the Bankruptcy Act, allowances for such fees *cannot and should not* approximate what attorneys might or would receive, under similar circumstances, for services to private persons."[43]

With the 1929 crash, and the onset of the New Deal, reform was in the air:

> In 1934, Congress enacted section 77B of the Bankruptcy Act for the reorganization of financially embarrassed corporations, in order to prevent on the one hand, "rigid and often wasteful" liquidation in bankruptcy, and on the other hand, the flourishing of the "equity receivership," which had sometimes been "used as an instrument of fraud or covin" and which sometimes "had a tendency to intrench delinquency in power, and to stifle inquiry into acts of waste or spoliation."[44]

This added sections 77B(c)(9) and 77B (c)(11) which provided:

> Upon approving the petition or answer or at any time thereafter, the judge, in addition to the jurisdiction and powers elsewhere in this section conferred upon him. . .may allow a reasonable compensation for the services rendered and

> reimbursement for the actual and necessary expenses incurred in connection with the proceeding and the plan by officers, parties in interest, depositaries, reorganization managers and committees or other representatives of creditors or stockholders, and the attorneys or agents of any of the foregoing and of the debtor . . . .[45]

Section 77B was soon replaced by Chapters X and XI of the Chandler Act, which would remain in effect until the enactment of the Bankruptcy Code in 1978.

Chapter X was intended to be the provision that dealt with large corporate debtors, even if it did not always turn out that way.[46] One practitioner summarized the control of costs under that chapter thus:

> The judge may allow reasonable compensation for services rendered by attorneys for the trustee and other officers, for the debtor and for the petitioning creditors, in obtaining approval of the petition and in obtaining appointment of the trustee, and by attorneys for indenture trustees, depositaries, reorganization managers, and committees or representatives of creditors or stockholders (except attorneys for the Securities and Exchange Commission). Similarly attorneys may receive reasonable compensation who represent creditors and stockholders in connection with the suggestions or proposals for a plan or in connection with objections by them to the confirmation of a plan. Here the judge must consider only services which contributed to the plan confirmed or to the refusal of confirmation of the plan or were beneficial in the administration of the estate. Even counsel for intervenors can be compensated. In the field of bankruptcy, economy is still the lodestar.[47]

By and large, the SEC, which was given a prominent role in Chapter X cases, had a large say in what appropriate compensation should be in corporate reorganization cases.[48]

The modern approach to overseeing corporate bankruptcy costs was taking shape, as an inevitable part of federalizing the system of corporate reorganization.[49] Small businesses might have liquidated with but a trustee and a referee, but large corporate enterprises employed many more professionals to achieve the task of reorganization.

But it was a gradual process, as the courts continued to hold that reorganization professionals were court officials, acting under court designation, and thus there was no reason for "vicarious generosity" in determining compensation.[50] Indeed, until the enactment of the 1978 Code, it was often stated that bankruptcy professionals should be paid something less than market rates, to promote thrift in insolvency.[51] This, of course, simply created a distinct market in bankruptcy.[52]

While corporate bankruptcy was increasingly federalized after the New Deal, and thus the regulation of fees was increasingly subject to the standard of frugality imposed by the federal courts, before the

New Deal corporate reorganization had been largely a matter of equity receiverships.[53] In these cases, regulation of professional fees was left to the sound discretion of the court.[54] In consensual receiverships, the receivers' costs were entitled to priority treatment.[55]

But the receivership courts also regulated fees in ways that would be understandable to modern Chapter 11 practitioners. For example, courts disallowed compensation for receivers when receivers were guilty of misconduct or acted negligently in rendering services.[56] Courts also disallowed compensation where services were duplicated.[57]

Indeed, modern practice under the 1978 Bankruptcy Code seems to draw more from these cases than those under the amended 1898 Bankruptcy Act, with their extreme focus on "economy of the estate."[58]

In particular, the retention of a professional, or at least any key professional, is subject to prior approval by the bankruptcy court.[59] The retention application must include the terms of the retention arrangement, including important facts like the rates to be charged.[60]

After work has been done in the case, all professionals retained by either the debtor or an official committee – most often a creditors committee – must file fee applications with the court before they can be paid from estate funds.[61] A similar rule applies to professionals retained by examiners or trustees.

A strange system then prevails in which the old ways are rejected in favor of the market, but the market is regulated by the bankruptcy court and the United States Trustee, a government position newly created by the 1978 Code, who acts as bankruptcy "watchdog."[62]

This fee system collects a large amount of the "in bankruptcy" costs of Chapter 11, while bankruptcy-related professional fees incurred in the days just before the bankruptcy filing are reported on the debtor's Statement of Financial Affairs.

Professional fees incurred by creditors who have a contractual right to charge such fees to the debtor – such as secured lenders, and even unsecured lenders with fee provisions in their contracts – are not included in most studies, inasmuch as these sorts of reimbursement obligations are not subject to section 330 of the Bankruptcy Code and are therefore not subject to express disclosure, except if separately itemized on a proof of claim.[63] Nonetheless, it should be noted that these fees, while not regulated, still contribute to the direct and indirect costs of corporate bankruptcy.

Thus, it is possible to obtain a reasonably good, if not fully complete, picture of the direct costs of American corporate bankruptcy. Unfortunately, it is difficult to obtain comparable data for out-of-court workouts, exchange offers, and other substitutes for bankruptcy. The next section thus takes up the broader question of studying corporate bankruptcy costs.

But as this brief historical review has indicated, it is not clear that the legal mechanisms for overseeing the direct costs of bankruptcy cases are the result of thoughtful design. Instead, historical accretion may explain the bulk of the current structure. And frequently there has been little consideration if regulatory concepts developed in "straight bankruptcy" – i.e., Chapter 7 – translate into the realm of corporate reorganization.

THE STUDY OF BANKRUPTCY COSTS

Studies of the direct costs of corporate reorganization in the United States date to the Great Depression.[64] Between the 1930s and the enactment of the current United States Bankruptcy Code in 1978, the most important study of direct costs was Jerold Warner's examination of railroads that had filed under section 77 of the Bankruptcy Act between 1933 and 1955.[65] Warner's study continues to make occasional appearances in the literature,[66] despite its exceedingly small sample size,[67] its focus on an industry that was in many ways atypical of corporate bankruptcy practice under the old Bankruptcy Act,[68] and its use of a sample that was arguably already out of date when published in 1977.[69]

The first important study of professional fees under Chapter 11 of the 1978 Bankruptcy Code was Weiss, who studied a sample of 37 publicly traded firms that filed for bankruptcy between 1979 and 1986.[70] This study found costs to be, on average, 3.1% of the book value of debt plus market value of equity at the end of the fiscal year preceding bankruptcy, which was noticeably less than the 4% to 25% that prior studies had reported.[71] Weiss ultimately concluded that Chapter 11 direct costs "will have little or no impact on the pricing of claims prior to bankruptcy."[72]

More recently, this author, in an LL.M. thesis using data from Warren and Westbrook's Business Bankruptcy Project, set out to consider assertions that direct costs of Chapter 11 were "excessive."[73] I conducted a study of 22 corporate bankruptcies and reported evidence that the direct costs of Chapter 11 were in fact nominal, both empirically and analytically, that is, "not only on a simple percentage basis but also in relation to other significant corporate transactions."[74]

Lubben (2000) turned out to be the opening act in a multitude of empirical legal studies of business bankruptcy costs over the next decade. That same year, Lawless and Ferris reported on their study of small business Chapter 11 costs.[75] Studying multiple judicial districts, the authors reported median costs of 3.5% of debtor assets. The authors concluded that whether "measured by total distributions or total assets, Chapter 11 costs are of a relatively low magnitude and at a level consistent with studies of large corporate bankruptcies."[76]

In 2004, Lynn LoPucki and Joseph Doherty reported on "one of the most extensive studies to date of the professional fees and expenses awarded by U.S. bankruptcy courts in the reorganization of large, public companies."[77] LoPucki and Doherty studied the professional fees and expenses awarded by U.S. bankruptcy courts in 48 Chapter 11 cases involving large, public companies whose plans were confirmed between 1998 and 2002.[78]

Among other things, LoPucki and Doherty reported that:

1. Four factors determined the amounts of fees and expenses. In declining order of importance, they are firm size (measured by assets reported on the petition), time elapsed from filing to plan confirmation, the number of professional firms authorized to incur fees, and whether the case proceeded in the Delaware Bankruptcy Court.
2. The ratio of fees to assets is subject to a scale effect. As the size of the case increases, the ratio of fees to expenses declines.
3. The total fees and expenses in the 48 cases studied were 1.4 percent of the debtors' total assets as reported in the bankruptcy files at the beginning of their bankruptcy cases. The average ratio of the fees and expenses paid by a company to total assets of the company was 2.2 percent; however, removal of a single outlier reduced it to 1.9 percent.[79]

Shortly thereafter, this author published a two-part article looking at the internal mechanics of attorney fees in Chapter 11.[80] Using the billing records of a large corporate law firm in a single Delaware Chapter 11 case, I demonstrated that more than 60% of the attorneys were not bankruptcy specialists, suggesting that a good deal of the costs that appear on fee applications may be exogenous to the Chapter 11 process. Since this data suggests that the direct costs of Chapter 11 itself might be even lower than previously reported, I concluded by noting the challenge that this presented for those who argue that Chapter 11 has a substantial effect on *ex ante* debt prices. Once discounted by the probability of default and time until such default, such small amounts would only be important in highly efficient markets, of which the debt markets are unlikely examples.

In 2006, Bris, Welch and Zhu published a study of almost 300 corporate bankruptcies filed in Arizona and New York from 1995 to 2001.[81] The sample was comprised of 225 Chapter 11 cases and 61 Chapter 7 cases.

As with the LoPucki and Doherty, and Lubben studies, the authors found that courts rarely deny fee applications. They also noted that bankruptcy costs are highly sensitive to the size of debtor being measured and how size itself is measured, both in terms of which metric is used (assets, debts, etc.) and the source of the data being used.

In 2008, LoPucki and Doherty returned to their original model and compared it with a new model, that the asserted better represented pure case complexity.[82] Describing the difference between the two regression models as the "billing opportunity" presented by a case, the authors asserted that professionals routinely overcharged for Chapter 11 work.

In the same year, this author produced the American Bankruptcy Institute Chapter 11 Fee Study,[83] and published a related article setting forth the results of that study.[84] The study examined a total sample of 1,026 cases filed in 2004 as 945 Chapter 11 cases were pooled into a "random" sample and 99 cases were considered in a "big case" dataset. The average firm in the big case dataset had scheduled assets of $423.4 million and scheduled liabilities of nearly $776 million, while the average firm in the random sample had scheduled assets of $21.2 million and scheduled liabilities of more than $37 million. Lubben found that for both samples professional fees totaled 4 to 4.5 percent of the bankrupt firms' assets and liabilities, but cautioned against reporting cost in relation to size, since the data evidenced significant economics of scale.[85]

While partially confirming prior studies, such as LoPucki and Doherty, Lubben also found that time spent in Chapter 11 was not a significant predictor of overall cost once case complexity was fully modeled. Lubben found the addition of other variables, such as looking at a bankrupt firm's assets and debts, presence of official committees and whether there were "first day motions" filed in a case, were better predictors of the costs involved in a Chapter 11 case. The study also found no indications that filing in Delaware or New York resulted in greater cost.[86]

Also in 2008, LoPucki and Doherty examined the growing role of investment bankers in modern Chapter 11 practice and constructed regression models for specific bankruptcy professionals.[87] The primary findings of this paper largely track those of its earlier companion papers, although the authors did note that "the fees of financial advisors grew at the rate of 25% per year, as compared with an increase in all professional fees and expenses of 7% per year." They also separately modeled the costs of lead debtor's attorneys, finding that Skadden, Arps, a leading New York corporate law firm,[88] was substantially more expensive than other debtor's firms. They concluded "Skadden Arps representation cost more in these cases because Skadden Arps billed more hours."

In their 2011 book, which revisits many of their earlier studies, LoPucki and Doherty revisited their earlier models, and dropped their earlier claims regarding Skadden, Arps.[89] Instead, in their predictive model they report that debtors' attorneys fees and expenses are a function of size, whether the case was prepackaged or prenegotiated, the year the case was filed, whether the case was filed away from the debtor's "home" district, and whether the case was filed in Delaware. In their evaluative models, they consider alternative factors like the duration of the case and whether the debtors hired particular investment bankers.

In their final model the authors explain some 90% of variance in debtor attorney costs with a model comprised of size, the year the debtor's plan was confirmed, the number of days the debtor spent in Chapter 11, the number of cases in which the attorney appears in the database, whether Lazard or Rothchild were the debtor's lead financial advisors, and a somewhat confusing set of interaction variables.[90] Specifically, the authors use (a) the number of docket entries in the case, (b) whether the case was filed in the Southern District of New York, and (c) an interaction of the first two variables, which captures something like the length of the docket conditional on the case being in New York, since the jurisdictional variable is a simple yes/no factor.[91]

The authors do not fully explain how to interpret these variables, especially the non-interacted variables in light of the interaction term in the model, but the negative coefficient on the interaction term might suggest that complex cases are cheaper when filed in New York. This would seem to be in tension with the authors' frequent thesis that Chapter 11 costs are driven by the tendency of big cases to file in New York and Delaware. They also provide little explanation for why the hiring of a particular investment banker should influence cost, and it may be that these are simply proxies for some unmodeled factor that influences attorney costs.

This overview is somewhat summary, and necessarily omits studies of specific types of professionals,[92] and studies of costs outside the United States,[93] as well as a host of older studies in the finance literature.[94]

But on some level, more descriptive reports on the cost of Chapter 11 or any other reorganization system are of little utility. What is really needed is context, and that is quite often lacking.[95]

We now know that Chapter 11 cases typically involve direct costs somewhere between two and three percent of pre-bankruptcy assets – and that smaller cases cost somewhat more, relatively speaking, than bigger ones.[96] That is, Chapter 11 seems to have economies of scale.

Is the cost too high? Is it low? We do not really know, because there is little agreement on the appropriate basis of comparison.

One approach might be to consider the issue from a marginal creditor's point of view. Being in Chapter 11 means that creditors' recovery on their claims moves from zero to some higher amount.[97] The professional fees are

Table 12.1 Recent measures of direct costs

Source	*What Measured*	*Measure*	*Of . . .*
LoPucki and Doherty (2004)	Overall cost of big cases	1.4%, but subject to strong scale effects	Debtor's assets
Lubben (2008)	Overall cost of big cases	For the smallest debtor quintile, 5.49% For the next smallest quintile, 5.19% For the median quintile, 5.49% For the second largest debtor quintile, 4.46% For the largest debtors, 1.97% Overall, 4.53%	Debtor's assets plus debts
LoPucki and Doherty (2011)	Overall cost of big cases	"6% for a $100 million company, 2% for a $500 million dollar company, 1% for a $2 billion company, and 0.5% for a $5 billion company"	Debtor's assets
Lubben (2012)	Overall cost of big cases	Standardized Chapter 11 cost by size quartiles: 1 (smallest) 10.10% 2 8.90% 3 4.20% 4 2.10%	Average of debtor's assets and debts
Lubben Attorneys (2012)	Attorney cost in big cases	Standardized Chapter 11 cost by size quartiles: Debtor's counsel (total) 1 (smallest) 4.90% 2 3.70% 3 1.00% 4 0.80% Lead debtor's counsel 1 (smallest) 4.80% 2 3.40% 3 0.90% 4 0.70% Committee counsel (total) 1 (smallest) 2.90% 2 1.50% 3 0.50% 4 0.30% Lead committee counsel 1 (smallest) 2.80% 2 1.40% 3 0.50% 4 0.30%	Average of debtor's assets and debts
Lubben (2011)	Financial advisor cost in big cases	Turnaround consultants, 17.27% Financial advisors, 17.05% Combined with bankruptcy attorneys, 71%	Total cost

the cost of moving to that higher recovery. The notion that money paid to professionals belongs to creditors is true only if the creditors could realize that value without the professionals.

But even liquidation does not happen by itself.[98] Indeed, only abandonment of a distressed firm might be costless – if we limit our conception of cost to actual "out of pocket" expenditures by the debtor-firm,[99] but that obviously ignores the larger costs to society.

The real policy question then is whether creditors are paying too much to go from a 0% recovery in Chapter 7 to a 40% recovery in Chapter 11, to put some rough numbers on the question. This is a question about the efficiency of the market for bankruptcy professionals, because if that market is efficient the professionals are limited in their ability to overcharge. If the market is inefficient, it is primarily a distributional question as to whom between the creditors and the professionals should grab the extra recovery afforded by Chapter 11.

Overheated rhetoric about the hourly rates of the professionals in question and the millions of dollars requested in fee applications do nothing to advance our understanding of these key issues. It is implausible that the same caliber of bankruptcy professionals would work for little or substantially reduced compensation, or that artificially capping bankruptcy costs would not have an effect on how Chapter 11 cases played out.[100]

For example, if a debtor could find cheaper bankruptcy counsel, are we sure that creditor recoveries would go up, as the conventional wisdom often implies, or will recoveries go down, because the cheaper firm is too inexperienced or too small to handle the case? Sometimes it is true that you get what you pay for.

Instead, the focus must be on identifying how much Chapter 11 costs, how much value Chapter 11 generates overall, and how those figures compare to the available alternatives, such as state debtor-creditor law, corporate insolvency systems used in other jurisdictions, or theoretical alternatives to Chapter 11, if the costs of the same can be fully understood. Simply declaring that Chapter 11 costs are "outrageous" is no more helpful from a policy perspective than any other soapbox declaration of one's personal beliefs. The important question is "why?" And that can only be answered by providing context.

* * *

One reasonable response might be that bankruptcy is indeed different. True, all corporations suffer from a separation of ownership and control. Thus, shareholders out of bankruptcy, like creditors in bankruptcy, lack insight into whether or not professionals are providing value to their corporate client, and whether that value is being provided in the most efficient manner.

But outside of bankruptcy most legal departments in corporations manage the external counsel engagements and are very focused on external counsel budgets. There is some agency risk here, but all indications are that general counsel offices do a good job monitoring their outside advisors.

But most legal departments – especially outside of financial institutions – have very little bankruptcy expertise. This places the debtor in a position of dependence on its bankruptcy counsel: the debtor's in-house counsel will have to trust their bankruptcy counsel, and will have little insight into which matters are truly important, and which matters might be ignored.

There is also an important change in the bargaining power dynamic between corporations and their counsel once bankruptcy is on the table. While previously the corporation may have had the power to demand discounts off of the law firm's stated billing rates, upon bankruptcy, the power returns to the attorneys' and few if any discounts will be available.

And debtor's counsel has incentives to over-prepare the case. For example, some bankruptcy judges are known for chastising counsel who are unprepared to discuss an issue, no matter how tangential or trivial. The debtor's general counsel may not know if the company is receiving efficient representation by reviewing time records of bankruptcy attorneys, but she could well draw conclusions about counsel's competence after seeing such an exhibition play out in open court. Debtor's counsel then has strong incentives to over prepare for hearings before the judge and avoid such a fate.

Committees, both official and ad hoc, who have an expectation of having their costs reimbursed by the debtor, will use their lawyers as a resource and litigation tool without too much thought about fee accruals. After all, while in some abstract sense greater Chapter 11 cost means less recovery for unsecured creditors, the cost is spread across such a large body of creditors that few individuals will be sensitive, or motivated enough to object.

Doing more, rather than less, mitigates risk because the less chance the professional will miss something or be surprised by something. There is no penalty for waste and there is actually a reward beyond the fees insofar as counsel leaves no stone unturned, and thus feels more prepared and less vulnerable heading into a hearing.

Fees are transparent in bankruptcy, in the sense that total amounts billed and time records must be disclosed. But are the reviews of massive fee applications really likely to disclose inefficiency in the case?[101]

There are good reasons to doubt it. In particular, without a deep understanding of the case, which in general will be inconsistent with the attorney-client privilege, it will often be unclear if time spent on particular issues was well spent.[102]

Thus, the objections to fees that usually surface through the Bankruptcy Code's system are typically trivial. Indeed, it is an old joke among bankruptcy attorneys that the United States Trustee, the government official charged with reviewing fees, spends so much time worrying about attorneys who spend $500 upgrading to business class on their flights, that they miss the $500,000 spent researching and briefing an irrelevant issue.

In short, the obvious mechanisms to control costs in Chapter 11 might not function properly, and without any evil intent, fees might be systematically higher in Chapter 11.

This is a possible thesis.[103] The problem is testing it. Bankruptcy fees are somewhat transparent, but most other fees are not. Again, the problem of context comes to the fore.

One possible approach is to consider American corporate reorganization as compared with systems in other jurisdictions. There have been a few attempts at this,[104] but comparative work in this area suffers from several problems.

First, many jurisdictions do not require similar degrees of transparency with regard to professional fees. In addition, even when fees are disclosed, the types of fees that might be disclosed are often not comparable to those disclosed in the United States. And while much scholarship on American corporate restructuring focuses on large, publicly traded debtors, few jurisdictions have sufficient cases of similar size to facilitate easy comparison. Nonetheless, there would appear to be some opening here for some Canadian, Australian and British comparative scholarship, given that those jurisdictions would seem to have fewer differences than most.

An even more difficult task is considering the costs of Chapter 11 relative to some, as yet hypothetical, alternative reorganization system.[105] The proper consideration is the incremental difference between the direct and indirect costs of both the proposed system and the extant system. For reasons already identified, in reality at most one of those four costs is likely to be known with any certainty.

It is probably not a coincidence that the production of elaborate, academic alternatives to Chapter 11 has greatly diminished since the publication of Weiss and the studies that followed. At the very least those studies suggested that the room for improvement on the direct cost front was relatively small. And it can be argued that indirect costs, or at least the bulk of indirect costs, are more of a function of financial distress in general, than any particular insolvency system.

It will also be equally difficult to test the opposite thesis: that the "public shaming" of having a fee application denied holds down costs of court supervised professionals. If true, this would suggest that an attorney representing a creditor will charge more – however measured – than a similar attorney representing a creditor's committee. But again, the general opacity of professional fees outside of those subject to disclosure under the Code represents a real challenge.

CONCLUSION

Ultimately there remains a broader question of whether the costs of Chapter 11, or any corporate reorganization system, actually matter. Or, more precisely, do costs matter once they are within some range of reasonableness, which is apt to be found in any developed economy?

It is often suggested by academics that bankruptcy costs have strong *ex ante* effects. In simple examples this seems quite intuitive: if the costs of insolvency will reduce my recovery, I should account for that in the price I charge up front.

But in the real world, the factors that go into setting an interest rate are myriad. And the probability of default is often quite small, especially outside of a few specialized contexts, like distressed lending. Thus, it seems that bankruptcy costs would have to be extreme to have a perceptible *ex ante* effect.

Ex post may be a different story.

On the very eve of bankruptcy, bankruptcy costs might well have a significant effect. The probability of default is high, and the influence of other, long-term factors will wane in the face of a probable bankruptcy filing. The market for distressed debt would then be the place to look for the real effect of bankruptcy costs.

Namely, distressed debt investors should pay less for claims that will be resolved in more costly jurisdictions.

The challenge will be finding debtors who are otherwise of equal risk, where the choice of jurisdiction is clear. Large corporate debtors have many choices of where to file within the United States, and also have some ability to file in foreign jurisdictions. The liquidity of the market for distressed claims also presents another possible confounding factor. Again, many jurisdictions will not have sufficient numbers of distressed debtors to support a liquid market in claims.

In the end, after several decades of study, the question of corporate bankruptcy costs remains rather unsettled – probably more unsettled than generally acknowledged.

We generally know what the direct costs of American corporate bankruptcy cases are, while the indirect costs remain a bit more vague. And the importance and effect of those costs remains the subject of yet to be completed research.

Until that work is done, it is difficult to know if the existing system of cost oversights works or is justified. But it seems likely that there must be a better way, given the substantial administrative burdens imposed by the current system and the dubious efficacy of the same.

NOTES

* Harvey Washington Wiley Chair in Corporate Governance & Business Ethics, Seton Hall University School of Law. Many thanks for the helpful comments provided by Oscar Couwenberg, Richard Levin, and Michael Simkovic.

1. 3A Collier on Bankruptcy ¶ 62.02[1], pp. 1390–91 (14th ed. 1975).
2. *See, e.g., Bankruptcy Jurisdiction*, 19 L. Rev. & Q.J. Brit. & For. Jurisp. 325, 327–8 (Nov. 1853–Feb. 1854); *Suggestions Regarding the Poor Law Amendment Act and New Bankruptcy Act*, 13 Law Mag. Quart. Rev. Juris. 274, 275 (1835). In a 1916 speech before the Commercial Law League, Samuel Untermyer complained that professional fees in railroad receiverships were "easily ten times as large as in any other country and necessarily so because of the complications of the procedure." The Bulletin of the Commercial Law League of America, Volume 21, at page 591.
3. Lynn M. LoPucki, Courting Failure: How Competition for Big Cases Is Corrupting the Bankruptcy Courts 141 (2005).
4. The key sections of the current Bankruptcy Code dealing with professional retention can be found at 11 U.S.C. §§ 327, 328, 330.
5. Alyeska Pipeline Service Co. v. Wilderness Society, 421 U.S. 240, 247 (1975). *See also* Samuel Berger, *Court Awarded Attorneys' Fees: What is "Reasonable"?*, 126 U. Pa. L. Rev. 281, 281–2 (1977).
6. John D. Ayer, *The Role of Finance Theory in Shaping Bankruptcy Policy*, 3 Am. Bankr. Inst. L. Rev. 53, 83 (1995).
7. The United States Trustee Program is a component of the Department of Justice that monitors bankruptcy cases for fraud and the like. It is distinct from the bankruptcy trustee appointed in all Chapter 7 and some Chapter 11 cases.
8. Gregor Andrade & Steven N. Kaplan, *How Costly is Financial (Not Economic) Distress? Evidence from Highly Leveraged Transactions that Became Distressed*, 53 J. Fin. 1443 (1998) (finding that most of the indirect cost of financial distress seems to be incurred before bankruptcy).
9. As noted by an earlier commentator in a related context:
   There is a common tendency to view bankruptcy as an "either-or" situation. Either the firm is solvent and there are no costs or the firm is bankrupt and there are costs. In fact, for indirect costs, there is usually a continuum of costs that increase at an accelerating rate as exposure to bankruptcy increases . . .
   Bernell K. Stone, *Bankruptcy Costs: Some Evidence: Discussion*, 32 J. Fin. 366, 367 (1977). *See also* R.A. Haugen & L.W. Senbet, *Bankruptcy and Agency Costs: Their Significance to the Theory of Optimal Capital Structure*, 23 J. Fin. & Quant. Anal. 27 (1988).
10. Depending on the basis of comparison, the indirect costs could thus be negative.
11. Edward I. Altman, *A Further Empirical Investigation of the Bankruptcy Cost Question*, 39 J. Fin. 1067 (1984) (measuring indirect costs by consideration of comparable company sales, but without specifying what portion of said costs are attributable to the bankruptcy system and what portion might be the result of general financial distress);

Andrade & Kaplan, *supra* note 8; T.C. Opler & S. Titman, *Financial Distress and Corporate Performance*, 49 J. Fin. 1015, 1040 (1994).

12. Heitor Almeida & Tomas Philippon, *The Risk-Adjusted Cost of Financial Distress,* 62 J. Fin. 2557 (2007).
13. *See, e.g.*, Barry E. Adler, *Bankruptcy and Risk Allocation*, 77 Cornell L. Rev. 439 (1992); James J. White, *Harvey's Silence*, 69 Am. Bankr. L.J. 467 (1995).
14. For a general history of bankruptcy in the United States, see Stephen J. Lubben, *A New Understanding of the Bankruptcy Clause*, 64 Case W. Res. L. Rev. 319 (2013).
15. Owen, *Treatise on the Law and Practice of Bankruptcy*, Appendix pp. 19–23.
16. *Id.*, at 12–13.
17. *Id.*, at 238.
18. Edward J. Balleisen, *Vulture Capitalism in Antebellum America*, 70 Bus. Hist. Rev. 473, 485 (1996).
19. 14 Stat. 517, 521 (1867).
20. *In re* Williams, 29 F. Cas. 1324, 1325 (D.S.C. 1868). Note the interesting reference to the "estate of the creditors."
21. *In re Curtis,* 100 F. 784, 792 (7th Cir. Ill. 1900).
22. Hon. Prudence Carter Beatty, *Judging at the End of the Millennium,* 18-9ABIJ 28 (1999).
23. Referees' Salary Act, 60 Stat. 323 (1946).
24. *In re* Fielding, 96 F. 800, 801 (W.D. Mo. 1899) ("It may be conceded that said section 65(a), strictly speaking, does not undertake to define what a dividend is, but it unmistakably indicates what, in the legislative mind, was meant by the term 'dividends.' It is an express declaration that in this respect claims having priority are identical with secured claims, neither of which is subject to a declaration and payment of the equal per centum."); *see also In re* Mammoth Pine Lumber Co., 116 F. 731, 736 (D. Ark. 1902). Following the 1903 amendments, trustee and referee compensation was based on both secured and unsecured claims.
25. *In re* Mammoth Pine Lumber Co., 116 F. at 734. *See also* §64b: order of payments: first taxes then priority claims; see also 30 Stat. 563 §65a "dividends of an equal per centum shall be declared and paid on all allowed claims, except such as have priority or are secured."
26. 30 Stat. 563 §64b.
27. Other clauses of §64b have been amended at various times, but the dates listed are those that pertain to §64b(3) as it discusses compensation for attorneys in bankruptcy proceedings.
28. 30 Stat. 563 §64b
29. James B. Hirsch, *Bankruptcy Fee Applications: Compensable Service or Cost of Doing Business,* 58 Fordham L. Rev. 1327 (1990); *see also In re* Nat'l Department Stores, Inc., 11 F. Supp. at 638: "where numerous persons participate in rendering one service susceptible of being rendered by one person, needless duplication results which should not form the basis of compensation."
30. Almost, but not exclusively. *See, e.g.*, 8 Women Law. J. 3, 21 (1919) (noting the appointment of Mrs. H.M. Linney as bankruptcy referee in Arizona).
31. Hirsch, *supra* note 29 at 1327.
32. 30 Stat. 562 §62: Expenses of Administering Estates a) The actual and necessary expenses incurred by officers in the administration of estates shall, except where other provisions are made for their payment, be reported in detail, under oath, and examined and approved or disapproved by the court. If approved, they shall be paid or allowed out of the estates in which they were incurred.
33. Hirsch, *supra* note 29 at 1327.
34. *In re* Consolidated Distribs., 298 F. 859, 863 (2d Cir. N.Y. 1924).
35. *In re* Poe, 1 F. Supp. 658 (D.N.Y. 1932).
36. 30 Stat. 563 §64(b)(3). See Duties of a bankrupt 30 Stat. 548 §7a: The bankrupt shall (1) attend first meeting of creditors; (2) comply with lawful court orders; (3) examine the validity of all proofs of claims filed against it; (4) produce and deliver requested papers;

(5) hand trustee all foreign properties; (6) inform trustee of an invasion by creditors to violate this act; (7) disclose any knowledge to trustee regarding false claims against his estate; (8) prepare a schedule of his property; (9) submit to court at meetings of his creditors an examination of his business.

37. *In re* Curtis, 100 F. 784, 786 (7th Cir. Ill. 1900).
38. 11 U.S.C. §330(a)(3).
39. 30 Stat. 563 §64b(3) "as the court may allow."
40. *In re* Anderson, 103 F. 854, 859 (D.S.C. 1900). (The court stated that "no allowance should be made for services rendered in defending the bankrupt from charges of fraudulent conduct or concealment of property"); *see also In re* Rosenthal & Lehman, 120 F. 848, 849 (D. Mo. 1902) (difficulties may arise in distinguishing purely personal services from those that benefit the estate).
41. *In re* Woodward, 95 F. 955, 956 (D.N.C. 1899).
42. Rosenthal & Lehman, 120 F. at 850.
43. *In re* Owl Drug Co., 16 F. Supp. 139, 144 (D. Nev. 1936) (emphasis added), *aff'd sub nom.* Cohn v. Edler, 90 F.2d 823 (9th Cir. 1937).
44. David Ferber et. al, *Conflicts of Interest in Reorganization Proceedings under the Public Utility Holding Company Act of 1935 and Chapter X of the Bankruptcy Act*, 28 Geo. Wash. L. Rev. 319, 326 (1959) (quoting Duparquet, Huot & Moneuse Co. v. Evans, 297 U.S. 216, 219 (1936)).
45. 48 Stat. 917 §77B(c)(9)–(c)(11)
46. As a general rule, corporations (and their managers) preferred to file under Chapter XI, when possible. The potential that Chapter XI would undermine Chapter X was recognized quite early. *Corporate Reorganization-Jurisdictional Scope of Chapters X and XI*, 17 N.Y.U. L. Q. Rev. 254 (1939).
47. Herbert U. Feibelman, *The Allowance and Reasonableness of Attorneys' Fees in Bankruptcy*, 15 Bus. Law 889, 896 (1960) (footnotes omitted). *See also* Alfred T. Tallakson, *Compensation of Attorneys in Bankruptcy Proceedings*, 32 Alb. L. Rev. 410 (1968).
48. Scribner & Miller v. Conway, 238 F.2d 905, 907 (2d Cir. 1956) (The "recommendation for allowances of the S.E.C., made by this responsible and disinterested public agency after close familiarity with the entire proceedings and careful study and report, should be followed unless the reorganization judge showed reasons otherwise based on specific findings."). *See also* Richard V. Bandler, *Securities Trading and Fee Sharing under Chapter X of the Bankruptcy Act*, 15 Rec. Ass'n B. City N.Y. 230, 250 (1960).
49. West v. Fradenburg, 86 F. 2d 318, 320 (8th Cir. 1936).
50. *In re* Paramount-Publix Corp., 12 F. Supp. 823, 828 (D.N.Y. 1935).
51. Massachusetts Mutual Life Insurance Company v. Brock, 405 F.2d 429, 432–3 (5th Cir. 1968).
52. Tallakson, *supra* note 47, argued in 1968 that

    Merely reiterating the "economy" principle in bankruptcy proceedings solves nothing. While it is true that preservation of the estate is to be kept in mind when awarding compensation to attorneys, the award ought not to be so small that attorneys refrain from representing trustees, receivers and petitioning creditors.

    Id. at 415.
53. Stephen J. Lubben, *Railroad Receiverships and Modern Bankruptcy Theory*, 89 Cornell L. Rev. 1420, 1440–41 (2004).
54. Sullivan Timber Co. v. Black, 159 Ala. 570, 588–99 (Ala. 1909).
55. Central Trust & Sav. Co. v. Chester County Electric Co., 9 Del. Ch. 247, 254 (Del. Ch. 1911) (citing Makeel v. Hotchkiss, 190 Ill. 311, 315 (Ill. 1901)).
56. Higgins v. Shield, 151 Ky. 227, 229 (Ky. 1912).
57. Conover v. W. Jersey Mortg. Co., 96 N.J. Eq. 441 (Ch. 1924).
58. *In re* M.R. Wright & Bro., 18 F.2d 686 (W.D.S.C. 1926).
59. 11 U.S.C. § 327.

60. Although courts have been known to approve retention applications that fail to meet these standards, making the investigator's work all the more difficult.
61. 11 U.S.C. § 330. *In re* Mirant Corp., 354 B.R. 113, 125 (Bankr. N.D. Tex. 2006).
62. *In re* Drexel Burnham Lambert Grp., Inc., 133 B.R. 13, 20 (Bankr. S.D.N.Y. 1991).
63. *See In re* Borders Grp., Inc., 456 B.R. 195, 203 (Bankr. S.D.N.Y. 2011).
64. Thomas Clifford Billig, Equity Receiverships in the Common Pleas Court of Franklin County, Ohio (1932); Israel Treiman, *An Analysis of the Statistical Data on Receivership Suits Filed in the St. Louis Circuit Court 1925–32 Inclusive*, 19 St. Louis L. Rev. 87 (1933). *See* Stephen J. Lubben, *Railroad Receiverships and Modern Bankruptcy Theory*, 89 Cornell L. Rev. 1420, 1452 (2004) (noting that one railroad paid attorneys alone more than $900,000 during the reorganization, which represented approximately 3.5% of its pre-receivership assets); *see also* Churchill Rodgers & Littleton Groom, *Reorganization of Railroad Corporations Under Section 77 of the Bankruptcy Act*, 33 Colum. L. Rev. 571, 571 n.2 (1933) (citing Paxton, *Railroad Receiverships and Reorganizations* (1933) 1 Ed. Research Rep., No. 2; Moulton and Associates, The American Transportation Problem (1933) *333 et seq.*; Chicago, M. & St. Paul Reorganization, 131 I.C.C. 673, 699 (1928)) ("The reorganization of the Wabash, 1911–1916 [was] reported to have cost $3,449,500; Pere Marquette, 1912–1917, $2,769,000; Western Pacific, 1915–1916, $2,000,000; Chicago, Milwaukee & St. Paul, 1925–1928, in excess of $5,000,000.").
65. Jerold B. Warner, *Bankruptcy Costs: Some Evidence*, 32 J. Fin. 337 (1977) (finding that professional fees averaged four percent of total assets). There is also some information on bankruptcy costs in the 1960s contained in David T. Stanley & Marjorie Girth, Bankruptcy: Problem, Process, Reform (1971).
66. Arturo Bris, Alan Schwartz, & Ivo Welch, *Who Should Pay for Bankruptcy Costs?*, 34 J. Legal Stud. 295, 296 n.1 (2005).
67. Eleven cases.
68. Only railroads could reorganize under section 77, railroads were not permitted to liquidate, and the railroads' proceedings were subject to oversight by the Interstate Commerce Commission.
69. Perhaps as a result of the fact that section 77 railroad reorganization typically took many years to complete. Richard W. Jennings, *Mr. Justice Douglas: His Influence on Corporate and Securities Regulation*, 73 Yale L.J. 920, 957 (1964).
70. Lawrence A. Weiss, *Bankruptcy Resolution: Direct Costs and Violation of Priority of Claims*, 27 J. Fin. Econ. 285 (1990). There were other studies of bankruptcy costs between 1978 and 1990, but often these papers used multi-year samples that failed to note the enactment of a new Bankruptcy Code in 1978, or assumed, sometimes only implicitly, that cases filed under the old Bankruptcy Act were relevant to determining the cost structure of cases under the new Code. *See, e.g.*, S. Ang et al., *Administrative Costs of Corporate Bankruptcy: A Note*, 37 J. Fin. 219 (1989) (studying cases from before the enactment of the 1978 Bankruptcy Code).
71. *Id.* at 286.
72. *Id.* at 299.
73. Stephen J. Lubben, *The Direct Costs of Corporate Reorganization: An Empirical Examination of Professional Fees in Large Chapter 11 Cases*, 74 Am. Bankr. L.J. 509, 510 (2000) (hereinafter "Lubben (2000)") (citing Sol Stein, A Feast for Lawyers: Inside Chapter 11 – An Expose (1989); Lynn M. LoPucki, *The Trouble with Chapter 11*, 1993 Wis. L. Rev. 729 n.6; Alexander L. Paskay & Frances Pilaro Wolstenholme, *Chapter 11: A Growing Cash Cow – Some Thoughts on How to Rein in the System*, 1 Am. Bankr. Inst. L. Rev. 331 (1993)).
74. Lubben (2000), *supra* note 73, at 511.
75. Stephen P. Ferris & Robert M. Lawless, *The Expenses of Financial Distress: The Direct Costs of Chapter 11*, 61 U. Pitt. L. Rev. 629 (2000). The authors had previously studied small business Chapter 7 costs. Robert M. Lawless & Stephen P. Ferris, *Professional Fees and Other Direct Costs in Chapter 7 Business Liquidations*, 75 Wash. U. L.Q. 1207

(1997). *See also* Robert M. Lawless et al., *A Glimpse at Professional Fees and Other Direct Costs in Small Firm Bankruptcies*, 1994 U. Ill. L. Rev. 847.
76. Ferris & Lawless (2000), *supra* note 75, at 651.
77. Lynn M. LoPucki & Joseph W. Doherty, *The Determination of Professional Fees in Large Bankruptcy Reorganization Cases*, 1 J. Emp. L. Stud. 111, 111 (2004).
78. *Id.*
79. *Id.*
80. Stephen J. Lubben, *The Microeconomics of Chapter 11*, Part 2, 4 Int'l. Corp. Rescue 87 (2007); *The Microeconomics of Chapter 11*, Part 1, 4 Int'l. Corp. Rescue 31 (2007).
81. Arturo Bris, Ivo Welch & Ning Zhu, *The Costs of Bankruptcy: Chapter 7 Liquidation Versus Chapter 11 Reorganization*, 61 J. Fin. 1 253 (2006).
82. Lynn M. LoPucki & Joseph W. Doherty, *Professional Overcharging in Large Bankruptcy Reorganization Cases*, 5 J. Empirical L. Stud. 983 (2008).
83. The ABI Chapter 11 Fee Study is available online (http://ssrn.com/abstract=1020477).
84. Stephen J. Lubben, *Corporate Reorganization & Professional Fees*, 82 Am. Bankr. L.J. 77 (2008).
85. *Id.*
86. *Id.* LoPucki and Doherty, *supra* note 77.
87. Lynn M. LoPucki and Joseph W. Doherty, *Rise of the Financial Advisors: An Empirical Study of the Division of Professional Fees in Large Bankruptcies*, 82 Am. Bankr. L.J. 141 (2008).
88. Skadden, Arps, Slate, Meagher & Flom LLP. www.skadden.com.
89. Lynn M. LoPucki and Joseph W. Doherty, Professional Fees in Corporate Bankruptcies: Data, Analysis and Evaluation 100–07 (2011).
90. Lynn M. LoPucki and Joseph W. Doherty, *supra* note 90, at pages 102–05. All factors positively effect attorney cost, save for the two investment bankers and the interaction of New York and the docket length, discussed in the next paragraph of the text.
91. It does not appear that these variables were mean-centered, but the book is written for a general audience, so this may have been omitted.
92. *See, e.g.*, Stephen J. Lubben, *The Chapter 11 Attorneys*, 86 Am. Bankr. L.J. 447 (2012) (Lubben Attorneys (2012)); Stephen J. Lubben, *The Chapter 11 Financial Advisors*, 28 Emory Bankr. Dev. J. 11 (2011) (Lubben (2011)).
93. *See, e.g.*, John Armour et al., *Corporate Insolvency in The United Kingdom: The Impact of the Enterprise Act 2002*, 5 European Co. & Fin. L. Rev. 135 (2008); Oscar Couwenberg & Abe de Jong, *Costs and Recovery Rates In The Dutch Liquidation-Based Bankruptcy System*, European 26 European J. L. & Econ. 105 (2008); Timothy C.G. Fisher & Jocelyn Martel, *The Irrelevance of Direct Bankruptcy Costs to the Firm's Financial Reorganization Decision*, 2 J. Emp. L. Stud. 151 (2005).
94. Many of these are collected in Avner Kalay et al., *Is Chapter 11 Costly?*, 84 J. Fin. Econ. 772 (2007).
95. And even when available, it can be quite difficult to ensure an "apples to apples" comparison. Robert G. Hansen & Randall S. Thomas, *Auctions in Bankruptcy: Theoretical Analysis and Practical Guidance*, 18 Int'l Rev. L. & Econ. 159, 167 (1998).
96. Stephen J. Lubben, *What We "Know" About Chapter 11 Cost Is Wrong*, 17 Fordham J. Corp. & Fin. L. 141, 167 (2012).
97. Stephen J. Lubben, *Business Liquidation*, 81 Am. Bankr. L.J. 65 (2007) (finding that the average Chapter 7 pays unsecured creditors nothing).
98. *See* Donald R. Korobkin, *The Unwarranted Case Against Corporate Reorganization: A Reply to Bradley and Rosenzweig*, 78 Iowa L. Rev. 669, 720 (1993).
99. *Cf.* Lisa E. Waisbren, *Abandonment of Toxic Wastes Under Section 554 of the Bankruptcy Code*, 71 Marq. L. Rev. 353 (1988).
100. Jay L. Westbrook, *Fees and Inherent Conflicts of Interest*, 1 Am. Bankr. Inst. L. Rev. 287, 296 (1993).
101. Cynthia A. Baker, *Fixing What's Broken: A Proposal for Reform of the Compensation System in Bankruptcy*, 5 J. Bankr. L. & Prac. 435, 480 (1996).

102. Nancy B. Rapoport, *Rethinking Professional Fees in Chapter 11 Cases*, 5 J. Bus. & Tech. L. 263, 276 (2010).
103. Another, largely contrary thesis might be that fees are in fact too low, or more precisely, that unsecured creditors and other junior claimants should be granted more ability to spend estate funds in an effort to push against the obvious power of senior creditors in modern Chapter 11. Such senior creditors have little incentive to maximize the going concern value of debtor-firm.
104. *See, e.g.*, Oscar Couwenberg & Stephen J. Lubben, *The Costs of Chapter 11 in Context: American and Dutch Business Bankruptcy*, 85 Am. Bankr. L.J. 63 (2011).
105. *See* Douglas G. Baird, *Revisiting Auctions in Chapter 11*, 36 J. Law & Econ. 633 (1993) (arguing in favor of auctioning off the debtor's assets to avoid the unwarranted costs of reorganization).

13. The Chrysler and General Motors bankruptcies

Todd J. Zywicki

In Spring 2009, after decades of challenges and years of hemorrhaging money, Chrysler and General Motors filed bankruptcy within weeks of one another, thereby initiating two of the most notorious bankruptcy proceedings of all time. Filed against the backdrop of the global financial crisis that came to a head in fall of 2008 and simultaneously the transition from the George W. Bush Presidential Administration to that of Barack Obama, the automaker bankruptcies were unique for their combination of size, speed, and high political profile. These two cases pushed prior bankruptcy law and practice to their limit and, as many have argued, well-beyond, into the realm of lawlessness. Indeed, the controversy did not end with the successful emergence of the companies from bankruptcy in 2011. It still remained a vital issue in the 2012 Presidential election, with some believing that President Obama's support for the auto bailouts and subsequent intervention in the bankruptcy proceedings contributed positively to his re-election that year.

The cases have spawned reams of analysis by judges, law professors, economists, politicians, and even participants in the high-profile cases. Yet the unique historical, political, and economic context of the cases has also led to great uncertainty as to their long-term impact on bankruptcy doctrine and practice, and the extent to which the cases should be treated as merely one-off *sui generis* cases or valid precedents shaping future law. The decision of the Supreme Court of the United States to subsequently vacate the Chrysler decision further confounds matters. Still, a leading critic of the Chrysler decision has argued that the case has already borne fruit in the controversial decision to approve the reorganization plan of the City of Detroit. Finally, supporters of the government's intervention—most notably from former President Barack Obama—have seen the cases as both an economic and, perhaps more importantly, political success, because these cases have raised the possibility that despite the dubious legality of the cases, political leaders might look to the cases in the future as a template for similar interventions in other industries, especially those involving powerful political interest groups.

This essay will review the course of the automaker bankruptcies to assess these cases' long-term legal, economic, and political impacts on bankruptcy law and practice. However, in the assessment of the cases, a crucial analytical distinction must be kept in mind throughout the entire discussion that follows: namely, the distinction between the narrow case for *some* limited government intervention to facilitate what could have otherwise been relatively ordinary bankruptcy cases, versus what *actually* transpired cases, which essentially became a political free-for-all that may have actually reduced the effectiveness of the long-needed company reconstruction.[1] Indeed, as will be seen, the majority of the most controversial and troubling aspects of the cases had little to do with the actual economic and financial reorganization of the companies. However, analyses of the cases tend to conflate these two issues, treating the cases as essentially all-or-nothing, take-it-or-leave-it packages of multiple different financial and political elements. Distinguishing these two basic elements is essential, however, to assessing the long-term lessons of the cases.

I. THE DESCENT INTO BANKRUPTCY

The road to the Chrysler and GM bankruptcies was many years in the making, but was precipitated by the financial crisis that rocked global markets in 2008. The impact of that crisis not only shaped the descent of Chrysler and GM into bankruptcy, but also was crucial to the debate over the unprecedented role of the United States government in its decision to intervene in the cases in the first place.

A. The Prelude to Bankruptcy

The descent of Chrysler and General Motors into bankruptcy was long in coming and resulted from decades of mismanagement, uncompetitive employee wage and benefit structures, and failure to adjust to the changing consumer demand and foreign competition. Moreover, as illustrated by the contrary experience of Ford, bankruptcy was far from inevitable.

In 1980, for example, General Motors possessed 45% market share in the U.S. auto industry. By 2009, however, that number had shrunk to 19.5%. Over this period, Ford and Chrysler also suffered erosion of market share. Yet much of the cost structure and dealer network of the U.S. 'Big Three' in the auto industry was set during those high-flying years, including extremely generous wage and benefit contracts. Goolsbee and Krueger, who participated in the auto bailouts as members of the Obama Administration, report that the hourly compensation of workers at the Big Three automakers was almost 25% higher than for transplants.[2] After including the legacy costs of retirees, they estimate that average labor costs for the Big Three were almost 45% higher. They conclude that the only way for American automakers to become competitive would be to reduce the fixed costs associated with retirees, the uncompetitive compensation levels for existing workers, and the heavy interest payments that they owed to bondholders.

Moreover, American automakers struggled with extraordinarily uncompetitive, collectively-bargained labor contracts that were a legacy of flush times. For example, under collectively-bargained UAW contracts, laid-off workers received 95% of their normal pay. Because union employees were effectively paid the same no matter whether they worked or were idle, labor was effectively a fixed cost for the firms.[3] 'With fixed costs so high, they had an incentive to build as many cars as possible so as to reduce the average cost per car. Similarly, with variable costs relatively low, additional cars could be made without much additional expense.'[4] These peculiar incentives led the automakers to focus on increasing output and sales volume, which in turn led to their extreme dependence on discounts and incentives to sell unwanted cars. As Rattner concludes, 'The end result was what no businessperson would want—a low-margin business that is vulnerable to any slackening in consumer demand.'[5] Also, this heavy fixed-cost structure made the American automakers particularly vulnerable to demand fluctuations over time.

In addition, UAW workers had the opportunity to retire at an early age and the UAW was notorious for its generous retiree benefit plan, which essentially provided free medical and dental care and prescriptions for life.[6] In 2007, Chrysler agreed to create a Voluntary Employee Beneficiary Association ('VEBA'), which was directly provided and funded by the auto companies and would assume responsibility of retiree health care benefits. Under the plan, Chrysler was committed to make a one-time $8.8 billion contribution to the VEBA, and in return it would have no further obligation. Thus, if the $8.8 billion turned out to be inadequate to fund the VEBA, responsibility for the shortfall would rest on the shoulders of the VEBA–UAW and the workers.

By the time of the financial crisis that began in 2008 and the ensuing recession, both GM and Chrysler were in dire financial straits. In 2007, GM lost $40 billion and suffered losses of $15 billion in the first three quarters of 2008.[7] Market share fell precipitously for both GM and Chrysler during that time as well. Despite their massive losses, both companies repeatedly claimed that it was not realistic for them to file bankruptcy because doing so would scare off consumers who would fear that they would not have their warranties honored and their cars serviced.[8] As a result, they insisted that the only option was a taxpayer-funded bailout and that bankruptcy was not a viable option to save the companies. Indeed, at the time when GM first approached the government for a bailout it had expressly refused to make contingency plans for a bankruptcy filing if no bailout was forthcoming.[9] As Steven Rattner subsequently observed, the refusal to make preparations for bankruptcy 'would add materially to the cost of the eventual rescue.'[10]

By the end of the process, American taxpayers had committed $81.8 billion total to auto-related bailouts.[11] This includes $49 billion to GM, $12 billion to Chrysler, $1.5 billion to Chrysler Financial, over $17 billion to GMAC (General Motors Acceptance Corp.), $600 million to support the consumer warranties on GM and Chrysler vehicles during the bankruptcy processes, and $400 million to supply-chain providers of auto parts (although $5 billion was committed only $400 million was drawn).

GM and Chrysler's failure and subsequent demand for bailouts contrasted with the actions of Ford during that same period.[12] Ford had suffered many of the same market dynamics as GM and Chrysler during that period. Unlike their rivals who were beset by poor management and inability to reform internally, Ford's management underwent a painful internal restructuring from 2006. It sold off non-core product lines such as Land Rover, Aston Martin, and Jaguar, unlike GM and Chrysler. Therefore, Ford did not end up having to file bankruptcy.

B. The Dubious Legality of Using TARP Money for Auto Bailouts

The legality of using TARP money to bail out the auto companies has been highly contested. Steven Rattner reports that when GM first lobbied the White House seeking to have TARP funds provided to bail out the auto companies, then-Secretary of the Treasury Hank Paulson opined that TARP was 'intended to stabilize the financial system, not bail out industrial companies.'[13] He then reportedly added, 'You're not going to be able to use it. . .. You will probably need to go to Congress.'[14] Paulson's skepticism was well-founded, as subsequent analysis by law professor Gary Lawson of the statutory text and authority granted by the TARP concluded that despite the extreme vagueness of the statute, the TARP legislation permitted those funds to be used only for 'financial institutions,' not car companies.[15]

Consistent with Paulson's admonition, the auto makers turned to Congress for a grant of bailout funds. Perhaps the most obvious evidence that the TARP was not intended to be used for the auto bailouts is the fact that Congress actually felt that it was necessary to consider separate legislation on the question of bailing out the automotive industry. As noted, that legislation passed the House of Representatives in December 2008, only to fail in the Senate. Had Congress believed that it had already authorized TARP funds to bail out the auto industry, it seemingly would have been unnecessary to consider special legislation doing just that. In fact, following President Bush's decision to allocate TARP funds to the automotive industry, irate Senators who had just voted down the very action then taken by the President sent a sharp letter to the President stating that 'Congress never voted for a federal bailout of the automobile industry, and the only way for [TARP] funds to be diverted to domestic automakers is with explicit congressional approval.' Ironically, the measure failed in the Senate because the appropriation lacked adequate safeguards to protect the bill from turning into a pure bailout that would not have required the automakers to engage in greater restructuring of UAW wages and benefits to bring them into parity with transplant automakers, a measure pushed by Senator Bob Corker of Tennessee, a state with numerous auto transplant factories.[16] The UAW refused the demand for wage concessions as a concession for receiving taxpayer money. As with GM itself, whose refusal to prepare for a bankruptcy filing was a game of chicken designed to force the Bush Administration into a bailout, the UAW refused concessions knowing that even if the negotiations in Congress failed, the Bush Administration would likely provide a bailout anyway in the short-run, which left the UAW to revisit the issue under the incoming labor-friendly Obama Administration.[17]

Once the measure failed in Congress, however, President Bush announced the unilateral diversion of TARP funds to the automakers. But he did not provide any legal justification for that decision.[18] Although the use of TARP funds was challenged by some of Chrysler's creditors, the bankruptcy court ruled that they lacked standing to raise the claim. The Supreme Court subsequently ruled all further challenges to be moot.

C. The Road Not Taken

Many assessments of the wisdom and efficiency of the auto bailouts conflate two distinct elements of the issue.[19] In so doing, the analysis obscures clear understanding of the nature of the controversies those cases engendered.

The first option that the government could have followed would have been to provide financing to the auto companies in order to effectuate their reorganization, either directly or through a guarantee to a private lender, but otherwise allow the bankruptcy process to proceed in an ordinary fashion according to the established rules and priorities of the bankruptcy process. This intervention in the process could have been extremely limited at addressing the continued disruptions in credit markets that had begun in 2008 and persisted through the period of the auto bailouts. Under this targeted intervention, the government's limited and passive role would have enabled the bankruptcy judge to pursue the ordinary goals of a bankruptcy proceeding—restructuring the firms' operations and balance sheet to maximize financial viability going forward.

The second option, which the government pursued instead, was to leverage the limited need for assistance to credit markets in order to provide debtors in possession financing to alter the bankruptcy process and accomplish other goals, such as to pursue politicians' political goals or to alter bankruptcy practice and priorities to advantage politically-powerful stakeholders in the bankruptcy process. In particular, under this more interventionist approach, the bankruptcy-bailout combination permitted politicians and interest groups to pursue aggressive redistributive and political goals instead of narrow economic goals. In a sense, the government was able to use the limited need for assistance to stabilize credit markets as a wedge into the cases that subsequently opened up very large opportunities to accomplish other goals.

The essence of bankruptcy reorganization turns on a distinction between two concepts: financial distress and economic failure.[20] In turn, these concepts turn on whether a firm is fundamentally worth more alive than dead—i.e., whether the current deployment of the human, physical, and financial capital assets kept together as a going-concern is worth more than the opportunity cost of those assets if the firm was liquidated and redeployed elsewhere in the economy.

Under this fundamental bankruptcy analysis, normally GM would have been the prototype for a firm that would be easily reorganized in bankruptcy, as it was clearly financially distressed rather than economically failed. Despite its longstanding struggles, it seems obvious that GM was worth more as a going-concern, at least in some configuration, than it would have been had it been liquidated and its assets redeployed elsewhere in the economy. These assets included a highly skilled workforce, firm and industry specific physical equipment and plants, several valuable models and nameplates with high consumer loyalty, and the potential for a positive cash-flow business that could provide returns to investors who invested. In this conventional analysis, GM was an easy case for bankruptcy reorganization. Under normal circumstances, it could have filed bankruptcy and reorganized without much difficulty. Indeed, similar reorganizations are commonplace in the American economy today: department stores, hotels, and even airlines, all are consumer-facing industries that have had numerous bankruptcy filings in recent years.

By contrast, Chrysler presented a more difficult call as to whether it was merely financially distressed or economically failed. An economically failed firm is one for which the current deployment of human, physical, and financial capital is lower than the opportunity cost of redeploying those assets elsewhere in the economy. As the smallest of the Detroit Three, Chrysler was in the weakest competitive position to remain viable going forward as an independent concern. Moreover, analysis by the Obama Administration suggested that much of Chrysler was in direct competition with other American automakers, especially GM, for market share. As a result, one likely consequence of Chrysler's liquidation would have been to strengthen GM's competitive position as it was poised to pick-up much of Chrysler's lost sales.[21] According to Steven Rattner, one option that was considered regarding Chrysler was a merger with GM. In the end, of course, Chrysler's assets were sold to the Italian automaker Fiat, a result which was consistent with the notion that the company was not viable as a stand-alone entity going forward.[22]

Where a firm is merely financially distressed, an efficient chapter 11 bankruptcy reorganization can restructure the balance sheet so as to create positive cash flow for the firm and to pay pre-bankruptcy creditors more than they would receive if the firm was liquidated instead. It follows from this positive cash-flow position that for such a firm, post-bankruptcy debtor in possession financing should be readily available to the firm. With respect to an economically failed firm, however, the lack of a viable path to solvency and viable cash flow going forward makes such loans highly risky.

This analysis suggests that, under normal circumstances, certainly GM and probably Chrysler would have been able to attract debtor in possession financing to fund their reorganization proceedings. However, at the time of their insolvency in late-2008 and early-2009, credit markets were still not functioning effectively, which suggested that they might have been unable to attract short-term credit because of liquidity conditions in markets, not because they were fundamentally failed as economic enterprises. If this were so—and there is little evidence to support or contradict the claim other than the self-serving testimony of Bush and Obama Administration officials—this reality could have arguably supported a limited role for government intervention to unclog credit markets. In that case, the government arguably could have stepped forward with limited and targeted debtor in possession financing, or even to merely guarantee private investment, which would have delivered the needed capital to reorganize the firm.[23] For example, at the time, future Republican candidate for President Mitt Romney argued that it would be appropriate for the federal government to 'provide guarantees for post-bankruptcy financing and assure car buyers that their warranties [were] not at risk.'[24] If this strategy had been pursued, the government could have limited itself to providing short-term, targeted financing but otherwise allowed the bankruptcy process to run its ordinary course.

Instead, the government chose the alternative path of a comprehensive intervention and aggressive control of the bankruptcy reorganization process. Seizing on the alleged need for a guarantee of debtor in possession financing or direct provision of financing, the government used that as a wedge to exert active control over the whole process, including controversial steps to arguably rearrange established bankruptcy priorities, to change the firms' management and dictate the firms' business plans and priorities, to strong-arm creditors into going along with the government's schemes, to reward and protect powerful political allies, and to accomplish political goals that had little to do with furthering GM and Chrysler's economic viability going forward and in many ways impeded it. As discussed in greater detail below, these decisions included large wealth transfers to members of the United Auto Workers union to protect them from the typical pain of bankruptcy, protection of politically-powerful auto franchise dealers from being closed, and the use of the government's influence to incentivize the increased production of environmentally friendly vehicles by Fiat-Chrysler, independent of the economic efficiency of that business strategy.

Contrary to standard bankruptcy analysis, these interventions and others like them—i.e., protecting the UAW from significant wage reductions, protecting inefficient dealers from downsizing, and providing incentives to manufacture unprofitable small cars—did *not* aid GM and Chrysler in reorganizing to become more viable as competitors. Instead, they did exactly the *opposite*—each of these interventions, which were imposed upon the firms and the bankruptcy judge by the government, actually *reduced* the going-forward economic competitiveness of the firms by limiting their discretion to make the necessary cost adjustments and improvements that would have made them more effective competitors over the long run. In other words, far from helping to save or reorganize the companies, these particular elements of the auto bailouts were like barnacles strapped to the companies' hull that they were forbidden to remove and instead continued to drag down their efforts to effectively reorganize.

The government thus confronted two different paths. On one hand, the government could have provided a limited intervention targeted to address the particular problem of poorly-functioning credit markets that otherwise would have provided liquidity to the firms, thereby leaving the basic bankruptcy process intact and focusing on reorganizing the companies into more efficient and viable competitors. On the other hand is the path actually pursued by the government—to use the limited need for assistance to provide liquidity to capital markets to drive a process heavily focused on *redistributive* and *political* goals and not merely the economic viability of the firms themselves. By pursing this path instead, the government implicitly chose to subordinate the goals of economic efficiency and competitiveness to multiple other goals that contradicted those goals.

This analysis suggests that an important threshold conceptual point to keep in mind in assessing the auto bailouts is that, simply because it might have been efficient for a limited government intervention to address the problems in credit markets, that does not necessarily imply that it is necessary to accept all of the political and redistributive elements of the case as efficient as well.

The Obama Administration has justified some of its decisions, such as the preferential treatment afforded to the UAW, as appropriate to advance efficiency goals of reorganization because the failure to do so could have led the UAW to strike, thereby resulting in the liquidation of the companies. In particular, the Obama Administration's decision in the Chrysler case to provide debt and equity to the underfunded UAW health care VEBAs while leaving the secured creditors incomplete was justified by the alleged fear that a failure to do so could prompt UAW workers to strike, thereby leading to the collapse of the companies; or as Rattner writes, 'you need workers to make cars.'[25]

Yet neither Rattner nor any other member of the Auto Task Force provides any evidence to support the assertion that career GM and Chrysler employees would strike the companies into liquidation instead of accepting wage and benefit concessions that would bring them into line with foreign transplants but still far exceeded the wages of most U.S. manufacturing workers. Moreover, in other analogous cases where unionized workers have been asked to take wage and benefit reductions, such as in airline bankruptcy cases, I have located no instances where workers have responded to demands for wage and benefit reductions by striking the company into liquidation. The Administration's willingness to take this assertion at face value and require no concrete justification is especially striking in light of the Auto Task Force's hardline approach to creditors, where the government rejected as implausible the creditors' claim that they would walk away instead of taking the government's offer. To the extent that the government's justification for favoring retired UAW workers over other retirees (including the Indiana teachers and police retirement funds) relates to the purported need to prevent UAW workers from striking, that justification appears to be somewhat specious and unsupported. Thus, as discussed below, this decision to spare UAW workers much of the pain absorbed by other stakeholders in the case appears to pit against one another the two contrary goals of economic efficiency and the desire of the Administration to reward a powerful political interest group.

II. THE BANKRUPTCY CASES

Chrysler filed its bankruptcy cases in the Southern District of New York on April 30, 2009, before Bankruptcy Judge Alberto Gonzalez. GM filed its bankruptcy on June 1, 2009, and the case was assigned to Bankruptcy Judge Robert Gerber. Although the two cases differed significantly due to the differences between Chrysler's and GM's situations at the time, the cases are very similar in many ways, including certain important aspects.

A. Chrysler

1. The case

On April 30, 2009, Chrysler LLC and 24 of its domestic subsidiaries filed bankruptcy. According to the bankruptcy court, in calendar year 2008 Chrysler recorded revenues of $48.5 billion, with assets of approximately $39.3 billion and liabilities of $55.2 billion.[26] As a result, Chrysler's net loss was $16.8 billion in 2008 alone.

When Chrysler filed bankruptcy, 80.1% of the equity of Chrysler Holding LLC (Chrysler's parent) was owned by Cerberus Capital Management, L.P. and its affiliates, and 19.9% was owned by Daimler AG. Chrysler also had several different groups of creditors. The largest one was approximately $6.9 billion, which was owed to a syndicate of lenders and secured by a first-priority security interest in substantially all of Chrysler's assets. Chrysler also owed $2 billion to affiliates of Cerberus, secured by a second-lien security interest in those same assets. In addition, Chrysler owed $4.27 billion to the U.S. Treasury Department in connection with the loan it received from the TARP in the prior fall, which was secured by a first-priority lien on any unencumbered Chrysler assets and the inventory of Chrysler's MOPAR parts division, as well as a third-priority lien on any assets already encumbered with first and second priority liens. Chrysler also had approximately $5.34 billion in unsecured trade debt. Finally, Chrysler owed $10 billion to a voluntary employee benefit association ('VEBA') that had been established in 2008 to provide healthcare benefits to union retirees.[27]

Chrysler filed a pre-packaged bankruptcy plan. Under the proposed plan, the old Chrysler sold substantially all of its operating assets to a newly-formed entity, New CarCo Acquisition LLC ('New Chrysler') for $2 billion in cash from New Chrysler and its assumption of some liabilities of Old Chrysler (including the obligations owed to the VEBA). The $2 billion that was received was distributed to the first-priority secured lenders, who thus received about 29 cents on the dollar for the $6.9 billion that they were owed, and consuming all of the revenue from the asset sale. This left no assets for the second or third priority lienholders for unsecured creditors. The first-priority creditors also received no unsecured deficiency claim and existing equity holders received nothing.

New Chrysler's asset purchase and operating expenses were financed by $6 billion in new secured credit from the U.S. Treasury from the TARP. The Canadian government also provided financing to New Chrysler's Canadian affiliate. The U.S. Treasury also received an 8% equity stake in New Chrysler and the Canadian government received 2%.

Most of the newly-issued equity in New Chrysler, however, was issued to two parties that provided no cash to New Chrysler. The majority position—55%—was provided to the VEBA. Along with $1.5 billion in cash and an unsecured note for $4.6 billion, this equity, cash, and debt replaced the $10 billion unsecured debt owed to the VEBA. Finally, Fiat S.p.A. was initially issued 20% of New Chrysler's equity but could receive 'up to 35%' of the equity of New Chrysler in exchange for providing technology (primarily related to the manufacture of smaller, fuel-efficient vehicles), distribution, and other things to Chrysler, if certain performance metrics were met, including fuel-efficiency metrics.

2. The criticisms

The rushed and irregular procedures followed in the Chrysler case have resulted in widespread criticism and confusion regarding the precedential implications for future bankruptcy cases. Because of the basic structural similarities between Chrysler's and GM's cases, many of the criticisms are consistent across the two; but distinctions between the two cases also raise particular issues unique to each case.

As a matter of bankruptcy law and policy, the Chrysler case occasioned greater controversy and concern than the GM case, not only because it was filed first but also because some controversial features of the Chrysler plan were absent in the GM case. Those criticisms can be captured under three basic headings.[28] First, Chrysler and GM broke with established bankruptcy law and practice: the two cases essentially permitted the effective reorganization of the entire companies through the mechanism of a sale of the whole company, rather than proceeding through the standard practice of a Chapter 11 reorganization process. In addition, the ostensible sale terms also explained how the proceeds of the sale would be distributed, rather than following the priority scheme laid out by the Bankruptcy Code. The comprehensive nature of the sale and dictating of the distribution of the proceeds, it is argued, constituted the equivalent of a plan of reorganization or a so-called *sub rose* plan. Second, even if the sale was appropriate in general, the process used to conduct the sale—and in particular the lack of competing bids—was highly irregular. Finally, the plan itself provided that, not only would secured creditors fail to receive full payment on their claims but also unsecured creditors with junior priority—the UAW VEBAs—would receive larger distributions in the case (44 cents on the dollar of their claims) than the secured creditors (which would receive only 29 cents on the dollar). In the following part of this chapter, I examine each of those claims in turn.

a. Was the Chrysler case a sub rosa plan of reorganization? From a bankruptcy perspective, the cornerstone of the Chrysler and GM cases was the novel use of sections 363 and 1129 of the Bankruptcy Code, which authorizes the debtor to sell assets as part of the bankruptcy case. Section 1129 permits the debtor to sell assets as part of a confirmed plan of reorganization. Section 363(b), by contrast, permits the debtor to sell assets and only requires the approval of the bankruptcy court after notice and hearing, and it does not require a confirmed plan of reorganization for the sale. As a practical consequence, this means that a §363 sale can be conducted much more rapidly and without the myriad procedural protections of a sale as part of a confirmed reorganization plan. Over time, it has become more common to sell the debtor's assets pursuant to §363 while distributing the proceeds of the sale to creditors in accordance with the Code's priority scheme.

Although §363 sales have become a more common element of bankruptcy cases, the sale in the Chrysler and GM cases was nevertheless highly irregular and controversial. First, the sale was unusual in that the entire sale process was essentially orchestrated to favor one bidder (the United States government) and did not invite competing bidders that could have bid up the price of the company for the benefit of creditors. In addition, no competing estimates of the value of the company's assets were solicited. Second, the sale was also irregular in that the purchaser was not a new arm's-length owner, but was essentially a continuation of the preexisting company and management that remained almost identical. Third, the purported sale was controversial in that the proceeds were not distributed in accordance with the priority scheme of the code but that as a condition of the sale dictated that preference should be provided to the UAW VEBA's unsecured claims instead of the secured claims of bondholders.

More generally, it has been argued that the assets sales in both cases were not really merely asset sales at all but rather de facto or *sub rosa* plans of reorganization, as they sold essentially all of the debtors' assets as a going concern and provided a distribution and priority scheme for the proceeds. As David Skeel has demonstrated, the Bankruptcy Code's Chapter 11 reorganization rules were designed to prevent the sort of arrangement that Chrysler (and later GM) would follow.[29] As Skeel observes in the early

20th century, 'large troubled corporations did not file for Chapter 11 like they do today. They used a process known as "equity receivership," which involved an artificial "sale" of the company to a new entity set up by the debtor and the investment banks who represented its bondholders and stockholders.' Moreover, like the Chrysler case, 'The new entity was the only bidder at the sale, and creditors who were unhappy with the terms of the reorganization had very little opportunity to interfere.'

Skeel notes that the use of a §363 sale had become common at the time of the auto bankruptcies. But Chrysler was distinct from this sale in that there was effectively no competitive bidding and that the 'sale' also included within it seeming alterations to bankruptcy priority rules by giving certain unsecured creditors (namely the UAW VEBA plans) a substantial stake in New Chrysler, while largely freezing out existing creditors. As Skeel writes, 'What makes the Chrysler plan unique, and makes it similar to the receiverships of the New Dealers' era, is that it is not really a sale at all. It is a pretend sale and its main purpose is to eliminate the pesky creditors who might otherwise interfere with the government's plan.'[30]

During the New Deal, therefore, the Bankruptcy Act was amended to address these practices. In particular, a more transparent and inclusive reorganization process was mandated to prevent insider enrichment and safeguards against unfair treatment were issued. Although some of the more stringent provisions were relaxed in the Bankruptcy Code, the modern bankruptcy process still places limits on what can be done through a §363 sale and requires large-scale restructuring in bankruptcy to be conducted according to the Chapter 11 process.

Permitting the debtor to conduct a sale of virtually all of the debtor's assets, especially when combined with dictates on the distribution of the proceeds that alter the Code's priority scheme, can enable a debtor to avoid all of the Code's built-in procedural protections within the Chapter 11 plan process, including the disclosure, voting, and plan confirmation requirements. As a result, courts have consistently held that they should be vigilant to ensure that a purported asset sale does not amount to 'sub rosa plan' that effectively resolves a case in the fashion of a confirmed plan of reorganization but without the procedural protections of that section.[31]

In the Second Circuit, where the Chrysler case was filed, the prevailing law was provided by the *Lionel* case, decided in 1983.[32] Under *Lionel*, a court can permit an asset sale outside the ordinary courts of business if there is legitimate business reason for the sale. In the *Chrysler* case, the bankruptcy court found that Chrysler's proposed asset sale would preserve Chrysler's going concern value, which was a good business reason for approving the proposed §363 sale.[33] In particular, the bankruptcy court concluded that the proposed transaction was the only viable alternative to liquidation of the company, because despite extensive efforts to find alternatives, no other option had been forthcoming. Moreover, the unusual speed of the sale was justified because several of Chrysler's factories were closed pending resolution of the case and Chrysler was burning through cash, resulting in an ongoing reduction in Chrysler's going-concern value.

b. Procedural requirements: competitive bidding and valuation According to the bankruptcy court, the sale of Chrysler for $2 billion was warranted because the company was valued at zero to $800 million, according to expert testimony presented at the case. As a result, the Obama Administration claimed that the $2 billion paid by the taxpayers to purchase Chrysler's assets was actually substantially more than the market price of the company, which is also a highly contested claim.

According to Roe and Skeel, the initial valuation submitted by Chrysler's experts gave a range of $900 million to $3.2 billion, with a likely recovery to the first liens of between $654 million and $2.6 billion,[34] which was subsequently revised downward to reflect changing conditions with the passage of time.[35] Moreover, although it is true that the experts retained by Chrysler presented the only valuation to the court, this is likely because the court did not provide objecting creditors with sufficient time to present an alternative valuation from their experts or provide for a competing valuation that would be paid for by the bankruptcy estate.[36] As a result, the court only received evidence from Chrysler's valuation expert and only with respect to the limited valuation scenarios described therein.

As to the inference that the absence of competing bids indicates that the government's plan was the only viable plan for Chrysler, this ignores the highly irregular nature of the bid solicitation process in the case. Indeed, as Roe and Skeel observe, 'The courts' deference to the sale proponents' weak market test was the single most disturbing feature of the Chrysler bankruptcy.'[37] In particular, they argue that in light of the tainted nature of the consent of a majority of the creditors because of their TARP entanglements, the lack of competing valuation opinions and the large uncertainty of the valuation opinion provided, and the fact that the court was circumventing the procedural protections of a standard Chapter 11 case by approving a sale that was effectively a reorganization, it was particularly important for the court to provide a market test. As they argue, '[T]he market test was the key way by which the Chrysler plan could have fully justified itself, removing the taints. But it did not.'[38]

However, the requirements that had to be met to qualify as a competing bidder were novel and conditioned on multiple conditions that had nothing to do with maximizing the value of competing bids or revealing Chrysler's underlying value. As David Skeel observes,

> The government proposed that no bid be allowed unless the bidder promised to protect precisely the same favored creditors as were protected by the government's bid. In Chrysler, for instance, bidders would be required to assume the approximately $5.3 billion of trade claims and offer stock and a nearly $4.6 billion note to retirees. A bidder could not simply bid, say, $2.5 billion, for Jeep, even though such a bid would provide more proceeds than the government's bid.[39]

To be a qualified bid, any competing bids had to promise to assume Chrysler's collective-bargaining agreements and products liability claims as well.[40] Douglas Baird has similarly observed that by only permitting bids that valued Chrysler as a going-concern, the court foreclosed potentially higher bids that would have contemplated a piecemeal sale of Chrysler, including the separate sale of Jeep and various real estate holdings.[41] 'In short,' Baird argues, 'the key question in Chrysler is not that there was a sale, but enough was done to look at sales that took different forms.'[42] As Roe and Skeel observe, the case was merely 'marketing valuations of the bankruptcy plan actually used, one that didn't separate Chrysler's assets from its largest preexisting liabilities. As such, their efforts were efforts to market the plan they preferred, not the alternative plans the Code requires the court to test.'[43] Moreover, the Court only gave competing bidders a week to place bids, which made it difficult to conduct due diligence or obtain financing for a bid.[44] Given the irregular nature of the case, Roe and Skeel argue that the court should have been especially vigilant to require a 'robust market test, not a weak one.'[45]

c. Did the plan violate absolute priority? Perhaps the most controversial element of the Chrysler bankruptcy case was the potential violation of the absolute priority rule, a standard bankruptcy principle that typically requires senior creditors to be paid in full before any distributions are made to junior creditors. In the Chrysler case, it was proposed that secured creditors with senior priority would be paid only 29 cents on the dollar on their claims, while the claims of the UAW's VEBA were paid at approximately 44 cents on the dollar.

According to the *Chrysler* bankruptcy court, however, the proposal did not violate absolute priority because the UAW supposedly would not be receiving any payments on account of its pre-petition claims against Old Chrysler.[46] Instead, the payments to the VEBA arose from new value provided to *New* Chrysler to facilitate the reorganization and from negotiations between the VEBA and New Chrysler. According to the bankruptcy court, therefore, the transfer of this new value to the VEBA 'was neither a diversion of value from the Debtors' assets nor an allocation of the proceeds from the sale of the Debtors' assets.'[47] The Second Circuit eventually affirmed the conclusion that all of the money paid to the UAW VEBA was from new value, not in payment of the UAW's prepetition claim. As a result, the proposal did not violate bankruptcy priority rules and did not constitute a *sub rosa* plan as it was not an effort to override the Code's priority scheme.

Steven Rattner has also argued that the preference for junior creditors was justified by the new value exception to the absolute priority rule, which awards discretion to those who provide new funds to a bankrupt company to direct those funds as they see fit. Rattner argues that the new value exception justified the government's decision to give away Chrysler's equipment to Fiat for nothing except the provision of technology and management.[48] The Administration also pointed to the fact that even though warranty holders were unsecured claimants as well, they received full payment, as did many suppliers, and that there was a valid business reason for treating the UAW VEBA accordingly.[49]

One unusual aspect of the case was the willingness of Chrysler's secured bondholders to consent to their treatment in the case instead of fighting the government's proposal. This consent came about through an unusual process. Under the terms of their credit agreement, the first-priority secured lenders agreed to appoint an administrative agent who had authority to represent the creditors as a group and the creditors agreed to be bound by the actions that the agent took as instructed by a majority of the indebtedness in the case.[50] In the Chrysler case, 92.5% of the indebtedness supported the agent's actions; as a result, the trustee's release of the lender's liens in the case was determined to be binding on the first-priority secured lenders.[51] On the other hand, while the vote of the creditors' trustee outside might be binding outside bankruptcy, it is not clear that that should bind parties within bankruptcy, where the Code provides its own voting rules.

The willingness of so many creditors to go along with the Chrysler plan is puzzling at first glance in that much of Chrysler's debt was held by substantial and sophisticated financial institutions, such as JPMorgan. This peculiarity might have several explanations. First, a large amount of Chrysler's debt was held by a number of large financial institutions that had received TARP funds from the government, and thus were unusually vulnerable to political pressure from Washington. Citigroup, JPMorgan Chase, Goldman Sachs, and Morgan Stanley—which together received $90 billion in bailout funds from the U.S. Treasury—held 70% of the dollar amount of the claims against Chrysler.[52] In addition to the direct leverage provided by the TARP, those banks also faced other governmental pressures, as the government was actively considering nationalizing some or all of them and displacing their management. As Roe and Skeel observe,

'Bank executives had reason to be wary, as Treasury-induced management changes of compensation mandates were being discussed. Senior bank management had good reason not to annoy the Treasury.'[53] Some critics of the cases have argued that because of their compromised positions they lacked the ability to vote independently, which is problematic in that through their votes they were able to bind other creditors who were not similarly compromised. Some commenters have gone so far as to argue that the votes of those bondholders should be disqualified because of their compromised position or that they should have been segregated into a separate class for voting purposes.[54]

In an additional extraordinary twist, President Obama and the White House intervened to strong-arm and intimidate nonconsenting bondholders to compromise their positions. President Obama held a nationally televised press conference where he excoriated those holders of Chrysler secured debt who refused to accept the government's treatment that provided them with 50% less of distribution than junior unsecured debt.[55] In addition, one investor claimed that the White House threatened to 'destroy its reputation' by turning the White House press corps against the bank if they did not drop their opposition.[56] Notably, among those who objected to the Administration's treatment and the §363 sale included the pension plans for the Indiana State Teachers and Police retirement funds, who eventually appealed the case all the way to the Supreme Court.[57]

According to the Administration, the arrangement in the Chrysler case did not violate the absolute priority rule because in receiving 29 cents on the dollar on their claims, the secured creditors received all that they were properly entitled to in bankruptcy—namely, the liquidation value of the company's assets.[58] As noted above, however, no independent valuation or competitive bids for the company's assets were permitted in the case.[59]

In addition to alleging that the plan violated the absolute priority rule, Chrysler's senior creditors had another complaint, namely that since they were not paid in full on their secured claims in the case they should have been entitled to a deficiency claim as an unsecured claim in the case as well. Instead, they were provided with a secured claim of 29 cents on the dollar but received nothing on the additional 71 cents that seemingly should have been paid as an unsecured claim even though the UAW VEBA received approximately 44 cents on the dollar for their unsecured claim. But the Bankruptcy Code requires that reorganization plans must be fair and equitable to all parties, which among other things requires that similarly-situated creditors be treated similarly. Thus, it seems to follow that even if they did not receive full payment on their secured claims, the bondholders should have received an unsecured deficiency claim for the remainder.[60] The bankruptcy court rejected this argument on the basis that, because the money that was transferred to the UAW came from new value provided by the government to New Chrysler and was not on account of the UAW's claim against Old Chrysler, the secured creditors had no right to those funds, nor could they complain of unfair discrimination.

B. General Motors

1. The case

GM filed bankruptcy on June 1, 2009, when GM employed approximately 235,000 employees worldwide. Among the 91,000 employed in the United States, 61,000 employees were represented by the UAW.[61] As of March 31, 2009, GM had reported assets of approximately $82 billion worldwide and liabilities of $172 billion.

Among GM's liabilities was $19.4 billion owed to the U.S. Treasury under the TARP, which was secured by a first-priority security interest in intellectual property, real property, cash, and equity, and a second-priority security interest in other assets. Unlike Chrysler, most of GM's debt was unsecured, amounting to approximately $117 billion, including $21 billion owed to GM's UAW VEBA and over $27 billion in outstanding bonds. GM also owed $3.9 billion to a group of creditors led by Citicorp US, Inc., $1.5 billion to a group led by JPMorgan Chase, $400 million to Export Development Bank Canada, and $125 million to Gelco Corporation. Those loans were secured in part by GM's inventory, equipment, and equity. Upon filing bankruptcy, GM received debtor in possession financing from the U.S. Treasury ($30.1 billion) and the Canadian government ($3.2 billion with $6 billion to be provided later).

The basic structure of the GM bankruptcy followed that of Chrysler. A newly-formed entity named Vehicle Acquisition Holdings LLC ('New GM') purchased almost all of Old GM's assets and assumed some of its liabilities, most notably the obligations owed to UAW VEBA. In exchange, New GM issued 10% of its common stock to Old GM and two separate warrants to purchase 7.5% of the post-closing outstanding shares of New GM at different levels of equity valuation. The U.S. Treasury and EDC, which had lent over $50 billion to GM in combined pre-petition and post-petition secured financing, assigned their loans to new GM, which then credit bid for the assets of Old GM.

New GM then issued 60.8% of its common stock to the U.S. Treasury, along with $2.1 billion of its preferred stock, and a $6.7 billion note. To EDC, GM issued 11.7% of its common stock, $400 million of its preferred stock, and a $1.3 billion note. Other first-priority secured lenders of Old GM (other than the U.S. Treasury and the Canadian government) were repaid their $6 billion in full by New GM. Curiously, therefore, secured creditors of Old GM were paid in full—unlike the secured creditors in Chrysler, which received only 29 cents on the dollar. Unsecured creditors received from Old GM the 10% equity stake in New GM, an additional 2% of New GM's stock if general unsecured claims against Old GM exceeded $35 billion, and the warrants to purchase an additional 15%. Old GM's shareholders received nothing. As part of the plan, the UAW agreed to make concessions to New GM on employee compensation and benefits and on retiree healthcare. Moreover, the plan proposed to create a new UAW VEBA, which would provide 17.5% of New GM's common stock, $6.5 billion in preferred stock, and a 6-year warrant to acquire 2.5% of New GM's common stock.

GM's plan had many of the same essential characteristics as Chrysler's. According to the bankruptcy court in GM's case, the sale again was warranted as it concluded that the only alternative to the §363 sale was liquidation and that the estate would benefit from a quick §363 sale; therefore, there was an adequate business reason to support the proposed sale.[62] Nor was the bankruptcy court persuaded that the sale amounted to a *sub rosa* plan, as the sale did not alter creditor priorities and that creditors received the full amount to which they were entitled.

One striking distinction between the Chrysler and GM cases is that whereas the secured creditors in Chrysler received a major haircut, Old GM's secured creditors were paid in full. There is no obvious reason why secured creditors were treated differently in the two cases, leading to the supposition that the differential treatment was one of convenience, rather than principle—that in Chrysler, which had a large amount of secured debt, it was necessary to stiff secured creditors in order to ensure adequate funds were available to transfer to the UAW, whereas in GM, the amount of secured debt was relatively small and as a result it was not necessary to squeeze secured creditors in order to transfer wealth to the UAW.

2. The criticisms

Many of the criticisms of the GM case are similar to those in the Chrysler case and will not be rehashed here—most notably the claim that the sale of the entirety of GM's assets as a going concern, without truly competitive bidding, and the instructions on how to distribute the proceeds, constituted a *sub rosa* plan. Moreover, because GM's plan paid secured creditors in full, it did not raise the issues of possible violation of the absolute priority rule in order to make payments to the UAW VEBA. Most of GM's bondholder debt was unsecured, not secured, and thus of equal priority at the UAW.

On the other hand, GM's plan proposed to pay a much larger percentage of the unsecured claims of the UAW VEBA than the unsecured claims of the company's bondholders. This implicated a different provision of the Bankruptcy Code, the requirement that creditors of similar priority should be treated similarly and not suffer unjust discrimination. Under this principle, it is presumptively the case that all creditors of similar priority—such as all general unsecured creditors—should share equally in the pro rata distribution of the estate's assets. Instead, the unsecured claims of the UAW VEBA received a much higher percentage distribution than the unsecured bondholders, who received about 10 cents on the dollar.

C. The Precedential Value of the Chrysler and GM Bankruptcies

The Chrysler and GM bankruptcies raised multiple novel issues of bankruptcy law and policy and broke substantial new ground with respect to the question of the degree to which debtors could use the procedure of a §363 sale to circumvent the process and protections of Chapter 11.[63] After the Second Circuit affirmed the Chrysler sale, a group of disappointed creditors petitioned the United States Supreme Court to stay the sale pending appeal. After initial hesitation and issuance of a stay, the Supreme Court refused the request for a stay and allowed the sale to proceed.[64]

After the stay was denied, the objecting creditors eventually returned to the Supreme Court and asked it to review the case on the merits. The Supreme Court responded by first granting *certiorari* on the case but then remanded the case to the Second Circuit with instructions to dismiss the appeal as moot.[65]

The Supreme Court's unusual action of granting certiorari and then dismissing the case as moot—instead of merely refusing the grant of certiorari in the first place—is significant for understanding the precedential role of the cases. This unusual procedural gambit effectively has only one important effect—by first accepting the case for certiorari this had the effect of vacating the lower court's opinion approving Chrysler's sale, thereby vacating its precedential value. It is therefore unclear what the continued precedential value of the cases is and whether they are valid to be relied upon in future cases.

In its short opinion, the Supreme Court cited *United States v. Munsingwear, Inc.*[66] Joseph Warburton notes that *Munsingwear* stands for the proposition that taking a case on certiorari and dismissing it as moot is done 'to prevent a judgment, unreviewable because of mootness, from spawning any legal consequences.'[67] By doing so, the action 'clears the path for future relitigation of the issues between the parties.'[68]

III. THE ROLE OF POLITICS

A defining element of the auto bailouts was the important role played by politics throughout the process. Times of economic and financial crisis are times in which the rule of law is most needed but also most likely to be relaxed in the face of political pressure and seizure of authority by the government to engage in discretionary decision-making.[69] Relaxing the rule of law can provide discretion to government officials to respond positively to emergent, unexpected problems; on the other hand, relaxing the rule of law can provide a rent-seeking opportunity to interest groups and politically-opportunistic politicians. Government-driven bailouts, such as those of banks during the financial crisis or the auto companies, invariably will be riddled with political bargains designed predominantly to further redistributive and political goals rather than economic efficiency.[70]

The political dynamics of the auto bailouts may be best summarized in a comment by South Dakota Senator John Thune to GM and Chrysler executives once they received government funding, 'You find yourself with a board of directors of essentially 535 members.'[71] At the same time, the auto companies found themselves responding to the particular political desires of the Obama Administration—namely the desire for greater production of green and smaller cars—regardless of effect of those policies on the bottom line. In turn, Democratic politicians were seeking to protect and reward political allies from organized labor, auto dealerships, and other interest groups.[72] The overall effect of these political pressures was to interfere with the bankruptcy and to weaken the needed restructuring of the companies.

The most notable beneficiary of the auto bailouts was the UAW. Indeed, as noted, the bankruptcy court concluded that the funneling of money to the UAW VEBAs instead of secured creditors did not violate the absolute priority rule because all of the funds that the government provided post-petition were designed specifically to enrich the UAW, without any claim that the UAW was entitled to those funds on account of its preexisting claim.

In fact, analysis by James Sherk and Todd Zywicki concluded that the entirety of the taxpayers' losses on the Chrysler and GM cases was attributable to preferential treatment given to the United Auto Workers in the bankruptcy cases as compared to similarly-situated parties in analogous cases, such as airline bankruptcies.[73] In all, Sherk and Zywicki estimate that the subsidies transferred to the UAW amounted to $26.5 billion, greater than the $23 billion loss that taxpayers suffered as a result of the bailouts. Most notably, the UAW's underfunded health care plans were treated far better than other unsecured creditors in similar cases.

Moreover, mechanics and airline pilots have been forced to make wage concessions to bring them into line with prevailing market rates in order to make the firm competitive. In the auto bailouts, by contrast, existing UAW workers were asked to make minimum concessions, as all pay cuts were to be borne by new hires. Steven Rattner later admitted, 'We asked all the stakeholders to make very significant sacrifices. We should have asked the UAW to do a bit more. We did not ask any UAW member to take a cut in their pay.'[74] In his memoir of the experience, he states that he 'felt a little bit of buyer's remorse about the Chrysler-UAW contract,' and that the failure to take a harder line in the Chrysler case had been a missed opportunity to increase Chrysler's overall competitiveness.[75] Beyond the direct transfers to the UAW's underfunded health care plans the Obama Administration's auto task force even approved the diversion of $1 billion of bailout money to 'top off' the pensions of the UAW members at the bankrupt auto parts manufacturer Delphi, which had been spun off from GM years before GM's bankruptcy and was merely one of many GM parts suppliers. At the same time that the auto task force transferred funds to Delphi, the auto task force forced the termination of the pension plan for Delphi's white collar workers and pointedly refused to include in its largesse blue-collar members of smaller, less-powerful unions.[76] And while these various transfers aided UAW members and retirees it should be remembered that among the holders of Chrysler's secured bonds were the Indiana police and teachers pension funds, thus the case may have been one of simply transferring wealth from a group of retirees with less political clout to one that was more powerful.

The cases were also characterized by a substantial amount of political meddling by Democratic members of Congress seeking to protect and enrich favored local interest groups and constituencies. Most notably, although a primary purpose of the bankruptcy filings was to enable GM and Chrysler to trim their overextended dealer networks, members of Congress intervened to aggressively protect auto dealers in their various districts.[77] Other politicians pressured the companies for special treatment for home-state suppliers of raw materials or intervened to prevent the closure of certain manufacturing facilities.[78] These interventions on behalf of politically-powerful interests were counterproductive to the companies' efforts to reduce costs and improve their competitive position.

IV. THE AFTERMATH

The auto bankruptcies were no ordinary bankruptcy cases and the implications of the cases have resonated well beyond that of the typical bankruptcy case. The legacy of the Chrysler case has turned out to be particularly contentious as a result of the controversy surrounding the decision to pay secured creditors less than in full while simultaneously providing the unsecured claims of the UAW VEBA with 50% more than secured creditors received, which arguably violated the absolute priority rule.

A. Effect on Credit Markets

The criticism of that element of the Chrysler case was immediate and heated.[79] Warren Buffett, for example, warned that it would 'disrupt lending practices in the future.'[80] He stated, 'If we want to encourage lending in this country, we don't want to say to somebody who lends and gets a secured position that that secured position doesn't mean anything.'

Empirical studies of the long-term impact of the Chrysler case have produced mixed results. Anginer and Warburton examined the impact of the Chrysler case on bond market prices for highly unionized companies and found no evidence that the Chrysler case led to higher risk premiums for bonds issued by heavily unionized companies.[81] Subsequent analysis by Blaylock, et al., by contrast, found that firms in more unionized industries experienced lower event-window abnormal bond returns, higher abnormal bond yields, and lower cumulative abnormal bond returns.[82] The authors also found that those effects were greatest for firms that are closer to distress.

B. Effect on the Automotive Industry

Since the auto bailouts, the Big Three automakers have recovered well and returned to profitability. Supporters of the government's actions point to the auto bailouts as a cause of this development. Another unusual aspect of the auto bailouts was the Obama Administration's decision to seize the opportunity to engage in government industrial planning, especially with respect to its emphasis on using the leverage of the bailouts to push for increased manufacturing of smaller cars, as exemplified by the decision to essentially give Chrysler to Fiat in exchange for small-car technology and the built-in financial incentives for Fiat to increase the average gas mileage of Chrysler's fleet. In one famous exchange on the verge of bankruptcy, President Obama asked his advisors 'Why can't they make a Corolla?'[83] Astonishingly, his advisors replied 'We wish we knew.'[84]

In reality, the explanation as to why American automakers 'can't make a Corolla' is quite simple—because the high labor costs of Detroit automakers renders doing so infeasible to manufacture smaller cars such as Corollas, i.e., high-volume, low-margin cars. The problem of high cost was exacerbated by the persistent gap held by consumers in the perceived quality of American products and that of the imports. Thus, Steven Rattner reported that a GM 'premium compact' sold for $3,814 less than a Toyota, 'a stunning gap for car prices at less than $20,000.'[85] And whereas 77% of Toyota's cars were on the 2009 *Consumer Reports* recommended list, only 21 of GM's cars made the list, and *zero* of Chrysler's offerings.[86] As Rattner concluded,

> [A]s much as the Detroit Three had been pilloried for missing the small-car market, their failure wasn't due to complete stupidity. If it costs $1,000 more in extra labor expenses to build a car that could be sold for only $16,000—nearly $4,000 less than its competitor—it would be impossible to make a profit. So why build it?[87]

Given this, it is not surprising that of the best-selling cars (excluding light trucks) in the United States, the most popular ones are Japanese cars, including (in order) the Toyota Camry, Honda Civic, Toyota Corolla, Honda CR-V, Toyota RAV4, Honda Accord, Nissan Rogue, Nissan Altima, all before any American car appears on the list (the Ford Escape).[88]

However, this ignores a more important story—the top-three best-selling vehicles in the United States are three pickup trucks: the Ford F-Series, Chevrolet Silverado, and RAM Trucks. And although Toyota sold 360,000 Corollas in the United States in 2016, Ford sold 820,000 F-Series trucks, making it the best-selling consumer vehicle in the United States for the 35th year in a row.[89] In contrast, in 2016 GM sold 24,739 Chevy Volts, despite major tax incentives.[90]

In short, to the extent that the American automakers have returned to profitability following the auto bailouts, it is precisely because they *ignored* the pressure of the Obama Administration to try to manufacture Corollas and other small cars, but instead have prospered by building larger, higher-priced vehicles where Detroit's higher labor costs can be recouped by higher prices. In addition, an extended period of low interest rates on car (and other) loans (thereby making more expensive cars more affordable) and low gasoline prices have made consumers more willing to purchase those vehicles. This suggests that the efforts of the Obama Administration to use the bankruptcy process as an opportunity to engage in larger industrial planning may have been misguided.

C. Other Effects

The auto bankruptcies have also had effects that ripple beyond their particular impacts on credit and auto markets. Many of these effects have been completely unexpected but suggest the complexity of containing the full reach of such a dramatic action.

David Skeel has argued that the effect of the courts' approval of the controversial aspects of the Chrysler case was to pave the way for even more dramatic actions in the city of Detroit's bankruptcy case in 2013. The controversy in the Detroit case focused on the disposition of the art and other assets of the historic Detroit Art Museum that were owned by the city. Under standard principles of bankruptcy, the DAM's art collection would have been sold for maximum value in order to pay off the claims of the city's creditors. In that case, however, the court supervised a 'Grand Bargain' that provided that the museum's collection be purchased and donated to a private trust, with the funds to be provided by a combination of state funding and private contributions. This would enable the collection to be maintained intact and retained in the city of Detroit. In turn, the funds received by the bankruptcy estate would be earmarked to pay the claims of the city's retirees and pensioners, rather than distributed to general creditors.[91]

As David Skeel observes, the Grand Bargain 'cleverly' resolved two of the key issues in the case. 'The only concern with the Grand Bargain,' he notes, 'was that it did not appear to be legal.' Moreover, he points to the Chrysler and GM sales as the conceptual foundation of the scheme, 'relying as they did on a fictitious sale that was designed to favor some groups of creditors over others.'[92] In fact, he adds, 'With both of its key features, the fictitious sale and the favoring of one group of creditors, the Grand Bargain was in some respects even more audacious than Chrysler or GM.'[93] He concludes, 'Indeed, it seems unlikely that the Grand Bargain would ever have been tried if it were not for the carmaker bailout precedent.'

Another unexpected issue that arose from the auto bailouts related to the use of the government's leverage *after* the bankruptcy filing was completed but while the U.S. Government still owned a controlling stake in Ally Financial, formerly GMAC, the vehicle finance arm of GM.[94] In addition to transferring TARP funds directly to GM and Chrysler, the government's bailout plan also provided funds to GMAC and Chrysler Financial (which later merged into Ally) and took a majority ownership stake in Ally. One of the major new institutions created by the Dodd-Frank Financial Reform legislation was the creation of the Consumer Financial Protection Bureau, which inherited enforcement responsibilities for fair lending laws. One early priority of the CFPB was to pursue claims of alleged racial discrimination against auto dealers and auto lenders. The CFPB chose Ally Financial as one of its first major targets.

According to a report of an investigation by the House Financial Services Committee, the CFPB chose Ally as one of its first cases not because Ally had done anything provably wrong or was particularly egregious in its behavior, but among other reasons because the government held 73.8% of the bank (and still held 63.4% at the time the case was actually settled).[95] The government's control of Ally placed it in a particularly weak position to fight a different arm of the federal government. For that reason, along with others, Ally was unable or unwilling to fight the federal government and settle the case. In addition, Ally needed regulatory approval from other governmental agencies that the CFPB was able to hold up.[96] As a result, Ally capitulated, eventually paying $98 million.

A final issue regarding the long-term legacy of the auto bailouts was the scandal involving GM's ignition switch litigation. One of the key provisions in the approval of the bankruptcy plan by the court was the provision that the 'sale' to New GM would be free and clear of all claims. Under normal circumstances, this provision would prevent creditors that could have brought their claims prior to the bankruptcy from doing so after the bankruptcy against the purchaser of the assets. All creditors, including tort creditors, whose claims arose prior to the bankruptcy case, would normally be required to assert those claims against the estate of the bankrupt debtor (Old GM) and would not be able to assert those claims against the new owner.

In March 2014, however, New GM announced for the first time that there were serious defects in the ignition switches used in many of its cars that could result in accident, property damage, personal injury and even death.[97] The defective parts had been installed going back to the 2005 model year and had persisted during the period that the U.S. government owned GM. As of the time of the litigation to determine whether those claims could be asserted against New GM, over 140 class action cases had been brought for the defective parts and the overall economic loss was estimated to run from $7 billion to $10 billion.

The Bankruptcy Court had originally barred many of the claims from going forward against New GM, holding that they arose from actions taken prior to the bankruptcy case and thus should be asserted against Old GM. On appeal, however, the Second Circuit held that because GM knew about or should have known with reasonable diligence the flaw before it filed bankruptcy and did not provide notice, customers' claims survived the bankruptcy filing.[98] As the Second Circuit wrote, 'New GM essentially asks that we reward debtors who conceal claims against potential creditors. We decline to do so.'[99] In addition, the Court specifically rebuked GM for not bringing the matter to light during the period of the government's ownership of the company.[100]

V. CONCLUSION

As a result of the unprecedented intervention of the U.S. government, the bankruptcy cases of Chrysler and General Motors pushed bankruptcy law to the limit, and many would say beyond. Absent the federal government's interference, the cases themselves raised no inherently novel or unusually difficult issues—they could have proceeded as conventional Chapter 11 cases. General Motors would have almost certainly reorganized successfully, with a new capital structure, more realistic labor agreements, a leaner dealership network, and shorn of money-losing product lines. The fate of Chrysler, the smallest of Detroit's 'Big 3' automakers, was less certain, but the eventual acquisition of the company by Fiat was one plausible scenario. With respect to the unique circumstance of their filings having occurred at the height of the financial crisis, the federal government arguably could have played a role in providing liquidity directly to the companies or in guaranteeing a private lender's extension of capital to make that possible.

Instead, the federal government launched an intervention that was unprecedented in its scope and unprecedented in the challenges that it raised to bankruptcy doctrine. The cases challenged core bankruptcy practices, such as the traditional requirements for fair sales processes as well as the distribution of sales proceeds. Although the sales were upheld by the bankruptcy courts and Courts of Appeals, when the Chrysler case finally reached the Supreme Court the Justices took the cases on *certiorari*, thereby dismissing the cases, only to immediately dismiss the case as moot. As a result, the continued legal validity of the actions taken in those cases remains open to question.

Despite the continued questions regarding their legal authority, the real-world consequences of the Chrysler and GM bankruptcies is unquestionable. Not only did the approval of the cases enable the companies to go forward, the courts' decisions arguably played a role in Barack Obama's successful 2012 re-election campaign, and the creative nature of the plans arguably served as a crucial precedent in the later bankruptcy filing by the City of Detroit. Finally, for one of the first times in American history, the cases introduced a new notion of 'political risk' into otherwise predictable bankruptcy proceedings, creating ripple effects across the economy. While the short-term consequences of the cases are now complete, the long-term story is yet to be written.

NOTES

1. *See* Todd Zywicki, *The Corporatist Legacy of the Auto Bailouts*, Liberty Law (January 13, 2014), http://www.libertylawsite.org/2014/01/13/the-corporatist-legacy-of-the-auto-bailouts/; Todd J. Zywicki, *The Auto Bailout and the Rule of Law*, 7 Nat'l Affairs 66 (Spring 2011).
2. Austin D. Goolsbee & Alan B. Krueger, *A Retrospective Look at Rescuing and Restructuring General Motors and Chrysler*, 29 J. Econ. Persp. 3 (2015).
3. Paul Ingrassia, Crash Course: The American Automobile Industry's Road to Bankruptcy and Bailout—and Beyond 7 (2011). In fact, unemployment benefits were so generous that eventually they gave rise to the phenomenon known as 'inverse layoffs,' in which senior workers volounteered to be laid off (at 95% salary) and thus bumped junior workers back onto the assembly line. *Id.*
4. Steven Rattner, Overhaul: An Insider's Account of the Obama Administration's Emergency Rescue of the Auto Industry 87 (2010).
5. *Id.*
6. *Id.* at 153.
7. *See id.* at 20.
8. *Id.* at 23.
9. *Id.* at 27. One reason for refusing to make bankruptcy preparations might have been to ensure a messy bankruptcy if no bailout was forthcoming, thereby essentially creating a moral hazard problem or chicken game to force the government's hand on a bailout.
10. *Id.*
11. *Id.* at 297.
12. *See id.* at 205–7.
13. *Id.* at 23–4.
14. *Id.*
15. *See* Gary Lawson, *Burying the Constitution Under a Tarp*, 33 Harv. J.L. & Pub. Pol'y 55 (2009). *But see* Congressional Oversight Panel, September Oversight Report: The Use of TARP Funds in the Support and Reorganization of the Domestic Automotive Industry 4 (2009) (noting that the legality of the auto bailouts was subject to 'considerable debate' and that there was 'ambiguity' in the legislative language and congressional intent).
16. *See* Rattner, *supra* note 4, at 35–7.
17. *Id.* at 38.
18. *See* Lawson, *supra* note 15.
19. Goolsbee and Krueger, for example, assume that accepting the wisdom of a government role for financing in the auto bankruptcies implies that one must accept the full range of government activity in the cases. *See* Austin D. Goolsbee & Alan B. Krueger, *A Retrospective Look at Rescuing and Restructuring General Motors and Chrysler*, 29 J. of Econ. Perspectives 3 (2015).
20. *See* Zywicki, *Auto Bailout*, *supra* note 1.
21. *See* Goolsbee & Krueger, *supra* note 19.
22. Douglas Baird has claimed that the sale to Fiat was really a way of 'allow[ing] Chrysler to fail slowly over the course of several years in a way that coincided with Fiat's entry into the U.S. market,' instead of closing Chrysler immediately. *See* Douglas G. Baird, *Car Trouble* 4 (Univ. of Chi. Law & Econs., Olin Working Paper No. 551, 2011). 'With luck,' he writes, 'Fiat could make its cars at factories that had been producing Chryslers while taking advantage of part of Chrysler's existing distribution system.'
23. *See* Zywicki, *Corporatist Legacy*, *supra* note 1.
24. Mitt Romney, *Let Detroit Go Bankrupt*, N.Y. Times, Nov. 18, 2008, at A35.
25. *Id.*
26. *In re* Chrysler Llc, 405 B.R. 84, 89 (Bankr. S.D.N.Y. 2009).
27. *See* A. Joseph Warburton, *Understanding the Bankruptcies of Chrysler and General Motors: A Primer*, 60 Syracuse L. Rev. 531 (2010).

28. A useful summary of these and other issues in the Chrysler case can be found in Mark J. Roe & David Skeel, *Assessing the Chrysler Bankruptcy*, 108 Michigan L. Rev. 727 (2010).
29. David Skeel, *Why the Chrysler Deal Would Horrify a New Dealer*, The American (May 8, 2009).
30. *See also* Ralph Brubaker & Charles Tabb, *Bankruptcy Reorganizations and the Troubling Legacy of Chrysler and GM*, 2010, U. of Ill. L. Rev. 1375 (2010) (arguing that the structure of the GM deal was similar to that of the equity receiverships that courts eliminated during the late 19th century).
31. *See* Pension Benefit Guar. Corp. v. Braniff Airways, Inc. (*In re* Braniff Airways, Inc.), 700 F.2d 935 (5th Cir. 1983).
32. Comm. of Equity Sec. Holders v. Lionel Corp. (*In re* Lionel Corp.), 722 F.2d 1063 (2d Cir. 1983).
33. *In re* Chrysler Llc, 405 B.R. 84, 96 (Bankr. S.D.N.Y. 2009).
34. *See* Roe & Skeel, *supra* note 28, at 742 n.39.
35. *Id.* at 742.
36. Chrysler's expert was paid $10 million to prepare its opinion. *See* Baird, *supra* note 22.
37. Roe & Skeel, *supra* note 28, at 746.
38. *Id.*
39. David A. Skeel, Jr., *From Chrysler and General Motors to Detroit*, 24 Widener L.J. 121 (2015).
40. Roe & Skeel, *supra* note 28, at 747.
41. *See* Baird, *supra* note 22, at 13.
42. *Id. See also* Barry E. Adler, *A Reassessment of Bankruptcy Reorganization After Chrysler and General Motors*, 18 ABI L. Rev. 305; Roe & Skeel, *supra* note 28.
43. Roe & Skeel, *supra* note 28, at 747.
44. *Id.* at 749.
45. *Id.* at 748.
46. *In re* Chrysler Llc, 405 B.R. 84, 99 (Bankr. S.D.N.Y. 2009).
47. *Id.*, 405 B.R. at 99.
48. *Id.*
49. *Id.* at 181.
50. *Id.* at 96.
51. Warburton, *supra* note 27, at 543.
52. *See id.* at 552.
53. Roe & Skeel, *supra* note 28, at 743.
54. *See* Adler, *supra* note 42, at 310; Roe & Skeel, *supra* note 28, at 744.
55. *See* Rattner, *supra* note 4, at 178. President Obama made similar statements against GM's bondholders that objected to their treatment.
56. *See* Warburton, *supra* note 27, at 552.
57. *See id.* at 544.
58. Rattner, *supra* note 4, 180. Rattner argues that even though the $2 billion that Chrysler's secured creditors received was less than the face value of their loans 'it represented more than 100 percent of the Chrysler's assets, as the company's liquidation value indicated.'
59. Warburton, *supra* note 27, at 543.
60. *See id.* at 555–6.
61. *In re* General Motors Corp., 407 B.R. 463, 475 (Bankr. S.D.N.Y. 2009).
62. *Id.* at 491–3.
63. There has been some debate over how novel the GM and Chrysler cases were. *Compare* Stephen J. Lubben, *No Big Deal: The GM and Chrysler Cases in Context*, 83 Am. Bankr. L. J. 101 (2009) (not novel) *with* Mark J. Roe & Joo-Hee Chung, *How The Chrysler Reorganization Differed from Prior Practice*, 5 J. of Legal Analysis 400 (2013).
64. Ind. State Police Pension Tr. v. Chrysler, LLC, 129 S. Ct. 2275 (2009).
65. Ind. State Police Pension Tr. v. Chrysler, LLC, 130 S. Ct. 1015 (2009).
66. United States v. Munsingwear, Inc., 340 U.S. 36 (1950).

67. Warburton, *supra* note 27, at 575–6 (quoting *Munsingwear*, 340 U.S. at 41).
68. *Id.* at 576 (quoting *Munsingwear*, 340 U.S. at 40); *see also* Fred N. David, *Interpreting the Supreme Court's Treatment of the Chrysler Bankruptcy and Its Impact on Future Business Reorganizations*, 27 Emory Bankr. Dev. J. 25 (2010) (discussing possible interpretations of the Supreme Court decision).
69. *See* Todd Zywicki, *The Rule of Law During Times of Economic Crisis*, *in* Economic and Political Change after Crisis: Prospects for Government, Liberty and the Rule of Law 36 (Stephen H. Balch & Benjamin Powell (eds), 2017).
70. Todd J. Zywicki, *Rent-Seeking, Crony Capitalism, and the Crony Constitution*, 23 S. Ct. Econ. Rev. 577 (2016).
71. *See* Jim Puzzanghera & Ken Bensinger, *GM, Chrysler Defend Slashing Dealerships*, Los Angeles Times (June 4, 2009), http://articles.latimes.com/2009/jun/04/business/fi-autos-congress4.
72. *See* Zywicki, *Auto Bailout*, *supra* note 1.
73. *See* James Sherk & Todd Zywicki, *Auto Bailout or UAW Bailout? Taxpayer Losses Came from Subsidizing Union Compensation*, Heritage Foundation Backgrounder No. 2700 (June 13, 2012).
74. Alex Nishimoto, *Rattner Says UAW Wages Should Have Been Cut During Bailouts*, Motortrend (Dec. 16, 2011), http://www.motortrend.com/news/rattner-says-uaw-wages-should-have-been-cut-during-bailouts-147425/.
75. Rattner, *supra* note 4, at 226.
76. *See* Special Inspector General for the Troubled Asset Relief Program, Treasury's Role in the Decision for GM to Provide Pension Payments to Delphi Employees (August 15, 2013).
77. *See* Zywicki, *Auto Bailout*, *supra* note 1 (listing examples).
78. *Id.*
79. *See* Todd J. Zywicki, *Chrysler and the Rule of Law*, Wall St. J., May 13, 2009, A19.
80. Lou Whiteman, *Buffett warns of Chrysler cramdown ramifications*, TheDeal.com (May 5, 2009) (quoted in Roe & Skeel, *supra* note 28, at 729).
81. Deniz Anginer & A. Joseph Warburton, *The Chrysler Effect: The Impact of Government Intervention on Borrowing Costs*, 40 J. Banking & Fin. 62 (2014).
82. Bradley Blaylock, Alexander Edwards & Jared Stanfield, *The Role of Government in the Labor-Creditor Relationship: Evidence from the Chrysler Bankruptcy*, 50(3) J. Fin. & Quantitative Analysis 325 (2015).
83. Rattner, *supra* note 4, at 44.
84. The following paragraphs are drawn from Zywicki, *Corporatist Legacy*, *supra* note 1.
85. *Id.* at 75.
86. *Id.*
87. *Id.*
88. *See* Benjamin Zhang, *The 20 Best-Selling Cars and Trucks in America*, Businessinsider.com (Jan. 7, 2017), http://www.businessinsider.com/best-selling-cars-trucks-vehicle-america-2016-2017-1/#20-hyundai-elantra-208319-sold-during-2016-down-138-over-2015-1.
89. The relevant others were Silverado (574,000) and RAM (489,000), leaving the Camry a distant fourth on the overall list at 388,000.
90. Jeff Cobb, *Chevy Bolt Sales Begin; Volt Smashes Sales Records*, www.hybridcars.com (Jan. 4, 2017), http://www.hybridcars.com/chevy-bolt-sales-begin-volt-smashes-sales-records/.
91. *See* Skeel, *supra* note 39, at 141.
92. *Id.*
93. *Id.*
94. *See* Todd J. Zywicki, *The Dodd-Frank Act Five Years Later: Are We More Stable?*, 43 J. Fin. Transformation 58 (2016).
95. Republican Staff of H. Comm. on Fin. Servs., 114th Cong., Unsafe at Any Bureaucracy: CFPB Junk Science and Indirect Auto Lending (2015).
96. Zywicki, *supra* note 94.

97. *In re* Motors Liquidation Co., 529 B.R. 510 (Bankr. S.D.N.Y. 2015).
98. *In re* Motors Liquidation Co., 829 F.3d 135 (2d Cir. 2016).
99. *Id.* at 160.
100. *Id.* at 165.

14. Cross-border corporate insolvency in the era of soft(ish) law*

John A.E. Pottow

Multinational firms follow markets more than national borders. Consequently, the financial distress of these businesses raises not just complex questions of jurisdictional doctrine but of corporate bankruptcy policy more generally. Scholars, policymakers, and judges alike all continue to struggle with how most efficiently and fairly to resolve these "cross-border" or "transnational" insolvencies. It is a fascinating area of corporate insolvency law because it is in such flux. This moving target has led to a paradoxical role for corporate bankruptcy scholars. On the one hand, because of the novelty of each new case that raises international concerns, academic work, even the deeply theoretical, has enjoyed considerably more attention than its traditional cobweb level of engagement in the domestic arena (hope you are enjoying this book!).[1] On the other hand, because international law involves international diplomacy and reveals the influence of other extra-legal and peri-legal considerations, what one might euphemistically call more "pragmatic" concerns frequently carry the day.[2] Thus, the purest academic theories are often ignored in this most unprincipled but necessary world, making scholarly relevance all the more challenging.

This chapter introduces the reader to the messy world of cross-border corporate insolvency. While it is mindful of the overarching goal many advocate (its author included) of reducing the cost of credit as a worthy foundation of corporate insolvency law, it cautions at the outset that a pragmatic, at times atheoretical sensibility guides this field.[3] This messiness stems in large part from the fractured (and fractious) nature of bankruptcy. Different nations have not just different bankruptcy laws but different conceptions about the desirability of unifying cross-border law. This divide has stymied historical efforts to craft international treaties related to bankruptcy.[4] Until recently, there wasn't even that much cross-border bankruptcy "law." After centuries of mistrust, however, international bankruptcy has reached a conceptual breakthrough just within the last two decades. The lynchpin to this success was the abandonment of conventional international law (conventions) and the rise of "soft law" instruments, such as, principally, UNCITRAL's Model Law on Cross-Border Insolvency.[5] UNCITRAL's Model Law (and the cognate EU Insolvency Regulation)[6] not only radically altered the international bankruptcy landscape but has now set the stage for what is going to be the next wave of reform that is presently unfolding. And it is this soft law status that gets all the credit.

This chapter will proceed as follows. First, it will introduce the reader to the academic theories dominating transnational bankruptcy law in order to set the stage for the explication of the Model Law. Next, it will explore the Model Law and show how its soft status enabled its embrace by multiple jurisdictions around the globe. Third, it will examine some of the important case law that has emerged under the Model Law with an eye to gauging the success of the instrument. Finally, it will critique the new proposals emerging as the "next wave" of international insolvency reform to see how they fit within the soft law approach and underlying academic theories.

I. CROSS-BORDER INSOLVENCY THEORY

For better or worse, scholarship in the transnational corporate insolvency arena has shifted to "second-order" considerations (or, in some instances, "third-order" considerations). So, too, has law-making. But because first-order consideration should anchor an analysis of second-order arguments, we should start (dear reader) by examining the dominant normative theories over the design of an optimal cross-border insolvency regime. Then we can relax the assumptions of theoretical purity for greater reality.

One of the canonical theoretical conceptions of corporate insolvency is collective-action based.[7] This widely accepted view imposes a "statist" solution to financial distress through reorganization or liquidation. "Statist" intends to convey the idea that a compulsory, public process is deployed as a concession to the likely impossibility of ad hoc contractual solutions that the parties would hypothetically prefer to remedy these collective action concerns but cannot achieve on their own. Hence, the U.S. Bankruptcy Code has an automatic stay and a bankruptcy judge blocking the atomistic conduct of self-interested creditors.[8] The statist solution enhances welfare by preserving value (especially going concern value), with the concomitant attribute of lowering credit costs. Higher insolvency-state distribution should translate to lower aggregate credit costs. ("Aggregate" because an efficient individual collector knowing it could reap the fruits of its rapaciousness might not like the forced *pari passu* collectivism in the statist approach of cross-subsidizing its less efficient brethren, but including all the uncertain, risk-averse, and/or lemon-concerned creditors makes the aggregate claim plausible.) The necessary foundation of the statist approach, therefore, by literal definition, is a *state*, replete with the sovereign's law-making and law-enforcing power.

In the international realm there is no state and hence no possible statist solution. This demoralizes the credit-cost-minimizing theoretician, who bemoans this lack of law. Of course, binding international law can be made by sovereign consent through treaty execution. Yet corporate insolvency – all insolvency – has until recently by international law standards remained stubbornly resistant to treaty enactment. Why is this so? Wise scholars have suggested that the challenge is due both to the invasive and to the normatively contested nature of bankruptcy law.[9] Consider invasive. Bankruptcy law is what might be considered "trans-substantive" because it overlaps and displaces other discrete domains of substantive law. For example, one can consider the law of patents as prescribing a set of rules governing certain intellectual property rights. But bankruptcy law dangles an asterisk over that field, cautioning that all bets might be off when a corporate debtor seeks relief from creditors.[10] Almost no area of substantive law is immune from trumping in bankruptcy, both vertically in a federal system and horizontally in terms of pre-emption of sister regulatory regimes.[11] In the United States, the pages of the bankruptcy reporters are flush with enraged lawyers for the IRS, EPA, and NLRB, not to mention scores of states attorneys general, who are routinely on the losing end of a scope question of bankruptcy law.[12] (The automatic stay shunting those lawyers into oft-unfamiliar bankruptcy courts to make their losing claims rubs salt in the wound.) Thus, one reason treaties are difficult – with their inherent cession of sovereignty – is that bankruptcy law can have wide-sweeping and deep-reaching effect.

The second reason is that bankruptcy laws have thick normative content. For example, consider the priority provisions.[13] Yes, priority rules can be dismissed as the spoils of domestic rent-seeking contests (and they often are), but they also do represent deeply held policy beliefs on the sensitive distributional choices that arise in financial failure. Take, for example, the security-trumping labor claim priorities of many domestic insolvency regimes.[14] Having to yield on those matters by treaty to a foreign country's laws is not an easy sell. It is no surprise that bankruptcy for a long time eluded international lawmaking.

Cognizant of these constraints, international bankruptcy scholars divided into opposing camps for two theoretical models of the optimal cross-border insolvency law. The first, *universalists*, took a "one law" approach and argued that both the principles of cost minimization and the fairness-animated justification for *pari passu* distribution militated in favor of one substantive bankruptcy law to govern a multinational's financial assets, regardless of their jurisdictional location.[15] Cost minimization would obtain, they argued, via at least three avenues: (a) reduction in monitoring costs, where creditors would not have to follow a debtor's assets as they crossed national borders to see which new substantive bankruptcy consequences would result; (b) reduction in fragmentation costs, as creditors would not have to open duplicative and wasteful proceedings in each jurisdiction that contained assets of the debtor; and (c) going-concern preservation, with one binding law able to prevent the destructive, territoriality-based liquidation of an enterprise whose going-concern value required coordinated utilization of assets in multiple countries (mimicking the statist approach).[16] Undergirding the universalists' cost-minimization arguments were also robust fairness concerns: that the recovery of a creditor should not depend upon the random happenstance of asset location on the day of bankruptcy. If a debtor happened to have a bounty of assets in Country X and a paucity in Countries Y and Z, then the X creditors should not have a windfall when the going-concern value is spread evenly over the three jurisdictions.[17]

Universalists (perhaps ironically) do not command universal support. *Territorialists*, as their name implies, oppose what they see as universalist pipe-dreaming on both cost-minimization arguments and their own fairness grounds.[18] On the cost front, they complain that whatever monitoring costs universalism saves might well be offset by non-diversification and forum-shopping costs. That is, because universalism puts all the distributional eggs in one nation's basket by global application of that one nation's bankruptcy laws, favored creditors will jockey to have their nation be the selected hegemon, just as jilted creditors will litigate vociferous opposition to bowing to that nation's rules. Forum shopping will follow as a matter of course, racing to the bottom or top (depending on one's views) as fast as the much-analysed corporate charters are drafted at U.S. state law. As such, no stable rule will ever evolve to select the "winning" jurisdiction, as perceived losers will either not acquiesce *ex ante* or will undermine *ex post*.[19] As for fragmentation costs, absent a pan-global adjudication system of cross-border bankruptcy tribunals, enforcement would fall to local courts, in which case multiple proceedings would have to be opened anyway, just with different substantive laws.[20] Finally, regarding the destruction of going-concern value, territorialists retort that nothing prevents creditors in diverse jurisdictions from cooperating ad hoc when to do so would be in the collective benefit.[21]

But even more than the cost arguments, deeply held beliefs of sovereignty and vested rights exercise the territorialists. Territorialists complain that creditors (more specifically, local creditors) lend to a debtor on the expectation that they have certain rights under local insolvency law. To pull the rug out from under them and apply a foreign bankruptcy law – because their debtor is a multinational – runs roughshod over these expectations. Worse, because of the normative content of bankruptcy law discussed above, application of this foreign law requires subjugation of the careful domestic policy balance of insolvency priorities in favor of some foreign jurisdiction's tastes. No country would—or should—accept this emasculation.[22] As such, territorialists contend, good borders make good neighbors, and allowing each nation to govern the adjudication of assets within its jurisdiction in the event of a multinational's bankruptcy is the best way to address general financial default.

It is fair to say that as an academic matter, the universalists have won the upper hand in terms of followers.[23] But the burden is on them, so to speak, because the dictates of sovereignty are that absent international agreement, territorialism is the status quo. The universalism-territorialism debate has been well ventilated academically, and so the reader of this chapter will have to join its author's theoretical stipulation that universalists have the better theoretical argument, especially when viewed through the lens of corporate insolvency law's interest in minimizing the *ex ante* cost of credit.

II. THE RISE OF SOFT LAW (AND, CONSEQUENTLY, UNIVERSALISM)

As alluded to above, recurrent attempts to execute an international convention on insolvency law have failed, which is not surprising given the hotly contested differences of universalists and territorialists. (Different countries map to different proclivities; the United States is a leading universalist jurisdiction, whereas Japan, although now improving, was widely known for its territorialism.) A couple of historical developments – perhaps aided by the backdrop of ever-increasing globalization of business – broke the historical logjam on international bankruptcy cooperation. Likely inspired by the landmark restructuring of Maxwell Communications,[24] a global publishing conglomerate, and certainly facilitated by the unfolding institutional apparatus of the European Union, the 1990s saw the drafting of a European Insolvency Regulation and concomitant Model Law on Cross-Border Insolvency promulgated by UNCITRAL. It is not an overstatement to say these were watershed innovations in cross-border insolvency that brought the first real semblance of coherence to the international bankruptcy scene. Because the EU has sovereignesque authority to bind member states directly to Directives and Regulations, its task (as a positive law matter, not necessarily as a political matter) was somewhat easier than UNCITRAL's.[25] Relatedly, the binding consequence of the EU

Regulation is stronger than the UNCITRAL Model Law. Both regimes, however, advanced the agenda of universalism.

A. Introduction to the UNCITRAL Model Law

Although these two instruments developed in tandem, for ease of exposition we will focus on the Model Law championed by UNCITRAL. This document's success was principally due to its "soft" status and departure from the traditional international document of the multi-state convention (treaty). Here, "soft" is being used as a term of art, and the reader is spared the voluminous literature on the constitution of "soft" law.[26] Relevant for purposes of this chapter is a working definition of "soft law" that means not only non-binding compulsion (the absence of legislation), an essential attribute of soft law, but a further, substantive dimension. Perhaps more accurately characterized as "incomplete" or "unspecified" law, the content of the Model Law, wholly apart from (actually, intrinsically related to) its non-binding nature, is notable for its careful failure to engage the most contentious substantive legal bankruptcy issues. It is thus both "positively" and "substantively" soft, which will be how "soft" law is used in this discussion.

Thus, UNCITRAL's Model Law sought to blunt the opposition of the two fervent camps of universalists and territorialists by carving a non-committal fine line down the middle to secure maximal buy-in. That is, the Model Law nominally purports to address matters of bankruptcy procedure (opening and recognition of proceedings, etc.) *without* comprehensively resolving the difficult distributional questions attendant with choice of bankruptcy law raised by the universalist-territorialist divide.[27] This might be considered its "substantive" softness, as opposed to its "positivist" softness, mentioned above. Some if not most commentators assessed this aspect of the Model Law (perhaps decried it) as milquetoast reform at best that did not advance the field significantly. Others have taken a more nuanced view. For them, the Model Law was not pussyfooting but intentionally reticent. And in being so, the Model Law exploited its soft law nature to advance the cause of universalism considerably and should thus be celebrated, not bemoaned, by bankruptcy scholars seeking to minimize the cost of credit.

How does a self-described (and other-described) middle-ground instrument that eschews the universalism-territorialism theoretical minefield manage to advance the cause of universalism? This chapter will not summarize the Model Law in all its glory and leaves interested readers referred elsewhere.[28] But it will highlight two broad ways in which the Model Law advances the universalism cause notwithstanding its middle-road substantive softness. First, the instrument does so mechanically. Specifically, the Model Law contains important procedurally focused grants of authority that allow enacting jurisdictions to cooperate, coordinate, and communicate with sister jurisdictions jointly seized with the administration of a cross-border corporate bankruptcy. For example, many countries have constraints on the abilities of their courts to contact foreign tribunals (think letters rogatory and other such barnacles), and so the Model Law makes clear that to the extent not incompatible with their local domestic due process norms, these courts can and even should reach out and to a certain extent "co-adjudicate" with foreign peers bankruptcy questions.[29] In a similar vein, Article 8 of the Model Law (codified as section 1508 in the U.S. Bankruptcy Code) instructs domestic courts to consider foreign law in rendering their decisions under the instrument, commanding that "regard is to be had to its international origin and to the need to promote uniformity in its application and the observance of good faith."[30]

B. The Model Law's Universalism: Doctrinal Anchors but "Substantive" Softness

Second, and perhaps even more importantly, beyond these cooperation-facilitating mechanical rules, the Model Law helps erect the doctrinal foundations for a universalist system. That is, for a pluralist universalist system to function, two conceptual pillars must be established. First, a jurisdiction-selecting rule must be propounded to designate the substantive bankruptcy law that will control the one, "universal" rules of priority, distribution, and the like that will transcend national borders. Second, there must be what universalism's chief proponent calls "an acceptance of outcome differences," meaning deferring or ancillary states must be willing to subordinate their own (normatively rich) distributional rules for the greater good of system efficiency.[31] The Model Law (just as the EU Insolvency Regulation) advances both of these constructs.

As broad overview, the general structure of the Model Law envisions a domestic court considering a request for assistance from a foreign bankruptcy proceeding representative. For example, a British bankruptcy administrator may open a proceeding in an Australian bankruptcy court to seek turnover of Australian-situated assets for purposes of transferring them to the U.K. proceeding for liquidation there. Alternatively, a Canadian order confirming a corporate reorganization proceeding under the Companies' Creditors Arrangement Act may be brought down to a U.S. court for enforcement to enjoin American creditors to comport with the plan. Thus, the Model Law is generally directed at "receiving" courts: it delineates the scope of cooperation and deference they should accord "requesting" courts in a multi-jurisdiction insolvency.[32] Against this backdrop, the Model Law reveals two universalist-leaning attributes.

First, the Model Law doctrinally deploys a jurisdiction-selecting rule. That rule is the Centre of Main Interests ("COMI," as it is now called around the world, itself a worthy sidebar discussion of legal nomenclature).[33] Several legal concepts coalesce ("principal place of business" in U.S. parlance, "real seat" from the French, etc.) to confirm that the jurisdiction with the greatest connection to the corporate debtor will be accorded the most control under the Model Law system in receiving assistance.[34] More specifically, the Model Law designates an insolvency proceeding afoot in the corporate debtor's COMI as a "foreign main proceeding," and contrasts it with other proceedings not so situated (and for the most part designated "foreign non-main proceedings").[35] While the Model Law requires enacting jurisdictions to recognize requests for assistance from foreign bankruptcy representatives coming from abroad to lay claim to domestic assets, the assistance granted to those shepherding foreign main proceedings is greater. Specifically, the domestic courts enter an automatic stay upon such a request from a foreign main proceeding.[36] While they can also stay domestic collection actions at the request of a foreign non-main proceeding's insolvency representative, that relief is purely at the discretion of the local court.[37] Thus, in according (at least some) automatic relief to a foreign main proceeding, the Model Law seeks to enshrine one court – the COMI – with greater legal authority over all others. This essence of "jurisdictional hierarchy" thereby erects this first pillar of universalism: selection of a dominant forum worthy of legal deference.[38]

The second universalism-fomenting feature is somewhat touchier. For a completely universalist system to get off the ground, the deferring or ancillary states have to be willing to suppress their home-state insolvency rules in favor of the COMI court's rules, a tough sell to the sovereignty-conscious. This, the Model Law (by design) does not do. A full analysis of the Model Law's capacity nonetheless to acclimate ancillary states to the imposition of COMI bankruptcy law is beyond the scope of this discussion. (The mechanisms are subtle and the subject of other work to which the interested reader is referred.)[39] A broad generalization can be made that suffices for purposes of this discussion: the Model Law facilitates that application of COMI state law by offering its potential application in a non-threatening (i.e., "soft") manner. What the Model Law does is suggest a framework, perhaps even a presumption, of that deference to COMI bankruptcy law, but then claws back that seemingly universalist proclivity with unambiguous territorialist retrenchments.[40] This is where we see pragmatism creeping its way into the theoretical purity of cross-border insolvency law. Specifically, the Model Law approach does not force wholesale "export" of the COMI state's bankruptcy laws to the ancillary jurisdictions as universalism would counsel. Rather, it permits, but for the most part does not require, its exportation. That is, while true the Model Law contains a jurisdictional hierarchy favoring the COMI state, it still leaves cooperation up to the cooperating states.[41] Some have called this "modified universalism," because the injection of discretion diminishes the universalist application of one substantive bankruptcy law. It "modifies" (better, "softens") universalism's unitary aspect by allowing some territorial concessions. This modification was likely necessary to get the law past territorialist states that would otherwise have balked at the cession of sovereignty from more full-throated universalism.[42]

The Model Law's balancing act is careful and delicate. That is, on the one hand it offers modified universalism and the ability of a foreign representative to take assets away from a local jurisdiction and deploy them under foreign distributional rules.[43] On the other hand, it qualifies those seemingly universalists powers by three important concessions to territorialists (wholly apart from the baseline discretionary power to cooperate with the request for assistance). Namely, the Model Law contains three principal "claw-backs" toward territorialism from its universalist inroads. First, although the recognition provisions accord relatively automated and mandated cooperation to the foreign insolvency representative (the local courts are commanded to "recognize" the foreign representative if a check list of factors is satisfied, and moreover to specify whether they are recognizing a foreign main or non-main proceeding),[44] the relief provisions are separated out for different treatment. Bluntly, recognition does not mean relief. Once recognized, the foreign insolvency representative must still ask the local court for specific bankruptcy-related relief. While some relief is awarded automatically (e.g., the stay to a foreign main proceeding), most relief is discretionary.[45] The Model Law grafts three constraints onto the exercise of that discretion.

Consider the most poignant of all relief requests: expatriation of local assets to the foreign main proceeding, which the Model Law explicitly countenances.[46] This is the essence of universalism. The Model Law envisions a domestic court ordering turnover of locally situated assets to the COMI court to share with COMI creditors and distribute under the substantive rules of COMI bankruptcy law. Local creditors are unlikely to welcome the departure of such assets that would otherwise be available to satisfy local claims. This is especially so for local creditors who are protected by local priority rules, such as, e.g., U.S. fishermen under the U.S. Code.[47]

Recognizing this territorialist tension working against its quintessentially universalist provision for discretionary relief, the Model Law spells out safeguard considerations that must be undertaken by a local court before assets can be turned over to the COMI tribunal.[48] One of those expressly states that the interests of local creditors must be "adequately protected."[49] To be sure, the Model Law intentionally and delphically leaves this standard undefined, but the idea is surely to offer the aggrieved local creditor ammunition to deny turnover and loss of domestic bankruptcy favoritism. Indeed, an overly robust form of interpreting "adequate protection" would deny any turnover unless the local creditors would receive at a minimum their precise entitlement under local law (a standard auguring poorly for the acceptance of outcome differences necessary to buttress universalism), but courts have for the most part not fallen into this trap.[50] Rather, the idea has been interpreted to allow something of a "margin of appreciation,"[51] and thus a loose recognition of "adequate protection" has been seen that requires only general respect of entitlements or assets without assuring perfect concordance.[52] A survey of the case law is beyond the scope of this analysis (although a flavor can be divined from the public policy cases discussed below). Still, however "strictly" or "loosely" the standard is interpreted, the point remains that the local creditor safeguard of adequate protection is a significant retrenchment toward territorialism contained within the universalist-inclined Model Law.

The second significant territorialist concession of the Model Law – whose inclusion was likely a *sine qua non* for hesitant states to join – was the supremacy of local bankruptcy proceedings. Recall that the archetypal Model Law application is to an ancillary proceeding lending assistance to a foreign main proceeding. But nothing in the Model Law precludes (indeed, specific provisions explicitly affirm) the ability of uncooperatively inclined local creditors to open a full "plenary" proceeding (for example, in the United States, a Chapter 11 reorganization) under local law to govern local assets. There, the world shifts back to the pre-Model-Law, comity-dependent State of Insolvency Nature, with courts negotiating ad hoc for cooperation, complete with the prospect of dueling and conflicting court orders. Although there are provisions that blunt the territorialist consequences of such a local creditor veto,[53] the fact remains that a territorially inclined creditor can drop the opt-out bomb at any time and have local law reign supreme.

The third concession to territorial sovereignty is the least surprising because it replicates the "escape clause" found in many international instruments involving recognition of foreign judgments and choice of foreign law.[54] It provides that the cooperating court may always refuse to grant relief – even purportedly automatic relief – if to do so would violate "fundamental public policy" of the recognizing jurisdiction.[55] This assuages the "little states" that they will not be hegemonically commandeered by the possibly offensive bankruptcy laws of the COMI jurisdiction. With these three carveouts/claw-backs toward territorisalism, the Model Law was able to advance a "proto-universalist" policy of a COMI-centered regime that defers, in some limited respects, to COMI-state bankruptcy laws but that backtracks in important ways from that promise. This middle-ground stance of the Model Law – at best a soft nudge toward universalism – was instrumental to its passage. A more brazen attempt toward universalism would likely have faltered given the sovereignty-consciousness of many states.

C. The Model Law's "Traditional" Softness (It's Not Law!)

Equally important to the passage of the Model Law as substantive softness, namely, its delicate middle-ground posture between universalism and territorialism (although leaning clearly universalist), was as a positivist matter its mode of implementation, namely, as a model law. While prior attempts at international agreement through the treaty mechanism tried and failed – repeatedly and spectacularly – the model law document allowed ultimate say on whether and how to enact the legislation up to each individual state, piecemeal and on its own timeframe. Model laws are thus soft laws. More precisely, they might be called "softish," because of course if and when the law becomes implemented as domestic legislation it crystallizes into hard law. As mentioned, this softness of the Model Law was another necessary condition to its acceptability by deeply hesitant and skeptical states.

But there are degrees of softness, and the Model Law, while soft, is far from the soft end of the spectrum. While soft enough to win over doubting states, it still tilts hard in several respects. For example, there are various provisions that are drafted with specific alternatives (i.e., Alternative A, Alternative B), such as the rules on foreign tax claims.[56] This format serves an agenda-setting function of cabining the perceived areas of legitimate differences of opinion and focuses dissent onto a few areas, rather than suggesting clause-by-clause consideration of each provision was appropriate by a state weighing enactment. Also, as an empirical matter, for the most part, this hard tilt of the softish law has worked. Many states that have enacted the Model Law have made only minor alterations at most to its text.[57] More importantly, the Model Law seems to be catching on. Leaving aside Europe, where its enactment rate is respectable but less urgent given the overlay of the EU Insolvency Regulation, the Model Law has been embraced by Canada, the United States, Mexico, Australia, Japan, and South Africa, to name just a few. There are some conspicuous omissions (the South American uptake has been slow), but for the large part, it is taking hold.[58] The uniformity (i.e., minimal deviations) of the enacting states doubtless accelerates this effect, as each successive country takes stock of how the law was deemed to be acceptable to the one before.

The model law construct is not new and shows the success of pan-governmental organizations, such as UNCITRAL, in capitalizing upon a soft law approach to international law. While treaties are far from foreign to UNCITRAL's tool kit, it shepherded through the model law approach – radically softer than a treaty – perhaps because it sensed the fragile negotiating environment on cross-border insolvency. And this model law, in particular, was substantively soft, likely further respectful of this environment. For example, the conspicuous omission of choice of law rules was another likely intentional stance.[59] UNCITRAL is especially well situated to gauge the level of comfort with member state delegations on account of its working group format. These working groups are deeply consensus driven. Formal votes are eschewed in lieu of a sometimes-painstaking process that encourages cross-delegate engagement. (Coffee breaks are intentionally generous.) The idea of "stretching" or trying to cram down one approach over the consternation of minority state delegations is just not how the operation works, and so its legal product hides from firm pronouncements and frequently contents itself with generalized principles or standards that leave some room for the eyes of the beholders. Here, too, the description of "soft" law is apt: not just non-binding but non-specifying.

D. More Soft(ish) Law: The EU Insolvency Regulation

Worth a brief discussion in comparison with the UNCITRAL Model Law is the EU Insolvency Regulation. The Regulation allows bankruptcy proceedings opened in one of the member states at the COMI of the debtor to be recognized automatically in other member states, such as an "ancillary" jurisdiction where cooperation by the COMI insolvency representative is sought.[60] But the EU Regulation goes further than the Model Law's tentativeness on choice of law matters such as priority, distribution, and the like. The Regulation provides a presumptive choice of law rule of COMI law (*lex fori concursus*). Under this presumption, COMI state law applies extraterritorially to all cross-border proceedings occurring within the Union.[61] That is, for a foreign main proceeding opened in the United Kingdom, UK bankruptcy law presumptively governs the distribution of assets of the debtor located in France (including the British rules of distribution). Needless to say, such a COMI-centered choice of law regime is deeply universalist and doesn't seem that soft at all.

Nevertheless, territorialists persist in Europe as elsewhere, and so there are indeed territorialist retrenchments, just as with the Model Law. Thus, although the Regulation is hard as a traditional matter (binding Union-wide, although Denmark did opt out originally),[62] it remains "substantively soft," following the lead of the UNCITRAL Model Law. First, the *lex fori concursus* rule is tempered by a laundry list of "carveouts" from the choice of law presumption, ranging from laws governing labor agreements to laws governing secured transactions.[63] So, for example, if the COMI bankruptcy law treats employee wages as general unsecured claims but an ancillary jurisdiction would give them a priority, the ancillary jurisdiction may not need to follow the *lex fori concursus*'s ranking rule but can instead apply its own *lex secondus* (actually, *lex laboris*) that elevates the labor claim's rank.[64] Given the breadth of these carveouts, it is understandable that the Insolvency Regulation is rarely described as universalist but rather "modified universalist" at best.

A second retrenchment toward territorialism is the ability to open secondary proceedings. Much like the veto local creditors hold under the Model Law to open parallel plenary proceedings under domestic law in the face of a COMI foreign main proceeding, so too does the EU Regulation allow local creditors (technically, any creditors) to open "secondary proceedings" under local insolvency law (per the above example, a French insolvency proceeding after the UK-COMI-ed debtor's main proceeding).[65] These secondary proceedings apply their own substantive bankruptcy laws of distribution and the like, further muting the universalist inroads of the Regulation. (The Regulation also has a standard public policy "escape clause" mirroring the Model Law.)[66]

III. ASSESSING THE ROLE OF SOFT LAW IN ADVANCING UNIVERALISM

The state of affairs of the cross-border insolvency legal system as it now stands is thus "somewhat" universalist – certainly dramatically more so than before the roll-out of the Model Law and the EU Regulation. But there is a deliberately vague, inchoate nature to the state of the law (demonstrating the rub of soft law). The parameters of the public policy carveout, the definition and application of "adequate protection," and so forth have been left unspecified, for courts and parties to hash out in litigation (or render moot by settlement on the courthouse steps). This might be considered yet another aspect of "softness" of the law. A key theme to the acceptability of the Model Law has been leaving difficult questions unanswered to assuage passage. Leaving questions vaguely answered constitutes a friendly amendment to that approach. (As discussed below, however, it is not without risk.)

A. Public Policy (Not) Gone Wild

The success of this nascent regime has seen fits and starts but for the most part has been encouraging. Two questions might be asked to test this encouragement: first, have cross-border restructurings been facilitated since the completion of these instruments; and second, have those restructurings evinced a universalist bent? The first question is hard to answer empirically, but certainly on an anecdotal review of headlines and war stories, the cooperation in multinational corporate insolvencies has been widespread and highly visible.[67] The second question is closer, but signs nevertheless augur positively.

One useful metric for the second question whether the Model Law regime has allowed its incipient universalism to take flight is to look at the usage of the public policy exception. Territorialists might opine that in any case in which there is even a marginal difference of dividend based on substantive law (or asset concentration) a local court will try to shoehorn a foreign request for assistance into the public policy exception and deny assistance, thereby protecting the local players (and local turf). By contrast, universalists hope for restrained application of the public policy escape. Whose predictions have been borne out?

Consider first the historical backdrop using the United States as an example. Before the Model Law, comity was king, albeit semi-codified in the U.S. Bankruptcy Code through former section 304.[68] There, U.S. bankruptcy courts were allowed to offer assistance to foreign proceedings on a discretionary basis and pursuant to a list of factors enumerated by statute.[69] One of them, 'distribution of assets substantially in accordance with the provisions of this title,' presented a similar question.[70]

Would courts find any trivial deviation in distribution from U.S. law fatal, or would they take a more permissive (perhaps "cosmopolitan") approach? On its strictest read, any deviation from U.S. law would preclude cooperation with a foreign representative, and so a universalist approach would be impossible absent substantive convergence of bankruptcy laws, a fantasy not yet achieved but a topic for another chapter perhaps.[71] Although there were some notable exceptions,[72] U.S. courts for the most part were willing to defer to foreign insolvency cases even when to do so resulted in differing creditor outcomes.[73]

Thus, the historical practice suggests a predisposition to take the universalist invitation of the Model Law and run with it (at least in the United States). There might have been backlash, but the initial reports indicate that the public policy clause has not been a rule-swallowing exception. Deployment has been restrained. Sticking to the U.S. experience, we can look at an important exemplar, *Mansfield*. In a seminal case stemming from the market collapse of the commercial paper-lending markets and a Canadian-COMI-ed restructuring proceeding under the CCAA, a Canadian representative tested U.S. willingness to allow departure from its own substantive bankruptcy laws in aid of enforcing a comprehensive reorganization designed in Canada.[74] There, the Canadian debtor secured multiple constituency buy-in for a plan, but because of the inter-connectedness of the commercial paper market participants, a global release was sought by non-debtor, third-party financiers not themselves in bankruptcy. The issue was fully litigated in the Canadian courts (up through appeals) and eventually resolved in favor of the debtor's plan and the non-debtors' releases, finding sufficient flexibility in the substantive provisions of the CCAA to permit the plan's unusual terms of discharging non-debtors from liability.[75]

When matters came down to New York for enforcement by injunctions of the releases against parties with U.S. connections through Chapter 15, objectors implored the U.S. court to find the third-party releases violative of public policy. The court would have none of it. Expressly discussing the necessity of comity and appreciation of foreign insolvency law and its differences, the court made clear that the mere impermissibility of the non-debtor releases under U.S. domestic bankruptcy law (actually a source of some contention and circuit division)[76] was not an impediment to the enforcement of the Canadian orders as appropriate relief under the Model Law.[77] Put another way, mere deviation from substantive U.S. bankruptcy law – even with distributional consequences (profound ones – discharge, no less!) – did not equate to a transgression of fundamental public policy worthy of triggering the escape clause. In crafting its holding, the U.S. court underscored both the need for a procedural focus (remarking at how the Canadian proceedings were cognate common law ones with full and fair trial and appellate procedure) and on the need to accept substantive differences of law in the international bankruptcy context and the related need to cabin the public policy exception of section 1506 strictly.[78]

Mansfield is a representative U.S. case in terms of the strict construction of the public policy exception. Contrary examples are few, but exist. For example, in the *Toft* case, the court found a violation of public policy by a German insolvency representative's request to get access to the debtor's email, which may have triggered criminal liability in the United States.[79] *Toft* was almost apologetic in its refusal to cooperate with the German representative and shows how courts are striving for limiting principles, not stretching for plausible grounds to dig in territorialist heels.[80] That said, the U.S. record is not unblemished. In one much-discussed U.S opinion, *Qimonda*, the trial court held that a German insolvency representative's request to enforce an order rejecting executory intellectual property licenses (as licensor) of U.S. licensees would violate fundamental public policy because the aggrieved licensees would only have an ordinary claim for damages as opposed to the special quasi-property remedy accorded under Section 365(n) of the U.S. Bankruptcy Code (which effectively allows the licensees to "reject the rejection" in part and continue exercising certain rights under the license).[81] The opinion delved into congressional history and divined an intent to foster entrepreneurial activity through protection of intellectual property licensees, elevating such incentivizing to fundamental U.S. policy. The opinion was ridiculed by most U.S. bankruptcy commentators as expanding the public policy exception to near-comical extent,[82] and its reasoning (although not its ultimate holding of non-cooperation) was abandoned on appeal.[83] All in all, it is fair to say the public policy exception has been interpreted narrowly in the United States, vindicating the Model Law's soft law potential to advance true deference to foreign insolvency laws by U.S. courts hosting ancillary proceedings. Harder law requiring cooperation was not necessary, and indeed could have proved destructive.

B. Beyond (and Avoiding) Public Policy: Adequate Protection with Restraint

Going beyond the public policy question to other territorialist safeguards, the U.S. experience has been similarly cooperative, for the most part restricting non-relief to egregious cases and not, as territorialists may have feared (or hoped), running wild with excuses to reject requests for relief.[84] A good example of the facts warranting non-cooperation involves the Mexican reorganization ("concurso") of Vitro, S.A.B. de C.V.[85] In *Vitro*, a Mexican-COMI-ed glass company sought to restructure its debt through a Mexican consensual, super-majoritarian voting regime analogous but far from identical to U.S. Chapter 11. A group of dissident bondholders based in the United States voted no and launched numerous objections in Mexico, complaining bitterly. Faring poorly in Mexico, they waged a more successful home court campaign in the United States, striving to convince the U.S. bankruptcy court in Chapter 15 neither to recognize nor to offer relief to the Mexican insolvency representative from the foreign main proceeding. They lost on the first front – it was, after all a foreign main proceeding afoot in the debtor's COMI under the Model Law – and so the U.S. court recognized the proceeding and opened up a Chapter 15 case.[86] But when it came time to enforce the *concurso* (through injunctive relief to bind the U.S. creditors and administer the U.S.-based property), the U.S. bankruptcy court balked, siding with the bondholders.[87]

Among the grounds argued to deny cooperation was, first, violation of fundamental policy. The section 1506 argument was launched on two general grounds: fundamental bankruptcy policy and fundamental due process. The gist of the latter assault was that the Mexican system, at least in this specific case, was crooked. Colorful facts about the questionable process used in the appointment of the insolvency representative and judicial ex parte procedures were all trotted out to disparage the result of the vote.[88] The gist of the first attack was directed to the voting rules that enabled the *concurso* to pass the Mexican thresholds for acceptance in the first place. Specifically, the company had (allegedly) manufactured inter-corporate debt owing from the debtor to affiliates sufficient to make those affiliates dominate the creditor vote and pass the plan. Worse, the corporate affiliates had guaranteed bondholder debt, and the *concurso* sought to dissolve those guarantees (a development the affiliates enthusiastically supported in casting their dominating votes to approve the plan). All these attributes were on the heels of a distribution proposal that offered equity around 50% of its stake while bypassing the creditors.

The *Vitro* U.S. bankruptcy court denied cooperation in light of these facts in finding a violation of bankruptcy policy.[89] But, again, the pains the court underwent to constrain the scope of its grounds for non-cooperation were striking—they come off as genuine, not feigned. For example, it assiduously avoided even engaging the corruption-based challenges (doubtless in the service of international diplomacy) and instead anchored its refusal to cooperate on the perversion of bankruptcy policy resulting from equity holders stripping off guarantees on the premise of a "consensual" waiver of the absolute priority rule by affiliated insider-creditors who were the obligors on the guarantees.[90] Thus, while *Vitro* nominally stands as an American example of non-cooperation under the Model Law regime, its opinion is intentionally narrow and draws attention to the case's specific and egregious facts (and even throws in some platitudes about Mexican insolvency law generally).[91] Indeed, on direct affirmance, the Court of Appeals downscaled the case even more, noting that the public policy clause did not even need to be reached because whatever the definition of "adequate protection" of creditors requires, this surely was not it.[92]

Vitro is an important U.S. precedent under Chapter 15, not just in its holding but its analysis, because it shows how rarely courts want to deny cooperation, and when they do, how they want to avoid suggesting another country's bankruptcy laws violate public policy.[93] The opinion is sensitive to distributional differences and sensitive to cabining (or avoiding) the public policy out. Its facts were truly striking, and for the most part it does not seem to have set the international community on edge about a U.S. backslide toward parochial territorialism.[94] Accordingly, *Vitro* is generally accepted and drew little of the scorn reserved for *Qimonda*. And taking

Vitro and the public policy cases collectively, the soft law gamble of the Model Law (at least in the United States) seems to have paid off. By leaving wide latitude for courts to cooperate, or not, it took a risk that the virtues of the universalist system would attract states not to unravel the regime through territorialist interpretations and exploitations of the slack in the system. That has happened, with universalist cooperation increasing.[95]

C. Universalism Doctrine Strengthening: COMI Construction

Developing alongside these heady delineations of the public policy exceptions to cooperation and the giving of content to the adequate protection of creditors standard has been seemingly more workaday but equally important precedent-building on the doctrinal constructs that operationalize the Model Law's soft law regime. The easiest example of this is the COMI concept. Cases both under the EU Regulation and the Model Law have had occasion to weigh in on what "COMI" means, such as how and when its presumption of registered office should be rebutted. The *Bear Stearns* case, for instance, established that the Model Law's presumption of registered office being the COMI is not a burden of persuasion that if unchallenged by the litigants will ripen into a finding of fact. The opinion holds, on the contrary, that a recognizing judge has an independent obligation (or at least prerogative) to assess the bona fides of COMI and allow the court to deflate the presumption sua sponte in the instance of a true "letter box" corporation that is officially registered in one jurisdiction but has no operational or other significance there.[96] *Bear Stearns* and its progeny put meat on the bones of COMI. EU Regulation cases have done so too, such as the famous *Parmalat* case,[97] which cross-fertilize the Model Law jurisprudence due to the same COMI standard and the injunction under 11 U.S.C. § 1508 to consider the foreign origins of Chapter 15. Ancillary doctrines are also being worked out in the case law, such as timing rules for determining COMI when there is COMI migration.[98]

D. Toward (But Not Yet) Distributional Universalism: *Nortel*

The most dramatic recent deployment of the Model Law's soft law regime has been with the sprawling *Nortel* bankruptcy.[99] Nortel Networks was a Canadian-COMI-ed telecommunications behemoth with arms spread all around the globe, including a good chunk of assets and operations in the United States. When the company collapsed, it had viable business lines and attractive IP portfolios. Under a strictly territorialist system, it is deeply implausible this value could have been preserved as assets would be carved up jurisdiction by jurisdiction at the behest of local creditors.

Recognizing this, and using the procedural tools offered by the Model Law in the various relevant jurisdictions, the stakeholders entered into a comprehensive protocol to coordinate treatment of the debtor's assets.[100] To be clear, this was not the archetypal universalist response. That is, they did not open a foreign main proceeding in Canada and ancillary proceedings (e.g., Chapter 15) in other jurisdictions to seek cooperation with that Canadian COMI proceeding. This decision was likely for a couple of reasons. First, the corporate group network of Nortel contained individual corporate affiliates – and not just shells, but real, thickly capitalized subsidiaries – that were COMI-ed outside Canada. Thus, for example, Nortel's U.S. subsidiary was very likely COMI-ed in the United States. Because the Model Law at present does not have rich tools for dealing with corporate groups, it is not clear there was anything much better that could be done than different proceedings in the different COMIs. The second reason is that there was likely too much money at stake for non-Canadian creditors to sign on up front to ancillary treatment when the COMI issue was up for grabs.[101] That said, the *Nortel* bankruptcy did deploy the procedural framework of the Model Law to implement a worldwide approach to maximizing value of the assets: essentially an agreement to permit a worldwide sale of the assets irrespective of national borders. This was effected through the execution of "protocols" signed by the insolvency representatives and debtors of the respective jurisdictions and ratified by courts conducting proceedings where necessary.[102] The non-Canadian proceedings were thus "parallel" plenary proceedings.[103]

Critical to the success of the *Nortel* protocols was taking a page from the incrementalist, soft law handbook of the Model Law. Specifically, the multinational agreement deferred resolving questions of allocation of the sale proceeds (i.e., the ever-vexing distributional question), and instead focused on the value-maximization question, garnering consensus that the assets should be sold as going-concerns whenever possible. This plan worked with remarkable success: complete business lines were sold from the *Nortel* estates, and a syndicate of suitors ended up buying the residual IP portfolio that remained after the business line sales.[104] Had the stakeholders insisted on hammering out an allocation rule of which creditors would get which share of the proceeds up front, the contentiousness of that issue would likely have doomed the cooperative impulses necessary to get the worldwide sale approach off the ground.

Act II of the *Nortel* proceedings, however, was less glamorous. Under the terms of the protocols, the stakeholders after sale were to mediate a mutually acceptable allocation of the sale proceeds to the local bankruptcy estates around the world. That mediation failed spectacularly. Legions of lawyers and experts tore through hundreds of millions of debtor assets in a mad squabble over who should get what.[105] Because the protocol planned for the worst, it instructed that if the stakeholders could not agree in mediation, the matter would be litigated in all relevant courts, which is what came to pass, with full-blown trials. The soft law of the Model Law had nothing to say on distribution, and so *Nortel* appeared to demonstrate the best potential of the Model Law at the outset of the case but then the limitations of its softness as the mediation unraveled in Act II.

But that recast is too negative. In fact, even though the mediation failed and the Model Law had no fast rule for allocating proceeds (universalist or otherwise), its procedural mechanisms helped coordinate the disputed parallel proceedings, with the Canadian CCAA judge and U.S. Chapter 11 judge conducting, effectively, a "joint trial," with simultaneous broadcasts and inter-judge conferences. Indeed, the two courts coordinated their decisions to be handed down at the same time. While the Model Law did not force the issue of choice of law, it at least facilitated a mechanism by which two judges who had no obligation to defer to one another could think and work together on judicial questions commended to their own sovereign courtrooms. Lo and behold, they arrived "independently" at the same decision on the merits of allocation (each venting with some chiding at the necessity for a litigated resolution).[106] And moreover, that decision was to share the assets internationally, regardless of territorial location.[107]

The quasi-paradoxical outcome of the *Nortel* case is thus fairly seen as yet another (partial) triumph for universalism. For although the ability to launch parallel plenary proceedings was earlier described as a territorialist concession to local creditors necessary to pass the Model Law,[108] the outcome of the *Nortel* "distribution" dispute lurched unabashedly universalist.[109] What both the Canadian and American judges concluded, after hearing an onslaught of experts and parties testify on the appropriate way to carve up the spoils, was that the assets should be presumptively shared on a worldwide pro rata basis – the crux of universalism – albeit on an "estate by estate" basis.[110] This solution can perhaps be seen as 2/3 universalist (evincing more incremental universalism). The foundation of the judges' reasoning was that substance should dominate over form and that Nortel's intellectual property assets were the result of an interconnected worldwide research web of corporate affiliates. Therefore, although, for example, many of the patents were held in a Canadian parent, that consolidation of title holding served purely logistical purposes and it would be neither a fair nor sensible way to divide the gain to suggest the Canadian estate should get 100% of the IP sale proceeds. The courts emphasized, for example, that the intellectual property accrued from research labs around the world.[111] (The Canadians were not alone in their self-serving allocation proposal. So too did U.S. creditors argue that the proceeds should be allocated on the basis of national proportionate revenue to the Nortel network, a metric that to nobody's surprise skewed strongly American.)[112]

Recall that universalism's insistence on the application of one substantive corporate bankruptcy law worldwide is premised on reducing credit costs. Its principal cost concern – that creditors should not squander resources monitoring asset movement across borders (or hamstring debtors with covenants) – translates into a distributional proposition that creditors' payouts from a multinational debtor should not depend on the possibly random situation of assets in one country over another. *Nortel*'s repudiation of strict territorial location – rejecting nearly out of hand the formal situation of the IP assets in Canada – is a telling embrace of universalism by judges forced to examine the pragmatics and function of an actual modern cross-border conglomerate. The U.S. court's focus on actual creditor reliance as opposed to presumed reliance based on formalism was revealed in comments noting that while creditors who had relied on distinct corporate entities could be protected, most likely knew they were dealing with one big beast.[113] Those familiar with the American doctrine of substantive consolidation might find this vector of analysis familiar. Interestingly, however, the U.S. court, mindful of governing appellate precedent, tripped over itself to insist it was *not* effecting substantive consolidation. (This is why the case was only 2/3 universalist.) Rather, the court said it was pooling the assets globally but then dividing those assets pro rata (by claims allowed) into the respective national (territorial) bankruptcy estates.[114] So, as a simplified example assuming only two countries, if there were $X in claims lodged in the U.S. proceeding and $2X in Canada, 2/3 of the proceeds would go to the Canadian creditors and 1/3 to the U.S. ones. In a world where creditors are sophisticated enough to file in either jurisdiction, however, this essentially *is* universalism for purposes of asset allocation. But where there is a difference in distributional rules, then the allocation does have contra-universalist tension. For example, if a favored class of creditors has priority under Canadian law, but not U.S. law, then they do better by having their priority attach to 2/3 of the debtor's assets. This is worse for the Canadian creditors than pure universalism, in which their Canadian priority would be exported to all the debtor's assets worldwide, but better than a situation in which assets physically within Canada constituted less than 2/3 of the worldwide pot. Thus, the *Nortel* case can only be described as "mostly" universalist but not completely so. (Accordingly, 2/3 seems like a helpful if arbitrary characterization.)

The "estate by estate" qualifier on the global sharing of assets was not the only holdback from full universalism in *Nortel*. For example, the courts also carved out cash on hand from the global consolidation and said each jurisdiction's cash on hand would stay within its estate, a clearly territorialist outcome – and somewhat odd given the findings of fact regarding interrelated cash management practices that treated the conglomerate as one giant entity.[115] Moreover, to defuse any concerns of substantive consolidation, the courts held that inter-corporate debt would be recognized as claims (and join the pro rata distribution) as would cross-corporate guarantees, outcomes that might not obtain under substantive consolidation.[116] On balance, however, the joint judicial opinions tilt unambiguously universalist, albeit tentatively and incrementally so: world-wide sharing of assets and pro rata distribution of spoils, but still ultimate allocation to territorial estates for distribution.

* * *

Taking all these case law data points together, culminating in *Nortel*, we can conclude that the Model Law has been developing a rich precedent book to flesh out some of its (deliberately) unspecified areas in a polycentric and non-binding incrementalist fashion. This success has vindicated its soft law approach. By allowing the content of the law to be worked out over time in a "jurisprudentially market-tested" manner rather than hammered out *ex ante*, the Model Law elided likely disagreements that were surmountable over time. This approach capitalizes upon the "dynamic" nature of cross-border insolvency law. The dynamic prediction is that the resistance of territorially inclined states is not static but likely to erode over time. This is not just because territorialist states are mistaken not to embrace the normative superiority of a universalist system (some commentators have gone so far to cast territorialist states as "troglodytes"),[117] and the passage of time will allow them to see the errors of their ways, but because part of their resistance to universalism is an unfounded risk aversion to the consequences of ceding some jurisdictional autonomy to foreign insolvency law. One Japanese commentator noting Japan's historically territorial mood has evocatively described this territorialist characteristic as "fear."[118] Acclimation and repetition are both means by which the reflexive fear of foreign law will dissipate. Thus, by skipping over some of the tough bits and deferring to follow-on explication through a developing casebook, the Model Law wisely allowed the confrontations to be put off to a time when the fear index of universalism would be lowered. This gambit paid off as seen by the increasing accommodation of foreign cooperation.[119] The soft law approach seems to have thus been a success for universalism.

IV. THE RISK OF SOFTNESS AND UNIVERSALISM'S FUTURE: WHITHER THE NEW REFORMS?

The *Nortel* case is important in showing the ascent of universalism under the present regime. But it also reveals what might be considered both the rosy and dark narratives that can flow therefrom. The happy story is one of directional incrementalism: that through case-by-case development of the contours of the Model Law regime, the system will be fleshed out to be increasingly universalist as time progresses. The mechanisms of that advancement will be case law at first but ultimately amendments and revisions to the underlying documents. (Indeed, the EU has just concluded its self-mandated review of the Regulation and enacted amendments.)[120] "Modified" universalism will relax its need to modify the universal application of one substantive bankruptcy law and eventually give way to the enlightened world of full universalism. That is the happy story.

There is, however, another version of the future. The sadder version is that the reason the Model Law was a compromise between universalism and territorialism is that there are certain bridges that sovereignty-conscious territorialist states will never cross, and full universalism is just untenable absent radical changes in legal cultures and domestic insolvency laws. If that is so, there is no incrementalist path at all – or at best univeralism will incrementally ascend the asymptote of Zeno but never arrive at its quixotic goal. On this view, future reform efforts will sputter if pushed toward further universalism, much to the dismay of those seeking to reduce the costs of corporate credit. Even the past success of the soft law approach – as mutual fund prospectuses counsel – is no assurance of future results.

How are we to know which narrative is more likely? We might be able to gather some evidence on which path is unfolding because we are in the midst of a new wave of reform on the first-round regime of the Model Law and EU Insolvency Regulation. That is, UNCITRAL is considering new model laws on further insolvency-related matters, some of which may be implemented by way of amendments to the Model Law itself.[121] And the EU Insolvency Regulation has undertaken a round of just-enacted amendments (in the middle of 2015).[122] Complementing these are other soft law efforts, most notably the Global Principles joint project of the ALI and III,[123] which includes a path-breaking choice-of-law annex that tackles some of the thorniest issues in cross-border insolvency.[124] Thus, to see the new directions of cross-border insolvency law – and whether the universalist promise of the soft law regime is being realized – we must look at these reform efforts to see whether they are trending universalist or have hit a territorialist stalling point.

The starting point with gauging the vector of these current reforms is to understand what is at play, i.e., what has been attracting clamor for change. Several clusters of insolvency law come to the fore. First, widespread consensus, even by the most enthusiastic defenders of the Model Law, is that it provides no clear guidance on what to do with corporate groups.[125] How to deal with the insolvency of a multinational corporation's often-integrated web of corporate subsidiaries and affiliates, especially when those affiliates if taken on standalone bases are COMI-ed in different jurisdictions, remains a difficult puzzle. Second, there is the oft-avoided question of choice of law and its distributional consequences that proved so intractable in *Nortel*. Third, there are the more mechanical issues, such as the previously discussed contours of the definition of COMI, that hunger for elaboration. Finally, there are the general communication and cooperation provisions that are purely procedural. Here, too, stakeholders have pressed for more.[126] Each of these "reform clusters" can be assessed in turn.

Taking the simplest first, the procedural provisions continue the march toward greater communication between courts, which surely is consistent with the advance of universalism. (Greater communication yields greater acclimation.) The EU Insolvency Regulation further encourages communications and in some instances lands affirmative obligations on courts or insolvency representatives to communicate.[127]

Second, the mechanical definitions are being similarly refined to flesh out the COMI construct. For example, the Insolvency Regulation amendments take a stance on the timing issue for COMI migration and formalize what had been the dominant test in case law (itself taken from a form of quasi-official preamble text)[128] that turns on creditor reliance and objective expectations of corporate seat.[129] All this augurs well for universalism and vindicates the incrementalist approach.

But this is the lowest hanging fruit. What of the distributional rub, namely, choice of law? UNCITRAL has yet to touch it with a ten-foot pole in its Model Law.[130] The revisions to the EU Insolvency Regulation have also for the most part been underwhelming, although there has been some movement. The revised instrument still recognizes the carveout-based system but has now focused carveouts on the "major" areas, such as labor law, secured credit rights, set-off, and the like.[131] Most tantalizing and candid is a concession and aspiration in the amendments' preamble stating that substantive bankruptcy law remains too divergent and sensitive to roll out universalism at present and so the carveouts must remain.[132] It is paired with an expressed hope that the next time around when reconsideration is mandated the carveouts might be ready for retirement.[133]

Other universalist inroads have been made in this current round of reform. For example, although too technical for the scope of this chapter, there have been modifications to secondary proceedings, the territorialist veto entitlements under the Regulation.[134] In brief terms, there are some universalist steps forward and backward but mostly forward on secondary proceedings. Secondary proceedings can now be used to support a corporate reorganization (not just liquidation),[135] and a sort of jurisdictional hierarchy is emerging whereby the insolvency representative of the secondary proceeding is partially beholden to COMI court insolvency representative.[136] Finally, the COMI court is now allowed to defer to the substantive bankruptcy law (e.g., priority) of the secondary proceedings in crafting a plan in the main proceeding.[137] This final addition might sound like a step backward toward territorialism by elevating the non-COMI (*lex secondus*) bankruptcy law to receive even greater effect in the multi-jurisdictional proceeding than it currently receives, but that is misleading. The concession is made with the over-arching goal of *reducing* the incidence of secondary proceedings with their disruptive transaction costs and parochial expressive costs.[138] These secondary proceedings revisions, while not earth-shattering, do seem consonant with (and indeed incrementally advance) the universalist agenda. Moreover, as alluded to briefly above, the even-softer ALI/III Global Principles (softer because they are just academic recommendations and do not even have the governmental imprimatur of UNCITRAL) go further and suggest reducing the number of carveout areas from *lex fori concursus*.[139] They may well have an effect on future reforms.

Finally, the corporate groups issue is being advanced more in the UNCITRAL domain than in the EU amendments. There, UNCITRAL is presently wrestling with an addendum to the Model Law that would deal with "group solutions" to cross-border defaults.[140] While the project is still in formation, proposals have been put forward by the UNCITRAL Secretariat to enable a "group representative" to design a "group solution" for a corporate bankruptcy, and, importantly, to allow corporate subsidiaries to participate in the group solution without necessarily having to open individual insolvencies in their own COMI jurisdictions.[141] As mentioned, it is early days, so nobody knows yet where this might go. The relevant point for this analysis of the soft law approach's success is that where law is softest – UNCITRAL and model laws – it seems to be tackling the most urgent and difficult subjects in cross-border insolvency reform. (On "the merits," the proposals are universalist in ceding more jurisdictional autonomy to other jurisdictions, here, the "group solution" court.) Incrementalism thus seems to have taken a foothold and blazed a path which may well now prove dependency-attracting. Specifically, crafting an international treaty on the treatment of corporate groups in cross-border insolvency now appears to be a methodological non-starter. Rather, due to the success of the Model Law, the logical starting point is building upon the soft law scaffolding already laid down by UNCITRAL.

In sum, the direction of current reforms seems to continue toward universalism, an important development for those who believe corporate insolvency law should strive to reduce credit costs. Those reforms themselves have been incremental, and their vitality builds upon the success of prior efforts. Transformative among these has been the UNCITRAL Model Law, with its deliberately soft(ish) law approach, both methodologically of avoiding a comprehensive treaty, and substantively in terms of its incomplete resolution of all possible bankruptcy law issues. By recognizing the likely dynamic nature of amenability toward cross-border cooperation in insolvency law, the UNCITRAL approach has used discretion as the better part of valor and led, perhaps somewhat serendipitously, to an ultimately more universalist system than we might otherwise have ever dreamed were possible. And the current round of reforms seems to be taking this potential and running with it (or at least walking with it). While universalism remains modified, and its ultimate realization a long way off, the soft law approach continues to reap success and move the ball further up the normatively desired field.

NOTES

* The author appreciates the seemingly endless research assistance from James Thurman, Michigan J.D. Class of 2015, whose work on two articles transcended his graduation. Due to the ever-shifting law in this field, this chapter has not incorporated analysis of its most recent developments, including, for example, UNCITRAL's 2018 completion of a Model Law on Recognition and Enforcement of Cross-Border Insolvency-Related Judgments (and the judicial decisions of some jurisdictions that served as its inspiration).

1. For example, the concept of "synthetic secondary proceedings," arising from my work and that of Ted Janger, found its way into the EU's recent amendments to its landmark Insolvency Regulation. *See* Regulation 2015/848, of the European Parliament and of the Council of 20 May 2015 on insolvency proceedings, art. 36, 2015 O.J. (L 141) (EU), http://eur-lex.europa.eu/legal-content/EN/TXT/PDF/?uri=CELEX:32015R0848&from=EN [hereinafter EU Insolvency Regulation]. *See generally* John A.E. Pottow, *A New Role for Secondary Proceedings in International Bankruptcies*, 46 Tex. Int'l L.J. 579 (2011); Edward J. Janger, *Virtual Territoriality*, 48 Colum. J. Transnat'l L. 401 (2010).
2. *See* Bob Wessels & Ian Fletcher, Int'l Insolvency Inst., Global Principles for Cooperation in International Insolvency Cases 151 (2010) (noting the pitfalls of compromise by saying "the best should not be allowed to become the enemy of the good").
3. For example, in amending its Insolvency Regulation, the E.U. championed the theory of universalism but bemoaned the necessary concessions to praxis: "This Regulation

acknowledges the fact that as a result of widely differing substantive laws, it is not practical to introduce insolvency proceedings with universal scope throughout the Union." EU Insolvency Regulation, *supra* note 1, at 22nd Recital.

4. *See* Jay Lawrence Westbrook, *Theory and Pragmatism in Global Insolvencies: Choice of Law and Choice of Forum*, 65 Am. Bankr. L.J. 457, 487 (1991) (discussing the Strasbourg Convention and the failed Brussels Convention); Todd Kraft & Allison Aranson, *Transnational Bankruptcies: Section 304 and Beyond*, 1993 Colum. Bus. L. Rev. 329 (1993) (discussing the challenges facing adoption of the International Bar Association's largely ignored Model International Insolvency Cooperation Act).
5. *See* U.N. Comm. On Int'l Trade Law, Model Law on Cross-Border Insolvency with Guide to Enactment, U.N. Sales No. E.99.V.3, art. 25 (1999) [hereinafter Model Law].
6. *See* EU Insolvency Regulation, *supra* note 1.
7. *See* Thomas H. Jackson & Robert E. Scott, *On the Nature of Bankruptcy: An Essay on Bankruptcy Sharing and the Creditors' Bargain*, 75 Va. L. Rev. 155, 158–60 (1989).
8. 11 U.S.C. § 541 (2012).
9. *See e.g.*, John A.E. Pottow, *Procedural Incrementalism: A Model for International Bankruptcy*, 45 Va. J. Int'l L. 935, 942 (2005).
10. *See e.g.*, *In re* Telegroup, Inc., 237 B.R. 87 (Bankr. D. N.J. 1999) (denying patent holder relief from stay to sue debtor for alleged post-petition patent infringement).
11. *See e.g.*, 40235 Washington St. Corp. v. Lusardi, 329 F.3d 1076, 1084 (9th Cir. 2003) (holding that conflict preemption precluded application of California statute governing validity of tax deeds because the statute conflicted with the automatic stay provision of the Bankruptcy Code); Walls v. Wells Fargo Bank, N.A., 276 F.3d 502, 510–11 (9th Cir. 2002) (holding that remedies for violation of discharge injunction under 11 U.S.C. §524 precluded claims under the federal Fair Debt Collection Practices Act). Criminal law probably fares best against bankruptcy. *See* 11 U.S.C. § 362(b)(1) (2012).
12. *See, e.g.*, *In re* Bristol Convalescent Home, Inc., 12 B.R. 448, 450 (Bankr. D. Conn. 1981) (holding that, contrary to the IRS's insistence, money owed to the debtor which the IRS had levied upon was in fact property of the debtor's estate and therefore subject to turnover under § 542).
13. *See e.g.*, 11 U.S.C. § 507 (2012).
14. *See* Andrew Guzman, *International Bankruptcy: In Defense of Universalism*, 98 Mich. L. Rev. 2177, 2196–8 (2000) (noting that although all regimes surveyed gave priority status to employee claimants, the status and amount of those claims varied country to country).
15. Jay Lawrence Westbrook, *A Global Solution to Multinational Default*, 98 Mich. L. Rev. 2276, 2284–5 (2000).
16. *See* Guzman, *supra* note 14, at 2199–204.
17. *See* Westbrook, *supra* note 15, at 2309. Indeed, pari passu distribution (tempered by voluntary contractual priority rearrangement) is likely the outcome of an approach focused on capital cost minimization, because, unless the parties have an affirmative reason to deviate from a ratable return, the avoidance of priority conflict and its attendant cost is a savings.
18. Lynn M. LoPucki, *The Case for Cooperative Territoriality in International Bankruptcy*, 98 Mich. L. Rev. 2216, 2239–42 (2000).
19. *See* Lynn M. LoPucki, Courting Failure: How Competition for Big Cases Is Corrupting the Bankruptcy Courts 217–21 (2006); Lynn M. LoPucki, *Universalism Unravels*, 79 Am. Bankr. L.J. 143, 143–4 (2005).
20. *See* Janger, *supra* note 1, at 409.
21. *See* LoPucki, *Universalism Unravels*, *supra* note 19, at 143–4. This argument ignores the collective action concerns animating the creditor's bargain theory of a statist solution, but such critique is beyond the scope of this discussion.
22. Professor Rasmussen has offered a third approach, "contractualism," which leaves the choice of law decision to the debtor, allowing corporate entities to select the regime to govern their insolvency proceeding in their corporate charters, but this contribution

is beyond the scope of our present focus. *See* Robert K. Rasmussen, *Resolving Transnational Insolvencies Through Private Ordering*, 98 Mich. L. Rev. 2252, 2254 (2000).

23. Pottow, *supra* note 9, at 947; *see generally* Frederick Tung, *Is International Bankruptcy Possible*, 23 Mich. J. Int'l L. 31 (2001); Guzman, *supra* note 14; Westbrook, *supra* note 15.
24. *In re* Maxwell Commc'n. Corp. plc, 93 F.3d 1036 (2d Cir. 1996).
25. The EU is not, strictly speaking, a sovereign entity because EU member states retain the power to opt out of EU regulations. Still, the Insolvency Regulation was adopted by all member states other than Denmark. *See* Westbrook, *supra* note 15, at 2280. Though beyond the scope of this chapter, it is notable that the Insolvency Regulation began as a convention but later took the form of a regulation due to the United Kingdom's sensitivity over mad cow disease. *See* E. Bruce Leonard, *The International Scene, The International Year in Review*, 2001 Am. Bankr. Inst. J. 34, 34.
26. *See, e.g.*, Andrew Guzman & Timothy Meyer, *Soft Law*, *in* The Research Handbook on the Economics of Public International Law 123 (Eugene Kontorovich & Francesco Parisi (eds), 2016).
27. The Enactment Guide states that the Model Law's "scope [is] limited to some procedural aspects of cross-border insolvency cases." *Guide to Enactment of the UNCITRAL Model Law on Cross-Border Insolvency*, ¶ 8, *reprinted in* 6 Tul. J. Int'l & Comp. L. 415 (1998). Additionally, commentators have noted that the Model Law does not even use the words "territorialism" or "universalism." *See* Pottow, *supra* note 9, at 961 n.106.
28. *See* Andre J. Berends, *The UNCITRAL Model Law on Cross-Border Insolvency: A Comprehensive Overview*, 6 Tul. Int'l & Comp. L. 309 (1998).
29. *See* Model Law, *supra* note 5, art. 25. The U.S. Bankruptcy Code mirrors the language of the Model Law. 11 U.S.C. § 1525.
30. Model Law, *supra* note 5, art. 8; *accord* 11 U.S.C. § 1508.
31. Jay Lawrence Westbrook, *Theory and Pragmatism in Global Insolvencies: Choice of Law and Choice of Forum*, 65 Am. Bankr. L.J. 457, 458 (1991).
32. *See generally* Model Law, *supra* note 5, arts. 25–7; 11 U.S.C. §§ 1525–15.
33. *See* Jay Lawrence Westbrook, *Chapter 15 at Last*, 79 Am. Bankr. L.J. 713, 719–20 (2005); Model Law, *supra* note 5, art. 17(2)(a); 11 U.S.C. § 1502(4).
34. *See* Miguel Virgos & Etienne Schmit, *Report on the Convention on Insolvency Proceedings*, arts. 16–148, 6500/96 (1996) ('Since the main proceedings can be opened only if the debtor has his centre of main interests in the State of the opening . . . the decision of the law of that state . . . should be respected by the other Member States, whose connection with the debtor is restricted to the existence of an establishment or assets.').
35. *See* Model Law, *supra* note 5, art. 2(b)-(c); 11 U.S.C. § 1502(4)-(5). "Main" and "non-main" do not exhaust the universe of cross-border insolvency proceedings. There is a third class of proceedings for debtors that do not meet the "establishment" requirement for a non-main proceeding. These oddities are beyond the scope of this enquiry. *See* Pottow, *supra* note 1, at 581.
36. *See* Model Law, *supra* note 5, art. 20 § 1(a)-(b); 11 U.S.C. § 1520(a)(1).
37. *See* Model Law, *supra* note 5, art. 21(1)(a)-(c).; 11 U.S.C. § 1521(a)-(c).
38. *See* Pottow, *supra* note 1, at 583 (defining "jurisdictional hierarchies" as systems "designed to subordinate the secondary proceeding and make them, aptly, secondary"). The selection of forum is not set in stone; the presumption of COMI is rebutted when the incorporation location is merely a sham, which serves as a proxy for forum shopping. *See* John A.E. Pottow, *Forum Shopping in Transnational Insolvency*, 32 Brook. J. Int'l L. 785, 793 (2007).
39. *See* Pottow, *supra* note 9, at 980–96 (discussing, among other things, notice provisions and the presumption of insolvency).
40. *See id.* at 969 ("[T]he Model Law, on the surface, appears to be a hybrid of sorts: partially universalist in outreach, but partially territorialist in retrenchment.").

41. *See* Model Law, *supra* note 5, arts. 25-26; 15 U.S.C. §§ 1525-27.
42. *See* Jay Lawrence Westbrook, *Multinational Enterprises in General Default: Chapter 15, The ALI Principles, and the EU Insolvency Regulation*, 76 Am. Bankr. L.J. 1, 17 (2002) (noting that Articles 28 and 29, which allow local proceedings to trump foreign proceedings under certain circumstances, were *sine qua non* of passing the Model Law).
43. *See, e.g.*, Model Law, *supra* note 5, art. 21(1)(e); 11 U.S.C. § 1521(a)-(b).
44. *See* Model Law, *supra* note 5, art. 17(1)-(2); 11 U.S.C. § 1517.
45. The automatic stay for foreign main proceedings arises from Article 20(1)(a), while discretionary interim relief, post-recognition relief, and relief under laws of the enacting state arise from articles 19, 21, and 7, respectively.
46. *See* Model Law, *supra* note 5, arts. 21.1(e)-21.2.
47. 11 U.S.C. § 507(a)(6) (2012).
48. Model Law, *supra* note 5, art. 22(1)-(2). The discretionary nature of the relief is not on its own enough to assuage territorially inclined states. This is because of agency costs and the possibility of renegade judges. The mere possibility that the Model Law could allow a judge to "go wild" would terrify policymakers from these states, and so the specific provisions built into the Model Law were necessary for their appeasement wholly apart from the discretionary nature of many of the relief provisions.
49. *See* Model Law, *supra* note 5, art. 21, ¶ 2; 15 U.S.C. § 1522(a). Note, this "adequate protection" is not coextensive with the safeguard for secured creditors under U.S. bankruptcy law. Congress used the term "sufficiently protected" here to avoid confusion. H.R. Rep. No. 109-31(I), at 115 (2005).
50. Some have. The recent U.K. case of *Cosco Bulk Carrier Co Ltd v. Armada Shipping SA*, [2011] EWHC 216 (Ch), 2011 WL 398130, casts some worry that even respected courts may fall victim to expansive insistence of foreign concordance with local law and even evince hostility to foreign procedures. The *Cosco* court held that a London arbitration between a Swiss debtor in a recognized foreign main proceeding from Switzerland and a British shipping company should continue over the foreign representative's objection and request for a stay. Referring to his discretion under the Model Law, the judge relied on the fact that the dispute would be governed by English shipping law and that London arbitrators would be more qualified. The court discounted the expense and delay of the arbitration, complaining that "the only reason why that has not occurred is because of the [foreign representative's] preference for some other, probably Swiss, method of dispute resolution." *Id.* at ¶¶ 52–60.
51. While there is no canonical definition of "margin of appreciation," the term generally refers to the latitude given to member states in observing conventions, initially applied to the European Convention on Human Rights. The term did not appear in the text of the Convention, but was first used in the Cyprus Case. *See* Greece v. the United Kingdom (The Cyprus Case) 2 Y.B. Eur. Conv. on H.R. 172 (1958–59) (Eur. Comm'n on H.R.).
52. *See e.g.*, *In re* Schimmelpenninck, 183 F.3d 347, 364 (5th Cir. 1999); *In re* Sivec SRL, 476 B.R. 310, 324 (Bankr. E.D. Okla. 2012); *In re* Petition of Garcia Avila, 296 B.R. 95, 112 (Bankr. S.D.N.Y. 2003).
53. For example, the parallel domestic plenary proceeding is restricted to assets within that country's territorial jurisdiction. *See* Model Law, *supra* note 5, art. 28; 11 U.S.C. § 1528. The Model Law thus cabins worldwide bankruptcy jurisdictional pretensions, such as found in the U.S. Code. *See* 11 U.S.C. § 541 (incorporating definition of "property of the estate" to include all property "wherever located and by whomever held").
54. *See, e.g.*, Restatement (Third) of Foreign Relations Law § 482(2)(d) (Am. Law Inst. 1987) ("A court in the United States need not recognize a judgment of the court of a foreign state if . . . the cause of action on which the judgment was based, or the judgment itself, is repugnant to the public policy of the United States or of the State where recognition is sought . . .").
55. *See* Model Law, *supra* note 5, art. 6; 11 U.S.C. § 1506.
56. *See e.g.*, Model Law, *supra* note 5, art. 13, note b.

57. *See* Pottow, *supra* note 9, at 986.
58. UNCITRAL maintains a list of the states that have enacted the model law, which now includes twenty-two states. *See* U.N. Comm'n on Int'l Trade Law, Status: UNCITRAL Model Law on Cross-border Insolvency (1997), http://www.uncitral.org/uncitral/en/uncitral_texts/insolvency/1997Model_status.html.
59. *See* U.N. Comm'n on Int'l Trade Law, Working Group V (Insolvency Law), Rep. of the Fourth International Insolvency Law Colloquium (Vienna, 16–18 December 2013), July 7–18, 2014, U.N. Doc. A/CN.9/815 (May 2, 2014) ("[P]rocedural centralization leaves open the issue of which legal question will be determined by the choice of forum (lex fori) and which will be left to the ordinary choice of law principles (lex situs). The Model Law is silent on this question . . .").
60. EU Insolvency Regulation, *supra* note 1, arts. 3, 19.
61. *Id.*, art. 7.
62. *See* EU Insolvency Regulation, *supra* note 1, at 33rd Recital.
63. *See* EU Insolvency Regulation, *supra* note 1, arts. 8-18.
64. *See id.*, art. 13. Because the operative section of Article 3, paragraph 2, only explicitly refers to laws 'applicable to the contract of employment' and confers power on courts in ancillary proceedings to "terminate and modify" them, the example above is merely an expository illustration.
65. EU Insolvency Regulation, *supra* note 1, art. 34.
66. *See id.*, art. 33.
67. The insolvency proceedings following the collapse of Lehman Brothers is a notable example. *See* Joseph Checkler, *Lehman Australia Files Chapter 15 Bankruptcy Petition in US*, Wall St. J. Blogs: Deal Journal Australia (Jan. 10, 2012, 4:40 PM), http://blogs.wsj.com/dealjournalaustralia/2012/01/10/lehman-australia-files-chapter-15-bankruptcy-petition-in-us/; Michael J. Fleming & Asana Sarkar, *The Failure Resolution of Lehman Brothers*, Fed. Res. Econ. Pol'y Rev., Dec. 2014, at 175, 175 ("More than eighty jurisdictions' insolvency laws applied to the non-U.S. Lehman Brothers entities . . .").
68. 11 U.S.C. § 304 (repealed 2005).
69. The factors courts considered under § 304 included just treatment of all holders of claims; protection of U.S. claim holders against the prejudice and inconvenience of foreign proceedings; prevention of fraudulent transfers; substantial accordance with U.S. bankruptcy distribution; comity; and opportunity for a fresh start for the individual whom the foreign proceeding concerns. *See* § 304(c); *cf.* 11 U.S.C. § 1507(b) (preserving [many of] these considerations in gauging certain discretionary relief).
70. *See* 11 U.S.C. § 304(c)(4).
71. *See* LoPucki, *supra* note 18, at 2217.
72. *See e.g.*, *In re* Treco, 240 F.3d 148 (2d Cir. 2001). Guided by the startling fact that the Bahamian administrators had devoured $8 million (USD) in fees on an estate of $10 million, the court denied deference to a Bahamian main proceeding under § 304(c)(4), on the appeal of a secured creditor founded solely on differential payout. *See id.* at 159–61.
73. *See e.g.*, *In re* Bd. Dirs. Telecom Arg., S.A., 528 F.3d 162 (2d Cir. 2008). Here, the court upheld the lower court's recognition of an Argentinian proceeding under § 304, despite the creditor's claim that Argentina's insolvency regime lacked protections available to creditors under U.S. law. *Id.* at 176 n.9.
74. *In re* Metcalfe & Mansfield Alt. Invs., 421 B.R. 685 (Bankr. S.D.N.Y. 2010).
75. *See id.* at 694.
76. The Second Circuit holds that bankruptcy courts may approve non-debtor releases under some circumstances by exercising their broad equitable powers under 11 U.S.C. § 105. *See In re* Drexel Burnham Lambert Grp. Inc., 960 F.2d 285 (2d Cir. 1992). In *In re* Zale Corp., 62 F.3d 746 (5th Cir. 1995), the Fifth Circuit distinguished *Drexel*, holding that, while temporary injunctions of third-party actions may be appropriate if the debtor and non-debtor enjoy an identity of interest or when the third-party action

would have an adverse effect on the ability of the debtor to reorganize, 11 U.S.C. § 524(e) does not permit permanent discharge of non-debtor liabilities because the statute extends only to discharge of claims against the debtor, and the proscription cannot be overcome by section 105. *See In re Zale Corp.*, 62 F.3d 746.

77. *See In re Metcalfe*, 421 B.R. at 694–700.
78. *See id.* at 697–8; *see also In re* Epherdra Prods. Liab. Litig., 349 B.R. 333, 336 (S.D.N.Y. 2006) (holding that Canadian court's order approving claims resolution procedure was entitled to recognition in part because the foreign procedure afforded claimants a fair and impartial proceeding).
79. *In re* Toft, 453 B.R. 186 (Bankr. S.D.N.Y. 2011).
80. The court noted that the powers sought by the foreign representative "go far beyond the powers that have traditionally been afforded to a U.S. estate representative." *Id.* at 198.
81. *In re* Qimonda AG, 462 B.R. 165 (Bankr. E.D. Va. 2011), *aff'd on other grounds*; Jaffe v. Samsung Elecs. Co., Ltd., 737 F.3d 14 (4th Cir. 2013).
82. *See e.g.*, Elizabeth Buckel, *Curbing Comity: the Increasingly Expansive Public Policy Exception of Chapter 15*, 44 Geo. J. Int'l L. 1281, 1301–03 (2013).
83. *See Jaffe*, 737 F.3d at 32. The Court of Appeals actually affirmed the lower court's decision on its finding of inadequate protection under § 1522 and thus declined to rule on the issue of the public policy exception. The Court of Appeals did concede that its decision indirectly furthered the public policy underlying 365(n). *See id.*
84. The general trend of cooperation between jurisdictions is borne out by the data and reflected in the literature. *See, e.g.*, Jay Lawrence Westbrook, University of Western Ontario, An Empirical Look at Chapter 15, 3 (2011). ("The data show that the United States courts are very strongly inclined to defer to foreign main proceedings within the intent of the Model Law and Chapter 15. Of the 253 cases that we found had reached a clear result, 237 resulted in recognition and only 12 in a denial of recognition."); Leah Barteld, *Cross-Border Bankruptcy and the Cooperative Solution*, 9 BYU Int'l Law & Mgmt. Rev. 27, 38 (2012) ("In addition to the regional arrangements now in existence in Southeast Asia, Latin America, Northern Europe, and Central Africa have structures in place for some form of cooperation."). I have not done my own recent study, but my intuition is that this cooperative trend is accelerating.
85. *In re* Vitro S.A.B. de CV, 701 F.3d 1031 (5th Cir. 2012), *aff'd on other grounds*, *id.*
86. *See In re* Vitro S.A.B. de C.V., 470 B.R. 408, 409 (Bankr. N.D. Tex. 2012), *aff'd*, 701 F.3d 1031 (5th Cir. 2012).
87. *In re* Vitro, S.A.B. de C.V., 473 B.R. 117, 133 (Bankr. N.D. Tex. 2012), *aff'd* 701 F.3d 1031 (5th Cir. 2012).
88. *See id.* at 132.
89. *See id.* at 133.
90. Responding to the bondholders' charges of corruption, the court made clear, "[T]his court has not seen evidence that the Mexican Proceeding is the product of corruption or that the LCM[*concurso*] is a corrupt process." *Id.* at 131. Instead, the court grounded its refusal on the fact that the plan provided for "drastically different treatment [from that given in a Chapter 11 proceeding] in that the bondholders receive a fraction of the amounts owed under the indentures from Vitro SAB and their rights against the other obligors were cut off." *Id.* at 132.
91. *See id.* at 133. ('Generally, reorganization pursuant to the LCM is found to be a fair process, worthy of respect.').
92. *See In re* Vitro S.A.B. de CV, 701 F.3d 1031, 1069–70 (5th Cir. 2012).
93. See *In re* Yukos Oil Co., 321 B.R. 396 (Bankr. S.D. Tex.) (finding cause to dismiss Chapter 11 case filed by Russian company under 11 U.S.C. § 1112 due to the company's minimal contacts with the United States).
94. *See e.g.*, Ramona Ortega, *A Cross-Border Insolvency Showdown:* Vitro's *Mexican Restructuring Plan Denied Comity in U.S. Bankruptcy Court*, Fordham J. Corp. L. Fin. Blog (July 13, 2012), https://news.law.fordham.edu/jcfl/2012/07/13/a-cross-border-insol

vency-showdown-vitros-mexican-restructuring-plan-denied-comity-in-u-s-bankruptcy -court/ ('Despite the Bankruptcy Court's refusal to extend comity, its decision seems to be influenced more by the specific terms of the reorganization plan rather than a revival of territorialism . . . .').

95. *See In re* Rede Energia S.A., 515 B.R. 69, 98–9 (Bankr. S.D.N.Y. 2014) (declining to apply public policy exception despite potential distributional differences because 'Brazilian bankruptcy law meets our fundamental standards of fairness and accords with the course of civilized jurisprudence.'). The scorecard is not perfect, of course. *See* Rubin v. Eurofinance SA [2012] UKSC 46, ¶ 130 (refusing to enforce a foreign avoidance action because such action 'would be only to the detriment of United Kingdom businesses without any corresponding benefit.'). *Id.*
96. *See In re* Bear Stearns High-Grade Structured Credit Strategies Master Fund, Ltd., 374 B.R. 122, 125–6 (Bankr. S.D.N.Y. 2007).
97. *See* Case C-341/04, *In re* Eurofood IFSC Ltd., 2006 E.C.R. I-3813, 3868, ¶¶ 34–5 (May 2, 2006) (citing a shell company's not carrying out business in the territory of the state of the registered office as a circumstance that would rebut the COMI presumption).
98. *See In re* Fairfield Sentry Ltd., 714 F.3d 127, 137 (2d Cir. 2013) (holding that a debtor's COMI should be determined based on its activities at or around the time the Chapter 15 petition is filed . . . [but] a court may consider the period between the commencement of the foreign insolvency proceeding and the filing of the Chapter 15 petition to ensure that a debtor has not manipulated its COMI in bad faith). *But see In re* Suntech Power Holdings Co., Ltd., 520 B.R. 399 (Bankr. S.D.N.Y. 2014) (holding that a foreign debtor's COMI at Chapter 15 filing was the Cayman Islands, despite the debtor's not having conducted any business there before filing).
99. *In re* Nortel Networks, Inc. 532 B.R. 494 (Bankr. D. Del. 2015); *In re* Nortel Networks Corp., 2015 CANLII 2987 (Can. O.N.S.C.), http://canlii.ca/t/ghtd6.
100. *See In re Nortel Networks, Inc.*, 532 B.R. at 531; *In re Nortel Networks, Corp.*, 2015 ONSC at ¶¶ 4-5.
101. The patent sale alone generated $4.5 billion, and the sale of Nortel's business lines netted another $3.285 billion. *In re Nortel Networks, Inc.*, 532 B.R. at 512-514; *In re Nortel Networks Corp.*, 2015 ONSC at ¶ 3.
102. *See In re Nortel Networks, Inc.*, 532 B.R. at 531–44; *In re Nortel Networks Corp.*, 2015 ONSC at ¶¶ 4–5.
103. *Cf.* 11 U.S.C. § 1528 (anticipating such proceedings).
104. The gargantuan asset portfolio was purchased by a consortium of tech giants Apple, Microsoft, Ericsson, Blackberry, Sony, and EMC. *See In re Nortel Networks, Inc.*, 532 B.R. at 502; *In re Nortel Networks Corp.*, 2015 ONSC at ¶ 41.
105. *See In re Nortel Networks, Inc.*, 532 B.R. at 550–51 ('The variance of the positions is of such magnitude that highly capable and responsible attorneys were unable, or in the heat of the fight were unwilling, to find a middle ground despite three extensive and costly mediations.').
106. *See id.* at 500 ("The Court can only speculate why the parties, all represented by the ablest of lawyers and sparing no expense, were unable to reach a settlement on allocation.").
107. *See id.* at 532; *In re Nortel Networks Corp.*, ¶ 258.
108. *See* Westbrook, *supra* note 42.
109. Quotation marks are used because technically ultimate distribution is left for each judge in his or her own jurisdiction to administer, presumably, but not necessarily, under local bankruptcy priority rules. This distinction might matter in instances of divergent priority rules. *See In re Nortel Networks, Inc.*, 532 B.R. at 534 ("[T]he Court is not ordering a consolidated or coordinated global distribution . . . Each Estate will distribute as appropriate, through a plan process within the bounds of the applicable law."). For detailed discussion of the universalist consequences of this seemingly territorial aspect of the *Nortel* case, see John A.E. Pottow, *Two Cheers for Universalism:*

Nortel's *Nifty Novelty*, *in* Annual Review of Insolvency Law 333 (Janis P. Sarra & Barbara Romaine (eds), 2015).

110. *See In re Nortel Networks, Inc.*, 532 B.R. at 532–50.
111. *See id.* at 500; *In re Nortel Networks Corp.*, 2015 ONSC at ¶ 16.
112. *See In re Nortel Networks, Inc.*, 532 B.R. at 547–9.
113. *See id.* at 522, 531, 559.
114. *See id.* at 534.
115. *Compare id.* at 532, 506 n.38 (presenting documents detailing debtor's "Global Cash Pooling," but nonetheless refusing to substantively consolidate so court could "respect the corporate separateness of the [subsidiaries] by recognizing cash in hand"), *with In re Nortel Networks Corp.*, 2015 ONSC at ¶¶ 218, 258(4) (noting also 'the existence and operation of a centralized cash-management system,' but equally holding each estate should 'continue to hold that cash and deal with it in accordance with its administration.').
116. *See In re Nortel Networks, Inc.*, 532 B.R. at 534; *In re Nortel Networks Corp.*, 2015 ONSC at ¶ 214.
117. *See* Pottow, *supra* note 9, at 992.
118. Sohsuke Takahashi, The Reality of the Japanese Legal System for Cross-Border Insolvency – Driven by Fear of Universalism 67–72 (March 14, 2011) (unpublished manuscript) (on file with the International Insolvency Institute).
119. *See e.g.*, *In re* Cozumel Caribe, S.A. de C.V., 508 BR. 330 (Bankr. S.D.N.Y. 2014) (rejecting a creditor's motion to terminate a recognition order as violative of public policy despite serious doubts as to the propriety of the actions of the foreign representative); *In re* Irish Bank Resolution Corporation Ltd., 538 B.R. 692 (D. Del. 2015) (holding Irish proceeding qualified for recognition as foreign main proceeding and that creditor's unsubstantiated claims regarding deprivation of due process and aggrandizement of debtor, a bank nationalized by the Irish government, was insufficient to satisfy the narrow public-policy exception).
120. *See* EU Insolvency Regulation, *supra* note 1.
121. *See generally* U.N. Comm. On Int'l Trade Law, Rep. of Working Group V (Insolvency Law) on the work of its forty-seventh session (New York, May 26–29, 2015), June 29–July 16, 2015, U.N. Doc. A/CN.9/835 (June 9, 2015) (summarizing developments).
122. *See* EU Insolvency Regulation, *supra* note 1. A list of amended provisions and the amendments thereto can be found at Annex C.
123. A.L.I. & International Insolvency Institute, Transnational Insolvency: Global Principles for Cooperation In International Insolvency Cases (2012) [hereinafter Global Principles].
124. *See id.* at 200–56.
125. *See e.g.*, Irit Mevorach, *Cross-Border Insolvency of Enterprise Groups: The Choice of Law Challenge*, 9 Brook. J. Corp. Fin. & Com. L. 107, 128 (2014) (noting that "The Model Law does not provide rules for groups."); U.N. Comm. On Int'l Trade Law, UNCITRAL Legislative Guide on Insolvency Law, U.N. Sales No. E.12.V.16, 84 ¶ 3 (2012) ("In the international context, the models that have been created to address cross-border insolvency issues have always stopped short of dealing satisfactorily with enterprise groups").
126. *See* U.N. Comm'n On Int'l Trade Law, Working Group V (Insolvency Law), Draft Notes on cooperation, communication, and coordination in cross-border insolvency proceedings, May 18–22, 2009, U.N. Doc. A/CN.9/WG.V/WP.86/Add. 1 (March 6, 2009).
127. EU Insolvency Regulation, *supra* note 1, art. 42.
128. *See* Virgos & Schmit, *supra* note 34, ¶¶ 73–5.
129. EU Insolvency Regulation, *supra* note 1, art. 3(1).
130. Model Law, *supra* note 5, at 3rd Recital ('The Model Law respects the differences among national procedural laws and does not attempt a substantive unification of insolvency law.').

131. EU Insolvency Regulation, *supra* note 1, arts. 8–18.
132. *Id.* at Recital 22. ("[A]s a result of widely differing substantive laws it is not practical to introduce insolvency proceedings with universal scope . . . The application without exception of the law of the State of the opening of proceedings would, against this background, frequently lead to difficulties . . .").
133. *Id.* ("At the next review of this Regulation, it will be necessary to identify further measures in order to improve the preferential rights of employees at European level.").
134. *Id.* at arts. 34–51.
135. *See id.* at arts. 41, 47.
136. See *id.* Article 41 mandates cooperation between representatives in the main and secondary proceedings, and Article 47 empowers the main proceeding representative to propose a restructuring plan if restructuring is allowed by the laws of the member state housing the secondary proceeding.
137. *See id.* at art. 36(1)-(2).
138. *See generally* Pottow, *supra* note 1, at 582, n.23 and accompanying text (describing traditional, if overblown, antipathy towards secondary proceedings being grounded in differences in priority rules: "those pesky normative distributional differences that the cynical cast as rent-seeking outputs of domestic lobbying efforts and the naïve see as the culmination of a thousand flowers of important socio-cultural differences blooming").
139. *See* Global Principles, *supra* note 123, at 253–5 ("[T]he question is whether it is currently appropriate, or acceptable, to eradicate virtually all exceptions to the application of the *lex fori concursus*, or whether a number of specific exceptions should be introduced, and if so, which ones . . . In these Global Rules, we have limited ourselves to those exceptions for which, both in the global domain of the relevant literature and also in the opinion of a large portion of the Advisers to the project, general consent is expressed.").
140. *See* U.N. Comm. On Int'l Trade Law, Working Group V (Insolvency Law), Facilitating the cross-border insolvency of multinational enterprise groups, May 26–29, 2015, U.N. Doc. A/CN.9/WG.V/WP128 (March 13 2015).
141. *See id.* at ¶¶ 19–23.

EDITOR'S NOTES

Since this chapter was drafted, the United Nations Commission on International Trade Law ("UNCITRAL") has supplemented its Model Law on Cross-border Insolvency with The Model Law on the Recognition and Enforcement of Insolvency-related Judgments. The supplement is consistent with, and evinces the insights of, the approach to cross-border insolvency described in this chapter.

15. Bankruptcy related contracting and bankruptcy functions

*Alan Schwartz**

1. INTRODUCTION

The Bankruptcy Code takes state law rights as it finds them, and contract is the primary source of commercial rights. Thus, a lender could have a property right in the borrower's property only if the borrower gave the lender a security agreement or a mortgage. That bankruptcy law respects state law rights and that states freely permit agents to create rights apparently implies that agents can freely contract about the insolvency related aspects of their relationship. On the other hand, bankruptcy exists to break contracts: when a debtor files, creditors no longer can freely enforce their agreements. Thus, the actual, and ideal, relation between freedom of contract and the imperatives of a bankruptcy code are, and continue to be, complex and contested issues.

In understanding these issues, it is helpful to begin with the standard justification for a collective bankruptcy procedure. The consensus goal for the procedure is to save firms with positive going concern values and to liquidate the rest. The market cannot achieve this goal unaided, it is said, because there is a conflict between collective and individual rationality: creditors as a group would do better satisfying their claims out of going concern value, when it exceeds liquidation value, but, without a public procedure, the individually rational creditor strategy is to attempt to collect regardless of the borrower's economic situation. In the most reasonable equilibrium, both viable and unviable firms are liquidated.[1]

This standard justification for a collective procedure applies after debtors become distressed, but restrictions on ex ante contracting also are necessary to permit the procedure to work as intended. For example, a borrower would get better terms from a creditor if the borrower agreed not to raise a bankruptcy defense to the creditor's collection efforts, but if every borrower made this contract with every creditor, the credit market would replicate the "everyone collects" equilibrium the bankruptcy procedure was designed to avoid.[2] Hence, contracting out of bankruptcy is not permitted.

There is a difficulty with the standard justification; it assumes but does not explain the debtor's capital structure. In that capital structure, firms have two investor types: equity and a widely dispersed symmetric set of creditors. Each of these creditors holds a claim that is small in relation to the total debt. The collective action problem exists as a result because no such creditor could internalize enough of the gain from coordinating a private restructuring to justify the cost. Capital structures are endogenous, however, so there is an economic question: why would debtors create a capital structure that makes a bankruptcy procedure necessary? This question lacks a good answer. It is difficult to find optimality justifications for the structure in the literature, and the data suggest that the structure is seldom seen in nature. Rather, capital structures that concentrate creditors are prevalent in the theory and appear common in fact.

There has been a mismatch, from the beginning, between the standard justification for a collective procedure and the motivations of the agents who sought one. The 1898 Code was the first Federal bankruptcy law to last. Creditors then did not seek a Federal law to solve a collective action problem. Instead, "What unsecured creditors most wanted in the nineteenth century was a uniform bankruptcy law that prohibited debtors from making preferential pre-bankruptcy transfers to family members and local creditors. Although the 1898 act seemed too generous to debtors, it gave creditors the basic protections they felt they needed."[3] Similarly, in the 1930s, firms that ran railroad and similar private bond restructurings asked Congress for help, but they did not seek a law that resembles today's Chapter 11. Rather, the lenders and bankers wanted majority (or even super-majority) voting rules that would bind all creditors to the private restructurings the professionals conducted.[4] The normative question a review of the modern literature thus raises is what kind of bankruptcy law is needed to enforce the capital structures that actually exist.

This essay raises that question but, in the short space of a review, cannot attempt a well-developed answer. Part 2 below takes the current Bankruptcy Code as given and asks whether parties should be able to contract to escape the procedure, or affect how parties behave in the procedure, or choose which of the "sub-procedures" – Chapter 7 or Chapter 11 – they will use. All of these contracts are unenforceable today. Part 2 argues that only the last prohibition is necessary to protect a procedure whose economic premise is the semi-mythic capital structure that the standard justification presupposes. Part 3 then reviews the capital structure literature to exhibit the difference between the imagined capital structure and structures that seem theoretically optimal and empirically present. This literature is too large to review comprehensively; Part 3 focuses on its bankruptcy related aspects. Part 4 extends the discussion by showing how creditor concentration enables creditors to control their debtors and restructure them privately. Consistent with the parties' ability to restructure privately, Part 4 shows that relatively few insolvencies eventuate in a Federal bankruptcy proceeding.

Parts 2–4 of this essay thus show that, while the law restricts "bankruptcy contracting" – contracting that regulates how agents use the public procedure – the law allows considerable freedom to "bankruptcy related contracting" – contracting that structures the relationships between creditors and debtors, and so has bankruptcy consequences. Bankruptcy related contracting has been a neglected area of bankruptcy scholarship. Part 5 is a conclusion that also speculates briefly about the tasks a bankruptcy law that regulates today's capital market should perform and calls for more collaborative work between the capital structure theorists and the bankruptcy theorists.

2. BANKRUPTCY CONTRACTING REVIEWED

2.1 Contracting to Escape the Procedure[5]

The standard justification for a collective procedure holds for creditors: that is, agents whose performances for the debtor are complete and so are owed money. These agents are debt investors or suppliers that have delivered goods or performed services. If the debtor files, the creditors must participate in the procedure to recover anything. After filing, however, some suppliers may play two roles: as a creditor for goods already shipped or services already provided and as *a contract partner* for goods or services the supplier has agreed to provide. The standard justification for bankruptcy apparently cannot support requiring agents, in their role as contract partners, to participate in the collective procedure because these agents are not attempting to collect debts.

To sharpen the distinction between creditors and partners, let firm S agree to supply j goods to firm B. The goods' production cost per unit is c(j) and the contract is to run for five periods: $t^1 - t^5$. Firm S is in a competitive market so the price per unit is p = c(j). Suppose that firm B becomes insolvent during period t^3. S is a creditor for goods supplied but not paid for; *but* S is a partner as regards goods to be supplied in periods t^4 and t^5 because S is contractually bound to supply those goods. In the usual case, a seller will believe that it is more risky to deal with an insolvent debtor than with a solvent debtor. Using our notation, S's cost of dealing with B thus increases to $c_B(j) > c(j)$. Because price equals cost, the seller would incur a loss if it must continue to perform at price p. B would want S's performance to continue, however, whenever B's monetary benefit from receiving goods for periods t^4 and t^5, v(j), exceeds the contract price (i.e., when $p < v(j)$). But it is possible for the buyer's return both to exceed the price and also to be below the seller's post-distress cost of supplying goods: that is, it is possible for $p < v(j) < c_B(j)$ to exist. The first half of this inequality says that B would derive a benefit from performance that would exceed the contract price he would have to pay; the second half of this inequality says that performance would be inefficient because B's benefit would be below S's cost of supplying the goods.

A seller is not excused from performance because its cost has risen above the price. If S anticipated the possibility of insolvency, however, the parties' contract could contain a term that would define B's insolvency as a breach of contract.[6] S would then have a contract right to discontinue its performance. If the contract were efficient to perform, however (value would exceed cost), the parties would renegotiate to perform it. Hence, sellers would only exercise their contract right to exit when the contract would be inefficient to perform, such as the contract illustrated here. And consistent with this reasoning, every US bankruptcy law until the 1978 revision required suppliers such as S to participate in B's bankruptcy *as creditors* but permitted suppliers to escape bankruptcy in their role as partners when a supplier had a contract right to exit.[7] The 1978 bankruptcy code changed this rule by making S's right to cancel its contract in the event of insolvency unenforceable. This change permitted B to "assume" the contract – i.e., to enforce the unperformed part. Suppliers thus may have to be partners.

A version of the standard justification for bankruptcy is said to justify the new rule: if every supplier exited, even viable debtors would have to be liquidated. This version seemingly cannot go so far, however, because *if* the debtor's continuation value exceeds its liquidation value, at least a majority of its contracts would be efficient to perform, and so the parties would voluntarily renegotiate to perform them. Hence, the Code primarily requires suppliers to perform inefficient contracts, whose value to the estate is less than the cost of performance. The second common justification for not enforcing contractually created exit rights is that the buyer would only assume contracts that would be profitable to the bankruptcy estate (here, $v(j) - p > 0$). This justification also is unpersuasive without a distributional reason to shift wealth to the buyer (and its creditors) from the seller (and its shareholders).[8] This essay next reviews a paper that shows, in a more complete framework, that the 1978 revision is both ex post inefficient, as has been argued here, and ex ante inefficient because the revision reduces B's incentive to invest in the transaction.[9]

To begin, let the parties function in the pre-1978 world and suppose that the buyer has a right to specific performance. The monetary benefit if the buyer's project succeeds is denoted v_S and the benefit from project failure is v_F ($v_S > v_F$). Assume that the failure return is less than the buyer's debt so the buyer is solvent only if the project succeeds. Project success depends on the buyer's effort, e, and the ex post state of the world. If B works hard – e_H –, the probability of success is ψ_H; if B does not work hard – e_L – the probability of success is $\psi_L < \psi_H$. It is assumed to be efficient for B to work hard.[10] The buyer derives a private benefit b from performance of the contract, whether the project succeeds or not. Thus, specific performance gives the buyer the power either to compel the seller to perform whether the project is successful or not, and so the buyer always receives the private benefit, or to exact a renegotiation rent for permitting the seller to exit if the project fails. The contract price will reflect the possibility that the seller either will have to perform inefficiently in the failure state or have to pay to leave.

Now let the parties include an ipso facto clause in their contract. This clause would increase the buyer's incentive to work hard for two reasons. First, the buyer could only realize his private benefit if the project succeeded because the seller would exit in the failure state. Second, because the seller will not produce unless the buyer can pay – the buyer's project succeeds – the price will be lower. Therefore, the buyer's net gain from project success – the difference between return and price – increases. The ipso facto clause thus increases the buyer's incentive to work hard in order to realize the private benefit and also to capture the larger net gain.

This example assumes that, without an ipso facto clause, the buyer could specifically compel the seller to perform. Even when, in the pre-1978 world, that assumption did not hold, the seller could have to perform when performance would be ex post inefficient. This is because, if the court can err in finding damages, the expected damages from breach against which the seller must optimize when making its exit decision would exceed the actual damages it might have to pay.[11] The difference between the seller's expected damages and the actual damages functions is a penalty on exit. Given the penalty, again in some states of the world a seller would perform inefficiently; in others, it would pay a renegotiation rent to exit. The price will reflect the expected cost of these outcomes.

Turning to the contracting stage, the ipso facto clause permits the seller to exit costlessly and so faces the buyer with a lower price. On the other hand, the clause eliminates the buyer's ability to compel the seller to perform inefficiently, and thus deprives the buyer either of the private benefit or the renegotiation rent. Hence, buyers before 1978 traded off the benefits of a better ex ante deal against the possibility of a higher ex post payoff. The ubiquity of ipso facto clauses suggests that buyers often resolved this tradeoff in favor of a better deal.

To summarize, the bankruptcy code's refusal to enforce ipso facto clauses sometimes permits insolvent buyers to compel inefficient performances and other times to exact renegotiation rents. As a consequence, solvent buyers pay higher prices and have worse incentives to invest in the transaction. Also, because the likelihood that a buyer will assume a contract is increasing in contract length, the 1978 Code creates an artificial incentive for suppliers to use short term contracts. In sum, while the case for requiring participation in the bankruptcy procedure is strong *for creditors* – agents that have completed their performances for the debtor – the case for requiring participation is weak for *contract partners* – agents with performances still to render.[12]

2.2 Contracting to Affect the Procedure

Creditors cannot escape the bankruptcy procedure but they may have preferences over how the procedure functions in particular cases. Bankruptcy systems commonly have two procedures: liquidation and reorganization. Creditor preferences over these procedures can be implemented ex post, ex ante, or in the interval between lending and insolvency. In the first case, creditors and the firm can renegotiate to have the insolvent firm choose the ex post efficient procedure, if the firm would otherwise choose the other procedure; in the second case, creditors may demand (or accept) lending agreements that induce or require the insolvent firm to choose the ex post efficient procedure; in the third case, the parties may renegotiate the lending agreement to require a solvent but shaky debtor to choose a particular procedure if its affairs deteriorate further. This section considers ex ante contracts.

These "bankruptcy contracts" can be efficient in a partial equilibrium framework – one debtor and a homogeneous set of creditors.[13] Consider a firm that raises money from a competitive credit market to fund a project that costs k. The firm's managers faithfully represent its shareholders, so agency costs only exist between the firm and the creditors. The firm's utility function is $U_F = y + b(a_i, \theta)$. The firm derives utility from project success – the y term – and from a private benefit that depends on the action a_i the firm takes when insolvent – i = liquidate or reorganize – and the ex post state of the world θ. If the project fails, the first term drops out: the managers, that is, then care only about the private benefit b.[14] The creditors' utility function is $U_C = F + v(a_i,\theta)$. The first term is the debt, which the creditor receives in the success state; the second term is the return the firm earns in bankruptcy (to which the creditors are entitled), which depends on the action the firm takes and the state of the world. There are two ex post states: in one, liquidation maximizes y (denoted θ_L); in the other, reorganization maximizes y (denoted θ_R). Private benefits are always greater when the firm chooses the reorganization procedure because the managers operate the firm for a longer period and because the firm may survive. In contrast, the creditors have ex ante preferences over the firm's later bankruptcy action. They prefer the insolvent firm to choose the procedure that maximizes y, whatever that procedure turns out to be. If so, the creditors' bad state return is maximized and the interest rate would fall.

At the lending stage, the firm can offer creditors two contracts. One contract would permit the firm to choose its preferred procedure ex post; the other contract would bribe the firm to choose what turns out to be the optimal procedure. Because the unconstrained firm would always choose reorganization, whether it was optimal or not, the creditors need not bribe the firm if reorganizing the firm in case of financial distress is likely to be optimal. When this condition is satisfied, the first contract is best: it restricts the firm to its private benefit and lets the creditors take the entire monetary return $v(\theta_R)$.

The second contract, which requires creditors to bribe the firm to make an ex post efficient choice, is optimal if the parties are uncertain regarding what the best ex post procedural choice would be or if they think that liquidation is likely to be that choice. The optimal bribe would pay the firm *the same* percentage share of the bankruptcy return regardless of the procedure the firm chose. Because the share is constant and because the liquidation return is higher than the reorganization return when liquidation is optimal, the managers do better financially by making the optimal choice. The bribe, however, must be set high enough to ensure that the managers are compensated for foregoing the larger private benefits that reorganization makes possible.[15]

This analysis supposes that the parties are symmetrically informed about the variables of interest, the creditors have identical preferences and the creditors lend at the same time. Because the parties are risk neutral, they only have to predict the mean of the various distributions, and contracts can update to include later arriving creditors. Creditor preferences may conflict, however. A trade creditor thus may prefer a suboptimal reorganization procedure if the profits the creditor earns by continuing to deal with the firm during the reorganization exceed the reduction in its return from pre-bankruptcy debts. These creditors will be willing partners during the reorganization because they can contract on current risk-adjusted terms. Creditor conflicts are handled within bankruptcy by requiring only two thirds (in amount) of the debt to approve a reorganization plan. A similar requirement can be applied to bankruptcy contracts; they would become optimal if a majority subscribes to them. Because bankruptcy contracts are unenforceable today, it is a matter of speculation just how strong the obstacles to them actually are. Opening up the contracting space, however, seems costless.[16]

2.3 Contracting to Choose the Procedure

The prior papers assumed that the bankruptcy menu – liquidation or reorganization – is mandatory: the parties could not agree, in their lending agreements, to require the borrower to use one or the other procedure, or to permit the borrower to choose from the menu ex post. Rather, the parties could only influence the insolvent debtor's ex post procedural choice by giving the debtor the efficient share of the bankruptcy return. This share, however, would reduce the estate available to creditors. Therefore, the option of letting parties make the bankruptcy chapter choice ex ante deserves consideration.

In the models considered here, agents are assumed to be informed, sophisticated and rational. Free contracting is optimal under these conditions unless agents' contracts would create externalities. There is a well-known externality in insolvency contexts: if many creditors liquidate the debtor's assets at the same time, the assets may bring "fire sale" prices.[17] A corollary to this possibility also should hold: if many debtors *agree* in their lending agreements to permit creditors to liquidate their assets in the event of insolvency the ensuing liquidation sales also may bring fire sale prices. The following paper shows that, over plausible parameter regions, many debtors would contract to require liquidation.[18]

In the model, there are two bankruptcy chapters, a large number of creditors and debtors,[19] and each debtor has a set of managers who would derive private benefits b from continuing the firm in Chapter 11 rather than liquidating it. Debt is productive because it permits firms to pursue projects.[20] Reorganization is costly while liquidation is costless: the liquidation value L, however, falls as more insolvent firms liquidate and as a debtor's assets are more specific.[21] The debtor chooses its debt level with knowledge of how many other firms also are choosing debt, but the debtor cannot affect the choices the other firms make.

A firm that is free to choose the bankruptcy procedure ex ante could contract only to have reorganization; only to have liquidation; or to have a menu (which lets the debtor choose the procedure ex post). The latter two choices dominate the first. Because the managers derive private benefits from reorganization, they will want to continue the debtor too often. Hence, if the managers could choose whether to liquidate or not, and actually choose liquidation, the creditors always would prefer liquidation as well. The parties therefore would want to give managers the option to liquidate. In a free contracting world, the issue thus is whether the equilibrium contract would *require* the debtor to liquidate or let the debtor choose from the menu.

Debtors often collectively are better off with a menu if debt is productive. Intuitively, firms can incur more debt when there is a reorganization procedure. The procedure absorbs some firms, which reduces the number of firms that liquidate and so raises liquidation values. As a consequence, all firms can borrow more. Hence, although managers choose Chapter 11 too frequently, because it yields them private benefits, firms collectively would be better off with a menu when debt is sufficiently productive.[22] If a menu were the optimal contract, however, firms apparently would choose it; there would be no need for a mandate. There are plausible equilibria, however, in which firms would contract away from a menu code, though collectively they would be better off in it.

To see why, let all firms contract for a liquidation insolvency code, thereby creating the possible fire sale externality. A lender and borrower nevertheless would not defect to contract for the menu code when the managers would derive high private benefits from reorganization and reorganization would be very costly. When these conditions are met, unconstrained managers would exploit the menu to choose reorganization too often, thereby imposing high reorganization costs on the debtor and, in anticipation of them, high interest rates. Because the lender and borrower would not defect from a liquidation only choice when the large private benefit and high reorganization cost conditions obtain, a contract requiring the insolvent firm always to liquidate could exist in a contracting equilibrium. But now let every firm contract for a menu. The *same conditions* that would cause firms to stay with a liquidation only choice – high private benefits and high reorganization costs – could cause parties to write contracts that defect from a menu choice: that is, to contract for liquidation. Hence, the unique equilibrium contract could permit creditors to liquidate ex post. As a consequence, free contracting could result in the fire sale externality.[23]

The state thus could increase welfare by mandating the menu code. And this is what the U.S. and other bankruptcy codes do. This result is important theoretically because it shows that preserving ex post choice by constraining ex ante choice can be efficient even for sophisticated contractors.[24] The result should not be overstated, however. Initially, the model presupposes that firms choose capital structures that make the fire sale externality possible, but does not justify that choice. Also, the law requires menus to be mandatory over the entire parameter space, not just the space for which a mandatory menu code would be optimal. For example, if reputational constraints would restrict managerial consumption of private benefits in bankruptcy, firms could trust managers to make the ex post choice: a mandate would be unnecessary. Also, reforms that reduce reorganization costs would make free contracting more attractive relative to mandates.

To summarize, restrictions on contracting about bankruptcy are inefficient when they (a) prevent solvent suppliers (of goods or services) from canceling their contracts when the debtor experiences distress; and (b) prevent creditors from bribing debtors to choose the ex post efficient bankruptcy chapter. But it is efficient not to enforce contracts that would eliminate the debtor's freedom (subject to being bribed) to choose ex post which bankruptcy procedure to access. This essay next turns to lending agreements that do not expressly concern bankruptcy, but that affect how debtors and creditors respond to the debtor's distress.

3. BANKRUPTCY RELATED CONTRACTING

The analysis begins with a deeper look at the canonical law and economics model of bankruptcy. The model begins with a liquidity constrained distressed debtor, who has $N >> 1$ symmetric, unsecured creditors, each of whom holds a small amount, d, of the total debt D (*i.e.*, $d = D/N$). There is no bankruptcy procedure in place. Hence, creditor collection efforts cannot be stayed, and payments for actual debts cannot be reversed. The debtor's liquidation value is L and its going concern value is V. That $L < V < D$ is assumed. Therefore, the efficient equilibrium would continue the debtor.

At t^0, creditors learn of the firm's distress. At t^1, the firm makes a take it or leave it workout offer W under which each creditor would get its pro rata share in a bankruptcy: $W = d(\frac{V}{D})$.[25] This offer would save creditors the costs of collecting in bankruptcy. The insolvent firm conditions the offer on $N - n$ of the debt accepting; if fewer than this number accept the workout offer, collection efforts will cause the firm to fail. It is not an equilibrium for every creditor to accept the debtor's offer. If a creditor believes that everyone but it will accept, this creditor has an incentive to defect: that is, to sue its debt to judgment. The creditor can infer from the firm's offer that the firm has enough money to pay at least one creditor in full. Because creditors are symmetric, however, other creditors likely will reason in this way and also reject the firm's offer. It is an equilibrium for everyone to reject the offer, however. A creditor that believes every other creditor will reject knows that the offer will fail (it is conditioned on $N - n$ accepting). Hence, accepting the offer would yield a creditor zero while rejecting it and attempting to collect may have a positive payoff.

Nevertheless, it is possible, though highly unlikely, for the firms' workout offer to succeed. A particular creditor may reason in this way: if n +

1 other creditors will reject the offer and attempt to collect their debts, the offer and thus the firm will fail; on the reasoning above, this creditor should attempt to collect as well. On the other hand, if no more than n – 2 other creditors will accept, the firm will survive whether this creditor collects or not. Thus, this creditor again would do better rejecting the offer and attempting to collect its full debt d. The illustrative creditor has a real choice only if it is pivotal: that is, if exactly n – 1 other creditors will accept. Then the firm's offer succeeds if the creditor accepts it and fails if the creditor rejects. The creditor will do better if it accepts. Accepting yields the pro rata payoff d(V/D) for every creditor, including the pivotal creditor, without incurring litigation costs. Rejection yields the pro rata payoff for every creditor, including the pivotal creditor, but every creditor would incur litigation costs. Hence, the pivotal creditor will accept the workout offer.[26]

When the debtor has many symmetric small creditors, as in the model, the probability that a creditor is pivotal is vanishingly small, however. Therefore, the only reasonable equilibrium has every creditor rejecting the firm's offer and attempting to collect. The offer thus fails and the debtor is liquidated. This is inefficient because $L < V$ is assumed.

The canonical, or creditor's bargain, model is a simultaneous move game. In this game, no creditor will coordinate creditor collection efforts because each creditor holds a small fraction of the debt so the active creditor would have to share the gain with many other creditors, but bear the full coordination cost itself. The cost commonly would exceed the gain. Debtor initiated renegotiation could not solve the coordination problem for two related reasons. First, the debtor would have to renegotiate with many creditors because each creditor holds little debt relative to the total. Hence, settling with one or a few creditors would not materially improve the debtor's prospects. The second reason is that the likelihood that a creditor will hold out for full payment increases with the number of creditors that already have settled. This reduces the debtor's incentive to renegotiate with anyone. As a consequence of these concerns, the debtor is passive and each creditor in the canonical model chooses its strategy – to collect or to accept – taking the choices of other creditors into account but being unable to influence them. The most reasonable equilibrium of this game, as shown, is the debtor's liquidation regardless of its economic state. A bankruptcy procedure thus is needed to stay creditor collection efforts and to coordinate post-distress bargaining.

There are two difficulties with this coordination failure account of the parties' pre-bankruptcy behavior. Beginning with the facts, the model predicts that, in a no bankruptcy system world, creditors would not monitor debtors (monitoring would be a public good); lending agreements would not contain covenants (because no creditor would have the incentive to create or enforce them); debt would never be renegotiated; and every insolvent firm would be dismembered. As is shown below, in our actual world creditors monitor; covenants are ubiquitous; debt is commonly renegotiated; and efficient firms often are continued. To be sure, bankruptcy is the legal default influencing these private efforts, but it cannot completely account for them. Creditor monitoring efforts and private attempts to restructure were common in the nineteenth century, before there was a comprehensive bankruptcy code.

Turning to theory, the model *assumes* that firms create the capital structures that make ex post creditor coordination impossible. Suppose instead a case where the debtor firm has one creditor who holds a substantial fraction of the firm's debt, and a group of creditors with small claims. The large creditor likely could internalize the cost of coordinating the creditor side. The creditor side and the debtor then will bargain and, on the parameters assumed above, probably split the surplus from continuing the firm. Importantly, a borrower could ensure itself of this outcome at the lending stage by *choosing* to finance its projects with a single dominant creditor. The bankruptcy analyst, that is, cannot assume a particular capital structure when analysing bankruptcy issues but rather must explain, and then work with, the capital structures on which bankruptcy law is likely to operate.

At this point, the law and economics literature runs out. As just shown, bankruptcy models do not endogenize the debtor's capital structure choice while debt models seldom take bankruptcy into account.[27] This essay next reviews some prominent debt models. The review illustrates the theoretically optimal and some of the actual capital structures a bankruptcy system could see.

3.1 Contracting that Shapes the Procedure

As said, the capital structure the canonical model presupposes is difficult to find in the theoretical or empirical debt literature. Theoretical papers that consider capital structure commonly predict a single dominant creditor, or a syndicate. A still current paper recites: "The most common financing pattern consists of senior bank debt with public debt subordinate to it. . . . [S]enior bank debt usually has a shorter maturity and a more restrictive set of covenants than junior public debt."[28] In this paper's model, the debtor, after borrowing, can choose a safe project or a risky project with a higher upside than the safe project but with a negative expected value.[29] Investors cannot observe the debtor's project choice so moral hazard has the debtor choosing the risky project (or managing the project in the more risky way).

The more likely, or the more severe, moral hazard is expected to be the worse lending terms the debtor gets, but creditor monitoring can detect and ameliorate moral hazard. Therefore, the debtor has an incentive to offer contracts that maximize the lender's incentive to monitor.

The senior debt chooses its monitoring intensity at the outset, when the creditors do not know which project the debtor will choose, or how the debtor will manage the project. In the next period, creditors can observe the probability, p, with which the debtor chose the safe project. Because creditors know initially that they will be able to observe this probability later, the lending agreement will contain covenants, denoted p^c, that are triggered if the debtor made the risky choice. In equilibrium, the covenants are very tight, so that the debtor *necessarily* will violate them. Because the dominant creditor has control when covenants are violated, it will liquidate the risky project if the project's expected value is less than the liquidation return; otherwise, the parties renegotiate to let the debtor continue to the last period. Monitoring enables a creditor to identify the debtor's project, and to liquidate the project if it is bad.

The interesting result is that, in this setup, the optimal capital structure has a single senior lender, who commonly would be a financial intermediary, and one or more junior creditors. A lender's incentive to monitor is maximized when it appropriates the full return from monitoring. It follows that for a lender to have optimal incentives there must be no lender senior to it. The lender's claim also *must be impaired*: that is, the claim must exceed the value of the collateral devoted to it. If the lender's claim is less than the project's liquidation value, the lender would liquidate every project type.[30] Impairing the senior lender gives it a stake in the firm's continuation value. Hence, the senior contributes the largest amount that will keep it impaired by liquidation and the juniors contribute the rest. The juniors do not monitor, though their claims are very risky, because the point of monitoring, as said, is to identify the debtor's project and liquidate it if it is bad. The juniors have no incentive to undertake this task: because the senior's claim is impaired, the juniors would get nothing on liquidation.

The debtor wants to give the senior lender control because control maximizes the lender's incentive to monitor; the lender uses its control to make the efficient liquidation versus continuation decision. Because the debtor will be liquidated when the continuation value of its project is less than the liquidation value, the debtor has the strongest incentive to choose the safe project (or to manage its project safely). Strong covenants are the debtor's commitment device.[31]

Relating this model to the canonical model, here the parties continue projects whose going concern value exceeds their liquidation value. The mechanism through which the parties coordinate on the efficient choice is to create an impaired senior lender with the power to monitor the debtor and shut it down. A collective bankruptcy procedure is unnecessary.

More recently, Gennaioli and Rossi derived a similar result.[32] In their model, the debtor can dedicate physical assets to creditors, but the debtor cannot fully commit to pledge cash flows. To pledge an asset (or cash) is meant to make the asset invulnerable to later appropriation by the debtor. The model assumes that the debtor can pledge $0 < \alpha \leq 1$ of cash flows: the smaller α is, the greater is moral hazard, which takes the form here of tunneling (consuming pecuniary private benefits). The debtor offers contracts to creditor investors that maximize the assets that creditors can reach in the event of financial distress, and therefore increase the amount the debtor can borrow.

The model has three periods. Parties contract at t^0. There are three possible future states: denoting a state as ω, in the model $\omega \in (G, U, B)$. At t^1, the debtor's project can turn out to be good (G): the project generates positive cash flow at t^1 and t^2 (the end). The project also can be underperforming (U) or bad (B); neither project type generates positive cash flow at t^1, so the firm is distressed then. A U project generates high cash flows at t^2 while a B project generates low cash flows. A firm with a U project thus is in financial distress; a firm with a B project is in economic distress. Because cash flow from the U and the B projects is zero at t^1, the creditor has the right, under the lending agreement, to liquidate both of them. Efficiency, however, requires B projects to be liquidated at t^1 and U projects to be continued to t^2, at which time the debtor is reorganized.

Importantly, at t^0 the creditor does not know ω, so parties cannot contract on the state of the world.[33] Parties, however, can observe cash flows. Hence, the investor can identify a G project at t^1 because only G projects generate a positive cash flow then. Lending agreements therefore can specify the amount the debtor borrows, a repayment schedule for a G project, the allocation of control between the investor and the debtor for the other projects, and the payments to creditors when the debtor is liquidated or reorganized. Because the court also cannot observe ω, the liquidation payment must be independent of the t^1 state. On the other hand, because the t^2 cash flow is observable, the reorganization payment the investor gets can be structured to induce the investor to continue the U project but to liquidate the B project. The issue is how best to do this.

The optimal contract discourages strategic default for a G project by authorizing the creditor to liquidate that project at t^1 if the debtor does not make the agreed payment.[34] The issue is how to induce the creditor to make the efficient decision for the other projects. The contract creates optimal incentives by pledging to the creditor the reorganization proceeds (which are observable) *and* a specified fraction, *less than one*, of the liquidation proceeds. Just as in the model above, the senior investor is impaired in the liquidation state. To see why here, the creditor has a liquidation bias when the expected period two cash payment is less than the period one liquidation value. An unimpaired lender would liquidate even a U project in this case. But because it is efficient to reorganize U projects, the creditor must be given a stake in the continuation value of the debtor; under-collateralizing the creditor creates that stake, thereby inducing the creditor to continue the debtor with a U project to t^2.

The optimal contract depends on the quality of investor protection in the relevant legal system. There is no need to liquidate a debtor who can fully pledge cash flows. As the debtor's ability to pledge falls – i.e., as investor protection declines – the probability of liquidation must increase. Put another way, when tunneling is a serious problem, the investor will not supply funds unless it can deter strategic behavior by liquidating even financially distressed firms, but then in order to induce the investor to continue such firms there must be under-collateralization.

The paper's central result is that the optimal capital structure has a senior creditor with control rights and a junior creditor (or creditor class) that lacks them. When a junior class is present, there is an additional gain from under-collateralizing the senior. The difference between the full liquidation proceeds and the senior's claim can be redistributed to the juniors. This maximizes the debtor's repayment to creditors and therefore the debtor's borrowing capacity. This structure creates another moral hazard concern, however: the senior may try to consolidate junior claims and then, when it is fully collateralized, liquidate both the economically and the financially distressed debtor. To avoid this concern, the junior debt should be widely dispersed. Then no junior would sell its claim to the senior for less than the fractional liquidation value that it holds, which implies a zero return for the senior's consolidation effort.[35]

Debtor moral hazard in these papers is increasing risk after a loan or consuming pecuniary private benefits. In both cases, the solution is the same: to impair the senior lender, who then will monitor and continue only efficient projects. There also should be a widely dispersed junior class with a positive expected insolvency payoff. Importantly, creditors make the efficient continuation or liquidation decision privately; there is no need for a collective procedure.[36] Moreover, the capital structure that is optimal in the models is widely observed.[37] The models are incomplete in an important respect, however. In both, and in similar analyses, it is the senior creditor's credible threat to liquidate the debtor that deters moral hazard. The concern is that insolvency often is positively correlated within an industry, and sometimes across industries. In these cases, liquidation may yield only fire sale prices.[38] This possibility may reduce the credibility of the liquidation threat.

As suggested above, these and similar analyses have a bankruptcy implication. Recall that in the canonical model there is no senior creditor with strong control rights. In that model's world, a bankruptcy system is necessary to avoid inefficient liquidations. The canonical model, however, presupposes a capital structure whose optimality has not been demonstrated and that seldom is seen. This essay thus next asks whether the models analyzed here have empirical support.

3.2 Data

The data do not test the theoretical models. Rather, the empirical papers are largely atheoretical.[39] Nevertheless, the papers offer some support for the theory. A recent paper studied the relation between a debtor's capital structure and bankruptcy.[40] Perhaps the most significant findings are that the traditional capital structure where a single bank is senior is becoming less common (though it is far from extinct). Rather, loans either are syndicated or packaged as collateralized loan obligations (CLOs). Loans are syndicated among banks (4:1 banks to a syndicate) and institutional lenders (15 to a syndicate). The paper finds "a positive and significant relation between reliance on traditional bank funding and the likelihood of successful restructuring outside of bankruptcy. . .. We find a negative and statistically significant relation between the likelihood of an out of court restructuring and reliance on institutional loans. . ..."[41]

The likelihood of restructuring outside of bankruptcy thus varies inversely with the number of creditors, but there are other structural impediments to restructuring arrangements. Consistent with the theory, "unimpaired senior secured lenders have little incentive to scale down their claims or modify key terms of the loan agreement. . .. Secured lenders are only likely to modify key terms of the loan contract when they are impaired. . ..."[42] Otherwise, creditor conflicts and the law increase the likelihood of formal bankruptcy. CLOs are less likely to be privately restructured because the law prevents parties to these loans from providing additional financing and because senior tranches are less likely to be impaired. Institutional syndicated loans are less likely to be privately restructured when, and apparently because, the lead arranger often is a relationship lender, and thus has a stake in the continuation value of the firm while the other syndicate members do not. In these cases, the unanimity requirement for many modifications precludes settlements. Despite these concerns, much debtor distress is resolved privately. Restructurings and prepackaged bankruptcies account for over 68% of the paper's sample.

Because some unanimity requirements are imposed by law, private solutions would probably increase if the law were modified.[43]

There is a gap between the theory and the data, however. The theory does not explain why traditional bank loans are becoming less common, and why some firms issue difficult to restructure debt – CLOs. On the other hand, the data show that debtors have few senior lenders, the lenders often are impaired, and coordination among creditors apparently is not a serious problem.

A paper using German data reports similar results.[44] The paper finds that "bank borrowing is very often concentrated": 'more than half the German firms borrow from one bank."[45] Concentration is facilitated by (main bank) low monitoring costs and a concentrated local credit market. This is not a theoretical paper, but it does observe that though the main bank lender gets informational rents, it can use its knowledge to prevent premature liquidation.

Another recent study (988 issuers during 1993–2007) is largely consistent with the earlier results.[46] Riskier firms use bank and other private debt: "we find that . . . private issuers are relatively younger, smaller, and have lower asset tangibility, profitability and credit ratings, as well as higher earnings volatility and growth opportunities."[47] These firms are more likely to engage in asset substitution – i.e., to increase risk – or to underinvest. Private lenders, especially banks, have an advantage over public lenders in monitoring such risky debtors. Public borrowers, in contrast, are older, larger and more profitable. Nevertheless, "large and mature firms have an average of 51% in bank debt, 38% in public debt and the remainder in nonbank private debt."[48] Interestingly, issuers with high earnings volatility – the more risky firms – prefer borrowing privately, but not from banks. All in all, firms that are more likely to experience financial distress are more likely to choose capital structures that facilitate renegotiation and private restructuring.[49]

Consistent with this finding, Colla et al. studied the capital structures of 3,296 firms between 2002 and 2009.[50] While large public firms used different kinds of debt, as in the Khang paper, 85% of the firms in the Colla sample financed with only one debt source. Also, two thirds of their firms used senior debt and notes. Firms that are likely to incur high bankruptcy costs and that are more opaque were more likely to use a single source. As in the theory above, the paper speculates that firms simplify their capital structures in order to facilitate creditor monitoring and to reduce the costs of financial distress.

4. CONTRACTING TO PROTECT DEBT VALUE[51]

4.1 Covenants: Theory

Theory and data suggest that debtors commonly have a major creditor or borrow from a small loan syndicate.[52] The ubiquity of covenants is consistent with this story. Covenants would not exist if creditors would not monitor to enforce them. In the canonical model set out above, monitoring the debtor is not done because it would be a public good.[53] Rather, a creditor will monitor only if its debt claim is large enough for the creditor to internalize a substantial part of the gain from better control of the debtor.

Covenants are commonly explained as responses to two types of debtor moral hazard, both of which require the debtor to have more than one creditor. First, consider a debtor with long-term debt outstanding that is held by several creditors. The debtor approaches one creditor to roll its contract over to short-term debt. The creditor likely will agree. If positive information about the default probability is revealed at the rollover date, it is cheap for the creditor to roll the debt over. But if negative information about the probability of debtor default is revealed, the now short-term creditor will increase the face value of its claim or take similar steps to protect itself.[54] The short-term creditor's actions will dilute the value of the other long-term creditors' claims because they will recover less in the event of default. The other creditors thus have an incentive also to convert their contracts into short-term debt as well. Hence, an all long-term debt capital structure would not appear in equilibrium.[55]

The second moral hazard story begins with a firm that has one project financed by one lender. The riskiness of the project is given by the "project beta", which is a function of the variance of the project's cash flows and the extent to which the lender is impaired.[56] A solvent debtor would take a second positive value project although it was riskier than the first. If the first project represents fraction z of the debtor's value and the second project represents (1 – z), the firm's risk is $\beta_{firm} = z\beta_1 + (1 - z)\beta_2$. There is moral hazard – i.e., debt dilution – if $\beta_2 > \beta_1$; taking the second debt-financed project increased the debtor's riskiness and thereby reduced the value of the initial lender's claim.[57]

There are two related solutions to these debt dilution stories. First, because both stories rely on externalities among creditors, reducing the number of creditors reduces the externality. And because a dominant creditor will monitor, these two stories are consistent with the theory set out above. The second solution is loan covenants. Regarding the first story, the debtor may offer, or creditors may request, covenants that prevent the move to roll overs. Regarding the second story, covenants commonly restrict or ban later debt. These stories do not fully cover the ground, however, because they assume that debt contracts are complete. This essay thus turns to the incomplete contract literature and to the data.

4.2 Covenants and Renegotiation

In the story to here, covenants help to prevent moral hazard. Covenants also help to complete incomplete contracts. A recent paper analysing private debt explains:

> . . . agents would design a contract in which inefficient outcomes can arise [because of] contractual incompleteness. Contracts could contain gaps, missing provisions, and ambiguities arising from bounded rationality, transaction costs, and non-verifiability of information. In this case, inefficient outcomes arise not from explicit punishments in the contract but from contingencies not explicitly addressed in the contract. As such, contractual incompleteness puts renegotiation at the fore of resolving inefficient outcomes under the contract.[58]

The covenants this paper studies (which are typical) give the lender strong control rights throughout the parties' relationship, "which suggests that information asymmetry about the investments, if not the borrower, is persistent."[59]

Turning to the data, borrowers initiate most renegotiations. Only 28% of the loans in the paper's sample are renegotiated because of covenant violations, though 75% of covenant violations lead to renegotiation. The typical loan in the sample had a 4.5 year term, and was renegotiated almost five times.[60] This history suggests that agents renegotiate away from outcomes that would be ex post inefficient under the contract as written in light of changed circumstances. Renegotiations yielded "economically large" changes in the pricing, amount and maturity of the debt. Also, 46% of renegotiations modify the covenant package. The most frequently changed terms are accounting measures (the net worth and other ratios) and the interest rate. Unsurprisingly, weaker borrowers renegotiate because of, or to prevent, covenant violations. "As leverage increases and credit quality declines, the probability of modifying a covenant increases. This is precisely when covenants are most likely to be violated and when agency problems are at their worst. Thus, covenant modifications are necessary to pre-empt or to address technical default."[61]

Earlier papers tell a similar story. Borrowers are assumed to have better information about their future – their possible projects and investment opportunities – than lenders do.[62] As in the theory, covenants are deliberately tight, but are relaxed if favorable information about the debtor is revealed. "[T]ight covenants effectively grant creditors substantial veto power over future investment and financing decisions."[63] The covenants this paper studies restrict capital investment and set the debt to EBITDA ratio. The creditor refuses renegotiation when the debtor has poor prospects but will renegotiate to relax covenants when information is favorable. When investment restrictions are relaxed, the debtor has good opportunities and increases investment, and when the EBITDA covenant is relaxed the debtor's liquidity problem is temporary. As in the Roberts paper, renegotiation is triggered more by anticipated than by actual covenant violations. And the covenants' function is the same: "Our findings are consistent with the view that covenants serve as important trip wires that facilitate the transfer of substantial control rights to creditors as the likelihood increases that existing covenants will be breached."[64] Also here renegotiation is common: 60.6% of the contracts in this paper's sample are renegotiated, many more than once.[65]

Covenants also are tightened when debtor bad behavior comes to light.[66] Bad behavior here is engaging in asset substitution or paying bonuses to managers or dividends to shareholders in bad states. Creditors materially tighten investment covenants for such firms when they are found out.[67] And to sound a familiar theme, "The vast majority of correctly identified distressed firms conducted some sort of debt restructuring before bankruptcy . . . companies usually had to restructure their debt again, often numerous times."[68]

An earlier study of covenants yielded similar results.[69] More than 40% of the firms in the paper's sample violated a covenant. Small firms are more likely to trip covenants but 25% of firms with assets over $5 billion also violated a covenant. These violations usually occurred when the firm was solvent but its performance was deteriorating. Following a violation, firms immediately "move to a more conservative financial policy . . . new expenditures on property, plant and equipment and acquisitions decline significantly, and violating firms begin to shed assets through sales and disposals."[70] There also is a statistically significant increase in CEO turnover.

Consistent with these results, debtor performance often improves after covenant violations and consequent renegotiations: "both operating performance and equity-market valuation improve, on average, following a covenant violation. . . . Most of the improvement in operating performance comes through a reduction in operating expenses, rather than increases in revenue . . . ."[71] The paper concludes: "The performance results suggest that creditor-led interventions are associated with a "turn-around" in company performance that improves firm value and benefits the shareholders of violator firms."[72]

To summarize, the capital structure that the creditors' bargain model assumes – equity and a single class of highly dispersed debt – is seldom seen in the theoretical and empirical literatures. Rather, theoretically optimal and observed capital structures commonly concentrate creditors. The creditors engage in extensive monitoring, which produces numerous renegotiations and frequent privately run restructurings. In turn, restructurings are attempted because optimal lending agreements give dominant creditors a stake in the debtor's continuation value. The common assumption that dispersed debt, such as bonds, cannot be privately restructured also seems questionable. Rather, history and current events suggest that private bond debt restructurings are frequent, and that the principal barrier to them is the hold out problem, which the Trust Indenture Act prevents the private agents from solving efficiently.[73] The data and theory also suggest that just about everything that could be done to save a viable debtor has been done before bankruptcy.

The infrequent use of the Federal Bankruptcy Code, relative to the occasions on which it could be used, is consistent with this conjecture. Morrison reports that 540,000 small businesses failed during 2003 but only 34,000 (6%) filed under the US Code.[74] More recent data are consistent with these facts. For example, there were 34,591 commercial bankruptcy filings in 2015, of which 5,188 (15%) used Chapter 11. Also, a substantial portion of public filings ratify privately arranged restructurings.[75] In addition, the average number of Federal business bankruptcies per year, between 2000 and 2014, was 36,277.[76] The number of distressed firms in the entire economy in each of these years is larger, by orders of magnitude, than the failures that eventuate in a Federal procedure.

Analysis and data thus raise two related, and novel, questions: (a) Are there systematic differences among the debtors, or the debtors' circumstances, between the relatively few firms that use the Federal procedure and those that do not? (b) What functions should a bankruptcy system perform when the system is not solving a coordination problem among creditors?[77] To ask these questions more concretely, let a debtor consider defaulting strategically to get better terms from its creditors. A bankruptcy law may function as a strong disagreement point for the debtor in renegotiation bargaining, skewing results in the debtor's favor, because creditors incur substantial costs if bargaining fails and the debtor files.[78] A law whose principal effect is to facilitate strategic behavior is unnecessary. Does the current Bankruptcy Code largely serve a redistributional function?

5. CONCLUSION

The standard justification for a bankruptcy law holds that the law exists to solve a coordination problem among the numerous small creditors of an insolvent firm. In the absence of a law, creditor collection efforts will cause the liquidation of both potentially viable and unviable debtors. Moreover, the law's shape is a function of the need to respond to the uncoordinated creditor collection problem. [79]

Part 2 of this essay takes the current bankruptcy structure as given and asks whether certain mandatory bankruptcy rules should be relaxed. The Part reviews papers that argue that the Code's refusal to enforce contract terms that would permit solvent parties to cease dealing with insolvent debtors and the refusal to enforce ex ante contracts that would induce debtors, after filing, to choose the bankruptcy chapter that would maximize the insolvency return given the ex post state both are inefficient, but efficiency is likely enhanced by the rule that prevents parties from choosing in the lending agreement the procedure that will operate if the debtor becomes insolvent. Rather, the parties should be required to make this choice ex post. Bankruptcy law, in sum, could be improved by opening up the contracting space, even if the law itself is largely shaped as a response to what apparently is not the actual insolvency problem.

Part 3 then reviews the theoretical and empirical capital structure literature as it relates to bankruptcy issues. This literature suggests that creditors seldom face a serious coordination problem, which helps to explain why creditors seemingly never asked Congress to solve one. Rather, theory and the data suggest that it is optimal for borrowers to have one or a few lenders, and to give these lenders the incentive and the power to liquidate unviable debtors and to continue the others. The "core function" of the current bankruptcy law – saving good and liquidating bad firms – can be and apparently commonly is privately achieved. Part 4 next reviews literature showing that creditors exercise control over debtors with tight covenants. The ubiquity of these covenants is consistent with the theory and the data. Covenants are enforced by monitoring, which requires one or a few dominant creditors, but no one monitors in the standard story because there are no such creditors. It is covenants that give creditors the power to shut down economically distressed firms and to continue the solvent ones. And to summarize, theory and data raise the question of what a bankruptcy law that is not solving a coordination problem should look like.

A very tentative suggestion is that a Bankruptcy Code should perform a subset of the functions it now performs, though these functions may need to be altered. The most important such functions are: (i) to facilitate liquidity by ameliorating the debt overhang problem. Bankruptcy permits debtors to strip liens, to sell assets free of liens[80] and less commonly to make super-priority loans; (ii) to perform the law's original function of ensuring that workout agreements or repayments respect the debtor's capital structure. Creditors thus can be given the right to challenge payments to insiders and fraudulent conveyances; (iii) to require majority voting rules for contractual restructuring arrangements;[81] (iv) to police auctions of all or part of the debtor for collusion or other irregularities.[82] Objecting creditors thus should be permitted to have a court review these sales.

An efficient bankruptcy code apparently need not perform more than these four functions. On the other hand, there has been almost no serious analysis regarding what a bankruptcy law that did not have to solve coordination problems should look like. Hence, a better view may hold that who actually uses the current code and what a modern bankruptcy code should look like are open empirical and theoretical questions. Thus, there is much to be gained by more collaboration among the lawyers and the finance scholars.

It may be helpful to end this essay with one more question, which may lead to one more research proposal. Chapters 7 and 11 regulate all business bankruptcies, but there is a question whether one size should be made to fit all. Between 2011 and 2014, billion dollar bankruptcies accounted for a yearly average of 16.075% of public company bankruptcies, but also accounted for a yearly average of 84.55% of the total assets under bankruptcy court control.[83] Coordination costs among creditors probably are increasing in the size of the assets that a bankruptcy procedure must manage and distribute. The data thus suggests that the canonical model may describe the bankruptcies of very large firms, a conjecture that is consistent with some anecdotal data but that has not been systematically tested. The data also raise a question whether there should be different bankruptcy procedures for such very large distressed firms than for other distressed firms, small in percentage but nontrivial in number, that also file. The reforms this Conclusion suggests may be apt in the small firm procedure, but something quite different may be needed in a very large firm procedure.

NOTES

* Sterling Professor of Law and Professor of Management, Yale University. Barry E. Adler, Douglas G. Baird, Alvin Klevorick, Robert Rasmussen, David Skeel and Mark Roe made helpful comments on a prior draft. Some footnotes below may clarify results for technical readers but can be skipped without losing the argument.

1. Part 3 formalizes this justification.
2. Part 2.3 infra reviews a model that expands this justification for contracting restrictions.
3. David A. Skeel, Jr., Debt's Dominion 84 (2001). See also Jeffrey T. Ferriell & Edward J. Janger, Understanding Bankruptcy 112 (3rd ed. 2013) ("Creditors, especially commercial creditors, wanted an involuntary act that could be initiated by creditors and used to pry assets out of recalcitrant deadbeats.").

4. See Skeel, supra note 3, at 105. The 1920s and 1930s restructurings are described in Harold Halbhuber, Debt Restructurings and the Trust Indenture Act, 25 Am. Bankr. Inst. L. Rev. (2017) (manuscript at 17, 31–2, 35) (https://papers.ssrn.com/sol3/papers.cfm?abstract_id=2782290), who reports: "What caused the most frustration with the [private restructuring] technique among reorganizers was its inability to bind dissenting minorities. . . . Opposition from dissenting minorities was not uncommon, and reducing their hold-up value was one of the main drivers behind the reenactment of the reorganization amendments to the [1938] Bankruptcy Act . . . Only the bankruptcy court's approval of the plan was capable of binding dissenters and forcing them to accept securities in the reorganized company."
5. The agents in the models discussed below are assumed to be sophisticated and risk neutral.
6. Such terms were called ipso facto clauses.
7. The state law default also permitted suppliers to exit if the debtor became bankrupt. See U.C.C. § 2–609.
8. Another way to put this point is that an insolvent buyer could not compel a firm to enter into a new supply contract with it even if the contract would benefit the buyer's bankruptcy estate. There does not seem a normative difference between a potential supplier's property right not to deal and an actual supplier's contract right not to deal.
9. Yeon-Koo Che & Alan Schwartz, Section 365, Mandatory Bankruptcy Rules and Inefficient Continuance, 15 J.L. Econ. & Org. 441 (1999).
10. $\varphi_H v_S - \varphi_L v_F > e_H - e_L$. This says that the marginal expected gain from the buyer's project if the buyer exerts high effort exceeds the marginal cost.
11. This is a technical note. Actual buyer damages are the maximum of v – p or zero. In the example above, the court must find v. Court errors on the low side are truncated at zero because the buyer does not pay negative damages, but court errors on the high side are unbounded. Hence, with positive probability the seller would face damages that exceed v by, say, the sum x; and with complementary probability the seller would face damages that are below v by, say, the sum y, where x > y. The damage distribution thus is skewed to the high side. For readers helped by a more technical discussion, let the probability that the court accurately finds damages be α, so that $\beta(v-p) = \alpha \max(v - p, 0) + (1-\alpha) E_\varepsilon[\max\{v - p + \varepsilon, 0\}]$, where the second term characterizes an inaccurate court and the error term $E_\varepsilon[] = 0$. The function max[•] – the second term – is convex in ε. Then, by Jensen's inequality – the value of the expectation of a convex function is larger than the expected value – $\beta(v - p) = \alpha \max (v - p, 0) + (1 - \alpha)E\varepsilon[\max\{v - p + \varepsilon), 0\}] > \max (v - p, 0)$ for any $\alpha < 1$. The expected damages – β(v – p) – exceed the actual damages that a court could later find – max(v – p, 0) – when the court can err and negative damages are not awarded.
12. There are two other ways agents could avoid the bankruptcy procedure. I have argued that parties should be free, in the lending agreement, to require private workouts that would replicate the expected bankruptcy priority order. See Alan Schwartz, Bankruptcy Workouts and Debt Contracts, 36 J.L. & Econ. 595 (1993). The parties' goal would be to have the Chapter 11 result without the Chapter 11 costs. These contracts too are unenforceable. Agents today, however, sometimes can avoid bankruptcy by partitioning debtor companies into distinct legal entities some of which the bankruptcy system could not reach. See Douglas G. Baird & Anthony Casey, No Exit? Withdrawal Rights and the Law of Corporate Reorganization, 113 Colum. L. Rev. 1 (2013). In the procurement contexts that Che and Schwartz analyze, a contract term seems a lower cost way for firms to escape the public procedure.
13. See Alan Schwartz, Contracting About Bankruptcy, 13 J.L. Econ. & Org. 127 (1997); Alan Schwartz, A Contract Theory Approach to Business Bankruptcy, 107 Yale L.J. 1807 (1998). Rasmussen also argued that the parties should have choices over the bankruptcy procedure but, in his story, the debtor would make the choice in its corporate charter, and creditors could sign on to it (or not). Because charters are difficult to amend, parties could not conveniently condition the bankruptcy chapter they used on

the ex post state. See Robert K. Rasmussen, Debtor's Choice: A Menu Approach to Corporate Bankruptcy, 71 Tex. L. Rev. 51 (1992).

14. The model assumes that the equity's monetary return is zero. For recent data that this is commonly the case, see Vedrun Capkun & Lawrence A. Weiss, Bankruptcy Resolution and the Restoration of Priority of Claims (Jun. 20, 2016) (research paper, HEC Paris), ACC-2016-1160, https://papers.ssrn.com/sol3/papers.cfm?abstract_id=2795069.
15. Denoting the bribe share as s, where $0 < s < 1$, the managers will choose L when L is optimal if $sv_{LL} + b_{L,L} > sv_{L,R} + b_{L,R}$. The first term on the left hand side is the firm's share of the monetary return when it chooses the optimal procedure L; the second term is the private benefits the managers receive in L. The first term on the right hand side is the firm's share of the monetary return if the firm chooses reorganization when liquidation would be optimal and the second term is the private benefits the managers receive when they choose reorganization. The optimal bribe satisfies $s = \frac{b_{L,R} - b_{L,L}}{v_{L,L} - v_{L,R}}$. The optimal bribe is increasing in the difference between the private benefits the two procedures make possible and is decreasing in the difference between the monetary returns the two procedures generate.
16. The debtors' managers today have an incentive inefficiently to delay filing, and thereby dissipate assets, if they expect to be treated badly in bankruptcy. For data showing that inefficient delay occurs, see Barry E. Adler, Vedran Capkun & Lawrence A. Weiss, Value Destruction in the New Era of Chapter 11, 29 J.L. Econ. & Org. 461 (2012). Paying a bribe to the distressed firm would ameliorate this behavior – see Paul Povel, Optimal "Soft" or "Tough" Bankruptcy Procedures, 15 J.L. Econ. & Org. 659 (1999) – but bribe contracts are unenforceable.
17. For a general review, see Andrei Shleifer & Robert Vishny, Fire Sales in Finance and Macroeconomics, 25 J. Econ. Persp. 29 (2011).
18. Antonio Bernardo, Alan Schwartz & Ivo Welch, Contracting Externalities and Mandatory Menus in the U.S. Bankruptcy Code, 32 J.L. Econ. & Org. 395 (2016).
19. The model assumes a capital structure similar to the structure in the standard justification.
20. In the model, debt of D yields λD, where $\lambda > 1$ is the productivity parameter.
21. The value of firm i in reorganization is $Vi - \varphi(D - Vi)$, where φ is a cost parameter: reorganization costs thus increase in how deeply the firm is under water. The value of firm i in liquidation is $L - \kappa\alpha$, where L is the liquidation value if no other firm liquidated or if the assets were put to another use. The liquidation value falls in α, which is the fraction of other firms that liquidate at the same time, and falls in κ, which indexes asset specificity.
22. The model derives a cut off value for λ, the productivity parameter, above which firms are better off with the menu bankruptcy code.
23. Formally, the liquidation only choice is the equilibrium contract when $(\frac{b}{\gamma\lambda})^2 > (\frac{1 + \varphi}{\varphi})$. The RHS is decreasing in φ, the reorganization cost; the LHS is increasing in b, the managers' private benefits, and decreasing in λ, the productivity of debt. Intuitively, both high private benefits and low project productivity make liquidation optimal, as do high reorganization costs. It had previously been shown that there is a fire sale concern, even with a mandatory menu, when industry-wide distress exists. See Viral V. Acharya, Sreedhar T. Bharath & Anand Srinivasan, Does industry-wide distress affect defaulted firms? Evidence from Creditor Recoveries, 85 J. Fin. Econ. 787, 819 (2007) ("Our main finding is that industry conditions at the time of default are robust and economically important determinants of creditor recoveries. In particular, our evidence suggests that recoveries fall during industry distress not only due to a downward revision in the economic worth of firm's assets, but also because of the financial constraints that industry peers of the defaulted firms face . . . ."). We thus show that under free contracting an "everyone liquidates" equilibrium would worsen an already bad situation.
24. Schwartz, supra note 12, summarized above, is complementary to this analysis. In the model there, a mandatory menu is assumed but managers are bribed to choose liquidation when liquidation would be optimal. The optimality of the liquidation choice is

falling in the number of other firms that are liquidating contemporaneously. Because the ex post chapter choice is state contingent, the optimal bribe therefore would have debtors choosing reorganization to avoid the fire sale danger when it would exist.

25. This Part formalizes the standard justification for a bankruptcy code. The justification has a name, attributed to Thomas Jackson, "the creditors' bargain." In Jackson's original story, the firm does not offer creditors the choice of a workout. Rather, every creditor somehow learns the debtor is distressed and begins to collect. See Thomas H. Jackson, Bankruptcy, Non-Bankruptcy Entitlements and the Creditors' Bargain, 91 Yale L.J. 857 (1982). The analysis here adds realism; distressed debtors commonly make workout offers. An equilibrium similar to the one immediately described below, though set in a different context, is characterized in Barry E. Adler, A Re-Examination of Near Bankruptcy Investment Incentives, 62 U. Chi. L. Rev. 575 (1995).
26. To see this, let x be the number of creditors that can be paid in full and let l be the creditor's litigation costs. The probability that a particular creditor is paid in full, when all of them sue at once, is x/N. The remaining creditors are not paid in the "everyone attempts to collect" equilibrium. Therefore, the pivotal creditor will accept the workout offer if the offer exceeds the expected value of suing to collect: that is, if $(\frac{V}{D})d > (\frac{x}{N})d - l$, or if $(\frac{V}{D}) > (\frac{V}{Nd}) - l$. Because Nd = D and l > 0, this inequality must be satisfied; the pivotal creditor accepts the workout offer W.
27. As a prominent example, Jean Tirole's excellent finance book does not discuss bankruptcy at all.
28. Cheol Park, Monitoring and the Structure of Debt Contracts, 60 J. Fin. 2157 (2000).
29. Another interpretation is that the debtor can manage its project in a more or less risky way.
30. The senior creditor's incentive to liquidate is analysed in Kenneth Ayotte & Edward Morrison, Creditor Control and Conflict, 1 J. Legal Analysis 511 (2009).
31. A contemporaneous paper that analyses bank borrowing also shows that it is optimal to have a single senior lender (or a cohesive group) whose role is to monitor the debtor and to liquidate the debtor if moral hazard is severe. Junior creditors exist in the model but do not monitor. See Gary Gorton & James Kahn, The Design of Bank Loan Contracts, 13 Rev. Fin. Stud. 331, 333 (2000) ("The social gain from bank loans comes from the enhanced ability to thwart inefficient risk taking [by the debtor] and to liquidate bad projects.") Consistent with this analysis, the premium on a firm's bonds increases when the firm defaults or trips covenants because the likelihood of creditor control increases. See Peter Feldhutter, Edith Hotchkiss & Oguzhan Karakas, The value of creditor control in corporate bonds, 121 J. Fin. Econ. 1 (2016).
32. Nicola Gennaioli & Stefano Rossi, Contractual Resolution of Financial Distress, 26 Rev. Fin. Stud. 602 (2013).
33. This assumption implies that parties cannot write a contract that requires liquidation at t^1 for a B firm and reorganization for a U firm.
34. The investor can identify a G project at t^1 because only it generates positive cash flow. Liquidation would be inefficient because the continuation value of a G project exceeds its liquidation value, but the investor must have the right to liquidate in order to deter strategic default. In equilibrium, G projects are continued.
35. It is difficult to know the extent to which senior creditors actually are impaired, but there is suggestive evidence. A recent paper that studied the lending behavior of a large Swedish bank found a mean ratio of collateral to debt for a senior lender of around 47%. See Geraldo Cerqueiro, Steven Ongena & Kasper Roszbach, Collateralization, Bank Loan Rates, and Monitoring, 71 J. Fin. 1295 (2016). The authors did not consider a ratio this low to be remarkable. In Capkun and Weiss's extensive data set, secured creditors recover the full value of their security in 77% of the cases but unsecured creditors recover the full value of their claims in 5% of the cases. Capkun & Weiss, supra note 14. This data implies that a creditor who is under-collateralized will almost always be impaired in bankruptcy. Finally, a paper by two bankruptcy practitioners suggests that impairment may be common: "Today, as a result of the increase of secured debt and the

proliferation of security interests covering the entire enterprise value of the borrower, secured creditors again must choose among foreclosure, inadequate third-party bids or becoming the owners of their collateral to avoid liquidation and devastatingly low recoveries." Randall Klein & Danielle Juhle, Majority Rules: Non-Cash Bids and the Reorganization Sale, 84 Am. Bankr. J. 297, 298 (2010).

36. In all of the papers so far, part of the senior lender's role is to liquidate bad projects. In perhaps the earliest paper in this optimal contract literature, debtors with relatively poor projects have a single lender and debtors with better projects have two (or more) creditors. And consistent with the above, "The main function of the optimal contract is that there is liquidation when the [debtor] firm's first period performance is poor." Patrick Bolton & David S. Scharfstein, Optimal Debt Structure and the Number of Creditors, 104 J. Pol. Econ. 1, 7 (1996).
37. See infra Part 3.2. A recent paper qualifies the theoretical results slightly, showing that after the debtor files for bankruptcy, the senior lender will agree to restructure when the firm's continuation value is positive and the senior's claim is strongly impaired. When the debtor's continuation value is barely positive, and the lender's claim is barely impaired, the senior lender may inefficiently liquidate the debtor. Inefficient bankruptcy liquidations occurred in 8% of the cases in the study but lost value was only 0.28% of going concern value on average. See Mark Jenkins & David C. Smith, Creditor Conflict and the Efficiency of Corporate Reorganization (May 29, 2014) (unpublished manuscript) (https://papers.ssrn.com/sol3/papers.cfm?abstract_id=2444700).
38. See Douglas Gale & Pierro Gottardi, Capital Structure, Investment, and Fire Sales, 28 Rev. Fin. Stud. 2502 (2015).
39. A recent entrant in this debate, however, studied the effect on over 35,000 Italian small and medium-size enterprises of a reform that increased the ability of debtors to pledge cash flows. The results supported the prediction that firms have a senior lender or a few seniors and a set of juniors, and that the junior set expands in the ability of the debtor to pledge cash flows. See Giacomo Rodano, Nicolas Serrano-Velarde & Emanuele Tarantino, Bankruptcy Law and Bank Financing, 120 J. Fin. Econ. 363 (2016). "First, we turn to the Gennaioli and Rossi (2013) theoretical finding that, as cash flows' verifiability increases, the two-tier debt structure with a class of non-controlling creditors should be observed. This prediction is confirmed in our data set. The relation between the number of firm-bank relations and the efficiency of judicial administration is positive and statistically significant." Id. at 379. A majority of firms in their sample used more than one bank, but the study measured total firm/bank relations, not how many banks a firm used to finance a project. The latter number is unlikely to be large because, in their sample, 94 banks lent to 35,041 firms.
40. Cem Demiroglu & Christopher James, Bank Loans and Troubled Debt Restructurings, 118 J. Fin. Econ. 192 (2015). Their sample had 171 out of court restructurings and 165 Chapter 11s. That parties use Chapter 11, however, does not imply the absence of private restructuring. In addition to pre-packaged bankruptcies, parties today use "restructuring support agreements" between the senior debt and the debtor under which the parties agree among themselves regarding ultimate payoffs and how the Chapter 11 is to be conducted. See Douglas G. Baird, Bankruptcy's Quiet Revolution (University of Chicago Law School, Working Paper No. 755, 2016), https://papers.ssrn.com/sol3/papers.cfm?abstract_id=2767057; Robert K. Rasmussen, "The End of Bankruptcy" Revisited 7–8 (USC Center for Law and Social Science, Research Paper No. CLASS 16-26, 2016).
41. Demiroglu & James, supra note 40, at 193. Loan syndicates are described in Amir Sufi, Information Asymmetry and Financing Arrangements: Evidence from Syndicated Loans, 62 J. Fin. 629 (2007).
42. Demiroglu & James, supra note 40, at 201–02.
43. An argument to this effect is Mark Roe, The Voting Prohibition in Bond Workouts, 97 Yale L.J. 232 (1987). More recently, see Harold B. Groendyke, Note, A Renewed Need for Collective Action: The Trust Indenture Act of 1939 and Out-of-Court

Restructuring, 94 Tex. L. Rev. 1239, 1239 (2016) (The Act "may needlessly push some financially distressed companies into bankruptcy.").

44. Steven Ongena, Gunseli Tumer-Alkan & Natalja Westernhagen, Creditor concentration: An Empirical Investigation, 56 Eur. Econ. Rev. 830 (2012). An earlier paper found that German companies sometimes borrow from several banks. These banks commonly form "pools" after the debtor's distress manifests, and these increase the likelihood of a successful private restructuring. Although several banks are involved in a pool, "We find no evidence of creditor runs before or during the distress episodes experienced by the companies in our sample." Antje Brunner & Jan Pieter Krahnen, Multiple Lenders and Corporate Distress: Evidence on Debt Restructuring, 75 Rev. Econ. Stud. 415, 416 (2008).
45. Ongena, Tumer-Alkan & Westernhagen, supra note 44, at 838, 845. Morrison's study of small business (less than 500 employees) insolvencies reports a similar result. Edward R. Morrison, Bargaining Around Bankruptcy: Small Business Workouts and State Laws, 38 J. Legal Stud. 255, 284 (2009) ("most businesses maintain a relationship with a single bank")
46. Kenneth Khang, Tao-Hsie, Dolly King & Hung Nguyen, What determines outstanding corporate debt mix? Evidence from fractional multinomial logit estimation, 48 Applied Econ. 276 (2016).
47. Id. at 277.
48. Id. at 280.
49. Short term debt is easier to restructure than long term debt. The use of long term debt varies inversely with the strength of creditor protection. This is an agency cost story: the stronger are creditor rights, the more likely are managers to lose their jobs if the firm enters the bankruptcy system. Firms respond by choosing capital structures that are easier to restructure privately. See Seong-Soon Cho, Sdkok El Ghoul, Omrane Guedhami & Jungwon Suh, Creditor Rights and Capital Structure: Evidence from International Data, 25 J. Corp. Fin. 40 (2014). This paper thus complements the findings in Adler, Capkun & Weiss, supra note 16.
50. Paola Colla, Filippo Ippolito & Kai Li, Debt Specialization, 68 J. Fin. 2117 (2013).
51. Covenants are used to control the investment behavior of the borrower as well as to protect the value of the debt. See Yuqi Gu, Connie X. Mao and Xuan Tian, "Bank Interventions and Firms' Innovation: Evidence from Debt Covenant Violations", 60 J. Law & Econ. 637 (2018) (after covenant violation, creditors induce borrower to engage in less but more valuable innovative projects); Daniel Saavedra, "Debt Maturity, Investments, and the Choice of Covenants", Manuscript (2018). (Covenants allocate control rights over borrower's investments conditional on borrower performance.)
52. There is a theoretical reason for firms to issue too much debt. Each additional dollar of debt from creditor A increases the default probability on loans from creditors B, C and D, but the debtor does not internalize this effect. See Anthonio Bernardo, Marco Pagano & S. Piccolo, Multiple Bank Lending and Information Sharing, 19 Rev. Fin. 519 (2015). Effective covenants, discussed next, may mitigate this effect.
53. Recall that in the canonical model, each symmetric creditor holds a debt claim that is small in relation to the total debt. Parties also can reduce the need for a collective procedure by issuing debt that can be converted into equity upon the happening of certain events, especially the materialization of financial distress. There are a variety of such debt instruments. For recent analyses, see Dandan Song & Zhaojun Yang, Contingent Capital, Real Options, and Agency Costs, 16 Int'l Rev. Fin. 3 (2016); Christian Dorion, Pascal Francois, Gunnar Grass & Alexandre Jeanneret, Convertible debt and shareholder incentives, 24 J. Corp. Fin. 38 (2014). The original idea is Barry E. Adler, Bankruptcy and Risk Allocation, 77 Cornell L. Rev. 439 (1992) and Barry E. Adler, Accelerated Resolution of Financial Distress, 76 Wash. U. L. Q. 1169 (1998). Convertible instruments are beyond this essay's scope, but there seems an open question regarding when agents prefer them to other forms of debt or equity.
54. See Douglas Diamond & Zhigo He, A Theory of Debt Maturity: The Long and Short

of Debt Overhang, 69 J. Fin. 719, 723 (2014) ("Short-term debt provides discipline in part because short-term lenders do not sit idly while a borrower misbehaves – they demand payment on maturity.")

55. For this story, see Markus K. Brunnermeier & Martin Oehmke, The Maturity Rat Race, 68 J. Fin. 483 (2013).
56. Formally, $\beta_{project} = \beta_{revenue}(1 + \frac{d}{v})$ where d is debt and v is the value of the project.
57. This story is modeled in Alan Schwartz, Priority Contracts and Priority in Bankruptcy, 82 Cornell L. Rev 1396 (1997).
58. Michael R. Roberts, The role of dynamic renegotiation and asymmetric information in financial contracting, 116 J. Fin. Econ. 61, 67 (2015). The paper concludes that "Renegotiation is also a means to dynamically complete contracts which are inherently incomplete." Id. at 77. To the same effect, see Christophe J. Godlewski, The Certification Value of Private Debt Renegotiation and the Design of Financial Contracts: Empirical Evidence from Europe, 53 J. Banking & Fin. 1, 2 (2015) ("We can consider that renegotiation leads to more efficient or more complete contracts as it translates new information into an updated contract."). Covenant violations are common, as are covenant violation induced renegotiations. See Jing Wang, Debt covenant design and creditor control rights: Evidence from the tightest covenant, 44 J. Corporate Finance 331 (2017). A comprehensive review of covenants now in common use is William W. Bratton, Bond and loan covenants, theory and practice, 11 Capital Markets Law Journal 461 (2016).
59. Roberts, supra note 58, at 62–3. Borrowers also provide accounting information to facilitate creditor monitoring. See Richard Carrizosa and Stephen G. Ryan, "Borrower private information covenants and loan contract monitoring", 64 J. Accounting and Econ. 313 (2017).
60. Almost a quarter of publicly traded firms experience covenant violations. This also is consistent with frequent renegotiations. In Jing Wang's sample "32% of the contracts experience at least one covenant violation, and half of the sample experience at least one covenant renegotiation before the stated maturity date." Wang, supra note 58, at 332.
61. Id. at 70. Also, "renegotiations arise quickly to address potential moral hazard problems among financially weak borrowers." Id. at 75. Roberts and Sufi found consistent results. Their study of covenants shows that covenant violations routinely are followed by renegotiations that lead to material reductions in debtors' leverage ratios. See Michael R. Roberts & Amir Sufi, Control Rights and Capital Structure: An Empirical Investigation, 64 J. Fin. 1657 (2009).
62. This assumption motivated the model in Schwartz, supra note 57.
63. David J. Dennis & Jing Wang, Debt Covenant Renegotiation and Creditor Control Rights, 113 J. Fin. Econ. 348, 365 (2014). Baird and Rasmussen informally discuss the function of covenants to transfer control to creditors when firms become distressed. See Douglas G. Baird & Robert K. Rasmussen, The End of Bankruptcy, 55 Stan. L. Rev. 751 (2002).
64. Dennis & Wang, supra note 63, at 365. See also Wang, supra note 58, at 350: ". . . the primary mechanism of debt governance through strict covenants is to assist creditor control after the lending relationship is under way."
65. In an earlier paper, Roberts and Sufi show that over 90% of long term contracts are renegotiated at least once. Renegotiations are triggered by poor debtor performance and by covenant violations. See Michael R. Roberts & Amir Sufi, Renegotiation of Financial Contracts: Evidence from Private Credit Agreements, 93 J. Fin. Econ. 159 (2009). The number of lenders in a syndicate does not predict the likelihood of renegotiation which, as said, is triggered by the debtor's behavior.
66. See Oksana Pryshepa, Kevin Aretz & Shantanu Banaerjee, Can investors restrict managerial behavior in distressed firms?, 23 J. Corp. Fin. 222 (2013).
67. "There are significantly more restrictive capital expenditure covenants in the debt contracts of correctly identified distressed firms than in those of incorrectly identified ones." Id. at 232. Also, a covenant violation in a prior loan contract results in stricter

covenants in subsequent contracts. See Felix Freudenberg, Bjorn Imbierowitz, Anthony Saunders and Sascha Steffen, "Covenant violations and dynamic loan contracting," 45 J. Corp. Fin. 540 (2017).

68. Id.
69. Greg Nini, David C. Smith & Amir Sufi, Creditor Control Rights, Corporate Governance and Firm Value, 25 Rev. Fin. Stud. 1713 (2012).
70. Id. at 1716.
71. Id. at 1716–17.
72. Id. The major creditor in this paper's study is a bank (or banks). The paper notes that hedge funds achieve similar results, but function during the bankruptcy. For recent evidence supporting this view, see Jongha Lim, The Role of Activist Hedge Funds in Financially Distressed Firms, 50 J. Fin. & Quantitative Analysis 1321 (2015). For additional evidence, see Stephen A. Karolyi & John Sedunov, Operating Risk and the Scope of Lender Control Rights 4 (November 1, 2016) (unpublished manuscript). (https://papers.ssrn.com/sol3/papers.cfm?abstract_id=2799915) (When lending syndicates have low coordination costs, "we find that borrowers reduce operating risk-taking following covenant violations, corresponding to a marginal decrease in the probability of experiencing financial distress within one year by as much as 10% . . . our estimates are quantitatively similar when we replace our measure of covenant breaches with material covenant violations sourced directly from SEC filings.").
73. See sources cited supra notes 4, 43; Mark J. Roe, The Trust Indenture Act of 1939 in Congress and the Courts in 2016: Bringing the SEC to the Table, 129 Harv. L. Rev. 360 (2016). That private restructurings of public debt are common is indirectly evidenced by the white paper that twenty eight leading law firms recently created to guide themselves as to when an unqualified opinion that any such debt restructuring is legal can be given and when not. See Opinion White Paper (April 25, 2016), http://www.debevoise.com/~/media/files/insights/publications/2016/04/opinion_white_paper.pdf. The signatory list begins with Baker Botts LLP and ends with Weil, Gotshal & Manges LLP. Other signatories include Cravath, Swaine and Moore, LLP, Davis Polk & Wardwell LLP, Kirkland & Ellis LLP and Skadden, Arps, Slate, Meagher & Flom LLP. Id. See also Marcel Kahan, "The Scope of Section 316(b) after Marblegate", NYU Law & Econ. Research paper Series Working Paper No. 18-01 (2018).
74. Morrison, supra note 45, which also reports that 16% of the corporate and 20% of the non-corporate debtors in his sample of failed small Chicago firms used the Federal procedure.
75. The data is reported in epiqsystems.com. See supra note 40.
76. 2015 Bankruptcy Yearbook & Almanac 4 (2015).
77. This Review does not discuss how financial contracting can mitigate conflicts among investors over the debtor's investment policy. For an introduction and analysis, see Dirk Hathbarth & David C. Mauer, Optimal Priority Structure, Capital Structure and Investment, 25 Rev. Fin. Stud. 747 (2012).
78. This use of the current Code is analysed in Schwartz, supra note 12. Morrison argues that this is the primary function the Code serves for small businesses. Morrison, supra note 45.
79. For representative statements: 'Non-bankruptcy rules are premised on individual creditors pursuing their own remedies. When a debtor has many creditors, the actions of each creditor often run counter to what is in the interest of creditors as a group. Bankruptcy law, in the first instance, responds to this collective action problem, a problem akin to the one that exists when individuals, pursuing their own interest, graze too many cattle in a common pasture. Solving this collective action problem gives the Bankruptcy Code much of its complexity.' Barry E. Adler, Douglas G. Baird & Thomas H. Jackson, Bankruptcy: Cases, Problems, and Materials 3 (4th ed. 2007); ". . . creditors . . . face a coordination problem. If each acts individually to enforce, this will very quickly result in the break-up of the firm's business. When the firm's assets are worth more kept together than broken up, this is an inefficient outcome and creditors would collectively be better

off by agreeing not to enforce, and instead to restructure the firm's debts. Each creditor nevertheless has an incentive to enforce individually: those who do so first will get paid in full rather than a less-than-complete payout in a restructuring. Resolving these problems is bankruptcy's core function." John Armour, Gerard Hertig & Hideki Kanda, Transactions with Creditors, in The Anatomy of Corporate Law: A Comparative and Functional Approach 115, 121–2 (2nd ed. 2009). The text next briefly speculates about what a bankruptcy law should look like when it need not, "in the first instance', respond to a collective action problem or when resolving that problem is not 'its core function." Id.

80. For a detailed explanation, see Kenneth Ayotte & David A. Skeel Jr., Bankruptcy Law as a Liquidity Provider, 80 U. Chi. L. Rev. 1557 (2013).
81. There in effect is a unanimity rule for private restructurings because a dissenting creditor has the right to sue its debt to judgment. The Trust Indenture Act also requires unanimous creditor consent to important loan contract modifications. Prepackaged bankruptcies illustrate the text's point: their appeal is that the new capital structure the professionals prefer is assessed under the Bankruptcy Code's voting rules.
82. Many of these irregularities are summarized in Alan Schwartz, A Normative Approach to Business Bankruptcy, 91 Va. L. Rev. 1199, 1243–8 (2005).
83. For this data, see references cited supra note 73.

Index